The Writings of William Walwyn

William Walwyn

The Writings of
William Walwyn

Edited by

Jack R. McMichael

and

Barbara Taft

Foreword by

Christopher Hill

THE UNIVERSITY OF GEORGIA PRESS

Athens and London

© 1989 by the University of Georgia Press
Athens, Georgia 30602
All rights reserved

Frontispiece: Portrait of William Walwyn is reproduced from
the frontispiece to his *Physick for Families*, London, 1681.
(William Andrews Clark Memorial Library,
University of California, Los Angeles)

Designed by Kathi L. Dailey
Set in Mergenthaler Palatino
Typeset by The Composing Room of Michigan
Printed and bound by Thomson-Shore
The paper in this book meets the guidelines for
permanence and durability of the Committee on
Production Guidelines for Book Longevity of the Council
on Library Resources.

Printed in the United States of America

93 92 91 90 89   5 4 3 2 1

Library of Congress Cataloging in Publication Data

Walwyn, William, b. 1600.
The writings of William Walwyn/edited by Jack R.
McMichael and Barbara Taft; foreword by Christopher Hill.
p.   cm.
Includes index.
ISBN 0-8203-1017-4 (alk. paper)
1. Levellers.   2. Great Britain—Politics and government—
1642–1660 —Sources.   3. Great Britain—Church history—
17th century—Sources.   4. Medicine—Great Britain—
History—17th century—Sources.   I. McMichael, Jack R.
II. Taft, Barbara.   III. Title.
DA407.W35A2   1989
941.06—dc19   87-18162
                         CIP

British Library Cataloging in Publication Data available

All times have produced men of several wayes, and I believe no man thinkes there will be an agreement of judgement as longe as this World lasts: If ever there be, in all probability it must proceed from the power and efficacie of Truth, not from constraint.

[William Walwyn], *The Compassionate Samaritane*

Contents

Medical Writings, 1654–1696

Appendixes

Foreword

William Walwyn is in many ways the most attractive figure among the leaders of the Levellers—the democratic party which appeared in London and in the New Model Army during the English Revolution of the seventeenth century. Walwyn was a sophisticated reader of Montaigne, and a much better writer of English prose than the verbose and self-advertising Lilburne; he seems to have been a warmer and more genial personality than Richard Overton, who was an equally brilliant writer, or than the sharp legal intellectual John Wildman. So it is splendid to have this edition of all the writings attributed to Walwyn. Now at last it will be possible for historians of political thought, of religious toleration, and of English prose to see him whole and give him his rightful place. He should rank much higher than he does at present in all three areas.

Historians of English literature will henceforth have no excuse for neglecting this subtle satirist, whose gentle irony conceals strong moral passion, and whose use of dramatic dialogue anticipates Bunyan hardly less than does Overton's. Walwyn is an important figure in the origins of democratic thought in the modern world. It will now be easier to relate his political thinking and his ideas about liberty of conscience to those of his better-known contemporaries—to Milton, for instance: *Areopagitica* will no longer seem an isolated document, nor Milton a cloistered and bookish academic. Milton was, as he very well knew, only one of the "pens and heads . . . musing, searching, revolving new notions and idea's . . . disputing, reasoning, reading, inventing, discoursing . . . things not before discourst or writt'n of."* Walwyn was another.

This edition will help us to become conscious of the wealth of speculation and controversy which was released by the collapse of the censorship in 1640; and this in its turn should help us to see Caroline

---

* John Milton, *Areopagitica* (1644), pp. 31, 33.

literature in a new perspective. Printed books contained what the
censor permitted men to say, not necessarily what they wanted to say.
Making Walwyn accessible to a general public is a very great service.
It is sad that Professor McMichael, whose initiative got the project off
the ground, did not live to see its completion. But he, Dr. Taft, and
their publishers have put all historians greatly in their debt, and all
those interested in English literature and democracy. Merely sorting
out the disputed questions of what Walwyn wrote must have been a
great labor. But here it is, for students to absorb and profit by—and
above all to enjoy. Walwyn is always entertaining. He clearly enjoyed
writing, and conveys to us across the centuries his zest, his indignation, his exuberance, his wide human sympathies and wisdom. It is
good to encounter a man who entered so wholeheartedly into the
fight for good causes, and yet remained witty, sceptical, and widely
tolerant of everything but the shams and humbug of the godly.

Christopher Hill

Preface

Among the books and pamphlets that flowed from the presses after 1640 the writings of William Walwyn are distinctive for the reach of their revolutionary proposals and the charity of their judgments. Toleration of every religious belief, civil liberties for every freeborn Englishman, representative governments democratically elected, an end to harsh and futile treatments for the sick: all these Walwyn advanced with unqualified conviction and enduring optimism as he appealed to the power of love and the evidence of reason.

Walwyn's writings are the principal source of knowledge about his life and character. None of his manuscripts or personal papers appears to have survived, and apart from sparse references to him in official records, the only contemporary observations about him are the denunciations of his opponents, the defenses of his son-in-law, and an occasional comment by a Leveller colleague. Two tracts published by Walwyn while he was in prison in 1649 include autobiographical material; earlier pamphlets explain his religious awakening and his commitment to revolutionary reforms. Beyond this, his writings have a coherence that reveals a close correspondence between the writer and his works. From his first religious pamphlets through his medical treatises decades later, Walwyn writes with the assurance of a man at one with his message.

Walwyn's quiet prose and quiet way of life set him apart from the many flamboyant radicals of the years of revolution. Amid increasingly apocalyptic rhetoric Walwyn continued to speak softly, rarely permitting bitterness to direct him and never abandoning his belief in the force of reasonable discourse. He was an early and eloquent exponent of individual liberty and true democracy—and his writings demonstrate that a revolutionary can advocate radical change without surrendering civility or grace.

This volume includes reprints of all Walwyn's acknowledged writings and thirteen anonymous pamphlets attributed to him. The texts are complete, except for the deletion of repetitious passages in some of the medical works. The Introduction traces Walwyn's life and the development of his thought, and with the Headnotes preceding each writing, places the religious and political tracts in the context of events. The Headnotes and the Appendix on Walwyn's canon present evidence for the inclusion of unacknowledged writings. The Appendix also explains the rejection of eleven anonymous writings previously attributed to Walwyn.

Jack McMichael conceived of an edition of Walwyn's writings some years ago. His study of Walwyn began as a doctoral dissertation at Columbia University and his thesis identifies a previously unattributed medical treatise as Walwyn's work. Thereafter, while teaching in departments of philosophy and religion, Jack continued his study of Walwyn and transcribed his known and possible writings with care and precision.

In 1981 Jack asked me to assist him with an introduction to Walwyn's collected works. Without Jack's knowledge of theology and understanding of the religious origins of Walwyn's convictions and conduct the Introduction would be seriously deficient. We were considering the Headnotes to the writings and conclusions about the canon at the time of Jack's death in 1984. We worked together harmoniously, for Jack was always open-minded, good-humored, and generous. Like Walwyn, he was a reasonable man.

Jack died before we had resolved all our questions. I completed the Headnotes, editing, Appendix on the canon, and final version of the Introduction with Jack's views very much in mind. Ultimate decisions, however, have necessarily been mine, and I am responsible for the choice of unacknowledged tracts that have been included and excluded.

During the years he studied Walwyn and his writings Jack McMichael was encouraged and counseled by many people. Acknowledgment of those whose names I have been able to recover is coupled with a request for forgiveness by any who may have been overlooked. John Herman Randall, Jr., gave valuable guidance during the writing of Jack's dissertation, and William Haller was interested and helpful. French Fogle, who suggested the study of Walwyn, continued to advise and encourage. Don M. Wolfe endorsed the projected edition of the works and his continuing interest was a lasting stimulus. More recently, Charles C. Dickinson III, Byron Nelson, and George Huntston Williams tendered friendly advice and support.

Dorothy McMichael, Jack's wife, gave essential help to both of us.

She encouraged Jack in his endeavors and appreciated his admiration for Walwyn and his writings. She eased the way when I assumed responsibility for the edition and welcomed me with true hospitality when I journeyed to West Virginia, where she gave me the run of Jack's papers. It was a great kindness and remains a warm memory. Steady support has been provided by my husband, William Taft. He has leavened traditional assistance with cheerful complaints about long absences for research and affable acceptance of short temper during composition. The combination has been more stimulating than he may realize.

Neither Jack nor I could have gone any distance without the skillful assistance of the staffs of many libraries and institutions. Jack began his research in the friendly milieu of the Huntington Library in San Marino. He was also welcomed at the William Andrews Clark Memorial Library, University of California, Los Angeles; the Sutro Branch of the California State Library in San Francisco; the Union Theological Library in New York; the Historical Medical Library at Yale; and the British Library and the Public Record Office in London. I, too, have received generous assistance from the staffs of these libraries, and ready help has also been forthcoming at the Library of Congress, the National Library of Medicine in Bethesda, the Beinicke Library at Yale, the Bodleian at Oxford, the Worcester Record Office, and the Guildhall Library and Dr. Williams's Library in London. Permission to reproduce title pages of tracts has been granted by: the Houghton Library, Harvard University (No. 2); the British Library (Nos. 5, 10, 17); the Rare Book and Special Collections Library, University of Illinois at Urbana-Champaign (No. 18); and the Folger Shakespeare Library in Washington (Nos. 4, 11, 21, 25, 26, 31). A special word of thanks is owed to the Folger. It is there that Jack McMichael and I came to know each other, and there that I have long enjoyed ideal conditions for research, the ever-cheerful support of an imaginative staff, and lively discussions with scholars who are ploughing adjacent fields.

Friends and fellow scholars have aided and encouraged me during my years with Walwyn and it is pleasant to express my gratitude to them. Caroline Robbins, who introduced me to William Walwyn many years ago, advised me to work with Jack McMichael and has assisted me with advice and the gift of valuable sources. Carol Biba generously offered to check proof with her expert eye. Linda Levy Peck read an early draft of the Introduction and made thoughtful comments. In all seasons I have been inspirited by the counsel and enthusiasm of Lois G. Schwoerer, who read the Introduction and the essay on the canon with unfailing care. I am deeply indebted to Austin Woolrych, who read the Introduction, the essay on the canon, and many of the Headnotes more than once and urged me forward at every stage. He and Professor Schwoerer made a number of valuable suggestions and saved me from several slips. For errors of commission or omission that remain, I, of course, am responsible.

Barbara Taft

Washington, D.C.
1988

Editorial Note

The texts are reprinted from seventeenth-century editions. The spelling, capitalization, and punctuation of the original printings have customarily been retained. Erratic punctuation has occasionally been altered; random words all in capitals have been lowercased; confusing misprints and intermittent errors in pagination have been silently corrected. Passages and random words in italics have usually been changed to roman type. Italics have been retained for titles of works, foreign phrases, quotations, and clarification. Marginal notes have been placed at the bottom of the page, with asterisks indicating where the marginalia occur in the original.

The Introduction and Headnotes obviate the need for extensive notes to the texts. The few explanatory notes are at the bottom of the page; unless an authority is cited these are marked: (Editors' Note). In the notes to the Introduction, Headnotes, and Appendixes all page references to the writings are to the original page numbers, which have been inserted in the texts in square brackets. Walwyn's infrequent use of square brackets for parenthetical remarks is not confusing. Throughout the Headnotes and the notes, dates of tracts in square brackets without question marks are from George Thomason's MS dates of acquisition on the copies in his collection in the British Library. Capitalization and punctuation of titles cited in the Introduction, Headnotes, Appendixes, and notes have been standardized.

All dates, unless otherwise indicated, are Old Style in accordance with the Julian Calendar used in seventeenth-century England. New Year's Day was celebrated on 1 January, but the official year began on 25 March. From 1 January through 24 March the form 1640/1 has been used.

Introduction

The Life and Thought of William Walwyn

William Walwyn was born in 1600, a younger son of a landed gentry family in Worcestershire. "Newland, a mile from Great Malvern . . . ," wrote a contemporary, "was the lands of the Walwyns."[1] William's father, Robert Walwyn, was a man of "Repute" in his county, with "between three and four hundred pounds Annual Estate."[2] Robert's second wife, William's mother, was Elizabeth, daughter of Herbert Westphaling, Bishop of Hereford.

As a younger son William Walwyn would not inherit land; nor did he follow his brother to Oxford or travel and study abroad. He never expressed resentment over his lack of privilege and praised his parents for being "both generous, as the world accounts; and ingenuous too, as wise men judge."[3] His mother may have been illiterate,[4] and Walwyn's early education was entrusted to tutors of whom he had a poor opinion. He knew no language other than English and declared that he would have learned Latin "(for my parents, I thank them, were not wanting) but for the tediousnesse, and impertinency of my teachers." He was no less critical of the education of others, contending that it too often made men "artificial and crafty, rather than truly wise and honest."[5] Walwyn's own learning was moral as well as intellectual, and for this he primarily honored his parents, "to whose exemplary virtue I owe more, then for my being." He recalled his Worcestershire "birth and breeding" with gratitude and warmth, writing with particular love of his "dear and ancient Mother."[6]

In 1619, like many younger sons of gentry families, Walwyn was bound apprentice to a London merchant. He lived with his master, a silk merchant in Paternoster Row, for seven years, during which his life was closely ordered and he received rigorous training as a craftsman.[7] Soon after he was released from his articles "William Wallwine weaver" married Anne Gundell in the parish of St. James Garlickhythe, 17 April 1627.[8] Subsequent entries in the parish register record many baptisms, and some burials, of sons and daughters.[9] An entry of 27 February 1628/9 again terms Walwyn "weaver," and the next entry, 24 February 1629/30, refers to him as "free of the weavers." Later entries confirm that Walwyn was a master, able to employ servants of his own, and on 4 August 1632 he was described as a merchant, having been "made Free of the Merchant Adventurers Company." The Merchant Adventurers held a monopoly on the export of cloth to the staple towns in the Netherlands and Germany. Membership assisted Walwyn's ability to support his wife and some twenty children "in a middle and moderate but contentful condition."[10]

The Walwyns lived in the parish of St. James Garlickhythe for fifteen years. Until 1633, at least, they lived in the Thames Street house of Anne's father, William Gundell, a chandler.[11] Walwyn was an active member and lay leader of his parish church, a member of the vestry, and spokesman for the committee for the poor.[12] When the Long Parliament began clearing the way for reformation of the established religion, Walwyn moved for reformation in the parish of St. James Garlickhythe yet labored to secure the well-being of the "out of order" minister.[13] Walwyn remained a member of his parish congregation, and while he was tolerant of a range of beliefs he rejected accusations that he was "a Seeker" who posed questions designed to weaken men's faith. He wished only, wrote Walwyn, "to know and understand all the severall doctrines and waies of worship . . . and for that have taken liberty to hear and observe all."[14]

By 1643 Walwyn was able to move his family to Moorfields, a pleasant area north of the City wall. There, he enjoyed a garden and a library which he shared with visitors and friends. He did love, he confessed, "a good Book, or an honest and discoursing Friend," and his enemies regarded his skill in dialectic as a root cause of his evil influence. Humphrey Brooke, Walwyn's son-in-law, after "8 yeers abroad" with the family wrote with admiration of Walwyn's goodness, simplicity, and delicacy, describing a loving marriage and family.[15] Walwyn continued to live in Moorfields until his death in 1680/1.[16]

1. Education of the Theorist

Walwyn's education was enriched when he moved to London. He seldom traveled, never going beyond or even to the sea, and except for occasional visits to Worcestershire he rarely left London.[17] His reading was as wide as his movements were limited. Early in his apprenticeship he became a serious and assiduous student, concentrating first on the Bible and the works of theologians: William Perkins, George Downham, Richard Hooker, Joseph Hall. He soon broadened his reading to include classical and more recent secular authors. Condemned in 1649 for his pursuit of pagan writers and his disturbing habit of taking a firsthand look into unorthodox religious sects and views, Walwyn made no apology. He acknowledged that he had been reading "humane authors" for twenty years, although "always in their due place; being very studious all that time in the Scriptures, and other divine authors."[18]

There is no indication that Walwyn read John Calvin's writings, but Perkins and Downham systematized the Geneva doctrine and anyone who attended a parish church in Jacobean England was assailed with Calvinist theology. Salvation, contended Calvinists, is solely a matter of God's election without which one is certain to suffer the eternal torments of hell. There were no other requisites for salvation, and as there were no external marks of election men desperately strove or waited for inward assurance. Walwyn describes his own "extream affliction of mind" as he vainly sought to save himself by anxious works of supererogation until the Scriptures, "void of glosse," came to his assistance and "by the cleare light whereof, I saw the enemies I feared vanquished."[19]

Walwyn could not have been unaware of Arminianism, which rejected Calvinist predestination for a belief that God's saving grace was available to all believers who steadfastly sought it. Arminianism spread rapidly in England after 1620, and Laud forbade predestinarian teaching in the Church of England after he became Archbishop in 1633. Walwyn does not mention Arminianism as an influence, an omission that confirms his need to find release from the terrors of Calvinism through his own scrutiny of Scripture. In 1643 he cautioned his readers "not to trust to the authority of any man, or to any mans relation." Everyone, he believed, must be "perswaded in his owne minde of the lawfulnesse of the way wherein he serveth God."[20]

Walwyn may have been assisted in the formulation of his creed of love, salvation, and tolerance by his reading of "those peeces annexed to Mr. Hookers *Ecclesiastical pollicy.*" Haller notes that the tractates appended to some editions of Hooker's work include "A Learned Discourse of Justification," which states that faith should not be separated from hope and charity and contends that "they are not all faithlesse, that are weake in assenting to the truth, or stiffe in maintayning things in any way opposite to the truth of Christian doctrine."[21] In his first pamphlet, *A New Petition of the Papists,* Walwyn cites Hooker to support toleration of "the Church of Rome" as he asks that everyone be permitted to "follow his owne Religion."[22]

Walwyn owned a translation of Benedetto da Mantova's *Benefite of Christs Death,* which maintains that Jesus' crucifixion ensures salvation for all men.[23] Martin Luther's *Freedom of a Christian* also was in Walwyn's library, and Walwyn notes that Luther followed the Word and "invited" men to live righteously in thankfulness for so great a benefit as "the Doctrin of free Justification by Christ alone."[24] Walwyn must also have known Laurence Sanders' *Fulnesse of God's Love,* for he gave bond to release Sanders from custody.[25] All these works would have nourished Walwyn's doctrine of free grace bestowed by a loving God. Walwyn observes that this doctrine was "called then, Antinomian,"[26] but he had nothing in common with mystical Antinomians who, certain of salvation, contended that they had no obligation to obey moral law. Walwyn held fast to the Word of God revealed in the Scripture.

The Bible, for Walwyn, was "the Book of Books,"[27] and the New Testament was his principal guide. Most of his quotations are from the King James version, new in his lifetime, but he occasionally quoted the Geneva Bible and his familiarity with the Elizabethan Bishops' Bible may be assumed. Walwyn was appalled at charges made in 1649 that he wished to have all the Bibles in England burnt, that he valued "Heathen Authors above the Scriptures." All who knew him, he insisted, could testify that he revered the Scriptures and had always maintained that "Reason and Philosophy could never have discovered peace and reconciliation by Christ alone, nor do teach men to love their enemies; doctrines which I prize more than the whole world."[28]

Although he never equated them with the Bible, Walwyn valued books of history and philosophy and believed that people would advance their knowledge and freedom by reading them. Thucydides, Plutarch, Seneca, Lucian, and Pierre Charron are named as authors

Walwyn enjoyed, but he most extensively quotes Montaigne.[29] Montaigne's questing mind, judicious temper, and inclusive tolerance enduringly attracted Walwyn, whose views were rooted in a Christian humanism similar to Montaigne's. "To learn civility, humanity, simplicity of heart; yea, charity and Christianity," Walwyn sent Independents to the "honest Papist," Montaigne, or to the "innocent Cannibals" praised by Montaigne.[30]

Pierre Charron, like Seneca, placed a value on reason that spoke to Walwyn. Charron's last work, *Of Wisdome,* makes points that Walwyn would stress in similar language half a century later:

> The true office of a man [wrote Charron] . . . is to judge. Why is he a man . . . but to understand, to judge of all things. . . .
>
> Why should it not be as lawfull to doubt, and consider of things as doubtfull . . . as it is to them to affirme? . . .
>
> . . . Every man calleth that barbarous that agreeth not with his palat and custome, and it seemeth that we have no other touch of truth and reason, than the example and the Idea of the opinions and customes of that countrie where we live.[31]

Islam, suggests Walwyn, could teach English churchmen the value of a "Law against Lying," and he recommends "a little Book, called the *Life of Mohamet.*" It would also be well, wrote Walwyn, if Englishmen regarded their own ancestors' avoidance of extreme laws concerning treason, and he cites passages from Sir Edward Coke that "are worth yours, and every mans knowledge."[32]

By his own account, Walwyn's critical judgment developed slowly. In his first signed tract he recalls his long inability to judge without the approbation of unnamed teachers and authors who "had captivated my understanding both in things morall, politique, and religious."[33] Liberated by "that pearle in the field, free justification by Christ alone," Walwyn became master rather than slave of whatever he read in divine or humane authors.[34] Criticism is evident in all Walwyn's writing, not excepting the medical works he published after 1650, wherein he attacks many prevalent medical practices. Independence of thought brought Walwyn personal fulfillment—and much opposition.

2. Religious Beliefs

Walwyn's conversion from the judgment-threatening doctrine of Calvinism to a religion of free grace, accepting love, and inner peace occurred before he wrote his 1641 plea for inclusive toleration, *The New Petition of the Papists*. Two years later he described the grace of God that brings salvation to all men: God's love can be neither earned nor compelled; salvation lies in acceptance and forgiveness, grace and free will. Men are not, he assures his readers, "under the law, but under grace: the law was given by Moses, whose Minister I am not: but grace and truth came by Jesus Christ, whose minister I am."[35] Walwyn recounts his religious emancipation in *A Still and Soft Voice*, describing a peace that came "after so many sad conflicts of distracted conscience, and wounded spirit, that it is to me a heaven upon earth." The law vainly taught that righteousness could effect salvation. In truth, salvation, assured by Christ's death, effects righteousness. Walwyn wished to know "nothing save Jesus Christ and him crucified: accounting all things as losse and dung, that I may be found in Christ, not having my own righteousnesse which is of the Law, but the righteousnesse which is of God in him."[36]

Walwyn's creed was grounded in Scripture, and he disapproved of those who neglected Scripture for wild notions that they claimed were transmitted to them by the Spirit of God. At the same time, Walwyn's respect for Scripture was far removed from fundamentalist literalism. He rarely refers to the Old Testament. His focus is on New Testament teachings that give him an ease and freedom denied to those who "were entangled with those yokes of bondage, unto which Sermons and Doctrines mixt of Law and Gospel, do subject distressed consciences."[37] He disregarded most of the textual wranglings of his time, considered many sermons trivial or misdirecting despite their Biblical contexts, and was indifferent to the Bible's obscurities and apparent contradictions. There is much in the Bible "that concerned only or chiefly, the times wherein they wrote, and the places and persons to whom they wrote." Many things are beyond understanding, and preachers too often focus on "nice & difficult questions" that are neither essential nor important. Emphasis should be on those passages that are spiritually saving and ethically effective—passages that enhance a peace rooted in charity, justice, and love. There is, wrote Walwyn, but "one universall Doctrine," easily understood: Jesus' crucifixion "is the propitiation for our sins, and . . . the sins of the whole world, . . . even when we were enemies, Christ dyed for us." Additional points in both Testaments might interest and inform, but they are spiritually and ethically unnecessary. The knowledge of "Jesus Christ and him Crucified" is the jewel for which the wise merchant "sould all that ever he had to purchase it."[38]

Walwyn presents the ethical message of the crucifixion with equal clarity: "We should love as Christ hath loved, . . . so that if we would try each others Faith, we are to consider each others love; . . . extending it self to the fatherles and to the Widdow; to the hungry, the naked, sick, and imprisoned."[39] Good works are a rightful duty of any Christian, but works motivated by fear will neither please God nor deliver anyone from misery. Walwyn admired Luther's portrayal of a free Christian's works of love without self-ends, directed solely and charitably toward a neighbor's good. Such works are spontaneous, natural expressions of gratitude for the love that God has given freely. "This Evangelicall truth of its own nature," wrote Walwyn, "would instantly set men on work to do the will of him, that hath so loved him, and constrain him to walk in love as Christ hath loved."[40]

Love, contended Walwyn, is essential to justice and identical with charity. One may hate sin, but not the sinner, hate error, but not its perpetrator. "I am one that do truly and heartily love all mankind," wrote Walwyn. ". . . I never proposed any man for my enemy, but injustice, oppression, innovation, arbitrary power, and cruelty, where ever I found them I ever opposed my self against them."[41] Love is the heart of Walwyn's responses to Thomas Edwards's denunciations of sectaries and toleration. In his first response Walwyn prescribes love as "a balsame that often, and well rub'd in, may Cure your *Gangraen.*"[42] Some months later, writing with rare irony, Walwyn put into the mouth of Edwards a speech of repentance and love: "Should I not love him that hath loved me, and shewed mercy unto me, for so many thousand sinnes, shall not his kindnesse beget kindnesses in me, yes love hath filled me with love."[43] Finally, in the delightful, Bunyan-like *Parable* Walwyn portrays Edwards as a patient treated by physicians: Truth, Patience, Justice, and Love. After a decisive dose of love cures Edwards of his distemper he preaches a sermon in which "the whole commandement is fulfilled in this one word, LOVE."[44]

Walwyn conjoined his belief that a loving God would not, in reason, deny anyone salvation with a belief that Scripture presaged happiness on earth. Rejecting the orthodox view of Adamic corruption and damnation, Walwyn believed that man created by God was joyous, good, loving, honest, and brotherly. A loving God had not made man damned and miserable but saved and happy. In man's natural state human understanding and "all things whatsoever that are necessary for the use of mankinde" are available. Their use is readily understood, and as they are ready to hand or easily found it is apparent, wrote Walwyn, "that God ever intendeth unto man a pleasant and comfortable life."[45]

Admiring Montaigne's primitive tribes that put "civilized" Christians to shame as did other pagans near the state of nature, Walwyn paints a blissful picture of primitive life—familial, communal, cooperative—and concludes that man's fall was due to the corruptions of civilization—private property, competition, lying, greed, vanity—which are akin to the superfluous fruit in the Garden of Eden. God made man righteous, but "he sought out unto himselfe many inventions: inventions of superfluous subtilities and artificiall things" which caused his fall from a naturally loving, truthful life to the selfish, dishonest life of civilization.[46]

Walwyn's view of the Genesis story sprang from his fundamental belief in God's universal, saving mercy. In spiritual as in natural things God dealt abundantly with man, offering easily understood ways to happiness and salvation. Man, however, adds dismal doctrinal "inventions" to the Word as to his life, neglecting "the plaine and evident places of Scripture manifestly declaring our peace and reconciliation with God."[47] Scripture shows the way to happiness on earth and salvation for men of every age and religion through the redemptive love of God.

3. Religious Toleration

Religious toleration was a major concern of Englishmen throughout the seventeenth century. In the early decades the common doctrine of Calvinism supported an uneasy peace among Protestants, whether Anglicans or Dissenters; differences were largely concerned with ceremonies and church government. The fragile accord was shattered by the Arminian challenge to predestinarian theology that culminated in Archbishop Laud's Arminianization of the Church of England in the 1630s. The Arminian bishops attempted to redefine Puritanism as Calvinism, particularly offending Calvinists within the established church. Calvinists, on the other hand, viewed Arminianism as a road to Rome. Most Calvinists believed, as Nicholas Tyacke states, that the basic issue "between Protestantism and Catholicism was that of divine determinism versus human freewill."[48]

When the Long Parliament assembled in November 1640, attacks on the Laudian hierarchy began within a week. Calvinist members of the Commons and petitioners throughout England demanded the extirpation of episcopacy with all its "roots and branches." At the same time, responsible men in and out of Parliament considered properly tuned pulpits essential supports of the state. The church must be reformed, but many sought a course between Arminian uniformity and the drastic demands of "root and branch" men.[49] If membership in a state church was not a prerequisite for loyalty to the state, a national church, regulated by authority, was essential to order in the state. In the event, the Anglican church was proscribed bit by bit. Throughout the first Civil War, while the Westminster Assembly of English divines, laymen from the Lords and Commons, and Scotch commissioners labored to construct a religious settlement acceptable to Parliament and the Church of Scotland, a series of parliamentary ordinances dismantled the established Church of England. In June 1646—four months before the office and authority of bishops were finally abolished—Parliament authorized a form of worship and church government deplored by the Scots as "Erastian."[50] English Presbyterians, the Scots had learned, were rarely, in the Scotch sense, Presbyterians at all. It should not have surprised them; until 1642 English Presbyterians had conformed even as they protested within the established church.

Long before the reformed establishment was in place the public practice of religion was profoundly altered. The collapse of discipline that followed the 1640 attacks on episcopacy permitted the open practice of religion by Dissenters hitherto confined to conventicles. While the Westminster Assembly labored to reach agreement, Independents, Baptists, and more radical sectaries gathered their separate churches. Throughout the first Civil War, assisted by the exigencies of wartime as well as the disputes over reformation, the gathered churches suffered little if any harassment. Many separatists added social and political programs to their religious doctrines. Nothing aroused more anxiety than demands for toleration. Some opposed any indulgence. Opposition to Popery was overwhelming. Very few favored unrestricted sufferance of Dissent, fearing that unchecked religious pluralism would lead to chaos. For many revolutionaries the question became: how much religious diversity is compatible with the good of the state?

William Walwyn had no doubts. His advocacy of unqualified toleration was rooted in his conviction that it was the way of Jesus Christ.
Love and Scripture, he believed, demanded that Christians seek freedom for all beliefs, respecting the right of every man to make his own
decision, however the belief might differ from one's own. Jesus and
the Apostles, observed Walwyn, possessed an infallibility of judgment not shared by others, yet they never used pressure or coercion
to secure conformity to their beliefs. They relied on loving persuasion, seeking free assent, requiring "that every man should be fully
perswaded in his owne minde of the lawfulnesse of that way wherein
he served the Lord." Jesus and his Disciples did not revile the Sadducees, who denied the resurrection of the dead. They answered
them gently, "using no means but argument and perswasion to alter
or controle their judgements."[51] Jesus sought "to remove errour by
the sword of the Spirit and soundnesse of argument." He sought always to convince, not to compel, "to conquour the under standing by
the glorious and shining brightnesse of truth." Jesus resisted hypocrisy, oppression, and cruelty, whether political or religious. "For Matters of opinion there was a toleration . . ." for "in matters of Religion,
no sort of men have no just power to determine for another."[52]

In addition to his primary contention that religious liberty was the
doctrine of Jesus, Walwyn advanced philosophic and pragmatic arguments for toleration: the golden rule of reason and nature; human
fallibility; the inevitability of ideological differences; the triviality of
many disputes; the political benefits of freedom; self-interest; the sinful results of coercion.

The golden rule, which "tells me I must doe as I would be done
unto," is described by Walwyn as a "rule of reason and pure nature"
as well as a rule of Scripture.[53] Men of many beliefs had hazarded
their lives and estates in defense of freedom and just government;
whether termed "Anabaptists, Brownists, Separation, Independents,
or Antinomies" they must not be restrained or molested for their
beliefs. "If any sort of them were greater in number than we, and
had authority to countenance them, we should esteem it hard measure, to be restrained from exercising our Religion according to our
consciences."[54] In the speech of recantation that Walwyn ascribes to
Thomas Edwards he states: "I have been too too cruel and hard
hearted against men for erors in religion, . . . though I my selfe have
no infallible spirit to discern between truth and erors, . . . yet have I
(as the Bishops were wont) argued them of obstinacy, and in stead of
taking a christian-like way to convert them, have without mercy cen-

sured, some of them worthy of imprisonments, and some of death, but I would not be so used, nor have I done therein as I would be done unto my selfe."[55]

Walwyn's commitment to reason did not blind him to reason's limitations. He was skeptical of presumed certainties and denied the efficacy of rational "proofs" for religious beliefs. Responding to those who called him an atheist, he asserted his own belief in God and Scripture but repeated that reasoned arguments could prove neither the existence of God nor the divine origins of Scripture. It was presumptuous to deny the possibility of error; all erred and many changed opinions. Persecutors were often among the most fallible: "Who are so forward to judge and comptrole therein, as meere smatterers and such as have least experience."[56] Everyone must be free to determine his own belief, for "no man, nor no sort of men can presume of an unerring spirit: . . . one sort of men are not to compell another, since this hazard is run thereby, that he who is in an errour, may be the constrainer of him who is in the truth."[57]

Observing that men had ever disagreed, Walwyn concluded that religious diversity is inevitable. He witnessed ideological differences—sometimes within a single congregation—in his wide reading and during his visits to a variety of churches. Even Thomas Edwards, wrote Walwyn, "cannot be ignorant how disputable all the parts of Divinity are amongst the most learned, how then can he judge it so horrible a thing . . . for men to differ." Deliberate, willful ignorance should never be excused. Honest difference, sincerely conceived, must be mutually respected and accepted. So long as knowledge is imperfect, "men must differ."[58]

Walwyn believed that men reached their religious convictions in two ways: reason and God's revelation. His own belief "that there is a God" was not based on "any natural argument or reason I ever heard or read." Nor was his belief "that the Scriptures are the Word of God" supported "by force of any argument I have ever heard or read." These truths, like New Testament teachings that Walwyn prized— free justification by Christ's gift and the doctrine that we must love our enemies—could not be reached by reason. They were disclosed by divine revelation.[59]

Toleration is equally essential for truths attained by reason and truths revealed by God. "Whatsoever a mans reason doth conclude to be true or false, to be agreeabe or disagreabe [*sic*] to Gods Word, that same to that man is his opinion or judgement, and so man is by his own reason necessitated to be of that mind he is."[60] Differences in revealed knowledge are no less inevitable. Salvation, contended Calvinists, is God's gift and the saving truths are given by God to whom he chooses and when he chooses. Walwyn rejected Calvinism for himself but built on the concept of God's gift to argue that as saving truths come not by a man's choice but by God's revelation a man cannot choose to reject them. It is beyond a man's control to follow "other mens Judgements and not his owne in a matter of so great importance as that of his salvation."[61] And if, contends Walwyn, he should "call him an heretique who differs from me, I doe but provoke him to call me so, for he is as confident of his, as I am of my judgement."[62] Coercion and punishment, appropriate in the realm of moral actions, are intolerable in regard to religious beliefs dependent on God's revelation. Diversity is unavoidable; toleration is essential. "Things supernaturall, such as in Religion are distinguished by the title of things divine; such, as the benefit and use thereof, could never have beene perceived by the light of nature and reason: . . . such things are not liable to any compulsive government, . . . therein every one ought to be fully perswaded in their owne minds; because whatsoever is not of faith is sinne."[63]

Walwyn considered the triviality of many differences that provoked religious coercion a subsidiary argument for toleration. Among the disputes he dismissed as absurd were laws prescribing places of worship. It is of no importance, wrote Walwyn, where one worships—in the mountains or the fields, on the water or the shore, in the synagogue or a private house. "All is one, . . . in every place he that lifteth up pure hands is accepted."[64] Only the spirit is important and the spirit must spring from within; it cannot be forced from without or compelled by external rites. As for the varied practices of Arminians, Puritans, Papists, and all others, Walwyn had one reply: "Let them alone."[65] He considered it "madnesse . . . for men to stand in strife about petty opinions."[66] His indifference to disputes about ceremonies and deep concern about fundamental beliefs is akin to Paul's: it is neither circumcision nor uncircumcision that avails, but the "new Creature" of faith working through love.[67]

The political benefits of religious liberty were evident to Walwyn. The state that accorded religious freedom to its citizens could expect from those citizens appreciation, affection, and support, whereas people denied that freedom would never be peaceful or content. Forced conformity, wrote Walwyn in 1641, "will breede in all a generall discontent, . . . and consequently must needs follow a mighty confusion." Let everyone follow his own belief and the king and the state will be rewarded with peace and love. Walwyn named Holland, Germany, France, and Poland as countries that permitted religious pluralism and enjoyed such "concord" that "they say with the Prophet David, *behold how good and pleasant a thing it is for Brethren to dwell together.*"[68] In 1642 the political disadvantages of intolerance formed the core of *Some Considerations,* and Walwyn repeated the argument throughout the first Civil War.[69] If, he wrote in 1646, Parliament "sheweth no disrespect to any honest religious person" great quietness would follow, "your warre would be at an end; your peace would be sure, and all the people safe and happy."[70]

Walwyn also suggested that intolerance could prove self-destructive. Recalling the old tale of the wolves who persuaded the sheep to call off protecting dogs in exchange for peace, Walwyn observed that the wolves then destroyed the sheep. Should "honest Presbyters" be persuaded to abandon and molest "valiant and assured friends of other judgements" they would be but wolves. It could prove unwise; Presbyterians might find that "the rod they provide for their discenting brethren to day, may whip them tomorrow."[71] Only universal freedom could protect every man's own future.

Walwyn's belief that toleration was the way of Christianity was equaled by his belief that coercion involved two great sins. As freedom of judgment is a corollary of "free justification by Christ alone" it is the greatest of sins to compel a man to profess beliefs of which he is not persuaded in his own mind. Scarcely less sinful is the hypocrite who yields to coercion and conforms against his convictions. To compel a man against his conscience is to compel him to sin: to "believe as the Synod would have us . . . [is to] become, as said an honest man, not the Disciples of Christ, but of the Synod."[72]

While he insisted on every man's right to worship as he believed, Walwyn did not question the right of the state to establish a church. He abetted the reformation of his own parish church and accepted the *Solemn League and Covenant,* which committed Parliament to the reform of religion, explaining that he understood the Covenant to mean—as it said—reformation "according to the word of God." This meant, he continued, "no compulsion or molestation for Conscience sake, . . . the word of God being clear and evident in that point." It did not mean the uprooting as heretics and schismatics of all who forsook the established church.[73] He accepted "a necessary use of a publick ministry, and parish Congregations," but rejected the use of tithes to maintain the public ministers. "Enforced maintenance," wrote Walwyn, is "contrary to the rule and practice of the Apostles" and violates the conscience of those compelled to support teachings that they do not believe.[74] A year later, the Large Petition of March 1646/7, which was probably drafted by Walwyn, asked that tithes be "for ever abolished, and nothing in place thereof imposed." All ministers should be paid by those who voluntarily contribute to their maintenance or choose them and contract for their labors.[75] Walwyn's last written word on the subject is included in the final Agreement of the People, signed by Walwyn and three other Levellers. This Agreement would forbid the Parliament to continue tithes, name any ministers, or bar anyone from office for "any opinion or practice in Religion"— excepting only those who maintained the supremacy of the Pope or any other foreign power. Every congregation should be free to select or dismiss its own pastor and should secure or withhold the means of his support.[76]

Walwyn always distinguished ideas, which should be freely conceived and expressed, from deeds, which should be curbed and punished when they injure others. "Let the strictnesse and severity of law be multiplied tenfold against all manner of vice and enormity."[77] Religious persecution was a deed most harshly condemned by Walwyn, a "disquieter and disturber of mankind, the offspring of Satan . . . contrary to God, to reason, to the well-being of States." Persecution by any group must be restrained and "is most especially to be watcht, and warily to be circumscribed . . . by the wisdome of the supream power in Common-wealths."[78] Years later Thomas Hobbes would contend that the myriad interpretations of Scripture that resulted from the availability of the Bible in English were a root cause of the English revolution.[79] To Walwyn, individual interpretation and judgment were essential to religious integrity and the right to exercise them must be rigorously protected. In contrast, all deeds "palpably vitious" must be restrained by "the greatest punishments."[80]

Walwyn's discovery that he was redemptively loved "wrought a real thankfulnes in me toward Christ . . . as I set myself daily more and more to do his will: and that in a more publick way."[81] His most precious public cause was religious liberty. In 1641 his first known pamphlet—A New Petition of the Papists (also issued without variation as The Humble Petition of the Brownists)—asked toleration for "all professions whatsoever," specifically naming for inclusion in this freedom: Anglicans or "Arminians," anti-Anglican Puritans, Brownists, separatist Independents, Socinians, nudist Adamites, Papists, and members of the Family of Love.[82] Between 1641 and the close of 1645

Walwyn published six anonymous tracts in which he reiterated his arguments for toleration. The closing weeks of 1645 witnessed his deepening involvement in the emerging battle for civil as well as religious liberty but his unceasing commitment to absolute liberty of conscience was manifested in every piece he wrote from 1641 to 1650.

Humphrey Brooke described Walwyn's pioneering work for inclusive toleration as "hazardable."[83] Clearly, his concept of toleration was too extensive for all but a very few. The regiments of the New Model army were filled with religious enthusiasts, but the army never demanded a limitless toleration. In January 1648/9 the Council of Officers version of the Agreement of the People promised freedom of worship to all Christians—although not necessarily "to Popery or Prelacy."[84] The Instrument of Government of the Cromwellian Protectorate was equally restrictive.[85] John Milton was a great advocate of religious liberty, but his last tract, published in 1673, continued to deny toleration to Roman Catholics.[86] Still later, John Locke urged wide toleration—yet he not only excluded Papists because they were primarily subjects of the Pope, but asserted that "those are not at all to be tolerated who deny the Being of a God."[87] More than forty years before, Walwyn had written that "it cannot be just, to set bounds or limitations to toleration," not even, he concluded, to exclude a man "whose mind is so far mis-informed as to deny a Deity, or the Scriptures."[88]

In the 1640s appeals for unlimited toleration for the sectaries provoked the widest fear and opposition. Although radical sectaries called for a toleration only less sweeping than Walwyn's, prominent Independents, whose churches were also newly gathered, favored a more limited indulgence. In 1643/4 five Independent divines addressed *An Apologeticall Narration* to Parliament—the ultimate court of appeal for opponents of rigid Presbyterianism. The *Narration* distanced Independents from strict separatists—"Brownists"—who not only withdrew from parish churches but considered them spurious. "We beleeve," stated the treatise, "the truth to lye and consist in a middle way betwixt that which is falsly charged on us, Brownisme; and that which is the contention of these times, the authoritative Presbyteriall Government in all the subordinations and proceedings of it."[89] It was a reasonable position for men who sat in the Westminster Assembly and had gained an important victory when leading divines in the Assembly subscribed to *Certaine Considerations to Disswade Men from Further Gathering of Churches in This Present Juncture of Time.* The statement asked ministers and people "to forbeare" further gathering of separate churches until the Assembly and Parliament had time to establish a reformed church and arrange for "such whose Consciences cannot in all things conforme to the publicke Rule." As Murray Tolmie notes, by emphasizing their rejection of extreme separatism Independents not only helped themselves but "secured a practical freedom for all the separate churches."[90]

An Apologeticall Narration prompted a flood of discordant opinion. John Goodwin led Independent supporters of the apologists. On the left, Roger Williams and the Baptists were ready for the total separation of religion from the state. At the other extreme, fears that the Independent position did, indeed, open the way to a limitless toleration inspired dire warnings about the consequences, not only from the Scots at the Westminster Assembly but from such English proponents of an unforbearing discipline as Thomas Edwards and William Prynne.[91]

Walwyn rejected any suggestion of a "middle way" toward toleration and denounced the *Narration* as the disappointing fruit of an alliance of Independents and Presbyterians. All separatists, wrote Walwyn, are innocent, honest citizens, wholly loyal to Parliament's cause, who have been "left in the lurch" by the apologists. As for Thomas Bakewell's *Confutation of the Anabaptists,* which asserted that Baptists were professed enemies of civil government, Walwyn dismissed it as "non-sense."[92] Some months later, in 1644/5, Walwyn defended Independents—particularly John Goodwin and Henry Burton—in his response to two tracts by Prynne that attacked Independency and contended that a religious discipline approved by Parliament must be obeyed without exception. Walwyn's *Helpe to the Right Understanding* rejects any restrictions on tolerance as it defends Independents and all separatists. The tract marks an advance in Walwyn's presentation. Skillfully printed to mimic Prynne's pamphlet format, the prose is both trenchant and gentle as Walwyn concludes that Prynne, having suffered persecution himself, may yet be persuaded into righteous ways.[93]

By the spring of 1646 Parliament's forces had essentially defeated or destroyed all the Royalist armies and garrisons—and the settlement of religion and the settlement of the government had become increasingly entwined. Richard Baxter greatly exaggerated when he stated that a visit to the regiments after the great victory at Naseby revealed that Oliver Cromwell's favorites were "hot-headed Sectaries . . . [who] plainly shewed me, that they thought God's Providence would cast the Trust of Religion and the Kingdom upon them as Conquerours."[94] In fact, not until the spring of 1647 would the New Model concern itself with politics. The victories of the New Model did, however, encourage many Independents and sectaries in London to believe that they were destined to reform religion and the state. On 2 April 1646 Hugh Peter, radical Independent, preached a fiery thanksgiving sermon before both Houses, the Lord Mayor and the London Aldermen, and the divines from the Westminster Assembly. God, said Peter, had preserved the faithful by assisting them to defeat the King's forces. But the work of the Lord was far from finished and the King could not be trusted. Now was the time for Parliament and the City to cleave together to perfect the religious and social reformation so gloriously begun.[95] Few in Peter's audience concurred with his view. At the time he spoke Parliament was seeking a middle way—accommodation with the King and a religious settlement that would unite the bulk of its partisans—while the City was eager for a speedy peace, a rigid Presbyterian establishment, and the suppression of the "swarm of sectaries" who filled the pulpits and enjoyed public office.[96]

Rising fears of the "swarm of sectaries" and their increasingly alarming convictions fired the controversy over toleration that swamped the presses in 1646. Many sober men regarded proposals for extensive toleration as dangerous if not subversive while attacks on tithes were looked on as a threat to all property. The most notorious—and most effective—opponent of any toleration was Thomas Edwards, whose *Gangraena: or A Catalogue and Discovery of Many of the Errours, Heresies, Blasphemies, and Pernicious Practices of the Sectaries of This Time* appeared in three long parts between February and December 1646. To Edwards, toleration was the greatest of evils, and he spoke for and to those who truly feared that "pretended liberty of Conscience" such as "Master Walwyn" urged would "lead to treason, Rebellion, and all kind of wickednesse." Some women "would not pray with their husbands, and some not sit at table when they gave thanks . . . and servants would not joyne in prayers with their Masters, nor hear them repeat the Sermons, and . . . many of them have cast off all duties in their families."[97] In the 1640s the threat to patriarchal authority aroused real panic among those who feared it presaged the disintegration of all social order.

Walwyn recalled 1646 as a time when, while the army was victorious "through the union and concurrence of conscientious people, of all judgments, and opinions in religion; there brake forth here about London a spirit of persecution; whereby private meetings were

molested, & divers pastors of congregations imprisoned, & all threatened; Mr. Edwards and others, fell foule upon them, with his Gangreen after Gangreen, slander upon slander."[98] Walwyn's five responses to *Gangraena* stand out among the many responses and are
among Walwyn's most attractive pieces. The contrast to Edwards's
relentless censure is highlighted by Walwyn's steady appeal to reason, frequent flashes of humor and irony, and ultimate reliance on
love.[99] The initial reply, with its softly subtle title, *A Whisper in the Eare
of Mr. Thomas Edwards,* is the first tract that Walwyn published over
his own name. Except for *A Parable, or Consultation of Physitians upon
Master Edwards,* which Walwyn later acknowledged as his, he henceforth signed all his writings except those that endangered him because of the severity of his criticism of those in positions of authority.

In addition to his five replies to Edwards, Walwyn wrote at least
four more tracts in 1646, three of which were primarily concerned
with toleration. In January he produced a swift refutation of the *Letter*
of the London ministers who particularly attacked Independents as
they rejected toleration.[100] Four months later a second edition of Walwyn's *A Word in Season* was "handed about" in Westminster hall by
John Lilburne the day a City *Remonstrance* was presented. *A Word in
Season* did not state that it was a response to the *Remonstrance*—which
strongly urged Parliament to establish Presbyterianism and suppress
the sectaries—but Thomason's note on the earlier edition of Walwyn's
tract asked: "Was this book Intended against the Remonstrance now
in hand?"[101] In October Walwyn joined opponents of a proposed ordinance that threatened heretics with death. Walwyn's insistence on
toleration for all beliefs was inevitably among the most extreme positions as he listed "Turkes and those that believe in strange gods"
among those who must be permitted to worship as they are persuaded is right.[102]

In the spring of 1647 Walwyn published *A Still and Soft Voice from the
Scriptures, Witnessing Them to Be the Word of God.* He prepared the pamphlet in the hope that a careful account of his belief in the Scriptures
would persuade his Independent critics that "they had nothing to
object against me." The tract did not achieve this immediate objective,
for Walwyn could not stay away from a defense of the need to reach
truth through "tryalls and examinations" of all views. He wrote
harshly of those whose "customary or superstitious Religion" ignores
Scripture, yet he concludes, as always, with a commitment to absolute toleration: "I have no quarrell to any man, either for unbeleefe or

misbeleefe, because I judge no man beleeveth any thing, but what he cannot choose but beleeve."[103]

In fact, although the many ordinances about religion that passed in 1645 and 1646 said nothing about toleration or the relief of tender consciences, throughout the Interregnum peaceful Christians enjoyed a *de facto* toleration. The settlement of the church was finally approved in June 1646 but neither the liturgy nor the discipline had wide support and the new establishment never took root. Variations within parish churches were rarely rebuked; separatist congregations continued to flourish; under the Commonwealth and Protectorate, Anglicans and English Papists were largely unmolested. It was, as Claire Cross observes, an interval when, "virtually for the first time, the generality of Englishmen had the liberty to choose their own form of Christianity."[104] It was not Walwyn's ideal, but it was a considerable achievement.

4. Leveller Leader

Walwyn's political activities were inspired by his belief that love, as described by Paul (I Corinthians 13), is the heart of true religion. The effects of true religion, Walwyn contended, are seen in good works, particularly on behalf of the poor and suffering. "Pure and undefiled Religion" accords dignity and respect to every man, is the foe of pride, demands justice and equality, and "will empty the fullest Baggs" by impelling the privileged to share with those in need.[105] It is only possible to serve God by loving and serving our neighbors, and as he did "truly and heartily love all mankind," Walwyn was much grieved by cruelty and injustice. "It is from this disposition in me, that I have engaged my self in publick affairs, and from no other."[106]

With the outbreak of the Civil War Walwyn found his public cause and moved rapidly leftward. In November 1642, three months after the war began, Lord Mayor Isaac Penington appointed Walwyn the Vintry ward member of a committee to collect assessments to support the war.[107] His second tract, *Some Considerations Tending to the Undeceiving Those, Whose Judgements Are Misinformed,* was published the same month. The avowed purpose of the pamphlet was to expose "cunning adversaries" who deluded good men into working against the country's good by dividing them religiously. Thus, "the Puritan and Sectaries, as they are called, are more odious to the Protestant, then the Cavalier, Malignant, or Papist." With equal vigor, Walwyn assailed those who endeavored to "take away our courages and dull our resolutions" by commending peace—which is of no value if unaccompanied by "liberty which we may now if we will our selves obtaine."[108]

Walwyn's political goals, like his actions, were rooted in his theology, which was complemented by his understanding of natural law: "the common Law of equitie and justice."[109] Combining the fundamental drive for religious freedom with the doctrine of natural law, he contended that religious liberty was but one—albeit the crucial one—of man's native rights. He had no interest in reclaiming England's "ancient constitution" and rejected the misty vision of an idealized past. He desired a new polity with equal protection for the rights and liberties of everyone. To these ends, after the reform of his parish church, his "next indeavours" assisted the election of strong proponents of Parliament as aldermen, common councillors, and other officers of the ward. In the spring of 1643 Walwyn also joined "with many others, in a remonstrance to the Common Councell, to move the Parliament to confirm certain infallible maximes of free Government." The Remonstrance, primarily concerned to prove the supremacy of Parliament, stated that supreme power lay in the people and in the Parliament that the people delegated to exercise it. The power of calling and dissolving Parliament and approving bills was merely a "matter of form annexed" to the office of king and "not left to his will." His absence, therefore, was no obstacle to the making of laws. Concluding demands asked that only "trustworthy" persons be given public office and asserted that no settlement should be made with the King that would "involve us and our posterity in perpetual thraldom." Walwyn stated that had the Remonstrance not been "stifled in the birth" few men would have taken part against Parliament "through error of judgement."[110] The conclusion is questionable. It is notable, however, that the 1643 Remonstrance presented a radical delineation of the distinction between the power of Parliament and the king's office. The revolutionary claim that supreme power resided in the people became the bedrock of Leveller ideology.

More than three years would pass before the Leveller party came together, and Walwyn did not encounter John Lilburne until 1645. Throughout much of the first war Walwyn was involved in "the proceedings of Salters hall," where the headquarters of a subcommittee to raise volunteer forces was established in April 1643. The Hall soon became a meeting place for separatists and political radicals, and there and at the Windmill Tavern Walwyn worked for goals he judged "right: and tending to the publike good."[111] Until the autumn of 1645 his efforts were largely concerned with the defense of those subjected to religious persecution, and as he published anonymously he worked unobtrusively, shunning publicity and open controversy. "All the war I have made," wrote Walwyn in 1646, "hath been to get victory on the understandings of men."[112]

By the time Walwyn made that statement he had met John Lilburne and was moving forward in the expanding crusade for the religious, civil, and political liberties of every Englishman. The two men may have met at the Windmill Tavern, center of Lilburne's political activities after his departure from the army in the spring of 1645. They certainly came together at Westminster Hall on 19 July when Walwyn and a deputation from Salters' Hall came to the door of the House to accuse Speaker Lenthall and his brother of correspondence with Royalists and the King. Lilburne, as so often, was in the Hall, waiting to be called by the Committee of Examinations to answer charges about illicit tracts. He promptly allied himself with the group attacking the Speaker and was taken into custody the same day.[113] Walwyn came to Lilburne's defense in *Englands Lamentable Slaverie*, remarking the differences between them "in matters of Religion"—Lilburne was a separatist and a Calvinist—and stating that religious differences in no way diminished his concern for Lilburne's, or any man's, sufferings. Commending Lilburne for insisting on his constitutional rights against the Parliament, Walwyn chided him for basing his stand for liberty on Magna Carta, for "calling that messe of pottage the birthright . . . of the people." Imprisonment without cause, asserted Walwyn, is "against all reason, sense, and the common Law of equitie and justice." Although Magna Carta had been "wrestled out of the pawes of those Kings" who ever held the people in bondage, it does not define these irrevocable rights, and the nation is free "to alter and change the publique forme, as may best stand with the safety and freedome of the people. For the Parliament is ever at libertie to make the People more free . . . but in things appertaining to the universall Rules of common equities and justice, all men and all Authority in the world are bound."[114] Walwyn's ideology was more advanced than Lilburne's and his mind was more perceptive, but he was captivated by the younger man's purpose and enthusiasm and they would work together to advance the Leveller movement.

Outwardly, they were an unlikely combination. Lilburne, fifteen years younger than Walwyn, had grasped the value of public confrontation as early as 1638 when, whipped through the streets for distributing a book against the bishops, he harangued the crowds as he stood in the pillory in New Palace Yard.[115] It was the beginning of a lifetime of outrage. In prison or out, Lilburne published scores of pamphlets that delineated his own sufferings as a symbol of persecution at the hands of arbitrary authority, inflaming followers who made sure that he was rarely seen without a throng of applauding admirers. It is difficult to conceive of a greater contrast than the self-effacing Walwyn, publishing anonymously throughout 1645, relying on the power of reason and love. John Bastwick, once Lilburne's mentor, later his target and opponent, described the meeting he had witnessed in Westminster Hall: Lilburne and his "complices, all that Rabble rout, tagragge and bobtaile, that followed him in these his needlesse and sought for troubles . . . if ever you had . . . heard their confused, hiddious noyses, calling for the liberties of the Subjects, and for the benefit of Magna charta, and the Petition of Right, and for a publike hearing, you would have thought your selfe in the very Suburbs of Hell." Walwyn, continues Bastwick, was "one of the properest Gentlemen amongst them all . . . in a great white and browne basket-hilted beard, and with a set of teeth in his head, much like a Pot-fish, all staring and standing some distance one from another, as if they had not been good friends."[116] However different in style, Walwyn and Lilburne were at one in their dedication to equal rights for everyone, and with Richard Overton they developed a new revolutionary program. Walwyn's vision was delineated in his defense of Lilburne in the autumn of 1645. Lilburne was released in mid-October and soon expanded his "tagragge" following by bringing disaffected sectaries together in the Windmill Tavern. It was the beginning of the Leveller movement.

Levellers, as they were later nicknamed by their opponents,[117] were the only proponents of modern democracy in revolutionary England. As trailblazers in the quest for individual liberty that illuminated the appeals of democratic revolutionaries for the next three centuries they command a unique place in the world's pursuit of freedom. Nevertheless, the attraction of their well-stated aspirations should not blind twentieth-century enthusiasts who share these aspirations to the limited appeal of the Leveller program for their contemporaries. In the 1640s Levellers proposed things that had never been proposed before: unqualified religious liberty and the abolition of tithes; reform of the legal system to make it more equitable and less confusing for the uninformed; a wider franchise and representatives more responsive to their electors; an end to monopolies; reform of discriminatory taxes; proper care for the poor. The demand for religious liberty was the most frightening to most Englishmen, but some other Leveller demands were no less alarming to thoughtful men who feared that the abandonment of traditional ways could cause the tragedy of civil war to be followed by the disaster of anarchy.

Support for the Levellers was neither broad nor deep, yet on several occasions during the uneasy years when the defeated King refused to deal honestly with Parliament, Levellers had an impact inversely proportional to their following. The rise of the movement—and to a considerable degree its demise—were due to the skills and characters of the leaders. Lilburne, charismatic, courageous, and confident, was the central figure without whom the Leveller following would have been much smaller. Overton, known to few "but by his Pen," was a conceptual thinker and a gifted satirist. With Walwyn, whom opponents considered the most cunning and dangerous of the three,[118] the leadership was an unrivaled combination of fervor, reason, and polemical talent. Lilburne and Overton, members of separatist congregations,[119] brought vital supporters to the movement, and the hard core of the Leveller following was always provided by the tradesmen, craftsmen, and apprentices who populated sectarian congregations. Walwyn, involved in leftwing politics at Salters' Hall since 1642, reached out to City radicals and employed his talent for organization to promote political action.

Until 1647 radicals invariably appealed to Parliament for the implementation of their proposals. Parliament, they contended, was supreme, its power bounded only by the Commons' position as delegates of the supreme people. Walwyn participated in the 1643 Remonstrance that asserted this doctrine, and throughout the first war he gave unreserved support to the Parliament—even as he noted the limits of its power. In February 1644/5, replying to Prynne's proposal to establish a national religion, Walwyn asserted that liberty of thought and conscience were beyond the regulation of any elected body. "The people of a Nation in chusing of a Parliament cannot confer more then that power which was justly in themselves: . . . therefore no man can refer matters of Religion to any others regulation."[120] Eight months later, denouncing the Commons' imprisonment of Lilburne, Walwyn wrote that Parliament could not do anything that made the people less free or safe than it found them.[121] In 1646 Walwyn countered City pressure for the enforcement of Presbyterianism and the suppression of the sects with praise for Parliament as the vigilant guardian of the people's interests, with a delineation of its powers, and with a strong expression of confidence in the members' awareness of their obligations to all the people.[122] Before the end of June Walwyn reiterated his faith in the Commons in a tract urging them to free Lilburne from his recent imprisonment by the Lords.[123] Lilburne was not released, and the first week in July Overton, with some assistance from Walwyn, published a wider appeal in *A Remonstrance of Many Thousand Citizens . . . Occasioned through the Illegall and Barbarous Imprisonment of . . . John Lilburne.*

A Remonstrance was the first of the great Leveller petitions—and the first coordinated statement of the movement's philosophy and goals. Most of the writing is characteristic of Overton's style but passages that are all but certainly Walwyn's work underline the likelihood that the two men consulted closely. Addressed to "their owne House of Commons," *A Remonstrance* reminded members that they held their trust from the people: "Wee are your Principalls, and you our Agents." Parliament is rebuked for carrying on "as if it were impossible for any Nation to be happy without a King"; the new religious establishment is condemned as no more than a change of bondage. Religious freedom must be absolute; the press must be free to all; monopolies and discriminatory taxes should be eliminated; unjust laws must be revised in accordance with "common equity, and right reason." Kings—"the continuall Oppressours"—and the House of Lords must be abolished.[124] It was the first public demand for the abolition of the monarchy.

The summer of 1646 was an apposite time for new demands. The war had finally come to an end, and while the City pressed Parliament for peace with the King at almost any price and the King played his duplicitous games, "the poore, and men of middle quality"[125] looked to Parliament for an improvement in their lot. Religious liberty led the list of concerns, and at times Independents and Levellers were mutually supportive. Throughout the spring such group pressure as existed had been largely directed by Independent churchmen. In May, John Goodwin's church contributed fifty shillings toward the printing of ten thousand copies of Walwyn's *Word in Season,* [126] and on 2 June "many thousands" of Londoners replied to the Common Council's 26 May petition with a plea that the House govern by its own wisdom and not permit freeborn Englishmen to be enslaved. Edwards reported that Hugh Peter, the Independent divine, did much to secure signatures to the petition. Parliament accepted the appeal, thanked the petitioners, and took no action.[127]

The July *Remonstrance*, peremptory and revolutionary, provoked inevitable divisions between its proponents and substantial Independents in City congregations. Walwyn noted two petitions, drawn up by "divers of the Churches, my self, and other friends," that were suppressed because Goodwin and "some other of the Independent Churches" believed that it was not "the season." Presumably, these City Independents opposed the petitions because they embraced the tone and some of the specifics of the July *Remonstrance*, and Walwyn claimed that, despite the support of "multitudes," at a final meeting—apparently at Lilburne's old headquarters, the Windmill in Lothbury—"shamefull" aspersions on Walwyn's character caused the second petition to be demolished. The dates of these petitions are unknown, but Walwyn noted the hostile investigation of his activities by a committee of Independents in 1646, and it can be deduced that the Windmill meeting took place in the autumn of that year. Within a few months the hostility of "Goodwins people" proved less meaningful to the Leveller movement than the growing support of many separatists: "Anabaptists and Brownists . . . [and] all sorts of conscientious people."[128]

Opponents concluded that Walwyn, rather than Lilburne or Overton, was the intellectual leader of the Levellers. They detailed his "crafty" methods of attracting a variety of men to his banner and assailed the provocative style of his petitions.[129] The interpretations and implications were malicious, but Walwyn's enemies were well informed. There can be little doubt that from August 1646 until November 1647 he played the leading role in the coordination of the Levellers as a distinct party with a program and an organization to advance it. Overton was arrested five weeks after the publication of *A Remonstrance*, and, like Lilburne, he was a close prisoner until the autumn of 1647.[130] Lilburne held indignation meetings with sympathetic visitors and issued passionate tracts recounting his sufferings. The organization and promotion of petitions and pressure was mainly the work of Walwyn.

The stimulus to the Large Petition of March 1646/7—which Walwyn subsequently implied was his work[131]—was the increasing harassment of the sects by High Presbyterians in the City. Walwyn's principal allies appear to have been the General Baptists. His religious neutrality was regarded with suspicion by many sectaries as well as Independents, but Overton was a member of the evangelical congregation that gave a lead to other sectaries and provided steady support for the appeals of March–June 1647.[132] The first—the Large Petition—outlined a program for the reforms requested in the 1646 *Remonstrance*. Again addressing only the Commons, the "supreame Authority of this Nation," the petitioners demanded: an end to any negative voice on decisions of the Commons; comprehensive law reform published in plain English, speedy justice and humane treatment of prisoners; dissolution of the Merchant Adventurers and all other monopolies; full religious toleration and the abolition of tithes.[133] Nothing was said about kingship. Parliament was the target, and the sweep of the demands revealed a new determination to force a showdown with the House.

Printed copies of the petition were circulated for subscription and one copy was seized at Thomas Lambe's Baptist meeting place on Sunday, 14 March. The next day the House referred the paper to Colonel Edward Leigh's committee of examinations and two promoters of the appeal were imprisoned. On the 20th "many well-affected Citizens" presented another petition that asserted the right of petition and asked that the prisoners be released and the Large Petition be received. On 20 May a third petition, after protesting the arbitrary arrests and the Commons "prejudging" of petitions, again asked for the right to present the Large Petition for due consideration. The House replied by ordering both the March and the 20 May petitions burnt by the hangman. Before the end of the month, alarmed by the growing power of High Presbyterians, the purge of Independent officers from the London militia, and Parliament's contemptuous treatment of petitioners, the "uppermost Independents" joined Walwyn's "meetings and debates"—which included at least one friendly meeting of John Price, Walwyn, and Oliver Cromwell. The upshot was a fourth petition—"the last and most sharp of any"—that conjoined the grievances of proponents of the Large Petition, concerned Independents, and opponents of summary disbandment of the army. On 2 June the petition was read and laid aside by the House.[134] Within a fortnight Walwyn reprinted all the appeals with a four-page preface in which he recounted their history and concluded that no good could "be expected from those that burn such Petitions as these."[135]

Petitions were a device for publicizing statements that were primarily manifestoes designed to bring dissident radicals together. Walwyn later denied that the instigators had "petitioned for such things as we did hope the Parliament would not grant," although he conceded that "we had cause to doubt" they would agree.[136] Those who doubted included Lilburne and Overton in their prison cells and young John Wildman, who, with Walwyn, would appear at army headquarters at Reading in July. Presumably, he was close to the Levellers much earlier. How far the movement progressed toward the status of a party in the spring of 1647 is not known, but the rapid distribution of printed petitions and pamphlet propaganda, the speed with which thousands of signatures to petitions were secured, and the evident ability to muster crowds of supporters to appear in Westminster all suggest that the money, manpower, and management that distinguished the lively organization described at year's end began to take shape the preceding spring. Walwyn's enemies were almost certainly correct when they named him as the man in charge.

It is also probable that Walwyn did much to prepare the way for the General Council of the Army's consideration of Leveller proposals in the autumn of 1647. Lilburne is frequently identified as the most influential Leveller in the months before the debates at Putney that began 28 October. But Lilburne remained in prison until 11 November and his tracts leave no doubt that his attacks on "great ones" and his "vigorus and strong attempt upon the private Soldiery" were prompted by concern for his own freedom.[137] Walwyn, Wildman, and Maximilian Petty are the only civilian Levellers included in a 1647 cipher key listing symbols for the King, Parliament, regiments, and officers from General Sir Thomas Fairfax to the Leveller colonels Thomas Rainsborough and William Eyres.[138]

The Commons' order to burn the Leveller petitions completed Walwyn's disillusionment with the existing House and he turned to the political forces emerging in the army. The "most sharp" petition of 2 June asked for consent to the just desires of officers and soldiers,[139] and Walwyn visited Cromwell often "about that time" in pursuit of the common goals of Levellers and the army. It was Walwyn, according to his account, who "perswaded" Cromwell to leave Parliament in early June and join the regiments at Newmarket.[140] In all probability the collapse of negotiations between Parliament's commissioners and the army, Cornet Joyce's seizure of the King from the custody of Parliament, and the threat of arrest by the Presbyterians who dominated the House were more compelling reasons for Cromwell's action, although there is no reason to doubt that Walwyn added his voice.

The rendezvous near Newmarket marked the army's entry into politics. The action was not inspired by the Levellers, who did not mention the army before the petition of 2 June. The politicization of the regiments was the result of Parliament's unsatisfactory response to petitions for relief of their professional grievances. Until the end of May the primary concerns of the rank and file were material: arrears of pay; indemnity; free quarter; summary disbandment. In March soldiers and officers had appealed to Parliament for redress of their grievances. The Parliament responded with a Declaration (30 March) asserting that those who persisted in such petitions would be "proceeded against, as Enemies of the State."[141] The threat caused the regiments to add the right of petition to their demands, and eight cavalry regiments selected two agents each to transmit grievances to their commanders. The agents—or "agitators"—included men who were members of or close to separatist churches that provided much of the Levellers' support, and papers that circulated in the regiments in May included Leveller proposals[142] whose influence was barely evident. Professional concerns continued to be the major complaints presented by twelve regiments in mid-May, although objections to religious intolerance were voiced by three regiments and two statements reflected Leveller objectives in identical protests against laws "in an unknowne Tongue."[143]

Within a fortnight news that Parliament had ordered disbandment of the New Model foot with minimal payment of arrears moved officers and soldiers to political action.[144] On 5 June the regiments assembled at the rendezvous near Newmarket subscribed *A Solemne Engagement* not to disband until the army's previously expressed grievances were redressed and the soldiers and officers were secured against punishment for their resistance to disbandment by the removal from power of those who had abused the army. To ensure these demands the *Engagement* established a Council of the general officers together with two commissioned officers and two soldiers from each regiment. Nine days later, in *A Declaration, or, Representation*, the army delineated a political program that included some important concerns of the Levellers. Asserting the duty of citizen-soldiers to secure "our owne and the peoples just rights, and liberties," the manifesto demanded: the removal of unfit members from the Parliament; an end to the present Parliament and elections to future Parliaments of limited duration; guarantees of the right of petition; prompt justice under law; an act of oblivion; religious liberty; and—in the Cambridge edition—a reapportionment of seats to make distribution more equal.[145] Like the *Solemne Engagement*, the *Declaration* was all but certainly drafted by Henry Ireton, Commissary-General of horse, member of Parliament, and son-in-law of Oliver Cromwell. Senior officers, like their subordinates, had concluded that the army would have a voice in the settlement of the state.

Walwyn, close to Cromwell and city Independents since late May, wrote that "very good Friends we were all; and I was by very eminent persons of the Army, sent for to Reading, to be advised withall touching the good of the people."[146] Army headquarters moved to Reading on 3 July and it is probable that Walwyn was there well before the meetings of the General Council on 16 and 17 July. In addition to such "eminent persons" as Cromwell and Ireton, Walwyn must have seen the agitators at Reading. On 6 July the agitators presented Lord General Fairfax with a paper protesting the imprisonments of Lilburne, Overton, and Nicholas Tew, who had been jailed in March because of his association with the Large Petition. A second paper protested the disposition of the London militia, and John Wildman made his first recorded appearance with his presentation of a similar protest from "the well affected of London" on or about the same day.[147]

Leveller influence was underlined as soon as the General Council assembled on 16 July. The agitators immediately submitted a "Representation" that demanded a march to London unless Parliament disabled eleven members impeached by the army, placed all forces under Fairfax, paid army arrears, and released and indemnified all illegally held prisoners. The prisoners specifically named included Lilburne, Richard Overton's wife and brother, the Leveller printer William Larner, and Nicholas Tew. Strong speeches in support of the "Representation" were made by Major Alexander Tulidah, jailed in March for advancing the Large Petition, and by Lieutenant Edmund Chillenden and William Allen, agitators associated with Baptist congregations in London. The next day, after Ireton submitted *The Heads of the Proposals*—an outline of the plans of the army commanders and their Independent allies for the settlement of the kingdom—Allen observed that it was work that "wee all expect to have a share in, and desire that others may alsoe."[148] It was an attitude that Walwyn would have approved and may have encouraged.

Walwyn's shaky accord with City Independents collapsed in mid-August. The army entered London on the 6th, escorting the Speakers and Independent members who had fled to the army during the counter-revolution of the High Presbyterians and Peace Party men in London. Fairfax established new headquarters in Kingston, whither Walwyn journeyed with allies from London, Southwark, and adjacent places to urge Fairfax to put the Tower under the charge of London "Citizens" rather than a new regiment. Independent leaders urged otherwise, and given the situation in the City in the summer of 1647, Fairfax wisely came down on the side of the beleaguered Independents. Harsh attacks on Walwyn's character again circulated in Lon-

don and there was "a great falling out" amongst Levellers and Independents—a falling out, wrote Lilburne subsequently, that extended
to "the grand Officers" who had failed to bring about the release
of imprisoned Levellers.[149] Certainly Walwyn did not thereafter record any meetings with "eminent" army persons, although unlike
Lilburne and Overton he never published personal attacks on the
generals.

By late September some regiments evinced increasing disapproval
of Cromwell's and Ireton's continued traffic with the King and growing dismay at their generals' inability to secure more than piecemeal
responses to army grievances.[150] Levellers, perceiving opportunity,
moved forward. Although Lilburne first proposed naming new agitators,[151] it is probable that John Wildman and the Leveller agitator
Edward Sexby arranged the selection and persuaded the new agents
to advance the Leveller program presented to Fairfax on 18 October.
The Case of the Armie Truly Stated, published over the names of self-
styled "Agents of five Regiments of Horse," was primarily the work of
Wildman. Condemnation of the failure to secure the army's demands
was followed by a restatement of the soldiers' grievances and new
demands for the dissolution of the present Parliament and the establishment of an unalterable "law paramount" ensuring biennial Parliaments elected by manhood suffrage. Old agitators from the five regiments disclaimed *The Case* and discounted its adherents as "a small
party," but the General Council agreed that it should be discussed at a
Council meeting on 28 October.[152] Walwyn is unlikely to have played
any part in the selection of the new agents or the drafting of *The Case*.
The constitutional proposals in the pamphlet accord with his views
but the slashing argument in the first sixteen pages is contrary to his
approach and the use of irregular agents was a divisive and dangerous tactic alien to Walwyn's convictions and conduct.

Walwyn must, however, have participated in preparations for the
debates that began in Putney Church on 28 October. The tone of the
Leveller speakers is very different from the tone of *The Case*, and Walwyn's influence if not his hand is discernible in the agents' reply to
the Council of the Army's objections to *The Case*. Much of the language is too overblown to be Walwyn's, but the conclusion denies any
thought of dividing the army and urges a return to "first principles"
wherein all engaged not to divide "untill the common rights of the
souldiery & people were setled." The paragraph has a quiet appeal
and a trust that "the all-seeing God will beare witnesse to the simplicity of our intentions"[153] that reflect Walwyn's expressed beliefs.

Walwyn's influence is also evident in the *Agreement of the People* that replaced Wildman's militant *Case* as the central document during the debates.[154] The *Agreement*'s proposals for regular and reapportioned Parliaments concurred with *The Heads of the Proposals,* and the "native Rights" beyond Parliament's power to infringe were common to the Levellers by 1647. Still, content as well as style indicate that Walwyn had more than a little to do with the drafting. Inflammatory demands such as manhood suffrage were avoided and the language is at once temperate and eloquent. Walwyn had edged toward a "bill of rights" two years before, writing that men must learn "what the Parliament may doe, and what the Parliament (itselfe) may not doe."[155] In the *Agreement*'s list of things that the Parliament may not do, the restriction forbidding interference with anyone's religion "because therein wee cannot remit or exceed a tittle of what our Consciences dictate to be the mind of God, without wilfull sinne" is an echo of Walwyn's repeated insistence that "to compell me therefore against my conscience, is to compell me to doe that which is sinfull."[156] Content, style, and the anonymity of the *Agreement* are all characteristic of Walwyn—and it would have been like him to believe that a proposal as rational as the *Agreement* could gain the support of fair-minded men in search of a settlement.

Spokesmen for the Levellers included Colonel Thomas Rainsborough, the agitator Edward Sexby, and two civilians, Maximilian Petty and Wildman. Wildman described himself as the "mouth" of the new agents. The *Agreement* said nothing about the franchise, but perhaps because Wildman was the principal Leveller spokesman and was regarded as the author of *The Case of the Armie*—which had demanded manhood suffrage—Ireton concluded that the article on reapportionment implied an inclusive suffrage. Levellers contended that voting was a birthright, although it was evident that they did not entirely agree about which people had forfeited their birthright. Ireton repeatedly reverted to property rights and those who had a "fixed interest" in the kingdom. Cromwell, who presided, agreed with Ireton and stated that the result, if not the intention, of a greatly extended franchise would be anarchy. Leveller agitators claimed that on 5 November they secured agreement for a general rendezvous of all regiments. This is unlikely, but however conciliatory the generals may have appeared on the 5th, three days later they confronted the Levellers and carried Cromwell's proposal to send officers and agitators back to their regiments.[157]

Attempts to force adoption of the *Agreement* by a mutiny during the first of three scheduled rendezvous were a dismal failure. At the meeting of nine regiments near Ware on 15 November the insurgents were easily quelled by firm commanders and the manifest loyalty of seven of the regiments. Two subsequent rendezvous were untroubled, and all the regiments subscribed to a new *Remonstrance* that condemned the new agents' actions and secured a pledge of obedience to Fairfax and his commanders, who promised that they would "live and die with the army" to secure redress of the soldiers' professional grievances and would strive for the earliest safe dissolution of the present Parliament and the election of more representative Parliaments at fixed intervals.[158]

There is no indication that Walwyn had anything to do with plans for the mutiny, which was evidently the brainchild of Lilburne, Wildman, and a few militant associates. Lilburne had been released from custody on 9 November and was waiting at Ware when the regiments gathered at Corkbush Field. He never appeared among the troops and slipped quietly back to London at the end of the day.[159] The failure of the mutiny was at once a clear indication of the limited influence of the Levellers among the rank and file of the army and a crucial victory for Fairfax and a united army. A month later the King signed the Engagement with the Scots and the second Civil War soon followed. Had the army been split in mid-November it would have proved disastrous for all revolutionaries.

Any hope Walwyn harbored that equity and "right reason" would persuade a united army to advance a constitution securing the rights and liberties of all the people proved as illusory as the belief of Lilburne and Wildman that attacks on Cromwell and Ireton would persuade the rank and file to "create new officers" who would bring justice and freedom "to all sorts of peaceable people."[160] After the failed mutiny Leveller influence in the regiments faded rapidly. It is unlikely that their ideology ever permeated the ranks to a significant extent. It was too complex for private soldiers whose material grievances could most effectively be alleviated by the pressure of their commanders on Parliament. Junior officers, on the other hand, absorbed much of the Leveller doctrine—as would be apparent during the debates on the second Agreement in December 1648.

With the collapse of the Ware mutiny Leveller leaders returned to their London constituents and to the employment of petitions signed and presented by multitudes. On 23 November a brief petition "To the Supream Authority" asked the Commons—who had condemned the *Agreement* as destructive to the kingdom—to review it "impartially" and by ratification deliver the people from tyranny and oppression.[161] The public appeal appended when the petition was published carries the tone of Lilburne, and although the petition itself is quieter, Walwyn's direct influence is less likely than his participation in the November campaign to secure thousands of signatures in support of the *Agreement*—which became a propaganda device rather than an end in itself.

There is no record of Walwyn's activities during the winter of 1647–48, although by the turn of the year the party structure adumbrated during his petitioning campaign the previous spring was revealed. There can be little doubt that Walwyn continued to play a major role in the management of an organization that had most of the elements of a modern political party: leadership; a program; a central committee; local chapters with weekly subscriptions collected from the members; agents to secure signatures to petitions and distribute pamphlets.[162] Lilburne and Wildman, provocative and deliberately visible, were imprisoned in January for promotion of a peremptory petition to the Commons and they remained in jail until the following August. Walwyn escaped any notice. His name was not mentioned in contemporary accounts of Leveller activities and he apparently published nothing during the first seven months of 1648, although the blasphemy and heresy ordinance passed on 2 May defined errors and prescribed penalties—including death—that were a natural target for Walwyn's pen.[163]

The second Civil War, which had begun in the spring with Royalist risings in Wales, roused Walwyn to ill-considered anger against Parliament and senior army officers. In August *The Bloody Project* revealed his temper in its title and advanced from the premise that the war was the "causelesse" promotion of "Grandee Factions" to a denunciation of the deaths of thousands who had never been told the goals for which they fought. Parliament had not only been less than specific about "the Libertyes of the People" but had betrayed basic rights anticipated by the foot soldiers: a representative and supreme legislature; religious freedom; reformed justice; relief from unfair taxes and tithes. Only the "great ones" found war an advantage; the only quarrel thus far had been "whose slaves the people shall be." There could be no project more bloody, concludes Walwyn in a brief Postscript, "then to engage men to kill one another, and yet no just cause declared." If the peace of the nation could not be secured without the King, let him return speedily with his power "declared and limited by Law." If the present Parliament could not secure the peace,

let a new Parliament be called with its power declared and limited.[164]
The Postscript not only foreshadowed the postwar Leveller program
but presented a solution to the monarchy that would be realized before the end of the century. It was a pragmatic coda to a tract that was
largely negative—and less than fair in its untempered condemnation
of those resisting insurgent Royalists in a war that neither Parliament
nor army had instigated or desired. As the short, bitter conflict
ground on through the summer, officers and men became increasingly angry as they struggled to hold London against the Cavaliers
and prepared for a Scottish invasion in the North.[165] Walwyn neither
commented on their difficulties nor appeared to consider what the
position of the Levellers would be if Parliament and the army had
failed to take up arms or were defeated by the Royalists in the field.

By the end of August definitive victories of Parliament's forces at
Preston and Colchester cleared the way for a new settlement of the
state. The Levellers moved forward, and although Walwyn denied
playing a major role in the preparation of the Leveller petition of 11
September, he praised its particulars and the mild style suggests the
Walwyn of 1647. Like the Large Petition—which was reissued on 19
September 1648—the petition of 11 September demanded far-reach-
ing reforms in conciliatory language. Rejecting any treaty with the
King, the petitioners demanded religious freedom, equal justice, and
an end to oppressive taxes and tithes, but, unlike the 1647 *Agreement*,
the petition said nothing about native rights or a paramount law restricting the magistrate and nothing that implied a drastic reform of
the franchise.[166] Levellers were no less committed to these concepts.
They had apparently concluded—for the moment, at least—that a
less peremptory approach would better serve their purpose.

The ensuing weeks exposed crucial divisions among the Round-
heads. Within the Parliament, the majority supported new negotiations with the defeated King. More radical revolutionaries included
five identifiable factions: incipient Commonwealthsmen who held a
small power base in the Commons and desired the abolition of king-
ship and the establishment of a legislative republic; embittered army
officers paced by Henry Ireton; the Levellers; self-styled Saints in the
army and separate churches who rejected earthly monarchy and en-
visaged a theocracy governed by godly men; City Independents who
again were moving leftward. It is possible that Ireton, who had long
since abandoned his support of King Charles, encouraged Cromwell, who was in the North, to instigate the London meetings that

took place between leading Levellers and City Independents in November.[167]

Levellers were the constructive leaders in the series of conferences that produced the draft constitution submitted to the Council of Officers in December. Proposals presented at Putney had matured into a comprehensive plan of government, and Leveller leaders advanced their constitution with confidence. They also had a clear concept of the most desirable sequence of events. Levellers had long urged the abolition of monarchy and the dissolution of the existing Parliament. They wished, however, to retain King and Parliament as a "balancing power" against the army until a new constitution was in place.[168]

Stormy meetings in London in mid-November persuaded "Gentlemen Independents" to accept Lilburne's proposal that four Levellers and four Independents work together to produce "some Heads" for an Agreement of the People. Walwyn was one of the four Levellers, but his sometime ally, John Price, refused to meet with him. Lilburne protested, and ultimately Price and Walwyn both withdrew. The remaining committee of six met on 15 November at the Nag's Head and agreed that the date of Parliament's dissolution ought to be part of an Agreement "above Law" that would be drawn up by representatives from the army and "the well affected" in every county. By the end of the month, recognizing that nothing could stop the army's imminent march to London to prevent the King and Parliament from concluding a treaty, Lilburne scrapped his plan for a country-wide constitutional assembly and secured Ireton's acceptance of the Leveller proposal for an Agreement drawn up by a committee composed of four men from each of four radical factions: the Council of Officers; the City Independents; the "honest men" in the House; and those "nick-named Levellers." Walwyn, Wildman, Petty, and Lilburne were selected by the Levellers and proceeded to Windsor where all sides met at the Castle. Henry Marten and the four Levellers withdrew to prepare a working draft of the constitution while the army moved to purge the Parliament—which journey, wrote Lilburne, "was very much opposed by M. Walwyn, and many reasons he gave against their march to London at all."[169] Neither Walwyn nor Lilburne revealed how they would have dealt with the Parliamentary majority poised to surrender much that they had fought for in order to conclude a treaty with the King.

During the first ten days in December, amid the army's march into London and Colonel Pride's purge of the Parliament, the committee met at Whitehall and considered the Leveller draft. Ireton led the officers' delegation, and after long and difficult arguments, "sometimes whole nights together, Principally about Liberty of Conscience, and the Parliaments punishing where no law provides," Lilburne believed that consensus was reached among the committeemen.[170] The completed draft: set a date for dissolution of the present House; prescribed biennial Parliaments and a Council of State whose members were debarred from the next Parliament; extended the franchise to adult, male householders who paid poor relief and subscribed to the Agreement; reapportioned the seats in the House. The core of the document is the section reserving eight explicit rights to the people. The Representative (as Parliaments again were styled) was forbidden to: (1) interfere with the religious practice of "any persons professing Christianity"; (2) impress for service in war; (3) call any person to account for actions during the late wars, except for Royalists designated by the present House and persons accountable for public money; (4 and 5) enact or continue any law or privilege that did not apply equally to all persons; (6) interfere with the execution of declared law; (7) name its members to lucrative office; (8) "take away, any of the foundations of Common right, liberty, or safety contained in this Agreement."[171]

The draft was submitted to the Council of Officers on 11 December and during the ensuing five weeks the Council spent many hours considering and altering the proposed constitution. Lilburne, Overton, and Wildman spoke during the first debate on the religious reserve (14 December), and Walwyn and Wildman are recorded as present on the 18th.[172] No Levellers are known to have been in attendance thereafter, and Lilburne published his version of the committee text on 15 December. The officers' text was submitted to the Commons on 20 January.[173] The advantages and disadvantages of the officers' alterations are arguable, but Lilburne considered them highly "dis-satisfactory" and bitterly denounced Ireton for permitting the officers to alter the committee draft at all.[174]

The attendance of Walwyn and Wildman at at least one meeting of the Council of Officers after Lilburne withdrew and published his text of the Agreement suggests a sharp difference of opinion within the Leveller leadership. Walwyn had nothing to do with the only petitions prepared in December and January,[175] and after the 19 January appeal a rare silence afflicted all Levellers. They mounted no campaign in support of the Agreement published by Lilburne, and the great events of late January and early February—the trial and execution of the King, the establishment of a republican Commonwealth—excited no Leveller comment. Lilburne subsequently stated that he had been so disheartened by the actions of the purged Parliament that he resolved to abandon the struggle and remain at home, "in solitarinesse there to abide."[176] Lilburne's retirement was exceedingly brief. On 26 February he led yet another delegation to the bar of the House with the petition published as *Englands New Chains Discovered*. It was the opening shot in the Levellers' last campaign to enlist the soldiers under their banner.

Walwyn played no part in Leveller activities from mid-December through the month of March. On 28 March the government responded to the publication of *The Second Part of Englands New-Chaines* by arresting Lilburne, Overton, Thomas Prince, and Walwyn. Lilburne was astonished that Walwyn was among them. Having understood, he wrote, that they were seized because of the new petition, "we could not but wonder at the apprehending of M. Walwin about that, he having for some months past (that ever I could see, or hear of) never bin at any of our meetings, where any such things were managed."[177]

Walwyn's withdrawal is explicable. He was fundamentally optimistic, believed in the power of reason and persuasion, and frequently revealed an inclination toward compromise. He had signed the *Solemn League and Covenant*, he never expressed the hostility toward Cromwell and Ireton that colored many of Lilburne's writings, and his attendance at the Council of Officers after Lilburne published his version of the Agreement suggests an open-minded approach to an agreed constitution. Support for this view may be found in Walwyn's subsequent observation that, despite its shortcomings, if the officers' Agreement had "been put in execution, we should scarcely have interrupted the proceedings thereof, since therein is contained many things of great and important concernment to the Commonwealth."[178]

Walwyn may also have suspected that the army's promise of toleration for peaceable Christians (excepting Papists and Prelatists)[179] would persuade sectaries to join City Independents in support of the new regime. If Walwyn's perception was this acute he could have concluded that he would best serve his cause by exposing the extremism of the wilder sectaries and the pretensions of Independent clerics who appeared to be gaining power in the new republic. Within a month of the establishment of the Commonwealth, Walwyn published *The Vanitie of the Present Churches*. The tract rejects "mock

Churches" as guardians of morality in the state, censures mystics
who replaced Scripture with "the spirit," and harshly attacks Independents for their narrow tolerance and their lack of social concern,
"true piety or reall Christian vertue." The sweeping severity of the
condemnation is scarcely mitigated by a conclusion that, free from
"Church-bondage," all will become loving Christians as they discover
God within themselves.[180]

Walwyn ultimately concluded that his arrest—less than three
weeks after the publication of *Vanitie*—had been incited by his adversaries in John Goodwin's congregation.[181] Imprisonment was a severe
shock to Walwyn. Unlike his fellow prisoners he had experienced neither prison nor army service—had never known so much as "a minutes restraint by any Authority." Maintaining the low profile of a man
who abhorred public confrontation, he had so ordered his political
activities that his family life had been quite undisturbed. The pre-
dawn invasion of house and garden by a party of soldiers threw his
family into a panic, although Walwyn himself reacted with dignity
and asked the commanding officer to subdue the soldiers, in order
that Walwyn might "preserve my credit (a thing sooner bruised than
made whole)."[182] The careful merchant was never far from the radical
revolutionary.

The imprisonment of the Leveller leaders hastened the disintegration of their movement. Their encouragement of mutiny in the army
had prompted their seizure, and while agitation in the regiments did
not immediately cease it had only a few weeks to run. As always, the
soldiers' primary grievances were material. Pressed by senior officers,
the Rump improved pay and payment of arrears,[183] and Leveller influence in the regiments all but vanished with the defeat of a mutiny
at Burford in mid-May. Walwyn had played no part in Leveller efforts
to incite the lower ranks to mutiny, and while it is probable that
prison and reunion with old allies deepened his understanding of
their denunciations of the Commonwealth and the "great Officers"
who supported it, his subsequent writings and actions reveal that he
never lost his gentle tolerance or his faith in the power of reasonable
appeal. Walwyn would have concurred with the opposition to the
Irish invasion and the emphasis on individual responsibility that run
through *The English Souldiers Standard*, but its encouragement to mutiny and the intemperance of the language belie suggestions that it is
his work.[184]

The party's London organization—in disarray since December—
collapsed within days of the leaders' arrest. The withdrawal of Wal-

wyn and Wildman had weakened the secular wing of the party and the silence of Lilburne and Overton during the crucial events of January and February had left their sectarian supporters adrift. They drifted toward the new government. Two or three days after their arrest, Lilburne, Overton, Prince, and Walwyn were visited in the Tower by Samuel Richardson, pastor of a Particular Baptist congregation. Stating that the Levellers were widely regarded as "grand disturbers . . . that would center no where, but meerly laboured to pul down those in power," Richardson urged the leaders to abandon their attacks on the Commonwealth. They refused, unless the government agreed to all their principles.[185] The Baptists' response was swift and definitive. On 2 April William Kiffin led a deputation of Baptist pastors to Parliament with a petition that repudiated *The Second Part of Englands New-Chaines Discovered*, denied any intent to "intermeddle with the ordering or altering Civil Government," and urged Parliament to take effective action against loose-living men who provoked God's wrath against the realm.[186]

Lilburne and Overton replied with characteristic asperity.[187] Walwyn, although he believed the petition had been designed "to rivet us in,"[188] prepared *A Manifestation* signed by the four prisoners which calmly and sadly remarked the desertion of "such as we took for Friends, our brethren of severall Churches; and for whom with truth of affection we have even in the most difficult times done many Services." The prisoners denied any association with Royalist agents, atheists, Jesuits, or men who sought "Levelling . . . an equalling of mens estates." They sought only the welfare of the people, and to secure an end to "Burdens and Grievances" they promised a revised version of the Agreement of the People.[189] The final *Agreement*, like *A Manifestation*, was signed by Lilburne, Walwyn, Prince, and Overton. Only the opening "Preparative to all sorts of people" bears unmistakable marks of Walwyn's style. The constitution itself is the conjoint work of men more concerned with restraints on the state than with the structure of government. It postulates an all but powerless executive, a severely restricted legislature, and a vast transfer of power from the central government to the local communities with popular election of all administrative, judicial, and religious officials—and all military officers except general officers.[190] It is less a constitution for a nation than a manifesto of utopian individualists who no longer had any reason to equivocate.

The prisoners were not without friends, but the desertion of the Baptists was a severe blow. Petitions reportedly signed by thousands

asked for fair trials and release, "but the seven Churches," wrote Walwyn, "were got before them, and had so much respect, that our
Friends found none at all."[191] The position of the separatists was underlined with the publication of *Walwins Wiles* in late April.[192] The
principal if not the sole author was John Price, the lay preacher in
Goodwin's church who had begun collecting disparaging information
about Walwyn in 1646.[193] Independents had long been uncertain allies, but the seven men who subscribed the tract included William
Kiffin and Edmund Rosier, lay pastor of Lilburne's separatist church.
Having broken with the Levellers, separatists joined the move to destroy them.

   Walwins Wiles ignores Overton, dismisses Lilburne and Prince as
"simple-headed" dupes, and concentrates its fire on Walwyn as the
wily leader who corrupted honest men in a movement designed to
destroy "the Interest of England." In addition to vicious attacks on his
character, conduct, and "Atheisticall" principles, the tract denounces
his social objectives and his attitude toward Ireland. He had, wrote
Price, diligently fomented "consideration of the disproportion and
inequality of the distribution of the things of this life" and wished to
so alter the economic course of the nation that a few "valiant spirits
may turn the world upside down." More specifically, the accusation
states that, when "discoursing of the inequality and . . . conditions
of men," Walwyn contended that "it would never be well untill all
things were common." As for Ireland, Walwyn is accused of sympathy for Irish Catholics in his condemnation of an Irish invasion as
unlawful, "cruel and bloody work to go to destroy the Irish Natives
for their Consciences . . . and to drive them from their proper natural
and native Rights."[194]

   Three pamphlets were published in Walwyn's defense. The first, by
his son-in-law Humphrey Brooke, concentrates on the goodness of
Walwyn's way of life and the "Christian fortitude" with which he
endured the slanderous attacks of lesser men.[195] Two days later, on 30
May, Walwyn published *The Fountain of Slaunder Discovered*. Largely
drafted before the appearance of *Walwins Wiles*, *Fountain* is primarily a
defense of Walwyn's life style and morality and an account of his arrest and imprisonment. The concluding pages explain that publication has been prompted by "the corrupt Fountain of Slander, . . . a
foggy mist of lies, invectives and slanders" perpetrated by the authors
of *Walwins Wiles*.[196]

   Within little more than a month Walwyn completed a direct response to Price's charges. A long, self-justifying tract, *Walwyns Just De-*

fence recounts the vacillation of Independent leaders during their intermittent accords with the Levellers since 1646, contrasting it with the conduct of the Levellers whose steady pursuit of a fair Commonwealth led to honorable imprisonment while Independents remain at liberty by bending to the political winds. Independents, wrote Walwyn, published a *Declaration* in the autumn of 1647 in order to make him "odious" by "vindicating your selves in those things whereof no man suspected you"—anarchy, equalization of property, and polygamy—"in a time when you had freshly & falsely asperst us, to be opposite to you in all these." Attacks in *Walwins Wiles* on his immorality and irreligion are refuted in great detail as Walwyn proclaims himself a man of extraordinary "plainnesse and openheartednesse" who commands none of the political arts and wiles described by his adversaries.[197]

Walwyn's manifest integrity and commitment to justice and fair dealing leave no room for the monster described in *Walwins Wiles*. At the same time, his portrayal of himself as an ingenuous innocent is less than convincing, unsupported by his writings or his known activities. He was, as he contended, a man who believed in absolute toleration and the power of reason to secure his ideals. He was, as Humphrey Brooke stated, a good and gentle man who treasured his quiet family life yet was compelled by his conscience to work for the liberties of all men. He was also a shrewd politician who, as draftsman, organizer, and fomenter of action, for many months kept a small, visionary faction in the vanguard of revolutionary movement.

Independents knew and feared Walwyn's political abilities and they were more right than wrong about aspects of his program. He made no comment at all about Price's accusation that he opposed invasion of Ireland and he probably concurred with the condemnation of invasion in *The English Souldiers Standard*. His reply to the charge of desiring to make "all things . . . common" is at best incomplete. "In so fruitful a land," countered Walwyn, government should provide that those who work should eat, "but for my turning the world upside down, . . . it's not a work I ever intended, as all my actions, and the Agreement of the People, do sufficiently evince."[198] Still, while Walwyn co-signed an Agreement that forbade levelling by "any Representative" and all but destroyed the central government, he never denied that his ideal was economic as well as political and legal equality, and the passages in *Walwins Wiles* reporting his conversations on the subject have the rhythm of his phrasing and the temper of his discourse. It is possible to argue that the comments reflect no more than an intellectual ideal inspired by admiration for the communal spirit of early Christianity and the innocence of primitive tribes. It is not possible to conclude that the reports had no basis in fact.

Evidence that Walwyn looked favorably on a more equitable distribution of wealth may be found in his writings. As early as 1643 *The Power of Love* extolled the sharing practiced by early Christians when "the multitude of beleevers had all things common."[199] In 1649 *A Manifestation,* even as it denied any intent of "equalling of mens estates," noted that it would be injurious "unlesse there did precede an universall assent thereunto."[200] Walwyn wrote more urgently than other Leveller penmen of "one main end of Government, to provide, that those who refuse not labour, should eat comfortably," and he did not join Lilburne's repudiation of the avowed communism of Gerrard Winstanley and his "True Levellers."[201] On the other hand, there is no evidence that Walwyn gave Winstanley any support, and in 1652 "W Walwins Conceptions; For a free Trade" delineates the essence of capitalism in arguing for open competition in a free market.[202] It is possible that he assisted a communal plan projected by Peter Cornelius Plockhoy in 1659, but the evidence is tenuous and Walwyn made no direct statement on the subject after the appearance of *A Manifestation* in the spring of 1649.

By the time the four Levellers were released on 8 November the party they had created was shattered. Old allies in the separate churches were supporting the new republic and many social and economic reformers were attracted to the "True Levellers" led by Winstanley. Walwyn wrote of economic equality, Overton demanded the return of enclosed land to the community, and the harsh effect of indirect taxes and tithes on the very poor was frequently deplored.[203] No plans, however, were advanced to alleviate the lot of laborers and wage earners. By and large, Leveller economic proposals to end customs and excise taxes, monopolies in foreign trade, and restrictions on independent tradesmen and craftsmen were addressed to "men of middle quality" who were urban, literate, politically aware—and soon recognized the futility of following men who refused realistic compromises with well-intentioned revolutionaries in the power centers: the army, the City, the Parliament.

The brevity of the Levellers' tenure as political activists cannot detract from the importance of their proposals for genuinely representative government and the protection of enumerated native rights. These proposals had a positive impact during the political uncertainties of

1647 and 1648. Some of the legal and electoral reforms advanced by the Levellers influenced legislation in the 1650s. Their economic demands were reiterated by reformers throughout the Interregnum. At the same time, the rapid decline of their movement when the Commonwealth was established reveals that Levellers had a tenuous hold on much of their following, while the ease with which the Leveller program was displaced by demands for godly government indicates that the Levellers' deepest messages reached a smaller audience than their abundant propaganda suggests.

5. Interregnum and Restoration

The decade that began with the republican Commonwealth and closed with the return of the King witnessed six changes of government. Political conspiracies harassed every administration, and individual Levellers were involved in most of them—from Royalist plots to restore the King to Fifth Monarchy intrigues to destroy secular government and prepare for Christ's kingdom on earth. As a party, Levellers never regained their cohesion, and after the Restoration the name itself passed into limbo.

Walwyn, forty-nine years old when he left prison, returned to Moorfields and the way of life that had been interrupted by seven months in the Tower. He had taken the Engagement to be loyal to the Commonwealth when he was released from custody[204] and resumed his trade as a merchant. He did not abandon his concerns for toleration and equal justice, but there is no evidence that he again associated with political dissidents and the only policy pamphlet he published includes an expression of confidence in the parliamentary republic.

In December 1651 Walwyn broke "a silence . . . equal to his that was born and continued dumb, till his father was in danger of being murthered." *Juries Justified* was provoked by Henry Robinson's proposal that juries be replaced in small jurisdictions by judges appointed by Parliament. The proposal was directly contrary to the Levellers' 1649 Agreement, which required judgment "onely by twelve sworn men of the Neighbor-hood; to be chosen in some free way by the people." *Juries Justified* is a masterful defense of this "fundamental essential liberty." Robinson's "seven Objections" are refuted one by one as Walwyn staunchly upholds the willingness of freeborn Englishmen to serve and their ability to judge fairly. He concludes that his observations probably are unnecessary "for certainly Juries cannot in time of Parliament be in any danger."[205]

Five months later Walwyn came forward in defense of free trade. It was a basic Leveller tenet, and if it was some distance from freedom of religion in Walwyn's roster of reforms, it is notable that during a controversy between free traders and the Levant Company commercial freedom was championed by a successful merchant who owed much of his prosperity to membership in a monopolistic company. But where reason led, Walwyn followed: freedom to trade was one of man's natural rights. In May 1652 Walwyn presented the Committee for Trade and Foreign Affairs with a well-stated argument for the abolition of all monopolies and trading restrictions. Free trade, he contended, is a common right conducive to the common good. It might not immediately "produce so many wealthy men, as have been in the same time by Companies, . . . yet it will produce Thousands more of able men to beare publique Charges or what other Publique occasions they may be called unto." The company presented an effective defense, which concluded with specific replies to Walwyn's paper. The government, as in other disputes between monopolies and free traders, came down in favor of the company.[206] Nevertheless, the committee's consideration of Walwyn's arguments supports a judgment that he neither took nor was suspected of taking any action hostile to the Commonwealth.

During the uncertain months between the destruction of the Commonwealth and the establishment of Cromwell's Protectorate the interim Council of State ordered Walwyn committed to prison. The summer of 1653 was filled with real and imagined conspiracies and the authorities were exceedingly apprehensive. Lilburne, banished on pain of death in 1651/2, returned to England in June 1653, two months after the eviction of the Rump. He published an open letter to Cromwell from "my present Lodging in little Moor-fields," but there is no hint that he saw Walwyn there. Lilburne was jailed less than thirty-six hours after he reached England, and tracts, petitions, and deputations protesting his imprisonment again became the order of the day.[207] By August frenetic millenarians in Barebone's Parliament heightened doubts about the government's stability. Suspects of every shade were rounded up, and fears of a Royalist-Leveller alliance reached a peak during the mob scenes surrounding Lilburne's trial. On 20 August Lilburne was acquitted "of any crime worthy of death"—and on 27 August he was sent to the Tower "for the peace of this Nation." Two

days later the Council of State issued an order "to commit Wm. Walwyn prisoner in the Tower."[208] Walwyn, unlike Overton and Prince,
was not among those recorded as attending Lilburne in jail or at his
trial, but Independents who dominated the Council of State had long
been fearful of Walwyn. There is no record of his arrival at the Tower
and no record of his release. While it is possible that Walwyn was in
custody until Cromwell's more confident Protectorate assumed power
in December, it is more probable that the order was never executed.
There is no hint that Walwyn had any other brush with officials.

In 1658, a few months before Cromwell's death, an idealistic
Dutchman, Peter Cornelius Plockhoy, came to England to organize a
cooperative commune in which the idle poor could work and put an
end to their poverty. Plockhoy was given a courteous hearing by the
Council of State but received no practical encouragement. After
Cromwell's death Plockhoy published a tract that included letters to
Cromwell, Parliament, and Richard Cromwell. A second tract, *A Way
Propounded*, is more revealing of Plockhoy's philosophy. Like Winstanley, he believed the law of nature entitled all persons to a means of
subsistence and considered private property a root cause of poverty and corruption. He outlined plans for communal living, cooperative farming, and social services provided by the state.[209] In 1948
Wilhelm Schenk noted that Plockhoy's basic ideas and English style
were very close to Walwyn's. Both men found the heart of Christianity in "brotherly love and unitie" and linked a true Christian life
with the simplicity described in primitive lands. Both were outspoken
opponents of intolerance and injustice. Both believed in the power of
reason to persuade. Inferring that it is unlikely that Plockhoy wrote
his English pamphlets unaided, Schenk concluded that he may have
been helped by Walwyn.[210] In 1952 Leland and Marvin Harder reprinted Plockhoy's tracts and noted that the Appendix to *A Way Propounded* included "W.W." as the donor of £20 in a list of seven London
contributors to Plockhoy's project.[211] Walwyn's connection to
Plockhoy is unproved, but it is a plausible theory—and if he contributed £20 he was still prospering as the Interregnum neared its end.

James Harrington's Rota Club, which met at the Turk's Head in the
autumn of 1659, would have been a natural milieu for Walwyn's discourse, but there is no suggestion that he ever attended. Nor can he
be linked with the Rota's predecessor, a club that assembled at John
Wildman's Nonsuch House in Bow Street. In June 1659 the Nonsuch
group published a broadsheet listing more than a hundred persons to
be added to a committee appointed by the House to consider Har-

rington's proposals for settling the government. "Mr. Walwin" is included in the list, but it is such an unlikely assortment of names that it cannot be taken seriously.[212]

Walwyn's name was last mentioned in a political context during the anarchy that preceded the Restoration. Captain William Bray, a steady Leveller who had been jailed at least three times between 1647 and 1655, produced two of the few Leveller tracts that appeared during the chaotic winter of 1659–60. *A Plea for the Peoples Fundamental Liberties and Parliaments,* drafted during the weeks of army rule in the autumn, condemned the interruption of the Parliament and included Walwyn among those who championed free Parliaments bound to comply with "the Fundamentall Lawes and Liberties of the Nation."[213]

The return of King Charles II confirmed the extinction of the Leveller movement. The Act of Indemnity and Oblivion was practical and purposeful, excepting only regicides and twenty additional men considered dangerous to the state. No Leveller had supported the trial of Charles I; nor was any Leveller considered for inclusion among the twenty who were not regicides.[214] Ultimately, Leveller ideology would become a vital part of the liberal canon. Neither unrestricted toleration nor constitutional democracy had any constituency in Restoration England.

6. Medical Practitioner

Some years before the Restoration, Walwyn became a medical practitioner. The precise date of this change in occupation is not known, but he was making and dispensing medications by 1654, when he wrote that he had been studying things appertaining to health "for many years."[215] The abandonment of his trade as a silk merchant may not have been his decision. As a member of the Merchant Adventurers he had taken an oath of loyalty to a company that enjoyed privileges of monopoly, yet the dissolution of the Merchant Adventurers was advocated in the 1646/7 Large Petition that Walwyn not only praised but declined to repudiate as his work. He repeatedly joined Leveller attacks on monopolies in general, and in 1652 he carried the banner of free trade before the Council of State's committee. If Walwyn had not already retired from the Adventurers it is unlikely that the company would have overlooked this public attack on a monopoly akin to its own. Whatever the reasons for Walwyn's move into medicine, he continued to prosper,[216] and his first medical treatise states that he had never taken "so much satisfaction in minde, in any thing wherein I ever exercised my self, (next the things of everlasting concernment) as I have done in this employment."[217]

Walwyn was peculiarly qualified for the role of lay physician. His medical judgment was grounded in his philosophy of love and his natural humanity assisted the thoughtful intelligence with which he considered the needs of the sick. The writings reveal his wide reading in medical texts as well as his bold advocacy of new ideas. Unimpressed by tradition and convention, he condemned practices which would not be discarded for more than a century. In medicine, as in religion, politics, and social justice, Walwyn was humane, imaginative, and enduringly hopeful of persuasion by reasonable argument.

Initially, Walwyn's medicines were dispensed from the Aldgate house of his son-in-law, Dr. Brooke, a professional physician who presumably gave Walwyn some technical guidance. Both men were concerned with prevention as well as cure, and Walwyn advises a sensible diet according to individual experience and recourse to a "conscionable Physitian" for physic in time of sickness.[218] Walwyn's first medical treatise, *Spirits Moderated*, reveals his temperate approach in the title. He used "Chymistry and Distillation" to combine and adapt spirits which are repeatedly described as "milde and pleasant."[219] Compassion, wrote Walwyn in *Physick for Families*, is essential for physicians. Nothing should be given to the sick that may not safely and profitably be taken by those in health, and such "molesters of the sick" as clysters, bleeding, purging, vomiting, sweating, and blistering ought to be "laid asleep forever." Physicians should be obliged to take as much opium as they prescribe, and occult elixirs are denounced as "vapouring Fancies." The sick, wrote Walwyn in a later edition of *Physick*, should be protected from "busie talkers" and "dejected visitants" and treated at all times with kindness, quietness, and hopefulness.[220]

By 1661 Walwyn was dispensing his medicines at the Star in the Postern Street joining little Moorfields,[221] and the potions were still advertised for sale in Moorfields after his death two decades later. During the great plague of 1665 he moved his family to temporary refuge in Sutton, Surrey, where they remained through the spring of 1666. Walwyn took care that his medicines continued to be available at the Star in the Postern Street during his absence, noting that he "had long declined Practice" and had published the uses and virtues of all his spirits.[222] The posthumous 1681 edition of *Physick* names Walwyn's son-in-law, Richard Halford of Finsbury, little Moorfields, as the dispenser of the medical recipes.[223]

Halford was named executor of Walwyn's estate in the will that Walwyn executed the same month that he died. Apparently, Walwyn had no financial difficulties at any time. He left bequests of £200 to one son-in-law and to three granddaughters. The will also reveals Walwyn's innate optimism and the joyous expectation of "Redemption by Christ." Looking beyond death, he asked "that no mourning be worne for me."[224] Walwyn had rejected both Calvin's predestination and the mortalism of Richard Overton, who contended that, as man is "wholy mortall," the belief that the soul goes immediately to Heaven or Hell is "a meer Fiction." The soul dies with the body and remains dead until the final resurrection, which, wrote Overton, "is the beginning of our immortallity, and then Actuall Condemnation and Salvation, and not before."[225] Walwyn, rejecting the remote judgment of the Last Day and irretrievable damnation at any time, believed that bodily death would be followed by a life of the spirit in the presence of a loving God.

All that we know of Walwyn denies his belief in an eternal Hell. His enemies charged that he rejected the concept absolutely, quoting alleged conversations in which he stated that Hell was within "an ill mans conscience in this life" and asked if it were possible to conceive "that God should cast a man into everlasting burnings . . . for a little time of sinning in this world?"[226] Humphrey Brooke attempted to refute the charge of unorthodoxy.[227] Walwyn himself did not deny it and his writings indirectly support it. Freed from the prevailing view of an angry God, as early as 1643 he stressed the universalist view that however sinful men may be they cannot frustrate God's all-conquering love or the salvation freely given to all men. No subsequent treatise modified this concept and Walwyn's last religious pamphlet, *The Vanitie of the Present Churches*, reiterated his belief that only reasonable and comforting Scripture was essential, that no doctrine should be irrational or absurd.[228] Walwyn did warn of social and national ruin and of individual degradation and disaster, especially for the misguided and oppressive. He believed in the Hell of societies and individuals who betrayed their fellows, their God, and their call to live in love—but he considered fear of eternal damnation contrary to the knowledge that Christ died that all men might be saved by God's love.[229] He did not believe in an angry God or a fiery Hell.

7. Perspective

Walwyn was a man of his revolutionary century who looked and pointed beyond it. He was actively involved in the great controversies of his time and nation, and as the Levellers led the agitation for democratic reform Walwyn led the Levellers in their progression from proponents of religious freedom to champions of all civil liberties and precursors of the movement for constitutional democracy. Rejecting reliance on existing and ancient English law, Walwyn asserted the universality of justice, the limited power of the people's representatives, and the need for a paramount law defining and restricting the powers of government. In their own time the Levellers witnessed no victories. Religious freedom and political democracy would be achieved in England in the ensuing centuries. Precepts delineated in the Leveller Agreements of the People would reappear in the Constitution of the United States. No connections can be established but the similarities are striking.

In religion, as in politics, Walwyn was a pioneer—although perhaps an unwitting one. He was active in the reformation of his parish church, yet he suspected that dogma, liturgy, and church ceremonies could impede true religion. He grounded his faith in Scripture, which led him to a loving, individualist Christianity manifested by concern for the welfare of the afflicted and oppressed. Many of his beliefs anticipated those of the emerging Society of Friends. From their stormy beginnings to the present, the Friends have been notable for their freedom from dogma, their compassion, and their social egalitarianism. The pacifism that became Quaker doctrine in the 1660s had been part of Walwyn's thinking more than a decade before, and the Friends came close to Walwyn's ideal of reason as they moved from evangelical strife to religious gatherings governed by quiet discourse, respectful listening, and freedom for any participant to speak as he was moved.

Christianity and the law of nature were the wellsprings of Walwyn's ideology, and there can be little doubt that he looked beyond the capitalistic system that served him so well to an ideal state akin to his perception of the selfless and sharing life of early Christians and men in the original state of nature. At the same time, his observation that to attempt an equaling of estates "is most injurious, unlesse there did precede an universall assent thereunto from all and every one of the People"[230] suggests that Walwyn perceived a conflict between the authoritarian control essential to an egalitarian state and his commitment to a limited government empowered by consent and ensuring individual liberties.

Walwyn's gentry origins and economic prosperity abetted his intellectual development. He had time and opportunity for wide reading and thoughtful reflection. To his opportunity he brought a questing mind: open to new ideas, skeptical of the traditional and established. His rationalism was tempered by a spiritual as well as a humane charity, yet he was always a Socratic searcher for truth who subjected conclusions to the light of reason.

Although Walwyn never left England and expressed some scorn for those who traveled abroad,[231] he was well informed about past and present practices of the larger world. Like many English radicals, he admired republican Holland; from his reading of Montaigne, he found much good in remote primitive tribes; admiration for Luther enabled him to relate to the Reformation and Germany; sympathy for those who fled to attain religious freedom enlarged his awareness of the New World; his medical studies informed him of an aspect of India and China.[232] He knew much about Greece and Rome through his reading of the classics, while from his basic dependence on the Bible Walwyn found his primary mentors among the ancient prophets and early Christians of Israel. Broadly read and deeply thoughtful, Walwyn expounded religious, political, and social principles that were as bold as any concepts of his revolutionary generation.

Perceptive as well as principled, Walwyn was rarely unreasonable or unjust. During the 1648 War that he described as "causelesse" he ignored the consequences of a Royalist victory as his diminishing hopes for reform released unwarranted criticism of erstwhile allies and revealed his deep aversion to violence and bloodshed.[233] A few months later, Walwyn's relentless attack on the Independents' shortcomings failed to recognize that they had done much to secure a toleration for Christians that was as extensive as most Englishmen would accept.[234] These lapses suggest that despair over a second bloody conflict and disillusionment with allies who did not share his religious concepts caused this very reasonable man to become on occasion somewhat less reasonable.

Overall, Walwyn was notably fair-minded. Unlike many idealists, he was as concerned with individuals as with their abstract liberties. His avoidance of public notice as he adroitly advanced unwon causes is indicative of the contented domesticity that is confirmed by his son-in-law's account of a loving family life. A compassionate concern for the sick was the foundation of his medical advice, and his religious and political works are as revealing of his character as of his depth as a theorist and skill as a polemicist. He was often subtle, sometimes ironic, and his generosity and humor are particularly notable in some of his responses to Thomas Edwards. All that we know of his life supports the evidence of his writings: he was a man of compassion and good humor. Above all, he was a reasonable man, ready to give courteous attention to others. There is nothing, Walwyn believed, "that maintaines love, unity and friendship in families, Societies, Citties, Countries, Authorities, Nations; so much as, a condescention to the giving, and hearing, and debating of reason."[235]

Religious and Political
Writings, 1641–1652

1

A New Petition of the Papists

1641
Reprinted from a copy of the tract in the Thomason Collection in the British Library

A New Petition of the Papists was also issued as *The Humble Petition of the Brownists*. Both versions were published anonymously, without imprint, "in the yeare 1641"; Thomason did not date either version. The typography is identical; only the title pages differ. Neither "Papists" nor "Brownists" so described themselves and the titles may have been the printer's bids for attention. The first page is headed by the meaningful title: "The Humble Petition of the Afflicted Brethren."

In 1916 T. C. Pease noted that Humphrey Brooke stated that the first book written on behalf of liberty of conscience "since these Troubles" owed much to Walwyn. Pease, discarding the view that Brooke's reference was to *Liberty of Conscience* (March 1642/3), averred that Brooke referred to *The Humble Petition of the Brownists,* and he concluded that the author was all but certainly William Walwyn.[1]

In 1934 William Haller observed that *A New Petition of the Papists* is identical in content to *The Humble Petition of the Brownists,* but he doubted the attribution to Walwyn, suspecting "some Catholic hand." Four years later Haller stated that he was "now inclined to agree with Pease."[2]

Pease cites evidence for his attribution. Rejecting the opinion that the tract is a satire,[3] he argues that it was serious in intent and points to the similarity of the *Petition's* appeal for Brownists, Socinians, Arminians, Papists, Familists, Puritans, and Adamites to a passage in Walwyn's signed tract, *A Prediction of Mr. Edwards.*[4]

Additional evidence of Walwyn's authorship is available. *The Petition of the Papists'* statement that no man who professes a religion should "be forced to follow other men Judgements and not his owne" and the supporting reference to Romans 14 are repeated in most of

Walwyn's acknowledged writings on religious liberty.[5] The belief that religious liberty is the most prized of freedoms was one of Walwyn's basic tenets,[6] and his belief that the place of worship "doth not import" is stated in the *Petition* and reiterated in *Prediction*.[7] The contention that toleration would be conducive to "the quiet of the state" and "breede . . . love, loyalty and affection" for those who ruled is found in Walwyn's signed and admitted tracts.[8] Toleration for Papists is supported in the *Petition* by a reference to Richard Hooker's five "bookes of Ecclesiasticall policy"—which conforms with Walwyn's later statement that these were among the works he particularly studied.[9] Passages in the text of the *Petition* referring to "Protestant" (i.e., members of the established church) suggest that the author was within the established church—a point that Walwyn's acknowledged works reiterate.[10]

Specific points indicating Walwyn's authorship of the 1641 *Petition* are complemented by the quiet conviction and appeals to Scripture and reason that pervade all of Walwyn's pleas for unqualified toleration. There is no reason to question Pease's conclusion: "The internal evidence all points to its [the *Petition*'s] composition by a man mentally nearer like Walwyn than any other writer of the day."[11]

A New Petition of the Papists is reprinted for the first time in this volume.

A NEW PETITION OF THE PAPISTS.

Printed in the yeare 1641.

THE **HUMBLE PETITION** OF THE *AFFLICTED BRETHREN.*

Humbly shewing,

That whereas there are so many different Religions now professed in England; as your Honours well know, and that with griefe no doubt, casting your eyes upon the great confusion that thereby ariseth in the common wealth; every one hoping and expecting that theirs alone shall be received and established by this present and powerfull high Court of Parliament and all others to bee cast forth abolished and prosecuted, which certainely would cause (if it be once Decreed) a farre greater confusion and discontentment.

For the timely prevention of which danger many hold it necessarie, and humbly desire, that you would take it into your deepe considerations and profound Judgements, whether it were not more convenient for this State, and more gratefull to the subjects to tollerate all professions whatsover, eve- [A2] ry one being left to use his owne conscience, none to be punished or persecuted for it.

There is no man that professeth a Religion, but is in conscience perswaded that to be the best wherein to save his soule, & can give no doubt some reason, yea, and alleage some authority out of the word of God for it, which is an argument that not his will, but his Judgement is convinced, and therefore holds it unreasonable, to be forced to follow other mens Judgements and not his owne in a matter of so great importance as that of his salvation is, which is the onely marke his tender soule aymes at in his Religion, and for which hee reades the word daily, and hourely sucking from thence sweet and holy Doctrines as Bees doe honey from sweet flowers in the Spring time.

It may be objected that this Tolleration would breede a greater confusion, but wee which know wee have the Spirit, beleeve the contrary; for the establishing of onely one, and suppressing all others, will breede in all a generall discontent, jarring, rayling, libelling, and consequently must needs follow a mighty confusion, where contrarywise, if all were permitted, all would bee pleased all in peace, and their obligation and love would be farre greater to the King and State for so great a benefit as the freedome of conscience, which to all men is the most gratefull thing in the world, more for the better maintaining of peace with each other, differring in Religion, how easie a matter it were considering the good natures and sweet dispositions of our English nation, who willingly would embrace a law en- [2] acted to that effect that were upon some penaltie to be imposed, should affront or upbraid the other for his Religion. This in divers well governed Countries is permitted, as Holland, Germanie, France, and Polonia, &c. where though their Religion be as opposite as Heaven to Hell, yet their concord is so great, that they say with the Prophet David, *behold how good and pleasant a thing it is for Brethren to dwell together,* Psal. 132.

If therefore the Brownists upon scruple of their tender conscience, and grounded upon the word, will separate themselves, and not go to the Church with Protestants,* let them alone, give them free leave to exercise their Religion where they please without disturbance, the place where doth not import, they not daring to adde or diminish any thing in the written word.

If the Puritants will not use the Service Booke, Corner Cap, Surplesse, or Altar, nor bow at the name of Jesus, their pure hearts esteeming it Idolatrie, let them alone, they are great readers of Gods booke, and if they bee in errour, they will sooner finde it, having liberty of conscience, then being oppressed with the Tyranny of the High Commission Court or other kindes of persecutions which disquiet their consciences and troubles their patience.

If the Socinians will not subscribe to the 39. Articles nor credit more then by Naturall force of their best witts they can reach unto, let them alone, they professe that if any man can give them a better reason, or confute them by the word, they are rea- [3] dy every hower to change their opinions, of such soft and pliable natures they are.

If the Arminians will have Bishops, Altars, Lights, Organs, hold Free-will, merit of good workes, and divers other points with Papists, though as yet no sacrifice with them, upon their Altars, let them alone, let them use their ceremonies without sacrifice, *let every spirit praise the Lord*, Psal. 150.

If the Papists will have Altars, Priests, Sacrifice and ceremonies, and the Pope for their supreame head in Spirituall affaires, seeing they affirme so confidently they have had these Sixteene hundred and odde yeares, let them alone with their pretended prescription, and let every Religion take what Spirituall head they please, for so they will, whether wee will or no, but the matter imports not, so they obey the King as temporall head, and humbly submit to the State and civill Lawes, and live quietly together.

Let the Adamits Preach in vaults & caves as naked as their nailes, and starve themselves with cold, they thinke themselves as innocent as Adam and Eve were in their nakednesse before their fall, let them therefore alone till some innocent Eve bee so curious as to eate forbidden fruit, and then they will all make themselves aprons of figge leaves perceiving their nakednesse.

Let the Family of Love meete together in their sweet perfum'd Chambers, giving each other the sweet kisse of peace; great pitty it were to hinder their mutuall charity; let them alone: [4] Lastly the same wee desire for all professors of the Gospel, *Let every one abound in his owne sence*, Rom. 14.

---

* Protestants: in this tract, members of the established church. Cf. No. 2, p. 1. (Editors' note)

Now were this freedome permitted, there would not bee so many idle scandalous pamphlets daily cast abroad to the great vexation of each other, & trouble to the whole Realme, every one labouring to preferre his owne Religion.

A Tolleration therefore would hinder all this strife and discontentment, but if oppressed with persecution they will cry out of the word of God, *We will render to Caesar, the things that are due to Caesar, and to God that which is due to God,* Marke 12. If Tollerated, more promptly will they obey the King and State, if troubled or molested, they will cry, *Wee must obey God rather then men,* Acts 5. and so remaine discontented and afflicted in spirit.

Neither doth a Tolleration seeme dissonant, but rather concordant with the Doctrine of the most learned Protestants: First the Primate of Ireland Doctor Usher, in a Sermon before King James at Wansted 1624. admittes all Christians into the Church of what Religion soever, good soule! hee will have none persecuted, his tender heart drawes all to Heaven, Muscovites, Grecians, Ethiopians, all reformed Churches even from Constantinople, to the East Indies, none! none by him are excluded from Paradise, as you may reade in the 10. and 11. page of his aforecited sermon, his pitifull heart cannot passe such a bloody sentence upon so many poore soules; nay hee will pull in the [5] very Jewes and Papists, for the Ethiopians though they baptize with us, yet they circumcise also both male and female, and in all other things joyne hands with the Pope, as in the confession of their faith sent to Gregory the 13. is manifest, this learned Doctor being so gracious and mercifully pittifull, how can wee Imagine that your clemencies will persecute those in earth which are esteemed worthy of Heaven. Master Hooker in his five bookes of *Ecclesiasticall policy,* page 138. affirmes the Church of Rome to be part of the house of God, a limbe of the visible Church of Christ, and page 130. he saith, we gladly acknowledge them to bee of the family of Jesus Christ: now if the family of the Roman Church bee of the family of Jesus Christ, then I hope you will not deny other professors of the Gospel to be of the family of Christ, if they be of the family of God, others are not of the family of the Divell, no, all servants of Christ, brethren of Christ, all according to Doctor Ushers doctrine shall bee saved: why then should any bee persecuted, shall the servants of the same family persecute their fellow servants, this must needes bee greatly displeasing to the Master of the family, let therefore none of the servants of the familie bee persecuted for the love and honour you beare to the Lord and Master.

Seeing therefore in the opinions of these and divers other learned

Protestant Doctors which you know well, the Papists may be saved, and as Doctor Some saith, in his defence against Master Penrie. Page 164. 182. and 176. that it is absurd [6] to thinke the contrary yee will without question thinke it more absurd to hold either professors damned, then it followes that it is most absurd to persecute any whose names are written in the book of life, never to bee blotted out, if they persevere and live the life of the righteous.

Let every one therefore follow his owne Religion so hee bee obedient to the State and temporall lawes certainely, that which is erroneous will in time appeare, and the professors of it will bee ashamed, it will perish and wither as a flower, vanish as smoake, and passe as a shadow.

The Apostles of Christ preaching (Acts. the 5.) the Jewes hearing these things it cut them to the heart, and they consulted to kill them; but as the same Chapter relates verse 34. one of the counsell rising up, a Pharisee called Gammaliell, a Doctor of the Law honorable to the people commanded the men to bee put forth a while, and then he said to them, you men of Israel what meane you to your selves for before these dayes there rose Theodus, saying he was some body, to whom consented a number of men, above 400. who was slaine, and all that beleived him were dispersed, and brought to nothing. After this fellow there rose Judas of Galilee, and drew away the people after him who were dispersed.

And therefore I say to you, depart from these men, and let them alone, for if this councell or worke be of men, it will be dissolved, but if it be of God, you are not able to dissolve them, least per- [7] haps you bee found to resist God also. And they consented to him, here is a president, here is an example even from the Scripture it selfe, follow it wee beseech you, give your consents, agree, vote it, that every man may have freedome of conscience, let them alone; you desire nothing but the truth by this freedome and connivency truth will at last appeare, that which is of men will be dissolved, that which is of God will continue and remaine for ever, now many men are wavering what to follow, what to embrace, neither will they bee contented with any thing that shall bee established by Act of Parliament, were it never so good, onely freedome will in time cause the truth to shine upon them.

The matter therefore of so great importance and consequence, we prostrate; leaving to your honours profound and deepe Judgements, humbly requesting and imploring againe and againe, that for the quiet of the state, for the comfort of the subject, and for the love of truth, you cause and proclaime a tolleration, that for Religion none shall bee persecuted, but every one shall freely enjoy his conscience.

This is every mans case, this would bring Joy to all, discontent to none; this would breede the hartiest love, loyalty and affection to our dread Soveraigne, our gratious King, this would cause all dutifull and loving respects to you, right honorable and noble Peeres of the upper House of Parliament, and no lesse to the most noble Knights, [8] Citizens and Burgesses of the Honorable House of Commons, the carefull watchfull, and painefull laborers, and endeavourers in this, behalfe for the good of the Common wealth, and the comfort of afflicted soules and consciences, grant therefore this Petition, and for ever you will eternize your names.

And so praying to the Lord that hee would endue your hearts with the spirit of true wisedome and clemency towards your poore servants and brethren in the Lord, and grant their humble petition, we cease.

FINIS [9]

2

Some Considerations Tending to the Undeceiving Those, Whose Judgments Are Misinformed

[10 November] 1642
Reprinted from a copy of the tract in the Huntington Library

Some Considerations was published anonymously, without separate title page, imprint, or date. Haller identifies it as Walwyn's work on grounds of its characteristic "personality, style and point of view." Walwyn, states Haller, reiterates "his belief in love and reason, his anticlericalism, his practice of inquiring into the beliefs of men whose religious convictions he does not share."[1]

Haller's judgment is supported by specific references, phrases, and attitudes in *Some Considerations* that are repeated in Walwyn's acknowledged writings. The author of *Some Considerations*, like Walwyn in *A Helpe to the Right Understanding* and *A Whisper in the Eare*, indicates that he is not a sectary but a member of his parish church.[2] The warning that, despite their loyal contributions to the cause of the Parliament, "evill Counsellors" in church and state strive to divide good men by making "the Puritan and Sectaries" odious to the "Protestant" (i.e., member of a parish church) recurs in other contexts in *Helpe, Antidote,* and *Parable*.[3] Toleration is supported by Scriptural references to Walwyn's favorite Romans 14,[4] anticlericalism pervades the tract,[5] and although *Some Considerations* is primarily concerned to reconcile "Protestants" and Puritans, the tract begins a characteristic listing of afflicted brethren: Puritan, Sectary, Brownist, Anabaptist.[6] One phrase—"what more seasonable councell can there bee to all sorts of men"—anticipates the title of Walwyn's acknowledged work, *A Word in Season: To All Sorts of Well Minded People*.[7] *A Word in Season* also points up precepts that Walwyn advances in *Some Considerations:* men should "dive into the reasons of things," should "inquire" for themselves rather than accept secondhand views, should "examine all not timorously, nor prejudicially, but impartially by that uncorrupt rules [*sic*] of reason."[8] And, as *Some Considerations* observes that a man may alter his judgments "upon better reasons which as yet he sees not," *A Word in Season* notes that Parliaments have altered their decisions "upon further or better information."[9]

Some Considerations appeared in November 1642, the same month that Walwyn was named the Vintry ward member of the London committee to collect assessments to support the war, which had begun the preceding August.[10] *Some Considerations* includes political as well as religious concerns and emphasizes the political benefits of toleration[11] as well as Walwyn's fundamental conviction that it is the way of reason and Christian love.[12]

Some Considerations is reprinted for the first time in this volume.

SOME CONSIDERATIONS

Tending to the undeceiving those, whose judgments are misinformed by *Politique Protestations, Declarations, &c.*

Being a necessary discourse for the present times, concerning the unseasonable difference between the *Protestant** and the PURITAN.

The end of the Parliaments consultations, and actions, is to free the Kingdome (the care whereof is to them by the Kingdome committed) from all those heavy tyrannies and oppressions which for many yeares, against expresse Lawes, and cautions to the contrary, have surrounded and overwhelmed the Kingdome, all which, if wee have not a desire to let them slip our memories, the Parliaments first Remonstrance** will fully present unto us. Those men that do oppose the Parliament, are generally such as some way or other have thrived under those pressures, as being made instruments

---

* Protestant: in this tract, a member of the established church. (Editors' note)

** The Grand Remonstrance, 1641. (Editors' note)

SOME

CONSIDERATIONS

Tending to the undeceiving thofe,
whofe judgements are mifinformed by *Politique Proteftations, Declarations, &c.*

Being a neceffary difcourfe for the prefent times, concerning the unfeafonable difference between the *Proteftant*
and the P u r i t a n.

HE end of the Parliaments confultations,
and actions, is to free the Kingdome (the
care whereof is to them by the Kingdome
committed)from all thofe heavy tyrannies
and oppreffions which for many yeares,
againft expreffe Lawes, and cautions to
the contrary, have furrounded and over-
whelmed the Kingdome, all which, if wee
have not a defire to let them flip our memories, the Parliaments
firft Remonftrance will fully prefent unto us . Thofe men that do
oppofe the Parliament, are generally fuch as fome way or other
have thrived under thofe preffures, as being made inftruments
and actors in them, or elfe being addicted to vice and loofeneffe,
found that connivence and indulgence, then which, in times more
reformed they cannot expect. Thofe men that doe now fide with,
and affift the Parliament, are fuch as in thofe corrupt times were
trodden under foot, fuch as were vext and impoverifht by infult-
ing Courts, and Court-officers, forc't againft confcience to per-

A   fwade

Title page of *Some Considerations Tending to the Undeceiving
Those, Whose Judgements Are Misinformed,* 1642.
(Houghton Library, Harvard University)

and actors in them, or else being addicted to vice and loosenesse, found that connivence and indulgence, then which, in times more reformed they cannot expect. Those men that doe now side with, and assist the Parliament, are such as in those corrupt times were trodden under foot, such as were vext and impoverisht by insulting Courts, and Court-officers, forc't against conscience to per- [1] swade to the breach of the Sabbath, compelled to flie their Countrie, or separate from the Church, by inducing vaine and empty Ceremonies, which direct our mindes from consideration of Gods love to us in Christ, and are utterly inconsistent with the true, and spirituall worship of God; and indeed therefore pressed upon us, that thereby their friends might be knowne from their foes, the easie to be abused from the more difficult, that they might be imbraced, and have all encouragements both from the Minister, and men of high places; and these disgraced, prosecuted, and though of never so honest lives, yet if in all things not conformable, scandalled, and made odious: Ceremonies were therefore too pressed upon us, that by them the Church becomming more pompous, and outwardly specious, the Clergy (by whom the Statesmen were especially to doe their ill intended worke) might win greater esteeme, and grow more and more reverenced by the people, who seldome they know dive into the reasons of things, but are usually carryed away by outward shewes and appearances. The Parliaments other friends are such as have beene tormented with the permitted corruption of Lawyers, those devouring Locusts, no lesse ravening then the Ægyptian ones that overspread that Land; such likewise as had lost the liberty of Trade, for the gaining of which, they served a long and tedious apprenticeship, by unlawfull engrossements, and Patents; and all the multitude of good men, who are sensible either by their owne, or their nighbours sufferings, of the injuries of former times, or desirous to prevent and divert our oppression and slavery for the future: Now as it is a notable policy of evill men, though of quite different and opposite conditions to combine and associate together against all that oppose them, bearing with, and passing by any thing for the present, though at other times much distastfull. So how much more does it behove the honest men of this Kingdome, who are likely to taste equally the sweetes of liberty, or the bitter pills of slavery, how ever they may be perswaded otherwise for the present, to unite themselves heart and hand, to joyne together as one man, against all those whom they shall discerne either to oppose the Parliament, or endeavour to raise divisions and differences among themselves. The only way for our enemies to doe their worke, is not by strength, and force of [2] Armes, for what ever their brags be, and how great soever their boasts by which they would seeme to have what they have not, that thereby they may encourage their party, and dishearten their adversaries, yet indeed their forces are but small, their provisions scanty, their meanes and mony only supplyed by rapine, which cannot be lasting, having neither Forts, nor Shipping, so that it cannot be that by strong hand they should have any hope to doe their worke: No certainly, and yet notwithstanding they still dare to hold up the Cudgels, seeme as confident as ever, beare up, as if the world were of their side; what should be the reasons hereof; reasons there are, we must perswade our selves, it is not to be supposed that they are foole-hardy, or that the sense of their many mischiefes have made them desperate, because past hope of recon- cilement (though they well may) their Councels are notable, and surely come not short of the most able the world affords, their sub- leties exceeds the Foxes, or the Serpents, Romes or Spaines; whose most damnable glory it is, that from meane beginnings they, by their wits especially, have raised themselves to the most extended tyran- nies in the Christian world: and why should our politique enemies then despaire? Since their wits are as quick, their consciences as deeply pained and sencelesse, many of our people as easie to be de- luded as ever men were, having the assistance of former contrivances in making men slaves, furnished with Machiavils, and* Staffords in- structions from Florence, with all the assistance Romes consistory, or Spaines can afford: and what force cannot doe, deceit may: a subtill deceitfull Declaration may doe much more mischief then an Army, the one kills men outright, and so leaves them unserviceable for both sides, but deceitfull words, when for want of consideration, unset- tlednesse of judgement, and weake information, they captivate men, they make them not only dead to good mens assistance, and their Countries service, but promoters likewise of their deluders interest, to the insensible ruine and slavery of their brethren, and in conclu- sion, of themselves. Deceits and delusions are the principall weapons with which the evill Counsellors now fight; by which they subdue and captivate the understandings and affections of men; to scatter these, they hurry about from one County into another, and there at Assises, and other forc't Assemblies [3] practise, in one place they colour and glose over their owne evill actions, with seeming pre- tences of Law, Religion: in another, they scandalize and traduce the

* The Author of the Machiavelian plot.

Parliament, for as they cannot want paint to make fowle and unsightly actions seeme faire and specious, so neither can they want dirt and mire to disfigure the best formed, and most honest enterprizes in the world; words are never defective to make evill seeme good, and good evill: what villany was there ever committed, or what injustice, but words and pretences might be found to justifie it: Monopolies were once pleaded legall, and very wholesome for the people, we were once perswaded Ship-money was lawfull, and now Commission of Array; if unjust things were offered to us, as they are, without disguise and artificiall covering, they would appeare so odious, as that each man would cry out upon them, and therefore it is a high point of policy to make the worst things shew fairest, speake best, when they intend most mischiefe. In other Counties the people were thanked for their affections and assistance, when they found them wiser then to yeeld any, and when they were driven by necessity to a place, they would seeme to be invited by love, and certainty of compliance, when God knowes in many places they found it much otherwise, and would likewise elsewhere too, but that the people were necessitated to their assistance by force, rather then forward, out of any liking. Well, their policies and delusions are most numerous, and every day increasing, and therefore it behoves every wise man to stand upon his guard, to be wary and watchfull that he be not apprehended by their subtilties: in nothing there is required greater care, their invasions being insensible, and having once seised upon a man, he no longer dislikes, but approves of them, they force a man to love what erewhiles he hated, what he but now cryed downe, to plead for, and not to observe, because his intentions are honest, and he meanes no ill, that he is even against his knowledge his Countries enemy: Hee that can give any cautions how to resist their wyles, or shew wherein we are already seduced by our cunning adversaries, doth doe very good service to his Country, and deserves to be heard; this discourse was written principally for that end, namely, to discover to all good men how they have suffered themselves to be wrought upon by the adversary in a case very considerable, and thereby, [4] though they observe it not, are become friends to their Countries chiefe foes, and foes to their principall friends. The worke of evill Counsellors, as it is to unite and joyne together their friends, so is it likewise to separate and divide their foes amongst themselves: all such are their foes as truly love their owne liberty, and desire to free themselves from their insulting tyranny: it must needs be very advantagious to them, if by any meanes they can divide these, for

being disjoyned, they cannot possibly be so powerfull against them
as otherwise they would be, did they continue at union: now
amongst many other wayes that they have used to accomplish this
end, there is not one hath been more effectuall then in raising, and
cherishing differences concerning formes and circumstances about
Religion, that so setting them together by the eares about shadowes,
they may in the meane time steale away your substance: there is no
difference they full well know is so permanent, as that which any way
touches upon Religion, and therefore like cunning Pioners, have
lighted upon what is likely to make the greatest breach, which by
continuall plying the work, the difference dayly increasing, it is much
to be feared that all the paines the Parliament takes, the assistance of
good men, the hazards of our resolute souldiers, or whatever endeavours else are used for the accomplishing of good mens desires, will by
this one difference, if continued, be utterly frustrate, and come to
naught: for it is almost come to that passe, that the Puritan and Sectaries, as they are called, are more odious to the Protestant, then the
Cavalier, Malignant, or Papist: all our discourses are diverted now by
the cunning practise of the Polititian from our forepast calamities,
plots, and conspiracies of lewd men, from thinking what will be the
best wayes to speed and advantage our undertakings for our liberty,
to raylings against the Puritan, to crosse and oppose the Puritan, to
provoke him by many insolencies, and affronts to disorders, and then
to inveigh with all bitternesse against his disorders: if at such times as
these, when so great a worke is in hand, as the freeing of us from
slavery, we can be so drowzily sottish as to neglect that, for the satis-
fying our giddy and domineering humour, what can be said of us, but
that our fancy is dearer to us then our liberty, that we care not what
goes to racke, though it be our substantiall Religion, Lawes, and Liberties, so we [5] doe but please our selves in crying downe our
Brethren, because they are either more zealous, or else more scrupulous then our selves: These things my friends, (for all good men are
such) doe shew that you are not considerate, nor doe not sufficiently
beare in mind what was told you in the Parliaments first Remonstrance, that it was (and still is) one of the principall workes of our
common enemy, to sow division between the Protestant and Puritan,
you have beene too easie, and quickly wrought upon by him for the
accomplishing that worke: I would to God you would lay it to heart;
the Puritan intends no mischiefe to any, you may assure your selves
he does not: if you inquire you shall finde that they had no hand in
our former oppressions, they were no maintainers of any unjust

courses, or Courts, unlesse by those many fines which were extorted from them, for that they of all men had the courage to withstand their injuries: wee heare of daily plunderings, rapes, and murthers of the Cavaliers, women with child runne through, and many other butcheries, and yet wee passe by these, as if by no interest they concerned us, and let flie our speeches only against the Puritan for plucking a raile downe, or a paire of Organs, a Surplice, Crucifix, or painted window, which are indeed no way conducible to the substantiall worship of God, and yet retained by the ill disposed Clergy, as fuell to yeeld matter to that discord they would continue amongst you: See how much too blame we are, see how exceedingly the polititian has deluded us, that we should doe thus, and yet see not that we doe unwisely. If thy brother bee weake and thou strong, beare with his weakenesse, or if the Puritan esteeme thee weake, and himselfe strong, it will be a good lesson to him; if wee be strong we should beare with them that are weake; if we are weake we should not judge them that are strong, it will be no shame for any one to take the Apostles advice; let not slight and indifferent things divide our affections; let them not especially when substantiall things lie at the stake; it is all one as if our enemy being in the field with full purpose and speed to destroy us, wee should turne aside to exclaime against a man that flung dirt upon us or laught at us: and wholly neglect altogether to defend our selves: what a shame will it be unto us, when hereafter it is said that the English might have freed themselves from oppression and [6] slavery, but that in the doing of it they neglected their common enemy, and fell at variance among themselves for trifles. Ceremonies and other things that occasion difference, are stickled for by the Protestant, not for that they thinke them necessary, for surely unlesse it be for some indirect end they cannot be urged to be so, but for that they are not yet taken downe by authoritie: The Puritan they would have them taken away for that they conceive them vaine, unwarrantable by Gods Word, reliques of the Romish Religion not throughly purged away, and therefore they desire they should be left off by us, which are the principall cause of their separation from us: In all differences to bee unwilling to reconcile, shewes not a spirit of love, which Christians should ever be possest withall, but of pride and contention, the Protestant hath not the engagements of conscience upon him, as the Puritan has, and therefore may the easier beare with the Puritans infirmities, if meat offend my weake brother I will eate no meat as long as I live, what an excellent thing were it if we could have that hold fast over our selves that the Apostle had to re-

fraine from any thing, how pleasant and deare soever unto us, rather
than give any offence, or occasion any difference betweene our selves
and weake brethren: let every man thinke of the answering this question to himselfe: whether if lewd men doe get the better over the
Parliament and honest men of the Kingdome, either Protestant or Puritan are likely to be any other but slaves: Certainly if any of them doe
perswade themselves otherwise, they are like the stiffe-necked and
unweildy Hebrewes, that wisht they were slaves in Egypt againe,
where the much loved Flesh pots were, for that it was troublesome
and dangerous passing through the Wildernesse into Canaan, a land
of plenty and lasting liberty. Be not deceived with deluding thoughts
of former times, when plenty covered our oppressions, and because
of peace wee could not see our slavery: it was a time when such as
Buckingham, Stratford, domineering Bishops, corrupt and lawlesse
Judges, grew rich and potent: when Courts Minions for no services
but slavery and luxury were exalted, when offices were not conferred
on foreseene vertue and honest desert, but were bought and sold;
when honours that ought to be the rewards of vertue, were by gold
purchased, and they onely deemed fit Subjects for both, that [7] were
easie to be corrupted, such as had stupid consciences, & would suffer
their masters to undertak any dishonest employment. He that wishes
for former times wishes for such times wherein it had beene much
better for a man to let goe his right or inheritance, though never so
apparantly his, to any varlet that would have laid but any colorable
claime to it, rather then have bin wurried by Court Mastives, & eaten
to the bare bones by griping Judges and avaritious Lawyers; wherein
a murder in one man was not so much punished as a word in another,
wherein a poore man was hanged for stealing food for his necessitie,
and a luxurious Courtier of whom the world was never like to have
any other fruits but oathes and stabbes, could be pardoned after the
killing the second or third man: wherein in a word, knaves were set
upon honest mens shoulders, all loosenesse was countenanced, and
vertue and pietie quite out of fashion: In these times, who kept themselves so steddy as the Puritan, who opposed against those exorbitant
courses, and by that meanes who smarted more then they: sure I
thinke their sufferings are yet in each mans memory, who but they, or
they especially withstood all Church innovations, and other taxes and
impositions, for which both the Bishops and Clergy, as also the corrupt Statesman, and Projector were their profest and open enemies,
and even then to make them odious, invented ridiculous names for
them, and studied scurrilous tales and jests against them, and ever

signed new devices concerning them, to direct our thoughts from our every dayes oppressions, to sport at the Puritan. The wayes of wicked men are like the way of a Ship in the Sea, so quick and speedily covered, that without much observancy we cannot trace them: So that we see these endeavors to make the Puritan odious is no new policy, nor yet the reasons why it is endeavored, and how great a blemish it is unto our judgement, that though this deceit hath beene so long in practise, and so apparently mischievous to good, and advantageous to bad men, we should not yet discover it, or being discovered and declared unto us, wee should not lay it to heart, and endeavor to avoid it. Sure I thinke there is no more evident marke of our disaffections to the Parliament, then our invectives against the Puritan, whom the Parliament and all good men ought in all reason to esteeme well of, for that they have beene so abundant in their [8] contributions, so forward in their services, so neglective of their private, to advance that necessary and most allowable work, both by God and all reasonable men in the world, of freeing us and our posterity from loathsome Tyranny and oppression: whatsoever faults the Puritan hath, this is not a time to cast them in his dish, neither are we certaine that they are faults, we have but so digested them to our selves, what he can say for himself, in his own justification, is not yet heard, nor is there yet a time of hearing: we may assure our selves that the Parliament will endeavour all that possible they can to give all sorts of men that will not prove obstinate, and unsatisfiable, the best and largest satisfaction: If they should now goe about it, or if they should at any time heretofore have enterprised it, they might in the meane time have had their throats cut, it is and hath been the endeavour of the Kings evill advisers, to urge them alwayes to the settlement of the Church, a worke they know requires much time for the performance of it, and so must of necessity have diverted all considerations and provisions for their safety, when in the meane time those advisers would have been most active and vigilant, losing no jot of time, nor balking no opportunity or advantage to have fortified themselves, made a prey of the Parliament, and in their ruines have buryed all thats neer & deer unto us: We see, that though the Parliament have only intended one business, the defence and preservation of themselves, and the Kingdome, so great opposition hath yet been made, and so difficult a worke have they found it, that there is no man can say they are too forward: and therefore if we will not willfully make our selves a prey to our common enemy, let us resolve for the time to come firmly to unite our affections beyond the policy of evill-witted

men to dissolve: let those whom the malignant and inconsiderate call
Puritans, endeavour all that they can possibly, to give no offence to
the Protestant, and let the Protestant be slow in taking any at the
Puritan: the Puritan indeed is too blame in his not observing all hee
can to win by love, gentle behaviour, such as differ from him in opinion, in not endeavouring all he can to bridle his passion, and not
suffer his different opinion to coole his love and affection to other
men: what? We have all need one of another, and till such time things
are throughly canvassed, and examined, how ever [9] each man concludes himselfe to be in the right (we know we are partiall to our
selves) he may be mistaken, and upon better reasons which as yet he
sees not may alter his judgement and be convinc't; let us unite together as one man to the extirpation of certaine and discovered enemies both of our substantiall Religion, our lawes, and liberties, that
so all being quiet, and wee assuredly free-men, all stratagems dissolved, and the Sunne of peace againe appearing, the Church may be
so purged and so religiously setled, that the Puritan may have no
cause of seperation (which cannot be according to his desire but that
to which by the instigation of his conscience he is necessitated too)
and so may be no longer an eyesore and distastfull to the Protestant,
but both may with mutuall joy and peace of conscience joyne together
in praises and thanksgivings to that God, who by the free, and alone
death of his Sonne attoned and reconciled us to himselfe, and in giving us his Sonne hath together with him given us all things also. But
to what purpose will this, or other discourses of this nature be, when
there is a sort of people in this kingdome, who make it their study
and bend all their endeavours for to encrease and enlarge this difference: and yet have full permission, and all opportunity that may be
to doe their worke; neither could the polititian have ever made this
breach or extended it to that businesse it is at, but for the certaine
assistance of the Clergy, who for that end bound them his instruments, by the liberall distribution of honours and preferments, by
enlargements of dignity & livings, by giving them power in Courts, &
letting them tast the sweets of domination: by authorising them in
their advance of tithes, multiplying their duties, favouring them in
their abundant differences, and restlesse lawsuits; and in all likelihood they must bee their servants who pay them such large wages;
insomuch that in all the time of this Kingdomes slavery and wicked
mens oppressions of us, who were greater promoters of both then the
Clergy; what was the politique subject of their Sermons then, and
discourses, but the advance of prerogative, and unlimited sway; the

gayning of estimation to themselves not by their doctrines or lives, for what could be more corrupt and scandalous, but by subtill delusions, and delusive sophismes; the fitting of our minds for slavery, the abasing of our courages against injuries in Church or State; by preaching for obedience to all commands good or bad, under [10] deceitfull termes of active and passive, by which meanes injurious men were heartned in induring mischiefes, and good men moap'd and stupified to a patient sufferance of them, their very tongues tied up and no libertie given so much as to motion against apparent injuries, or to discover to the world the iniquitie of them: This use is made of those most admirable guifts we admire the Clergy for, to this good end serves their great learning and excellent parts; and as in former times by these and many other wayes they onely employed their studies to make us apt and easie to admit our slavery without grudging or gainsaying, so doe they still continue the Statesmens hirelings, to further that difference betweene the Protestant and Puritan, which makes so much for their advantage: And that they may be truely serviceable, to this end they are brought up in the Universities fitted for the purpose; no man there countenanced unlesse he is like to prove a champion against the Puritan, the greater their abilities are that way, their preferments are answerable, insomuch, that generally those Ministers are onely good, that trusting onely to themselves, and not taking the pleasing course, could expect no encouragement from the Bishop or others in high places, but very contentedly did betake themselves to such places their honest friends and deserts obtained for them, whereas men of that other straine were almost courted into benefices, where the former benefits did not more sway with to justifie injustice, and sow division, then the longing expectation after greater and greater preferments; and what though some have refused preferments, and yet are zealous in your worke; it is well knowne yet that they live in abundance, drinke the sweet, and eate the fat of the Land, are recompenced with large gifts, and abundant Legacies; who by a cunning refusall of what they need not, and perhaps they thinke would be too troublesome, have taken so deepe root in unwatchfull mens minds, that there are none so great promoters of this worke as they; who likewise being the most subtill of all the tribe, order the businesse so, that what by their abilities of speech, reverent estimation men have of their persons, of their functions, of their sinceritie, they even delude them as they list, and have so farre fomented this fire of dissention, that it is to bee feared it will very shortly breake out into a flame: they have even heightned [11] this hatred to an insurrection, the people rise up one against another, grow into factions and acquaintances by wearing colours, and publike meetings, outfacing authority, and slighting the most soveraigne power, even of the Parliament it selfe; nor is this likely in short time to be entinguisht, though much care be used, and great paines taken for the doing it, so long as a cunning malicious sort of men are suffered without controule or just punishment to yeeld new matter to this destructive flame of contention; to curbe the licence, and punish the insolencies of those licentious Clergymen may very well be one of the principall workes of the Parliaments, whose earnest endeavours and noble undertakings doe find no greater opposition from any sort of men, no not from the Cavalier himselfe, or the Kings evill Councellors, then from these men of malice and dissention; many of them are Delinquents, and so voted, others likewise would appeare to be so, did the people thinke it a fit time to make their complaints, many of them are of scandalous and debaucht lives, all of them indeed are bound by the respects they have to their owne safetie to destroy the Parliament, by whom they know, were they at leasure they should be sifted, and their crimes censured, and to bring in againe the former government, wherein they found so great connivance in all sorts of vices whatsoever: And now what more seasonable councell can there bee to all sorts of men, then to try and examine all that they heare, to entertaine nothing for the opinion we have of the man, for the judgement is never so likely to be deluded as when the person is too highly esteemed, to see likewise in how many respects the Clergyman is bound to make the Puritan odious to the Protestant, and how greatly disadvantagious that is to the worke, all honest men are bound in conscience to further, and likewise to conclude those Clergy men disaffected that shall hereafter endeavour it, and to let both them and others in authority know it, to be firme in their affections to the Puritan, past all their subtilties to disunite them, that so all honest men being heartily united, the greater may be their force, and the kingdomes enemies the speedier subdued.

The Ministers under pretence of railing against, [the Puritan, Sectary, Brownist, and Anabaptists]* doe scandalize and defame all the honest men of the Kingdome, yea even [12] of the Parliament themselves: so that if we be not the more cautious we may be so farre deluded, as to disesteeme even their actions, not for that to any rea-

---

* The original tract mistakenly prints the words in brackets on the preceding line. (Editors' note)

sonable discreet man they can appeare to be any other then as the actions of the most wise should bee, but because they are approved of by the honest Puritan: It is not safe they thinke to rave against the Parliament point blanke, they would then indeed appeare so palpably malicious and villanously disaffected, that men would have much adoe to tarry their tryall by Law without doing present execution on them: & therefore like men full of subtlety, they wound the Parliament through the Puritans side, and therein take so vast a liberty, that almost provokes an honest hearted man beyond his patience; sometimes they speake in a doubtfull sense, so as that all who are misled by them can understand them, and yet they thinke that if they should be questioned, as out of guilt of conscience they cannot but expect if they shall bee able to give such an interpretation to their words, that thereby they can delude the holdfast of Law and the censure of justice: thus they provide an excuse before they act their villany, and proceed as farre as they imagine that will beare them out; what high time it is that these men should bee crushed, least in time they sow so many tares in the hearts of men, that no wisedome of man shall be able to plucke up, but that they choake even the seeds of good doctrine, and root out of our minds the very principles of reason: Another villanous worke they have in hand, is to take away our courages and dull our resolutions by commending peace unto us, when we are necessitated to take up our Swords; what fooles they imagine us to be, as if we did not know what were the sweets of peace, but then it must be accompanied with liberty, the bondman is at peace; there is peace, there is peace in a dungeon, yet I thinke no man can bee heartily in love with such kinde of peace, no certainly, if our liberty and our religion be much dearer to us then our lives, as I thinke they are to every wise man, then sure they must be dearer to us then our rest, our swords are drawne for them, and so long as they are violated, what peace? what peace? so long as the insolencies and conspiracies of unjust men, and their usurpations are so many? what peace? so long as those that would free us from former oppressions, and would provide for our future liberties, [13] are in no safety but in continuall hazard of their lives? were wee not necessitated to it, it were madnesse to thinke wee could take pleasure in shedding of our owne bloods: what shallow men doe they imagine us to be, that thinke, that through their sweet words, and smooth faces, we doe not see their fowle and mischievous intentions: yes to their griefe of heart and the joy of all good men they behold that, notwithstanding they have in many other things deluded us, in this they have not; the Militia is

setled in safe and trusty hands, the Forts and strong holds made
good, the Navy secured and commanded by a faithfull and coura-
gious lover of his country, that a strong and a welfurnished Army is a
foote to the terrour of wicked men and we hope to the suppression;
they are quite frustrate of their ends, all their cunning discourses and
subtle motions for peace, though delivered with never so much pretended piety, and seeming love to our safeties, come short of their
purpose, they have not thereby lulled us asleepe, and made us too
secure, no, we have the courages of men, of valiant provoked men
upon us, provokt by an insight into all our injuries, which are now
fresh in our memories, provoked by discovery of their delusions, and
animated by the amiable sight of liberty which we may now if we will
our selves obtaine, of which for many yeares we have beene deprived: and therefore it is not good nor honest that they continue
their invitations to peace, so long as the Parliament see it needefull to
provide for warre. This it is when they will be overwise and passe the
bounds of their office, nor are they more mistaken in this, then in
other matters, especially when they plead the Kings cause, their engagements and flatteries here make them starke blind, and let them
not see how under stickling for the Kings prerogative they com-
prehend under that such things, the obtayning whereof if duly considered would make his Maiesties office the most hazardous, and
fraught with least content of any one in the Kingdome. A negative
voyce they much stand for, a power of calling and likewise of dissolving Parliaments; these things because they carry power with them,
and seeme to adde much greatnesse and high prerogative to the
King, they stickling for them, and see not that if the King should have
them, he would be thereby ever liable to the blame, and censures of
the people; for if any thing should be consulted [14] of by the Parliament, and by them concluded to be safe and necessary for the Kingdome, and that the King by that power they claime for him, should
crosse it if the people should in the time to come by necessitie for the
want of what the Parliament would have provided for them, and the
King would not, whom have they then to blame but the King; and he
likewise must of necessitie lie under their hard opinions, should the
neglect of calling Parliaments bring oppressions upon the people: or
the too soone dissolving them without consent of the House before
their businesse were fully dispatcht. Both which in their booke of
Canons and constitutions ecclesiasticall, where without once mentioning the Parliament, they take liberty to make the Kings Prerogatives what they please, there I say have they peremptorily con-

cluded the power of calling and dissolving all assemblies to bee the Kings undoubted right, and would likewise have possest the people so by the quarterly reading of those decrees of theirs in Churches by their owne order: It is true indeed these commons are most justly damned by the Parliament, but by the remembrance hereof we may palpably observe, what a power they then usurpt to themselves, and how notoriously they abused that power to the prejudice of the King, his perpetuall hazard and disquiet: The King past all question saw all this when he so willingly assented to those two acts for the constant calling of Parliament, and not dissolution of this, both which the Clergy had no other meanes to disanull and make of no effect, then by infusing into his Maiesties eares, and insinuating to the people, that the King hath a negative voyce by which all that the Parliament shall doe comes to nothing, unlesse it pleases the King to assent, which is not like to be but when those that are so powerfull (his evill counsellers) over him shall give way to; by which meanes alone those evill men have a power of crossing and making voyd all the debates and conclusions of the Parliament, and though this bee in effect to make the safety and freedome of the people to depend upon one mans will & understanding, an absurdity in government; a man would think these men could not have the impudence to plead for, much lesse that the people should be so unadvised as to admit it to enter their thoughts as a thing just and reasonable, yet indeed so impudent are those as to plead for it, and so ignorant are the people, as [15] to admit it, which is the ground and occasion of all the evils and mischiefes which at this day threaten both his Maiesty and the whole people. So that wee see the King hath little to thank them for their too hasty forwardnesse in clayming what is so unsafe for him, and so likely to divide the affections of the people from him: But what care they, the King getting power, they get advancement, credit, honour, and what not? so little respect they what is safe for him or prejudiciall to the people, so their owne ends bee served; there comes no harme from good consideration, the advice then cannot be amisse, to wish every one to consider what they heare, to examine all not timorously, nor prejudicially, but impartially by that uncorrupt rules of reason, and to give no credit to what is spoken for the credit or estimation of the speaker, but because it is the truth, and nothing but the truth.

FINIS [16]

(3)

The Power of Love

[19 September] 1643
Reprinted from a copy of the tract in the Thomason Collection in the British Library

The Power of Love, published anonymously, was printed by "R.C." (unidentified) for John Sweeting, a bookseller in Popes-head Alley; it is dated 1643. There is no imprimatur from an official licenser as required by the ordinance regulating printing (14 June 1643).[1] Haller readily included the tract in Walwyn's canon, observing that only Walwyn would have conjoined "what purports to be a Familist sermon on *The Power of Love* with an evident free rendering from Montaigne's essay on cannibals of a passage on the state of nature."[2]

The central message of *The Power of Love* is the promise that God's grace assures salvation for all men. The pamphlet differs from most of Walwyn's religious writings in that it is neither a strong defense of toleration for harassed separatists nor a defense of Walwyn's own beliefs. It is a gentle discourse addressed "To every Reader" in the hope that men will be comforted and guided by awareness of God's universal love. Although the plea for toleration is mild,[3] the work is studded with contentions, phrases, and references that are unmistakably Walwyn's. The opening lines, which contend that "whosoever is possest with love" is "sure one of the Family of love," are echoed in Walwyn's signed *Prediction,* where he again makes it clear that the "Family" is God's family of "true Christian love."[4] Following a familiar listing of oppressed brethren—Anabaptists, Brownists, Antinomians[5]—*The Power of Love* urges every reader to "enquire into their doctrines your selfe, and so make your conclusion . . . stand cleare from all prejudging."[6] Romans 14 is again referred to,[7] and the limits of reason and the need for faith set forth.[8]

Scripture, states *The Power of Love,* plainly reveals "that God ever intendeth unto man a pleasant and comfortable life,"[9] and the description of man's natural state, where he has all things necessary for his well-being, paints a blissful picture of primitive life that owes much to Walwyn's admiration for Montaigne's essay on the "innocent cannibals."[10] There is a suggestion that the author of *The Power of Love*, like Walwyn, worshipped within his parish church.[11] In *The Power of Love*, *A Still and Soft Voice*, and *Vanitie of the Present Churches* accounts of the effects of "true religion" are presented as happy consequences of walking "as becommeth the Gospel of Christ."[12] *The Power of Love*'s observation that "true Christianity hates and abhorres tyranny, oppression, perjury, cruelty, deceipt, and all kinde of filthinesse" foreshadows the list of "enemies" enumerated in Walwyn's *Whisper in the Eare*.[13] The inevitability of error and differences while knowledge is imperfect is suggested.[14] The reference to the story of Diana and Demetrius (Acts 19: 24–38) is the first of many in Walwyn's writings,[15] while the warning against "Wolves in Sheepes cloathing" and the advice to be "wise as Serpents, . . . innocent as Doves" (Matthew 10:16) in dealing with deceivers are used in a similar context in *A Word in Season*.[16]

The *Power of Love* is reproduced in facsimile in *Tracts on Liberty*, ed. Haller, 2:271–304.

THE POWER OF LOVE.

LONDON, Printed by *R.C.* for *John Sweeting*, at the signe of the Angell in Popes-head Alley. 1643.

To every Reader.

For there is no respect of persons with God: and whosoever is possest with love, judgeth no longer as a man, but god-like, as a true Christian. What's here towards? (sayes one) sure one of the Family of love: very well! pray stand still and consider: what family are you of I pray? are you of Gods family? no doubt you are: why, God is love, and if you bee one of Gods children be not ashamed of your Father, nor his family: and bee assured that in his fa- [A3] mily, he regards neither fine clothes, nor gold rings, nor stately houses, nor abundance of wealth, nor dignities, and titles of honour, nor any mans birth or calling, indeed he regards nothing among his children but love. Consider our Saviour saith, He that hath this worlds goods, and seeth his brother lack, how dwelleth the love of God in him? Judge then by this rule who are of Gods family; Looke about and you will finde in these woefull dayes thousands of miserable, distressed, starved, imprisoned Christians: see how pale and wan they looke: how coldly, raggedly, & unwholsomely they are cloathed; live one weeke with them in their poore houses, lodge as they lodge, [A3v] eate as they eate, and no oftner, and bee at the same passe to get that wretched food for a sickly wife, and hunger-starved children; (if you dare doe this for feare of death or diseases) then walke abroad, and observe the generall plenty of all necessaries, observe the gallant bravery of multitudes of men and women abounding in all things that can be imagined: observe likewise the innumerable numbers of those that have more then sufficeth. Neither will I limit you to observe the inconsiderate people of the world, but the whole body of religious people themselves, and in the very Churches and upon solemne dayes: view them well, and see whether they [A4] have not this worlds goods; their silkes, their beavers, their rings, and other divises will testifie they have; I, and the wants and distresses of the poore will testifie that the love of God they have not. What is here aimed at? (sayes another) would you have all things common? for love seeketh not her owne good, but the good of others. You say very true, it is the Apostles doctrine: and you may remember the multitude of beleevers had all things common: that was another of their opinions, which many good people are afraid of. But (sayes another) what would you have? would you have no distinction of men, nor no government? feare it not: nor [A4v] flye the truth because it suites not with your corrupt opinions or courses; on Gods name distinguish of men and women too, as you see the love of God abound in them towards their brethren, but no otherwise; And for that great mountaine (in your understanding) government, 'tis but a molehill if you would handle it familiarly, and bee bold with it: It is common agreement to bee so governed: and by common agreement men chuse for governours, such as their vertue and wisedome make fit to governe: what a huge thing this matter of trust is made of? and what cause is there that men that are chosen should keepe at such distance, or those that [A5] have chosen them bee so sheepish in their presence? Come, you are mightily afraid of opinions, is there no other that you feare? not the Anabaptists, Brownists, or Antinomians? Why doe you start man? have a little patience, would you truly understand what kinde of people these are, and what opinions they hold? If you would; bee advised by

some learned man, and with him consult what hath learnedly beene
written of the most weake and vitious amongst any of them that
could bee found, and make your conclusion (according to custome)
that they are all such: but if you would free your selves from common
mistakes concerning those your bre- [A5v] thren, then acquaint your
selves with them, observe their wayes, and enquire into their doctrines your selfe, and so make your conclusion, or judge not of them;
visit them, heare them out, stand cleare from all prejudging: and then
see what dangerous people they are that are generally so called: particulars being absurd rules of judging; for so the Turke is misled in his
judgment of Christianity: and no marvaile since hee judgeth thereof
by the doctrine and life of the most superstitious, Idolatrous, and
vitious amongst them. Well, what next are you afraid of? for some
men take delight to be under the spirit of bondage, and doe not think
themselves in good [A6] estate except they be in feare: but come,
feare nothing, you are advised by the Apostle to try all things, and to
hold fast that which is good: to prove the Spirits whether they bee of
God or not: 'tis your selfe must doe it, you are not to trust to the
authority of any man, or to any mans relation: you will finde upon
tryall that scarcely any opinion hath beene reported truly to you: and
though in every one of them you may finde some things that you
cannot agree unto, you will yet be a gainer, by discovering many excellent things that you as yet may be unsatisfied in, and by due consideration of them all perfect your owne judgement. Reade the ensuing discourse impartially, and you will finde the minde [A6v] of him
that hateth no man for his opinion; nor would have any man troubled
for any opinion, except such, as make the bloud of Christ ineffectuall,
or such as would destroy all that will not submit to their opinions; hee
seemes to bee of the Apostles minde, that considered all other things
in love: (and that in matters of moment too, even where some observed a day unto the Lord, & others not observed) He bids you
walke in love, as Christ hath loved you, and gave himselfe for you, an
offering and a Sacrifice; you that love your brother so poorely, as that
you cannot allow him the peaceable enjoyment of his mind and judgment would hardly lay downe your life for him; let brotherly love
conti- [A7] nue, and let every one freely speake his minde without
molestation: and so there may be hope that truth may come to light,
that otherwise may be obscured for particular ends: plaine truth will
prove all, sufficient for vanquishing of the most artificiall, sophisticall
errour that ever was in the world; give her but due and patient audience, and her perswasions are ten thousand times more powerfull

to worke upon the most dull refractory minde, then all the adulterate
allurements and deceivings of art. What is here publisht is out of fervent love to the Communion of Christians: that they might tast and
see how good the Lord is, In whose presence [A7v] there is fulnesse
of joy, and at whose right hand there are pleasures for evermore.
Wherefore rejoyce in the Lord alwayes, and againe I say rejoyce: and
let your song bee alwayes, Glory be to God on high, in earth peace,
good will towards men. Let truth have her free and perfect working,
and the issue will bee increase of beleevers: let faith have her perfect
working, and the issue will bee increase of love: and let love have her
perfect working, and the whole world will be so refined, that God will
be all in all; for hee that dwelleth in love, dwelleth in God, in whom,
ever fare you well, and bee cheerefull. [A8]

THE POWER OF LOVE.

Tit. 2. 11, 12. The grace (or love) of God that bringeth salvation unto all men hath
appeared, teaching us to deny ungodlinesse and worldly lusts, and to live soberly,
righteously, & godly in this present world.

It is evident (though it be little regarded or considered, the more is the
pity) that in naturall things all things whatsoever [1] that are necessary for the use of mankinde, the use of them is to be understood
easily with out study or difficulty: every Capacity is capable thereof;
and not only so, but they are all likewise ready at hand, or easily to be
had: a blessing that God hath afforded to every man, insomuch, that
there is no part of the habitable world, but yeeldes sufficient of usefull
things for a comfortable and pleasant sustentation of the inhabitants;
as experience testifieth in all places; and Saint Paul witnessed that
God left himselfe not without witnesse, in that he did good, gave
them raine from heaven, and fruitfull seasons, feeding their hearts
with foode and gladnesse: by all which it plainely appeares that God
ever intendeth unto man a pleasant and comfortable life: you know it
is said, that God made man righteous, but he sought out many [2]
inventions: that is, he made him naturally a rationall creature, judging rightly of all things, and desiring only what was necessary, and so
being exempt from all labour, and care of obtaining things superfluous, he passed his dayes with aboundance of delight and contentment: until he sought out unto himselfe many inventions: inventions

of superfluous subtilities and artificiall things, which have beene multiplied with the ages of the world, every age still producing new: so
now in these latter times we see nothing but mens inventions in esteeme, and the newer the more precious; if I should instance in particulars, I should or might be endlesse, as in diet, your selves know to
your costs, (for it costs you not only your monyes, but your healths,
and length of dayes) that this fruitfull nation sufficeth not to furnish
scarce the [3] meanest meale you make, but something must be had to
please the luxurious palate from forraine and farre countryes: and
ever the farther the better, and the dearer the more acceptable; you
know likewise the excessive provision that is made for entertainments and set meetings, where all grosse meates (you know my
meaning) must be banished, and nothing admitted but what is rare
and fine, and full of invention, in the dresses, sauces, and manner of
service: where all the senses must be pleased to the heighth of all
possible conceipt. If I should reckon up your new inventions for
buildings, and furniture for your houses, and the common costlinesse
of your apparell, and should set before you the manifold vexations,
perplexities, distractions, cares, and inconveniences that accrew unto
you by these your vaine [4] and ridiculous follies, I might be endlesse
therein also, and lose my labour; for there is no hope that I should
prevaile for a reformation of these things, when your daily experience
scourges you continually therunto, in one kind or other, and all in
vaine; yet I shall take leave to tell you that in these things, you walke
not as becommeth the gospell of Christ, but are carnall and walke as
men, as vaine, fantasticall, inconsiderate men; such as very heathen
and meere naturall men would be ashamed of: their experience (that a
life according to nature, to be content with little, with what was ever
ready, and easy to be had, was the most pleasant life and exempt
from all vexations) was instruction sufficient unto many of them, to
frame themselves thereunto, and to abandon all kindes of superfluities, without retaining the [5] least; & thereby obtained a freedome
to apply themselves to the consideration and practise of wisedome
and vertue.

It is a wonderfull thing to my understanding, that men should call
themselves Christians, and professe to be religious, and to be diligent
readers of Scripture, and hearers of Sermons, and yet content themselves to bee indeed in many things carnall, and to walke as did the
most indiscreete and inconsiderate Gentiles. Doth the Scripture teach
no more then nature teacheth? though it doe infinitely, yet your practise compared with wise considerate naturall men declares it doth

not; how extreamely then (thinke you) doe you cause the name of God to be blasphemed? Doe you thinke it is sufficient that you are not drunkards, nor adulterers, nor usurers, nor contentious [6] persons, nor covetous? beloved, if you will truely deserve the name of Christians, it is not sufficient: but you are to abandon all superfluities, all poring after vaine superfluous things, and thereby to exempt your selves from all unnecessary cares that choake the Word, and bee at liberty to consider, and to apply your selves freely to the continuall contemplation of the infinite love of God, evidently and plainely set forth unto you in his blessed word: as in the words that I have read un[to] you: for as it is in naturall things, so holds it in spirituall: God hath dealt abundantly well with us; there being nothing that is necessary either for the enlightning of our understandings, or the peace of our mindes, but what hee hath plainely declared and manifestly set forth in his Word: so plainely, that the meanest capacity is fully capable of [7] a right understanding thereof, and need not to doubt but that he is so. I will not say that God is not more good unto us, then we are hurtfull to our selves, (for his goodnesse is more availeable to our welfare, then our evill can be to our misery) but wee are as evill to our selves in all things as we can be possible: and that not onely in naturall things, but likewise in spirituall and divine things too, for therein also we have our inventions; the plaine and evident places of Scripture and manifestly declaring our peace and reconciliation with God, is become nauseous to us: they make salvation too easie to be understood, and tender it upon too easie tearmes, and too generall: this Manna that comes to us without our labour, industry, study, and watching, is two fulsome, something that hath bones in it must bee found out, and will be- [8] come more acceptable: every child or babe in Christs Schoole can understand these: We are full growne men in Christ, wee have spent our time in long and painefull studies, and have full knowledge in all Arts and sciences: there is no place of Scripture too hard for us: shew us the mysteries we cannot reveale: the Parables that wee cannot clearely open: the Prophesies that wee cannot interpret: a word or Syllable that wee cannot fitly apply, or the most palpable seeming contradiction that we cannot reconcile; nay it is to be doubted (wee have seene the vaine humour of man puft so high, and the world so fill'd and pestered with works and labours of this vaine nature) lest there are some such daring undertakers, that like as Alexander the great is said to have wept that there were no more worlds to conquer, so these Cham- [9] pions are grieved that there are no harder places for their braines to worke upon: or (which is more to bee lamented) one would feare they are much troubled that the most necessary truths are so easie to be understood: for that when they treate upon some very plaine place of Scripture, even so plaine as this which I have read unto you, yet in handling thereof they make it difficult, and darken the cleare meaning thereof with their forced and artificiall glosses: but as I wish there were no such dealers in divine things, so have I in my selfe resolved to avoid these extreame evills: for as in naturall things I am fully assured there is nothing of necessary use but what is easily understood and even ready at hand, so also doth my experience tell me, that we have no bettering of our understandings, or quieting of our mindes (the end [10] for which God hath vouchsafed his word) from any places of Scripture that hath any obscurity in them, but from such as are clearely exempt from all difficulty. You know God frequently complaines by his Prophets, saying, My people will not consider, they will not understand: and when I consider that your owne experience schooles you not sufficiently against your dotage upon the vaine superfluities of this world, wherein you know your selves to be carnall, and to walke as men, heaping unto your selves vexation upon vexation; I doe wonder that it doth not stagger the Ministers of God in their publishing of things divine to a people so qualified, so extreamely inconsiderate: indeed it would make one to suspect that the doctrine that you continually heare, that it were not powerfull nor from heaven, but weake and fitted [11] to your corrupt humours, and customes, since after so long time, it hath not subdued your worldly mindednesse. Sure I am, and I must have leave to tell you, that there is utterly a fault amongst you, nay those expressions are too soft, you have almost nothing but faults amongst you, and you will not consider, which you must doe, and seriously too, or you will never reduce your selves into such a condition, as will be really sutable to the blessed name of Christians. Beloved I have seriously considered it, and it is not your case alone, but it is the universall disease. I know not any that is not infected therewith, nor to whom it may not be said, Physitian heale they selfe; the milke we have suckt, and the common ayre hath beene totally corrupted: our first instructions, and all after discourses have beene indulgent [12] flatterers to our darling superfluities: and therefore he that undertakes the cure, must bee sure to bee provided of a fit and powerfull medicine, and to be diligent and faithfull in his undertaking; it is a taske that I have proposed unto my selfe, and though I should meete with the greatest discouragements, (as, the world is like enough to furnish his utmost forces to preserve his Kingdome) yet considering whose service I have undertaken, and whose works it is, I shall not despaire of successe. I am not ignorant that this worke hath often-times beene attempted, and persisted in: but with little fruit; through the universall mistake, that men are sooner perswaded from their vanities, through pressures of the law, and affrighting terrors of wrath and hell, then by the cordes of love: which yet I abundantly preferre, as you may [13] perceive by this text which I have chosen: for when all is done, It is the love of God bringing salvation, that teacheth us to deny all ungodlinesse and worldly lusts, and to live soberly, righteously, and godly in this present world. I must entreate your most earnest attention, as being full of hope that I shall doe you much more good then you conceive: for I must tell you, I cannot cure you of your earthly mindednesse, of your dotage upon superfluities, till I have first showne you your peace and reconciliation with God, and have wrought in you (through the power of Gods word) peace of conscience and joy in the holy Ghost. You are then seriously to consider what is said, and understanding will succeed. The love of God I know is often spoken of: a theame that hath begotten abundance of bookes and discourses: yet [14] none in no comparison like the Scriptures: most (if not all) discourses, that ever I have read or heard, doe in some sense or other, or in some measure injure and wrong those blessed discourses therof.

The love and favour of God (saith David) is better then life it selfe; What man in the whole world doth not gladly heare the joyfull tydings of the love of God? But it is good that every man rightly understand, and mistake not himselfe in this so blessed and delightfull Subject. I shall lay downe therfore some infallible principles which concerne the same. And I shall tell you nothing but what your selves know: and that is, that God doth most vehemently hate all manner of sinnes, and that it is impossible for him to doe otherwise, as being directly opposite to his most righte- [15] ous nature: and to that righteous nature wherein at first man was created, for in the likenesse of God created he him; and whilst you consider this, I shall advise you not to flatter your selves as the Pharisee did, saying, Lord I thanke thee I am not as other men, extortioners, unjust, adulterers, drunkards, covetous, proude, or licentious; can you say you have noe sinne? if you should, the word of God would contradict you, which testifieth that he that saith he hath no sinne is a liar, and the truth is not in him; and if sinne be in every one, necessarily it followes where sinne is, there is Gods hatred; nor doeth it any whit excuse or exempt those from the hatred of God, that can say their sinnes are fewe in number, and of very meane condition compared to others: whosoever you are that are thus indulgent to your [16] selves, you doe but deceive your selves, for Gods hatred, his wrath and anger, is so exact against all and every sinne, and so odious it is in his sight, that he denounceth, saying, Cursed is every one that continueth not to doe all that is written in the booke of the law: So as every mouth must be stopped, and all the world stand guilty before God; and though the sense and deepe apprehension of this woefull condition, doe worke in you the deepest of sorrow, though you should spend your dayes in weeping, and your nights in woefull lamentation, though you should repent your selves in dust and ashes, and cover your selves with sackcloathes: though you should fast your selves into palenesse, and hang downe your heads alwayes: though you should give all your goods to the poore; nay, [17] though you should offer up the fruit of your bodies, for the sinne of your soules; all this and more could be no satisfaction for the least sinne, nor bring any peace to your mindes: but you must of force cry out at last, as Saint Paul did, (stating this sad condition of all mankind under the law) *Oh wretched man that I am, who shall deliver me from this body of death!* Justly is it called a body of death; for man is of a fraile and weake condition at the best: a considerate man hath death alwayes before him: What joy or comfort then can hee take all his life long; being in the hatred of God, a vessell of wrath, and liable to eternall death in hell fire for ever? What can he looke upon that can give him content? Present a man that walkes in the sense of his sinfull condition, with all the pleasures the world afford, [18] and his sad heart turnes all into death; his conscience continually afflicts him; terrours, and feares, and eternall torments are ever in his thoughts: and such a wounded Spirit, who can beare? My beloved, I would not be mistaken in what I have said of this woefull condition, as though I presented it to your thoughts, as a meanes to terrifie you from any your sinfull courses: I know full well it is not the way, it is not Gods way: nor doe I wish this sad condition to be any of yours: though happily it may be thus with many of you: many of you may through sense of sinne, and of wrath due for sinne, walke in a very disconsolate condition: feares and terrours may abound in you: to whom (I doubt not) though great heavinesse may indure for a night, yet greater joy shall come in the morning: which as much as in [19] mee lyes, I shall indeavour to produce in every one of you.

I have presented this woefull condition of all mankind under the law, thus sadly and truly, because I finde generally men doe not seriously consider the bottomlesse depth of the misery from the which they are redeemed: I am not a preacher of the law, but of the gospell;

nor are you under the law, but under grace: the law was given by
Moses, whose minister I am not: but grace and truth came by Jesus
Christ, whose minister I am: whose exceeding love, hath appeared:
and because I would have you fully to see and consider his love,
therefore did I shew the woefull condition, from which only by his love
you are delivered.

Another principle I shall pray you to consider, is that God loves
nothing but what is pure and holy, [20] without spot or blemish: so as
it is a vaine and delusive doctrin, to say that God passes by our daily
infirmities, accepting our wills for our performances: our desire to be
obedient to his Commandements, for obedience: for where there is
the least defect, God hates for that very defect, and loves not but
where there is perfect holinesse and righteousnesse: which makes
this truth appeare, that by the deeds of the law shall no flesh be justified in his sight: for by the law is the knowledge of sinne. It is a sad
favour that the law ever did unto mankinde, to make his sinne appeare out of measure sinfull, stopping every mans mouth, admitting
no plea or excuse on mans behalfe; And yet it is so naturall to thinke
that he is still bound to doe something for obtaining the love and
favour of God, that you will [21] finde it is the hardest thing in the
world to free your selves from it, though it be the grossest Antichristian errour that ever was, for if righteousnesse come by the law, then
Christ died in vaine; It is such an errour that untill it be removed out
of your mindes, it will be but labour lost to endeavour to worke any
truth upon your mindes; and I have much cause, to feare your mindes
are tainted therewith, because our publicke catechismes, bookes, and
Sermons are for the most part corrupted therewith, so as we sucke
this errour in even with our very milke, and it becomes one substance
with many of us even to our old age; It was so in the Apostles times,
as may be seene in Acts the 15, from the 5. verse to the end of the
chapter, where you shall find that some that beleeved affirmed that it
was necessary to circum- [22] cise, and to keepe the law: but you will
finde by the story it was their errour; Also in the second to the Corinthians, the third to the end, where you shall find the law stiled the
ministration of death, written in tables of stone (which was the 10
Commandements) and verse the 11. to be done away, and a more
glorious ministration to take place and remaine: and yet the breeding
of the Jewes being under the law, (though they did beleeve the comming of Christ) yet still (even to that day the Apostle wrote) their
minds were blinded, and the vaile remained at the reading of the old
Testament, which vayle is done away in Christ. These things (be-

loved) you are to consider seriously, for that untill you doe undoubtedly see your selves not to be under the law, no not in the least respect, you cannot see your selves to be under [23] grace: that is, in the
favour and love of God, untill when you cannot with sound judgment
affirme, that which my text affirmeth, that is, that the love of God
hath appeared: for he that in any measure conceiveth himselfe to be
under the law, doth not clearly discerne the love of god: for that
vayle is before his eyes; you all give credit to the word of God: let S.
Paul then be your guide to leade you out of this sad Ægyptian bondage who knew all things that concerned the law, yet cryes out, I account all things as losse and dung, that I may be found in Christ, not
having my owne (or mans) righteousnesse, which is of the law, but
the righteousnesse which is of God in him: make it your own cases by
sound consideration, for yee are all justified freely by his grace
through the redemption that is in Jesus Christ: your feares, [24] nor
sinnes, nor doubtings, cannot alter that condition which Christ hath
purchased for you, for though the sting of death be sinne, & the
strength of sin be the law, yet thankes be unto God, for he hath given
us the victory through our Lord Jesus Christ: so as you may all boldly
say, Oh death where is thy sting, O grave where is thy victory? And
that none of you may doubt of his exceeding love, and your perfect
reconciliation with God, I wil reade unto you certaine passages (in the
5 chapter, to the Romans,) which if well weighed, will leave you without all scruple, (verse, 6) When we were yet without strength in due
time Christ died for the ungodly: you see there that ungodlinesse did
not hinder, but that Christ died for thee that art ungodly: dost thou
stand amazed, and canst not throwly beleeve? the [25] Apostle grants
that to mans judgment it is incredible; for amongst men, scarcely for a
righteous man will one dye, yet peradventure for a good man one
would even dare to dye: but to confirme thy timerous heart (verse 8.)
God commendeth his love towards us, in that whilst we were yet
sinners Christ died for us, (v. 9.) much more being then justified by
his bloud we shall be saved from wrath through him, (v. 10.) for if
when we were enemies, we were reconciled by the death of his
Sonne, much more being reconciled, we shall be saved by his life: so
as now thou hast cause to joy in God through our Lord Jesus Christ,
by whom thou hast received the atonement: and to take from thee all
staggering (in the 18. v.) he confirmes thee, saying, As by the offence
of one, judgement came upon all men to condemna- [26] tion: even so
by the righteousnesse of one, the free gift came upon all men to justification of life: and (in the 20. vers.) because he knew thy pronenesse

to make questions still about the Law, he tels thee the Law entred that sinne might abound, but withall assures thee, that where sinne abounded, grace (or love) did much more abound: that as sinne had reigned unto death, even so grace (or love) might reign through right-eousnesse unto eternall life through Christ our Lord.

(Beloved) God by the power of his Word hath begotten so ful as-surance of these things in me, as that thereby he hath made me an able Minister of the New Testament: not of the Letter, (or the Law) but of the Spirit: for the Letter killeth, but the Spirit (that is the Gospel) giveth life. Nor doe I see any cause why any of you here present should [27] so much as doubt your salvation; I am a Minister of recon-ciliation, and am thereby bound to tell you (for woe is unto me if I preach not the Gospel, as in the 2 Cor. 5. 19.) that God was in Christ reconciling the world unto himselfe, not imputing their trespasses unto them: and hath committed unto us the Word of reconciliation; Now then we are Ambassadours for Christ, as though God did be-seech you by us, we pray you to be reconciled unto God; for he hath made him to be sinne for us, that knew no sinne, that we might be made the righteousnesse of God in him; so as (however we may vainely conceive to our owne prejudice) God considers us not as we see our selves full of sinne, full of iniquity, but as we should consider our selves, agreeable to all these passages of his blessed Word, fully and perfectly washed from all [28] our sinnes by the bloud of his Son (which every one of us doe beleeve, though we doe not consider) and then with unspeakable joy we shall see that we are reconciled to God by the death of his Sonne: that we are justified freely by his grace: that for our lost righteousnesse of the Law, we are made the right-eousnesse of God in him: having peace of conscience and joy in the holy Ghost, by whose word these blessed truths are declared unto us. Are these things so indeed, doth God accept me a poore miserable sinner, as righteous in his sight, and freed from sinne, from all sinne? Heare still the Word of God, he hath borne our sinnes in his body on the tree, and it is the bloud of Christ that cleanseth thee from all sinne: he by his one oblation once offered, hath made a full, perfect, and sufficient satisfaction, and sacrifice for the [29] sinnes of the whole world; and if we sinne, we have an Advocate with the Father, Jesus Christ the righteous: and he is the propitiation for our sinnes; and not for ours onely, but for the sinnes of the whole world. This worke of your redemption and reconciliation with God was perfected when Christ died: and nothing shall be able to separate you from his love then purchased: neither infidelity, nor impenitencie, nor un-thankfulnesse, nor sinne, nor any thing whatsoever can make void his purchase: no, though with the Jewes you should deny the Lord that bought you: so powerful was his bloud-shedding, and of so full value for discharging of all our debts, past, present, and to come; so infinite is his goodnesse, so free is his love, and so abundantly happy is our condition, though many of us have beene too [30] too ignorant thereof: and for want of this knowledge many of us have walked very uncomfortably, spending our time in fasting, weeping, and mourning; in praying, reading, and hearing, and in performance of other duties, as you call them, and all to get Christ: our feare distracts our judgements, that wee consider not what the Scripture sets forth unto us: if we did, wee should see aparently that it sets forth salvation wrought and perfected for ever: to whom doth it manifest the same? to sinners, to the ungodly, to all the world: a worke perfected, depending on no condition, no performance at all, What would people have to give peace to their mindes? you doe wrong your selves through nice distinctions: the word of God is given to declare these truths, and that he is our peace: the word of God you doe [31] beleeve, and so cannot but be comforted, the onely end for which it is preserved unto you: that you might reade, and know, and understand your blessed condition: for faith comes by hearing, and hearing by the word of God: and you are to looke for no other testimony: nor are you to doubt your selves: for though your present comfort depends upon your beleeving this word, yet the worke of Christ depends not on your beleeving: and though you should not beleeve, yet hee is faithfull and cannot deny himselfe to be your redeemer, your peace-maker, your Saviour. Men are not pleased except salvation be proved to be very difficult to bee obtained, it must still depend either on our beleeving, or doing, or repenting, or selfe-deniall, or Sabbath-keeping, or something or other, or else man is not pleased: [32] too easie? good God! that free love should be suspected; that because it is easie to be had, we should put it farre from us; why, God knew full well thou wert dead, he considered that thou wert but dust; suppose he had required any thing of thee, without which thou shouldst have no part in Christ, what a sad case hadst thou beene in? goe thy wayes, and with chearefulnesse possesse his infinite love, and declare unto thy brethren what the Lord hath done for al our souls; tel them that the love of God bringing salvation hath appeared, teaching us to deny all ungodlinesse, and worldly lusts, and to live soberly, righteously, and godly in this present world. And I shall desire to know of all that heare me this day, whereof some may happily be addicted to the corruptions of this world: for our times though we call [33] them times of light, yet do abound with gluttony, drunkennesse, and whoredome, usury, pride, oppression, and all kinde of wickednesse, such as is not to be named amongst Christians, (what shall I say to these things? it will be in vaine for me to reprove you for them: for men never reforme their vices, till first their judgements be well informed, and then they kindly reforme themselves) I shall onely demand whether the love of God doth more appeare unto you now, then it hath done formerly? surely it is impossible but you must be sensible of his love, it is so full and absolute, so free and unexpecting love. How is it possible you should heare and not consider? had it not beene for this unexpressible and unexampled love, you had beene eternally wretched and miserable, companions of Devils, and damned spirits in Hell for [34] ever, where the Worme never dieth, and the fire never goeth out; me thinkes you should embrace this love with open armes, and meditate thereupon day and night: it deserveth to be entertained with the greatest respect, and to be esteemed above ten thousand lives: for (beloved) though it comes freely to you, and costs you nothing, no not so much as a sigh or teare, yet if you read over the story of our Saviours passion, and sufferings, you will finde it was purchased at an excessive price, excessive paines, and excessive torments: nay it is even past wonder that he that thought it no robbery to be equall to God, should be in the forme of a servant, and become obedient to death, even the most bitter death of the Crosse for our sinnes: that he should be made sinne for us that knew no sinne, that we might be made the [35] righteousnesse of God in him; me thinkes these and the like considerations should be powerfull in your minds, that your spirits should even burne within you, untill you found out some way to expresse your thankfulnesse for so great, so infinite love. I cannot suspect the most vitious man in the world, but that hearing these things his heart will make strict enquiry, what he shall render unto the Lord for all his benefits? and his heart once moving in thoughts of thankfulnesse will instantly be inflamed with love, which in an instant refines the whole man. God is love, and love makes man God-like; and henceforth let me pray you to marke the workings of love in your owne soules, and you shall finde that when your long accustomed corruptions (by which you have wounded your owne consciences, [36] and brought dishonour to God, and reproach to the holy name of Christians) doe tempt to the like abominable actions, your love to God that so freely hath loved you, will be so prevalent with you, that you will resolve rather to lose your lives then to show your selves so basely ungratefull: the vanities you have delighted in will become odious unto you: all your labour will be that your conversation be as becommeth the Gospel of Christ, nay you will shunne the very appearance of evill: and if your brother offend you in any kinde whatsoever, you will finde no difficulty to forgive; if you doe, doe but thinke of the love wherewith Christ hath loved you, and nothing can be imagined so abominably injurious but you will gladly forgive. And if you have this worlds goods, and that brother lacke, you will rejoyce [37] that you have an occasion and means to make known unto the world how powerfully the love of God dwelleth in you: you will be able to doe all things through love that strengthens you. Love will be as a new light in your understandings by which you will judge quite otherwise of all things, then formerly you have don; the vanities and superfluities which in the beginning of my discourse I reckoned up unto you, will seeme odious unto you, and you will no longer fashion your selves like unto this world, but will walk as becommeth the Gospel of Christ: you will no longer minde high things, but make your selves equall to men of low degree: you will no longer value men and women according to their wealth, or outward shewes, but according to their vertue, & as the love of God appeareth in them: nay if you be studious in this worke of [38] love, nothing will be more deare unto you then the glory of God (who hath so infinitely loved you) so as you will be most zealously opposite to whatsoever is opposite unto God, you will finde it nothing to hazzard your lives for God, in defence of his truth from errour; in defence of your brother or neighbour from oppression or tyranny: love makes you no longer your owne but Gods servants, and prompts you to doe his will in the punishment of all kinde of exorbitances, whether it be breach of oathes, breach of trust, or any kinde of injustice in whomsoever, and to be no respecter of persons; nor will any ones greatnesse over-sway or daunt your resolutions, but you will be bold as Lions, not fearing the faces of men: you will when neede requires, that is, when tyrants and oppressors endeavour by might [39] and force to pervert all Lawes, and compacts amongst men, and to pervert the truth of God into a lie, interpreting his sacred word as patron of their unjust power, as if any unjust power were of God, and were not to be resisted: I say, such insolencies as these will inflame your zeale, and set you all on fire manfully to fight the Lords battell, and to bring into subjection those abominable imaginations and ungodly courses of men: your judgements will be so well informed, as you will know these things are by God referred unto you, and you will not resigne them up to him, but willingly sacrifice your lives and fortunes, and all that is neare and deare unto you, rather then suffer his name to be so blasphemed, or your innocent brethren, or your wives and children to become a prey to wicked and [40] bloud-thirsty men. The politicians of this world would have religious men to be fooles, not to resist, no by no meanes, lest you receive damnation: urging Gods holy Word, whilst they proceed in their damnable courses; but (beloved) they will finde that true Christians are of all men the most valiant defenders of the just liberties of their Countrey, and the most zealous preservers of true Religion: vindicating the truths of God with their lives, against all ungodlinesse and un-righteousnesse of men: making thereby the whole world to know that true Christianity hates and abhorres tyranny, oppression, perjury, cruelty, deceipt, and all kinde of filthinesse; and true Christians to be the most impartiall, and most severe punishers thereof, and of all kinde of wickednesse, of any men whatsoever. [41]

Great is the power of love, for love makes men to bee of one mind: and what can bee too strong for men united in love? and therefore I shall warne you to marke and consider those that make divisions amongst you. I pray mistake me not, I doubt you are too apt in this case to make a wrong application: I doe not meane that you should marke those, that are different from you in judgement, with any ridiculous or reproachfull names: but my advice is that you marke those that make divisions amongst you, and those are they that have invented a name of reproach for every particular difference in judge-ment: and in their publike Sermons and private discourses, endeav-our might and maine to keep at the widest distance, and by odious tales and false imputations make you irreconciliable: [42] nay make you even ready to cut one anothers throates; or by this division pre-pare you for your common adversaries to cut both yours and theirs too; difference in judgement there will be, untill love have a more powerfull working in our hearts: wee should therefore like wise men at least beare with one anothers infirmities: love will cover all that can bee called infirmity; but resolved malice love it selfe will punish. Such opinions as are not destructive to humane society, nor blaspheme the worke of our Redemption, may be peaceably endured, and consid-ered in love: and in case of conspiracy against our common liberty, what a madnesse is it for men to stand in strife about petty opinions? for who are all those that are so much railed at by our common Preachers? [43] who are they say they? why, they are the most dan-gerous Anabaptists, Brownists, and Separatists: that are enemies to all order and decency, that cry down all learning and all government in the Church, or Common-wealth. (Beloved) to my knowledg these things are not true of any of them: it is true, they cannot do al things so orderly and decently as they would, because they are hunted into corners, and from one corner to another, and are not free to exercise their consciences, as had they liberty they might, and would; And as for learning, as learning goes now adaies, what can any judicious man make of it, but as an Art to deceive and abuse the understandings of men, and to mislead them to their ruine? if it be not so, whence comes it that the Universities, and University men throughout [44] the Kingdome in great numbers are opposers of the welfare of the Common-wealth, and are pleaders for absurdities in government, arguers for tyranny, and corrupt the judgements of their neighbours? no man can be so simple as to imagine that they conceive it not lawfull, or not usefull for men to understand the Hebrew, Greeke, or Latine; but withall, if they conceive there is no more matter in one language then another, nor no cause why men should be so proud for understanding of languages, as therefore to challenge to themselves the sole dealing in all spirituall matters; who (I say) can blame them for this judgement? they desire that a mans ability of judge- [45] ment should be proved by the cleare expression of necessary truths, rather then by learning: and since the Scriptures are now in English, which at first were in Hebrew, Greeke, or Syriack, or what other language; why may not one that understands English onely, both understand and declare the true meaning of them as well as an English Hebrician, or Grecian, or Roman whatsoever? I, but saies some politick learned man, a man that doth not understand the Originall language, cannot so perfectly give the sense of the Scripture, as he that doth: or as one that makes it his study for ten or twenty yeares together, and hath no other employment: every man being best skilled in his owne profession wherein he hath been [46] bred and accustomed. I did well to say some politicke learned man might thus object: for indeed what is here but policie? for if it be as such men would imply, I pray what are you the better for having the Scripture in your owne language: when it was lock'd up in the Latine tongue by the policie of Rome, you might have had a learned Fryar for your money at any time to have interpreted the same: and though now you have it in your owne language, you are taught not to trust your owne understanding, (have a care of your purses) you must have an University man to interpret the English, or you are in as bad a case as before but not in worse; for, for your money you may have plenty at [47] your service, & to interpret as best shall please your fancie. Let me prevaile with you to free your selves from this bondage, and to trust to your own considerations in any thing that is usefull for your understandings and consciences: and judge more charitably of your brethren, & understand what learning is, and to marke those that cause divisions among you, and you shal finde that they are learned men, & not unlearned. The learned man must live upon the unlearned, and therfore when the unlearned shal presume to know as much as the learned, hath not the learned man cause to bestir his wits, and to wrangle too when his Copy-hold is in such danger? I pray what was the cause that Demetr. and the Craftsmen cried out, great is Diana of [48] the Ephesians, whom al Asia and the world worship? was it the love to the goddesse or her worship? no, we find it was their covetousnesse and particular gaine? What is it els to cry out, great is learning, great are the Universities, who shall answer an adversary? (money answereth all things) ambition, covetousnesse, disdaine, pride, and luxury are the things aimed at: and if it be not so, by the fruits you shall certainely know. As for government, those that are accused are not guilty, for they are enemies onely to usurpations, and innovations, and exorbitances in government: indeed they are haters of tyranny, and all arbitrary power, but no other: and therefore those that falsely accuse them, are [49] they that cause and foment divisions amongst you: therefore marke them, and be not deceived by their dissembled insinuations to hold you in division, whilst they have opportunity to make a prey of you. You know there are Wolves in Sheepes cloathing: be wise as Serpents, able to discover them, innocent as Doves, gently bearing with the infirmities of the weake, having nothing in more esteeme then love: thus you will answer love with love: that henceforwards your owne soules may constantly witnes to your selves (what this Scripture expresseth) *That the love of God bringing salvation to all men hath appeared, teaching you to live soberly, righteously, and godly in this present world:* Now unto him [50] that hath loved us, and washed away our sinnes in his owne bloud, be praise and glory for ever, Amen.

FINIS [51]

(4)

The Compassionate Samaritane

1st edition, [June–July?] 1644. This edition of 83 pages includes "Good counsell to
   all," pp. 72–83.
2d edition, "corrected and enlarged," [July?] 1644. This edition of 79 pages omits
   "Good counsell to all." Thomason's date of acquisition, 5 January 1644/5, is all
   but certainly well after publication in view of the appearance of Good Counsell
   to All as a separate tract more than five months before.
Reprinted from a copy of the 2d edition of the tract in the Thomason Collection in the
   British Library

The Compassionate Samaritane was published anonymously without
imprint or license. The 1st edition includes three parts: an introductory address "To the Commons of England"; "Liberty of Conscience
Asserted, and the Separatist vindicated"; "Good counsell to all," pp.
72–83 (12 pages). The 2d edition of Compassionate Samaritane does not
include "Good counsell to all," which was issued in July 1644 as a
separate tract of 14 pages, numbered 79–92.[1] The format and type
style of the two editions of Compassionate Samaritane are different, and
there are variations in paragraphing, capitalization, spelling, and
punctuation. The text of the 2d edition has a number of interpola-
tions—including the addition of "Finis" at the end of page seventy-
nine. Haller identifies the tract as Walwyn's and resolves the bibliographical problem of the two editions.[2]

   In general and particular Compassionate Samaritane has unmistakable
marks of Walwyn's mind and style. The central plea of the work is for
liberty of conscience for the separatists "left in the lurch" not only by
Presbyterians but by Independents who subscribed to the argument
of An Apologeticall Narration.[3] The author of Compassionate Samaritane
notes that he is not a separatist and indicates that he is within his
parish church. He speaks not in "mine own cause" but on behalf of
"harmlesse people" whose advocate he has become "after much inquiry and examination of their Tenets, and practice."[4] Intermittently

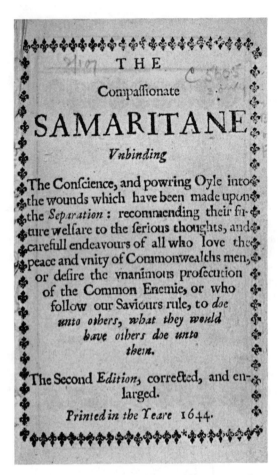

THE

Compaſſionate

SAMARITANE

Vnbinding

The Conſcience, and powring Oyle into
the wounds which have been made upon
the *Separation* : recommending their future welfare to the ſerious thoughts, and
carefull endeavours of all who love the
peace and vnity of Commonwealths men,
or deſire the vnanimous proſecution
of the Common Enemie, or who
follow our Saviours rule, to *doe
unto others, what they would
have others doe unto
them.*

The Second *Edition,* correƈted, and enlarged.

Printed in the Yeare 1644.

Title page of *The Compassionate Samaritane,* 1644.
(Folger Shakespeare Library)

resorting to a modified Socratic method, the tract repeatedly recalls the loyalty and assistance given by separatists to the cause of Parliament and the breaking of the "yoakes" that had also burdened the now reforming Presbyterians and Independents.[5] These divines, states Compassionate Samaritane, uses the new licensing ordinance to suppress separatist writings; the press should be free to all who write "nothing scandalous, nor dangerous to the State." In 1649 Walwyn would recall his early opposition to "the stopping of the presse."[6]

The golden rule (Matthew 7:12), which is repeated in several works known to be Walwyn's, is quoted twice in Compassionate Samaritane.[7] Walwyn's fundamental conviction that no man can follow other than his own belief is stressed,[8] as is his belief that, as long as knowledge is incomplete, diversity is inevitable and "no man, nor no sort of men can presume of an unerring spirit."[9] Anticlericalism occupies many pages,[10] and Diana of Ephesus is twice recalled.[11] Walwyn's favorite verses, 5 and 23, from Romans 14 are repeated.[12] The political advantages of peaceable people in a nation enjoying religious liberty are remarked,[13] and the importance of individuals reaching their own judgments is emphasized.[14]

The 2d edition of The Compassionate Samaritane is reproduced in facsimile in Tracts on Liberty, ed. Haller, 3:61–104.

THE Compassionate SAMARITANE

Unbinding The Conscience, and powring Oyle into the wounds which have been made upon the Separation: recommending their future welfare to the serious thoughts, and carefull endeavours of all who love the peace and unity of Commonwealths men, or desire the unanimous prosecution of the Common Enemie, or who follow our Saviours rule, to doe unto others, what they would have others doe unto them.

The Second Edition, corrected, and enlarged.

Printed in the Yeare 1644.

Si populus vult decipi, decipiatur.

To him that reads.

IF after this, when all the guiles,
That have misled you, and the wiles

Are manifested cleare as day,
So that you must say, these are they:
You yet will be befoold, you may.
Errours have some excuse, when they'r not knowne,
But being known once, wilfulnesse has none. [A2]

TO THE COMMONS OF ENGLAND.

To you whom the People have chosen for the managing of their affaires, I present this necessary Treatise without boldnesse and without feare: for I am well assured, that as it is mine, and every mans duty, to furnish You with what we conceive will advanse the Common good, or bring ease or comfort to any sort of men that deserve well of their Countrey (as You cannot but know the Seperation doe, if You consider with what charge [A3] and hazard, with what willingnes and activity they have furthered the Reformation so happily begun) so likewise it is, Your duty, to heare and put in execution, whatsoever to Your judgments shall appeare conducing to those good ends and purposes. I recommend here to Your view the oppressed Conscience, and the despised Separation: They have been much wounded (I believe every body can say by whom) and the people have passed by without compassion or regard, though they themselves must necessarily partake in their sufferings There are none left, to play the good Samaritanes part but Your selves, who as You have power; will, (I make no question) be willing too, when You have once well considered the matter, which this small Treatise will put You in mind to doe. It is not to be supposed, that You (who have so long spent Your time in recovering [A3v] the Common Liberties of England, should in Conclusion turne the Common into Particular; let the insinuations and suggestions of some in the Synod, be what they will, I make no question, but You will see both through and beyond them; and will never be swayed from a good conscience to maintaine particular mens Interests.

In the beginning of Your Session, when our Divines (as they would have us call them) wrote freely against the Bishops, & the Bishops made complaint to You for redresse; some of You made answer, that there was no remedy, for as much as the Presse was to be open and free for all in time of Parliament: I shall make bold as a Common of England to lay claime to that priviledge, being assured that I write nothing scandalous, or dangerous to the State, (which is justly and upon good grounds prohibited by Your Or [A4] dinance to that effect) only I humbly desire You to consider whether more was not got from You by that Ordinance then You intended, and that though it was purposed by You to restrain the venting and dispersing of the Kings writings and his Agents, yet it hath by reason of the qualifications of the Licensers wrought a wrong way, and stopt the mouthes of good men, who must either not write at all, or no more then is sutable to the judgments and interests of the Licencers. The Seperation (I guesse) would have tooke it for better dealing, if the Divines had in expresse tearmes obtained of You an Ordinance for suppression of all Anabaptisticall, Brownisticall, or Independant writings; then to have their mouthes stopt so subtlely, so insensibly, and their just Liberty in time of Parliament taken from them unawares. There can be no greater Argument, that [A4v] the Divines intend not well, then their taking uncough, and mysterious, subtile wayes to effect their ends; even such as far better become Polititians, then Ministers.

It is high time O Commons of England, to put an End to the sufferings of the Seperation, who have for many yeares been the object of all kind of tyranny, Papisticall, Prelaticall, and Regall: The first Foundation of honor, and respect was certainly from publike service and protection of the distressed: Make it Your worke, and assure Your selves, You will find not only the universall love of all good men accompaning You, but a quiet and cheerfull Conscience, which is above all honour and riches, Others may weary themselves in plots and contrivances to advance selfe-ends and interests, to the peoples dammage and molestations; sadnesse and distraction will be their [A5] companions for it. But make it Your businesse, Ye chosen men of England according to the trust reposed in You to protect the Innocent, to judg their cause impartially, to circumvent men in their wicked endeavours; and so You will become the beloved of God, the beloved of good men. [A5v]

LIBERTY of CONSCIENCE asserted, And the Separatist vindicated.

Having heretofore met with an Apologeticall Narration of Thomas Goodwin, Philip Nye, Sydrach Sympson, Jeremy Burroughs, William Bridge; I did with gladnesse of heart undertake the reading thereof, expecting therein to find such generall reasons for justification of themselves, to the world, as would have justified all the Separation, and so have removed by one [1] discourse those prejudices and mis-apprehensions, which even good men have of that harmelesse and well meaning sort of people: But finding contrary to that expectation that their Apologie therin for them selves and their Toleration was grounded rather upon a Remonstrance of the nearnesse between them and the Presbyterian, being one in Doctrine with them, and very little differing from them in Discipline, how they had been toler-ated by other Presbyter Churches, and indulgd with greater priv-iledges, then the Separatist, how they differed from the Separatist, and had cautiously avoyded those roks and shelves against which the Separatist had split themselves, confirming by these words, the peo-ples disesteem of Separatists, suggesting by that phrase of theirs, as if there were amongst the Separatists some dangerous by- [2] pathes or opinions, which they warily shund, though no mention be made what they are, which is the worst sort of calumny.

Finding to my hearts greife the Seperatist thus left in the lurch, and likely to be exposed to greater dangers then ever by the endeavours of these men, my heart abounded with greife, knowing the Innocency of their intentions, and honesty of their lives, that they are necessarily enforced to be of the mind they are, upon long examination of their owne tenents that they desire nothing more then that they should be publikely and impartially reasoned, knowing likewise their affection to the Common-wealth, their forwardnes of assistance in purse and person, knowing their Meetings to be so innocent, so far from confed-eracy or counterplots (though they are ve- [3] ry sensible of the sad and perplexed condition that they are in) that they have not yet so much as spoke ought in their owne defence, but trusting to the good-nesse of God, the equity of the Parliament, the simplicity and integ-rity of their owne wayes, doe quietly enjoy themselves and their wor-ship, let what will be brewing against them, being resolved like Hester to doe their dutyes, and if in doing thereof they perish, they perish: Me thinkes every man is bound in conscience to speak and doe what he can in the behalfe of such a harmelesse people as these: what though you are no Separatist (as I my selfe am none) the love of God appeares most in doing good for others: that love which aimes only at it selfe; those endeavours which would procure liberty only to them selves, can at best be called but selfe [4] love and selfe respects: 'Tis common freedome every man ought to aime at, which is every mans peculiar right so far as 'tis not prejudicall to the Common: Now because little can be done in their behalfe, unlesse Liberty of Con-science be allowed for every man, or sort of men to worship God in that way, and performe Christs Ordinances in that manner as shall appear to them most agreeable to Gods Word, and no man be punished or discountenanced by Authority for his Opinion, unlesse it be dangerous to the State: I have endeavoured in this Discourse to make appeare by the best reason I have, that every man ought to have Liberty of Conscience of what Opinion soever, with the caution above named: In doing whereof, I have upon occasion removed all prejudices that the people have concerning [5] the Separatist, and vindicated them from those false aspertions that are usually cast upon them to make them odious; wherein, my end, I make account, will evidently appeare, to be the peace and union of all, and to beget this judgement in the People and Parliament, that 'tis the principall interest of the Commonwealth, that Authority should have equall respect, and afford protection to all peaceable good men alike, notwithstanding their difference of opinion, that all men may be encouraged to be alike serviceable thereunto; liberty of Conscience is to be allowed every man for these following reasons

1. *Reason.* Because of what judgment soever a man is, he cannot chuse but be of that judgement, that is so evident in it selfe, that I suppose it will be granted by all, whatsoever a mans reason doth conclude [6] to be true or false, to be agreeabe or disagreabe to Gods Word, that same to that man is his opinion or judgement, and so man is by his own reason necessitated to be of that mind he is, now where there is a necessity there ought to be no punishment, for punishment is the recompence of voluntary actions, therfore no man ought to be punished for his judgment.

Objection. But it will be Objected, That the Separatists are a rash, heady People, and not so much concluded by their Reason, as their Fancie, that they have their Enthusiasms, and Revelations, which no body knowes what to make off, and that if they were a people that examined things rationally, the Argument would hold good for them. [7]

Ans. That I suppose this to be the Argument not of the present, but of the loose witted times before the Parliament, where some politike Bishop, or Dr. Ignorant University man, or knave Poet would endeavour by such a suggestion to the people to misguide their credulous hearts into hatred of those good men, who they knew to be the constant enemies to their delusions: but let all men now have other thoughts, and assure themselves that the Brownist and Anabaptist are rationall examiners of those things they hold for truth, milde discourseres, and able to give an account of what they beleive; they who are unsatisfied in that particular, may, if they please to visite their private Congregations which are open to all commers, have further satisfaction; perhaps here and there amongst [8] them may be a man that out of his zeale and earnestnes for that which he esteemes truth, may outrune his understanding, & shew many weaknesses in his discourse, I would the like frailty and inabilities were not to be found in many of us; but if the slips and wanderings of a few, and those the weakest, be an Argument sufficient to discountenance the Separation, and worke them out of the worlds favour, I pray God the same Argument may never be made use of against us; amongst whom, many, and they not esteemed the weakest neither, would give great advantages that way: In the mean time I wish with all my heart we could all put on the spirit of meeknes, and rather endeavour to rectifie by argument and perswation one anothers infirmities, then upbraid the owners of them with a visible [9] rejoycing that such things are slipt from them to their disadvantage.

One Custome they have amongst them which doth make even the generality of them able arguers in defence of their way, and that is either an use of objecting against any thing delivered amongst them, or proposing any doubt, whereof any desires to be resolved, which is done in a very orderly manner, by which meanes the weakest becomes in a short time much improved, and every one able to give an account of their Tenets, (not relying upon their Pastors, as most men in our congregations doe) which may serve to remove the objection, and put us to consider, whether the like custome be not wanting amongst us.

2. *Reas.* The uncertainty of knowledg in this life: no man, nor no sort of men can presume of an uner- [10] ring spirit: 'Tis knowne that the Fathers, Generall Councells, Nationall Assemblies, Synods, and Parliaments in their times have been most grosly mistaken: and though the present times be wiser then the former, being much freed from superstition, and taking a larger liberty to themselves of examining all things, yet since there remaines a possibility of errour, notwithstanding never so great presumptions of the contrary, one sort of men are not to compell another, since this hazard is run thereby, that he who is in an errour, may be the constrainer of him who is in the truth.

Ob. But unity and uniformity in Religion is to be aimed at, and confusion above all things to be avoyded, by Toleration new Opini- [11] ons will every day breake forth, and to the scandall of the Nation, we shall become a very monster in matters of Religion, one part being

Presbyter, another Anabaptist, Brownist another, and a fourth an Independent, and so divers according to the diversity of opinions that are already, or may be broached hereafter.

Ans. I answer, that in truth this objection appeares specious at the first glosse, and therfore is very moving upon the people, which the Bishops well knew, whose it was, and taken up as the fairest pretence for the suppression of those, who it is to be feared, will prove the suppressors. For answer whereunto I averre, that a compulsion is of all wayes the most unlikely to beget unity of mind, and uniformity in [12] practice, which experience will make evident. For,

The Fines, Imprisonments, Pillories, &c. used by the Bishops as meanes to unite, rather confirmed men in their judgments, and beget the abomination and odium which these times have cast upon the Hierarchie, being in the worst kind tyrannicall, as endeavouring by the punishment of the person, the bowing and subjecting of the Conscience. And if it be it instanced, that some there were that turned with the wind, and were terrified by feare of punishment into a compliance. I answer, that such men are so farre from being examples to be followed, that they may more justly be condemned for weathercokes fit (to be set up for men to know which way blowes the wind) of favour [13] delicacy, ease and preferment.

Secondly, The conscience being subject only to reason (either that which is indeed, or seems to him which hears it to be so) can only be convinced or perswaded thereby, force makes it runne backe, and strugle; it is the nature of every man to be of any judgment rather then his that forces. 'Tis to be presumed, that 'tis upon some good grounds of reason that a man is of that Judgement whereof he is. Wouldest thou have him be of thine? Shew him thy grounds, and let them both worke, and see which will get the victory in his understanding. Thus possibly he may change his mind, and be of one judgment with thee: but if you will use Club Law, instead of convincing and uniting, you arme men with prejudice against you, to conclude that you have no assurance [14] of truth in you, for then you would make use of that, and presume of the efficacy thereof, and not fight with weapons which you (doe or at least should) know not to be the weapons of truth. But I feare there is something more in it: I cannot thinke that the Bishops in their times used so many stratagems of vexation and cruelty against good people, to gaine them to be of their mind, they could not be ignorant that they set the Nonconformists of all sorts thereby at an irreconcilable hatred against them. No, there end rather was this, They had consulted who were opposite to their designes, and finding the Puritane and Sectary so to be, their interest was by all possible meanes to suppresse them, that so they might without opposition trample upon the people. And therefore in these times men should con- [15] sider what they doe. For if they who have the publique countenance doe beare themselves after the same manner towards the Anabaptists and Brownists, or whatsoever other sect there is, or may be, that cannot comply with them in judgement or practice (as by their beginnings we feare they will) what can we judge of them but that their ends and intentions are the same with the Bishops? For by their fruits (saith our Saviour) ye shall know them: we may be deceived by words their turnings and contextures are so infinite, that they may be framed so, as to make the worst seeme good. The actions of men are the best rules for others to judge them by. Now upon view of the actions of the Divines that are now in favour, men doe speake very strangly, some say the tyrannie over [16] conscience that was exercised by the Bishops, is like to be continued by the Presbiters: that the oppressours are only changed, but the oppression not likely to be removed. Others say, that the Anabaptist and Brownist are like to find harder masters, for that the Bishops made the punishment of them a matter of sport and profit to themselves, and reserved their punishments to be diversions of the peoples mindes from taking too much notice of their intrenchments upon the lawes and common liberty, suffering their societies notwithstanding to remaine, though so low and dejected that they were past feare of them. But the Presbiters, as it is conceived, will be more violent, as slaves usually are when they become masters: and thus talke not onely the Anabaptist and Brownist [17] and Antinomian (being chiefly in danger) but other the most moderate ingenious men, that are not swayed by the Divines interest.

They say too, that as it is not just, so neither is it politike, that in the beginnings and first rise, when the Divines are but laying the foundation of their greatnesse, wealth, and sway over the peoples consciences, and twisting their interest insensibly with the Parliaments, that in the infancy of their tyrannie they should carry themselves so high and presumptuous as they doe over other men, shewes that their wisedome here comes somewhat short of the Serpents, or else that they are so impatient at the not compliance of other men, that they break, out even against their owne interest. Nay some say further, that they did well indeed in being so zealous against [18] the Bishops, those Drones and Caterpillers of the Commonwealth, in making deservedly odious to the people their oppressive Courts,

Fines, Censures, and Imprisonments. But they begin to fear that some bad ends of their owne were aimed at herein, and not so much the liberty of the people, as that they might get up into the Chaire and become to them instead of a Lord Bishop, a ruling Presbytery, which they feare will bring in more rigidnesse and austerity, no lesse ambition and domination then the former.

And the reason they have to feare, is, because our Divines have not dealt clearely with us in many particulars, but continue certaine interests of the Bishops, which they find advantagious to advance their honour & esteeme with the people and [19] have entered already into many of their steps, which in them at first they did seem so much to abominate. That the interest only of the Bishop in particular, and of that sort of Prelates is exploded, but the generall interests of the Clergie, whereby another Prelacy may be erected, and the mystery of the Divines maintained in credit amongst the people, is still with all art and industry preserved. I will take the paines both to tell you what those generall interests are, and what in reason may be said against them.

I. Their first interest is to preserve amongst the people the distinction concerning Government of Ecclesiasticall and Civill, though upon consideration it will be found that two Governments in one Common-wealth hath ever been, and will ever prove inconsistent with [20] the peoples safety: The end of Government being to promote virtue, restraine vice, and to maintaine to each particular his owne, one sort of Government which we call the Civill, either is sufficient, or by the wisedome of the Parliament may be made sufficient for these ends. At the beginning of this Parliament it was confessed, that it was both too burdensome for the Divines, and too hazardous for the State, that they should bee trusted with any thing of Government, their preaching and instructing the people being, if well discharged, sufficient to take up the whole man. But the times change, and the men with them; the designe is feasible, and it must now againe be thought necessary that the Divines should have a stroake in the Government, and therefore [21] that distinction is againe maintained, which being taken up at first by proud Church-men for ambitious ends, is still continued for ends though not in every thing the same, yet differing (I feare me) rather in the degrees than nature of them, we cannot tell what else to thinke of it, but that finding our Divines aiming at authority and jurisdiction, have judged it most politicke to gaine a preheminence, (lesse stately and pompous, but) altogether as imperious and awfull over men as the former, which because it is not so garish outwardly as the Bishops, they may presume will therefore be the easier admitted, and prove of longer continuance.

II. The second interest of the Divine, is to preserve amongst the people the distinction of Clergie and Laity, though not now in those termes, because they have been un- [22] happily discovered. The Scriptures so evidently makeing the people Gods Clergy by way of distinction from the Ministers, I Pet. 5. 3. but never the Ministers by way of distinction from the people. And then for Laity, a people (as the word signifies) I hope the Ministers are such as well as any others. Well, the distinction by words is not so materiall, as a reall distinction with their interest is to preserve. They would not have us to thinke that a Minister comes to be so, as an other man comes to be a Merchant, Bookeseller, Taylor, &c. either by disposall of him by his friends in his education, or by his owne making choyce to be of such a Trade: no, there must be something spirituall in the business, a *Jure Divino* must be brought in, and a succession from the Apostles, and even as some would [23] have us thinke Kings to be annoynted of God, because the Israelitish Kings were by his command, so we are made to beleive, that beccause the Apostles were ordained by God to be Teacheers of the people, and endued with guifts for that end; that therefore there is a like divine, though secret ordination from God in making of our Ministers, and spirituall guifts & qualifications thereunto: Because otherwise, if the people did not beleive so, they would examine all that was said, and not take things upon trust from the Ministers, as if whatsoever they spake, God spake in them: they would then try all things, and what they found to be truth, they would embrace as from God, for God is the Authour of truth; what they found to be otherwise, they would reject, and then for the most part they [24] might spare their notings and repetions too, unlesse the more to discover the groundlesnesse of the doctrine, and the giddinesse of the Divinity which they generally heare. They would then handle their Ministers familiarly, as they doe one an other, shaking off that timorousnesse and awe which they have of the Divines, with which they are ignorantly brought up. He that bade us try all things, and hold fast that which was good, did suppose that men have faculties and abilities wherewithall to try all things, or else the counsell had beene given in vaine. And therefore however the Minister may by reason of his continuall exercise in preaching, and discoursing, by his daily study, and reading, by his skill in Arts and Languages, by the conceit of the esteeme he hath with a great [25] part of admiring people (in whom is truly fulfilled the prophecie of St. Paul, 2 Tim. 4.3.4.) presume it easie to possesse us, that they are more divine then other men (as they style themselves) yet if the people would but take boldnes to themselves and not distrust their owne understandings, they would soon find that use and experience is the only difference, and that all necessary knowledge is easie to be had, and by themselves acquirable: and that it is the Ministers interest, their living depending thereupon, to frame long methods and bodies of Divinity, full of doubts and disputes, which indeed are made of purpose difficult to attaine unto, that their hearers may be alwyes learning, and never come to the knowledg of the truth, begetting disquiet and unsetlednesse of mind, continuall controversies, sad- [26] nesse, and many times desperation: All which makes for them, for that upon all occasions men have recourse to them for comfort and satisfaction, which how weake and short soever it be in it selfe, must be currant, because from them: the Keyes of the Church (a prerogative which our Saviour gave to his Apostles,) they arrogate to themselves, a new Authority they make mention of in their Sermons, which they call Ministerial (though no such thing belongs to them, nor is yet setled upon them, nor I hope ever will be) thus their interest is to make of themselves a peculiar Tribe, of a nearer relation to God then other men: His more immediate Servants the Labourers in his Vineyard, the Co-workers with him, and all other titles they claime, given in Scripture to the Apostles, [27] though neither for their abilities, much lesse for their vertues or conversations, or in any other respect can be due unto them.

III. The third interest is to perswade the people, that the Scriptures though we have them in our owne tongue, are not yet to be understood by us without their helpe and interpretation, so that in effect we are in the same condition with those we have so long pitied, that are forbid to have the Scripturs in their own tongue: for 'tis all one not to have them in our own tongue, and to be made beleive, that we cannot understand them though we have them in our owne. Is the Cabinet open to us, and doe we yet want a Key? has so much labour been spent? so many Translations extant, and are we yet to seeke? Let us argue a little [28] with them: either the Scriptures are not rightly Translated, or they are: If they are not, why have wee not beene told so all this while? why have wee beene cheated into errours? If they are rightly Translated, why should not Englishmen understand them? The Idiomes and properties of the Hebrew, and Greeke Languages, which some say, cannot word for word be exprest in English, might all this while have beene Translated into as many English words as will carry the sence thereof. There is nothing in the Hebrew or Greeke but may be exprest in English, though not just in so many words (which is not materiall) so that it must be confest, that either we have not beene fairly dealt withall hitherto in the conveyance of the Scripture, [29] (a thing which few dare suspect) or else the Scriptures are as well to be understood by us, as by any Linguist whatsoever.

Well, notwithstanding all this how evident soever it be, a great part of us, people doe beleeve just as they would have us, and therefore silly men (as we are) in case of doubt to them we goe to be resolved: and hereby is maintained the necessity and excellency of learning, and the Languages, and so of Universities, and a supposall that the arts likewise are of necessity to a Divine: seven yeares at least are allotted for the attaining thereof, to fit and dispose men for the study of Divinity, the Arts being, as they say, handmaids and preparations to Theologie. But I heare wise men suspect all this, and say, that the Divines of what sort soever, have other [30] ends in urging all these things to be of necessity.

First, they have hereby made it a difficult thing to be a Minister, and so have engrossed the trade to them selves, and left al other men by reason of their other professions in an incapacity of being such in their sense.

And therefore, Secondly, if any doe take upon them their profession without University breeding and skill in the Arts and Languages (how knowing a man so ever he be otherwise) they have fastened such an odium in the hearts of most of the people against him, that a theif or murderer cannot be more out of their favour then he. Thirdly, they being furnished with these Arts and Languages, have a mighty advantage over all such as have them not, & are admirers therof, (as most men are) so that hereby they become masters [31] of all discourses, and can presently stop the peoples mouthes, that put them too hard to it, by telling them that it is not for Lay-men to be too confident, being no schollers, & ignorant of the Originall; That the Originall hath it otherwise then our Translations: And thus they keep al in a mystery, that they only may bee the Oracles to dispence what, & how they please: so that this third interest is of much concernment to them.

I know what the scruple of most men wil be, in reading of this last particular; almost all wil be the Divines Advocate for Learning, & have him in great hate & derision, that is an enemy thereto. For as

Diana was, so is Learning those Crafts-mens living & the peoples goddesse. However, I will make no Apologie for my selfe, but desire, that every man would give his reason scope, boldly to examine, [32] what it is, what good the World receives from it, whether the most learned, or unlearned men have been the troublers of the World. How presumptious and confident the learned Scribes, Priests, and Doctors of the Law were, that they best understood the Scriptures: How the poore and unlearned Fishermen and Tent-makers were made choyce of for Christs Disciples and Apostles, before any of them: How in processe of time they that tooke upon them to be Ministers, when they had acquired to themselves the mysterie of Arts and Learning, & confounded thereby the cleare streames of the Scripture, and per-verted the true Gospell of Jesus Christ, and by politicke Glosses, and Comments introduced an other Gospell sutable to the covetous, am-bitious, and [33] persecuting spirit of the Clergie (which their esteeme with the people made authentick) they then began to scorne the sim-plicity and meanesse of the Apostles, to call that the Infancy of the Church, and to engrosse great Livings, Lordships, Territories and Do-minions; to embroyle States in warres, to supplant one an other and divert the people from the prosecution of their owne interest, (which is their safety and libertie) to maintaine their quarrells, and erect that Governement the then rising part of them could agree upon. So that the Preists and Ministers of Christendome (though others have the name) yet they are indeed the Lords and leaders thereof, as at present by Englands sad experience may evidently appeare: For I would have all wise men consider, whe- [34] ther the party who are now in armes to make us slaves, consists not cheifly of such as have had esteeme for the most learned Arts men in the Kingdome; or of others, (who if not learned themselves) are admirers of such as are. Yea, to examine whence most of the warres of Christendome have sprung, and whether these artificiall Clergie men have not been the cheife causers and still are the grand Incendiaries of our present miseries which threaten our utter ruine, and although the Episcopall Clergie pretend to strive for the Regall Prerogative on the one side, and the Pres-biterian Prelacy for Reformation, and the Liberty of the Subject on the other side; yet both of these mainely intend their owne respective profits, and advancements; so that which side soever prevaile (if such may [35] have their wills, both aiming at their own greatnesse and Dominion over the consciences of their Brethren) extreamest miserie, and basest kind of slavery will unavoydably follow; whilst each of them by all slye insinuations and cunning contrivances seeke to obtaine authority to compell the whole Nation to be subject to their doubtfull, yea groundlesse determinations, which of all other is the greatest and worst sort of oppression and tyranny. The people may, if they please, dote upon that which ever hath been, and will be their destruction: It would be more safe for them (I am sure) to distinguish of Knowledge, and to reject what is uselesse (as most of that which hath hitherto borne the name of learning, will upon impartiall examination prove to be) and esteeme that only which is evi- [36] dently usefull to the people; to account better of them that having no by-ends or respects, have studied the Scriptures for their owne and others information, and doe impart the same to the people out of a desire of their good, for nothing, (as the Anabaptists doe to their Congregations) than of such men as use all meanes to augment their tythes and profits, who being rich and abundantly provided for, yet exact them from poore people, even such whose very bellies can hardly spare it; whose necessities ought to be releeved by them, and not the fruite of their labours so unreasonably wrested from them, as oft it is, and the same so superfluously spent, or so covetously hoarded up, as for the most part is knowne to be. When they commend Learning, it is not for Learnings sake, but their owne; her [37] esteeme gets them their Livings and preferments; and therefore she is to be kept up, or their Trade will goe downe. Have a care therefore O yee Clergie, as you esteem your honour and preferment, your profit and observance, that you keep this Diana of yours high in the peoples esteem: Rouze up your selves, and imagine some new wayes to quicken the admiration of this your Goddesse; for I can assure you, mens eyes begin to open, they find that she is not so beautifull as she once seemed to be; that her lustre is not naturall, but painted and artificiall: Bestirre your selves, or your Diana will downe. But why should I excite you, who I know are too industrious in the preservation of your owne interests.

Divers other interests they have plied, as to make themselves the only publike speakers, by which meanes [38] whome, and what they please they openly condemne, cry up, or cry downe, what makes for or against themselves: There they brand men with the name of Hereticks, and fasten what errours they thinke are most hatefull to the people, upon those men they purpose to make odious: There they confute all opinions, and boldly they may doe it, for as much as no liberty of reply or vindication in publike is allowed to any, though never so much scandalized by them. And that men may not vindicate themselves by writing, their next interest is to be Masters of the Presse, of which they are lately become by an Ordinance for licensing of Bookes, which being intended by the Parliament for a good & necessary end (namely) the prohibition of all Bookes dangerous or scandalous to the State, is become by [39] meanes of the Licencers (who are Divines and intend their owne interest) most serviceable to themselves (scandalous Books being still disperst) in the stopping of honest mens writings, that nothing may come to the Worlds view but what they please, unlesse men will runne the hazard of imprisonment, (as I now doe) so that in publike they may speake what they will, write what they wil, they may abuse whom they will, and nothing can be said against them: well may they presume of making themselves Masters of the people having these foundations laid, and the people generally willing to beleive they are good. I might proceed, to shew what usage wise men expect from their Government, being once establisht how rigid and austere some thinke they will prove, countenancing no recreations but what them- [40] selves are addicted to: how covetous others deem them, observing that they have more regard to the Benefice then the people, and doe usually change and shift upon proffer of a better Parsonage. Some say that they are a people sicke of the Pharises disease, they love to sit upermost at feasts, & to be reverenced in publike places, that their respects towards men are as they are rich and beneficiall to them, and that a pore man can hardly obtaine a visite, though at the time when the world conceives there is greatest necessity of it: that they hover about dying men for their Fee, and hope of Legacy, & many other things are commonly talked of them, which because I suspect to be true I will set myself hereafter more narrowly to observe.

The Objection wereupon all this (I hope) necessary digression [41] is built, was that men may be compelled (though against conscience) to what the Synod or present Ministery shall conclude to be good, and agreable to Gods Word, because unity and uniformity in the Church is to be endeavoured. To which I further

Ans. Answer, That to force men against their mind and judgment, to beleeive what other men conclude to be true, would prove such tyranny as the wicked Procrustes (mentioned by Plutarch) practised, who would fit all men to one Bed, by stretching them out that were too short, and by cutting them shorter that were too long. If we beleive as the Synod would have us, what is this but to be brought into their miserable condition that must beleive as the Church beleives, and so become, as said an honest man, not the Disciples [42] of Christ, but of the Synod?

3. *Reas.* The third Reason for Liberty of Conscience is grounded

upon these foundations, that whatsoever is not of faith is sin, and that every man ought to be fully perswaded of the truenesse of that way wherein he serveth the Lord: upon which grounds I thus argue, To compell me against my conscience, is to compell me against what I beleive to be true, and so against my faith; now whatsoever is not of faith is sin; To compell me therefore against my conscience, is to compell me to doe that which is sinfull: for though the thing may be in it selfe good, yet if it doe not appeare to be so to my conscience, the practice thereof in me is sinfull, which therefore I ought not to be compelled unto.

Againe I am counselled by the A- [43] postle to be perswaded in my owne mind of the truth of that way wherin I serve the Lord; I am not therefore to be compelled to worship God in such a way, of the justnesse whereof I am not yet perswaded, much lesse in such a way as is against my mind.

Ob. Nothing is more dangerous to a State, espeacially in these times, than division and disturbance by severall wayes of Brethren which have encreased our miseries, and therefore to avoyde division they who wil not of their own accords comply, are for the quiet of the state to be compelled and punished.

Ans. I Answer, that it is verily thought that the harshnesse only of this proposition hinders that it is not yet put in execution, till time & cunning have fitted it for the people; [44] for we are told in the last consideration tending to diswade from further gathering of Churches, that suffering is like to be the portion of such as shall judge the right rule not to be delivered to them. A man would thinke that those people that so lately were the sufferers, the noyse of whose exclamations against such courses, is scarce yet out of the peoples eares, that they should not so soone thinke of being the Tyrants. But to the Objection I answer, that the diversity of mens judgments is not the occasion of division, because the word division hath reference to a falling off from the Common cause. Now, though the provocations and incitements, against the Brownists, and Anabaptists and some of the Independents have beene many, yet their affections to the Publike [45] weale are so hearty in them, and grounded upon such sound principles of reason, that no assay of the Synod can make them cease to love and assist their Countrey; and it is more then evident by the prosperity of our neighbours in Holland, that the severall wayes of our brethren in matters of Religion hinder not, but that they may live peaceably one amongst an other, and the Spaniard will witnesse for them that they unite sufficiently in the defence of their common liber-

ties and opposition of their common enemies: Besides, its very materiall to consider, that it hath ever been the practice of those that are
countenanced by Authority to endeavor the suppresion of those that
are not: who is therefore in the fault? the quiet Separatist, who being
perswaded in his conscience of the truth of that way he [46] desires to
serve the Lord in, peeceably goes on to do his duty as he thinkes
himselfe bound to doe, or they who out of a lordly disposition care
not what injury they doe to others, though to the hazard of the Common-wealth, to advance themselves and their government, they defame the Separation in their writings and Sermons, bid their pros-
elites beware of them, as of a dangerous and factious people, stoppe
their mouthes, keep the Presse from them, provoake them by all
wayes possible, and then like the crafty Politian cry out upon them as
the causers of division.

I heare some men say, that it concernes the Minister so to doe,
because his living (depending upon his tythes and guifts) is the
greater, the more rich and numerous his audence is; and therefore
the Separatists [47] are not to be suffered, who they find by experience draw many people after them, and though not the devout honourable women, nor the cheife men of the City, yet many whose
number might much encrease the yearly revennue of the Minister,
and therefore you must thinke it has concerned them to meet together, and to say amongst themselves, *Sirs, you know that by this our
craft we have our wealth: moreover ye se & hear, that not alone at London, but
in most parts of the Kingdom these Separatists have perswaded & turned
away much people, saying that our Ministry is no true Ministry, our Church,
no true Church, our Doctrine in many things erronious, that our succession
from the Apostles is but a pretended thing, & as we our selves do derive it
descended for many 100. yeares through the detestable Papacy & Ro-* [48] *mish
Ministry, so that if these men be suffered our gaine, and the magnificence of the
Ministery, wich not England only, but all Christendome doth highly magnifie
and reverence, would quickly downe:*

For what other reason then this can be imagined, why the Separation should bee the eye-sore of our Ministers? It cannot be instanced
in one particular whereby the Common-wealth receives prejudice
from them: And then for the charge of Separating, for their making a
Scisme, which is endeavoured, to be cast so heavily upon them:

I answer, That by reason of the Church of Romes corruptions, the
Church of England did long since make a Scisme from the Church of
Rome, for [49] which cause likewise many of the present Ministers in
lieu of the Antichristian domineering Bishops thought it no robbery

to make scisme from England; and even this Idolizing Synod, which though not yet upon her Throne, sticks not to let her clients see *she sayes in her heart; Behold I sit a queen, I am no widdow, and shall see no sorrow,* Rev. 18.7. May not I say this, Reverend Synod: if to be proceeded against by such carnall sandy principles, such humane ordinances, by which the Separatists stand prejudiced, be legally found, to have made the greatest and most transcendent scisme which England ever knew or heard of, since the Papistrie was discarded; If then the Separation have gon a little further, and not only with the Bishops separated from Rome, with the Ministers from the [50] Bishops but by reason of some corruptions still remaining among the Ministers, are by their consciences necessitated to separate from them likewise: In all these separations there was difference in judgment; the Bishops differ in some things from Rome, our Ministers from the Bishops, and amongst themselves too, which differences by the Scriptures they cannot determine, as appeareth both by their writings and preachings, wherein with much vehemency they urge the same against other; of little force then will the major vote of a Synod be for the determining thereof, having so lately most notoriously discovered themselves to be men-pleasers and temporisers, by crying downe the things which but yesterday they so highly magnified in their Pulpits, and also practised with much devotion (at [51] least seemingly) and having withall their owne interests so much concerned therein (as is before in part declared.) And further, knowing that the same persons themselves, and their Tenets, (as well as the opinions of Independents, Brownists, and Anababtists, whom they oppose) doe stand condemned not by the major vote of divers Synods only, but by many generall Counsells also, (who are accounted to represent the whole Church upon Earth) no whit inferiour to them either in Arts or Learning, or any other qualification: Let it be then no wonder, nor so much as seem blameable hereafter, that the Separatists should differ in some Opinions from this present Synod, since the Ministers therein no little differ amongst them selves, much more than yet appeares, and will do so, while Sun and Moon [52] endures untill we have courage and strength enough to abandon all private interests and advantages.

All times have produced men of severall wayes, and I beleive no man thinkes there will be an agreement of judgement as longe as this World lasts: If ever there be, in all probability it must proceed from the power and efficacie of Truth, not from constraint.

Objection. An assembly of Divines, men that have imployed all their time in the study of Religion, are more likely to find out the truth, then other men, that have not so spent their time; who being now consulting, what Doctrines, and [53] what Discipline is most agreeable to the Word of God, it is but meet that all men should waite their leasure, till it be manifest what they shall produce.

Answ. To this objection I say first, That they being now in consultation, not for themselves, but as they say, for the whole people; it is but reasonable that they should publish to the world whatsoever is in debate amongst them, and invite every man to give them their best light and information, that so they may heare all voyces, and not conclude ought against mens judgments before it be heard what they can say for themselves: This might peradventure be a meanes to find out all truth, and settle things so as that every man might be satisfied. You will say, that they consider of all [54] objections amongst themselves. I reply, that is not sufficient, for 'tis a knowne case men are generally partiall to themselves and their owne judgments, urging the weakest objections, and that but slightly: and it can give no satisfaction to men to have their causes pleaded by their Adversaries.

Secondly, how palpable soever it appeare, that an Assembly of Divines are more likely to find out truth then other men; yet it is to be considered, that it will puzzle any man to instance when they did so. Besides, grant it be more probable, yet it may be otherwise, and 'tis well knowne hath proved so. The Liturgie was by universall consent approved, and by the Parliaments Authority authorised, particular men being for these many yeares averse [55] to it, and separating from the publike Congregations because of it: it now appeares who were in the right. How confident soever therefore the Divines (as they style them selves) are that they shall find out the right rule; yet since it may be, and hitherto hath been otherwise, it is but meet that they should decree only for themselves and such as are of their owne mind, and allow Christian Liberty to all their Brethren to follow that way which shall seem to them most agreable to truth.

Ob. But we are told in the Divines Considerations that all men must wait, otherwise the Parliament are like to be provoaked.

Answ. I marry Sir, this is a good strongue Argument, and speakes home to us: I cannot blame the [56] Separatists now for crying out, they feare your Club more then your Reason. I see what they might expect, if the sword and authority were in your hand, your nine Considerations informes me, wherin are these two suppositions. First, that the right rule may not be delivered us: And secondly, that then men may be called to suffer. It is a wonder to observe the wretched condition of man, and his foule ingratitude: Is it so long since the

yoakes were broaken off these mens necks, that they forget the burthen & injustice of them, or that assistance they had from their separatist Brethren in breaking those yoakes, that now so soone as they
are got into reputation, they should suppose a time of suffering for
their brethren for doing what to them appeares to be their duty! Regard O God, since man is become thus [57] forgetfull, take thy distressed Servants, the Separatists into thine owne protection: Thou O
Lord, that are the Judge of all the Earth, put into the hearts of the
Parliament to doe right in this cause, and to suffer those afflicted people no longer to endure reproach or molestation for doing of their
duties.

Ob. But some may say, I beat the Aire all this while, there is no
purpose in the Divines to force the conscience, they are sufficiently
informed that, the conscience cannot be forced, being in no wise subject to compulsion, only it concernes them they say to prevent the
grouth and encrease of errours, which cannot otherwise be done but
by punishing those that are the authors and maintainers of them, that
so truth only may flourish, and the Gospell with the Ordinances according to [58] the true institution of them, be maintained and practised by all the people of the Nation.

Answ. I answer, that though it were certaine that what they esteeme
truth were so indeed, and that the true Gospell and Ordinances were
in every part and circumstance of them that which they judge them to
be: however, though they are earnestly to endeavour by argument
and perswation to reduce all men to the same beleife and practice
with themselves, yet those that cannot be thereunto perswaded, they
ought not by any meanes to punish, for the first and third Reasons
afore given. But then for the assurance of the Divines that their conclusions and Articles are certainly true, if it be built upon certaine
foundations, they need not avoyde the combate with any [59] sort of
men of what opinion soever: Truth was not used to feare, or to seeke
shifts or stratagems for its advancement! I should rather thinke that
they who are assured of her should desire that all mens mouthes
should be open, that so errour may discover its foulnes and trueth
become more glorious by a victorious conquest after a fight in open
field; they shunne the battell that doubt their strength. Wise men are
at a stand to see that whilest the Presse was open no man undertooke
the Anabaptists, and that now their adversaries have bound their
hands they begin to buffet them; what can they doe else but necessarily suspect that our Divines have not the truth, nor by any evidence thereof are able to make good their owne standings or prac-

tices. To stop mens mouths or [60] punish men for speaking their mindes, was profitable indeed, and necessarie for the Bishopes who had proposed to themselves such endes as could endure no discourse upon them, and framed such constitutions, ceremonies and doctrines, as must be received without scanning, or else would appeare empty and groundlesse. But that the reforming Clergy, that pretend to have truth in its simplicity, and the Gospell in its purity, and seeme to abominate all by-endes or respects, should yet take the same course of prohibitions with the Bishops, locke up the Presse, and then vent themselves in a furious and (evidently) scandalizing way, as in their late preachings and Pamphlets against the Anabaptists, will make, I beleeve, all wise men suspect that either they doubt their [61] owne tenets, or know some grosse errours amongst themselves, which yet their interests and professions engage them to maintaine. To say they goe not about to compell the conscience, which is uncapable of compulsion, but will only punish the person, is as if they were sportfull in their cruelty, and shewes as if it proceeded from men setled, and long practised in tyranny, I could wish for Christianity sake they had more wisedome then to play with mens afflictions: I professe unto you, did I still dote upon the persons and seeming holynesse of our Ministers (as I have done) such carriage as this I thinke would open mine eyes, and make me see they are not the men they seeme to be, that in so short a time can grow so wanton with their owne estate and preheminence, as to gibe and scoffe at their brethrens miseries. Is it not a shame [62] to our profession, and scandall to our cause, that well affected men, reall, and irreconcileable enemies to tyranny, and our common Adversaries, should be necessitatd to leave their native Country, because they can hope nothing from you, our Divines, but to be imprisoned or punished for exercising their consciences, though by their helpe you should be setled in your liberties, I cannot tell what else to make of this for my part, but that you had rather be slaves to the King, and hazard the freedome of the whole Nation, then that these men should have freedome with you; yee may flatter your selves, that yee are rich in spirituall graces, and presume that you are in the right, and have found out the truth of the Gospell and Ordinances, but so long as yee want the maine evidences thereof, Love and lowlinesse of mind, [63] so long as yee propose dominion and the sway over your Brethren, which our Saviour said his followers should not doe, Matth. 20. 25. 26. Marke 10. 42. you must give men that are unwilling to be deceived leave to thinke that yee have yet but the forme and shew of Religion, but want the inward

sweetnesse and most excellent fruites and effects thereof; I could wish
I had no occasion for speaking thus much, but when sores begin to
fester, they must not be nourished and swathed, but lanc'd and cor-
raciv'd, 'tis no time to hide and excuse mens imperfections, when
they strive to take roote for perpetuity. Were it in mine own cause, I
could not speak so much, but in behalfe of such a harmelesse people
as I have found those of the Separation to be, after much inquiry and
examination of their Tenets, [64] and practice, I thinke my selfe bound
in conscience to breke silence and become their advocate.

Ob. There is one Objection more against the Anabaptists in particular, and that is, that they allow not of Civill government and therefore
not to be tolerated because they hold an opinion directly destructive
to the Common-wealth.

Ans. Who saies they hold this opinion? why the Divines commonly
in their Pulpits, and what ground have they for their so saying? They
find it in bookes that they who have written of them affirme that they
maintaine this opinion. But how if the societies of Anabaptists in this
Kingdome are most Zealous and rationall defenders of our Government? as to my knowledge they are, and that [65] experience can
testifie for them, that noe men have more forwardly and constantly
then they assisted the Parliament against those that would disolve
our free governement, and bring in tyranny; how is it true then that
the Anabaptists hold such an opinion? O then they tell us that our
Anabaptists are no Anabaptists: To what purpose then doe they exclaime against Anabaptists that have been of that opinion? (as they
say) (though for my part I beleeve neither them, nor the books that
tells them so) when they cannot but know, if they know any thing,
that the Anabaptists which now are, be not of that opinion; why for
this end and purpose, they resolve to make the Anabaptists odious to
the people, and nothing they thinke will sooner doe it, then by making the people be- [66] leeve that they are the harbourers of such an
opinion as would dissolve all societie, and bring into confusion the
state.

Now this they speake of the Anabaptists in generall, knowing that
the people will apply it to the Anabaptists in England, concerning
whom how true it is you may judge by that which followes.

The Anabaptists opinion concerning Government is, that the world
being growne so vitious, and corrupt as it is, there can possibly be no
living for honest men without Government: That the end of making
Government, is the Peoples quiet and safety, and that whatsoever
doth not conduce thereto is tyranny or oppression & not go- [67]

vernment, That the Government of England is of all others that they know the most excellent, the people by their chosen men, being the makers & reformers therof: That therein the Parliament is the supreme power, and that the King is accountable to them for the not performance of his Office, as all other Officers of the Common-wealth are: That the Parliament only are the makers and alterers of Lawes for the regulation and ordering of the people: That of right they are to be called by those Lawes they have made in that behalfe, and to dissolve when they themselves see good: that it is not at the Kings wil or pleasure to signe or refuse those Bills the Parliament shall passe, but that he is of duty to signe them: That all great Officers and Majestrates of the Kingdome are to be chosen by them: [68] That the King is to have his personall abode neer the Parliament, that they may have free conference with him at pleasure touching the former discharge of his Office, or the present state of the Common-wealth: That to Parliaments alone belong the disposall of Shipping, Forts, Magazines, and all other the Kingdomes strengths, both by Sea & Land: The making of peace & war, the pressing of souldiers, the raising of monie for the preserving or regaining the safety or freedome of the people, which for any other person to doe, is treasonable. These grounds & principles of our government they knowing, could not but see the exorbitances of the King, & whereto al his lawles courses & designes tended, & therefore have not ignorantly (as perhaps others) but upon these grounds assisted the Parliament, and will doe till the last. [69]

Judge by this then whether these men hold an opinion against government, or at what wretchlesse passe those men are that would make the people beleive they doe.

I might insist here upon a Booke called *The Confutation of Anabaptists* lately set forth, which saies, *They are absolute and professed enemies to the essentiall Being of Civill Government,* but I find people so little regard the Booke, it being so full of non-sence, and in this particular so evidently contrary to truth, and the experience of every man, that lookes abroad, and knowes any thing of the Anabaptists; that it will be but losse of time to take notice of it, only it were worth observation to see how easily it obtained an *Imprimatur,* and how open the Presse is to any thing [70] true or false, sence or non-sence, that tends to the Anabaptists scandall or disgrace.

In the beginning of the Parliament a Booke was published, called the History of the Anabaptists in High and Low Germany, the aime whereof was by fastning odious errours and feigned mutonies upon the Anabaptists to deter this present Parliament in their Reformation of Bishops, for feare, as the booke saies, least they who now cry out for Christs rule, strike not so much at the misrule of Episcopacy, as quarrell at all rules, so that what course was taken by the Bishops and their freinds to hinder the Reformation of that Hierarchie, namely, the affrighting the Reformers by airy and imaginary consequences, the [71] same are used by our Divines to prevent a through Reformation: of many erroures, and mistakes in our Clergie, which they exceedingly feare, and therefore they have, and doe continue early and late to render the Anabaptists as odious to the people as their wits and inventions can make them. But as the Bishops then failed of their ends by the wisedome of the Parliament; so I trust the present endeavoures of our Divines in striving to raise themselves upon their Brethrens disgrace and ruine, will by the continued courage and prudence of the Parliament prove vaine and fruitlesse.

They who echo the Kings words and take the Bishops course (I will not say have the Kings ends but) so farre doe the Kings worke. [72]

The King, I confesse, has reason to cry out upon the Anabaptists, because he knowes them to be enemies not of Government, but oppression in Government, and all those who intend to oppresse in any manner, ought, if they will be true to themselves to doe so too; for the Anabaptists are oppressions enemies, whoever be the oppressours.

And whereas they say, they find in Bookes, that the Anabaptists are enemies to all Government, it were well if they would consider who wrote those Bookes: it may be they were written either by mistake, or for the same end that they repeate them. We can shew you books too, that say the Parliament are Brownists & Anabaptists; And past all question, if the King should thrive in this unnaturall warre, this Parl. [73] should in their Court Histories, not only be called Anabaptists, but branded also to all posterity with that opinion falsly and maliciously fathered upon the Anabaptists, That they were enemies to Government, and went about to bring all into confusion. little credite therefore is to [be] given to Bookes in matter of obloquie and scandall: but the men, and their judgments in the times they live, are to be considered: And then I am confident it will appeare, that the Anabaptists be of well affected mindes: and peaceable dispositions, meriting a faire respect from the State, and may well challenge amongst others, the quiet enjoyment of themselves as they are men, and the ordinances of Christ as they are Christians.

I will adde one thing more to the [74] Brownists and Anabaptists glory; that in the times of the Bishops domineering, when many of the Presbyterians complyed, some to the very top of Wrens Confor-

mity, and preached for those things they now pretend cheifly to reforme, and the Independants fled to places where they might live at
ease, and enjoy their hundred pounds a yeare, without danger; the
Brownist and Anabaptist endured the heate and brunt of persecution,
and notwithstanding the severall wayes of vexing them, continued
doing their duties, counting it the glory of a Christian to endure trib-
ulation for the name of Christ: And the times altering the Presbyterian soon comes about, and the Independant comes over, to be
leaders in the Reformation, when forgetting the constancie and integrity of those who bore the heat [75] and burden of the day, they hold
the same heavy hand over them, that their fathers the Bishops did.
And as the Brownists & Anabaptists affection to the common good of
all, was then firme, & able to endure the triall of persecution, so hath
it in these present searching times continued constant & unshaken,
notwithstanding the many almost unsufferable Injuries & provocations of the Divines on the one side, & the faire promises & frequent
invitations of the King on the other; so that had any ends of their
owne beene aimed at, they could not have continued such resolved &
immoveable enemies of Tyranny, & freinds to their country: I beleeve
if we would suppose other men to be in their Condition, we could
hardly expect the like even & upright carriage from them, amidst so
many stormes and [76] temptations surrounding them. I hope all
good men will take all that hath been said into consideration, especially the Parliament who I presume are most ingenuous and impartiall of all others and whom it cheifly concernes, they being called
and trusted to vindicate and preserve the peoples liberties in generall,
and not to enthrall the Consciences, Persons, or Estates of any of
them unto a pregmaticall pretended Clergy, whether Episcopall, Pres-
biteriall, or any other whatsoever, The greatest glory of authority is to
protect the distressed; and for those that are Judges in other mens
causes to beare themselves as if the afflicted mens cases were their
owne; observing that divine rule of our Saviour, *Whatsoever yee would
that men should doe unto you, even so doe yee to them* And if to the Parl. it
shall appeare for the reasons given or other better reasons [77] they
can suggest to themselves, that it is most unjust, and much more un-
christian, that any man should be compelled against his conscience to
a way he approves not of, I doubt not but they wil be pleased for
Gods glory, and union sake and likewise for these good mens sake,
which for the present it principally concernes, at least for their owne
sakes (for who knowes how soone this may be his owne case) speedily to stop all proceedings that tends thereunto: and for the future

provide, that as well particular or private Congregations, as publike, may have publike protection, so that upon a penalty no injury or offence be offered either to them from others, or by them to others. That all Statutes against the Separatists be reviewed, and repealed, especially that of the 35. of Eliz. That the Presse may be [78] free for any man, that writes nothing scandalous or dangerous to the State. That so this Parliament may prove themselves loving Fathers to all sorts of good men, bearing equall respect to all, according to the trust reposed in them, and so inviting an equall affection and assistance from all: that after Ages may report of them, they did all these things, not because of the importunity of the people, or to please a party, but from the reason and justnesse of them, which did more sway with them, than a Petition subscribed with Twenty thousand hands could have done.

FINIS [79]

Good Counsell to All

First published as the third part of The Compassionate Samaritane, *1st edition,*
[June–July?] 1644, pp. 72–83.
Subsequently published separately, without title page and with pagination beginning
with page 79. Thomason's MS note on his copy states: "This is all of this booke
though it begins here. July 29 1644."
Reprinted from a copy of the tract in the Thomason Collection in the British Library

The format of the separate publication of *Good Counsell to All* is identical to the format of the 2d edition of *The Compassionate Samaritane.* Some of the capitalization, spelling, and punctuation in the separate issue of *Good Counsell to All* differs from the style in the third part of the 1st edition of *The Compassionate Samaritane;* the texts of the two versions are essentially the same. Haller identifies the work as Walwyn's.[1]

Good Counsell to All is replete with points of view and references that distinguish Walwyn's known works. It begins and ends with a familiar warning against those who seek to promote divisions within "the honest party" over religious differences.[2] "Despised Brethren" are listed and defended by the writer—who is not a sectary but a member of his parish church.[3] Antinomians are described as believing, as did Walwyn, that the love of God brings salvation to all men.[4] Romans 14:5 and 23 again support the need for each man to be "perswaded in his owne minde" of his religious beliefs.[5] Christ's gentle treatment of the Sadducees is cited as an example of toleration,[6] and the inevitability of human fallibility so long as knowledge is imperfect is reiterated.[7]

Good Counsell to All is reprinted for the first time in this volume.

this is all of this booke
though it begined 69

July-29 1644 London

Good counfell to all
thofe that heartily defire the glory of God, the free-dome of the Common-wealth, and the good of all vertuous men.

YOu are moft earneftly in-treated to take notice, and to be warned of a moft peftilent and dangerous defigne lately practifed by fome hellifh Polititians, tending to the dividing of the honeft party a-mongft themfelves, thereby to weaken them, and to give advan-tages to the Common Enemies.

E 4 The

Title page of *Good Counsell to All*, 1644. (British Library)

Good counsell to all

Those that heartily desire the glory of God, the freedome of the Commonwealth, and the good of all vertuous men.

You are most earnestly intreated to take notice, and to be warned of a most pestilent and dangerous designe lately practised by some hellish Polititians, tending to the dividing of the honest party amongst themselves, thereby to weaken them, and to give advantages to the Common Enemies. [79]

The ground of their designe is, The difference of judgement in matters of Religion amongst conscientious well minded people, occasion being taken from thence to make them not only to despise and hate one another, but as odious to the generality of good men as are theeves, murderers and harlots.

The means they use to promote their designe, is principally to broach some grosse and foolish errours; and then to father them on all those that are called Anabaptists, Antinomians, Brownists, Separatists or Independents:

Perswading and possessing the people:

First, concerning the Anabaptists, That they hold all government in the Commonweale to bee [80] unlawfull; which you are to know is most pernicious delusion, for they approve of, and doe submit unto all government that is agreed on by common consent in Parliament; and disapprove only of arbitrary and tyrannicall government, usurpations and exorbitances in Magistrates and Officers; and have disbursed their monies and hazarded their lives as freely for their just government, and liberties of this Nation, as any condition of men whatsoever.

Secondly, That the Antinomians doe hold, that a Beleever may live as he list! even in all licentiousnesse: which is most grossely false: there being no Scripture more frequent in their mouthes then this, namely, *The love of God bringing salvation to all men hath* [81] *appeared, teaching us to deny all ungodlinesse and worldly lusts, and to live righteously and godly, and soberly in this present world.*

Thirdly, That the Brownists, Separation and Independents doe hold that all other Protestants are in a damnable condition, who doe hold fellowship, Church society, and communion with grossely, vitious and wicked persons: which also is most notoriously false: for they doe not so judge of any; but doe judge that themselves having (to their apprehensions) grounds in Scripture, proving the un-

lawfulnesse of such mixt communions, may not, nor dare not so communicate: And as concerning others they judge (as themselves would
be judged) that they exercise their Religion in that way which ap- [82]
peareth to them most agreeable to the Word of God.

When these sowers of division have possest the people, that these
and the like absurdities are held by them: Then they advise them to
flye from them as from Serpents, and not to heare them or discourse
with them, as they tender the safety of their souls; & make them glad
& rejoyce when they heare any of them are imprisoned or silenced; or
their bookes (though slightly and absurdly) answered: and when they
heare that many of them are forsaking the Kingdome, and betaking
themselves to the West-Indies and other places for Liberty of their
Consciences (as void of all remorse) they cry out, Let them goe, a
good riddance, it will never bee well in England [83] (say they) so
long as these Sects are permitted to live amongst us; nor untill the
Parliament do set up one expresse way for exercise of Religion, and
compell all men to submit thereunto, and most severely to punish all
such as will not.

But you will finde that this is the very voice of Prelacie, and the
authours thereof to bee the very same in heart, what ever they are in
cloaths and outside— And that it is not the voyce of the Apostles,
who required that every man should be fully perswaded in his owne
minde of the lawfulnesse of that way wherein he served the Lord; and
that upon such a ground as no authority on earth can ever dispence
withall, namely, That whatsoever is not of faith (or full assurance of
minde) is sin. [84]

Our Saviour Christ did not use the Sadduces in so unkinde a manner, and yet they held more dangerous opinions then any that are
accused in our times; for they beleeved that there was no resurrection, and that there was neither Angell nor Spirit; though they came
to him in a kinde of insolent confidence in these their opinions, which
he knew sufficiently, He, neverthelesse both heard and answered
them gently; he did not revile them with reproachfull language, telling them that they were not worthy to live in a Commonwealth; nor
did he warne others to discourse with them; hee did not command
their persons to be imprisoned, nor declare their lives to be forfeited:
It is likely they lived quietly, and (in all civill respects) according to the
loves [laws] of [85] the Country, and were honester men then the
Scribes and Pharisees who were hypocrites: and so, as the true authour
of his Apostles doctrine, he allowed them to be fully perswaded in
their owne mindes, using no meanes but argument and perswasion

to alter or controle their judgements: He knew that men might live peaceably and lovingly together, though they differ in judgement one from another: Himselfe was composed of love, and esteemed nothing so pretious as love; His servant and Apostle Paul was of the same minde also, affirming that though hee had all faith and al knowledge, and understood all mysteries, though he could speak with the tongues of men and of Angels, and have not love, he is nothing, a meere sounding brasse or tinckling symball: he desires that those [86] who are strong in the faith, should beare with those that are weak, adviseth him that eateth that hee should not condemne him that eateth not: where one observed a day to the Lord, and others not (though a matter of great moment) yet he alloweth every one to be fully perswaded in his owne minde: Now if our Saviour and his Apostle, that could infallibly determine what was truth, and what was error, did neverthelesse allow every man to bee fully perswaded in his owne minde, and did not command any man upon their authority to doe any thing against judgement and conscience— What spirit are they of, whose Ministers are they, that would have all men compelled to submit to their probabilities and doubtfull determinations? [87]

The Apostle perswadeth those whom he instructed to try all things: These allow not things to be compared, they take liberty to speake what they please in publike against opinions and judgements, under what nick-names they thinke fittest to make them odious, and write and Print, and licence the same, wresting and misapplying the Scriptures to prove their false assertions; but stop all mens mouthes from speaking, and prohibit the Printing of any thing that might be produced in way of defence and vindication; and if any thing bee attempted, spoken or published without authority or licence, Pursuivants, fines and imprisonments, are sure to wait the Authors, Printers and publishers.

And though experience of all times under Popery and Prelacie, [88] have proved this a vaine way to bring all men to be of one minde, yet these men are not yet made wiser by the folly of others, but suffer themselves to be outwitted by the devillish policies of those that put them on in those compulsive and restrictive courses, as knowing it to be the only meanes to obstruct the truth, to multiply opinions, and cause divisions, without which they know they should in vaine attempt the bondage or destruction of the honest party.

Be you therefore wise in time, and speedily and freely unite your selves to those your brethren, though reproached with never so many nick-names, and use all lawfull meanes for their ease and freedome, and for protection from reproach, injury or violence, that [89] they may be encouraged to abide in, and returne unto this our distressed country, and to contribute their utmost assistance to free the same from the bloudy intentions of the common enemies, and give them assurance of a comfortable freedome of conscience when a happy end shall be given to these wofull times: you cannot deny but that they are to bee trusted in any imployment equall to any condition of men, not one of them having proved false hearted or treacherous in any pub-like employment: sticke you therefore close to them, they will most certainly sticke close to you; which if you doe, all the Popish and malignant party in the world will not be able to circumvent you: but if you suffer your selves to be so grossely deluded as to despise or re-nounce [90] their assistance and association, you shall soone perceive your selves to be over-growne with malignants (the taking of a Cove-nant will not change a blackamore) your bondage will be speedy and certaine: The ground upon which you renounce them is so unjust and contrary to the word of God, that God cannot prosper you; you have therefore no choice at all; but if you joyne not; you perish: Your de-struction is of your selves. (complaine of none else) your pride and disdaine of them will be your ruine.

Thus have you the faithfull advice of him who is neither Anabap-tist, Antinomian, Brownist, Separatist or Independent: But of one that upon good ground (as he conceiveth) holdest fellowship and communion with the Parochi- [91] all congregations, who observing with a sad heart the manifold distractions and divisions amongst his brethren about difference of judgement in matters of Religion; and finding the same fomented and made use of to the destruction of the common freedome of his deare Country: He could not forbeare to give warning thereof to all sorts of well-affected persons, hoping that they will labour to informe themselves more truly of the opinions and dispositions of those their too much despised Brethren; and (as him-selfe hath done) resolve henceforward to joyne heart and hand with them in all offices of love and mutuall assistance of the Common-wealth.

FINIS [92]

A Helpe to the Right Understanding of a Discourse Concerning Independency. Lately Published by William Pryn

[6 February] 1644/5
Reprinted from a copy of the tract in the Thomason Collection in the British Library

A Helpe to the Right Understanding was published anonymously, "Anno Dom. 1644," without imprint or license. The title page was so designed that it suggests that the tract is the work of William Prynne. Walwyn indirectly acknowledged the tract as his work in 1649.[1] Language, content, and style are characteristic of Walwyn, who again indicates that he worships within his parish church.[2]

Walwyn's short, trenchant rejection of any and all intolerance stands out among the various responses to Prynne's attacks on Independency.[3] In large part a defense of John Goodwin, Henry Burton, and the Independents, *Helpe* specifically counters two of Prynne's recent tracts.[4] Walwyn implies that the corrupting influence of practice as a lawyer may have affected Prynne, although, noting that Prynne himself suffered persecution, the tract suggests that misunderstanding may have misled him and ventures the hope that love and reason may persuade Prynne's followers to embrace the toleration essential to sound government.

A Helpe to the Right Understanding is reproduced in facsimile in *Tracts on Liberty,* ed. Haller, 3:191–201.

A Helpe to the right understanding of a DISCOURSE CON-
CERNING INDEPENDENCY.

Lately published by *WILLIAM PRYN* of *Lincolns Inne,*
Esquire.

PROV. 12. 13. *The evill man is snared by the wickednesse of his lips,*
but the just man shall come out of adversity.

Printed *Anno Dom.* 1644.

A helpe to the right understanding of a Discourse concerning INDEPENDENCY, &c.

As it is a very great benefit to the world when wise and considerate men, suffer for maintenance of a just cause: so also it
proveth often-times very prejudiciall to a Nation, when rash inconsiderate men, wise only in their owne strong conceits, doe suffer
though for a cause as just as common freedome it selfe: because suffering winneth reputation to the person that suffereth, whereby his
sayings, opinions, and writings carry authority with them: and
though never so much blended with slightnesse, arrogance, impurity,
violence, error, and want of charity: yet make they deep impression
in the minds of many well meaning people, and sway them to the
like, or dislike of things: not as they are really good, or palpably evill
in themselves, but according to the glosse, or dirt, that such men
through ignorance, impatience, or malice cast upon them.

For instance whereof, I am somewhat troubled that I must alledge
Mr. William Pryn, who to his great commendation in the late arbitrary
times suffered for the maintenance of the just liberties of his Country:
but in a great example of late it is too sadly proved that he that did the
greatest service, may live to doe the greatest mischiefe: and I am fully
instructed. That only perseverance in well-doing, is praise-worthy:
and therefore I conceive I may without breach of charity, be as bold
with him as with any other man whatsoever: that others may learne
by me to respect good men no longer then they continue so.

Of late he is fallen upon so unhappy a subject (The difference of
judgement in matters of Religion) and hath so totally engaged himselfe therein that even men who have formerly had him in great re-

pute for integrity, begin to doubt his ends; supposing that he strikes in with the rising party in hope to raise himselfe with them, and by them; and that he is carried away with that infirmity unto which men of his tribe have been much subject.

Others there are that conceive he is defective only in his understanding, and easily out-witted, and wrought to doe that, which he intended not to do, charitably hoping by his endeavours in the argument of Church government that he really intended the reconciling of all parties, and that he hath unhappily wrought a contrary effect, and made the division greater, through his want of judgement, and naturally passionate weaknesse: inconsiderately engaging, and (being engaged) and prosecuting with violence: and they argue it to be so, from his publishing Romes master-piece; and the Archbishops Diary; intending, no doubt, to blazon the vilenesse of that Arch Incendiary to the world; whereas to an advised Reader, it will be evident that the first is framed of purpose to lay the designe of all our troubles upon the Papists; and make the Archbishop such an enemy thereunto, as that they plotted to take away his life; as if Satan were divided against Satan; and his [1] Diary is so subtilly contrived, as that among those from whom he expecteth honour, it cannot faile to worke most powerfully thereunto, so great are his good workes therein expressed, so large are his pious intentions, so watchfull over his wayes, so seldome offending, so penitent after offences, so devout in prayer, so learned and patheticall in his expressions; that to any that are but tainted with the least Prelaticall superstition, he will appeare a Saint, if not equall to Noah, Lot and David, yet full parallel with the most holy Primitive Fathers; especially when they shall consider that these his works were published by his greatest enemy, which was the Archbishops Master-piece indeed, being both written of purpose to be published in their best season, and by a person that should most advantage the deceit: if it had not been so, they had easily been fiend [sic] or concealed, past his finding: no man can thinke the Bishop so impolitick, as after so long imprisonment, not to be warned concerning his notes.

Others judge him to be much of the Archbishops spirit, his late adversary, and feare that if he had equall power to that he once had, he would exceed him in cruelty of persecution; and their reason is, because he is so violently busie already, egging and inciting the Parliament, like their evill Genius, to acts of tyranny against a people he knows innocent: how much more would he rage against them had he

that command of censure, fine, pillory, imprisonment and banishment, which the Archbishop unjustly usurped; especially since his
rage against them has so exceeded all bounds of modesty already, as
to affirme that their writings are destructive to the very being of Parliaments, and as bad or worse then the Popish Gunpowder-plot, and
to tearme their honest and submisse demeanours, Insolencies, un-
paralleled publicke violations and impeachments of the rights and
priviledges of Parliament, and of the tranquility and safety of our
Church and State. I am at stand Methinks, and cannot but grieve
within my selfe to consider how full swolne with bitter malice, yea
and the very poyson of Aspes, that breast must needs be from
whence proceeds such malevolent and scandalous speeches, yet so
grossely untrue and unsutable to the spirits of the Independents.

Men likewise say that this must needs proceed from spleene: for if
he were a really conscientious man he would first pull the beame out
of his own eye, as he is a Lawyer, and examine his owne wayes in the
course of his practise, or set out something to set out the unlawfulnesse of tythes, as learned Mr. Selden hath done. Mr. Pryn professeth
the true Christian Religion, and that most zealously, yet continueth to
take fees for pleading mens causes, a thing that the vertuous men
amongst the very heathens accounted base, and would doe it gratis:
and what fees taketh he? no lesse then treble the vaine of what is
taken by pleaders in Popish Countries; but he taketh as little as any
man of his calling, and no more but what is lawfull for him to take:
therein, say they, consists the misery of the Common-wealth, with all
other the extreame abuses of our Laws, the very way of the ending of
controversies, being so totally pernicious and full of vexation: that
were he truly conscientious for the good of the whole Nation, as he
pretendeth, he would have laid open to the Parliament, how improper it is that our Laws should be writen in an un- [2] knowne
language, that a plaine man cannot understand so much as a Writ
without the helpe of Councell; how prejudiciall it is that for ending a
controversie, men must travell Terme after Terme from all quarters of
the Land to London, tiring their persons and spirits, wasting their
estates, and beggering their families; tending to nothing but the vexation of the people, and enriching of Lawyers; with a little labour had
he been so vertuously disposed, he could have discovered the corrupt
originall thereof, and have layed open all the absurdities therein, and
shewed the disagreement thereof to the rules of Christianity: he could
also have shewed to the Parliament what of our Lawes themselves are
unnecessary, what are prejudiciall to good men, and have moved for

reducing all to an agreement with Christianity: were he (say they) truly pious, and could deny himselfe, this he would have done, though he had thereby made himselfe equall to men of low degree, both in estate, food, and rayment: yea though for his livelihood hee had beene constrained to have laboured with his hands, &c. This indeed had beene a proper worke for him a Christian Lawyer in a time of Reformation: What needed he to have meddled against the Independent and Separation, there being so many learned Divines (as hee himselfe esteemes them) sitting in Councell so neare the Parliament, which shewes him to bee too officious?

And as concerning Church-Government: If hee had really intended the good of the Nation, and the weale of all peaceable minded men, he would have had in minde such considerations as these.

The Parliament are now upon setling the affaires of the Church, a thing of a very nice and dainty nature, especially being undertaken in a time of a homebred Warre: If it be not very advisedly and cautiously done, it may soone divide the wel-affected party within it selfe, then which nothing can be more pernitious and destructive: already I have seene some that have laid downe Armes, and many withdraw their persons and estates into forreigne parts, for no other cause but for being disturbed or discouraged in exercising of their consciences in matters of Religion: And it was but thus in the Prelaticall time. I finde by my selfe, that Christians cannot live, though they should enjoy all naturall freedome and content, where they are not free to worship God in a way of Religion: And I finde also by my selfe that Christians cannot worship God in any way but what agreeth with their understandings and consciences; and although I may be at liberty to worship God according to that way which the Parliament shall set up for a generall rule to the whole Nation; yet if I were not perswaded that I might lawfully submit thereunto, all the torments in the World should not enforce mee: and this I finde to bee the case of many conscientious people, very well affected to the Parliament and to common freedome: Men that have spent their estates, and hazarded their lives as freely in defence of just Government, as any men whatsoever; and whether they are under the names of Anabaptists, Brownists, Separation, Independents, or Antinomies; wee have had all their [3] most affectionate helpe in throwing down Episcopacy and arbitrary government: men they are that still remaine in most opposition to the Popish and malignant parties, somewhat we must doe for the ease of these our brethren, it must not be in the settlement of our Reformation that they remaine under the same restraint or molestation for

their consciences as they were in the Prelaticall time; we must doe as
we would be done unto: if any sort of them were greater in number
then we, and had authority to countenance them, we should esteem
it hard measure, to be restrained from exercising our Religion according to our consciences, or to be compelled by fines, imprisonments,
or other punishments, to worship contrary to our consciences, we
must beare with one anothers infirmities; no condition of men in our
dayes have an infallibility of judgment: every one ought to be fully
perswaded in his owne minde of the lawfulnesse of the way wherein
he serveth God; if one man observe a day to the Lord, and others not;
and both out of conscience to God, both are allowed by the Apostle;
and the one is not to molest, no not to despise or condemne, Rom. 14.
v. 3. much lesse compell the other to his judgement, because whatsoever is not of faith or full assurance of minde is sin: had Mr. Pryn
debated thus with himselfe, he had shewed himselfe a true Disciple
of Christ and his Apostle: differing opinions would not then have
appeared such abominable, damnable things in his sight: The dealing
of our Saviour with those most erronious Sadduces, would have come
into his mind, they beleeved that there was neither Angell nor Spirit,
and that there was no resurrection: Opinions as contrary to the current of the then Interpreters, as any in our time, and yet they professed it openly, as appeareth by their attempting our Saviour, and
were as unreproved of him as of authority; he resolves their question
by an answer which removed that absurdity which they thought impossible: briefly telling them, That they neither marry nor are married, but as the Angels of God in heaven; using them gently, without
threats or reproaches.

If Mr. Pryn had thought of this Subject, with such like considerations, he would soone have seen, That the people of a Nation in chusing of a Parliament cannot confer more then that power which was
justly in themselves: the plain rule being this: That which a man may
not voluntarily binde himselfe to doe, or to forbear to doe, without
sinne: That he cannot entrust or refer unto the ordering of any other:
Whatsoever (be it Parliament, Generall Councels, or Nationall Assemblies:) But all things concerning the worship and service of God, and
of that nature; that a man cannot without wilfull sin, either binde
himselfe to doe any thing therein contrary to his understanding and
conscience: nor to forbeare to doe that which his understanding and
conscience bindes him to performe: therefore no man can refer matters of Religion to any others regulation. And what cannot be given,
cannot be received: and then as a particular man cannot be robbed of

that which he never had; so neither can a Parliament, or any other just Authority be violated in, or deprived of a power which cannot be entrusted unto them.

That Emperours, and Kings, and Popes, have assumed an absolute power over Nations in matters of Religion, need not to have beene so laboriously proved; nor that Councels and Parliaments have done the like: the matter [4] is what they have done of right: who knowes not that all these have erred as often as they did so: our present Parliament have greater light then any former, and propose to themselves to abandon what ever former Parliaments have either assumed, or done upon mis-information: and have not yet declared themselves to dissent from the fore recited rule: and then Mr. Pryn may consider, whether he hath not extreamly mispent his time, and with much uncharitablenesse injured that faithfull servant of God, and sincere lover of his Country, Mr. John Goodwin, a man that to my knowledge, and to the knowledge of many, values neither life nor livelihood, could he therewith, or with losse thereof, purchase a peaceable liberty to his Country, or a just Parliamentary government; so far is he, or that other worthy man Mr. Burton; or any Independent, Anabaptist, Brownist, or any of the Separation now extant, from deserving either those slight, but arrogant expressions of his in his said Epistle, telling the honourable Parliament, That he knows not what evill Genius, and Pithagorian Metempsychosis, the Antiparliamentary soules formerly dwelling in our defunct Prelats earthly Tabernacles, are transmigrated into, and revived into a new generation of men (started up of late amongst us) commonly knowne by the name of Independents: such bumbast inckhorne tearmes, savouring so much of a meer pedanticke, as ill beseemeth his relation to that supream power of Parliament: And thogh those Independents, for the most part are such by his owne acknowledgement, whose affections and actions have demonstrated them to be reall and cordiall to the Parliament and Church of England, for which (saith he) and for their piety they are to be highly honoured, yet hath not he so much charity as to shew any inclination that they should be relieved in their just desire of Christian liberty; but prosecutes all those their severall judgements, as derogatory and destructive unto Parliament and Church in their Anarchicall and Antiparliamentary positions; for which, and for their late gathering of Independent Churches, contrary to Parliamentary injunctions (which were never seen) they are he sayes, to be justly blamed as great Disturbers of our publicke peace and unity: these his great words make a great noise, I confesse: a man that did not converse amongst these people, may easily be induced to believe them to be very dangerous. Mr. Pryn is of great credit with many in authority, and how far he hath therein done them wrong, his owne conscience will one day tell him to his cost.

If Mr. Pryn were a stranger to the Separation, and unacquainted with the innocency of their wayes and intentions, I might charitably judge him to plead for the persecution of Gods people ignorantly, as St. Paul did: but since he cannot but know that they are both in affection and action reall and cordiall to the Parliament, as himselfe confesses, and hath found them for his owne particular compassionate in his sufferings, and liberally assistant to him in his miseries: I professe, I can make no other construction of his so violent pleading for persecution, and incensing the Parliament against a People he knowes harmlesse, and modest and reasonable in their desires whose utmost end is only not to be molested in their serving of God: I can make no other construction of it, I say, [than] that engagement to the Divines, and some interest [5] of his owne hath begot a hardnesse over his heart, and clouded that noble courage and common spirit which did possesse him. If he wanted information, I would labour with him, but since I cannot doubt but that he hath sufficient of that, I will leave him till the truth and excellency of that freedome against which he fights, till the sincerity and uprightnesse of the Separation which he delivers up to the sword, in these words, *Immedicabile uninus ense recidendum est*, make him one day appeare even to his present admirers, the man he is indeed.

In the meanetime, I turne to the people, and desire them to enquire after the Separation, and have full knowledge of them: they will then finde they are extreamly misunderstood by authority, and all others that apprehend them to be any other then a quiet harmlesse people, no way dangerous or troublesome to humane society: I have found them to be an ingenious enquiring people, and charitable both in their censures of others, and due regard to the poore. I am become their advocate, out of no engagement or relation to them, I professe, more then what my knowledge of their sincerity and true affection to their Country hath begotten in me.

Mr. Goodwin, I need not speak much of, he is a man so well knowne, that Mr. Pryns so rigid urging of his expressions upon him, as he hath too largely and spleenishly done in his Epistle, making so unsavoury and utterly disproportioned comparisons betwixt him, and the malignant Prelats, and Antiparliamentary Cavaliers, that a man that knows the antipathy betweene them cannot but stand amazed thereat; and necessarily conclude that something hath blinded not only the light of Mr. Pryns conscience, but of his understanding also, and then after a most unchristian application, his sentence is in these dismall old Antichristian and Prelaticall tearms; if they will not be reclaimed, *fiat justitia*, better some should suffer then all perish: but happy it is, that the power of Parliament is not in Mr. Pryn: if it were (in the minde he is now in) 'tis much to be doubted, his part would differ little from Bonners or Gardiners in Queen Maries dayes: but blessed be God, it is otherwise; nor will that just Authority I presume be moved either with his fierce exclamations, or incomparable flatteries to doe any thing contrary to right reason and true Christianity: nor is there indeed (the fore mentioned rule holding) any cause why that supreme Authority should be offended: for all sorts of Independents, whether Anabaptists or Brownists, or Antinomians, or any other doe all agree, that in all Civill and Military causes and affaires, they have an absolute supreme power: And if they shall conceive it just and necessary for the State to propose one way of worship for a generall rule throughout the Land, and shall ingratiate the same by an exemption from all offence and scandall of weake consciences as far as is possible: The Independents, &c. have nothing to oppose against their wisdomes: and if the publicke way should be such as should agree with any of their judgments and consciences, they would most readily joyne in fellowship therein: but if their judgements and consciences should not be fully satisfied concerning the same, then whatsoever is not of faith is sinne; and they cannot but disjoyne: and in such a case, all good men that know them will shew themselves true Christians [6] indeed, in becomming humble suters to the Parliament, that as for convenience to the State they propose one generall publicke way: so for the ease of tender consciences, and for avoyding of sinne either in compelling of worship contrary to conscience, or in restraint of consciencious worship: they would be pleased to allow unto all men (that through difference of judgement could not joyne with the publicke congregations) the free and undisturbed exercise of their consciences in private congregations.

And if they should be pleased so to doe; it is but what is agreeable to common equity and true Christian liberty: It hath beene the wisdome of all judicious Patriots to frame such laws and government as all peaceable well minded people might delight to live under; binding from all things palpably vitious by the greatest punishments, and proposing of rewards and incouragements to all publicke vertue: but in things wherein every man ought to be fully perswaded in his particular minde of the lawfulnesse or unlawfulnesse thereof; there to leave every man to the guidance of his owne judgement; and where this rule is observed, there all things flourish, for thither will resort all sorts of ingenious free borne minds: such Commonwealths abound with all things either necessary or delightfull, and which is the chiefe support of all: such a government aboundeth with wise men, and with the generall affections of the people: for where the government equally respecteth the good and peace of all sorts of virtuous men, without respect of their different judgments in matters of Religion: there all sorts of judgements cannot but love the government, and esteem nothing too pretious to spend in defence thereof.

Who can live where he hath not the freedome of his minde, and exercise of his conscience? looke upon those Governments that deny this liberty, and observe the envyings and repinings that are amongst them, and how can it be otherwise, when as if a man advance in knowledge above what the State alloweth, he can no longer live freely, or without disturbance exercise his conscience? what follows then? why he takes his estate, and trade, and family, and removes where he may freely enjoy his minde, and exercise his conscience: and as this hath been the sad condition of this Nation to its extreame lesse divers wayes: so Mr. Pryn would have it continued for ought by his writings can bee discovered; nor is he any whit troubled in spirit to see at this day of Jubile, and of Reformation unto all just liberty: thousands of well-affected persons at their wits end, not knowing where to set their foot, for want of encouragement in the cause of conscience.

I but, sayes Mr. Pryn, our Covenant bindes us to maintaine an absolute Ecclesiastick power in the Parliament: it bindes us to maintaine their undoubted rights, power, priviledges: but Mr. Pryn must ever beare in minde, that what the people cannot entrust that they cannot have; which will answer all objections of that nature.

As for our Brethren of Scotland: there is no doubt, but they are sad observers of all the distempers and misunderstandings that are amongst us, and would be most glad that the wisdome of Parliament would minister a speedy remedy; although therein they should somewhat vary from their way of [7] Church Government; as well knowing there can be no greater advantage given to our common Enemy, then the continuance of these our divisions and disaffections.

And where Mr. Pryn may suppose all liberty of this kinde, would tend to the encreasing of erronious opinions, and disturbance to the

State; I beleeve he is mistaken; for let any mans experience witnesse whether freedome of discourse be not the readiest way both to give and receive satisfaction in all things.

And as for disturbance to the State: admit any mans judgement be so misinformed, as to beleeve there is no sinne; if this man now upon this government should take away another mans goods, or commit murder or adultery; the Law is open, and he is to be punished as a malefactor, and so for all crimes that any mans judgement may mislead him unto.

And truly you are to consider in reading his great Book (improperly entituled, Truth triumphing over falshood) that he acknowledges them to bee but nocturnall lucubrations, distracted subitane collections; and if you truly weigh them you will finde them very light, and little better compacted then meere dreams, or such fumes as men use to have betwixt sleeping and waking: and when you have viewed all those many sheets, consider them as in one, and it will resemble Saint Peters vision, a mixt multitude of unclean testimonies raked out of the serpentine dens of meer tyrannous Princes, Antichristian and Machivillian Councells, erronious Parliaments, and bloudy persecuting Councells and Convocations, which he hath produced, to be perswaders and controlers in these times of pure Reformation. Certainly if a man were not in a deep Lethargy, such a masse of so grosse excrements could not passe from him without offence to his owne nostrill; if it be his case, hee that scracheth him most, and handles him most roughly, is his best friend, there being no other remedy; when he is recovered and broad awake hee will thanke his Physitian: in the meane time thus much is presented to his admirers, to preserve them from that malevolent infection, unto which his writings and reputation of former sufferings might subject them unto; and this by one who is no more obliged to any Independent, Anabaptist, Brownist, Separation, or Antinomian, then Mr. Pryn himselfe; but hath taken paines to know them somewhat better, and cannot but love them for their sincere love to our dear Country, to the just liberties thereof, and to our just Parliamentary Government: most heartily wishing them their just desires and a peacefull life amongst us: That they might be encouraged to joyne heart and hand with us, in prosecution of the common Enemies, of our common liberties, knowing no reason why I should not love and assist every person that loves his Country unfeignedly, and endeavours to promote the good and freedome thereof, though of different judgement with me in matters of Religion; in which case I am not to judge or controle him, nor he me: and

I heartily wish all true lovers of their Country were in this minde: and when they are so, then the miseries of this Nation will soon be ended, and untill then, they will continue, as is too much to be feared: I could heartily wish that what is here written, might worke a good alteration in Mr. Pryn [8] but when I remember the story, That a certain Lawyer came to our Saviour, tempting him; I fear it is in respect of himself, but washing of a Blackamoore: self deniall, is too hard a lesson for him; and if so, you shall have him in some bitter reply instantly; for though he cannot out-reason men, yet if he can but out-write his opposers, he claps his wings and crows *victoria*, that he hath silenced them all. Truly for writing much, I verily believe that he out-does any man in England, which is no commodity at all to a State or the Truth, and then considering what free liberty he hath to Print whatsoever he writeth, discreet men will consider what a great advantage he hath therein, and will not deem it want of ability in his opposers, though they doe not see him presently answered to their full satisfaction; and yet I am confident his great Booke will be suddenly answered throughly: but if Mr. Pryn would deale upon equall tearmes, and use meanes that the Presse may be open for all Subjects, but for six moneths next comming free from the bonds of Licencers; if Mr. Pryn be not so silenced, as that all his former and late books doe not under sell browne paper; let me be henceforward esteemed as vaine a boaster, as now I esteem him: for his opposers, as in the justnesse of this cause they cannot regard his spleene; so nothing would be more welcome to them then his love, and change of minde, whereof some doe not dispaire: however, I end with his owne words, more justly applyed *fiat justitia;* better it is that he undergoe this my plaine dealing, then that either the Readers of his bookes should be seduced, or so many innocent well-affected persons be so grossely abused by him.

FINIS [9]

(7)

Englands Lamentable Slaverie

[11 October] 1645
Reprinted from a copy of the tract in the Thomason Collection in the British Library

Englands Lamentable Slaverie was published anonymously, without separate title page, imprint, or license. Thomason's date is supported by "Printed October, 1645" at the end of "The Printer to the Reader" in which the printer advises his "Courteous Reader" to read *Englands Birthright Justified*, which probably was published by William Larner's press at Goodman's Fields.[1] Comparison of the body of *Slaverie*—an open letter to "John Lilburn Prisoner in Newgate"—with the long title and the printer's concluding message reveals that the letter is from a different hand. The title and subtitle, like "The Printer to the Reader," are probably the work of the printer, who equally condemns kings, Parliaments, priests, and the "cowardlinesse of People."[2] Pease assigns the tract to Walwyn "at a guess."[3] Haller states that "internal evidence" and "attendant circumstances" confirm the attribution.[4]

    Englands Lamentable Slaverie was prompted by Lilburne's imprisonment by the Commons on 19 July, the day he and Walwyn met in Westminster Hall.[5] *Slaverie*'s response to the continuing imprisonment includes a clear statement of one of the natural rights of man— "for a man to be examined in crimminall cases against himselfe, and to be urged to accuse himselfe is as unnatural and unreasonable, as to urge a man to kill himselfe"—and a remarkable exposition of perceived limits of government suggested in Walwyn's *Helpe*, eight months before: "Parliament men are to learne . . . what the Parliament may doe, and what the Parliament (itselfe) may not doe," for the Parliament is empowered by the people and may justly act only for their safety and freedom.[6]

    Specific evidence of Walwyn's hand is recurrent. The treatise opens with the observation that Lilburne and the author differ "in matters of

Religion" and states that those who would divide men by fomenting such differences have failed with the author, who is concerned with the sufferings of any man.[7] The indication that this has been the author's practice for "almost a score of yeares . . . having read, observed, debated, and considered both ancient and latter times," accords with Walwyn's autobiographical statement that when the Long Parliament assembled he was "40 years of age, 20 of which I had been a serious and studious reader and observer of things necessary."[8] A characteristic reference to Diana of the Ephesians[9] introduces *Slaverie*'s dismissal of Magna Carta as "that messe of pottage"—a judgment reiterated by Walwyn in 1651.[10] The conviction that denial of religious liberty is denial of the most important freedom is expressed in positive terms in Walwyn's known works.[11] William Prynne's "swolne" malice toward Lilburne is condemned as "the Poyson of Asps"—the same words that Walwyn used in *A Helpe to the Right Understanding* to describe Prynne's attacks on the Independents.[12]

Englands Lamentable Slaverie is reproduced in facsimile in *Tracts on Liberty*, ed. Haller, 3:311–18, and is partially reprinted as Walwyn's work in *The Levellers in the English Revolution*, ed. G. E. Aylmer (London, 1975), No. 2.

ENGLANDS LAMENTABLE SLAVERIE

Proceeding from the Arbitrarie will, severitie, and Injustices of Kings, Negligence, corruption, and unfaithfulnesse of Parliaments, Covetousnesse, ambition, and variablenesse of Priests, and simplicitie, carelesnesse, and cowardlinesse of People.

Which slaverie, with the Remedie may be easily observed.

By the scope of a modest & smooth Letter, written by a true Lover of his Countrey and a faithfull friend to that Worthy Instrument of Englands Freedome, Lieuten. *Collonell Lilburn*, now unjustlie imprisoned in Newgate.

Being committed first, by Order and Vote of Parliament without cause shewed, and then secondly for refusing to answer some Interrogatories to their Committee of Examinations, Contarie to

1. The Great Charter of England.
2. The very words of the Petition of right.

3. The Act made this present Parliament; for the abolishing the Star-Chamber.

4. The Solomne Protestation of this Kingdom.

5. And to the great Vow and Covenant for uniting the two Kingdomes together.

The Copie of which Letter (with the Superscription thereof) hereafter followeth.

A private Letter of publique use, to the constant maintainer of the Just Liberties of the People of England, Lieuten. Coll. *John Lilburn* Prisoner in Newgate by command of Parliament.

SIR,

Although there is some difference between you and mee in matters of Religion, yet, that hath no white abated in me, that great love and respect justly due unto you, for your constant zealous affection to the Common Wealth, and for your undaunted resolution in defence of the common freedome of the People. [1]

The craft and delusion of those that would master and controle the People, hath not availed (by fomenting our differences in Religion, which is their common practice) to make me judge preposterously, either of your or any other mens sufferings.

We have a generall caution, that no man suffer as an evill doer; but if any suffer for well doing, who are they that would be thought Christians, and can exempt themselves from suffering with them? No certainly, it is neither pettie differences in opinions, nor personall frailties in sufferers, nor both, that can acquite or excuse us in the sight of God so we are not simplie to be spectators or beholders of them afar off (as too many doe) but if one suffer, all ought to suffer with that one, even by having a sympathie and fellow feeling of his miserie, and helping to beare his burden; so that he may be eased in the day of tentation; yea and the sentences both of absolution and condemnation shall be pronounced at the great day, according to the visiting or not visiting of Prisoners, and hearing of their mourning, sighs, and groanes.

This is my judgement, from whence hath issued this my practice, that when I heare of the sufferings of any man, I doe not enquire, what his judgement is in Religion, nor doe I give eare to any tales or reports of any mans personall imperfection (being privie to mine owne) but I presently labour to be rightly informed of the cause of his sufferings (alledged against him) whether that be evill or good, and of the proceedings thereupon, whether legall or illegall, just or unjust.

And this hath been my course and practice in things of that nature for almost a score of yeares, whoever have been the Judges, whether Parliament, King, Counsell-board, Starr-Chamber, High Commission, Kings-bench, or any Judicatory, yea what ever the accuser, or the accused, the judgement or punishment hath been; I have taken this my just and necessary liberty; for having read, observed, debated, and considered both ancient and latter times the variations and changes of Governments and Governors, and looking upon the present with an impartiall judgement, I still find a necessity of the same my accustomed watchfullnesse, it never being out of date; [the more my hearts griefe] for worthy and good men (nay the most publique spirited men) to suffer for well doing, unto whom only is promised the blessing and the heavenly Kingdome: Mat. 5. 10.

Your suffering at present, is become every good mans wonder, for they all universally conclude your faithfulnesse and zeale to the publique weale to be such, as no occasion or temptation could possibly corrupt, and the testimonies you have given thereof to be so great, as greater could not be. [2]

They observe likewise, the large testimonie given of your deserts, by your honourable and worthy Friend in the Armie, Lieuten. Generall Cromwell.

And therefore, that you should now be kept in safe custodie, was very sad newes to all that love you; knowing how impossible it was, to make you flee or start aside; but when they heard that you were sent to that reproachfull prison of Newgate, they were confounded with griefe.

It should seeme, that you being questioned by the Committee of Examinations stood upon your old guard alledging it to be against your liberty, as you were a free borne Englishman, to answer to questions against your selfe, urging MAGNA CHARTA to justifie your so doing; And complaining that contrary to the said Charter, you had beene divers times imprisoned by them.

Now it is not much to be wondred at, that this your carriage should be very offensive unto them; for you were not the first by divers, (whom I could name) that have been examined upon questions, tending to their own accusation and imprisonment too, for refusing to answer, but you are the first indeed, that ever raised this new doctrine of MAGNA CHARTA, to prove the same unlawfull.

Likewise, You are the first, that compareth this dealing to the crueltie of the Starre Chamber, and that produced the Vote of this Parliament against those cruelties (so unjustly inflicted on your selfe by that tyrannous Court) And how could you Imagine this could be indured by a Committee of Parliament? No, most Parliament men are to learne what is the just power of a Parliament, what the Parliament may doe, and what the Parliament (it selfe) may not doe. It's no marvell then that others are ignorant, very good men there be; who affirm, that a Parliament being once chosen, have power over all our lives estates and liberties, to dispose of them at their pleasure whether for our good or hurt, All's one (say they) we have trusted them, and they are bound to no rules, nor bounded by any limits, but whatsoever they shall ordaine, binds all the people, it's past all dispute, they are accountable unto none, they are above MAGNA CHARTA and all Lawes whatsoever, and there is no pleading of any thing against them.

Others there are (as good wise and juditious men) who affirme, that a Parliamentary authority is a power intrusted by the people (that chose them) for their good, safetie, and freedome; and therefore that a Parliament cannot justlie doe any thing to make the people lesse safe or lesse free then they found them: MAGNA CHARTA (you must observe) is but a part of the peoples rights and liberties, being no more but what with much [3] striving and fighting, was by the blood of our Ancestors, wrestled out of the pawes of those Kings, who by force had conquered the Nation, changed the lawes and by strong hand held them in bondage.

For though MAGNA CHARTA be so little as lesse could not be granted with any pretence of freedome, yet as if our Kings had repented them of that little, they alwaies strove to make it lesse, wherein very many times they had the unnaturall assistance of Parliaments to helpe them: For Sir, if we should read over all the hudge volume of our Statutes, we might easily observe how miserablie Parliaments assembled, have spent most of their times, and wee shall not find one Statute made to the enlargement of that streight bounds, deceitfully and improperlie called MAGNA CHARTA, (indeed so called to blind the people) but if you shall observe and marke with your pen, every particular Statute made to the abridgement of MAGNA CHARTA, you would make a very blotted booke, if you left any part unblotted.

Sometimes you shall find them very seriously imployed, about letting loose the Kings prerogatives, then denominating what should be Treason against him (though to their owne vexation and continuall danger of their lives) sometimes enlarging the power of the Church, and then againe abridging the same, sometimes devising punishments for Heresie, and as zealous in the old grossest superstitions, as in the more refined and new, but ever to the vexation of the people.

See how busie they have been about the regulating of petty inferiour trades and exercises, about the ordering of hunting, who should keep Deere and who should not, who should keep a Greayhound, and who a Pigeon-house, what punishment for Deere stealing, what for every Pidgeon killed, contrary to law, who should weare cloth of such a price, who Velvet, Gold, and Silver, what wages poore Labourers should have, and the like precious and rare businesse, being most of them put on of purpose to divert them from the very thoughts of freedome, suitable to the representative, body of so great a people.

And when by any accident or intollerable oppression they were roosed out of those waking dreames, then whats the greatest thing they ayme at? Hough with one consent, cry out for MAGNA CARTA, (like great is Diana of the Ephesians) calling that messe of pottage their birthright, the great inheritance of the people, the great Charter of England.

And truly, when so choice a people, (as one would thinke Parliaments could not faile to be) shall insist upon such inferiour things, neglecting greater matters, and be so unskilfull in the nature of common and just freedom, [4] as to call bondage libertie, and the grants of Conquerours their Birth-rights, no marvaile such a people make so little use of the greatest advantages; and when they might have made a newer and better Charter, have falne to patching the old.

Nor are you to blame others for extolling it, that are tainted therewith your selfe, (saving only that its the best we have) *Magna Charta* hath been more precious in your esteeme then it deserveth; for it may be made good to the people, and yet in many particulars, they may remaine under intolerable oppressions, as I could easily instance: And if there be any necessity on your behalfe, it shall not faile (with Gods grace) to be effected, let who so will be offended, but if there be not a necessity, I conceive it better (for this present age) to be concealed, then any wise divulged.

But in this point you are very cleare, that the parliament ought to preserve you in the Freedomes and liberties contained in *Magna Charta* at the least, and they are not to permit any authority or Jurisdiction whatsoever to abridge you or any man thereof, much lesse may they be the doers thereof themselves: Something may be done through misinformation, but believe it, upon consideration, they are to make amends. *Humanum est errare.*

But as Abraham reasoning with God, was bold to say to that Almighty power, Shall not the Judge of all the earth doe right? Much more may I in this your case be bold to say, shall not the Supreame Judicatory of the Common Wealth doe right? God forbid.

That libertie and priviledge which you claime is, as due unto you, as the ayre you breath in; for a man to be examined in crimminall cases against himselfe and to be urged to accuse himselfe is as unnaturall and unreasonable, as to urge a man to kill himselfe, for though it be not so high a degree of wickednesse, yet it is as really wicked.

And for any man to be imprisoned without cause declared, and witnessed (by more then one appearing face to face) is not only unjust, because expreslie against *Magna Charta* (both of Heaven and Earth) but also against all reason, sense, and the common Law of equitie and justice.

Now in such cases as these, no authoritie in the world can over-rule with out palpable sinne; It is not in these cases as it is in other things contained in *Magna Charta,* such as are the freedomes of the Church therein mentioned for some doe argue that their power must be above *Magna Charta,* or otherwise they would not justlie alter the Government of the Church, by ArchBishops and Bishops, who have their foundation in *Magna Charta.*

But such are to consider, that the Government of the Church is a thing [5] disputable, and uncertaine, and was alwaies burthensome to the people: now unto things in themselves disputable and uncertaine, as there is no reason why any man should be bound expresly to any one forme, further then his Judgement and conscience doe agree thereunto, even so ought the whole Nation to be free therein, even to alter and change the publique forme, as may best stand with the safety and freedome of the people, For the Parliament is ever at libertie to make the People more free from burthens and oppressions of any nature, but in things appertaining to the universall Rules of common equitie and justice, all men and all Authority in the world are bound.

This Parliament was preserved and established, by the love and affections of the people because they found themselves in great bondage and thraldome both spirituall and temporall; out of both which, the Parliament proposed to deliver them in all their endeavours, at least Declarations, wherein never was more assistance given by a people.

And for the first, it was a great thing, the exterpation of Episcopacie, but that meerly is not the main matter the people expected which indeed is, that none be compelled against Conscience in the worship of God, nor any molested for Conscience sake, the oppression for Conscience, having been the greatest oppression that ever lay upon religious people, and therefore except that be removed, the people have some case by removall of the Bishops, but rather will be in greater bondage, if more and worse spirituall taskmasters be set over us.

These were no small matters also, their abolishing the High-Commission, and Starre Chamber for oppressing the people, by imposing the Oath Ex Officio, and by imprisoning of men, contrary to law, equitie, and justice. But if the people be not totally freed from oppression of the same nature, they have a very small benefit of the taking downe of those oppressing Courts. Seeming goodnesse is more dangerous then open wickednesse. Kind deeds are easily discerned from faire and pleasing words. All the Art and Sophisterie in the world, will not availe to perswade you, that you are not in Newgate, much lesse that you are at libertie.

And what became of that common and threed-bare doctrine, that Kings were accountable only to God, what good effects did it produce? No, they are but corrupt and dangerous flatterers, that maintaine any such fond opinions concerning either Kings or Parliaments.

What prejudice is it to any in any authority, meaning well, to be accountable, for indeed and truth all are accountable, and it is but vaine, (if not prejudiciall) for any to thinke otherwise. Doth any man entrust, and [6] not looke for justice and good dealing from him he trusts.

And if he find him through weakenesse or wickednesse doing the contrary, will he forbeare to set him right (if he can.) Can he sit downe silently with injurie or prejudice? I could judge those people very neare to bondage, (if not to ruine) that could be brought to beleeve it, there be many instances both Forraigne and Domestick, which yet I forbeare to expresse.

The greatest safety will be found in open and universall justice, who relyeth on any other, will be deceived, Remember therefore (saith God) whence thou art falne and repent, and doe the first workes, or else I will come quickly, and will remove thy Candle sticke out of his place. March not so swiftly ye mighty ones, one single honest hearted man alone oftimes by unpleasing importunity, not only stayes, but saves a whole Army from inevitable danger; for better is wisdome then weapons of warre Ecclesiastes 9. 18. Timely mementoes and cautions to advised and modest men (howsoever uttered) are never without good effect. If godly David made some good use even of rash Simeis railing, then what happie use may the godly minded make of any faithfull mans words, which tend altogether, to justice, equitie, and reason?

Nor can I imagine any evill is now intended towards you for your faithfull and plaine dealings, except by some few, and those instigated by one onely, who (by his great successe, in getting out Mr. Henry Martine, that just and zealous Patriot of his Countrey, and some other prevalencies) hath swolne so big with confidence, of greater matters, that he thinkes Lilburns blood the next meat Sacrifice for Oxford, so that what the King could not doe to him (as one of the Parliaments best friends) when he was close Prisoner there, the Parliament themselves must endeavour to doe to him in his unjust prisonment here.

The Poyson of Asps is under that wicked mans tongue, with which he laboureth alwaies to poyson Scripture, (mixing it figuratively) in his discourse to corrupt, sinister, and unworthy ends, whose malice and hypocrisie (doubtlesse) will ere long discover him to all men.

And (I doubt not) but that same God that took a happie course with Haman, and delivered Mordicai and all his people, will in your greatest necessity and his fittest opportunity, fight against all your enemies, and deliver both you and all yours out of all your afflictions, at least so to mitigate and sweeten them (by supporting you under them, or rather bearing of them with you,) that this shall prove to be exceeding joyes and consolations, to you and all that love you.

The honest and plaine men of England in dispite of that mans mallice [7] shall be your Judges, and will spread forth in order (like King Ezekias letter) both before God and their owne consciences, what a world of injuries and miseries you (betweene 20. and 30. yeares of age scarcely to be paraleld any where in this age) have with great fidelity, magnanimitie, and constancie undergone, in the discharge of your conscience, and defence of the liberties of your native Countrey, and will not suffer a haire of your head to be touched, nor any reproach to be stucke upon your good name, but you shall live and be an honour to your Nation in the hearts of all honest and well affected men, which shall ever be the hearty desire of me.

Your faithfull Friend.

The Printer to the Reader

There is here a copie of an excellent letter, which comming to my hands, by the carefull meanes of a worthy friend, who is a Wel-willer both to his Countreys priviledges, and to those few who either stand for them, or for the truth, have thought it my dutie not to smother nor obscure such a needfull Epistle but rather (as times are) to manifest it to the world, according it came entituled to me, namely, *A Private letter of publique use:* Whereby it may appeare now in these dangerous dayes, both how the States and Clergie of this Kingdome have pittifully abused the people, even our antient predicessors for many ages, both in Church and Common wealth.

First, In bringing them with a high hand, under heavy thraldome and great bondage, and then keeping them in lamentable slaverie for many hundreds of yeares, as still their Successors the States men and Clergie of our dayes, doe with all their policie and machinations; and what designes they cannot thereby bring to passe, they endeavour by all possible meanes (whether directly or indirectly) even by open violence, without shewing any just cause, and yet all under the colour of lawes, when in the meane time they were called together, sworne, intrusted and commanded, both to rectifie whatever wicked decrees, Popish Cannons, Arbitrary, corrupt, or defective Lawes, their predicessors in the dayes of grosse ignorance and palpable darknesse, did establish.

Howsoever, the body of the Letter doth not specifie in plaine tearmes, what the title painteth out in lively colours, yet thou being judicious and industrious, may easily enough perceive the same by the full scope, true intent and meaning thereof, intimated to thy understanding, under the Authors modest and loving expressions, to this worthy instrument of Englands delivery, Lieuten. Collonell Lilburn, that he may see more cleerly, then (it may be) he did formerly, both how far short even those which we call our best lawes, commeth of the marke of perfection, justice, integrity, and reason, that the worthyes of Parliament, according to their duty unto the people, and the peoples due at their hands, may not only reforme what is amisse (and that now whiles they professe reformation) but likewise carrie that dutyfull respect unto him, as one of their most trusty servants, and that according to the degree, nature, and eminencie of all his faithfull services, and cruell sufferings, and that such others, (though these be few) may be rather encouraged to persist, then any wise being so rewarded, to desist. Fare you well.

Courteous Reader, I desire thee to read a late Printed Booke intituled, *Englands birthright justified, against Arbitrarie usurpation, whether Regall or Parliamentary, or under what Vizar soever.*

FINIS

Printed *October,* 1645. [8]

(8)

Tolleration Justified, and Persecution Condemned

[29 January] 1645/6
Reprinted from a copy of the tract in the Huntington Library

Tolleration Justified was published anonymously "in the Year, 1646" without imprint or license. The tract was prompted by *A Letter of the Ministers of the City of London . . . against Toleration* (1 January 1645/6), which attacked Independency as the great danger to the establishment of an unforbearing religious discipline. Haller, without explanation, places *Tolleration Justified* in Walwyn's canon.[1]

Evidence supporting the attribution is discernible in the persistent civility of *Tolleration Justified*'s point by point responses to the *Letter of the Ministers* as well as in the many contentions and references that are recurrent in Walwyn's acknowledged works. The golden rule of "our Saviour"—"do unto others, as we would be done unto our selves"—is reiterated in *Tolleration Justified*,[2] anti-clericalism is present throughout,[3] and the importance of individuals being "fully perswaded of the truth" of their beliefs is supported by Walwyn's favorite verses from Romans 14.[4] *Tolleration Justified* finds no reason to equate disaffection with diversity[5] and cites Matthew 5:44, in which Christ "bids us love our enemies."[6] The importance of conforming to Scripture—"the Word of God"—is emphasized,[7] and Walwyn's confidence that truth will defeat falsehood is stressed.[8] The familiar listing of sects—"Presbyters, Independents, Brownists, Antinomians, Anabaptists, &c."—appears,[9] and the author urges everyone to "examine" Independents, sectaries, and "all sorts of men and writings, as they are in themselves, and not as they are represented by others."[10] The loyal support of Independents and sectaries for the Parliament's cause is noted more than once,[11] the inevitability of diversity while knowledge is imperfect is stressed,[12] as is Walwyn's conviction that toleration breeds peace in the nation.[13]

There should be, states *Tolleration Justified*, no exceptions to toleration, not even atheists, and error should be countered by love, reason, and example, not by punishment, which is wrong and fruitless.[14] The appeal to Parliament for relief from the threat of an intolerant Presbyterian establishment had been adumbrated in *A Helpe to the Right Understanding*, as was the contention that there are limitations on a Parliament "chosen by the People to provide for their safety and Freedome,[15] whereof," adds *Tolleration Justified*, "Liberty of conscience is the principall branch."[16] In addition to the characteristic defense of toleration based on reason and Christian love,[17] *Tolleration Justified* includes Walwyn's distinctive interpretation of the *Solemn League and Covenant* of 1643. Walwyn had denied the "Presbyterian" interpretation in *Helpe* and in his subsequent tract, *A Word More*, he detailed the view supported by Romans 14 in *Tolleration Justified*.[18]

Tolleration Justified is reprinted in two collections published by the California State Library, Sutro Branch: (1) *Occasional Papers, English Series No. 6* (San Francisco, 1940), Part 3; (2) *Pamphlets on Religion and Democracy, 16th to 19th Centuries* (San Francisco, 1940), pp. 158–79.

Tolleration Justified, AND Persecution condemn'd.

IN An ANSWER or EXAMINATION, OF THE *London-Ministers Letter*

WHEREOF, Many of them are of the Synod, and yet framed this Letter at Sion-Colledge; to be sent among others, to themselves at the Assembly: In behalf of Reformation and Church-government,

2 CORINTH. 11. VERS. 14. 15. And no marvail, for Sathan himself is transformed into an Angell of Light. Therefore it is no great thing, though his Ministers transform themselves, as though they were the Ministers of Righteousnesse; whose end shall be according to their works.

LONDON, Printed in the Year, 1646.

THE LETTER OF THE LONDON MINISTERS TO THE Assembly of DIVINES at Westminster; against TOLERATION, mildly examined; AND The mistakes thereof friendly discovered; As well for the sakes of the *Independent* and *Separation,* as for the good of the COMMON-WEALTH.

When I call to minde the generall oppression (before the Parliament) exercised upon good people, conscientious in the practice of their religion; and that the Presbyters did not onely suffer as much as any therein, but exclaim'd, and labour'd as much as any there-against: It is a wonder to me, that now that yoke is removed, and a blest opportunity offered by Almighty God, to the people and their Parliament, to make every honest heart glad, by allowing a just and contentfull Freedome, to serve God without hypocrisie; and according to the perswasion of conscience: That one Sect amongst us, that is the Presbyters, that have been yoke-fellowes with us; should not rest satisfied with being free as their Brethren, but become restlesse in their contrivances and endeavours, till they become Lords over us. The wonder is the same, as it would have [1] been, had the Israelites, after the Ægyptian bondage, become Task-masters in the Land of Canaan one to another, but that is more in them who have been instructed by our Saviour in that blessed rule; of doing unto others, what they would have others doe unto themselves.

To discover the severall policies the Presbiters have used to get into the chayre they have justled the Bishops out of, whose example they have followed in many particulars; as especially in the politick and graduall obtaining the Ordinance for Licencing, upon a pretence of stopping the Kings writings, but intentionably obtained, and violently made use of against the Independents, Separation, and Commonwealths-men, who either sees more, or something contrary to the designes of the Licencer. To signifie to the People, how the Presbiters have laboured to twist their interest with the Parliaments, as the Bishops did theirs with the King, how daily and burdensomly importunate they are with the Parliament, to establish their Government, (which they are pleased to call Christs) and back it with authority, and a compulsive power, (which by that very perticular appeares not to be his) To lay open their private juncto's and councels, their framing Petitions for the easie and ignorant people, their urging them upon the

Common Councell, and obtruding them upou the chusers of Common Councell men, at the Wardmote Elections, even after the Parliament had signified their dislike thereof; to sum up their bitter invectives in Pulpits, and strange liberty they take as well there, as in their
writings, to make the separation and Independents odious by scandals and untrue reports of them, in confidence of having the presse in
their own hands, by which meanes, no man without hazard shall
answer them, to lay open the manner and depth of these proceedings, is not the intention of this worke; I only thought good to mention these particulars, that the Presbiters may see they walke in a net,
no 'tis no cloud that covers them, and that they may fear that in time
they may be discern'd as well by the whole People, as they are already by a very great part thereof.

The London Ministers Letter, contriu'd in the conclave of Sion Colledge, is one of the numerous projects of the Clergy: not made for the
information of the Sinod, but the misinformation of the People, to
prevent which is my businesse at this time; I will only take so much of
it as is to the point in hand, to wit, Tolleration.

Letter,

It is true, by reason of different lights, and different sights among Brethren,
there may be dissenting in opinion, yet why should there be any seperating
from Church Communion.

Why? because the difference in opinion is in matters that concerne
[2] Church Communion: you may as well put the question, why men
play not the Hypocrites? as they must needs do if they should communicate in that Church Society, their minde cannot approve of. The
question had been well put, if you had said, by reason of different
lights, and different sights, there may be dissenting in opinion, yet
why should our hearts be divided one from another? why should our
love from hence, and our affections grow cold and dead one towards
another? why should we not peaceably, beare one with another, till
our sights grow better, and our light increase? These would have been
questions I thinke, that would have pusled a truly conscientious man
to have found an answer for.

That which next followes, to wit, the Churches coat may be of divers colours, yet why should there be any rent in it: is but an old jing of
the Bishops, spoken by them formerly in reference to the Presbiters;
and now mentioned, to make that which went before, which has no
weight in it selfe, to sound the better.

Letter.

Have we not a Touchstone of truth, the good word of God, and when all things
are examined by the word, then that which is best may be held fast; but first
they must be knowne, and then examined afterward.

I shall easily concur with them thus farr, that the Word of God is the
Touchstone, that all opinions are to be examined by that, and that the
best is to be held fast. But now who shall be the examiners, must
needs be the question; If the Presbiter examine the Independant and
seperation, they are like to find the same censure the Presbiters have
already found, being examined by the Bishops, and the Bishops
found from the Pope: Adversaries certainly are not competent Judges;
againe, in matters disputable and controverted, every man must examine for himselfe, and so every man does, or else he must be conscious to himself, that he sees with other mens eyes, and has taken
up an opinion, not because it consents with his understanding, but
for that it is the safest and least troublesome as the world goes, or
because such a man is of that opinion whom he reverences, and verily
believes would not have been so, had it not been truth. I may be helpt
in my examination, by other men, but no man or sort of men, are to
examine for me, insomuch that before an opinion can properly be
said to be mine, it must concord with my understanding. Now here is
the fallacy, and you shall find it in all Papists, Bishops, Presbiters, or
whatsoever other sort of men, have or would have in their hands the
power of persecuting, that they alwayes suppose themselves to be
competent examiners and Judges of other men differing in judgement
from them, and upon this weake supposition (by no meanes to be
allowed) most of the reasons and arguments of the men forementioned, are supported. [3]

They proceed to charge much upon the Independents, for not producing their modell of Church-government; for answer hereunto, I
refer the Reader to the Reasons printed by the Independents, and
given into the House in their own justification, which the Ministers
might have taken notice of.

I proceed to the supposed Reasons urged by the Ministers, against
the Tolleration of Independency in the Church.

Letter.

1. *Is, because the Desires and endeavours of Independents for a Toleration, are*
at this time extreamly unseasonable, and preposterous For,

1. *The reformation of Religion is not yet perfected and setled amongst us, according to our Covenant. And why may not the Reformation be raised up at last to such purity and perfection, that truly tender consciences may receive abundant satisfaction for ought that yet appeares.*

I would to God the people, their own friends especially, would but take notice of the fallacy of the Reason: They would have reformation perfected according to the Covenant, before the Independents move to be tollerated: now Reformation is not perfected according to the Covenant, till Schisme and Heresie is extirpated; which in the sequel of this Letter, they judge Independency to be, that their charity thinks it then most seasonable, to move that Independency should be tolerated after it is extirpated: their reason and affection in this, are alike sound to the Independants. Their drift in this, indeede is but too evident, they would have the Independents silent, till they get power in their hands, and then let them talke if they dare, certainly, the most seasonable time to move for tolleration is while the Parliament are in debate about Church Government; since if stay bee made till a Church Government bee setled, all motions that may but seeme to derogate from that, how just soever in themselves, how good soever for the Common-wealth, must needs be hardly obtained.

And whereas they say, *Why may not Reformation be raised up at last to such purity and perfection, that truly tender consciences may receive abundant satisfaction, for ought that yet appeares.*

Observe, 1. That these very Ministers, in the sequel of their Letter, impute it as Levity in the Independents, that they are not at a stay, but in expectation of new lights and reserves, as they say, so that a man would think they themselves were at a certainty: But tis no new thing for one sort of men to object that as a crime against others, which they are guilty of themselves: though indeed but that the Presbiters use any weapons against the Independant's, is no crime at all, yea 'tis excellency in any man or woman, not to be pertinacious, or obstinate in any opinion, but to have an open eare for reason and argument, against whatsoever he holds, and to imbrace or reject, whatsoever upon further search he finds to be agree- [4] able to, or dissonant from Gods holy Word. It doth appeare from the practises of the Presbiters, and from this Letter and other Petitions expresly against Toleration, that unlesse the Independants and seperation will submit their Judgements to theirs, they shall never be tollerated, if they can hinder it.

Their 2. Reason is that it *is not yet knowne what the Government of the Independent is, neither would they ever let the world know what they hold in that point, though some of their party have bin too forward to challenge the London Petitioners as led with blind obedience, and pinning their soules upon their Preists sleeve, for desiring an establishment of the Government of Christ, before there was any modell of it extant.* Their 3d. Reason, is *much to the same purpose.*

I answer, 1. That the Ministers know that the Independent Government for the Generall is resolved upon by the Independents, though they have not yet modelized every perticular, which is a worke of time, as the framing of the Presbyterian Government was. The Independents however have divers reasons for dissenting from the Presbyterian way, which they have given in already. And though they have not concluded every perticular of their owne, but are still upon the search, and enquiry; yet it is seasonable however to move for toleration, for that the ground of moving is not because they are Independents, but because every man ought to be free in the worship and service of God, compulsion being the way to increase, not the number of Converts, but of hypocrites; whereas it is another case for People to move for establishing of a Government they understand not, having never seene it, as the London Petitioners did, that is most evidently a giving up of the understanding to other men, sure the Presbiters themselves cannot thinke it otherwise, nor yet the People upon the least consideration of it. Besides, the London Petitioners did not only desire, as here the Ministers cunningly say, an establishment of the Government of Christ, but an establishment of the Government of Christ (a modell whereof the reverend Assembly of Divines have fram'd, which they never saw) so that herein, the People were abused by the Divines, by being put upon a Petition, wherein they suppose that Government which they never saw, to be Christs Government. If this be not sufficient to discover to our Presbyterian Lay-Brethren, the Divines confidence of their ability to worke them by the smoothnesse of phrase and Language to what they please, and of their own easinesse, and flexibility to be so led, I know not what is.

2. The Ministers urge *that the desires and endeavours of the Independants for Toleration, are unreasonable, and unequall in divers regards.*

1. *Partly because no such toleration hath heitherto been establisht (sofar as we know) in any Christian State, by the Civill Magistrate.* [5]

But that the Ministers have been used to speake what they please for a Reason in their Pulpits without contradiction, they would never sure have let so slight a one as this have past from them: It seems by this reason, that if in any Christian State a Toleration by the Magistrate had been allowed, it would not have been unreasonable for our

State to allow it: The practice of States, being here supposed to be the rule of what's reasonable; whereas I had thought, that the practice of Christian States is to be judg'd by the rule of reason and Gods Word, and not reason by them: That which is just and reasonable, is constant and perpetually so; the practice of States though Christian, is variable we see; different one from another, and changing according to the prevalency of particular partees, and therefore a most uncertain rule of what is reasonable.

Besides, the State of Holland doth tollerate; and therefore the Ministers Argument, even in that part where it seems to be most strong for them, makes against them.

Again, if the practice of a Christian state, be a sufficient Argument of the reasonablenesse of a Tolleration, our State may justly tollerate because Christian, and because they are free to do what ever any other State might formerly have done. But I stay too long upon so weak an Argument.

2. Partly, Because *some of them have solemnly profest, that they cannot suffer Presbitary, and answerable hereunto is their practice, in those places where Independency prevailes.*

'Tis unreasonable it seems to tollerate Independents, because Independents would not if they had the power, suffer Presbyters. A very Christianly argument, and taken out of the 5. of Matthew 44. *Love your Enemies, blesse them that curse you, do good to them that hate you, and pray for them which hurte you, and persecute you:* What, were all our London Ministers forgetfull of their Saviours instructions? Does their fury so farre blinde their understanding, and exceed their piety? Which seems to be but pretended now, since in their practice they would become Jews, and cry out *an eye for an eye, and a tooth for a tooth.* Whosoever meddles with them it seems, shall have as good as they bring: Was ever so strange a reason urg'd by a Sect of men, that say they are Ministers, Christs Ministers, Reformers too, that would make the world believe they are about to reduce all matters Christian, to the originall and primitive excellency of Christ and the Apostles, and yet to speak and publish to the world a spleenish reason, so expressely contrary to the precepts, to the practice of Christ and his followers. To Christ I say, that bids us love our enemies, that we may be the children of our Father which is in heaven, who makes the Sun to shine on the evill and the good, and sendeth rain on the just and on the unjust. The Ministers should be like the Master, what a disproportion is here? As if the title were taken [6] up for some other end; we know the Apostle speaks of Ministers that could transform themselves as though they were the Ministers of Righteousnesse; I pray God our Ministers do not so, I would willingly suppresse those fears and suspitions; which, doe what I can arise in me, from their words and practice. Sure they had approved themselves better christians, if upon the discovery of so bad a spirit in any of the Independents; as to persecute, had they power (though I beleive, there are not any such) I say, it had been more Christ-like in our Ministers, to have disswaded them from so unmanly, so much more unchristianly a vice, then to have it made an argument for practice in themselves. They might by the same rule, be Jewes to the Jew, or Turke to the Turke, Oppressours to the Oppressour; or doe any evill to others, that others would doe to them: if other mens doing of it, be an argument of the reasonablenesse thereof. But I hope, our Ministers will be so ingenious, as when they see their weaknesses forsake them, it will be both more comfortable to all other sorts of men, and in the end more happy for themselves.

2. Again, I suppose your suggestion to be very false; namely, that the Independents if they had power, would persecute the Presbyters: though let me tell you of all sects of men, those deserve least countenance of a State that would be Persecutors, not because of their consciences in the practice and exercise of their Religion, wherein the ground of Freedome consists; but because a persecuting spirit is the greatest enemy to humane society, the dissolver of love and brotherly affection, the cause of envyings, heart-burnings, divisions, yea, and of warres it selfe. Whosoever shall cast an impartiall eye upon times past, and examine the true cause and reason of the subversion, and devastation of States and countries, will I am confident; attribute it to no other, then the Tyranny of Princes, and Persecution of Priests. So that all States, minding their true interests, namely the good and welfare of the people, ought by all meanes to suppresse in every sect or degree of men, whether Papists, Episcopalls, Presbyters, Independents, Anabaptists, &c. the spirit of Domination, and Persecution, the disquieter and disturber of mankind, the offspring of Satan. God being all Love, and having so communicated himselfe unto us, and gave us commands to be like him, mercifull, as he our heavenly Father is mercifull; to bear with one anothers infirmities: neither does reason and true wisdome dictate any other to us, then that we should do unto others, as we would be done unto our selves; that spirit therefore which is contrary to God, to reason, to the well-being of States, as the spirit of Persecution evidently is; is most especially to be watcht, and warily to be circumscribed, and tied up by the wisdome

of the supream power in Common-wealths. I speak not this to the disgrace of Presbyters, as Presbyters; for as such, I suppose they are not Persecutors: forasmuch as I know, some, and I hope there are many more of them, that are zealous and conscientious for that form of Government, and yet enemies to a compulsive power in matters of Religion. But for this end only, namely to beget a just and christian dislike in all sorts of men, as well Presbyters, as others; of forcing all to one way of worship, though disagreeable to their minds: which cannot be done, without the assistance of this fury and pestilent enemy to mankind, Persecution. I proceed to the Ministers third Reason. [7]

3. *And partly to grant to them, and not to other Sectaries who are free-born as well as they, and have done as good service as they to the publick (as they use to plead) will be counted injustice, and great partiality; but to grant it to all, will scarce be cleared from impiety.*

To the former part of this argument I gladly consent, that Sectaries have as good claimes to Freedome, as any sorts of men whatsoever; because free-born, because well-affected, and very assistant to their country in its necessities. The latter part of the argument is only an affirmation, without proof; the Ministers think sure it will be taken for truth because they said it, for such a presumption it seems they are arrived to. In the mean time what must they suppose the people to be, that do imagine their bare affirmations sufficient ground for the peoples belief; I would the people would learn from hence to be their own men, and make use of their own understandings in the search and beleif of things; let their Ministers be never so seemingly learned or judicious, God hath not given them understandings for nothing; the submission of the mind is the most ignoble slavery; which being in our own powers to keep free, the Subjection thereof argues in us the greater basenesse; but to the Assertion, that it will be impiety to grant it to all Sectaries.

I answer, First, that the word Sectary is communicable both to Presbyters and Independents, whether it be taken in the good sense for the followers of Christ; for such, all Presbyters, Independents, Brownists, Anabaptists, and all else, suppose and professe themselves to be: or in the common sense, for followers of some few men more eminent in their parts and abilities then other. And hereof the Independents and Presbyters are as guilty as the Separation, and so are as well Sectaries. Now all Sectaries, whether Presbyters, Independents, Brownists, Antinomians, Anabaptists, &c. have a like title and right to Freedome, or a Toleration; the title thereof being not any particular of the Opinion, but the Equity of every mans being Free in the State he lives in, and is obedient to, matters of opinion being not properly to be taken into cognisance any farther, then they break out into some disturbance, or disquiet to the State. But you will say, that by such a toleration, blasphemy will be broached, and such strange and horrid opinions, as would make the eares of every godly and christian man to tingle; what must this also be tolerated? I answer, it cannot be just, to set bounds or limitations to toleration, any further then the safety of the people requires; the more horrid and blasphemous the opinion is, the easier supprest, by reason and argument; because it must necessarily be, that the weaker the arguments, are on one side, the stronger they are on the other: the grosser the errour is, the more advantage hath truth over it; the lesse colour likewise, and pretence there is, for imposing it upon the people. I am confident, that there is much more danger in a small, but speciously formed error, that hath a likenesse and similitude to truth, then in a grosse and palpable untruth.

Besides, can it in reason be judged the meetest way to draw a man out of his error, by imprisonment, bonds, or other punishment? You may as well be angry, and molest a man that has an imperfection or dimnesse in his eyes, and thinke by [8] stripes or bonds to recover his sight: how preposterous would this bee? Your proper and meet way sure is, to apply things pertinent to his cure. And so likewise to a man whose understanding is clouded, whose inward sight is dimn and imperfect, whose mind is so far mis-informed as to deny a Deity, or the Scriptures (for we'l instance in the worst of errors) can Bedlam or the Fleet reduce such a one? No certainly, it was ever found by all experience, that such rough courses did confirme the error, not remove it: nothing can doe that but the efficacy and convincing power of sound reason and argument; which, 'tis to be doubted, they are scarce furnisht withall that use other weapons. Hence have I observ'd that the most weak & passionate men, the most unable to defend truth, or their owne opinions, are the most violent for persecution. Whereas those whose minds are establisht, and whose opinions are built upon firm and demonstrable grounds, care not what winds blow, fear not to grapple with any error, because they are confident they can overthrow it.

3. Independency is a Schisme, and therefore not to be tollerated.

The principall argument brought to prove it, is this; *Because they depart from the Presbyter Churches, which are true Churches, and so confest to be by the Independents.*

I answer, that this Argument only concerns the Independents, because they only acknowledge them to be true Churches. Whether they are still of that opinion or no I know not, 'tis to be doubted they are not, especially since they have discern'd the spirit of enforcement and compulsion to raign in that Church; the truest mark of a false Church. I believe the Independents have chang'd their minde, especially those of them whose Pastors receive their Office and Ministery from the election of the people or congregation, and are not engag'd to allow so much to the Presbyters, because of their own interest; as deriving their calling from the Bishops and Pope, for the making up a supposed succession from the Apostles, who for their own sakes are enforc'd to acknowledge the Presbyter for a true Church, as the Presbyters are necessitated to allow the Episcopall and Papist Church, true or valid for the substance, as they confesse in the ordinance for Ordination, because they have receiv'd their Ministery therefrom, without which absurdity they cannot maintain their succession from the Apostles. But that the Independents are not a schism, they have and will, I believe, upon all occasions sufficiently justifie: I shall not therefore, since it concerns them in particular, insist thereupon; but proceed to the supposed mischiefs which the Ministers say will inevitably follow upon this tolleration, both to the Church and Commonwealth. First, to the Church.

1. *Causelesse and unjust revolts, from our Ministery and Congregations.*

To this I say, that it argues an abundance of distrust the Ministers have in their own abilities, and the doctrines they preach, to suppose their auditors will forsake them if other men have liberty to speak. 'Tis authority it seems must fill their Churches, and not the truth and efficacy of their doctrines. I judge it for my part a sufficient ground to suspect that for gold that can't abide a triall. It seems our Ministers doctrines and Religion, are like Dagon of the Philistins, that will fall to pieces at the appearance of the Ark. Truth sure would be more confident, in hope to appear more [9] glorious, being set off by falshood. And therefore I do adjure the Ministers, from that lovelinesse and potency that necessarily must be in Truth and Righteousnesse, if they think they do professe it, that they would procure the opening of every mans mouth, in confidence that truth, in whomsoever she is, will prove victorious; and like the Suns glorious lustre, darken all errors and vain imaginations of mans heart. But I fear the consequence sticks more in the stomacks, the emptying of their Churches being the eclipsing of their reputations, and the diminishing of their profits; if it be otherwise, let it appear by an equall allowing of that to

others, which they have labour'd so much for to be allowed to themselves.

2. *Our peoples minds will be troubled and in danger to be subverted,* Acts
15.24.

A. The place of Scripture may concern themselves, and may as well
be urg'd upon them by the Separation or Independents, as it is urg'd
by them upon the Separation and Independents; namely, that they
trouble the peoples mindes, and lay injunctions upon them, they
were never commanded to lay. And 'tis very observable, the most of
those Scriptures they urge against the Separation, do most properly
belong unto themselves.

3. *Bitter heart-burnings among brethren, will be fomented and perpetuated
to all posterity.*

I answer. Not by, but for want of a Tolleration: Because the State is
not equall in its protection, but allows one sort of men to trample
upon another; from hence must necessarily arise heart-burnings,
which as they have ever been, so they will ever be perpetuated to
posterity, unlesse the State wisely prevent them, by taking away the
distinction that foments them; namely, (the particular indulgency of
one party, and neglect of the other) by a just and equall tolleration. In
that family strife and heart-burnings are commonly multiplied, where
one son is more cockered and indulg'd then another; the way to foster
love and amity, as well in a family, as in a State, being an equall respect from those that are in authority.

4. They say, the *Godly, painfull, and orthodox Ministers will bee discouraged and despised.*

Answ. Upon how slight foundation is their reputation supported,
that fear being despised unlesse Authority forces all to Church to
them? Since they have confidence to vouch themselves godly, painfull, and orthodox, me thinks they should not doubt an audience. The
Apostles would empty the Churches, and Jewish Synagogues, and by
the prevalency of their doctrine convert 3000 at a Sermon; and doe
our Ministers feare, that have the opportunity of a Church, and the
advantage of speaking an houre together without interruption, that
they cannot keep those Auditors they have; but that they shall bee
withdrawn from them by men of meaner lights (in their esteeme) by
the illiterate and under-valued lay Preachers, that are (as the Ministers suppose) under the cloud of error and false doctrine? Surely they
suspect their own Tenetss or their abilities to maintain them, that esteem it a discouragement to bee opposed, and feare they shall be
despised if disputed withall. [10]

5. They say, *The life and power of godlinesse will be eaten out by frivolous disputes and vain janglings.*

Answ. Frivolous disputes and vain janglings, are as unjustifiable in the people as in the Ministery, but milde and gentle Reasonings (which authority are onely to countenance) make much to the finding out of truth, which doth most advance the life and power of god-linesse. Besides, a Toleration being allowed, and every Sect labouring to make it appear that they are in the truth, whereof a good life, or the power of godlinesse being the best badge or symptome; hence will necessarily follow, a noble contestation in all sorts of men to exceed in godlinesse, to the great improvement of vertue and piety amongst us. From whence it will be concluded too, that that Sect will be supposed to have least truth in them, that are least vertuous, and godlike in their lives and conversations.

6. They urge, *That the whole course of religion in private families will be interrupted and undermined.*

Answ. As if the Independents and Separation were not as religious in their private families, as the Presbyters.

7. *Reciprocall duties between persons of nearest and dearest relations, will be extreamly violated.*

Answ. A needlesse fear, grounded upon a supposition, that difference in judgement must needs occasion coldnesse of affection, which indeed proceeds from the different countenance and protection, which States have hitherto afforded to men of different judgements. Hence was it, that in the most persecuting times, when it was almost as bad in the vulgar esteem to be an Anabaptist, as a murtherer, it occasioned dis-inheritings, and many effects of want of affection, in people of nearest relations; but since the common odium and vilification is in great measure taken off, by the wise and just permission of all sects of men by the Parliament, man and wife, father and son, friend and friend, though of different opinions, can agree well together, and love one another; which shews that such difference in affection, is not properly the effect of difference in judgement, but of Persecution, and the distinct respect and different countenance that Authority has formerly shewn towards men not conforming.

8. They say, That the whole *work of Reformation, especially in discipline and Government, will be retarded, disturbed, and in danger of being utterly frustrate and void.*

It matters not, since they mean in the Presbyterian discipline and Government, accompanied with Persecution: Nay, it will be abundantly happy for the people, and exceedingly conducing to a lasting

Peace (to which Persecution is the greatest enemy) if such a government so qualified be never setled. The Presbyters I hope, will fall
short in their ayms. 1. 'Tis not certain that the Parliament mean to
settle the Presbyterian Government, since they have not declared that
Government to be agreeable to Gods Word; although the Presbyters
are [11] pleas'd, in their expressions, frequently to call their Government, Christs Government. Howsoever, their determination (which
may well be suppos'd to be built upon their interest) is not binding:
They are call'd to advise withall, not to controul. 2. In case the Parliament should approve of that Government in the main, yet the Prelaticall and persecuting power of it, we may well presume (since they
themselves may smart under it as well as the rest of the people) they
will never establish.

9. *All other Sects and Heresies in the Kingdome, will be encouraged to
endeavour the like tolleration.*

Sects and Heresies! We must take leave to tell them, that those are
termes impos'd *ad placitum*, and may be retorted with the like confidence upon themselves. How prove they Separation to be Sects and
Heresies; because they differ and separate from them? That's no Argument, unlesse they can first prove themselves to be in the truth? A
matter with much presumption suppos'd, but never yet made good,
and yet upon this groundlesse presumption, the whole fabrick of
their function, their claim to the Churches, their preheminence in determining matters of Religion, their eager persuit after a power to
persecute, is mainly supported. If the Separation are Sects and Heresies, because the Presbyters (supposing themselves to have the countenance of Authority, and some esteem with the people) judge them
so: The Presbyters by the same rule were so, because the Bishops
once in authority, and in greater countenance with the People, did so
judge them to be.

And whereas they say, *That Sects and Heresies will be encouraged to
endeavour the like tolleration with the Independents.*

I answer, that 'tis their right, their due as justly as their cloths, or
food; and if they indeavour not for their Liberty, they are in a measure
guilty of their owne bondage. How monstrous a matter the Ministers
would make it to be, for men to labour to be free from persecution.
They thinke they are in the saddle already, but will never I hope have
the reines in their hands.

Their 10th. feare is the same.

2. *They say the whole Church of England* (they meane their whole
Church of England) *in short time will be swallowed up with distraction and
confusion.*

These things are but said, not proved: were it not that the Divines blew the coales of dissention, and exasperated one mans spirit against another; I am confidently perswaded we might differ in opinion, and yet love one another very well; as for any distraction or confusion that might intrench upon that civill peace, the Laws might provide against it, which is the earnest desires both of the Independents and Seperation.

2. They say, *Tolleration will bring divers mischiefes upon the Commonwealth:* For, [12]

1. *All these mischeifes in the Church will have their proportionable influence upon the Common-wealth.*

This is but a slight supposition, and mentions no evill that is like to befall the Common-wealth.

2. They urge *that the Kingdome will be wofully weakned by scandalls and Divisions, so that the Enemies both domesticall and forraigne will be encouraged to plot and practise against it.*

I answer, that the contrary hereunto is much more likely, for two Reasons.

1. There is like to be a concurrence, and joynt assistance in the protection of the Common-wealth, which affords a joynt protection and encouragement to the People.

2. There can be no greater argument to the People, to venture their estates and lives in defence of their Country and that government, under which they enjoy not only a liberty, of Estate and Person, but a freedome likewise of serving God according to their consciences, which Religious men account the greatest blessing upon earth; I might mention notable instances of late actions of service in Independents and Seperatists, which arising but from hopes of such a freedome, can yet scarce be paraleld by any age or story.

3. They say *it is much to be doubted, lest the power of the Magistrate should not only be weakned, but even utterly overthrowne; considering the principles and practices of Independents, together with their compliance with other Sectaries, sufficiently knowne to be antimagistraticall.*

An injurious, but common scandal, this whereof much use has been made to the misleading the People into false apprehensions of their brethren the Seperatists, to the great increase of enmity and disaffection amongst us, whereof the Ministers are most especially guilty: Let any impartiall man examine the principles, and search into the practises of the separation, and he must needs conclude that they are not the men that trouble England, but those rather that lay it to their charge: the seperation indeede and Independents are enemies to Tyranny, none more, and oppression, from whence I beleeve has arisen the fore-mentioned scandall of them: but to just Goverment and Magistracy, none are more subject, and obedient: and therefore the Ministers may do well to lay aside such obloquies, which will otherwise by time and other discovery, turne to their own disgrace.

In the last place they say, *'tis opposite to the Covenant, I. Because opposite to the Reformation of Religion, according to the Word of God, and example of the best Reformed Churches.*

I answer, 1, That the example of the best reformed Churches is not binding, further then they agree with the Word of God, so that the Word of God indeed is the only rule. Now the word of God is expresse for tolleration, as appeares by [13] the Parable of the Tares growing with the wheate, by those two expresse and positive rules, 1. Every man should be fully perswaded of the truth of that way wherein he serves the Lord, 2. That whatsoever is not of faith is sinne; and 3. by that rule of reason and pure nature, cited by our blessed Saviour: namely, whatsoever ye would that men should do unto you, that do you unto them.

2. *They say it is destructive to the 3. Kingdomes nearest conjunction and uniformity in Religion and Government.*

I answer, that the same tolleration may be allowed in the 3. Kingdomes, together with the same Religion and Government; whether it shall be Presbiterian, or Independent, or Anabaptisticall: Besides that I suppose which is principally intended by this part of the Covenant, 'tis the Union of the 3. Kingdomes, and making them each defensive and helpfull to the other, which a tolleration will be a meanes to further, because of the encouragement that every man will have to maintaine his so excellent freedome; which he cannot better do, then by maintaining them all, because of the Independency they will have one upon the other.

3. *'Tis expresly contrary to the extirpation of Schisme, and whatsoever shall be found contrary to sound doctrine, and the power of Godlinesse.*

I answer, That when it is certainly determined by Judges that cannot err, who are the Schismaticks, there may be some seeming pretence to extirpate them, though then also no power or force is to be used, but lawfull means only, as the wise men have interpreted it; that is, Schisme and Heresie, when they appeare to be such, are to be rooted out by reason and debate, the sword of the Spirit, not of the Flesh; arguments, not blowes: unto which men betake themselves upon distrust of their own foundations, and consciousnesse of their owne inability.

Besides, as the Presbiters judge others to be a Schisme from them, so others judge them to be a Schisme from the Truth, in which sence only the Covenant can be taken.

4. *Hereby we shall be involved in the guilt of other mens sinnes, and thereby be endangered to receive of their plagues.*

I answer, that compulsion must necessarily occasion both much cruelty and much Hypocrisie: whereof the Divines, labouring so much for the cause, which is persecution, cannot be guiltlesse.

5. *It seemes utterly impossible (if such a tolleration should be granted) that the Lord should be one, and his name one, in the 3. Kingdomes.*

I suppose they mean by that phrase, it is impossible that our judgements and profession should be one; so I believe it is, whether there be a Tolleration or no. But certainly the likeliest way, if there be any thereunto, is by finding out one truth; which most probably will be by giving liberty to every man to speak his minde, and produce his reasons and arguments; and not by hearing one Sect on- [14] ly: That if it does produce a forc'd unity, it may be more probably in errour, then in truth; the Ministers being not so likely to deal clearly in the search thereof, because of their interests, as the Laity, who live not thereupon, but enquire for truth, for truths sake, and the satisfaction of their own mindes.

And thus I have done with the Argumentive part of the Letter. I shall onely desire, that what I have said may be without prejudice considered: And that the People would look upon all sorts of men and writings, as they are in themselves, and not as they are represented by others, or forestall'd by a deceitfull rumour or opinion.

In this controversie concerning Tolleration, I make no question but the Parliament will judge justly between the two parties; who have both the greatest opportunity and abilities, to discern between the integrity of the one side, and the interest of the other. That the one party pleads for toleration, for the comfort and tranquility of their lives, and the peaceable serving of God according to their consciences, in which they desire no mans disturbance. That the other that plead against it, may (I would I could say onely probably) be swayed by interest and self-respects, their means and preheminence. I make no question but the Parliament, before they proceed to a determination of matters concerning Religion, will as they have heard one party, the Divines, so likewise reserve one ear for all other sorts of men; knowing that they that give sentence, all partees being not heard, though the sentence be just (which then likely will not be) yet they are unjust. Besides, the Parliament themselves are much concerned in this controversie, since upon their dissolution they must mixe with the people, and then either enjoy the sweets of freedome, or suffer under the most irksome yoke of Priestly bondage: and therefore since they are concern'd in a double respect; first, as chosen by the People to provide for their safety and Freedome, whereof Liberty of conscience is the principall branch, and so engag'd by duty: secondly, as Members of the Common-wealth, and so oblig'd to establish Freedome, out of love to themselves and their posterity.

I shall only add one word more concerning this Letter, which is this; That 'tis worth the observation, that the same men are part of the contrivers of it, and part of those to whom 'twas sent; Mr. Walker being President of Sion Colledge, Mr. Seaman one of the Deans, (observe that word) and Mr. Roborough, one of the Assistants, all three Members of the Synod: who with the rest framing it seasonably, and purposely to meet with the Letter from Scotland, concerning Church Government, may well remove the wonder and admiration that seem'd to possesse one of the Scotch grand Divines in the Synod, *at the concurrence of Providence in these two Letters:* of the politick and confederated ordering whereof, he could not be ignorant.

FINIS [15]

9

A Whisper in the Eare of
Mr. Thomas Edwards, Minister

[13 March] 1645/6
Reprinted from a copy of the tract in the Thomason Collection in the British Library

A Whisper in the Eare is the first tract published over Walwyn's name. The pamphlet was published without separate title page or license; the imprint appears on the last page, verso: "London, Printed according to Order, by Thomas Paine, for William Ley, at Paules-Chaine, 1646." It is the first of several tracts printed by Paine for Walwyn in 1646.[1]

Whisper is the first of five tracts Walwyn wrote in response to Thomas Edwards's *Gangraena.* The tracts reveal Walwyn at his best, and the reasonable, gentle, often loving though ironic replies are a potent contrast to Edwards's intemperate attacks on the "pernicious Practices of the Sectaries of this time." In the first part of *Gangraena,* [26 February] 1645/6, Edwards made a single comment about "one Mr. Wallin a Seeker, and a dangerous man, a strong head."[2] Walwyn seized the occasion to vindicate his life and character as he notes that "though I am not in fellowship with those good people you call sectaries, yet I joyn heart and hand with them in any thing that I judge to be right: . . . and love them as heartily as those that are one with me in judgement."[3] *Whisper* is of particular interest for its account of Walwyn's religious awakening, his discovery of love and toleration as the mainsprings of conduct, and his determination to do Christ's will in a "publick way."[4]

Whisper is reproduced in facsimile in *Tracts on Liberty,* ed. Haller, 3:321–36.

A *WHISPER* IN THE EARE

of Mr. *Thomas Edwards* Minister.

By *William Walwyn* Marchant.

Occasioned by his mentioning of him reproachfully, in his late pernitious booke, justly entituled the *Gangræa*.

Micah. 7. 2. *The good man is perished out of the earth, and there is none righteous among men: they all lie in wait for blood: every man hunteth his brother with a net.*

SIR, Your extream fury in driving on a work wherein no charitable well minded Christian takes any comfort, but rather an abundance of griefe, hath made me to conclude, that you are quite deaf on the right christian eare; deaf to all that is good: a man (I fear) altogether without Conscience, or sence of goodnesse: and that you have the use of hearing only on the left side of Machiavilian policy: just as Demetrius the silversmith, that opposed not the doctrine of Christ out of zeale to the Goddesse Diana as he pretended: nor out of any hatred to that doctrine, but as it tended to the losse of his craft and gain: even so you, (as I verily fear) do not indeavour to make odious the severall doctrines and practices of conscienscious people, out of true zeal to any thing you apprehend as truth; or out of hatred to any thing you apprehend as error: but because the doctrines and practices of those you term independents, [1] Brownists, Anabaptists, Antinomians, and Seekers: do all tend to the losse of your craft and gain: in that they all disallow of tythes, as ceremonious and popish, and all contracted for, or enforced maintenance for ministers under the Gospel, as disagreeing to the rule thereof: nay you have further cause against them, for they spoile you not onely of your gaine, but of your glory and domination, things dearer to you then your life: of your glory, in denying your ministry to be successive from the Apostles: of your domination, by denying unto you any more authority to judge of doctrines or discipline, then any other sort of Christian men: and to speak truly, these are sore temptations to such worldly minds as yours, who in your hopes had made your selves sure of the greatest part of all that was taken from the Prelats, and thereby of a foundation of advancing the honour, and splendour, and power, and profit of the Clergy once more in this Nation: It is confest that such provocations as these have not onely produced such reviling accusations, as you bring against conscientious well minded people, but a subversion of the calumniators: as it befell the late Prelats, whose railing, reviling, and molesting of the harmelesse faithfull puritan, under pretence of herisie, schisme, faction, sedition, and the like, being all contrary to every mans knowledge and experience of them: the issue was, the utter extirpation of their calumniators: and that so lately, as might be a warning to you, and such politique worldly men as you are; but that it is (through the wisdom and justice of God) the fate of policy and politique men not to be warned by other mens judgements, but to trust so much to the strength of their braines, that they fear not to trace those very steps that gradatim brought the last Arch bishop* to the block, making no conscience of vexing, disgraceing, and undoing of any man, nay thousands of men and families, standing twixt them and their unjust ends: and this too so madly and rashly, as to make themselves adversaries of such, as really aimed at their good, and to preserve them from those precipitations their folly and malice labours to hasten. And this is your case with me, for I am confident and well assured, that amongst all those whom in this your frantick booke you have named, there is not one that opposed your waies more out of love, and seriously for your good, then I have done: for what ever you through want of an experimentall knowledge of me, or upon mis-report may judge of me, I am one that do truly and heartily love all mankind, it being the unfeigned desire of my soul, that all men might be saved, and come to [2] the knowledge of the truth, it is my extream grief that any man is afflicted, molested, or punished, and cannot but most earnestly wish, that all occasion were taken away: there is no man weake, but I would strengthen: nor ignorant, but I would informe: nor erronious, but I would rectifie, nor vicious, but I would reclaim, nor cruel, but I would moderate and reduce to clemency: I am as much grieved that any man should be so unhappy as to be cruel or unjust, as that any man should suffer by cruelty or injustice: and if I could I would preserve from both; and however I am mistaken, it is from this disposition in me, that I have engaged my self in any publick affairs, and from no other, which my manner of proceeding in every particular busines wherein I have in any measure appeared, will sufficiently evince, to all that have without partiallity observed me: I never proposed any man for my

* William Laud, Archbishop of Canterbury. (Editors' note)

enemy, but injustice, oppression, innovation, arbitrary power, and cruelty, where ever I found them I ever opposed my self against them; but so, as to destroy the evil, but to preserve the person: and therefore all the war I have made (other then what my voluntary and necessary contribution hath maintained, which I wish ten thousand times more then my ability, so really am I affected with the Parliaments just cause for the common freedom of this Nation) I say all the war I have made, hath been to get victory on the understandings of men: accompting it a more worthy and profitable labour to beget friends to the cause I loved, rather then to molest mens persons, or confiscate estates: and how many true and thorow converts have been made through my endeavours: you tempt me to boast, were I addicted to such a vanity, or were I not better pleased with the conscience of so doing. Before this Parliament I was of full years to be sensible of the oppression of the times, being now forty five years of age, having accustomed my self to all kinds of good reading, and to the consideration of all things; but so, as for a long time I took not boldnesse to judge, but upon the approbation of some authors and teachers that had captivated my understanding both in things morall, politique, and religious: in the last of which, being very serious and sincere in my application of things to my own conscience, my grounds being bad, though much applauded, I found much disconsolation therein, great uncertainty, and at last extream affliction of mind, the law and Gospel fighting for victory in me, in which conflict, the Scriptures were taken in more singly, and void of glosse, to my assistance, by the cleare light whereof, I saw the enemies I feared van-
[3] quished, which wrought a real thankfulnes in me towards Christ, which increased with the increasings of faith: insomuch as I set my self daily more and more to do his will: and that in a more publick way then formerly: Whereupon an occasion being offered by this honourable Parliament, our minister and parish (James Garlick-hill London) being quite out of order: I, with others, moved for reformation, in doing whereof, how I laboured to have preserved the continuance and well being of our minister: himself, and the ancient that opposed our endeavours, I presume will testifie, but if they should not, there is enow that will, but he was a man that trusted to policy, which in the end failed him: our next indeavours were for the whole ward, wherein after much labour, we so prevailed, that the well affected carryed the choice of Alderman and common councell men, and all other officers in the Ward: my next publike businesse was with many others, in a remonstrance to the Common Councell, to move

the Parliament to confirm certain infallible maximes of free Government: wherein the power of Parliament was plainly distinguished
from the Kings Office, so plainly, that had it taken effect: few men
after due consideration thereof, would through error of judgement
have taken part against the Parliament, or have befriended arbitrary
power, as too too many did for want of light. but it was stifled in the
birth. I was also interrested in all the proceedings of Salters hall,
whence much good issued to the whole City and Kingdom; where I
beleeve it will be testified by all, I was never heard or observed to
propose or second a bad motion, nor far short of any in prosecution of
any thing that was good: and when the common enemy was at the
highest, and the Parliaments forces at the lowest, I with many others
petitioned the Parliament for the generall raising and arming of all the
well affected in the Kingdom, and though that also took not its proper
effect, and came not to perfection: yet it mated the common enemy,
and set all wheels at work at home, was the spring of more powerfull
motions and good successes: God so ordering things that no man
moves for good, but good in one kind or other comes thereof: and in
all that I have at any time done, I ever associated my self with persons
of known good affections to Parliament and Common-wealth: that it
is my extream wonder that any well-affected person should affirm me
to be a man dangerous: I have never shunned the light, all that I have
had a hand in hath come to the publick view and touch, and truly
there hath not been a just thing promoted or endea- [4] voured to be
promoted, that ever I was absent from, if I had a call thereunto: and
whereas I have addicted my selfe to know and understand all the
severall doctrines and waies of worship that are extant, and for that
end have taken liberty to hear and to observe all: it is that I might be
able to judge rightly of their differences, to vindicate them when they
are wronged: and to advise them for their good: in doing whereof, I
have gained much good, there being not any (how light esteeme
soever you make of them) but have somthing worthy the observation:
and this I must testify for all sorts of them, they are a people the most
ready to render love for love, that ever I met withall: and not apt to
render evil for evil: they are all universally faithfull to the Parliament,
friends to all just government, and enemies to all unjust: but yet there
is not any thing I have observed that hath prevailed with me to dis-
claim the publike ministry, or the parochial congregations & I have yet
some hopes to see them reduced into such a condition, as that all
things thereunto belonging, may without difficulty be justified: but
though I am not in fellowship with those good people you call sec-

taries, yet I joyn heart and hand with them in any thing that I judge to
be right: and tending to the publike good: and love them as heartily as
those that are one with me in judgement: sometimes I contest with
them somewhat vehemently in arguing, but it is as I conceive for
truth, and for their good: and they take it so, and bear with me as I
with them: and we meet and part in love, as becometh Christians, nor
doth this hinder, but that when any difference befalleth betweene
them and the publick ministers, but that I judge as clearly in such
cases, as if I had no difference with them, for I esteem it a high part of
true religion to promote common justice: and not to be a respecter of
persons in judgement, wherein the Scripture is my rule: and that
being on their side, I should take part with them therein against my
father, minister, or the dearest friend I have in the world: and from
hence it is, that when the question is about liberty of Conscience, the
Scripture tells me, every one ought to be fully perswaded in his own
mind, and that whatsoever is not of faith, is sin: it tells me I must doe
as I would be done unto: I would not be enforced to the Parish Congregations, then I must not force them to them, or from their owne:
God onely perswades the heart: compulsion and enforcement may
make a confused masse of dissembling hypocrites, not a Congregation of beleevers, that seeing our Saviour reproached not those that
denyed the resurrection, angels and [5] spirits, nay Joh. 12: 47, 48. &c.
he saith plainly (and that by authority from heaven, v 49,) *He that
refuseth me, and receiveth not my words, hath one that judgeth him: the word
that I have spoken, it shall judge him in the last day.* Also in Luke the 9: 54,
55, 56. Insomuch as I see no more warrant now to reproach or punish
any man for Religion, but rather that we are all bound in peace and
love to reclaime our brother from what wee judge an error in his way:
wherein the best and most knowing amongst men in our daies, may
be mistaken; being all liable to take truth for error, and error for truth,
and therefore there is no cause of strife or compulsion, except for
mastery: then which (as I conceive) nothing is more unchristian, neverthelesse I may see a necessary use of a publick ministry, and parish
Congregations, and it is my work to perswade others therein, and not
to speak reproachfully thereof, as they would not have their way reproached: but then when the question is concerning a maintenance
for these publick ministers: and that any shall insist for tythes, or an
enforced maintenance, truly in this case the Scripture manifesting to
my understanding, tythes to be ceremoniall and Jewish, and so to
cease at the comming of Christ: and that to enforce or enjoyn a maintenance though under any other notion, is as I apprehend contrary to

the rule and practice of the Apostles, how is it possible but I must adhere to them therein: but then that our publick ministers should have no maintenance, therein I wholy dissent, and as it hath been my endeavour to assist the one party to avoid the molestation of their consciences in tythes, & all enforced contributions so have I often proposed a way for the maintenance of the publick ministers, more certain, more quiet for themselves, and lesse irksome to the people, lesse disturbant to the Common-wealth: and thus you may see how through mis-information: you have taken me for an enimy, that have alwaies approved my self your reall friend in all things I apprehended just: and thus you may see how dangerous a man I have been that in all these publick differences have done no man hurt by word or deed: nay at all the meetings I have frequented, whether at Salters hall, the wind mill, or else where, I never heard any man named reproachfully, but I openly shewed the unfitnes thereof: alwaies advising that if any man had ought against any particular person, that he should make it known to those that by law had a right to take notice thereof, and that we should be very cautious in thinking evil of any man upon report and hearsay, especially of any in authority: The truth is, I have been and [6] am of opinion, that it is not good for the Common-wealth, that the ministers should have any power or jurisdiction put into their hands, or that it were good for the ministers themselves, the same having so often proved their ruine, and the disturbance of the people, but do conceive it more safe for them, and more for the quiet of the people, that they be freed from all other employments, except preaching and administring the publick worship of God, according as the Parliament shall ordain, for I look upon you as ministers ordained by the State, and so are to do as they conceive is most agreeable to the word of God, and most beneficiall to the generallity of the people: in setling whereof, you may advise, but are not to urge or be importunate for more power then they see good, and it lesse beseems you to grow passionate, and to move others to be importunate, and by preaching and printing to labour to make their faithfull friends odious unto them, and to magnifie your desires, above their own intentions, and so to beget emulations and parties, threaten judgements and desertions, and turning the scriptures against them and all others that oppose or fulfill not your will, as if they were opposers of the will of God, which you take upon you to know, with the same confidence as the bishops and prelates did, and in the very same manner, and application of Scripture. No interpretation was good but theirs, no ministers the ministers of Christ, but whom they ordeyned by imposition

of hands, no government, discipline, or worship, agreeable to the
Scriptures, but theirs, no opinion found, but what they allowed, all
were sectaries and hereticks, whom they pleased so to denominate:
those that opposed them were seditious: disturbers of the peace, a
viperous brood, enemies to the state, and subverters of all order and
government, and by all means to be extirpated: if any pleaded conscience, they conclude them obstinate, and thus it is with you expresly,
so as Mr. Edwards his *Gangraena,* is indeed but a new edition of
Prelaticall doctrine, with some additions appliable to the present
times, and his Clergies immediate interest: but trust me, this is extreamly prejudiciall to your party, for there is no moderate Presbyterian that can excuse this, and hath beene a hindrance to me in
arguing for a publick ministry, besides you soar so high in daring
expressions, as if you presumed upon some other way of obtaining
your desires, then by allowance of Parliament, which may loose you
many friends there, and occasion them to think they have through a
mistaken compassion, fostered a frozen snake in their bosomes, that
no sooner finds [7] heat and strength, but falls into his serpentine
hissing, and stinging his preserver, you have also lost many of your
friends abroad, by this unchristian nominating men and women in
your *Gangraena,* and many more you will loose, when they shall consider that you have not taken the known Gospel way of first admonishing of them, but upon bare report, as it were to post them reproachfully to the view of the world, they cannot deem this as the
proceeding of a minister of Christ, but rather as a violent hast to do
your owne work: trust me, I cannot but impute the great abatement of
your sect, the falling from you of so many judicious persons, and the
daily great increase of other sects, to no one thing more, then to your
inconsiderate rashnes, violent railing, and adventuring on unheard of
waies to compasse your ends, for when I have prevailed with some
(through debate and argument) to come to our publike Churches, and
to hear your sermons, they have found there such abundance of passion, sweat, and labour, not to beget children unto Christ, by preaching the sincere Gospel of Christ, but to revile and reproach, and make
odious conscientious well affected people, because of difference in
judgement, whereby they have been much discouraged from fre-
quenting those places, affirming that all the accusations you bring
against others, are expresly and visibly due to your selves if but indifferently weighed: as where you charge others with pride, ambition,
covetuousnes, effeminacy, obstinacy, cruelty, delicacy of pallate, and
the like; they have demanded of me with a positive vehemency,

whether these were not to be found in you, rather then in those you have condemned for those vices, blaming me very much for going about to excuse the same, insomuch as I verily beleeve, you have no enemy like your self, and am perswaded if you would forsake all corrupt interests, and would conscienciously set your selfe to do the worke of Christ, to labour in his word and Gospel, out of a pure mind, and not for filthy lucre, if you would make it evident by your actions, that you seek not ours, but to win us to God, that you would thereby prevaile more in one halfe year towards your owne comfortable establishment, then you shall in an age by all your by-waies and policies, therefore leave them, and betake your self to the work of Christ, whilst it is called to day: the night of ignorance I presume is past with you: O that truth and this my plain dealing might beget or awaken Conscience in you, and provoke you to cast of the works of darknes, and to put on the armour of light, and henceforth to walk honestly, and not in strife and [8] envying, but to walk in love as Christ hath loved nor is it meet you should esteeme your self a Christian, untill you find your soul possessed with the spirit of true Christian love, which doth no evil to his neighbour, and therefore is the fulfilling of the Law. What though you could prevail (as you endeavour) to work the ruine of all that oppose your judgement or ends? Would it be peace in the latter end? no, assure your self it would be a sulphurious bitternesse and horror of conscience, and therefore sit downe and seriously consider what you are resolved to do, weigh your intentions in the even scales of love, touch and prove them with the touch-stone of love, if you would be esteemed a disciple of Christ, it must bee knowne by love: now love suffereth long, and is kind; boasteth not it self, is not puffed up, doth not behave it selfe unseemly, seeketh not her owne, is not provoked to anger, it thinketh not evil, it rejoyceth not in iniquity, but rejoyceth in the truth: beareth all things, beleeveth all things, hopeth all things, endureth all things, this is that I would ever whisper in your ear, this being a balsame that often, and well rub'd in, may Cure your *Gangraen*, and though at first your distemper may cause you to loath it, yet take a little and a little of it, use inwardly and outwardly, constantly, and you will find your disposition to alter and change from one degree unto another, until you come to be a strong and healthfull Christian: of Saul a persecutor, you will become Paul a preacher of peace and reconciliation by Jesus Christ, and bee able to lay down your life for those Brethren you have so much dispised: then will you do as you would be done unto, and in all things disputable allow every one to be fully perswaded in their own minds, and then you will bee sencible, that *whatsoever is not of faith is sinne:* you will acknowledge it is God only that can perswade the heart, and (doing your duty) patiently waite his leisure for the conversion of your Brethren: the same mind and meeknes will bee in you, as was in Christ Jesus, and you will be mercifull as our heavenly Father is mercifull: you will not break the bruised reed, nor quench the smoaking flax; then you will see what pure religion and undefiled before God, even the Father, is: you will feed the hungry, cloath the naked, visit the sick, relieve the prisoner, deliver the captive, and set the oppressed free, especially the oppressed for Conscience sake: you will then see error in judgement or misapprehension in worship, to bee but a mote in your brothers eye, compared to a persecuting or mo- [9]* lesting, or the reproaching beame in your owne: in a word, would you seriously set your selfe to the studdy and practice of love, you would againe fill your Churches, and without the help of Jewish Tythes, or any unchristian or forced maintenance, preaching the Gospel, would live comfortably of the Gospel and draw all men after you.

As for those blemishes you labour by your *Gangreen* to stick upon mee, I beleeve your labour will be lost, except in the opinion of such as know me not: but to acquit my selfe farther, and to free them from prejudice, to what I have said I add thus much more.

In your 96. page, you have me in these uncharitable expressions, one Mr. Walwyn a seeker, and a dangerous man, a strong head: truely in the mind you were in, when you wrote this *Gangreen,* I am heartily glad I appeared not worthy of your Commendations, certainly you have been extreamly covetous of informations, you seeme to have suckt them in with greedinesse, and swallowed them without chewing; tis pitty an evil intent should be better served; your informations to my knowledge of many particulars as that of Mr. Lilburnes and others, and my self, have been such to you, as if they had been made of purpose to shame you to all the world, I a seeker, good now; whose your author? Am I one because I know many, and have been amongst them often, that I might know them fully; so have I been with all other judgements, but I carry with mee in all places a Touch-stone that tryeth all things, and labours to hold nothing but what upon plain grounds appeareth good and usefull: I abandon all nicities and uselesse things: my manner is in all disputes reasonings and discourses, to enquire what is the use: and if I find it not very materiall, I

---

* Beginning with page 9 all pages in the original tract are misnumbered and have been renumbered here. (Editors' note)

abandon it, there are plain usefull doctrines sufficient to give peace to my mind: direction and comfort to my life: and to draw all men to a consideration of things evidently usefull, hath been a speciall cause that I have applyed my selfe in a friendly manner unto all: but hence it is that some have said I am a great Anabaptist, others (upon as good ground) a great Antinomian: and you a seeker: mistake me not, I do not esteeme these as names of reproach, no more then to be called Presbyterian or Independent; nor doe I take upon me peremptorily to determine what is truth, and what is error, amongst any of them: all have a possibility of error: I judge all Conscienscious, and to hold their severall judgements upon [10] grounds of scripture: to them appearing, and so long cannot but hold them: and why any should controule another, I cannot discerne: had I all the power or strength in the World at my disposing, in cases of religion I conceive I should sinne, if I should do more then in a loving way offer my argument, and gently perswade to what I conceive is both evidently true, and really usefull: and thus have I done amongst those my loving friends, whom you judge seekers: for though I do fully assent with them that now in these times there is no such ministry as the Apostles were, endowed with immediate power from on high, by imposition of whose hands, the Holy Ghost was conferred, enabling to speak with tongues, and do miracles, in a most wonderfull manner, and to speake to all men, the infallible word of God: and that convincingly to the Consciences of gain-sayers: yet am I not thereby of opinion that we may not make use of those things they have left unto us in the scriptures of the mind and will of God; or that it is not profitable to follow their examples so far as we are able in all things, for what though the effects are now weake, in comparison of theirs, yet are they such as bring great satisfaction with them: I have often perswaded with them that they should not reject what they may with much comfort make use of, because they cannot find what they seek, & for ought I know are not like to find in this world: see now what a seeker you have found of me: I once heard you at Christ-Church, which few seekers will do, but never but once, for I was not so blind a seeker, as to seek for Grapes of thornes, or Figgs of thistles: and why I pray you a dangerous man? indeed, by some reall dangerous men, I have been accounted so some whereof are falne into the snare they laid for all the well affected in this City; but that ever I was accounted so by any that conversed with me, that was a knowing well-affected man, I do not beleeve, and I beleeve I could produce thousands of knowing well-affected persons, that if they heare I am engaged, and doe appeare in any publick businesse, though they know no tittle thereof, will adventure odds; it is both just and necessary, and therefore you incline me to beleeve that you labour for beliefe onely amongst the weake, ignorant, rash, or ill affected people, with whom Credit and repute is not worth the having: well, your last appellation you bestow upon me is a strong head, and what would you have understood by this? Would you have your disciples stand aloof and not dare to [11] hold discourse with me, lest I should open your designes, and make it appeare how much it concerns your corrupt interrest to keep their heads in ignorance and a superstitious weaknesse: is it because I know whose maxim, this is *Rustica gens, optima Flens, pessima ridens:* Is it because my hearing is so good as not to bee perverted by Glosing doctrines, or because my smelling serves my turne to smell a Fox, or Wolfe, though in Sheeps clothing, or is my seeing so strong that it dispels the magick mists of sophisticated art: or is it because my taste discerneth the brackishnesse of flattery, from the pure sweetnesse of plain dealing: or do you mean head strong, because I am not likely nor could ever be drawn to dance after your Pipe.

Doubtlesse these are the causes that any strong head troubles you: neverthelesse, as strong as it is, you see a small knock from your hard hand hath so opened it, that I can hardly shut it again, but Ile shut it presently, onely thus much, I cannot see how authority can passe over this unparaleld use of the presse which you have taken, to name in publike so many of their faithfull adherents in so reproachfull a manner, to tax their proceedings in the proceedings of their Committees, to affirme and declare to all the world, that the victorious successes of the Parliaments forces, is but the increase of errors and herisies, that sectaries of all sorts get places of profit and power, and be the men all in request for offices and employments: in the which, you make your self the judge of what is error and herisie, and who is a sectary: in all which you are as likely to be mistaken as any man: for none are such in your calender, but such (as at first I told you) who stand twixt you and your profit, glory and domination: so as a man may be a reall good Christian, and a most cordiall friend to the Parliament, and neverthelesse be exploded by you for a sectary, or an heretick: one thing more, you, and such as you are (if you be not changed since you wrote your *Gangraena*, as I heartily wish you were) doe extreamly abuse this Nation, in laying the main weight of the reformation (intended) upon the reduceing of mens judgements and practice in Religion to union and uniformity, whereas the main weight of all resteth, in extirpating the popish prelaticall spirit of persecution and molestation for conscience: as the main thing that oppressed all sorts of conscientious people before the Parliament, and since; and that which cannot fail to disturbe and vex any nation where it remaineth, but the truth is, without it you cannot keep your self aloft: with- [12] out it you cannot compell a maintenance: distinguish a Clergy, nor have power over mens persons by their consciences, but grant you the power you desire, and you are master of all, and then see who dares open his mouth, or move his pen in this argument: your present confidence proceeds from the mist you have raised, but it is not yet thick enough, nor will our english braynes prove so muddy as to afford matter for thickning, I beleeve and hope it is now at thickest, and when your hopes are greatest, you will find your self in a fogge: to hold men in ignorance or bondage is not a work either for honest men or good Christians, but abhorred by both, and beleeve it, truth is become too strong to admit of either in this age: and we trust the honourable Parliament that are chosen to preserve us from both, will not fail to preserve us, though you should do the worst you can, and whereas you commend them to the love of God and his truth, and the hating of all sects and schismes, I in all humility and true love to all that honour God, and desire the welfare of England, do most heartily pray, that they may hate all persecuting sects with a perfect hatred: all enforcing and compulsive schismaticks, as the onely cause of all trouble and distraction.

To conclude, If you be so ill as your word, and bring forth such evill fruit once every month, and that we whose names you have blasted, can find a licencer, (as we hope we shall) that will do but so much for Christ, as yours hath done for B. We shall I doubt not, find a new way of innocculation, and produce grapes out of your thorns, and figges out of your thistles, and fetch abundance of good out of your evil: but more happy will it be for you if you repent, (once a month shall I say) once every houre, and in token thereof, use your uttermost indeavour to promote this or the like petition to the honourable Parliament, whereby you will make some amends for the evill you have done by this your book.

Humbly sheweth,

That as with all thankfulnes we acknowledge your unwearied labours to remove the grievances and dangers of the Common wealth, so are we exceedingly grieved to observe the manifold unexpected difficulties which at severall times have obstructed your proceedings, amongst which we conceive the differences in Religion to be the greatest, and of most importance. [13]

In your considerations whereof, being an affair of so tender a nature, so apt to be mis-understood, and such as hath miscarried in all former Parliaments, to the great disturbance of this Nation, and to the great affliction of conscientious people, we humbly conceive you have not in any thing shewed greater regard to the glory of God or greater care of the welfare of the people, then in proceeding therein with so cautious and advised a deliberation: giving time and opportunity to your wisedoms, rightly to understand the word of God in that point which most concerneth tender consciences, to hear, try and examine all that can or may be said or writ thereof, and we trust you will in the end produce that which shall be agreeable to the will and mind of God, and to the quiet of all wel-affected people.

And although your progresse therein hath not been with so much speed, or such severity towards tender Consciences, as some importunely have desired, yet have we good cause to beleeve that you have been guided therein by the good hand of God, who in due time will (we doubt not) bring you to such an issue, as neither your selves, nor any others (well minded) shall have cause to repent, or ever to alter.

And therefore we most earnestly intreat that you will not through any importunity be induced to hasten your proceedings in this weighty cause (wherein least error may prove very prejudiciall) beyond what upon your mature deliberation shall appear to be just and necessary: there being as we humbly conceive, no greater breach of the priviledge or abatement of the power of Parliament, then for any to do more then humbly to informe or advise you in this, or any other negotiation.

Blessed be God though the differences are many in point of judgement throughout your quarters, as they have been alwaies throughout the world, and will be so long as knowledge is imperfect: yet being amongst conscionable, quiet, well-affected people, they are not properly to be called divisions, [14]

And though we cannot but fear there are some wicked Polititians that endeavour by all means to make them such, and thereby to distemper and distract all your undertakings, and to make the same advantagious to their unjust ends, yet are we confident (through Gods protection) their endeavours shall be fruitlesse (except to draw confusion on themselves) God having blessed the people in generall with a cooler spirit, and greater wisdom, then by dividing among themselves, or not adhering unto you, to become a prey to any enemy; and hath produced universally in them, as in us your humble Petitioners, a resolution to defend the just power and priviledge of this honourable House, against all delusion or opposition whatsoever, to the last penny of our estates, or last drop of our bloods, beseeching you to go on with the same caution and godly resolution, to perfect those just works you have undertaken, according as God shall direct you, both for the manner and the season: for his way is best, and his time most seasonable.

And as in duty bound, we shall ever pray, &c.

To conclude, if you shall do this conscionably and effectually, I am confident henceforward you will not be able to do any thing against the truth, but for the truth which is the unfeigned desire of him who cannot but earnestly desire your reformation, and eternall happinesse:

William Walwyn

FINIS [15]

LONDON, Printed according to Order, by Thomas Paine, for William Ley, at Paules-Chaine, 1646 [15v]

10

A Word More to Mr. Thomas Edwards Concerning the Nationall Covenant

[19 March] 1645/6
Reprinted from a copy of the tract in the Thomason Collection in the British Library

A Word More, "By William Walwyn, Marchant," was printed by Thomas Paine, 1645 [1645/6], without separate title page. It was not licensed.

Appearing within a week of *A Whisper in the Eare, A Word More* is an addendum explaining Walwyn's acceptance of the *Solemn League and Covenant* of 1643. Walwyn contends that the reformation of religion "according to the word of God"—as the Covenant states—is a clear mandate for freedom of conscience.[1] It was a reasonable argument, based on a phrase which, as a perceptive Royalist commented, made the oath to the Covenant "capable of a million of interpretations."[2]

A Word More is reprinted for the first time in this volume.

A WORD MORE to MR. *THOMAS EDWARDS* Minister,

By William Walwyn *Marchant,*

Concerning the Nationall Covenant.

Judge not according to appearance, but judge righteous judgement.

LONDON. *Printed according to order,* by Thomas Paine. 1646.

Sir,

Untill I perceive the contrary, I cannot but hope that I have prevailed something with you towards a change of your mind, and that you have begun to repent you of the evill you have done by publishing your book entituled the *Gangreen:* and doe wish my whisper had come so timely to your eare, as to have prevented the second edition, but repentance is ne- [1] ver too late, and I earnestly desire it may be hearty in you, for furtherance whereof, having in my last forgotten to declare my judgement concerning the Nationall Covenant, wherein either you are entangled, or whereby you entangle others, forcing such an interpretation thereupon, as to bind all that have taken the same, to endeavour the establishment of a compulsive Presbyterian Government: directly contrary to the whole scope of the new Testament.

To remove this error, if you be consciencious there in: or to prevent the evil intended, and to undeceive those that misunderstand the Covenant, I shall at this time manifest unto you in what sence I tooke the same: conceiving my self obliged so to do, chiefly in duty to the publick, but withall, in due respect to my own good name, having been questioned by some, how it could stand with my Covenant, that I should be opposite in my judgement and endeavours to the government you intended, or be so serious an Advocate for liberty of Conscience? and I discerned a necessity of doing hereof at this instant of time, by occasion of a sermon I lately heard at Pauls: wherein all were supposed to be breakers of the Covenant, that did not insist and be importunate for such a government, & so much power as the assembly of divines should think fit, or to that effect; urging with such vehemency of expression, the pursuance of the Covenant in that sence, with such threats of judgements, and strong provocations, that I was amazed thereat, and had more feared the issue, but that I knew those honourable persons to whom he spake, were endued with wisdom to discerne whose worke he did: though I confesse it was done so artificially, as to have deceived the very choisest of men. [2]

The two first articles of the Covenant, are only materiall to the point in question: and therefore I shall declare in what sence I took them, not medling with any other part thereof.

A VVORD MORE

TO

Mr. *THOMAS EDWARDS*

Minifter,

By

William VValwyn *Marchant,*

Concerning the Nationall Covenant.

Judge not according to appearance, but judge righ-
teous judgement.

LONDON,
Printed according to order, by Thomas Paine. 1645.

Sir,

Till I perceive the contrary, I cannot but hope
that I have prevailed fomething with you towards a change of your mind, and that you have
begun to repent you of the evill you have done
by publifhing your book entituled the *Gangreen* : and doe
with my whifper had come fo timely to your eare, as to
have prevented the fecond edition , but repentance is ne-

A   ver

Title page of *A Word More to Mr. Thomas Edwards*, 1645/6.
(British Library)

The first Article is thus, *That we shall sincerely, really, and constantly through the grace of God, endeavour in our severall places and callings, the preservation of the reformed Religion in the Church of Scotland, in doctrine, worship, discipline, and government, against our common enemies:* by this I did binde my self to indeavour in my place and calling, the preservation of the Reformed Religion in the Church of Scotland, in doctrine, worship, discipline, and government, *against our common enemies,* that is, that our common enemies shall not in any sort disturbe our brethren the Covenanters of Scotland, in the enjoyment of their Religion, and that form of Church Government which they conceived most agreeable to the Word of God: my bond being of force onely *against our common enemies,* and in no measure as justifying or judging of the form of government, be it Presbyterian, or any other. And I verily beleeve, thousands that chearfully took the Covenant in reference to mutuall aid and assistance of them *against our common enemies,* did not know or understand what their Government was, and should they alter their government to some other forme, I hold my self bound in duty to defend them therein *against our common enemy,* and do judg the honourable Parliament of Scotland as free to alter, as for ours to establish what God shall direct them, and the people there as free to move for the removall of any thing they find prejudiciall in their goverment, as we are here.

By the next words in the Covenant, I binde my selfe (in like manner) to indevour the reformation of Religion in the Kingdoms of England and Ireland, in doctrine, worship, discipline and Government, *according to the word of God,* and the example of the best reformed Churches: here the Word [3] of God is my particular and expresse rule, for the best Reformed Churches may need reformation, and can at best only minister an occasion of consideration of what is good in them, and agreeable to that word, but that word is still my unerring rule, and not reformed Churches. Withall, so farre as reformed Churches are in use in this case, I could not but esteem that Church the best reformed, where no coercive power is admitted, where there is no compulsion or molestation for Conscience sake, or matters of Religion, the word of God being clear and evident in that point. And truly so far as matters of Conscience and Religion can be intrusted (for I conceive no truly consciencious person in the world can absolutely intrust the regulation of his Conscience in the worship of God to any authority) but so far as it can, in this Nation of ours, I am certain it belongeth onely to the Parliament to judge what is agreeable to the word of God and not unto the Assembly, who were conveened by the

Parliament to hear their advice, but reserving all power of determination to themselves, as no wise delegable to any others, and God hath blessed all their undertakings in a wonderfull manner, by the hands of Conscienscious people, because of their just and tender regard unto their freedom in Religion, notwithstanding all importunity to the contrary.

And where in the next place I bound my self *to endeavour to bring the Churches of God in the three Kingdoms to the nearest conjunction and uniformity in Religion, confession of Faith, forme of Church goverment, Directory for Worship and Catechisme,* I conceive my bond is of force onely as I understand these or any of these to be agreeable to the word of God (which I must understand with my own understanding, and not by any others) and then also my endeavour for conformity, must be only by lawfull and just means, not by com- [4] pulsion or enforcement, but by love, light, and argument: which was the way of our blessed Saviour and his Apostles, and in so doing, wee and our posterity after us may live in faith and love, & the Lord may delight to dwell in the middest of us: for God is love, and he that dwelleth in love, dwelleth in God, and God in him: Nor do I conceive the Conscience of the Parliament to be any otherwise obliged, then a particular mans Conscience, their votes and results being issues of particulars, and as they only are intrusted, so I trust and am confident they will understand with their owne understandings, and preserve us in our liberties, not only as we are men, but (Christians namely, in a liberty to be fully perswaded in our own minds, in all things appertaining to Gods worship,) and protect us in the peaceable practice of our consciences, against all kinds of molestation.

And how strange soever this may seem to you, unto me it seemeth most equal: because otherwise, a consciencious man (that of all men is the most precious in the sight of God, and should be so in the judgement of law and authority) of all men would be the least free, and most liable to disturbance, for allow unto such a one all the comforts that this world can afford, and but abridge him of his liberty of worshipping God according to his Conscience, his life in an instant becomes burthensome to him, his other contentments are of no esteeme, and you bring his gray hairs with extreame sorrow to the grave: for of all liberty liberty of Conscience is the greatest: and where that is not: a true Christian findeth none.

In the second Article I bound my selfe to endeavour the extirpation of heresie, schisme and whatsoever shal be found contrary to sound doctrine &c. Whereby it is supposed and urged that I am expressely bound against liberty of Conscience; but as I said before: judge not according to appear- [5] ance, but judge righteous judgement: by heresie you understand all doctrines that are not agreeable unto yours: though you are not infallible: by schisme you understand the declining or forsaking the Presbyterian Government or congregations: in which sence you were a schisme from the Prelaticall Church: (but I entreat you speedily to explain by grounds of scripture what heresie is, and what schisme is: to which you will stand.) Most commonly by heresiy in the covenant, you understand heretick, and by schisme schismatick, and where in the covenant the word extirpation is applyed to heresie and schism, you apply it to the rooting up of hereticks: and schismaticks: but in all this I conceive you are extreamly mistaken.

However, when I tooke the Covenant I considered what heresie was, and I found that heresie is not: but where a man forsakes an infallible and knowne truth, and professeth the contrarie, for vile and worldy respects, as may appear by the words of the Apostle, to Titus, Chap. 3. v. 10:11, *A man that is an heretick, after the first or second admonition reject: knowing that he that is such, is subverted, and sinneth, being condemned of himselfe,* so as if I should know that you in the Bishops time did understand and beleeve upon sure grounds of scripture, that libertie of Conscience was due to every Christian, and in respect unto the truth thereof did plead and suffer for the same: and yet after that by the justice of this Parliament, you were delivered from that oppression and molestation for conscience sake: and stated in freedom: if after this, to gain honour profit or preferment, you shall be so subverted, as to practice the same oppression towards others, (that differ with you in judgement or way of worship) as was injuriously inflicted upon you: and strongly and clamourously, importune for power to suppresse consciencious people, this scripture as I conceive, judges you an [6] heretick: one that sinneth, and is subverted and condemned of himselfe: if your conscience condemne you, God you know is greater then your Conscience, and will not acquit you. I dare not peremptorily take upon me to judge you in this sad condition, but that error in judgement, or blindnes in understanding, though very erronious and grosse, is heresie, I do not beleeve, but do rather conceive it an invention of some corrupt Clergy-men (to cause hatred among the people about opinions, thereby to divide them in affection, it being their maxim, (as well as other polititians) divide and

master them,) and to have some colour of enforcing their interpretation of scripture as a rule upon all men, and to punish all opposers.
And truly you shal do a good office if you shall open the eies of your
friends in this particular, and not suffer them any longer to judge
according to the rule of corrupt prelats and persecuting bishops, nor
continue so violent against such as differ from them in judgment, but
to judge others to bee consciencious as well as themselves, and beare
with others, as they would be born withall themselves: being ever
mindfull that none are now infallible.

And as concerning schism, I judge it not to be, but where an un-
peaceable, and violent perversnesse appeareth, a disposition impossible to hold fellowship withall, and hee onely a schismatick that is
such, and not an honest quiet spirited person, that out of conscience
and difference in judgement, cannot walk in Church fellowship with
me, this being also another invention, (as I beleeve) of corrupt prelats
and persecuting bishops, to find occasion against Consciencious people, and by vexing them, to make them draw in their yoak, wherein
also you shall doe well to open the eies of your friends, and help them
to distinguish rightly of heresie and schisme, that so they may know
what they have covenanted to extirpate, and what not. [7]

And though I should find such heresies and schismes, and am
bound by my Covenant to extirpate them; I must doe it in a way that
is justifiable, I must not (as you seem to judge) endeavour to root out
the hereticks and schismaticks, by banishment imprisonment or
death, but by gentle and christian means: that is, by perswasion, admonition, and information endeavour to reclaime them, and when
that availeth not, I am only to reject them: or to hold no familiar society with them; According to this sence I took these two articles of our
Nationall Covenant, and so did divers others that I know, nor do I
discerne that I strained the naturall or genuine sence thereof in a tittle. If I am mistaken, I shall thank you or any other by grounds of
scripture to shew me my error, but if this sence be good, you had
need to warne your friends to take heed what they heare, for strange
inferences are made from those two articles in the covenant: but I
hope what I have said will satisfie all considerate consciences, and
suffice to acquit me from breach of covenant, though I earnestly endeavour for liberty of conscience, wherein I am fully perswaded, the
glory and truth of God, and good of all mankind is really involved;
otherwise I would never have moved my tongue or pen in this argument.

And if I shall be so happy by what I have done, as to bee an instrument to reduce you into a charitable demeanor towards tender Consciences, I shall rejoyce more then to see a miracle: for I still remaine most earnestly desirous of your reformation, and eternall happinesse.

William Walwyn

FINIS [8]

11

A Word in Season: To All Sorts of Well Minded People

1st edition [18 May] 1646; 2d edition [26 May] 1646
Reprinted from a copy of the 1st edition of the tract in the Thomason Collection in
the British Library

Both editions of *A Word in Season* were published anonymously and printed by Thomas Paine, 1646. The tract was licensed by John Bachiler and John Parker and entered in the Stationers' Register on 20 May 1646.[1] In 1649 Walwyn stated that "Mr Batcheler can tell who was Author of" *A Word in Season*. A few weeks earlier Walwyn had written that his "judgement concerning Civil Government" is evident in "my *Word in Season*."[2] Thomason, who collected both editions, wrote on the first: "written by Mr Sadler"—an erroneous attribution to John Sadler that is perpetuated in many bibliographies and catalogues.[3]

The formats of the two editions are different: the first edition is 9 pages; the second is 14 pages. The title page of the second edition adds "for the Publicke good" to the notation "Published by Authority"; locates Thomas Paine's printing shop precisely; omits the name and location of the seller. There are differences in spelling, capitalization, and punctuation throughout; there is one difference in paragraphing (p. 4, 1st edition; p. 6, 2d edition). The texts are identical.

A Word in Season was a response to the growing movement in the City and the London Common Council for peace with the King and the Scots, the establishment of Presbyterianism, and the suppression of the sects.[4] John Goodwin's Independent congregation contributed fifty shillings toward the printing of ten thousand copies of Walwyn's tract, which Lilburne distributed in Westminster Hall on 26 May, the day the Common Council presented its *Remonstrance* to Parliament.[5]

The central message of the tract is the importance of adherence to Parliament, guardian of the people's liberties.

A Word in Season is reprinted for the first time in this volume.

A word in season: TO ALL SORTS OF WELL MINDED PEOPLE IN THIS MISERABLY DISTRACTED and distempered nation.

Plainly manifesting, That the safety and well-being of the Common-wealth under God, dependeth on the fidelity, and stedfast adherence of the people, to those whom they have chosen, and on their ready compliance with them.

Also That the destruction and bondage of the Common-wealth in generall, and of every good minded man in particular cannot be avoided, if the people, through want of consideration, shall give eare *to any other counsel or counsellers.*

PROVERB. 2.11,12. *Discretion shall preserve thee, understanding shall keep thee, to deliver thee from the way of the evill man, from the man that speaketh froward things.*

Published by Authority.

LONDON, Printed by *Thomas Paine,* and are to be sold by *Edward Blackmoore,* at his shop in *Pauls* Church-yard at the Signe of the Angell. 1646.

A word in season; TO ALL SORTS OF WELL-MINDED PEOPLE IN THIS MISERABLY DISTRACTED AND distempered Nation.

SINCE, (as the Scripture speaketh) no man hateth his own flesh, but loveth and cherisheth it; and that naturally, every man seeketh his owne good: it is very strange, (seeing we have the helpe of reason, of experience, of the Word of God) that the right way, which leadeth to that end, should be so hard, and difficult to be

A word in feafon:

TO

ALL SORTS OF WELL

MINDED PEOPLE IN THIS
MISERABLY DISTRACTED
and diftempered Nation.

Plainly manifefting,

That the fafety and well-being of the
Common-wealth under God, dependeth on the
fidelity, and ftedfaft adherence of the people, to
thofe whom they have chofen, and on their
ready compliance with them.

Alfo

That the deftruction and bondage of the Common-wealth in generall, and of every good minded
man in particular cannot be avoided, if the people,
through want of confideration, fhall give eare
to any other counfels or counfellers.

PROVERB 2. 11,12.
Difcretion fhall preferve thee, underftanding fhall keep thee, to deli-
ver thee from the way of the evill man, from the man that fpeaketh fro-
ward things.

Publifhed by Authority.

LONDON,
Printed by *Thomas Paine.* and are to be fold by *Edward*
Blackmoore, at his fhop in *Pauls* Church-yard at the
Signe of the Angell. 1646.

Title page of *A Word in Season: To All Sorts of Well Minded People,* 1646.
(Folger Shakespeare Library)

found, certainly, it cannot be so in it self; God hath been more good to man, then to make things necessary hard to come by.

The difficulty will rather be found to arise by our own default, from our want of a patient, setled, serious, and religious consideration of things, wherby we are continually liable upon all occasions to be mis-led, either by our owne evill and eager desires, or by the evill exam-ples of others, or by evill (though long setled) customes; or by the perswasions of politique deceivers, into such wayes, which though they seeme to be strewed with Roses and perfumes, yet are the wayes of death, and when we least suspect, bring us to destruction.

Our blessed Saviour therefore bids us to be wise as Serpents, be-cause whilst we live in this world we have to do with Serpents, and to beware of wolves that come to us in sheepes clothing; To be innocent as doves, is a most blessed temper of spirit, but very unsafe and liable to e- [1] very ginne, and bird of prey, if the wisdome of the Serpent be not joyned therewith: Now all the helps of reason, of experience or the word of God, produce not this wisdom without consideration; advised, deliberate consideration, (such as few in this Nation are ac-customed unto) without which that which is called knowledg or un-derstanding, is not true knowledge nor understanding, serving to no publique use at all, except to distract and distemper, and vex and destroy a Nation. It is the voyce of God himselfe: *my People will not consider, they will not understand*, without consideration it is impossible to understand anything as we ought, & without understanding (true considerate understanding) man is like unto the beasts that perish: nor had this Nation ever been thus miserable as it hath bin, is, and is like to be, but for want of this kind of consideration, in the People; so that it may be as truly said of this, as of the pervers, rash, inconsiderat Nation of the Jewes; thy distruction is of thy self O England. And if ever there were a cause to study & put in practice the wisdom of the Serpent: to beware of foxes that come to us in sheeps clothing: if ever there were a time requiring the uttermost of wisdom and considera-tion in all sorts of people, rich and poore, high and low, one with another; now there is a cause, now is the time.

For never to this day, were those who are trusted with the care of the Common wealth, so beset and surrounded with difficulties; with unexpected appearances of strange thinges, such as no age can par-ralell, of so high and great concernment, as the least miscarriage therein, may in a moment of time make void all their long, their faithfull and painefull endevours, and involve us all into the most misserable bondage, that ever over-whelmed any People.

And therefore (however any sort of man may delude [2] them-selves) if we doe not all joyntly and unanimously (laying aside all disaffection for differences in Judgment in Religion) patiently, setledly and seriously, deliberate and consider what every one of us ought to doe, in reference to their preservation; abandoning all passion, and willfull prosecution of perverse and prepostrous things; all jarring and repining at their proceedings; this Nation cannot be safe or happy, nay cannot but be miserable and wretched.

For the greatest and most superlative freedome, of this Nation (and wherin the safty and well-being thereof doth reside) consisteth in this; That Lawes cannot bee made, Government (Ecclesiasticall or Civill) cannot be established or Altered: Warre cannot bee levied, nor Peace concluded, nor Monyes raised, nor any thing done, but by the Authority of those whom the people themselves doe chuse for Parliament: and entrust as their Commissioners, with full and compleat power for Their good. Had it not been by this just Authority, We had never been Freed, from the Tyranies, oppressions and cruelties of the High Commission, Star-Chamber, and Councel-board: from the bur-thenous Execution of the Forrest-law, Court of Honor, Commissions of Waste: from the Extortions, and Exorbitances, in the Courts of jus-tice, Chancery, Requests: from Ship-money (for remission wherof, no lesse than Twelve Subsidies were required) and from all those other innumerable Patents, Projects, Illegall warrants, and Imprisonments: Things which the whole Land long groned under; though (now re-moved) the benefit be unworthily forgotten, or misattributed to an Act of grace. Had it not been for this Authority; the Court of Wards had [3] never been abolished, and that for many Ages hath oppressed the Land.

Had not this Authority, opposed; the King had been furnished with monyes to have Warred upon our Brethern of Scotland, in his first attempt upon that Nation. This Authority, in the worst of all former Times, when the strongest Force and Power was upon them, ever stuck closest to the interest of the People, nor did the People, in the worst of Times, ever forsake them, but maintained Their power, and Priveledges, their Essence and authority, whensoever they called upon them for helpe and assistance, nor hath this just and powerfull Authority been more true to the Commons that chose them, then to those worthy Lords and Patriots, that at any time have assisted them for the common good of the Nation, preserving their Honours with as true affection as the liberties of the People; no man can name the time that (intentionally) this Authority ever did injury to any just intrest either at home or abroad, but have borne and suffered much, from those that have made an ill use of their lenity and credulity.

All which is necessary to be remembred, and seriously considered in this instant of time, because if these things be seriously laid to heart, it may happily expel those poysonous vapors, with which our ayre begins to be infected, we have a generation of forgetfull, ingratefull people, who because the Parliament cannot yeild unto all they desire, (without extreame thraldom to the people, in things Ecclesiasticall and Civill) are degenerate into a malevolent disposition, murmuring and repining at all their proceedings, and making hard constructions of their Just endevours; and by politique and subtill meanes, labour to [4] alienate the hearts of their friends from them, and to incline them to give eare to other Connsels, laying open their infirmities (which they should rather goe backward to cover) and would (if they could) possesse the world that there is a sort of men that would settle Religion more purely, performe and interpret the Covenant more exactly, and doe justice more speedily, and more sincearely then this just Authority, whom the people themselves have chosen; nay, there are fames abroad, that there are catalogues taken of any thing that may possibly beare a bad or sinister construction, to be shewed to the people, in the day of their extremity, if such a day can be procured.

And for what end all this? Why, you shall not faile to be told it is for the glory of God, the setting up of the Kingdome of Jesus Christ, and the everlasting Good of the soules of the people, and the like: but take yee heed how yee heare or give credit to these Syren songs; these charmes of Dalilah, are but to deprive Sampson of his strength, to rob the people of their Power: It is a sad proverb, but Court Logick hath proved it so frequently true, that it may be related without suspition of blasphemy, *In nomine Domini incipit omne malum*; When the Devill transformes himselfe into an Angell of light, to make his delusion currant, he is necessitated to use such language: For which cause our blessed Saviour advised us to be *Wise as Serpents*, lest wee bee beguiled by their subtill glosing dissimulations.

But as the Apostle saith in another case, *If an Angell from heaven preach any other doctrine, let him be accursed.* So in this case, if any, though in the shape of an Angell [5] of light, of strength, of powers, or dominations, shall endevour, by any meanes whatsoever, to divide you from those you have chosen, either in affection, or assistance, you are to hold them for the most accursed Traitors that ever trode upon English ground, and to use all lawfull meanes to bring them to condigne punishment; being well assured, that whatsoever is pretended; the intent can be no other then to extirpate for ever the foundation of the freedom and safety of the People: which once done, a ready way is made for any thing that can make a people wretched and miserable, without hope of remedy.

And therefore be advised in time, before you are engaged too farre, and be confident, those inconveniences you have fancyed to your selves (and wherein you are like enough to be mistaken) if they should indeed prove reall ones, yet were you better to have patience, and by loving discourses and prudent meanes endevour to worke a better information, (which time may produce, as by experience in your selves you cannot but know) rather then through impatience and violent importunity, to cast your selves upon a remedy that must necessarily be destructive to the whole people of the Land: For once suppose or admit that any (pretending whatsoever, piety or authority) may more properly judge of law (or religion so far as concerns the publick) or give interpretation of oaths or covenants, or treaties, or transactions, or any thing which is of public concernment, then those whom the people have chosen: and farewel common freedom for ever, who ever those are you would so prefer, as far as in you is, in so admitting or supposing, you betray the great freedome of the Nation, and set Masters over the Parliament, then which there can be no greater Treason. [6]

Be not flattered and deluded out of your birthright: Consider, whatever you are, you are but a part of the whole people, it is impossible that you can give the sense and mind of all the Commons of England: Nay, if you could, it is not lawfull for you to doe it, otherwise then by a becomming information, and to rest satisfied when you have so done: You are not entrusted by the People, you are not Chosen to that end: But this just Authoritie is a power chosen, and entrusted; and you are to know, that they are absolutely Free to follow the dictate of their own Understandings and Consciences, informed by the Word of God, by principles of right reason, and all other good meanes, as is most probable to conduce to the safetie and weale of the people; which they lately and worthily have declared to be the end of the Primitive Institution of all Government.

Whosoever shall tell you, that either themselves or any others will ever doe you more good then those you have chosen; make no scruple to owne them for deceivers, that Absolon-like, kisse and wooe you, of purpose, to enslave you.

What though some things may not be done so perfectly, or so inex-

cusably as you could wish: Consider, they are but men, subject to the
same passions and infirmities as your selves; they are not like some
ancient Fradulent great Councells, that have maintained the Canons
and Decrees thereof to be infallible: Nay, they are so farre from such
delusion, that they have many times altered their owne Orders, Ordinances, and Acts, upon further or better information, and doe not
refuse, nor reject Petitions and Informations [7] duely offered by any
peaceable persons, few, or many, and as readily follow the advices of
others (which they approve) as their owne immediate apprehensions
and Councells.

And, as a sure testimony of their faithfulnesse and sinceritie; doe
but seriously consider, how exceedingly God hath blessed them, *viz.*
with the affections of the people, with power and strength in the
field, with deliverance from many most desperate Plots, and out of
many sore and difficult exigents, that their enemies have bin as Chaffe
before their Armies: What force hath beene too mightie, or place too
strong for their Achievement? And now, that they have all, as it were,
in their owne command (by the same good providence of God) would
you now, because they cannot please you in every particular, except
they shall goe against their owne Consciences, gladly see them trodden upon and brought under: Surely, if you would but open your
eyes, you could not but see, that the hand of God is still with them,
and will not be shortned: He hath already brought low the mightie,
and reproved, vanquished even Kings for their sakes, and for theirs
whom they represent: And doe you now thinke, that any shall be able
to lay their honour in the dust? You cannot certainly be many, that
have beene thus blinded, or deluded: Nor can you possibly long continue in so bad a mind. A little consideration must necessarily change
your minds, and God I trust, will prevent you with his converting
grace, and will not suffer you to be tempted above your power. However, this is most visible to all considerate men, that there are multitudes of honest Religious peo- [8] ple that remain immaculate in their
affections to this Honourable Parliament, & are truly thankful for their
unwearied labors, in recovery of the long lost Liberties of this great
Nation, & stand firmly resolved to maintaine and defend with their
lives and estates, their just power and priviledges, against all opposition, circumvention, or delusion whatsoever; And those who shall
cease to doe this, through any conceived cause or provocation, they
shall esteeme them the most treacherous upon earth, and not worthy
the name of true Englishmen or Christians.

This, by generall discourse & observation, is found to be a knowne truth; and therefore, it is earnestly hoped, the Honourable Parliament will no whit abate of their resolutions, to make this Nation absolutely free and happie; notwithstanding the manifold new Discoveries of strange Apparitions, if they but please to consider seriously the true Englishmans temper, they will find, they have multitudes more with them then against them; and that in times to come this shall be an English Proverb, *As certaine to perish, as those that openly oppose, or would secretly undermine a Parliament.*

FINIS [9]

12

An Antidote against Master Edwards His Old and New Poyson

[10 June] 1646
Reprinted from a copy of the tract in the Thomason Collection in the British Library

An Antidote against Master Edwards, published over Walwyn's name, was printed by Thomas Paine, 1646. "Imprimatur, John Bachiler. May 26. 1646" appears on the last page and the tract was entered in the Stationers' Register on 10 June.[1]

Antidote is as readable as it is effective. Walwyn describes "Gangraena" Edwards as a desperately unhappy man who has become a malevolent investigator resorting to Machiavellian tactics of ugly rumors and lies to destroy loyal Independents, separatists, and political activists. It is evident from Walwyn's cautions to readers of Edwards's "next book" that the first sixteen pages of *Antidote* were written before *The Second Part of Gangraena* was published.[2] After seeing *The Second Part* Walwyn added a postscript, "A Graine More." He includes no specific replies to Edwards's extended attacks on himself[3] but with gentle irony suggests that those who read the new poison take a double dose of the preceding *Antidote* with a quantity of the Christian love vainly prescribed for Edwards: "either he will not use it, or takes not that paynes to rub it in which I advised."[4]

Antidote is reprinted for the first time in this volume.

An Antidote AGAINST MASTER Edwards HIS OLD AND NEW POYSON:

Intended TO PRESERVE THIS long distempered Nation from a most dangerous Relaps.

WHICH HIS FORMER, HIS later, and next Gangrenous Book is likely to occasion, if not timely prevented.

by WILLIAM WALWIN.

Deut. 22. 33. *Their Wine is the poyson of Dragons, and the cruell venime of Aspes.*

Rom. 3. 13. *Their throat is an open sepulcher, with their tongues they have used deceit, the poyson of Aspes is under their lips.*

Proverbs 22. 10. *Cast out the scorner, and contention shall go out: yea, strife and reproach shall cease.*

London, Printed by *Thomas Paine,* dwelling in *Red-Crosse-street,* in *Goldsmiths-Alley,* over-against the signe of the *Sugar-loafe.* 1646.

An Antidote AGAINST MASTER Edwards HIS OLD AND NEW POYSON.

Though God hath given unto Mr. Edwards, parts and abilities, wherewithal to acquire a comfortable life, in a just and good way, and wherein hee might bee helpefull unto many, and hurtfull unto none; neverthelesse hee seemeth unhappily to have placed his contentment in being a Master and Comptrouler of other mens judgements and practises in the worship of God, (wherein the Word of God and a mans owne conscience is only to governe): and thereupon (necessarily) finding opposition from al consciensious people, hee growes most passionately impatient, and even violently madd against all such as either plead their cause, or take their part; plainly manifesting, throughout [1] the whole course of his preaching and writing, that he would esteem it his greatest felicity, if he could prevaile with authority, or provoke any others to the perpetuall molestation and destruction, of all that will not (though against their consciences) submit to those rules which he approveth.

Now the piety and justice of this Honourable Parliament, having so lately freed this long oppressed Nation, from this very kind of Tyranny, in the Bishops and Prelaticall Clergy, and very many judicious, and considerate persons (through a blessed opportunity, freedome of discourse, and cleerer search of Scripture then heretofore) being fully satisfied in their understandings, that to compell or restraine, any peaceable person in matters of faith, and the worship of God, is as reall a sinne, and as odious in the sight of God as murther, theft or adultery, and thereupon engaging themselves in the just defence of liberty of conscience, Master Edwards his worke (of bowing all to his rule) falls out to be very difficult, and impossible (by any arguments drawn from the word of God) to be effected, or proved just.

And this also, insteed of qualifying his spirit, or stopping him in his race, hath set [2] him all on fire, that he rageth like an Irish, ravenous and hungry woolfe, deprived of his prey by generous and true English Mastives, that watch both night and day to save the harmlesse and benefitiall sheep (the Independants and Separatists) who from the begining of these our troubles, to this very day, have continually without repining contributed their fleece for clothing, and their limbes and lives for nourishment, and strength, to preserve not only their owne liberties, but the just liberties of this Nation; Yet nothing abateth the madnesse of this prophet; but even (as is to be feared) against his owne conscience, and as if hired thereunto by some politique Balacks, hee flieth from one hill to another, from authority to authority, hath his parables and his offerings, and Satan like, would tempt the Lord himselfe to fall downe and worship him, to go against his owne declared will, and to stir up a persecuting spirit in the Magistrate, against this his beloved Israel, to compell them to worship him (as doe the Hipocrites) against their minds and consciences, then which nothing could be more abominable in his sight.

And though he cannot but see the hand of God against him, and that notwithstan- [3] ding all his opposition, or any others, the numbers of them are daily increased, and that their faithfulnesse to the Parliament & common-wealth, hath caused them to grow in favor with al the People; though (if he would speak his heart) he must as Baalam, perforce acknowledge *there is no enchantment against Jacob, nor any divination against Israel;* no prevailing for a coersive power, against this good people, in a time of refreshment from any just Authority: Yet persists he in his ungodly resolution, and seeing and knowing that God will by no meanes answer his eager desire, of cursing this part of his people; he seemeth to grow desperate, and like as Saul when God had cast him off, and refused to answer him, either by Urim or Vision, betooke himselfe to the witch of Endor, even so this most unhappy man, betaketh himselfe to Machivillian policy, for execution of his cruel purposes against them: and finding no just or judicious party that will afford him any countenance, or assistance, he applyeth himselfe to any that hate them, though enemies to the common-wealth, hazarding the doing of their work, so that with them, and by them, he may but doe his owne, whereunto the weaknesses of many wel minded people ministreth to great [4] an advantage, their rashnesse and to easie credulity, being all the foundation which he hath now left, to build his hopes upon, for if these would but a while suspend their belief, and patiently consider the things he hath spoken or is about to publish, and would thereupon with-draw themselves from his wicked and delusive counsels, and insteed thereof would fall to councelling of him to forsake his violent Rayling, and reviling, of a people they know to be faithfull, it were then impossible for him to effect his unjust designes, wch also (if effected) must necessarily be the bondage or ruin of all sorts of wel minded people, as wel Presbiterians as others (however his charmings may for the present flatter them) that must and will be the conclusion, if they continue to take in his poysonous counsells, how pleasing soever they seem to a pallat corrupted by long custome; they are poysonous, and will in time both swell and destroy them.

And therefore unto this sort of people, doe I at this time principally addresse this discourse by way of *Antidote*, to prevent the working of his banefull Counsels, and to frustrate his accursed ends.

This unjust man, knoweth all just and [5] judicious men, cannot but oppose his unjust designes, and therefore it is, he hath denounced so many of them by name in his books, as his enemies, his ablest enemies they are, and the more powerfull, because they are all knowne to be really faithfull to the Parliament: In this case saith Machivel there is but one help, that is, they must be brought into disgrace, and disrepute, with the people, for if these remain in credit, the people will give eare unto them, be rightly informed by them & be in no capacity to be deceived: well saies Mr. Edwards, how shall they be sufficiently reproached: Why saies Machivel, seek out unto your ayd honest zealous persons of godly life, and good repute in the world, such as you know are fiery hot against errours and heresies so called, and unto them sadly complaine of the dayly infinite increase thereof, & intreat their assistance in the extirpation of them, & for that end desire them to collect their memories, what they have heard in any discourse, what they have any waies observed or knowne, to proceed from such and such men, naming divers, that are taken and reputed to be either grand Hereticks, and Schismatiques themselves, or the defenders and maintainers of them, by word or [6] writing, tell them you have heard that such and such, hold such and such blasphemous opinions, at such and such a time uttered, such & such horrible speeches, pray them to consider how exceeding necessary it is such things were knowne, and made publique to all the world, lest through ignorance such blasphemous and hereticall persons in time get into offices of Magistracy, if not into the Parliament it selfe; lay before them the danger if it should be so, and intreat them (for prevention) that they will thrust themselves into all meetings, companies, and societies, to provoke discourses, and to take notice of what they observe, or can any waies learne of any of them or any others, and it shall be your care to divulge them to the world, in the strongest colours your Art can give them: And (saith Machivel) as they through eagernesse, will over-heare and make things worse then they were either spoken or intended, so it must be your care to make them rather wors then better, then their relations, you must be sure to cast durt enough upon them, some will stick, and a little (amongst those you would pervert) will suffice to blemish the clearest and most able amongst them, and to deprive them of all credit and repute for ever. [7]

If you observe any man to be of a publique and active spirit, (though he be no Independent or Separatist) he can never be friend to you in your work, and therefore you are to give him out, to be strongly suspected of whoredom, or drunkennesse, and prophanesse, an irreligious person, or an Atheist, and that by godly and religious persons, he was seen and heard blaspheming the holy Scriptures, and making a mock of the Ordinances of Christ, or say he is suspected to hold inteligence with Oxford, or any thing no matter what, somewhat will be beleeved, you cannot be ignorant how much this hath prevailed against divers able persons.

If you see any such man but once talking with a Papist, or (though not) you may give out that very honest men suspect him to be a Jesuit: If any one but demand of you or any others, how you know the Scriptures to be the word of God, give it out for certain he denieth them, or if any put questions concerning God or Christ, or the Trinity, you have more then enough to lay accusations upon them, that shall stick by them as long as they live, if you will follow this my counsell throughly saith Machivel (as in part you have done) you cannot faile of your end, you can never want matter, you shall (amongst [8] those you deceive) be taken for a most zealous, holy, and religious man, you may write book upon book, great and large ones, and make good profit (or great renowne) by them, and in after ages, be recorded as a famous Author.

Moreover if you prosecute this course, you may haply hereby not only hold your friends firme unto you, ready upon all occasions to petition what you would have them, or to doe any thing you shall require them, but you shall be sure to hold them for ever devided from your adversaries, in all things, they shall not regard any thing, though never so just or good, if they see they have but a finger therein, nay if you work wisely, you need not dispaire of dividing your most powerfull adversaries amongst themselvs, doubts & jelousies being of great force:

And you know it is an undoubted truth, a house divided within it selfe cannot stand.

This is Machivels way; and this hath been Mr. Edwards his way; and in this way hee goeth on, but the way of God have they not knowne, or rather have they not despised the way of the Lord.

This is the Poyson by which he hath envenomed the hearts and understandings of thousands (in themselves) honest, religious [9] people, too too easily misse-led, for want of knowledge or consideration of these Machivelian courses; men that being sinceare in their owne intentions, are easily deluded by the least pretence of zeal and godlinesse.

And however his heart may be hardned that he will not regard any thing, that hath been written unto him; you that have been deceived by him, are not so farre gone but you may yet recover, & become untainted, with the least savour of his spirit, and in time abominate his waies:

But surely then you must consider things more seriously then hitherto you have done, you must suspect your owne waies, and compare them once more with the waies of God, commended to you in his holy Word; That is the only *Antidote* that is able to expell the Poyson you have taken, or shall be offered in his next book; you know the word of God is mighty to the casting down of strong holds, & to bring into subjection all Machivelian Imaginations.

I shall therefore pray you in reading his next book which (it is to be feared) is reserved for an accursed purpose, and to second some worke of Darknesse; that you will with open eyes see how farre, and how plausible Machivel may go with colours of reli- [10] gion transforming himselfe into an Angell of light.

Also that you will not hastily give credit to any thing spoken by him a professed adversary, lest in so doing, you become guilty of bearing false witnesse against your neighbour.

That you will consider and marke those that cause divisions and offences, contrary to *the doctrine which ye have learned*, and avoid them: *Rom.* 16. 17.

That you will mind a speciall part of that doctrine to be expressed in the fourteenth Chapter thorow-out, and the beginning of the fifteenth, which I entreat you to reade without prejudice or preoccupation of judgment; and then I cannot doubt, but liberty of conscience will appeare more just in your eyes, then it hath done, and confesse that your selves cannot live without it.

That you will lay to heart how dangerous it may prove to the Common wealth, and to the cause you have hitherto joyntly maintained, (God prospering you in so doing) if by any policies you should stand divided from those your brethren of other judgments; beleeve it, the hand of Joab is in all your divisions, what-ever you see or judge, your common enemy, is the fomenter of [11] them; and under what notion or colours soever they appeare, they are a common enemie to you both, that labour to divide you, and in the end, you will find it to be so to your cost, if not to your ruine.

An ancient Philosopher (somewhat to this purpose) hath a fable, That the Wolves being at long and deadly war with the sheep, and not prevailing by force; but contrary to their expectation almost vanquished: Resolved to try what they could doe by policie, and thereupon desired a treaty, which the sheep simply and easily granted: The principall thing in the treaty, which the Wolves insisted on, was, that the sheepe would but discharge & send away their dogs, and then there would be no cause of warre at all, but they should live quietly one by another, urging withall, that the dogs were of a quarrelsome disposition, had been the beginners and continuers of the war, that they were of a different nature & temper from the sheep, maintain'd the war only for their own ends, and in probability were like enough to make a prey of the sheep themselves, and the like; if they would discharge them, they would give them what security themselves would desire, for assurance of their peaceable neighbourhood. The poor sheep soon weary of [12] the charge and trouble of war, yeelded thereunto, and discharged their dogges, their strongest help, (whereby they had not only preserved themselves, but by many battels and maine force had even quite vanquished the Wolves) wch was no sooner done, but the Wolves in short time muster up their force, (the dogs being out of call) and when the sheep least suspected, fell upon them and destroyed them utterly.

I conceive this could never have been effected, but that the Wolves had conveyed some of themselves into sheepes cloathing, who by flattering and dissembling cariage, got themselves into credit with the sheepe, and so perswaded to this goodly treaty, and wrought them to those destructive conditions.

And (if well considered) this fable (though dogs and Christians hold no fit comparison) may demonstrate, that whosoever doth, or shall endevour to perswade the godly and honest Presbyters to abandon, discourage or molest their faithfull, helpfull, valiant and assured friends of other judgements (whom Mr. Edwards would have to be used worse then dogs) they are at best, but Wolves, or Wolves friends, and seek the destruction of all honest people, of what judgement soever. [13]

And whether Master Edwards do expresly ayme at so horrid an issue, or not; for certaine, his workes and endevours do mainly tend thereunto, and will help on the wicked purposes of any that intend the destruction of the sheepe.

But, blessed be God, we are not as sheepe without a shepherd, wee have had, and still have faithfull & resolved shepherds set over us by providence, in a most just and orderly way, a Parliament (the terror of the wicked, and comfort of the just) that for these 5 years and upwards, have been a strong Tower of defence! to the sheep of the Lords Pasture, to all the godly party in the Land: and though many of our froward and weak sheepe have many times been tampring & harkening after offers and conditions as dangerous to the whole flocke, as the discharging of that strength, the Wolves most feared; yet hath the wisdom of those our faithfull Shepherds hitherto prevented the same; and according to the true rules of wisdom have made most use of those whom the Wolves most feared.

And we trust the same God that endowed them with such a new modelising wisdome, as hath been successefull to the astonishment both of their friends and enemies, will still guide and direct them, when the policies of [14] the enemies, are most busie and strongly working; and when the weaknesse and frowardnesse of their friends are most troublesome & importunate for destructive things, yea though some should be wrought upon so farre, as to shew a wearisomnesse of these their Shepherds; the same God will then we doubt not, shew his mighty power and wisdome in them, and thereby preserve this whole Nation, from a most dangerous Relaps, which otherwise were to be feared:

The whole flock is their charge, God hath made them Overseers of the whole, and to our joy and comfort they have hitherto shewed, a greater care to preserve the whole People, then to please any part of them; in unreasonable things: and in so doing they have been (and cannot but be) blessed and prosperous:

And notwithstanding Mr. Edwards his venomous poyson, blowne abroad by his unhappy quill, to blast and destroy the repute of honest, religious, and faithfull men, yet (the tree being knowne by his fruite) the Parliaments wisdome expelleth his poyson and sheweth no disrespect to any honest religious person, and every juditious man followeth their worthy example therein: and when you that are weak and have been mis- [15] led, and tainted with his poyson, shall consider it, your judgments I trust will be rectified, and strengthened so sufficiently, that you will no longer judge of men according to his malitious accusations, but according to their workes and what you see them doe:

Which if you doe, wee shall have done with his poysonous, and scandalous bookes, which serve for nothing but to deceive and destroy the people; great quietnesse will follow thereupon, and you will soone finde a nearer way to a finall end of your troubles, then the wrangling way he hath proposed, for if once you were united you would have no enemies; your warre would be at an end; your peace would be sure, and all the people safe and happy;

Which is my only ayme in this work and my most earnest desire:

WILLIAM WALWIN [16]

A GRAINE MORE, And no more.

Observing by some passages and occurrences of late, that all the labour bestowed towards the conversion and reducing of Master Edwards into a truly, charitable, and Christian disposition, hath proved no other, then as the washing of a Blackamoore; and thereupon, daily expecting a poysonous issue from his infectious braine. To prevent the mischiefe that might ensue: I prepared this little *Antidote*, intending to have had it in such a readinesse, as that it should have met his poyson in the instant he first spread it, wherein I did my part, but the Printers mistake hindred it.

Those therefore that have read his new Gangrenous and scandalous book, and doe find themselves any whit tainted with the poyson thereof, and have slept upon it: My friendly advise is, that they take double the quantity of this *Antidote:* that they reade this little Treatise twise over, and consider every part of it seriously and deliberately, and if they are any thing farre gone, and in [17] danger: then it will be necessary they adde thereunto a good quantity more of true Christian love, it will be somewhat hard to find, there being abundance every where of that which is counterfeit, the best of which will do more hurt then good; and therefore it will be needfull you get the help of some that by experience can distinguish the true from the false, and such a one I can assure you is also very hard to find: but without it there is no hope, and with it there is infallible certainty of recovery.

If there were not much false and counterfeit love abroad, this wretched man with all his cursed diligence could never have been furnished with matter to have sweld his poysonous bulck to so vast a greatnesse.

And truly had those whoever they are that gave those malicious informations concerning me, as he reciteth them if they had had, but one scruple of true Christian love in them they never had administered to his (so unmanly) occasion.

I blesse God, I have through diligent seeking found this pretious liquor, and have enough to spare upon those his unadvised intelligencers, and through the power thereof can freely forgive their evill intentions, which my conscience assures me, I never de- [18] served from any, I ever conversed withall, or that ever knew me.

As for himselfe, if passion and fore-judging did not blind mens understandings, and that most men are transported with flashy fancies, and are unapt to consider things judiciously, it would evidently appeare, that he hath not in any measure answered, either my *Whisper* or the *Word more*, both which wil live in despite of his utmost venome, and wil concerne him, and all such deceivers as he is, being there set forth in their truest colours, nor is his neglect of them, any other but a device to keep mens eyes off from reading or regarding them, wherein he hath indeed dealt very pollitiquely, and like one fully possest with a true Machivillian spirit, which more evidently appeareth in laying his charge upon me in such subjects, as wherein he knoweth the presses in these times are not admitted the lest measure of freedome, & if I should insist upon the mistakes, & nullities in the charge, I should be inforc'd to use the names of some persons, I much esteeme for that publique affection I have seen in them, and for the un-interupted friendship l have had with them, which is no waies sutable to my spirit: insomuch as I [19] am yet unresolved what course to take, besides, since it concernes only my particuler, and that of necessity it will occasion a bulk in print beyond my temper, the world being also opprest with books of particuler contest, I beleeve I shall incline to forbeare, though I am not certaine.

As for those who know me, or throughly know him, with al those I shal remain unprejudiced in my repute, though he should have spet al his venome at once, and as for those that neither know him nor me, I shal (and I think may) safely trust my credit to the operation of my Antidote, & to the most powerful addition of true Christian love, wch (were there need in this cause) would cover abundance of evill: love is the balsome which in my Whisper I really commended to his use, but either he will not use it, or takes not that paynes to rub it in which I advised, but though I have cast my pearle amisse, and have sped accordingly; that shall not hinder or abate my esteem of so pretious a Jewell, it is the delight of life, and the joy of Heaven, and whilst I live I trust I shall live in love, and when I dye, that I shall dye in this love, and Rise and remain Eternally in love, that is in God (for God is love) in whose presence [20] there is fulnesse of joy; at whose wright hand there are pleasures for evermore; and full amends for all reproches.

WILLIAM WALWIN

FINIS

Imprimatur,
John Bachiler. May 26. 1646. [21]

13

The Just Man in Bonds

[29 June] 1646
Reprinted from a copy of the tract in the Thomason Collection in the British Library

The Just Man in Bonds was published anonymously, without separate title page, imprint, or date. The typography is similar to that of works printed by Thomas Paine—who printed the four tracts signed by Walwyn in 1646—and Haller places *The Just Man in Bonds* in Walwyn's canon without further comment.[1] Wolfe concurs, observing that the persuasive, unprovocative style "appears to be that of Walwyn."[2]

Circumstances and content support the attribution. On 6 June John Lilburne, who had distributed copies of Walwyn's *A Word in Season* in Westminster Hall on 26 May, published charges against Colonel Edward King and alluded slightingly to the Earl of Manchester. On 11 June Lilburne refused to obey a warrant from the House of Lords, contending that the Lords had no judicial authority over a commoner. Committed to Newgate, Lilburne continued his defiance and the Lords sent him to the Tower during the pleasure of the House.[3] *The Just Man in Bonds* opens with the warning that Lilburne's "case is mine, and every mans."[4] Reference to Lilburne as a "young man"[5] suggests the fifteen years between Lilburne and Walwyn, and the description of the Lords' power as "like a shallow, un-even water, more in noise than substance" is countered by the challenge to the Commons—"who are put in trust, and enabled with power to protect the people"—to put an end to the Lords' "usurpation of the Commons liberties" and Lilburne's "just cause."[6]

The argument of *Just Man* is narrower than Walwyn's defense of Lilburne's rights in *Englands Lamentable Slaverie*. *Just Man* focuses on Lilburne's deeds and courage in resisting injustice and cruelty, and two paragraphs advising the Commons that justice is pleasing to God reflect views expressed in *A Whisper in the Eare* and *A Still and Soft*

Voice.[7] *Just Man* introduces reservations about the value of enduring "the miseries of warre" if the result is a mere substitution of one arbitrary rule for another.[8] This possibility became a rising concern of the Levellers, who released the first coordinated statement of their goals the week after Thomason acquired *Just Man.*[9]

The *Just Man in Bonds* is reprinted for the first time in this volume.

THE JUST MAN IN BONDS.

OR Lieut. Col. *John Lilburne* close Prisoner in Newgate, by order of the HOUSE of LORDS.

Since this worthy gentle mans case is mine, and every mans, who though we be at liberty to day, may be in Newgate to morrow, if the House of Lords so please, doth it not equally and alike concerne all the people of England to lay it to heart, and either fit both our minds and necks to undergoe this slavery, or otherwise thinke of some speedy and effectuall meanes to free our selves and our posterity there from.

This noble and resolute Gentleman Mr. Lilburne, then whom his countrey has not a truer and more faithfull servant, hath broke the Ice for us all, who being sensible that the people are in reall bondage to the Lords (and that the Lawes and Statutes providing to the contrary, serving them in no stead) hath singly adventured himselfe a Champion for his abused country men, nothing doubting but that he shall thereby open the eyes, and awake the drowsie spirits of his fellow Commoners, or rather Slaves (as the case now stands) with them; and likewise animate the representative body of the people, to make use of that power wherewith they are trusted to free us, themselves, their and our posterities, from the House of Lords imperious and ambitious usurpation.

Object. Some through ignorance, or poverty of spirit, may (peradventure) judge Mr. Lilburne a rash young man for his opposing himselfe against so mighty a streame or torrent of worldly power, which the Lords now possesse. To such I answer, 1. That the power of the House of Lords, is like a shallow, un-even water, more in noise then substance; If we could distinguish between what is theirs of right, and what by incroachment, we should soone find that they have deckt themselves with the Commoners brave feathers, which being reassumed, they would appeare no better arrayed then other men, even equall by Law, inferior in uprightnesse, and honesty of conversation: We should then find that they are but painted properties, Dagons, that our superstition and ignorance, their owne craft and impudence have erected, no naturall issues of lawes, but the extuberances and mushromes of Prerogative, the Wens of just government, putting the body of the People to paine, as well as occasioning deformity, Sons of conquest they are and usurpation, not of choice and election, intruded upon us by power, not constituted by consent, not made by the people, from whom all power, place and office that is just in this kingdome ought only to arise.

2. Mr. Lilburnes opposing himselfe against this exorbitant and extra-judiciall power [1] of the Lords, ought rather to be admired by us a pitch of valour we are not yet arrived too, through the faintnesse of our spirits, and dotage upon our trades, ease, riches, and pleasures, then censured by us as rash or furious. He that dares scale the walls of an enemie, or venture himselfe upon the utmost of danger in the field, is not judged rash but a valiant man, unlesse by those low spirits that dares not doe as he hath done. Let us therefore rather blame our selves for want of fortitude, then accuse him, as having too much.

Consider I pray the great danger we are in, if the Lords thus presume to clap a Commoner of England in close prison, even now when the Commons of England are sitting in Parliament, who are put in trust, and enabled with power to protect the people from such bondage (yea and so suddainly after they have in effect declared, that they will doe it, in their Declaration of the 17. of April last) what injuries will not these Lords doe to us, when the Parliament is ended, and the people have none of their owne Commons nor Trustees to protect them, heare their cryes, nor redresse their grievances; What prison or dungeon will then be base enough, what punishment or torture great enough for them, that are not cowardish enough so to be slaves and bond-men? And so is not the last errour, like to be worse then the first?

Death it selfe is more tollerable to a generous spirit, then close imprisonment, besides the continuall feares that such an inhumane practice brings with it, of private murther or poisoning, as there are manifold examples of such cruelties, of which Overberies was not one of the least who was poisoned in the Tower, and to salve or colour that wickednesse, it was strongly given out and avouched that he murthered himselfe, though afterwards divers were hang'd for it, and the Earle of Somerset and his Countesse hardly escaped. Sir Richard Wiseman was moped and stupified with his close imprisonment, and what mischiefes (of divers sorts) may be done to honest and faithfull Mr. Lilburne upon this renued opportunitie by the Lords (as he had too much formerly by the Bishops, though contrary to all equitie and justice, yea and even to the Lords owne reparations which lately they voted and alotted to him) whiles he is now close prisoner in their owne hands, who know him to be their chiefest opposite in all their usurpations and encroachments upon the Commoners freedomes? doth it not concerne all the Commons of England to consider and prevent the same, especially their great and generall Counsell in Parliament assembled.

Lay to heart I beseech you o yee house of commons, that neither your selves nor your children can plead any immunitie or security from this cruelty and bondage of the House of Lords, if now yee be slack or negligent, but yee may justly expect and feele the smart thereof upon you and your posterity, as well as we upon us and ours, at least after you are dissolved, and dismissed from your Authorities. And is not this one of the maine points for which yee have put your selves, us, and so many of this Nation as stand in your defence, to the effusion and expence of so much blood and multituds of estates?

If yee did intend to expose this Kingdome to the miseries of warre for no other ends but that one kind of Arbitrary government, Starchamber, or High Commission Power, might be abollished, and others of these kinds established over us, why would yee not tell us in due time, that wee might have both spared our lives and estates, and not made so many souldiers, Widowes and fatherlesse to mourne at the Parliaments gates, for the manyfold wants occasioned by your service, and made us sooner like humble vassals, to present our selves like slaves upon our knees at the House of Lords Barre, and suffer our eares to be bored through with an aule, in testimony that wee are their bond-men for ever. [2]

But if yee would either free your selves of this suspition, or us of those just feares, then shew your selves to be such worthies as doe truly deserve that title, by using this happy oppertunity which God hath put into your hands, and making us free-men; it being the maine cause for which wee used and intrusted you; and as a present signe of your fidelity and magnanimitie, let your reall intentions in the generall appeare by the exactnesse and speedinesse of your delivering of this your owne, and his Countries faithfull servant Mr. Lilburn from prison with all due reparations.

Banish all base fears, for there be more with you then against you, and the justnesse of your cause will daylie increase both your number and power, for God is alwaies present where Justice is extant, and yee cannot but observe by manifold experiences that he not only loves and protects just men, but by his Almighty power so abaseth all their Enemies, that they shall flee before him and his, like the dust before the wind: If yee will but take example by the courage and justice of your owne Armies, and doe as they doe, doubtlesse the same God who hath prospered them will also prosper you, yea and be with you, in all your proceedings whilst yee are with him, but if yee forsake him, (by denying, selling, or delaying justice, contrary to your duties, Oaths, Covenants, Protestations, and declarations) he will also forsake you, as he hath in all ages (even his owne People for their injustice, sins, and abominations) and stirred up both forraigne and intestine enemies to revenge his just quarrell and true cause against them.

For more particular information, these ensuing lines will be a speciall meanes.

Upon the 22. of June 1646. the House of Lords sent an Order to the Keeper of Newgate, to bring Mr. Lilburn before them upon the 23. thereof at ten a clock, wherof he having notice that morning, wrot a letter to the said Keeper, declaring his just liberties and the House of Lords usurpation thereof, contrary to Magna Charta and other fundamentall Lawes of this, Kingdome and that he would not go to them willingly, but had appealed and petitioned to the House of Commons, and therefore he desired the Keeper to take heed what he did, lest he could not recall any violent action, not grounded upon Law:

And after Mr. Lilburn had sent the said letter by his wife, together with the printed coppy of his protestation against the House of Lords illegal proceedings against him as a Commoner, & his appeale & Petition to the House of Commons, as his competent Judges, but shee not finding the Keeper at Newgate prison, nor at his owne house, & the hour of his appearance before the House of Lords near aproching, shee delivered the same to the Sheriffs of London, being then in Guild-hall at the Court of Aldermen, where doubtles both the said letter and book were read, and as Sheriffe Foote informed her, that they sent a messenger to Newgate with their answer, what it was, is not yet knowne.

But if it came at all, it was not in due time, for after the deputy Keeper and his assistants had attended halfe an hour for Mr. Lilburns comming from his chamber to go with them before the House of Lords at the time appointed, and upon his constant refusing to go willingly with them (or so much as to open his Chamber doore, but shut it in token of his constant opposing so unjust a power over him a free borne English man) and before the messenger whom he sent to Guild-hall with their consent, had returned with an answer (and whose returning they promised to attend) [they brake open his doore, tooke him away to Westminster] and no messenger was sent (who yet wee have heard of) from the Court of Aldermen.

When they had brought him to the painted chamber next the House of Lords [3] doore, where he attended with his Keepers almost two houres before he was called in, (as it seemeth) the House of Lords servants and attendants, taking notice of the intercourse of Parliament men and others speaking to him told their masters thereof, and lest their usurpation of the Commons liberties, and his just cause should be manifested as well by word, as by writing, the Lords did call his Keepers and commanded them that they should speedily charge him to hold his peace, and speake with none at all; but to be altogether silent untill he was called in before them to answer their interrogatories.

Unto whom he returned this answer, and had them tell the same to the House of Lords who sent them, that he would not hold his peace, but speak with any man who in the way of love spake to him, so long as he had his tongue, except the Lords should put a gag into his mouth as their Fellow Lords the Bishops did to him 8 yeares agoe, on the Pillory at Westminster, after they had caused him to be whipt from the Fleet prison thither, and after he had told them their spirituall usurpations, as it doth these Lords their temporall encroachments on free mens liberties.

Then he being called into the House of Lords, was commanded by their Keeper of the Black-Rod to kneele before them, which he absolutely refused to doe, and after their still urging, and his constant refusing, they asked him the reason, he answered that he had learned both better Religion and manners then to kneele to any humane or mortall power how great so ever, whom he never offended, and far lesse to them whom he had defended with the adventure both of his life and estate, yea and withall the friends he could make: whereupon they not only returned him to Newgate prison, but commanded him to be kept close-Prisoner, as appeareth by these ensuing orders.

Die Lunae 22. Junij 1646.

Ordered by the Lords in Parliament assembled, that Lieu. Col. John Lilburne now a prisoner in Newgate, shall be brought before their Lordships in the [High Court of PARLIAMENT] *to morrow morning by ten of the clock: And this to be a sufficient warrant in that behalfe.*

To the Gent. Usher of this House, or his Deputy, to be delivered to the Keeper of Newgate or his Deputy.

Joh. Brown Cler. Parliamentorum.

Die Martis 23. Junij. 1646.

Ordered by the LORDS *in* PARLIAMENT *assembled, that* John Lilburn *shall stand committed close prisoner in the Prison of Newgate; and that he be not permitted to have pen, inke, or paper; and none shall have accesse unto him in any kind, but only his Keeper, until this Court doth take further order.*

To the Keeper of Newgate his deputy or deputies.

Joh. Brown Cleric. Parliamentorum.
Exam. per. Rec. Bristoe Cleric. de Newgate.

FINIS [4]

14

A Remonstrance of Many Thousand Citizens, and Other Free-Born People of England, To Their Owne House of Commons

[7 July] 1646
Partially reprinted from a copy of the tract in the Thomason Collection in the British Library

A Remonstrance of Many Thousand Citizens was published anonymously, without imprint, "in the Yeer. 1646." In 1914 Pease stated that, although it was "a mere guess," the "style, expression, and ideas" suggested that the tract was Richard Overton's or possibly Henry Marten's work. Haller assigns it to Overton, and Wolfe concludes that it was written "in the main" by Overton but that Marten and Walwyn collaborated, with Walwyn taking a special hand in the last seven pages.[1] C. M. Williams doubts that Marten had any part in a tract so critical of the Commons.[2]

Related events as well as the language and content support a judgment that Overton wrote most of *A Remonstrance* but that he and Walwyn consulted closely throughout the drafting. It is unlikely that Walwyn wrote the last seven pages in their entirety, but he probably proposed and amended several passages there and elsewhere, and the two excerpts reprinted here are at once so characteristic of Walwyn's civility and alien to Overton's aggressive tone that they strengthen the likelihood that Walwyn played an important role in the preparation of the manifesto.

A Remonstrance was secured by Thomason on 7 July, a month after
Lilburne's imprisonment by the House of Lords, a week after Thomason picked up Overton's defense of Lilburne in *A Pearle in a Dounghill,* and eight days after Thomason's date on Walwyn's defense in *The
Just Man in Bonds.*[3] The titles alone reveal the sharp contrast between
Overton's and Walwyn's styles. *A Remonstrance,* which is addressed to
"their owne House of Commons," states on the title page that it is
"occasioned through the Illegall and Barbarous Imprisonment
of . . . John Lilburne," and the frontispiece is a copperplate portrait of
Lilburne with bars before his face.[4] These may have been late additions, employed to rally attention. The only mention of Lilburne in
the body of *A Remonstrance* includes him among the "worthy Sufferers" imprisoned by the Lords.[5] The pamphlet is as critical of king-
ship as of the Lords and is only less critical of the Commons for failing
to take charge and relieve the people who empower them. The tract is
most notable because it presents the first comprehensive statement of
the Leveller program.[6] It is probable that the drafting was well along
before Lilburne was imprisoned, and it is likely that Overton and Walwyn paused to write their separate attacks on the Lords' action. Both
tracts include in their four pages concepts that are detailed in *A
Remonstrance.*

Ideas were widely shared by radical penmen by 1646, but Walwyn's
distinctive references and points of view abound in the passages of *A
Remonstrance* reprinted here. Romans 14 is quoted in the first and second paragraphs, as the Commons are assured that they have no
power to compel anyone in matters of religion.[7] Walwyn's acceptance
of an established church is reiterated,[8] but the House is warned
against coercion in words similar to those in *A Helpe to the Right Understanding:* "wee could not conferre a Power that was not in ourselves."[9]
The golden rule is implied in the statement that "we ought not to
revile or reproach any man for his differeing with us in judgement,
more than wee would be reviled or reproached for ours,"[10] the peaceful results of toleration are stressed,[11] and the need for all "to give an
eare," to hear "all voices" and "try all things" is a replication of Walwyn's belief that men should enquire for themselves instead of accepting the views of others.[12]

The second passage repeats Walwyn's dismissal of Magna Carta as
"but a beggarly thing"—an attitude, as Wolfe notes, that is contrary
to that of Overton, who praised Magna Carta three months later in *An
Arrow against All Tyrants.*[13]

A *Remonstrance* is reproduced in facsimile in *Tracts on Liberty,* ed. Haller, 3:351–70, and reprinted in *Leveller Manifestoes,* ed. Wolfe, No. 1.

A REMONSTRANCE of Many Thousand Citizens, and other Free-born PEOPLE of ENGLAND, To their owne House of COMMONS.

Occasioned through the Illegall and Barbarous Imprisonments of that Famous and Worthy Sufferer for his Countries Freedoms, Lieutenant Col. JOHN LILBURNE.

Wherein their just Demands in behalfe of themselves and the whole Kingdome, concerning their Publike Safety, Peace and Freedome, is Express'd; calling those their Commissioners in *Parliament* to an Account, how they (since the beginning of their Session, to this present) have discharged their Duties to the Universallity of the People, their Sovereigne LORD, from whom their Power and Strength is derived, and by whom (*ad bene placitum,*) it is continued.

Printed in the Yeer, 1646.

. . . .

And though it resteth in you to acquiet all differences in affection, though not in judgement, by permitting every one to be fully perswaded in their owne mindes, commanding all Reproach to cease; yet as yee also had admitted Machiavells Maxime, *Divide & impera,* divide and prevaile; yee countenance onely one, open the Printing-presse onely unto one, and that to the Presbytry, and suffer them to raile and abuse, and domineere over all the rest, as if also ye had discovered and digested, That without a powerfull compulsive Presbytry in the Church, a compulsive mastership, or Arristocraticall Government over the People in the State, could never long be maintained.

Whereas truely wee are well assured, neither you, nor none else, can have any into Power at all to conclude the People in matters that concerne the Worship of God, for therein every one of us ought to be fully assured in our owne mindes, and to be sure to Worship him according to our Consciences.

Yee may propose what Forme yee conceive best, and most available
for Information and well-being of the Nation, and may perswade and
invite thereunto, but compell, yee cannot justly; for ye have no Power
from Us to doe, nor could you have; for wee could not conferre a
Power that was not in ourselves, there being none of us, that can
without wilfull sinne binde our selves to worship God after any other
way, then what (to a tittle,) in our owne particular understandings,
wee approve to be just.

And therefore We could not referre our selves to you in things of
this Nature; and surely, if We could not conferre this Power upon you,
yee cannot have it, and so not exercise it justly; Nay, as we ought not
to revile or reproach any man for his differing with [12] us in judgement, more than wee would be reviled or reproached for ours; even
so yee ought not to countenance any Reproachers or revilers, or molesters for matters of Conscience.

But to protect and defend all that live peaceably in the Common-
wealth, of what judgement or way of Worship whatsoever; and if ye
would bend your mindes thereunto, and leave your selves open to
give eare, and to consider such things as would be presented unto
you, a just way would be discovered for the Peace & quiet of the land
in generall, and of every well-minded Person in particular.

But if you lock up your selves from hearing all voices; how is it
possible you should try all things. It is not for you to assume a Power
to controule and force Religion, or a way of Church Government,
upon the People, because former Parliaments have so done; yee are
first to prove that yee could have such a Power justly entrusted unto
you by the People that trusted you. . . . [13]

. . . .

Yee know, the Lawes of this Nation are unworthy a Free-People,
and deserve from first to last, to be considered, and seriously debated, and reduced to an agreement with common equity, and right
reason, which ought to be the Forme and Life of every Government.

Magna Charta it self being but a beggerly thing, containing many
markes of intollerable bondage, & the Lawes that have been made
since by Parliaments, have in very many particulars made our Government much more oppressive and intollerable. . . . [15]

15

A Prediction of Mr. Edwards His Conversion and Recantation

[11 August] 1646
*Reprinted from a copy of the tract in the Thomason Collection in the British
Library*

A Prediction of Mr. Edwards, "By William Walwin," was "Printed by
T.P. [Thomas Paine] for G. Whittington and N. Brookes," 1646. The
imprimatur of John Bachiler, 22 July 1646, is on the last page, verso.
   Prediction, Walwyn's fourth tract in reply to Edwards, adds parody
to irony. Edwards's violence of spirit, wrote Walwyn, surpasses Paul's
before Damascus, and conversion must be at hand. Anticipating "the
happy end of his unhappy labours," Walwyn gives Edwards a speech
of recantation in which he condemns himself and embraces all that is
good in all faiths. It is a splendid device for a brilliant vindication of
liberty of conscience.
   Prediction is reproduced in facsimile in *Tracts on Liberty,* ed. Haller,
3:339–48.

A PREDICTION of Mr. EDWARDS

HIS CONVERSION, and Recantation.

By William Walwyn.

London, Printed by *T.P.* for *G. Whittington* and *N. Brookes,* at
the signe of the Angell in Cornhill, below the Exchange. 1646.

A PREDICTION OF MASTER EDWARDS HIS CONVERSION and Recantation.

There hath of late so much labour, and so many good discourses beene bestowed upon Mr. Edwards, and with so pious and good intentions, that it is not to be supposed, so many precious endevours can be vaine or fruitlesse, in reference to his conversion.

In cases so desperate as his, the worst signes are the best; as wee use to say, when things are at the worst, they are nearest to an amendment.

To an impartiall judgement, that seriously considers the violence of his spirit, manifested against harmelesse, well-meaning people, that differ with him in judgement: [1] He cannot but seeme, at best, in that wretched condition, that Paul was in, when hee breathed out threatnings and slaughter, against the disciples of the Lord; and went unto the High Priest, and desired of him letters to Damascus, to the Synagogues, that if he found any of this way, whether they were men or women, he might bring them bound unto Jerusalem.

For certainly, had not Authority, in these our times, being endowed with much more true Christian wisdome then such teachers, and through the power thereof, had not restrained the bitternesse of his (and the like) spirits: we had had (before this time) multitudes of both men and women, brought from all parts of this Nation, bound, unto London, if not burned in Smithfield.

But many there are, that feare, his condition is much more sad, and desperate, then this of Pauls, (which yet the blessed Apostle was much troubled to thinke on, long after his conversion, accompting himselfe as one borne out of due time, and not worthy the name of an Apostle, *because he persecuted the Church of God.*) It being exceedingly feared that in all his unchristian writings, preachings, and endevours, to provoke Authority against conscientious people, that therein [2] he goeth against the light of his owne conscience, that he is properly an Heretique, one that is subverted and sinneth, being condemned of himselfe.

And indeed, who ever shall consider, the exceeding Light that hath been darted from so many Seraphick Quills, shining round about him; amidst his persecuting intentions, (all which he hath hitherto resisted) will find and confesse; there is cause to feare: So great a shining and a burning light, that it cannot be doubted, but that hee discerneth, how unreasonable a thing it is, that one erring man should compell or comptroule another mans practice, in things supernaturall: or that any lawes should be made for punishing of mis-apprehentions therein, wherein thousands are as liable to be mistaken; as one single person.

He must needs know, that, only things naturall and rationall are properly subject unto government: And that things supernaturall, such as in Religion are distinguished by the title of things divine; such, as the benefit and use thereof, could never have beene perceived by the light of nature and reason: that such things are not liable to any compulsive government, but that therein every one ought to be fully perswaded in their [3] owne minds; because *whatsoever is not of faith is sinne.*

He cannot be ignorant, how disputable all the parts of Divinity are amongst the most learned, how then can he judge it so horrible a thing as he seems to doe, for men to differ, though upon the highest points: he knowes every one is bound to try all things, the unlearned as well as the learned: now if there be different understandings, some weaker and some stronger, (as there are) how is it possible but there will (upon every tryall) be difference in degrees of apprehensions: and surely he will not say that weaknesse of understanding is sinfull where there is due endevour after knowledge: and though it should be sinfull in the sight of a pure God, yet will he not say it is punishable, by impure and erronious man: But,

To rayle revile, reproch, backbite, slander, or to despise men and women, for their weaknesses: their meanes of trades and callings, or poverty, is so evidently against the rule of Christ and his Apostles, that he cannot but condemne himselfe herein: his understanding is so great, and he is so well read in Scripture, that he must needs acknowledge, these cannot stand with Love: [4] that knowne and undisputable Rule.

Insomuch, as if bad signes in so desperate a case as his is, are the best, surely he is not farre from his recovery and conversion.

With God there is mercy, his mercyes are above all his workes, his delight is in shewing mercy: and the Apostle tells us *where sinne hath abounded grace* (or love) *hath super-abounded:* O that he would stand still a while, and consider the love of Christ, that he would throw by his imbittered pen, lock himselfe close in his study, draw his curteines, and sit downe but two houres, and seriously, sadly, and searchingly lay to heart, the things he hath said and done, against a people whom he knoweth, desire to honour God: and withal to bear in mind the infinite mercy of God, *that where sin hath abounded, grace hath over abounded:* certainly it could not but work him into the greatest and most burning extremity that ever poor perplexed man was in, such an extremity as generally proves Gods opportunity, to cast his aboundant grace so plentifully into the distressed soule, as in an instant burnes and consumes all earthly passions, and corrupt affections, and in stead thereof fills the soule with love, which instantly refineth and [5] changeth the worst of men, into the best of men.

May this be the happy end of his unhappy labours: it is the hearty desire of those whom he hath hitherto hated, and most dispitefully used; (nothing is to hard for God) it will occasion joy in Heaven, and both joy and peace in earth, you shal then see him a man composed of all those opinions he hath so much reviled: an Independent: so far as to allow every man to be fully perswaded in his owne mind, and to molest no man for worshiping God according to his conscience.

A Brownist: so far, as to separate from all those that preach for filthy lucre: An Anabaptist: so far, at least, as to be rebaptised in a floud of his owne true repentant teares: A seeker: in seeking occasion, how to doe good unto all men, without respect of persons or opinions: he will be wholly incorporate into the Family of love, of true Christian love, that covereth a multitude of evils: that suffereth long, and is kind, envieth not, vanteth not it selfe, is not puffed up, doth not behave it selfe unseemly, seeketh not her owne, is not easily provoked &c. And then: you may expect him to breake forth and publish to the world, this or the like recantation. [6]

Where have I been! Into what strange and uncouth pathes have I run my self! I have long time walked in the counsell of the ungodly, stood in the way of sinners, and too too long sate in the seat of the scornful!

O vile man, what have I done? Abominable it is!

O wretched man, how have I sinned against God! It shameth me: It repenteth me: My spirit is confounded within me.

I have committed evils, of a new and unparalelled nature, such as the Protestant Religion in all after-ages wil be shamed of. For I have published in print to the view of all men the names of divers godly well affected persons, and reproached them as grand Impostors, Blasphemers, Heretiques and Schismatiques, without ever speaking with them my selfe.

And though I am conscious to my selfe, of many weaknesses, and much error, and cannot deny, but I may be mistaken in those things, wherein, at present I am very confident, yet have I most presumptuously and arrogantly, assumed to my selfe, a power of judging, and censuring all judgements, opinions, and wayes of worship (except my owne) to bee either damnable, hereticall, schismaticall, or dangerous: And though I [7] have seene and condemned the evill of it in the Bishops and Prelates, yet (as they) have I reviled & reproached them, under the common nick-names of Brownists, Independents, Anabaptists, Antinomians, Seekers, and the like: of purpose to make them odious to Authority, and all sorts of men: whereby I have wrought very much trouble to many of them, in all parts throughout this Nation; and have caused great disaffection in Families, Cities and Counties, for difference in judgement, (which I ought not to have done) Irritating and provoking one against an other, to the dissolving of all civill and naturall relations, and as much as in me lay, inciting and animating to the extirpation and utter ruine one of another, in so much as the whole Land (by my unhappy meanes, more then any others) is become a Nation of quarrels, distractions, and divisions, our Cities, Cities of strife, slander, and backbiting; by occasion whereof, both our counsell and strength faileth, and all the godly party in the Land, are now more liable to abuse and danger, whether they are Presbyterians, Independents, or others, then they have been since the beginning of this Parliament; though many of them are so blinded by my writings and discourses, [8] and so perverted in their understandings that they cannot discerne it: And wherefore I have done all this, O Lord God thou knowest, and I tremble to remember, for I have done it out of the pride and vanity of my owne mind, out of disdaine, that plaine unlearned men should seeke for knowledge any other way then as they are directed by us that are learned: out of base feare, if they should fall to teach one another, that wee should lose our honour, and be no longer esteemed as Gods Clergy, or Ministers *Jure divino;* or that we should lose our domination in being sole judges of doctrine and discipline, whereby our predecessours have over ruled States and Kingdomes.

O lastly, that we should lose our profits and plentious maintenance by Tithes, offerings, &c. which our predecessours (the Clergie) for many ages have enjoyed as their proper right, and not at the good will of the owners, or the donation of humane authority: All this I saw comming in with that liberty, which plaine men tooke, to try and examine all things; and therefore being overcome with selfe-respect, and not being able to withstand so strong temptations, being also then filled with a kind of know- [9] ledge that puffeth up: I betooke my selfe to that unhappy worke, to make all men odious, that, either directly, or by consequence, did any thing towards the subversion of our glory, power, or profit.

In doing whereof: what wayes and means I have taken for intelligence: What treachery, inhumanity, and breach of hospitality, I have countenanced and encouraged; my conscience too sadly tels me, and my unhappy bookes (if duly weighed) will to my shame discover.

The most knowing, judicious, understanding men that opposed me, or my interest, I knew were those, that did and could most prejudice our cause; and therefore I set my selfe against them in a more speciall manner, labouring by any meanes to make them odious to all societies, that so they might not be credited in any thing they spake.

The truth is: In this my perverse and sad condition, whilst I stood for maintenance of my corrupt interest, it was impossible for me, truly to love a judicious or an enquiring man: I loved none, but superstitious or ignorant people, for which such I could perswade, and over such I could bear rule: such would pay whatsoever I demanded, and do [10] whatever I required: they spake as I spake, commended what I approved, &c reproached, as I reproached: I could make them run point-blanck against Authority, or fly in the face of any man, for these took me really for one of Gods Clergie, admired my parts and learning, as gifts of the Holy Ghost, and beleeved my erring Sermons to be the very word of God; willingly submitted their consciences and religion to my guidance.

Whilst (as indeed it is) an understanding enquiring man, studious in the Scriptures, instantly discerneth me to be but as other laymen, and findeth our learning to be but like other things that are the effects of study and industry, and that our preachings are like any other mens discourses, liable to errours and mistakings, and are not the very Word of God, but our apprehensions drawne from the Word.

I confesse now most willingly to my owne shame, that there was nothing which I conceived effectuall, to work upon the superstitious or ignorant, but I made use thereof as the Prelats had don before me, yea I strictly observed order in such things as few men consider, & yet are very powerful in the [11] minds of many; as the wearing of my Cloak of at least a Clergy-mans length, my Hat of a due breadth and bignesse, both for brim and crown, somewhat different from lay men, my band also of a peculiar straine, and my clothes all black, I would not have worne a coloured sute at any rate, that I thought enough to betray all, nor any triming on my black, as being unsutable to a Divines habit.

I had a care to be sadder in countenance and more sollemne in discourse because it was the custom of a Clergy man, this I did though I knew very well the Apostles of Christ, used no such vaine distinctions, but being not indeed unlike other men, through any endowments from on high, or power of miracles, and yet resolving to maintayn a distinction, (being unable to do it by any thing substantiall, I) concluded it must be done (as it long time had been, both in the Romish and Prelatique Church) even by vain and Fantastick distinctions, such as clothes and other formalities; and though I knew full well, that God was no respecter of persons, and that he made not choise of the great, or learned men of the world, to be his Prophets and publishers of the Gospel: [12] but Heards-men, Fisher-men Tentmakers Toll-gatherers, &c. and that our Blessed Saviour thought it no disparagement to be reputed the Sonne of a Carpenter: yet have I most unworthily reviled and reproached, divers sorts of honest Tradesmen, and other usefull laborious people, for endevouring to preach and to instruct those that willingly would be instructed by them, tearming them illiterate Mechanicks, Heriticks, and Scismaticks, meerly because I would not have my superstitious friends, to give any eare or regard unto them.

And for these respects, have I magnified our publique Churches or meeting places, and reproached and cryed out upon all preachings in private houses, calling them conventicles and using all endevours, to make all such private meetings liable to that Statute that was enacted, and provided to restraine and avoyd all secret plotings against the civill government, when in the meane time I knew the scriptures plainly shewed, both by the precepts and practices of our Saviour and his Apostles, that all places are indifferent, whether in the mountaine or in the fields, on the wa- [13] ter, in the ship, or on the shore, in the Synagogues Or, privat houses, in an upper or low-roome; all is one, *they went preaching the Gospell from house to house. Not in Jerusalem, nor in this mountaine, but in every place he that lifteth up pure hands is accepted. Wheresoever two or three are gathered together in my name, there* (saith our Saviour) *I will be in the midest of them,* all this I knew: yet, because the superstitious were (through long custom) zealous of the publique places, I applyed my selfe therein, to their humors and my owne ends, and did what I could to make all other places odious and ridiculous: though now I seriously acknowledge, that a plaine discreet man in a privat house, or field, in his ordinary apparell, speaking to plaine people (like himselfe) such things as he conceiveth requisit for their knowledge, out of the word of God, doth as much (if not more) resemble the way of Christ and the manner of the Apostles, as a learned man in a carved pulpet, in his neate and black formalities, in a stately, high, and stone-built Church, speaking to an audience, much more glorious and richly clad, then most Christians mentioned in the Scriptures: and may be as acceptable. I have most misera- [14] bly deluded the world therein, and those most with whom I have beene most familiar, and have thereby drawne off their thoughts from a consideration of such things as tended to love, peace and joy in the Holy Ghost, to such things as tended neither to their owne good nor the good, of others. I have beene wise in my own eyes, and despised others, but I must abandon all, I must become a foole that I may bee wise, hitherto I have promoted a meere Clergy Religion, but true Christian religion; pure religion and undefiled I have utterly neglected: I have wrested the covenant from its naturall and proper meaning, to make use thereof for the establishment of such a Church government, as would maintaine the power of the Clergy distinct from and above the power of Parliaments, and such as would have given full power to suppresse and crush all our opposers, but I now blesse God, the wisdom of Parliament discerned and prevented it.

I have been too cruel and hard hearted against men for erors in religion, or knowledge supernaturall, though I my selfe have no infallible spirit to discern between truth and erors, yea though I have seene them so [15] zealous & conscientious in their judgments (as to be ready to give up their lives for the truth thereof) yet have I (as the Bishops were wont) argued them of obstinacy, and in stead of taking a christian-like way to convert them, have without mercy censured, some of them worthy of imprisonments, and some of death, but I would not be so used, nor have I done therein as I would be done unto my selfe.

I have beene a great respecter of persons, for outward respects, the man in Fine rayment, and with the gold ring, I have ever prefered whilst the poore and needy have beene low in my esteeme.

I have too much loved greetings in the market place, and the uppermost places at feasts, and to be called Rabby.

And to fill up the measure of my iniquity: I have had no compassion on tender consciences, but have wrought them all the trouble cruelty and misery I could, and had done much more but that through the goodnesse of God, the present authority was too just and pious to second my unchristian endevours: My mercifull Saviour would not breake the brused reed, nor quench the smokeing flax, but my hard heart hath done [16] it. O that I had not quenched, that I had not resisted the Spirit, what fruit have I of those things whereof I am now ashamed; O how fowle I am, and filthy, yea how naked and all uncovered, my hidden sinne lyes open, I see it, and the shame of it, and how fowle it is; and the sight of it grieveth and exceedingly troubleth me. I would faine hide my selfe from mine owne sinne, but cannot; it pursueth me, it cleaveth unto me, it stands ever before me and I am made to possesse my sinne, though it be grievous and loathsome and abominable and filthy above all that I can speake, what shall I doe? whither shall I fly? who can deliver me from this body of death? my spirit is so wounded I am not able to beare: Can there be mercy for me? can there be balme for my wounded spirit, that never had compassion on a tender conscience? my case is sad and misserable, but there is balme in Gilead: with God there is mercy: with him is plenteous redemption, I will therefore goe to my Father and say unto him, Father I have sinned against Heaven and against thee, I am not worthy to be called thy child, make me as one of thine hired servants, I will faithefully apply my selfe to thy will, and to the [17] study of thy Commandements, yea I will both study and put in practice thy new commandement, which is love, I will redeem the time I have mispent: love will help me, for God is love, the love of Christ will constraine me, through love I shall be enabled to doe all things, should I not love him that hath loved me, and shewed mercy unto me, for so many thousand sinnes, shall not his kindnesse beget kindnesse in me, yes love hath filled me with love, so let me eate, and so let me drinke, for ever, love is good and seeketh the good of all men, it helpeth and hurteth not, it blesseth, it teacheth, it feedeth, it clotheth, it delivereth the captive, & setteth the oppressed free, it breakes not the brused reed, nor quencheth the smokeing flaxe, farewell for ever all old things, as pride envy coveteousnesse reviling, and the like, and welcome love, that maketh all things new, even so let love possesse me, let love dwell in me, and me in love, and when I have finished my dayes in peace, and my yeares in rest, I shall rest in peace, and I shall dwell with love, that have dwelt in love. [18]

May his meditations hence-forward, and his latter end be like unto this, or more exellent and Heavenly, which is all the harme I wish unto him, as haveing through Gods mercy, in some measure, learned that worthy and Heavenly lesson of my Saviour, *But I say unto you, love your enemies* etc. and may all that love the Lord Jesus, increase therein.

FINIS [19]

July 22. 1646. Imprimatur, JOHN BACHILER [19v]

16

A Demurre to the Bill for Preventing the Growth and Spreading of Heresie

[7 October] 1646
Reprinted from a copy of the tract in the Thomason Collection in the British Library

A Demurre to the Bill for Preventing the Growth and Spreading of Heresie was published anonymously, without separate title page, imprint, or date. Haller ascribes the tract to Walwyn, citing no evidence beyond its possible publication by Thomas Paine.[1]

The proposed ordinance against heresy and blasphemy was a likely target for Walwyn's pen,[2] and *Demurre* is typical of his thoughtful appeal to reason and studded with specific signs of his hand. The opening attack on the intolerant clergy includes a passage contrasting them with the Apostles of Christ,[3] and the demand for inclusive toleration is supported by confidence that truth will defeat error and a reminder of Christ's gentle treatment of the Sadducees.[4] The belief that religious conviction is "infused by God, or begotten in us by discourse and examination" reflects contentions set forth in *Prediction* and *A Still and Soft Voice*,[5] and the need for every man to reach conclusions by "meditation, and deliberate examination" is underlined.[6] The familiar listing of "the Independents, the Brownists, the Antinomians, the Anabaptists," who "hold fast that which they account good," is coupled with the reminder that "these sorts of men" did "venture their lives and estates for their Country."[7] "Every man," states *Demurre*, paraphrasing Romans 14:5, "is to satisfie his owne conscience, the best he can."[8]

Presbyters are warned that "no sort of men have no [sic] just power

to determine for another." Today's heresy may be tomorrow's truth—
"as what formerly was accounted errour is now esteemed truth"—
and the rod that Presbyterians "provide for their dissenting brethren
to day, may whip them tomorrow."9 Reminding Parliament of the
many perversions of laws by "crafty men," *Demurre* compares the
members of the Westminster Assembly with "subtill and bloody Simon & Levy" (Genesis 49:5–7) and concludes that the Parliament's
rejection of the Assembly's harsh proposals "would be their honour
to future generations: and is the most zealous desire of all those that
would gladly see the quietnesse and happinesse of Parliaments and
People."10

Demurre is reprinted for the first time in this volume.

A DEMURRE TO THE BILL FOR PREVENTING THE GROWTH AND SPREADING OF HERESIE.

Humbly Presented to the Honourable the *House of Commons*.

Wee beseech you for the great love you have from the people, that you will be cautious in determining any thing in this
businesse of blasphemy & heresie; and that you will resolve to doe
nothing therein, but what shall evidently appeare to be just and
agreeable to the word of God.

Our feares are great; that those who urge you so much to suppresse
heresies and blasphemies, have their own unjust ends therein, and
the enslaving of the people to their wils: To estrange their affections
from you; and to make them out of love with Parliaments.

For what is it you are urged unto; but in effect to establish a very
inquisition, to be as a curb to all those that oppose the doctrines and
oppinions of the ministers, or will not without reasonings or disput-
ings submit their faith, practise and purses to their wils.

It is not to be supposed but that these desires and motions, have
their rise and birth from them, whose purpose it is to make you Instruments of their cruelty; certainly they have digged deep, and are
grown confident you are fully underminded; they judge you believe
[1] you are; and that you are so fully captivated by their policies and
stratagems, that you dare not but doe what they desire? though never
so unjust or distructive to your selves.

It cannot be; they should think you so ignorant as to believe they make these desires out of zeale to God, to Christ or his word; they are assured, you not only doubt, but know they doe it only to make you instruments, to subject the people to their no lesse then popall tyrany, they know you know it to be so, and think they have you upon such a lock as you dare not deny them.

But will you now feare the power of a Clergy, so lately raised out of the dust by your selves; when neither the power of the Court; and a long setled Clergy united, hath been able to stand before you; there is nothing for this Parliament now to feare but God.

The Clergy doe but presume, and like the Prelates doe things hastily, that will speedily make them odious, and be their ruine.

The people already generally see through them, they have waighed them in the ballance and find them light, a delusive, covetous, violent, bloody, imperious sort of men, no more like the Apostles or Disciples of Christ, then Simon Magus was; there is nothing so much in discourse as their pride and coveteousnesse: That it is they who set Nation against Nation, and neighbour against neighbour, and to have their will, set even all the People together by the eares; their craft and pollicies are worne threed bare, and their credits and reputations is grown low in the Peoples esteem, and therefore doe they make hast unto you for some reall power.

And because they would prevaile, they seem to be advocates for God, for Christ, for his word, for the precious soules of men, transforming themselves into this shape of angels of light, in hope to deceive the very Parliament it selfe.

Wee beseech you to looke upon them without dread, without superstition; with open eyes, see through them to their ends, and you will see they mind only themselves, to set themselves above you, to trample upon the People, who yet trust you will preserve them from so great a bondage.

1. First for their desire concerning heresie: for I presume I may safely call them theirs first: for it is not probable they know any person that doe deny and maintaine there is no God, if any such were they would no doubt ere this time have been brought to light, by these searching inquisitive Church-men: their purpose in this parti-
[2] cular seems to be no other then to keep men in awe & feare of affrunting them in their arguments, to have advantages against any that hold any set discourses, and to beget in men a superstitious beliefe of any thing they say, without any examination of their grounds and reasons.

2. In case any being ignorant, maintaine the contrary, can it be judged in wisdome or justice, an equall thing that they should therefore be discharged? Would it not farre better become us to endevour the enlightening of their understanding. or to waite Gods leasure till he doe it in his due time, rather then by their death to make sure that it shall never be done.

3. Men are not borne with the knowledge of this more then of any other thing; it must therefore either be infused by God, or begoten in us by discourse and examination as other things are; if it be infused, we must waite Gods time; his season is not the same for all, though happily one mans understanding may be opened at the first or second houre, another may not till the eleventh or last houre.

If by discourse and examination; then every man must have liberty to discourse thereupon; to propose doubts, to give and take satisfaction, to scruple, argue, or doe any thing that may firmely establish our minds in this prime and fundamentall truth.

4. Wee beseech you let not God and the truth of this being, be so excessively disparaged as not to be judged sufficient to maintaine it against all gainsayers, without the help of earthly power to maintain it; Let Turkes and those that believe in strange gods, which are indeed no gods: make use of such poore and infirme supporters of their supposed deities; but let the truth of our God, the only God, the omnipotent God, be judged aboundantly; able to support it selfe; tis a tacite imputation of infirmnesse, to imagine it hath need of our weak and impotent assistance.

5. If there be any feare that for want of such a terrour and penalty as is desired, men will take greater liberty to be vicious; Let the strictnesse and severity of law be multiplied tenfold against all manner of vice and enormity: Let some course be taken and charge given to the publique speakers, that they spend lesse time about controversies and entrigate disputes; and divert the streame of their discourses against the uglinesse of vice, and let forth the lovelinesse and excellency of vertue and true piety; that so all men may be inamoured therewith, and hate whatsoever is vicious with a perfect hatred. [3]

Concerning those that deny the unity of God: His eternity, presence or omnipotency; the divinity of Christ the purity of his manhood: the distruction of the two natures: the sufficiency of his death, and suffering for the satisfaction for our sins: the Trinity: resurrection, or judgement to come: or any other position mentioned in the former part of the desired Ordinance.

Those Miserable men I say, that through ignorance maintain any of these particulers: must they therefore be put to death? Is there no way to cure the blindnesse of their understandings, but by taking away that and life together? Is it not misery sufficient to these unhappy men that they are deprived of that knowledge, which is the principle comfort of this life: a support to us in afliction, the joy and solace of our soules?

But must they for this their infirm filicity loose their lives also? What precept I pray have wee for so doing? What command or Authority from Scripture? Was there ever any injunction given by Christ or his Apostles for the extirpation of the Romans or any others that denyed our God; and multiplyed other feighned gods to themselves? Can we think the name of God was lesse precious to Christ or his Disciples then it is to us? The Apostles way was to make the unknowne God, to be known to ignorant men; to remove errour by the sword of the Spirit and soundnesse of argument; not by punishment or death: If worldly strength had been judged the best and meetest way for the implanting the Gospell, God would with a word have furnished his servants there with: He could have chose to him out of the greatest and most potent upon the earth, or have made the Apostles: which seeing he did not, it evidently sheweth that his truthes are not to be propagated by strength and the sword: Nay we see rather it was his way to give all errours the advantage of worldly power, and trust the establishment and support of truth to its own effecacy, upon assurance whereof, he sent it abroad by messengers of meane condition, of no power in the world, as proposing it as his end to convince, not to compell, to conquour the under standing by the glorious and shining brightnesse of truth: and not subdue it by force of armes, by fire and faggot, by the hatchet or halter: Christ and his Disciples were frequently with the Sadduces, that denyed the resurrection, and by consequence the Judgement to come: yet wee find not that they ever Instigated the Magistrate against them: and though there were heresies in their times, as many and as grosse as there are said now to be; [4] yet our blessed Saviour shewes no zeale against them; the most that ever he exprest was against hypocrisie: the oppression of the Pharises, the cruelty of Herod, the pride and imperious mastery of the Scribes and Doctors of the Law: for Matters of opinion there was a toleration no man was molested: and it is exceedingly to the honour of Christianity: Yet of it selfe notwithstanding its low beginnings and despicable appearance at first, through the inherent and essentiall excellency and power that inseperably accompanies it, it was able to erect it selfe, and spread its branches about a great part of the world:

let us not therefore make use of other meanes then Christ used; nor flee to those poore, refuges of civill power, which he purposely a-voided, let us not now cast a blemish upon our profession: Let us not now undervalue it, by thinking it cannot stand without crutches, or that errour unlesse the Magistrate assist, will be to hard for it.

For blasphemy, if thereby be ment, a reviling or speaking evill of God, his Christ or his word; It is but meet that some fit punishment (as the word clearly imparts 1. Tim. 1. chap. & 20 ver. compared with 2. Pet. 2.10. Judg. 8.10.) should be appointed for restraining thereof, as also for any other evill and reproachfull language, against either men or opinions: though reason and argument is allowable and nec-essary for the finding out of truth, yet reviling railing, bitter taunts, and reproches, tends to the disturbance of civill peace, and proceeds from a maligne and a distempered mind, and are therefore justly re-strainable; But surely the punishment mentioned of burning in the cheeke with a hot Iron, is to rigorous and severe, I shall not prescribe, but leave it to your discretion.

For the supposed errours summed up in the latter part of the de-sired Ordinance, though many of them are disallowed by all, yet some of them are esteemed truths by the Anabaptists, some by the Brownists; some by the Independents, some by the Antinomians, and some by all of them: And such truths as they doe as really esteem themselves bound to maintaine, as the Presbyterians doe any of their tenets, this Ordinance therefore is like a insurrection of one sort of men against another, the purport and desires thereof in effect being that all the Independents, the Brownists, the Antinomians, the Ana-baptists that have so much courage left, as to hold fast that which they account good, should be imprisoned till they can find two sub-sity men that will be sureties for them, that they shall never professe nor practice what they esteem truth any more. [5]

Have these sorts of men been invited (though indeed they needed no invitation) to venture their lives and estates for their Country; and is this the reward? What could these good mens persons have been worse, had they been conquered by the Enemy? Since if this Ordi-nance takes effect, they must lead the remainder of their lives in a prison; and after they have got the victory be cast into bonds: I cannot perswade my selfe but that the Presbyters themselves, the ingenious I meane and meekly disposed amongst them, must utterly dislike this motion, as savouring not only of ingratitude and inhumanity, but of injustice; neither can I think but that the Honourable House of Com-mons will shew tendernesse to those sorts of men, from whom they have had reall affection, assistance protection, besides many excellent services and performances: and expresse no other then a detestation of such imperious and unequall desires, evidently tending to enslave them.

Though wee will not contend who has done best service for their Country, in the time of its straites and necessities, yet the presbyters sure themselves will acknowledge with us, that these sorts of men have not been backward in emptying themselves here at home, and powring out their blood abroad, thinking nothing to deare for their Country, and all in hope that the worke being done, they should perticipate of its peace and freedome, but the enemy being subdued, and freedome being now expected of serving God according to conscience, as a recompence for all the miseries and calamities Independents and Separation have indured for their Country, and amongst others, for the Presbyters: And instead thereof, motions are made that they may be put out of all Offices and imployment in the common wealth (and not only so, but it is further intended) by this desired Ordinance that they may be put in prison.

1. If this dealing be just or any waies pleasing to Almighty God, let the Presbyters themselves judge? Let it be considered first, that in matters of Religion, no sort of men have no just power to determine for another: neither are the Presbyters computent judges of the Independents or Anabaptists &c. no more then they are of the Presbyters.

2. That those tenets which are now accounted heresies, may be in the countenanced truthes of the next age; as what formerly was accounted errour, is now esteemed truth; every man is to satisfie his own conscience, the best he can, and doing so, walking, likewise according to his light (which is now principally wanting) it is as much [6] as in equity can be desired; consider that though the bondage of the Presbyters seems not to be included within this Ordinance; yet being and setled, the Ministers having such a foundation to work upon, they will extend it to all, and the Presbyters themselves not complying in all things to their desires, shall by questioning, catechizing, or some other way, be look [sic] within in the verge of its power.

4. Our bretheren the Presbyterians, having no assurance that they shall not change their minds, and therefore it may so fall out, that the rod they provide for their discenting brethren to day, may whip them to morrow, and Mordecaies gallowes, may serve for Hamans execution.

5. We may very well dread the tendensie of the government wch in

its first desires is so rigid and bloody minded, what will it in time grow up to? what will its corruptions arise to? We see how frequent it hath been to pervert the end of Lawes, and extend them beyond the intentions of the Law-makers: The Law against meetings in private, was intended for the security of the Nation against conspiracies and traiterous plottings against the State: But is wasted by the malicious men, and made to serve their turne against the godly people, and men best affected to the State, meeting together to worship and to serve God: The Statute against Recusancy, was intended against Papists, but they frequently put it in execution against the Separation: So that it is very necessary to be provident and causious in making Lawes of this nature: since crafty men have devices in their braine that good men never dreames of; and though the glory of God be the pretence at present; yet upon very good grounds it is to be feared that the principle thing intended in these desires, is to lay ginnes and snares to intrap men with all, to terrifie men from a free and necessary search into the grounds and originall of things, and to dispose all men to an easie and apt beliefe of whatsoever the Synod and learned Church-men shall hold forth. It cannot be, Oh yee lovers of the People, but that you desire the People should be a judicious, knowing & understanding people; a people established and grounded upon solid principles, begotten by serious meditation, and deliberate examination: You cannot but abhor that most superstitious maxime to believe as the Church believes; O doe but consider; what the Clergy men desire; and see whether it amounts to lesse, then to barre all search, enquire, or examination, and in time to believe as the Assembly believes: at least to professe as they professe, or not the contrary upon paine of death, imprisonment, or other punishments. [7]

Certainly if there be need of any ordinance concerning the Assembly it is for their dissolution, and that the Parliament would be pleased to take a survey of their manifould attempts upon them, and that like subtill and bloody Simon & Levy, in the greatest exigents and difficulties of their waightiest affaires, as trusting rather to what necessity might enforce, then what justice would allow. They have been goads in your sides, & thornes in your feet, hindering by frequent & politique stratagems, your progression towards the peoples good and wealfare; be pleased therefore instead of complying with them in these vast and unreasonable desires; admonishing them to labour for humble and contented spirits: and to yeild ready obedience to the commands of Parliament, by whom they are ordained, and whose direction they are to observe without dispute; and that they would not spend their time, and stuffe their sermons with State affaires to beget parties, and factions to carry on their own ambitious designes.

If the Parliament would be pleased to answer their desires thus, and to forbeare to make either Ordinances or Lawes of that nature, which their crueltie hath prompted them to desire, it would manyfest so great a care of the quietnesse of the people as would cause them to blesse their remembrance for ever, and would be their honour to future generations: and is the most zealous desire of all those that would gladly see the quietnesse and happinesse of Parliaments and People.

FINIS [8]

17

A Parable, or Consultation of Physitians upon Master Edwards

[29] October 1646
Reprinted from a copy of the tract in the Thomason Collection in the British Library

A Parable, or Consultation was published anonymously. Printed by Thomas Paine for Giles Calvert, 1646, the tract was not licensed. Walwyn acknowledged the tract as his in 1649.[1]

In the last of his five tracts opposing Edwards, Walwyn employs a dramatic dialogue similar to that used by Richard Overton in *The Araignement of Mr. Persecution*, [8 April] 1645. Walwyn and Overton had collaborated in the drafting of *A Remonstrance of Many Thousand Citizens* in the summer of 1646[2] and it is a reasonable assumption that Walwyn was influenced by Overton's allegorical device. Both tracts are short on subtlety, although *Parable* is at once gentler and more ironic than *The Araignement*. Among the observers who summoned Doctors Love, Justice, Patience, and Truth to minister to Edwards, Walwyn may be discerned in the persona of Conscience whose dialogue provides rich evidence of Walwyn's good humor and generosity of spirit.

Parable is reprinted for the first time in this volume.

A PARABLE,

OR CONSULTATION OF PHYSITIANS UPON MASTER EDWARDS.

Doctors: Love. Justice. Patience. Truth.

Observers: Conscience. Hope. Piety. Superstition. Policie.

A
PARABLE,

OR
CONSVLTATION OF
PHYSITIANS VPON MASTER
EDWARDS.

| Love.
Juſtice.
Patience.
Truth. | } Doctors. | { | Conſcience.
Hope.
Piety.
Superſtition.
Policie. | } Obſervers. |

octob: 29

LONDON, Printed by *Thomas Paine*, for *Giles Calvert*, and are to be ſold at his ſhop at the Black ſpread Eigle, at the weſt end of Pauls Chuich. 1 6 4 6.

Title page of *A Parable, or Consultation of Physitians upon Master Edwards*, 1646. (British Library)

LONDON, Printed by *Thomas Paine*, for *Giles Calvert*, and are to be sold at his shop at the Black spread Eagle, at the west end of Pauls Church. 1646.

To the Reader

Men, for the most part, of all opinions, are bread up with so much feare and scrupulosity, that they no sooner arive to some measure of knowledge in their particular way, but they become meere Pedants; fierce and violent censurers of all things; they are not accustomed to themselves, instantly engaging, and condemning, before they have deliberately examined, or maturely debated the thing they judge: which is an evill and unhappy temper of mind, because unsociable: and proceedeth from want of that generall knowledge, which freedome of consideration would beget.

It is therefore worth our labour, to study how to reduce our minds into the most friendly disposition, to be ready, and alwayes provided of harmlesse and friendly thoughts of men and things, untill evident cause appeare to the contrary; not to looke with an evill or a growling eye, as if we desired to find matter to except against, it is a shrewd signe of disease, when the stomock hankers after unwholesome things. [A2]

It cannot proceed from true Religion rightly understood, to beget melancholly, moody, angry, frampoll Imaginations, for that rightly understood begets cheerfulnesse of spirit: which is ever accompanied with love, and maketh the best construction: for love thinketh no evill: but hopeth all things: and is very kind to all men.

The ensuing discourse, would not need this preparative, but that there is an aptnesse in the most to misconster; and a readinesse to give eare gladly to any that shall shew either wit, passion, or mallice, in finding fault: it is a pitie good people should so easily be deluded: or evill men so easily worke their ends upon them: or good intents be so easily frustrated: the unusualnesse of the Title and method of this discourse will minister occasion to the Weake and to the Perverse: but if the authority, antiquity and use of Parables, be considered with some ingenuity, the Author will not loose to end of his discourse, nor of this preface, which is, to worke amendment in some, where there is cause enough. [A2v]

A PARABLE. Or Consultation of Physitians upon Master EDWARDS.

Doctor Love: Mr. Edwards, I have knowne you long, and have considered your complextion, & inclination; & am no stranger to your alterations and changes: your turnings and returnings: your loathing, and againe liking, one and the same thing: and was alwaies willing to have advised you, to take some fit course in time; as being too well assured, you could not but fall into some desperate distemper; which now we all see hath proved too true: but you ever shunned my acquaintance; and at present, seem so little to regard my words, as if you wished my absence.

Doct. Patience, Sir, excuse him, you see his distemper is very violent.

Doct. Love, Nay Sir, it moves me nothing; nor shall not hinder me from doing him all the good I am able.

Mr. Edwards: Gentlemen, as desperately violent as you judge my distemper; I have not yet lost the use of my sences, I know you all; and have heard Mr. Loves wise exordium: I have known him as long as he has known me, but I was never yet so simple, as to think him wise enough to counsell me, in case I had needed any; nor doe I know by what strange meanes, he or any of you (of his politique tribe) thus thrust your selves upon my privacy.

Piety, Sir, it was my care, and their loves that brought them hither for in my apprehension, you are in a most dangerous condition: and the more, because you are altogether insensible thereof.

Truth, He is either very insensible as you say, or very obstinately desperate.

Mr. Edw. As for both your judgements, I value them no more [1] then I desire your companies: and as for you friend Piety, you and I of late have had no such great familiaritie that you should presume to be thus officious, and indiscreetly troublesome: you see I am not friendlesse, here are friends whose friendship and counsel I much esteem: Pray friends, what is your opinion of me, am I not as sound of wind and limme, as ever I was in my life? have I need think you of the counsell of these learned Doctors or not?

Superstition, Mr. Edwards, you know I am your faithfull friend, I have received much good by you, I would not for anything in the world, the least hurt should befall you: It is from you, I have received that little knowledge and comfort that I have, for which I have not been unthankfull; if it had not been for you, I might ere this have run into one strange Sect or other, but through your care, I keep close to my owne Church, and to the Churches Doctrine, through which I live quietly, and for which I am respected in the place where I live, and may in time be some body in my parish, if not in the City: and there-fore I love you, and will be plaine with you: I professe Sir, I judge the Doctors to be very simple persons, for it is as evident, as the light that is in me, that you are in as perfect a good condition as I my selfe am at this time, and I am confident you will say I were very unwise, to ask their advice.

Conscience. For all this Sir, you must know these Doctors, are of approved judgement and fidelity, and how ever you may desire to be flattered, you very well know, the ignorance and weaknesse of this your friend Superstition, whom yet you sooth and keep company with all, and make to much use off contrary to my counsell: you were better abandon him, and all the advantages you make of him: and whilst you have time, give eare to the counsell of these Doctors: if you neglect this opportunity, you are likely never to have the like.

Super. Sir, you are too rash in judgeing, but Mr. Edwards knows me, and I know him, better then to be estranged by you, or any such as you are.

Justice. By your favour Sir, you may sooner be too rash then he: for what he hath said wee shall find both just and true:

Policy. Truly Mr. Edwards, I am glad I have a further occasion to shew my love unto you at this time: you and I for some yeares now have been bosome friends; you cannot imagine, I meane any other-wise to you, then your owne heart; and I must needs tell you, I do [2] see some symtomes of disease upon you: but what it is, these learned men can best judge: and if I may perswade with you, you shall for your owne good; thankfully except their loves, and submit to their judgements, and directions: but this I must also say, that I evidently see there is no cause of hast, some few dayes hence may be time enough, in which time, you and I shall have setled that busines which you know I am now come about: A work gentlemen, that being finished, your selves will say, was worthy the hazard of his and all our lives; no lesse then the building of Gods owne house, sweeping out of hereticks & schismaticks, stopping the mouthes of illitterate mechanicall preachers: and beautifying this holy building, with the glorious ornament of uniformity, the Mother of peace and all blessed things.

And if it will please these worthy Physitions, and the rest of your friends, to give you and I leave for the present, to goe on with this pious work, and to repaire to you when you shall find cause to call upon them, I think they shall in so doing shew not only a care of you, but of the whole Church of God: nor shall I leave it only to your own care Mr. Edwards, for truly gentlemen, he is too apt to neglect his health and all that is deare unto him, for the good of his brethen: I speake my conscience, and the very truth from my heart and am confident no hurt can come to him, but a great deale of good to the publique; if you allow of this my counsell, and I judge you so prudent and pious, as to preferre the publique, before your owne private trouble.

Cons. Although (Mr. Edwards) when you and I, and your friend Pollicy, are together, and no body else, he alwaies overswaies you, ever proposing things sutable to your corrupted humours, yet now here are others present that can impartially judge betwixt us, and therefore I shall use my accustomed plainnesse, though I have never any thankes for my labour. (Pray Sir, turne not from me, but heare me, and let these worthy men judge betwixt my perswations, and the perswations of Pollicy) gentlemen, I pray observe well this darling of his: This is hee whose councell he hath long time followed, he it was that first inticed him to undertake this unhappy worke, which contrary to all reason and Religion, he calleth the building of Gods house, &c. though I shewed him plainly, he went about therein to destroy the living houses of God: the vexing and molesting of [3] his most deare (because most consciencious and peaceable) servants: though I told him plainly, any that differed with him, might as justly compell him to conforme unto them, as he could compell them: though I manifested that he was as liable to errour, as any that he complained off, and that therefore there was no reason why he should endevour to make men odious for opinions: I shewed him it was impossible, so long as knowledge was imperfect, but men must differ: I shewed how neverthelesse, every man was bound equally as himselfe, to worship God according to his own and not another mans understanding of the word of God. I told him he would bring upon himselfe, the odium of all judicious Religious people.

I put him in remembrance, how extreamly he himselfe complained of compulsion and restriction of worship; in the Bishops times: laid before him their miserable endes, and the great disturbances, that have arisen from thence to the Commonwealth, shewed how much it tended to devision, and confusion, to set up one way of worship and to persecute or dispise all others, that it was not Gods way to bring men to truth by force, but the devills and Antichrists, to fasten men in

errour: that there was no sin more unreasonable nor more odious in
Gods sight, then to enforce men to professe practice, or worship, contrary to knowledge and beleefe: and that to enforce is as justly
punishable by man, as any other violence.

This and much more I told him continually: yet this wretched Pol-
licie finding him ambitious, and covetous, applyed his arguments, to
these his corruptions; and in an instant, swayed him into an engagement: for he said no more but this: if conscience heere will undertake
to secure unto you the honour, domination and profit, due to you as
you are a Clergy man, then follow his councell: but if his, tend to
make you esteemed, but as a lay man, and (not regarding your learning and venerable calling) to mix you amongst the vulgar, and (in
effect) bidds you to labour with your hands the things that are lawfull,
that you may no longer be a receiver of tythes, offerings, &c. but from
your owne labours and sweat, to give to them that need: if he bids
you, having food and rayment be herewith content: and I shew unto
you a way to abound with superflueties, like the men of this world,
and to have a large share in controwling the unlearned, and shall
manifest unto you the [4] defects of the prelatick Clergy, and shall
supply you with rules that cannot faile to effect our desires: then let
you and I joyne our force and councell together.

And if we doe not in the end, share between us all the honours and
glories of this world, saye Machevill was not so wise as Ignatius
loyola the Father of the Jesuites: upon this they struck hands, and
ever since have plyed their work, and though successe hath failed,
and time hath produced contrary effects, those increasing in number,
and reputation, whom they labour to suppresse and defame; though
Mr. Edwards through malencholly, and vexation, be fallen into this
desperate condition, you now see him in: yet you see this wicked
Pollicy labours in a most cunning manner to diswade him from taking
your present councell, least you should direct him for his recovery,
into some such course, as would frustrate his wicked designe, and
deprive him of this his most speciall instrument: this is the intent of
this crafty pollicy.

And if you interpose not with your wisedome, he will prevaile, to
the ruine of this our distressed Friend, for a few houres more, in this
ungodly worke (falsly and deceitfully called the building of Gods
House) will put him past hope of recovery; therefore admit of no delay: but if Piety will help: you, and I, & he and hope: will thrust this
varlet Pollicy downe the stayers, and out of doores, and then I shall
not doubt but some good may be done; come, pray set your hands

too't, suffer him not to speake a word, for he will delude a whole nation, and make you beleeve no man is so godly, or so charitable as he——what a sturdy strong devil it is, you have had so good entertainement heere; you are loth to depart; stand too't Piety; Justice, Love, Truth, (Patience, where are you now; you will still befoole your selfe) down with him,——so out with him, and Ile shut the doore fast enough I hope, for his entrance heere any more: ———how this one ungodly wretch has made us all sweat; Superstition, I thought you would have been so vainly zealous, as to have helpt him, but an you had, you had gone too, but was well you were quiet, you shall now stay and see what usage your woefull friend here finds amongst us.

Love: Conscience, Let us sit still a while: I judge your violence against Pollicy, (being unexpected) hath put our distressed Friend here, into a kind of extacie; let us observe the issue: I doubt not after this, wee shall find him sencible of his distemper, draw the Curtaines close; if he rest twill do well. [5]

Justice, Conscience, I cannot but approve your faithfulnesse to your friend, in the course you have taken against Pollicy I must confesse, had not you by your pertinent discourse, kept my eyes open his subtill speech had deluded me, as I see it did Patience, who was at the doore to be gon, but it is: better as it is: let us consider what is to be done.

Truth, As old as I am, I confesse ingeneously I never yet was called to such a consultation, the distemper is of such a nature, as I have not seene the like, that a man should discourse, labour, studdy, watch, write, and preach, and all these to the continuall vexation of honest, religious, peaceable people, and yet seemeth not to be sencible of any evill he doth therein: though nothing in it selfe be more opposite to the true end of labour, study, writing, or preaching, and what to advise in this case, I professe I am at present to seeke.

Justice, What think you of an issue, if the humors be not too much setled, they may gently, and by degrees be so drawne from him.

Patience, Happily I may speake some what properly of his disease, because I have had much to doe with him of late: and it will be a good step to his cure if we can but discover his disease: All my reading will not furnish me with any definition or denomination I must therefore take the boldnesse to transgresse our common rules, and for your information; coyne a name and call it a fistula in the brayne: whose property is to open, and vent it selfe once a month, and though the matter it issues, be to a sound nostrill the most intolierably odious that can be imagined, yet to himselfe it is not so offensive; and the great profit he makes thereof, makes him beare with the stinke thereof.

For to such as this man is whom you call superstition, nothing sells at a deerer rate, nothing is more exceptable, it is their meat and drink, without it they are as dead men, with it, who but they: and this makes him instead of seeking after a remedy, to studdy how to increase the humour, and nothing shames or grieves him more then when it flowes not monthly having proclaimed a market once every month: as beggers live by their sores so doth he by this fistula, cure him and you undoe him: a Phisitian is as death to him, divers have undertaken him but all his study is how to mischeife them and he only, is welcome, that feeds his humour: I think he speakes pray let's listen. [6]

Mr. Edwards, Welcome Sir, you are very kindly welcome, pray sit downe, I see you faithfully labour, and take paines, in the sweeping of Gods house; come what Rubbish have you discovered—so, I have heard indeed, he is a stirring Sectarie,* but have you nothing else against him, but Rebaptizing and generall redempsion, I had as much before; and have publisht it, with as much reproach as I could, and yet I heare their numbers increase dayly, is there none amongst them, adicted to drunkennesse, or whoredome, or theivery—come, speak all you have, I can not be my selfe in every place, if you bring me not matter to reproach them and they thrive and increase, the fault's yours, and not mine— A Tayler and Porter Preach, whats this now adayes? tis nothing twill doe nothing; they are heard with as much respect as I am: for shame abroad againe, and bring some extreordinary matter, or all our labours lost?

O tis well yee are come—you spake with him your selfe you say, and provoak't him to discourse all you could; what, and bring away nothing? Devillish cunning indeed; ask't two questions, for you one; go, you are simple, and for want of wit, and dilligence, the Sectaries increase dayly, and will doe except you bring something dayly for me to make them odious withall; goe; mend for shame, and let not them out-strip you.

So. tis well you are come—I am almost out of breath, with chiding the simplicity of those I employ as intelligencers:—Your kinsman you say, dyn'de in your company; at your friends house, very familiar you were, and merry; he suspecting nothing, but friendship from you (an

---

* His Intelligencers are here supposed to bring him informations.

excellent oppertunity) well, and there he uttered the words in your note, which you say, you can safely swear to——Yes, you did say you could sweare to it? and why should you now scruple it, since you presume it is truth? Well leave me your note.

I shall now pay this great Favourorite of the Sectaries, your note shall not be lost, nor a little of it, never feare it: pray be continually watchfull in this great worke, you know your labour shall not be lost.

I thought I should have seen no body to day: I am glad yet you have not forgot the worke: A great meeting you say, and a Petition read, somewhat tending to liberty of conscience; and they talk of the [7] King, and the Parliament, and assembly, and Scots, and the Army, and you were there all the while: but whats all this, without some perticular words that can be taken hold off.

Ile not give a rush for such informations, can you make me believe, so many Sectaries could be together, and nothing to be, taken hold off; away for shame, be sure you be at next meeting, and take somebody with you, that is able to bring away somewhat to purpose; begon I say.

O come, I have been so vext, men bring a great deale of circumstance. but no substance at all: What is it you have got: —Mr. Peters you say, spoke the words in this paper: you are sure of it: and M. John Goodwin these in this paper: and Mr. Kiffen these: this the copy of a letter written from the North: A woman dipt, and dyed tenne daies after: and this the parties name that dipt her: An Anabaptists wife very well in health, and in five daies dead of the Plague: so, you have no more you say; truly yee have done very commendably; never feare the losse of your trade.

Ile take a care, some friends I have shall be better to you then twise your trade: Olack, I would not for any thing you had forgot it: is that active youth (say you) suspected to be a Jesuite; you say you have strong presumption of it; and what is said by him you wot on—How an Atheist and blasphemer—and the other a drinker, and loose companion: truly I am glad I know it: if I doe not set them out to the life; let me Perish: heres matter worth the publishing: this will be welcome newes to my deere friend Pollicy, who is now setting the greater wheeles a going, and hath prevailed very farre already; nor doe I doubt, but all will be as he and I doe wish; but I must be carefull to keepe all close from my busie companion Conscience, hee's one that knowes too much of my secrets, and I know not well how to be rid of him; I think Pollicy and I must cach him alone, and stifle him.

Love, How strangely his mind runnes upon the unhappy worke, he hath undertaken: if we interupt him not, he will spend all his spirits, and expire in this extacy: Conscience, pray take hold on this occasion, and speake to him.

Conscience, Mr. Edwards, I know all your proceedings, observe all your waies, and have ever faithfully advised you for your good to [8] leave the wayes of Pollicy, and to walke in the waies of Christ; but you are so farre from following my advice, that you lay plots to stifle me; but?

Truth, Conscience, save your labour: your voice no sooner sounded in his eares, but he fell fast asleep, tis wonderous sad to consider, but I hope the issue will be good.

Justice, Twere but just, he should never wake; I never observed the most wicked man in the world, delight in so abominable a worke.

Patience, Deare Justice, Let us take this oppertunity, to consult what may be done for his recovery? for that is now our worke.

Piety, I pray yee friends, bring the light and come hither, I begin to smell the most filthy savour that ever was smelt; see, see, what a black froth his mouth fomes with all; see, it riseth more and more, some thing must be brought to receive it from him: out upon't, I am not able to hold the light any longer, if it continue thus, we shall no be able to endure the roome.

Superstition, Pray let me doe that office, I wish I might never have a better sent, I am sure some of you smell of ranke heresie, if I mistake, not.

Truth, Wee must beare with your weaknesse, till you are better informed, how abundantly it flowes: he is now extreame weake: but were he in his wonted strength, with this most filthy Gangrenous matter, would he mix his inke, and whilst it were even hot, and boyling, fall to writing as he hath done lately, some huge volumne; with which he poysons the spirits of thousands (otherwise) well minded people; and fils them with a violent, musterfull disposition, with which they goe up and downe, vexing and molesting all they meet, if any man refuse to doe as they would have them, in the worship of God (though never so peaceable and well minded) him they revile, at him they raile, call him Anabaptist, Independent, Brownist, Seeker, Antinomian: worry and vex him, by all the waies and meanes they can: instigate the Magistrate, and rude people, to wearie them out of all societyes: and will joyne with their owne enemies, to their owne ruine, rather then these should have a quiet life amongst them: It flowes extreamely stoop him a little (humillity is alwaies good) I feare it will blister his mouth, it is so hot, but I hope it will all come from him, and then wee shall have no more to doe, but to get out the bagge for that must be done, other wise the humour will fill againe, and he will never be perfectly cured. [9]

Hope, Sir, the couler begins to alter from its blacknesse, and turneth red.

Patience, There is now some hope of a good event: it doth not smell so strongly:

Love, Pray hold this soveraigne Pomander to his nostrill, lest his spirits faint.

Piety, I should be exceeding glad to see his recovery, which if he doe, truly Conscience, you deserve the greatest thankes.

Justice, There comes now perfect blood; my opinion is, wee must instantly proceed to open his head, and take out the blader, and in roome thereof, to leave some ingredients, proper for rectifying the temper of the brain and to bring it into a good constitution. I have instruments ready, and he sleeps very soundly.

Love.	Wee all agree: but let us be very tender: Superstition,
Patience.	you had best withdraw a little, lest you fall into a sound, or
Truth.	your hand shake: give the light to Piety: Conscience and
	Hope, lend us your helpe: who should that be that knocks
	so loud, Conscience, pray step and see————

Conscience, What an inpudent wretch is this? who should it be but Pollicy, returnd in a grave Doctors habit, pretending to be sent hither, by a Colledge of friends, to lend his assistance: twas well I went to the doore, for he would have deceived any that had not knowne him so well as I, he was so like a Collegiate, sure his familier tels him, his agent is likely to be dispossest; but I have sent him packing, with a vengeance: pray goe on with your worke.

Justice, I pray bow him a little more to me-ward, so, give the pan to superstition, I am not able to stand neere it.

Piety, Rather let it be burnt, for Superstition is too much infected already.

Conscience, By no meanes, Ile keep it untill my friend wakes, that he may see, what filthy matter, his head was stuft with all.

Piety, It is well considered: and if he loath the avon [sic] himselfe, his cure will the better appeare to us to be perfect.

Love, Doe ye not lance too deep think you? Pray be very carefull.

Justice, Pray Piety hold the light neerer: come all hither, see what mighty large bag it is, I professe I never saw the like—except in the late head of great CANTERBURY; but it was not discovered till after his death: but the savour of this is much worse; what shall we doe with it, [10] now we have it out? sure it is best to reserve it, to shew him with the matter it contained, otherwise he will never beleeve it: and I pray be all ready, with your severall ingredients to fill up the empty place, that the humours may be rectified; and that thence may issue forth, no more such unsavory pestilent matter, odious to good men, but such as may bring honour to God, and peace to all good men: come let us see what wee have amongst us, for this work will admit of no delay.

Love, I have a most excellent powder, the maine agent therein, being the eyes of Turtle doves: and the property thereof, is to expell all sinister apprehentions, and hard constructions of men and things.

Justice, I have a balsome; approved by long experience, for the clensing, and drying, of all violent, hot, and grosse humours.

Patience, I have found much profit, by carrying about me the well known plant, called Al-heale: and I judge it very usefull in this cure.

Truth, I have an ingredient, which though of a strange nature, yet without it, I am parswaded the cure cannot be perfect: it is an extraction from the braine of a Serpent: which gives quicknesse of apprehension and foresight.

Justice, I pray you truth be carefull you ecceed not the just proportion, because if you should, yould marre all: Hope, what think you of our course.

Hope, I approve thereof, so farre as I understand: but here is Piety, is better able to judge.

Piety, I exceedingly approve of all: and if you please Ile mix them and work them into a body, and forme the same, fit for the place: and then Justice, when you please you may goe on with your worke.

Justice content:——so——tis very well he stirs not: Ile close up all, and wee will all with draw, and leave him to rest: for rest now will be his best friend: Conscience weele pray you to stay with him: if he stirre youle call us, weel be but in the next roome.

Love, This Conscience is of true temper to make a friend off, he neither flatters nor feares: no unkindnesse alienates him, nor danger affrights him, from doing the office of a true friend at all times: one would not be without such a friend, for anything in the world: this distressed man hath extreamly abused him; and yet you see with what fervency of affection he sticks to him.

Justice, I know abundance of the name, and of his kindred, and truly all the generation of them are such. [11]

Patience, Whence is hee, is he a Scholler? What profession is he off?

Truth, I never saw no signes of schollership in him; nor doth he make any profession (that I know of) of any one calling now in use: but he is of a wonderous publique spirit: you shall have him at all meetings, that are for publique good, finding fault with the lazinesse of one sort of men, with want of charity in another, with pride and disdaine in another: telling them they glory to be esteemed Christians, and talke much of Religion, go much to Church, heare and read, and pray, and fast frequently, because these are the cheapest parts of Religion; but to deliver the captive, and set the oppressed free, or to feed the hungry, cloath the naked, or visit the Fatherlesse Widowes, to all these they are very backward, when they are called to these, one hath a great family, another hath married a wife, another hath but one servant at home, & cannot be spared from his trade, & getting of mony; I says he, you are rare christians that can aboud in this worlds goods, & see your brother lack.

His dealing is so plaine, & to the point; that very few regard his company, and that's the reason, those great meetings produce so little good as they do; for without his company, you shall never see any effect worthy the name of Christian: he hath had no breeding, neither in the Universities, or Ins of Court: never was a Courtier, nor Trauailer; & yet he is ignorant of nothing: & speaks very shrewdly to purpose; owneth every just & publick cause, without respect to persons or opinions: he will not weare finer cloathes, if you would give them to him gratis: & yet to an ingenious & vertuous man, there is not a more pleasant companion.

Hope, Pray yee, what Religion is he off.

Truth, For matter of outward formes, he is very reserved, as if he were not fully satisfied; I have often heard him say, God is a Spirit, and will be worshipped in spirit and truth: but he professeth himselfe, to be clearely for liberty of worship; and the greatest enemy to compulsion or restriction that can be; affirming there is no sinne so unreasonable, or un-Christian, as for one man (especially one erring man) to persecute, punish, or molest another for matters of Religion, or to make Lawes, concerning any thing supernaturall: he saies it proceeds not from any savour of Christianity, that men doe so: but from an imperious domineering spirit, that takes it in foule scorne, that any man should doe any thing, but by Licence from him: I assure yee Conscience allowes no such dealing; and this is the maine quarrell twixt him, and our Patient Mr. Edwardse but I hope wee shall see them good friends againe. [12]

Superstition, Well, if this man dye under your hands, your lives shall go for his: Ile take my oath, you are the cause of his death. Piety, Spare your teares, Superstition, you shall find we have done him a good office, you will see him a new man: and your selfe too I doubt not ere long,

Conscience, Hoe, friends, pray yee all come in quickly.

Love. ⎫
Justice. ⎬ Whats the matter?
&c. ⎭

Conscience, Doe you see this posture wherein he lyeth? thus he hath layne about a quarter of an houre, his lips moving, his hands and eyes lifted up, just as if he were praying in the Pulpit.

Hope, It is very wonderfull: He takes notice of nobody, what will be the issue? See, he now strives as if he would raise himselfe, as if his prayer were ended, and he were preparing to Preach; Conscience, help to hold him up, and see what he will doe: certainly he supposeth himselfe to be in some great presence, for just thus is his manner at such times—peace, and listen for he begins to speake.

Mr. Edwards, Men of England, my purpose is not now (as formerly) to promote my owne work: but to prosecute what is just and necessary, without respect of persons, or opinions: which hath occasioned me to make choice of this place of Scripture.

The whole commandement is fulfilled in this one word, LOVE.

It hath often come to my thoughts why the Apostle Saint John is called in a peculer manner, the Disciple whom Jesus loved; but it never made so deep impression in me as at present: certainly there could be nothing more joyous to his own spirit, then to consider it; and my heart at present panting after the reason thereof: tels me that John certainly was of a mild, a loving, and tender disposition, more eminently then any of the rest; so soft, that our Saviour chose his brest, for a place of his repose: and I am strengthened herein, because I find it recorded of him, that when he was so old that he was hardly able to come in to the speaking place, or to speake, he prosecuted this most blessed and amiable theame: little children love one another, repeating it often, little children love one another: as having throughly disgested this lesson of his Masters: the whole commandement is fulfilled in this one word LOVE; Love is the true touch-stone of all Christian performances, it instantly manifesteth how things are; so much love, so much of God [13]

It is the surest guide in all private and publique undertakings; without a due regard to the rule of love, all things will goe wrong: observe it, & it will be like the North pole to the Marriners, to guide you to the quiet harbour of justice and peace: it is a rule easie to be understood, the meanest capacity is capable thereof, none can excuse themselves that swarve from this rule.

If you would know your duty to God, it will tell you that in equity you are to love, as he hath loved: hath he so loved, as to give himselfe an offering and a sacrifice for you, then ye ought to walke in love as Christ hath loved; would you know how you should manifest your love to Christ? Love will set before you the sick, the naked, the aged, and impotent; it will lead you to prisons, and houses of distresse, and shew you the captives, the widowes and fatherlesse Children, and it will assure you that in as much as you ministred to the necessities of these, you have done it unto him, but if you have this worlds goods, and see, and suffer these, or any of these to lack, there is not the love of God in you.

Would you have a rule for your conversations? Why, *the love of God which bringeth salvation to all men, hath appeared teaching us to deny all ungodlinesse and worldly lusts, and to live righteously, godly, and soberly in this present world:* Are yee publique persons? Are yee intrusted to judge righteously in all causes: Love is the best property even in a judge, for God is Love, who is the righteous judge of all the earth, and slayeth not the righteous with the wicked: Love (rightly so called) putteth no difference betweene high and low, rich and poore, but loveth all men (as they are men) alike: but the proper object of Love is vertue, the more vertuous, the more it loveth; the lesse vertuous, the lesse it loveth: what so ever justly deserveth the name of infirmity, Love can beare with all: but it is contrary to its nature to beare with wickednesse, because mercy to the wicked, tends to the ruine of the just, and so becomes the greatest cruelty: Love is just, as God is; spares not the greatest, for his greatnesse, nor the wealthy for his money, nor any for any by respect; so that hold but up your love to God, and you can never be partiall in judgement.

Love doth as it would be done unto, in which respect it is a motive to the compleat performance of trust: for would it not grieve you to have your love abused, in the trust you have given for your good: doubtlesse it would? Why then (sayes Love) grieve not those that have loved [14] and trusted you: but be watchfull for their safety; tender of their freedomes, and then you shall certainly reape the fruite of love, which is an aboundance of love and reall thankfulnesse.

Are you in dispute what you shall doe in matters of Religion! take Love along with you, to light you through this laborinth, whence never any Authority returned without prejudice? Say now, is Religion of that nature that you can referre it to him (whom you must love) to set you rules in such sort, as you can assure your selfe, you shall without sinne obay those rules.

Nay when your friend hath done all he can doe; are you not to follow your own understanding of the word of God & not his? and if you doe not so, doe you not sin? if so, how can any trust Religion? And if none can trust, none can be trusted? And love will never meddle with matters not intrusted, by way of injunction, but only by perswasion: whilst we live here knowledge will be imperfect, and whilest it is so, that which seemeth truth to one, seemeth an errour to an other: If I now shall be so unadvised, as to call him an heretique who differs from me, I doe but provoke him to call me so, for he is as confident of his, as I am of my judgement: and here the rule of Love is broken, that ought not to love in reference to opinion but according to vertue and godlynesse of conversation; for this were a way otherwise, to bring all into confusion, there being so many severall opinions; if one should revile and reproach another, with the names of Heretiques and schismatiques, Anabaptist, Brownist, Antinomian, Seeker, Sectarie, Presbyter, this tends to nothing but to devide the honest party, and to make way for your common enemy; for in whatsoever the true and evident rule of Love is broken, it tends to dissolution, it being love that preserveth all things.

Therefore my humble advice is in this great cause, (upon which more dependeth, then is presently seen) that you give not countenance to one before another, for that begets a high conceite in those you favour, and makes them dispise all others, though they may be as nigh the truth as those; in the one you beget pride, in the other feare; the fruit of both being the worst that can come to any people; none are now infallible, truth and errour are two easily mistaken; but love; is easily understood; to doe as you would be done unto, is a rule generally agreed on.

Let those that conceive they can justly submit their consciences to [15] others arbitration in the worship of God, give in their names for themselves and the places they represent; I beleeve upon a little consideration few would be found; tis not what formerly hath been done, but what may justly be done, that is to beare sway with all true reformers; No man hath been more earnest then I, for compelling all to uniformity, and for punishment of all contrary practisers, but I now see my errour; and will doe all I can to make amends for the evill I have done; the books I have written, I will burne with my owne hand: for I judge no opinion so evill as molestation for Religion.

What I have in hand, shall never see the light, because I now see it to be a work of darknesse, and I exceedingly rejoyce that I have this opportunity to declare thus much before you: if ever men shall kindly be brought to be of one mind, I see it must be by liberty of discourse, and liberty of writing; we must not pretend to more infallible certenty then other men, this distinction of Clergy and layety, how I loath it, Ile no longer abuse the world therewith, nor with any thing appertaining there unto, I will henceforth magnifie nothing but love: I am the devoted servant of Love, and his lovely companions, Justice, Patience, truth, Piety. and Conscience, shall be my fortresse to defend me from the wiles and force of Machiavilian Pollicy: O Love! how thou hast melted me, how thou hast refined me, and made me all new; perfect thy worke O! Love, that I may become all love, and nothing but love.

Piety, Here is a happy change indeed: certainly the cure is absolute, we have great comfort of our poore indeavours: how his discourse fell at last from the publique to his particular content: my advice is, that wee all silently depart, and let all things be removed as if no man had been here: as for you Conscience, I know you will not leave him, and when he wakes, your presence doubtlesse will be most acceptable.

FINIS [16]

18

A Still and Soft Voice from the Scriptures, Witnessing Them to Be the Word of God

[March–April?] 1647
Reprinted from a copy of the tract in the McAlpin Collection at the Union Theological Seminary

A Still and Soft Voice, signed "By William Walwyn, Merchant," was published without imprint "in the Yeare, 1647." The tract was not secured by George Thomason, but *Walwyns Just Defence* places the time of publication within a few weeks of the appearance of the Large Petition of March 1646/7.[1]

Walwyn wrote *A Still and Soft Voice* on the advice of Henry Brandriff, who, wrote Walwyn, was "my then intimate friend." Brandriff was also a member of John Goodwin's congregation, and he persuaded Walwyn that he could disarm his Independent adversaries by owning his belief in the Scriptures.[2] Walwyn believed that his treatise was well received by Goodwin's followers,[3] but it is not surprising that, in fact, it failed to reassure them. The tract not only reveals Walwyn's own religious creed: it defends the right of enquiry and examination of all beliefs and draws a sharp distinction between the joys of "true Religion"—which manifests itself in loving deeds "as becometh the Gospell of Christ"—and the mockery of "educated, customary or superstitious Religion"—which ignores Scripture and encourages bigotry.[4] The argument is rational, the tone is quiet, and in places Walwyn all but pleads for understanding.[5] At the same time, the unpleasant portrait of those who practice customary or superstitious religion foreshadows the harsh denunciations of many Dissenters in *The Vanitie of the Present Churches* (No. 21).

A
STILL AND SOFT VOICE
From the Scriptures,

VVitneffing them to be the VVord of God.

I Kings. 19. 11. 12.

And he faid (to Eliah) come out and ſtand upon the Mount before the Lord. And behold the Lord Went by, and a mighty ſtrong wind rent the Mountaines and brake the Rocks before the Lord, but the Lord was not in the Wind, and after the Wind came an Earth-quake, but the Lord Was not in the Earth-quake.

And after the Earth-quake came fire, but the Lord was not in the fire, and after the fire came a ſtill and ſoft voice. And when Eliah heard it, he covered his face With a Mantle, &c.

Printed in the Yeare, 1647.

Title page of *A Still and Soft Voice*, 1647. (Rare Book and Special Collections Library, University of Illinois at Urbana-Champaign)

A Still and Soft Voice is reprinted in Don M. Wolfe, *Milton in the Puritan Revolution* (New York, 1941), Appendix 2.

A STILL AND SOFT VOICE From the Scriptures, Witnessing them to be the Word of God.

I Kings. 19. 11. 12. *And he said (to Eliah) come out and stand upon the Mount before the Lord. And behold the Lord went by, and a mighty strong wind rent the Mountaines and brake the Rocks before the Lord, but the Lord was not in the Wind, and after the wind came an Earthquake, but the Lord was not in the Earth-quake.*

And after the Earth-quake came fire, but the Lord was not in the fire, and after the fire came a still and soft voice. And when Eliah heard it, he covered his face with a Mantle, &c.

Printed in the Yeare, 1647.

A Still and Soft Voice.

As he who is arrived to the full age of a man, and seriously considers, the severall passages and progresse of his fore past life: what he did or understood, when he was a child, a youth, a young man; a meere man, or before he came to be advised, and to consider all things by true rules of reason: is best able to deale with every one in every age and condition, to shew them their vanity, ignorance and mistakings: and to point them out the path of virtue. Experience making the best Schoole-master in things naturall and morall.

Even so is it in Religion, he only can best judge, advise and counsell others, who hath observed and most seriously considered the severall passages and progresse of his owne knowledge in things divine: yet who are so forward to judge and comptrole therein, as meere smatterers and such as have least experience.

I suppose it will be acknowledged, by all experienced Christians, that the greatest number of men and women in the world, are drawne into the consideration and Practice of Religion, by education, and custome of the place where they are bred: and that [3] many never have any other foundation, nor motive to continue therein, then the reputation it brings them: all other religions or wayes of worship being discountenanced and out of credit, such as these are Champions for whats in fashion: ever running with the streame, and crying downe all contrary minded; *Vox populi, Vox dei*, the Major voice (then which nothing is more uncertain in Religion) is to these as the voice of God: and when they are zealous for vulgar opinions they thinke they are zealous for God and his truth: when they revile, abuse, and hale men before the Magistrates, and even kill and destroy them, they think they doe God good service: being zealous of the traditions of the times: for though truth should be publickly professed: yet to such as hold it only by education and custome: it is in them traditionall, and they are not truly religious; but meere morrall christians: utterly ignorrant of the cleare Heavenly brightnesse, inherent, in pure and undefiled Religion.

But though it be evident, that there are too too many, who hold their religion, on this fraile foundation, yet it is very comfortable to behold, the sincerity of multitudes of good people in our dayes: who; not content to possesse their knowledg in a traditionall way: doe accustome themselves to try and examine all things.

Yet as it is a hard thing unto men, bred so vainly as most men are, to keepe the golden meane, in naturall or morrall Reformations: so is it difficult to preserve from extreames, in matters of religion, the reason is, because in our tryalls and examinati [4] ons, we have not that heedfull care, which is absolutely necessary, to free our Judgments from absurdityes or improper things: common and vulgar arguments catching fast hold upon us too suddenly; and so we engage over violently, averring and maintayning without giving due time to our consideration to worke and debate itselfe into necessary conclusions.

The first sort of these religious persons: are deadly enemies to examination and tryall of things, we (say they) are not fit to Judge of these matters *ne sutor ultra crepidam,* is commonly in their mouthes: the Cobler ought not to goe beyond his last: what are the learned for, if these high things fall within the compasse of our capacities, why chuse wee wise and juditious men, more able then our selves, but to reforme, and settle Religion: if you draw them into any discourse, and endeavour to shew them their weakenesse, their only aime is how to entrap you, in your words, and if it be possible to make you obnoctious to authority.

If their ignorance and superstition appeare so grosse and palpable, that (in loving tearmes, and for their better information,) you demand how they come to know there is a God, or that the scriptures are the word of God: their common answer is, doe you deny them: it seems you doe? otherwise why doe you aske such questions? if they offer to proove by some common received argument: and you shew the weaknesse thereof: they'le goe nigh to tell you to your face, and report for certaine behind your back, to all they know, or can know, that you are an Athiest, that you deny there is a God, and deny the [5] Scriptures to be the word of God: nor doe they hate any sort of men so much, as those who are inquisitive after knowledge, judgeing them as busie bodyes, men of unquiet spirits, that know not when they are well, or when they have sufficient: for their parts, they are constant in one, for the substance; their principles are not of yesterday but of many yeares standing: and the most learned and wise are of their way, and why should not others be as well content as they, is it fit (say they) that every one should follow his owne understanding in the worship of God, wee see what comes of it; when men once forsake the beaten Road (the Kings high way) in Religion, into how many by-pathes, doe they runne, nay, whether would they not runne, if our care were not to hedg and keepe them in.

And thus ignorance becomes many times Judge of knowledge: and the most grosse and slothfull; comptroler of the most active in Religion.

Of this sort of men there are very many; and they are made very much use of by worldly Pollititians, who have found by constant experience, that superstition is the easiest meanes to lead a multitude, this way, or that way as their occasions and purposes may require, and on the contrary, that true Religion is in it selfe as oppsite to their unjust ends, as it is to superstition and therefore if they observe any man who out of the principles of true Religion opposeth their ends; at him they let loose these ignorant and morrall christians, furnish them with reproachfull tales, and falshoods, against him, call him Athiest Infidell, Heritick, Scismatick, any thing: which is as eagerly effected, as wickedly devised: and how to stop these mens mouthes is in my apprehention [6] no lesse a worke then to make white a Blackamore.

Those others who are startled in their consciences, and roused by the word of God, out of this worldly way of religion, or running with the streame, it is a hard matter to hold them to a due pace, in the persute of necessary knowledge or to keepe them to a propper Method, or to obtaine this of them, that they receive nothing as a truth, which they see admiteth of an obsurdity.

But having broke loose from the bands of educated and customary religion, through necessity of conscience, and being anew to begin, they are apt hastily to take in, that which is first offered with any resemblance of truth, and so in an instant, fall into new entanglements.

For if hast, make wast in any thing, it is in pursute after knowledge: and though every considerate mans experience findeth this a truth: though it be confest by all, that there is nothing of greater concernment to man, then the truth of his Divine knowledge: though nothing doth more disturb the minde of man, then error and mistakeing in religion.

Yet is there not any thing wherein men: proceed more irregularly, or more impatiently: either they are over rash and sudden or over fearfull, and irresolute: they approach all discourse with prejudice, and a mind distempered, searching nothing throughly or orderly, but content themselves with an overly examination, and (in my apprehention) are not so disingenious in any thing, as in religion: willingly resigning and forfeiting their understandings, and Judgments, at a cheap rate then Esau did his Birthright: and so continue very long (not truly religious, [7] but) superstitious men, always amazed: neither remembring what themselves or others speake: he that once opposeth them, hath a Wolfe by the eares, hee can neither speake, nor hold his peace, without damage, they take allthings in the worst sence sigh, lament, pitty, or censure, all that sutes not with their opinion or practice: and talk or report of, any man, any thing that comes in their imaginations; those that come behind them in knowledge; are carnall: those before them desperate And therefore it may be very profitable; that the differences betwene true Religion and superstition, be made knowne to these times, more fully than it is, the one being commonly taken for the other.

Now both are best knowne by their effects: for true Religion setleth a man in peace and rest: makes him like unto the Angels, always praising God and saying Glory to God on High, in earth peace, Good will towards men, it is ever provided with good intentions and good desires, maketh the best construction in doubtfull cases, see how true Christian love is described by the Apostle in the 13. to the Corinths. and that is the true Religious mans Character.

On the contrary, superstition troubleth and makes a man wilde, a superstitious man suffereth neither God nor man to live in peace, (as one well observeth from experience) he aprehendeth God, as one anxious, spiteful, hardly contented easily moved, with difficulty appeased, examining our actions after the human fashion of a severe Judge, that watcheth our steps, which hee prooveth true by his manner of serving him, hee trembleth for feare is never secure, fearing he never doth well, and that he hath left [8] some thing undone, by omission whereof, all is worth nothing that he hath done.

But generally now a dayes, (contrary to former tymes) the superstitious mans devotion costs him litle, he hath somuch worldly wit in his zeale, as to save his purse, hot and fiery against heresie and blasphemy, (which are titles he freely bestowes on all opinions, contrary to his own, true or false), he will course his poor neighbour out of all he hath, yea out of the Nation, if he can not course him into his opinion: and all upon pretence of doing God service and for the good of his soule.

As for his body, or estate, thats no part of his care, hee is not so hasty to runn into his poore neighbours house, to see what is wanting there, hee may ly upon a bed, or no bed, covering or no covering, be starved through cold and hunger, over burthened with labour, be sick, lame or diseased: and all this troubles not the superstitious mans (nor the morall Christians) Conscience: he may through want and necessity goe into what prison he will, and ly and rott and starve there: and these kind of Religious people are not halfe so much moved at it, as if he goe to another Church or congregation, then what they approove: if hee doe so, upstarts their zeale; and after him, watch, spy, accuse and informe: and all for the good of his soule: and for the Glory of God.

One would not think it were possible man could be so blind, or so inconsiderate as to immagin, that God would be thus mocked, thus madly served, contrary to the whole tenor of the Scriptures, but such are the effects of educated, customary or superstitious Religion.

Whilst the effects of pure and undefiled Religion, are another thing: as Feeding the hungry, Cloathing the naked, Visiting the sick, the Fatherlesse, the Widdowes and Priso [9] ners: and in all things walking as becometh the Gospell of Christ: it will empty the fullest Baggs: and pluck downe the highest plumes.

And whoever serveth God sincerely in this Religion, shall be knowne by his fruites: his light shall so shine before men, that they seeing his good Workes, shall Glorify our Father which is in heaven.

But of these there are few to bee found; and as few that truly labour, to reclaime those many thousands of miserable people that are drencht all their life long in grosse ignorance, and notorious loathsome wickednesse: *Yet there is joy in heaven over one sinner that repen-*

teth, more then for ninety nine just persons that need no repentance: Why talke wee so much of Christianity, holinesse, and saintship, whilst wee neglect the lost sheep, or the recovery of our brethren from those Errors of their wayes.

The plain truth is, this grosse neglect of known duty herein, and the generall eagernesse in the lesse necessary parts of zeale and devotion, manifesteth the world is not subdued; that there is little selfe-deniall, little of pure and undefiled Religion as yet in the world: men content themselves with forms of godlinesse, but are regardlesse of the power thereof.

And therefore I have been the lesse troubled in my selfe; for the hard measure I have found: amidst so great a mixture of worldlinesse, ignorance, and superstitious zeale, why should one looke for much ingenuity, these times have but cast an eye towards the materiall parts of true Christianity: It is not yet knowne what it is, in its excellency, the end and issue thereof, is too good to bee deserved, or discerned, by a people that are not yet broad awake, they strike him that brings them more light; then they can well endure.

All the evill and reproach I have suffered, hath beene by occasion of my forwardnesse to do others good: my freenesse [10] in discourse, though harmlesse in it selfe, and intended for good, hath been perverted, misconstrued, and made use of to my prejudice.

I accompt nothing more vain, then to discourse meerly for discourse sake, nay, it is painfull and ircksome to me, to heare a discourse that is not really necessary and usefull, nor doe I know, that I have ever purposely set my self to debate any serious matter, slightly or carelessely, though cheerefully.

And my manner is, whatever is in debate, to search it thorowly, being of an opinion, that, what is really true, stands the firmer, for being shaken: like a house that is built upon a rock.

I have been much troubled, to observe men earnestly engage to maintaine the strongest maximes and principles by weak arguments; the weaknesse whereof, I have endevoured to manifest, that I might discover the weaknesse of such practises, and to make it evident, that fundamentall truthes support all things, and need no supporters: *Thou bearest not the root, but the root, thee.*

But this my free dealing (with uncharitable or superstitious people) hath found this evill returne, they have reported me, to deny that there is a God, when I have only denyed the validity of a weak argument, produced to prove that there is a God; it being too too common to insist upon meere notionall indigested arguments: so also have I been most uncharitably slandered to deny the Scriptures to bee the word of God, because I have opposed insufficient arguments produced to prove them such: and because at the same time I have refused to shew the grounds inducing me to beleeve them.

Now it hath been my lot to be drawne into discourses of this nature for the most part by timerous, scrupulous, people, in whom, I have discovered so much impatience, and discontent, at the shaking of their arguments, that I have not discerned any reason to open my selfe at that time; yet I never [11] parted with any of them, but I alwayes professed that I did believe, both that there is a God, & that the Scriptures are the Word of God, though I judged their grounds not good; and withall, that if they would be so ingenious as to acknowledge the weaknesse of their arguments, I would then shew them my ground of faith; or if at any time they stood in need, I would not be wanting to the uttermost of my power to supply them, but I have seldome found any, who in the heat of contest and prosecution of dispute, have been qualified, to receive, what I had to say, touching this matter, their apprehension and mine being at too great a distance therein.

But I blesse God it is not so ill with me, as some bad minded men desire, nor as some weak and scrupulous men imagin.

And there are some ingenious men, with whom I have daily converst, that know I doe acknowledge and beleeve there is a God, and that the Scriptures are the Word of God.

Yet the testimony of men in this case to mee is little; my owne conscience being as a thousand witnesses.

That there is a God: I did never beleeve through any convincing power I have ever discerned by my utmost consideration of any natural argument or reason I ever heard or read: But it is an unexpressible power, that in a forcible manner constraines my understanding to acknowledge and beleeve that there is a God, and so to beleeve that I am fully perswaded there is no considerat man in the world but doth believe there is a God.

And, *That the Scriptures are the Word of God*, I shall clearly make the same profession, That I have not beleeved them so to be, by force of any argument I have ever heard or read, I rather find by experience, most, if not all arguments, produced in prejudice thereof: (Art, argument, and compulsive [12] power, in this case holding resemblance with the mighty strong wind, the Earth quake and fire, distracting, terrifying and scorching the minds of men) but I beleeve them through an irresistible perswasive power that from within them (like unto the soft still voyce wherein God was) hath pierced my judgment and affection in such sort, that with aboundance of joy and gladnesse I beleeve, and in beleeving have that Peace which passeth all utterance or expression; and which hath appeared unto me after so many sad conflicts of a distracted conscience, and wounded spirit, that it is to me a heaven upon earth: It being now long since, I blesse God, that I can truly say, *My heart is fixed, O God, my heart is fixed, I will sing and give praise:* In other respects, I conceive the most holy upon earth, if they give impartiall eare to this voyce, will finde no cause to boast or to finde fault with others, but as Eliah to cover their faces with a mantle.

And truly were it not that too too many pretenders to Religion, are over apt to receive false reports (which is a most uncharitable disposition) and over prone to make the worse construction, which is altogether unchristian, it had beene impossible for any to have abused me in these or any other respects.

But it will be needfull for all such, seriously to lay to heart, *that they ought to do as they would be done unto in all things, that he who seemeth to bee religious and bridles not his tongue, that mans religion is vaine.*

That he who boasteth *to beleeve a God,* and *the Scriptures to be the Word of God,* and glorieth in his ability of exposition thereof: yet applieth it to the discovery of a mote in his brothers eye, rather then a beame in his own: he whose expressions and actions do demonstrate him to say within himselfe, *Lord I thank thee, I am not as other men, extortioners, unjust adulterers, nor as this Publican:* This man who ever he be, is not [13] yet got through the lesson of the Pharisies; that were wise in their owne eyes, and despised others.

But it would be much more profitable to society and good neighbourhood that there were a more exact accompt taken by every man of his owne wayes; it is verily thought most men neede not goe abroad for want of work, if either pride, covetousnesse, backbiting, unreasonable jealosy, vanity of minde, dotage upon superfluities: with hard heartedness to the poore: were thought worthy of Reformation.

To be zealous in lipp service, or to expresse our devotion, in censuring of others, yeelds neither honour to God, nor good to man.

Who were more blinde, then those who said are wee blind, also? the Angell of the Church of Laodicea, boasted that he was rich, and increased with goods and had neede of nothing: and knew not that he was wretched, and misserable and poor and blind and naked.

Wee have many now a dayes, who are doubly unjust and thinke

not of it: they are partiall and favourable in examining and corecting of themselves: and severe towards others, when as they ought to be severe towards themselves: and favourable towards others.

And it is a fault not easily mended: it requires a greater power of true religion to doe it, then the most have as yet attained, if one may judge by the Fruites: and therefore it will be good for every one to neglect that which is behinde, and to presse forward to the marke, for the price of the high Calling of God which is in Jesus Christ: either renounce the Name, or let your practice demonstrate, that you are a Christian.

Hee who greedily receiveth a hard report of his neighbour, is not provided of charitable and loving thoughts as he ought; and if he report any evill, before he be certaine of the [14] truth thereof, hee is a slanderer; and when hee is certaine it is true, if he report it with delight, it argues him of malice.

He who is glad of his neighbours defamation, would not be sory at his ruine: a slanderer would be a murderer but for feare: and therefore, every honest vertuous religious man should shun a slanderer, as he would shun a Serpent.

And thus having said enough to free my self from this slander (if religious people will but study ingenuity, which hath been too much wanting amongst them) the whole course of my actions, writings and discourses, evidencing the contrary to all that throughly know me: and this my profession being added to, satisfie those that know me but by hearsay: I have done: judging it a small thing to be judged of any, or of mans judgement; *Who art thou that judgest another mans servant, to his owne master, hee standeth or falleth.*

The liberty of my native Country, and the freedome of all consciencious people hath been, and still is pretious in my esteeme: nor shall I be discouraged (by any the unworthy slanders cast upon me) from a just and due prosecution of both, according to my place and calling: I shall make bold to deceive the deceiver and his instruments therein: I should be glad to see the Educated and customary morall Christians become Christians indeed, and cease to persecute: I should exceedingly rejoyce to see the superstitious, become really religious, and to see babes; become strong men in Christ, and all bend their endevours to deliver the captive, and set the oppressed free, to reclaime the vicious, and to labour the saving of the lost sheep of the house of England: To see Charity abound, and all envy, malice, and worldly mindednesse to cease for ever, and not to be named amongst us, as becommeth Saints indeed: to see all men ingenious, loving, friendly and tender-hearted one towards another: but I must neither be silent, nor slothfull till I see it, nor sorow as one with- [15] out hope of seeing it: but through evill report, and good report, do my duty? patiently expecting a good issue? laboring in all estates to be content; knowing there is no temptation hath taken hold upon others, but may befall unto me. In the mean time, knowing all terrestriall things to be but vain and transitory, my chiefest comfort is, that I desire to know *Nothing save Jesus Christ and him crucified:* accounting all things as losse and dung, that I may be found in Christ, not having my own righteousnesse which is of the Law, but the righteousnesse which is of God in him.

I have no quarrell to any man, either for unbeleefe or misbeleefe, because I judge no man beleeveth any thing, but what he cannot choose but beleeve; it is misery enough to want the comfort of true beleeving, and I judge the most convincing argument that any man can hold forth unto another, to prove himselfe a true sincere beleever, is to practice to the uttermost that which his faith binds him unto: more of the deeds of Christians, and fewer of the arguments would doe a great deale more good to the establishing of those that stagger: It being not the leaves but the fruit that nourisheth and carrieth the seed with it, Shew me thy faith by thy workes; If I have all faith and have not love, I am as sounding brasse, or as a tinckling cymball, if faith worke, it workes by love: Let us all therefore hence-forth walk in love, even as Christ hath loved, and hath given himselfe an offering and a sacrifice for us: to whom bee glory and dominion for ever. *Amen.*

By WILLIAM WALWYN, *Merchant:*   *(there being a Minister*
                                          of the same name.)

FINIS [16]

19

Gold Tried in the Fire; or, The Burnt Petitions Revived

[14 June] 1647
Reprinted from a copy of the tract in the California State Library, Sutro Branch, San Francisco

Gold Tried in the Fire was published anonymously, without separate title page, imprint, or date. It includes "A Preface" and copies of four petitions and a "Certificate" addressed to the House of Commons between March and 2 June 1647.[1] The version of the four petitions in *Gold*, the version in John Lilburne's *Rash Oaths Unwarrantable* ([25 June] 1647), and the separate issue of the Large Petition collected by George Thomason in September 1648 (E. 464 [19*]) vary in capitalization, punctuation, spelling, and paragraphing. There are also small differences in phrases, but the texts are essentially the same.

William Haller, unaware that the four petitions were published with the Preface, stated in 1934 that the Preface and the Large Petition (the first of the four) "were undoubtedly the work of Walwyn. No other writer among the Levellers could have put the case so clearly, so incisively, or with so much dignity and intelligence. At a later time, moreover, Walwyn said that his ideas on government would be found in 'that large petition that was burnt by the common Hangman.'"[2]

Haller's attribution is strengthened by attendant circumstances and the content of the Preface and the petitions. The account of events surrounding the petitions that is set forth in the Preface to *Gold* is paralleled in *Walwyns Just Defence* in passages in which Walwyn notes without denial that the Large Petition has been attributed to him.[3] Walwyn also states that John Price, "his Friends and mine," joined to advance the "last and most sharp" petition of 2 June.[4] Price subsequently published a harsh attack on Walwyn, finding "one of the great Masterpeeces of his craft and subtilty, viz. in the framing, ordering and managing" of Leveller petitions.[5] *Gold's* Preface and the 2 June petition oppose changes in the London militia that were further protested in July when Walwyn visited army headquarters at Reading.[6]

The Preface concludes with a judgment that no good can be expected from the Parliament as presently constituted. But even as he condemns "the sons of Zeruiah" the author emphasizes that "if the endeavours of the good Common-wealths-men in the House could have prevailed, these Petitions had not been burnt; nor the Petitioners abused." And he ends on a characteristic note of trust in God, confidence in the future, and a call to men to "not sorrow . . . nor be discouraged, but goe on and persist, for the just liberties of England."[7] Like the petitions published with it, the Preface to *Gold Tried in the Fire* is quintessentially Walwyn. No other Leveller, as Haller observes, could have put the case so well.

The Preface to *Gold* is reprinted as Walwyn's work in *Freedom in Arms*, ed. A. L. Morton (London, 1975), No. 4. A facsimile of Thomason's copy of the Large Petition (dated 19 September 1648) is reproduced in *Tracts on Liberty*, ed. Haller, 3:399–405. The same text is reprinted as "likely to have been" from Walwyn's pen in *Levellers in the English Revolution*, ed. Aylmer, No. 5. The version of the Large Petition published by Lilburne in *Rash Oaths Unwarrantable*, pp. 29–35, is reprinted as a collaborative work which was chiefly drafted by Walwyn in *Leveller Manifestoes*, ed. Wolfe, No. 2, and in *Freedom in Arms*, ed. Morton, No. 2.

Gold Tried in the Fire is reprinted in its entirety for the first time in this volume.

Gold tried in the fire, *or* The burnt Petitions revived.

A Preface.

Courteous Reader, I shall give thee a short Narative of some passages upon the following Petitions, first concerning the large Petition: Divers printed coppies thereof being sent abroad to gaine subscriptions, one whereof was intercepted by an Informer, and so brought to the hands of Mr. Glyn Recorder of London, and a member of the Commons House; who was pleased to call it a scandalous, and seditious paper: Whereupon it was referred to Colonell Leighes Committee (it being that Committee appoynted to receive informations against those men who preached without licence from the Ordainers) to finde out the Authours of the said Petition; upon this a certificate being drawn up, and intended by the Petitioners, to have been delivered to the said Committee, for vindication of the said Petition, as will appeare by the certificate herewith printed; and notice being taken of one of the petitioners named Nicholas Tue, who red the said certificate in the Court of Request; for the Concurrence of friends who had not formerly seen nor subscribed the certificate: and for his so doing he was sent for presently before the said Committee, and for refusing to answer to Interrogatories, was presently by them Committed, and still remaineth in prison, it being at the least three Moneths since his first commitment.

Likewise Major Tuledah, was upon complaint of that Committee, the next day committed by the House, but since discharged [A1] upon baile, without any just cause shewn for either of their Commitments: and others of the Petitioners abused, and vilified by that Committee; some of them offering to draw their swords upon the Petitioners. All which, with more was ready to be proved to the whole House, but could by no meanes be obtained, though earnestly desired, by a Petition, presently delivered into the House, humbly desiring the examination of these miscarriages; but after eight weekes attendance, with much importunity; after many promises and dayes appointed to take their Petition into consideration, they obtained a very slight answer: which was that they could not like of their Petition.

Occasion being taken sodainely after to commit one of the Petitioners named Mr. Browne to the prison of Newgate; for his importunity in desiring an answer to that Petition, after many promises and delayes. Shortly after the slight answer obtained to the said Petition, the Petitioners thought good to deliver a second Petition to the House, to see if it were possible to obtain a better answer to their just desires; hoping that they would better consider of things, but after attendance and importunity, they obtained an answer in these words. That the Parliament had Voted it a breach of priviledge, scandalous, and seditious, and that Petition, and the large Petition, to be burned by the hand of the Hangman; which was accordingly done by Order of the House, in these words.

Die Jovis 20 *May,* 1647,

Resolved &c. That the Sheriffes of London and Middlesex, be required, to take care that the Petition and paper be burnt, which accordingly was done, before the Exchange, two dayes after the said Vote and Order of the House.

And shortly after this the Petitioners prepared a third Petition, which is the last Petition herewith printed: and after much importunity with the Members of the House; after almost two dayes attendance, obtained so much favour from one of the Members, as to present that Petition to the House, and after all this could obtaine no other answer to that Petition; [A1v] but the House after long dispute thereupon passed this Vote.

Upon the 2d. of June 1647. That no answer shall be given to the Petition at the present: and two dayes after the Petitioners attended the House, for a further answer delivering copies of their Petition to the severall Members of the House, but could obtaine no further answer thereunto; but received many vilifying, and disgracefull speeches, from severall Members of the House: and so after a whole dayes attendance, departed without any hope, to receive any answer to their just desires in the said Petition.

And thus I have faithfully, and truly (though briefly) given ye an account of the proceedings upon the ensuing Petitions. Now let the judicious and considerate Reader judge whether the Petitioners have received equall and even dealing herein from this present Parliament: the Petitioners being such who have laid out themselves, both in their persons and purses, far above their abilities; who have not valued their lives, their childrens lives, nor their servants lives, nor estates, to deare for the service of the Parliament and Common-wealth.

And is this the reward they shall receive, after they have thus laid out themselves? Nay, they have just cause to feare that they and their friends are men appointed to utter ruine, and destruction; otherwise what meaneth all the rayling, reviling, and reproachfull speeches of their Ministers, and Agents, out of the pulpit and presse, to stirre up the rude multitude to fall upon them, and destroy them; is not this ingratitude in the highest degree, shall not the very Heathen rise up in judgement against such a generation, of degenerate men as these? Who could say, *Si ingratum dixeris, omnia dixeris.*

You cannot chuse but take notice of severall Remonstrances, and Petitions presented to the House from these men, who call themselves Lord Major, Aldermen and Commons, of the City of London in Common-councell assembled, what high affronts they have offered to the

Parliament; yet they have in some measure by steps, and degrees, answered the Remonstrances, and granted their Petitions, and you may observe what answer they have given to their last Petition, for raising of Horse, &c. (The tendencie whereof may be of very dangerous conse- [A2] quence if well weighed) which is thus. Mr. Speaker by command of the House, exprest unto them the true sense the House hath of their constant good affections to this Parliament; and that no alterations whatsoever can work any change in their duty, and love; for which he is to give them the hartiest thanks of this House.

I could enlarge my selfe, but I affect brevitie, and the judicious and considerate Reader may enlarge himselfe in his own thoughts: well weighing the matter in the said Remonstrances, and Petitions; and upon due consideration may judge whether their Petitions, or the Petitions burnt, vilified, and disgraced, deserve most thanks, or tend most to the safetie of the Parliament, and Common-wealth.

And will henceforth conclude, that as there is little good to be hoped for from such Parliaments, as need to be Petitioned; so there is none at all to be expected from those that burn such Petitions as these.

If the endeavours of good Common-wealths-men in the House could have prevailed, these Petitions had not been burnt, nor the Petitioners abused; but the sons of Zeruiah were to strong for them, that is to say, the Malignants, and Delinquents, the Lawyers (some few excepted) the Monopolising merchants, the sons and servants of the Lords; all these joyning together, over Voted them about 16 Voyces; but God in time, will we trust, deliver the people of this Nation, from their deceipt, and malice; and therefore let us not sorrow as men without hope, nor be discouraged, but goe on and persist, for the just liberties of England, a word to the wise is sufficient. Farewell.

By a well-wisher to truth and peace.

Printed in the yeere 1647.[A2v]

To the Right Honourable, and supreame Authority of this Nation, the COMMONS in PARLIAMENT Assembled.

The humble Petition of many Thousands, earnestly desiring the glory of God, the freedom of the Common-wealth, & the peace of all Men.

Sheweth,

That as no Government is more just in the constitution, then that of Parliaments, having its foundation in the free choyce of the people;

and as the end of all Government is the safety and freedome of the governed, even so the people of this Nation in all times, have manifested most hearty affection, unto Parliaments as the most proper remedy of their grievances; yet such hath been the wicked policies of those who from time to time have endevoured to bring this Nation into bondage; that they have in all times either by the disuse or abuse of Parliaments deprived the people of their hopes: For testimony whereof the late times foregoing this Parliament will sadly witnesse, when it was not only made a crime to mention a Parliament, but either the pretended negative voyce, (the most destructive to freedome) or a speedy dissolution, blasted the fruite and benefit thereof, whilst the whole Land was overspread with all kinds of oppression and tyranny, extending both to Soule and Body, and that in so rooted and setled a way, that the complaints of the people in generall witnessed, that they would have given any thing in the world for one six moneths freedome of Parliament. Which hath been since evidenced in their instant and constant readinesse of assistance to this present Parliament, exceeding the records of all former ages, and wherein God hath blessed them with their first desires, making this Parliament the most absolute and free of any Parliament that ever was, and enabling it with power sufficient to deliver the whole Nation from all kinds of oppressions and grievances, though of never so long continuance, and to make it the most absolute and free Nation in the world.

And it is most thankfully acknowledged that yee have in order to the freedome of the people suppressed the High-Commission, Starr-Chamber, and Councel-Table, called home the banished, delivered such as were imprisoned for matters of conscience, and brought some Delinquents to deserved punishment. That yee have suppressed the Bishops and Popish Lords, abolished Episcopacy, and that kinde of Prelatick persecuting government. That ye have taken away Ship-money, and all [1] the new illegall Patents, whereby the hearts of all the wel-affected were enlarged and filled with a confident hope, that they should have seen long ere this a compleate removall of all grievances, and the whole people delivered from all oppressions over Soule or Body: But such is our misery, that after the expence of so much precious time, of blood, and treasure, and the ruine of so many thousands, of honest families in recovering our Liberties, wee still finde this Nation oppressed with grievances of the same destructive nature as formerly, though under other notions; and which are so much the more grievous unto us, because they are inflicted in the very time of this present Parliament, under God, the hope of the oppressed. For, as then all the men and women in England, were made lyable to the Sommons, Attatchments, Sentences, and Imprisonments of the Lords of the Councell-boord, so wee finde by wofull experience and sufferings of many particular persons, that the present Lords doe assume and exercise the same power, then which nothing is, or can be more repugnant and destructive to the Commons just liberties.

As the unjust power of Star-Chamber was exercised in compelling of men and women to answer to Interrogatories tending to accuse themselves and others; so is the same now frequently practized upon divers persons, even your cordiall friends, that have been, and still are, punished for refusing to Answer to questions against themselves and nearest relations. As then the great oppression of the High Commission was most evident in molesting of godly peaceable people, for non-conformity, or different opinion and practice in Religion, judging all who were contrary minded to themselves, to be Hereticks, Sectaries, Schismaticks, seditious, factious, enemies to the State, and the like; and under great penalties forbidding all persons, not licenced by them, to preach or publish the Gospel: Even so now at this day, the very same, if not greater molestations, are set on foot, and violently prosecuted by the instigation of a Clergie no more infallible then the former, to the extreame discouragement and affliction of many thousands of your faithfull adherents, who are not satisfyed that controversies in Religion can be trusted to the compulsive regulation of any: And after the Bishops were suppressed, did hope never to have seen such a power assumed by any in this Nation any more.

And although all new illegall patents are by you abolished, yet the oppressive Monopoly of Merchant-adventurers, and others, doe still remain to the great abridgement of the liberties of the people, and to the extreame prejudice of all such industrious people as depend on cloathing, or other woollen manufacture, (it being the Staple-commodity of this Nation,) and to the great discouragment & disadvantage of all sorts of Tradesmen, Sea-faring-men, and hinderance of Shipping and Navigation. Also the old tedious and chargeable way of deciding controversies, or suits in Law, is continued to this day, to the extream vexation and utter undoing of multitudes of Families; a grievance as great and as pal- [2] pable as any in the world. Likewise, that old, but most unequall punishment of malefactors is still continued, whereby mens lives and liberties are as liable to the law, and corporall pains as much inflicted for small as for great offences, and that most unjustly upon the testimony of one witnesse, contrary both to the

Law of God, and common equity, a grievance very great, but little regarded. Also tythes, and other inforced maintenance are still continued, though there be no ground for either under the Gospel; and though the same have occasioned multitudes of suits, quarrels, and debates, both in former and later times. In like manner, multitudes of poore distressed prisoners for debt, lye still unregarded, in a most miserable & wofull condition throughout the Land, to the great reproach of this Nation. Likewise Prison-Keepers, or Gaolers, are as presumptuous as ever they were, both in receiving and detaining of prisoners illegally committed, as cruell & inhumane to all, especially to such as are wel-affected, as oppressive & extorting in their Fees, & are attended with under-officers, of such vile & unchristian demeanour, as is most abominable. Also thousands of men & women, are still (as formerly) permitted to live in beggery and wickednesse all their life long, and to breed their children to the same idle and vitious course of life, and no effectuall means used to reclaime either, or to reduce them to any vertue or industry.

And last, as those who found themselves aggrieved formerly at the burthens & oppressions of those times, that did not conforme to the Church-government then established, refused to pay Ship-money, or yeeld obedience to unjust Patents, were reviled and reproached with nicknames of Puritans, Hereticks, Schismaticks, Sectaries, or were termed factious or seditious, men of turbulent spirits, despisers of government, & disturbers of the publick peace; even so is it at this day in al respects, with those who shew any sensibility of the fore-recited grievances, or move in any manner or measure for remedy thereof, all the reproaches, evils, and mischiefes that can be devised, are thought too few or too little to be laid upon them, as Round-heads, Sectaries, Independents, Hereticks, Schismaticks, factious, seditious, rebellious, disturbers of the publick peace, destroyers of all civill relation, & subordinations; yea, and beyond what was formerly, Nonconformity is now judged a sufficient cause to disable any person, though of known fidelity, from bearing any Office of trust in the Common-wealth, whiles Newters, Malignants, and dis-affected are admitted and continued. And though it be not now made a crime to mention a Parliament, yet is it little lesse to mention the supreme power of this honourable House. So that in all these respects, this Nation remaineth in a very sad & disconsolate condition; & the more, because it is thus with us after so long a session of so powerfull & so free a Parliament, & which hath been so made and maintained, by the aboundant love and liberall effusion of the blood of the people. And therefore knowing no danger nor thraldome like unto our being left in this most sad condition by this Parliament, and observing that yee are now drawing the great and weighty affaires of this Nation to some kinde of con- [3] clusion and fearing that yee may ere long be obstructed by something equally evill to a negative voyce, and that yee may be induced to lay by that strength, which (under God) hath hitherto made you powerfull to all good works: whiles we have yet time to hope, and ye power to help, and least by our silence wee might be guilty of that ruine, and slavery which without your speedy help is like to fall upon us, your selves and the whole Nation; wee have presumed to spread our cause thus plainly and largely before you: And doe most earnestly intreat, that yee will stir up your affections to a zealous love and tender regard of the people, who have chosen and trusted you, and, that yee will seriously consider, that the end of their trust, was freedome and deliverance from all kinde of grievances and oppressions.

1. And that therefore in the first place, yee will be exceeding carefull to preserve your just authority from all prejudices of a negative voyce in any person or persons whomsoever, which may disable you from making that happy return unto the people which they justly expect, and that yee will not bee induced to lay by your strength, untill yee have satisfied your understandings in the undoubted security of your selves, and of those who have voluntarily and faithfully adhered unto you in all your extremities; and untill yee have secured and setled the Common-wealth in solid peace and true freedome, which is the end of the primitive institution of all governments.

2. That yee will take off all Sentences, Fines, and imprisonments imposed on Commoners, by any whomsoever, without due course of Law, or judgement of their equals; and to give due reparations to all those who have been so injuriously dealt withall, and for preventing the like for time to come, that ye will Enact all such Arbitrary proceedings, to bee capitall crimes.

3. That yee will permit no authority whatsoever, to compell any person or persons to answer to questions against themselves, or nearest relations, except in cases of private interest between party and party in a legall way, and to release all such as suffer by imprisonment, or otherwise for refusing to answer to such Interrogatories.

4. That all Statutes, Oaths, and Covenants may be repealed so farre as they tend, or may be construed to the molestation and ensnaring of religious, peaceable wel-affected people, for non-conformity, or different opinion or practice in religion.

5. That no man for preaching or publishing his opinion in Religion in a peaceable way, may be punished or persecuted as hereticall, by Judges that are not infallible, but may be mistaken (as well as other men) in their judgements, lest upon pretence of suppressing Errors, Sects, or Schismes, the most necessary truths, and sincere professors thereof, may bee suppressed, as upon the like pretence it hath been in all ages.

6. That yee will, for the incouragement of industrious people, dissolve that old [4] oppressive Company of Merchant-Adventurers, and the like, and prevent all such others by great penalties, for ever.

7. That ye will settle a just speedy playn and unburthensome way, for deciding of controversies and suits in Law, and reduce all Lawes to the nearest agreement with Christianity, and publish them in the English Tongue, and that all processes and proceedings, therein may be true, and also in English, and in the most usuall Character of writing, without any abbreviations, that each one who can reade, may the better understand their own affaires; and that the duty of all Judges, Officers and practisers in the Law, and of all Magistrates and Officers in the Commonwealth may be prescribed, and their fees limitted, under strict penalties, and published in Print to the view and knowledge of all men: by which just and equitable means, this Nation shal be for ever freed of an oppression more burthensome, & troublesome then all the oppressions hitherto by this Parliament removed.

8. That the life of no person may bee taken away, under the testimony of two witnesses at least, of honest conversation; and that in an equitable way yee will proportion punishments to offences, that so no mans life may be taken, his body punished, nor his Estate forfeited, but upon such weighty and considerable causes as justly deserve such punishments; and that all prisoners may have a speedy tryall, that they bee neither starved, nor their families ruined, by long and lingering imprisonment; and that imprisonment may be used onely for safe custody, untill time of tryall, and not as a punishment for offences.

9. That tythes and all other enforced maintenance, may be for ever abolished, and nothing in place thereof imposed; but that all Ministers may be paid onely by those who voluntarily chuse them, and contract with them for their labours.

10. That yee will take some speedy and effectuall course to relieve all such prisoners for debt, as are altogether unable to pay, that they may not perish in prison through the hard-heartednesse of their

Creditors; and that all such as have any estates, may be inforced to make payment accordingly, and not shelter themselves in Prison to defraud their Creditors.

11. That none may be Prison-keepers, but such as are of approved honesty, and that they may be prohibited under great penalties to receive or detain any person or persons without lawfull warrant; That their usage of prisoners, may be with gentlenesse and civility, their fees moderate and certain, and that they may give security for the good behaviour of their under-Officers.

12. That yee will provide some powerfull meanes to keep men, women, and children, from begging and wickednesse, that this Nation may bee no longer a shame to Christianity therein.

13. That yee will restrain and discountenance the malice and impudency of impious Persons, in their reviling and reproaching the wel-affected, with the ignominious titles of Round-heads, factious, seditious, and the like, whereby your [5] real friends have been a long time, and still are exceedingly wronged, discouraged, and made obnoxious to rude and prophane people, and that yee will not exclude any of approved fidelity from bearing office of trust in the Commonwealth for non-conformity; rather neuters, and such as manifest disaffection or opposition to common-freedome, the admission, and continuation of such being the chiefe cause of all our grievances.

These remedies, or what other shall seeme more effectuall to your grave wisdomes, wee humbly pray may be speedily applyed and that in doing thereof, yee will bee confident of the assistance of your Petitioners, and of all considerate well-minded people, to the uttermost of their best abilities, against all opposition whatsoever, looking upon our selves as more concerned now at last to make a good end, then at the first to have made a good beginning: For what shall it profit us, or what remedy can we expect, if now after so great troubles and miseries this Nation should be left by this Parliament in so great a thraldome, both of body, minde, and estate?

We beseech you therefore, that with all your might whilest ye have time, freedome and power, so effectually to fulfill the true end of Parliaments in delivering this Nation from these and all other grievances, that none may presume, or dare to introduce the like for ever.

And wee trust, the God of your good successe, will manifest the sincerity of our intentions herein, and that our humble desires are such as tend not onely to our own particular, but to the generall good of the Common-wealth, and proper for this Honorable House to grant, without which this Nation cannot be safe or happy; And that he will blesse you with true Christian fortitude, suitable to the trust and greatnesse of the worke yee have undertaken, and make the memory of this Parliament blessed to all succeeding Generations.

Shall ever be the prayer of your humble Petitioners.

To the Right Honourable, the Commons of England assembled in Parliament.

The humble Petition of divers well-affected Citizens.

Sheweth,

That as the oppressions of this Nation, in times fore-going this Parliament, were so numerous & burthensome, as will never be forgotten; so were the hopes of our deliverance by this Parliament, exceeding great and full of confidence, which as they were strengthened by many Acts of yours in the beginning, especially towards consciencious people, without respect unto their judgements or opinions; So did the gratitude [6] of well-minded people exceed all president or example, sparing neither estates, limbs, liberties, or lives, to make good the authority of this Honorable House, as the foundation and root of all just freedome.

And although wee many times observed to our griefe, some proceedings holding resemblance rather with our former bondage, then with that just freedome wee expected: yet did wee impute the same to the troublesomnesse of the times of warre, patiently and silently passing them over, as undoubtedly hoping a perfect remedy so soon as the warrs were ended: but perceiving our expectations altogether frustrate, wee conceived our selves bound in conscience, and in duty to God, to set before you the generall grievances of the Commonwealth, and the earnest desires of ingenious well-minded people; and for that end did ingage in promoting the Petition in question, in the usuall and approved way of gathering subscriptions, with full intention to present the same to this Honourable House, so soon as it should bee in readinesse: but as it appeareth, a Copy thereof was unduly obtained, and tendred to this Honourable House, under the notion of a dangerous and seditious Paper: Whereupon this House was pleased to order the Petition to the Committee, whereof Col. Lee is Chair-man; and Mr. Lambe, at whose House it was said to be found, to be there examined concerning the same.

Whereupon your Petitioners conceived it their duty to own and avouch the said Petition, and for that end, in a peaceable manner attended that Committee with this humble Certificate hereunto annexed, to bee offered to their wisdomes as opportunity should be ministred: but through some small miscarriage of some few persons (for which your Petitioners were much grieved) your Committee took so sudain and high displeasure, as to command your Petitioners to withdraw, threatning to remove them with a guard, before they had time to turn themselves.

Whereupon your Petitioners caused the Certificate to bee publikely read in the Court of Requests, to take the sense and allowance of many persons, who had not before seen the same, with intent still to present it; which though endeavoured to the utmost, was absolutely refused to bee received. But to our astonishment, occasion was taken against our friend that read the same, so farre, as that hee stands a prisoner to that Committee, and much harsh language, with threatenings and provocations issued from some of the Committee, towards some other of our friends, purposely (as we verily beleeve) to get some advantage, to present us odious to this Honourable House, whose persons and authority hath been as deare in our esteeme as our very lives. And therefore, wee have just cause to complaine to this Honorable House. [7]

1. Of unjust useage from those that indevoured to interupt the gathering of hands in a peaceable way, or to possesse this Honourable House with evill suggestions concerning the intention & purpose of the said Petition.

2. Of hard measure from your Committee in the particulars forementioned, contrary to what wee have deserved, or should have found in former times.

3. Neverthelesse, our liberties, to promote Petitions to this Honourable House, is so essentiall to our freedome, (our condition, without the same being absolute slavery) and our hope of justice from this Honourable House, [is so essentiall to our freedome, our condition, without the same being absolute slavery: and our hope of justice from this Honorable House,]* so great in protecting us therein, that wee are not discouraged by what hath passed; but in confidence thereof, do humbly intreat,

First, That ye will bee pleased to declare our freedome, to promote,

* The repeated passage within brackets is evidently a misprint. (Editors' note)

and your readinesse to receive the said Petition, which wee cannot but still looke upon, as tending the generall good of this Nation.

Secondly, That our friends may bee inlarged, and that Yee will discountenance the officiousness of such over-busie informers, as have disturbed the just progresse of that Petition.

Wee are not ignorant, that wee have been, and are like to bee represented unto you, as Heretickes, Schismatikes, Sectaries, seditious persons and Enemies to Civill-government, and the like: but our said Petition is sufficient to stop the mouthes of such Calumniators, and declare us to bee not only sollicitors for our own particulars, but for the generall good of the Common-wealth, and will minister a just occasion to suspect the designes of those, that so frequently asperse us, though their pretences bee never so specious. And trust your wisdomes will timeously discover and prevent any evill intended against us.

And whereas Major Tuledah stands committed by Order of this Honourable House, for some conceived misbehaviour towards some Members of your said Committee; we humbly intreat, that he may be forthwith called to your Barre, and be permitted to answer for himselfe, and that witnesses also may bee heard on his behalfe, that so this Honourable House may bee rightly and fully informed, concerning his cause and demeanour of those Members, the suddain imprisonment of our friends being very grievous unto us.

And your Petitioners shall pray. [8]

To the Honourable Committee of Parliament, sitting in the Queenes Court at Westminister, Colonell Lee being Chair-man.

The Humble Certificate of divers persons interested in, and avouching the Petition lately referred to this Committee by the Right Honourable House of Commons.

Humbly certifying:

That the Petition (entituled, The humble Petition of many thousands, earnestly desiring the glory of God, the freedome of the Common-wealth, and the peace of all men, and directed to the Right Honourable, and supreame authority of this Nation, the Commons assembled in Parliament) is no scandalous or seditious Paper (as hath been unjustly suggested) but a reall Petition, subscribed, and to bee subscribed, by none but constant cordiall friends to Parliament and Common-Wealth, and to bee presented to that Honourable House with all possible speed, as an especiall meanes, to procure the universall good of this long inthralled, and distracted Nation; and wee trust this Honourable Committee will in no measure dishearten the people from presenting their humble considerations, Reasons, and Petitions, to those whom they have chosen (there being no other due and legall way wherein those that are aggrieved can find redresse) but that rather you will bee pleased to give all incouragement therein: In assured hope whereof, wee shall pray.

To the Right Honourable, the Commons of *England* assembled in PARLIAMENT.

The humble Petition of divers well-affected people in and about the City of LONDON.

Sheweth,

That as the authority of this Honorable House is intrusted by the people for remedy of their grievances, so hath it been their accustomed and undoubted liberty in a peaceable manner to present unto this House whatsoever they deemed to be particular or generall grievances: And as yee gave encouragement unto others in the use of this just Liberty, reproving such as endeavoured to obstruct the peaceable promoting of Petitions, so did wee verily hope to have found the like Countenance and protection in promoting our large Petition: but no sooner was the promoting thereof discovered but Mr. Glin Recorder as is commonly reported, hastily & untimely brought it into this House, exclaiming against it, as a most dangerous and seditious Paper, and shortly after the Common-councell in like manner prejudged it, as guilty of [9] danger and sedition, though both without any grounds or reasons affixed, that wee know of.

And as the worke of Mr. Recorder was the occasion (as wee conceive) of an enquirie after the promoters, so also of the hard measure we found at Col. Lieghs Committee, where occasion was suddenly taken to threaten our removal by a guard, to imprison Nicholas Tew, one of the Petitioners, the rest being reviled with odious titles of factious and seditious sectaries, & Major Tulidah another of the Petitioners, not onely reviled and reproached as the rest, but violently hauled, and most boysterously used by Sir Philip Stapleton, and Col. Hollis, who made offer as if they would draw their Swords upon the Petitioners, and Sir Walter Earle lifting up his Cane in a most threatening manner, tooke another by the Shoulder: all which is ready to be certified by sufficient witnesses, and which wee do verily beleeve was done purposely, out of their hatred to the matter of the Petition, to render us as a turbulent people to this Honourable House, to beget a dislike of our Petition, and to frustrate our endeavours in promoting thereof.

Unto which their misinformation of this honourable House, as wee have cause to suspect, may be imputed the occasion of the sudden imprisonment of Major Tulidah without hearing of him, and our so long and tedious attendance for answer to our last Petition, and Certificate, and the misapprehension of this honourable House of our desires in that Petition: For we did not desire (as your answer importeth) that this House should declare their liking or disliking of our large Petition, being not then promoted nor presented by us, but that you will bee pleased to vindicate our Liberty, to promote that Petition, notwithstanding the hard measure we had found, and the aspersions cast upon it, to release the party imprisoned by the Committee, meaning Nicholas Tew, to discountenance those that obstructed the gathering of subscriptions, to call Major Tuledah to your Barre, and to heare witnesses on his behalfe, that so ye might also be rightly informed, as of his cause, so of the demeanour of some Members of that Committee.

Now for as much as the more wee consider the generall grievances of the Common-wealth, the greater cause wee still finde of Promoting the Large Petition, as not discerning any thing of danger therein, except to some corruptions yet remaining, nor of sedition, except as before this Parliament it be in some mens esteems seditious to move, though in the most peaceable manner for remedy of the most palpable grievances: and for as much as wee are hopefull this Honourable House will in due time have good use thereof, for discovery of such as are engaged either directly or by Relations in those corruptions, for removall whereof the Petition is intended, and not knowing for what end so great an effusion of the blood of the people hath been made, except to procure at the least the Particulars desired in that Petition, and that we might know our selves so farre at least to be free men and not slaves, as to be at Liberty to promote Petitions in a peaceable way, to be Judges of the matter thereof, and for our time of presenting them to this Honorable House, without let or Circumvention.

We humbly intreat that you will bee pleased

1. To weigh in Equall ballance the carriage of Mr. Recorder, and that of the Common-Councell in this weighty cause of prejudging Petitions; and to deale with them as the cause deserveth.

2. To consider of how evill consequence it is, for your Committees to assume a power of imprisoning mens persons, without your Commission, and that yee will not pass over this in this Committee. [10]

3. To receive the Testimonies concerning Sir Philip Stapleton, Coll. Hollis, and Sir Walter Earle, and to deale with them according to the ill consequence of their violent demeanour, and misinformation of this honourable House, tending to no lesse then the obstruction of Petitions, the greatest mischiefe that can befall a people in time of Parliament.

4. That Nicholas Tew may be wholly enlarged, and that no man may henceforth bee committed by an arbitrary power, as hee at the first was, nor without cause shewed, though by lawfull authority.

5. That yee will as yet suspend your sense of our large Petition, untill such time as the Petitioners shall judge it fit to present the same as a Petition unto your wisdomes.

And as in duty bound, wee shall pray &c.

To the Right Honourable the Commons of *England* Assembled in Parliament.

The humble Petition of many thousands of well-affected people.

Sheweth

That having seriously considered what an uncontroulled liberty hath generally been taken, publiquely to reproach, and make odious persons of eminent and constant good affection to Parliament and common-wealth, how prevalent indeavours have been, to withhold such from being chosen into places of trust or Counsell, how easie to molest, or get them into prisons, how exceedingly liable to misconstruction, their motions and Petitions in behalfe of the publique have lately been.

When we consider what grudgings and repinings, have sinistrously been begotten, against your most faithfull and successefull Army: what arts and devises, to provoke you against them, and to make you jealous of them; what hard measure some of them, both Officers and Souldiers have found in divers respects, in sundry places.

When we consider what change of late hath importunately (though causelessly) been procured of the Committee of Militia in the City of London, and how that new Committee hath already begun to remove from Command, in the Trained Bands and Auxiliaries, persons not to be suspected of disaffection or newtrality, but such as have been most zealous, in promoting the safety of Parliament and City.

When wee consider how full of Armies our neighbor Countries are round about us, and what threatnings of foraine forces, we are even astonished with griefe, as not able to free our selves from apprehensions of eminent danger but are strongly induced to feare some evill intentions of some desperate and willfull persons, yet powerfully working, to blast the just ends of this Parliament, and re-imbroile this late bleeding and much wasted Nation, in more violent wars, distempers and miseries.

And as our earnest desires of the quiet and safety of the Commonwealth, hath necessitated these our most sad observations: So are we constrained to beleeve, that so dangerous an alteration, could not so generally have appeared, but that there is some great alteration befalne, both in counsels and authorities throughout the Land: which we verily conceive ariseth from no other cause, but from the treacherous policy of Enemies, and weaknesse of friends, in chusing such thereinto, as having been unfit for those imployments, some whereof (as is credibly reported) having served the Enemy [11] in Armes, some with moneys; horse, ammunition, or by intelligence, some in commissions of Array, some manifesting constant malignity in their actions, speeches, or standing Newters in times of greatest triall, some culpable of notorious crimes, others lying under heavie accusations, some but are under age, or such who are at present engaged in such courses as in the beginning of this Parliament were esteemed Monopolies.

Now may it please this honourable House, if such as these should remaine, or may have privily crept into your Councels of Authorities (as by the forecited considerations, we humbly conceive cannot but bee judged) what can possibly be expected, by those who have been most active and faithfull in your service, but utter ruine, or the worst of bondage.

For prevention whereof, and of those dangers, warres and troubles that are generally feared, we are constrained earnestly to intreat:

1. That you will be pleased instantly to appoint a Committee of such Worthy Members of this honourable House, as have manifested most sincere affections, to the Well affected, and to authorize them to make speedy and strict inquirie after all such as are possessed of places of Councell, trust, authority or command, who according to law, Ordinance, Reason, or Safety, ought not to be admitted, and that

all persons without exception, may be permitted and encouraged to bring in accusations, witnesses, or testimonies for the more speedy perfecting of the Work: and that you will forthwith exclude all such out of all offices of Councell, Trust, Authority, or command, against whom sufficient cause shall bee proved, without which wee cannot see how it is possible for the well-affected to live either in peace or safety.

2. That you will countenance, protect, and succour the cordiall wel-affected in all places, according to their severall cases and conditions, especially in their addresses with Petitions.

3. That you will bee pleased to condesend unto all the just and reasonable desires of your Commanders, Officers & Souldiers, by whose courage and faithfullnesse, so great services have been performed, and severely to punish all such as have any way sought to alienate you from them.

4. That the Militia of London may bee returned to the custody and disposing of those persons of whose faithfullnesse and wisdome in managing thereof, you have had great experience, and that none may be put out of Command in the Trained bands or Auxiliaries, who have been and are of knowne good affection to the Common Wealth,

All which we humbly intreat may be speedily and effectualy accomplished, according to the great necessity and exigency of these distracted times, and as in duty bound, we shall pray, &c.

FINIS [12]

20

The Bloody Project; or A Discovery of the New Designe, in the Present War

[21 August] 1648
Reprinted from a copy of the tract in the Thomason Collection in the British Library

The Bloody Project, "By W. P. Gent.," was published without imprint "in this Yeare of dissembling, 1648." The tract is a direct contradiction of William Prynne's ideology and his initials may have been used ironically. Haller at first doubted but subsequently concluded that the tract is probably Walwyn's work.[1] Godfrey Davies, Joseph Frank, and A. L. Morton concur.[2]

Contemporary attribution, the correlation of Walwyn's state of mind with events in the summer of 1648, and the characteristic "Postscript" of *Bloody Project* support a judgment that Walwyn wrote the tract. Ten months after Thomason acquired his copy, a harsh attack on the four imprisoned Levellers was published as *The Discoverer . . . The First Part*. *The Discoverer* states that Walwyn was not "behinde hand" in calling "upon the Souldiers to mutinie" and supports the allegation by quoting a passage from *The Bloody Project*.[3] Three weeks later Humphrey Brooke published a broad defense of the Levellers in *The Crafts-mens Craft*. Brooke, who was Walwyn's son-in-law, states that the accusations of incitement to mutiny are supported by citations "out of some of our Books, [that] are cited but piecemeal, without the preceding and subsequent passages."[4] Brooke's point is well taken, but he does not deny *The Discoverer's* attribution of *Bloody Project* to Walwyn. Nor did Walwyn deny it.

Bloody Project, which was published shortly before the Royalist surrender at Colchester, apparently was written during the fiercest fighting of the second War. The tract opens with a bitter protest that men are killing and dying at the behest of "Grandee Factions" who are preventing "a just Peace, and promoting . . . a causelesse Warre." Those who do the fighting and dying have never been told the goals for which they engaged; "the Libertyes of the People" have not been specified by the Parliament and basic rights anticipated by the soldiers have been betrayed. King, Parliament, and leaders of the City and the army are equally condemned for seeking "Honor, Wealth and Power" only for themselves. "Soldiers and People," states *Bloody Project* in the passage cited by *The Discoverer*, should "let not the covetous, the proud, the blood-thirsty man bear sway amongst you" but should use "all the might you have to prevent a further effusion of blood."[5] If less than a clear call for regimental mutiny, the message is a considerable distance from Walwyn's 1642 tract, *Some Considerations*, in which he warned against precipitous peacemakers who would "dull our resolutions by commending peace unto us, when we are necessitated to take up our Swords."[6] In 1642 Walwyn had been filled with hope that grievances would be redressed and great reforms achieved. Throughout the first war he steadfastly supported Parliament, by which he soon came to mean the House of Commons. Prospects for real reform faded rapidly in the second half of 1646, and when the Commons burned the Leveller petitions in May 1647 Walwyn turned to the political forces emerging in the army.[7] Inevitably, the army, too, disappointed the Levellers—as *The Bloody Project* clearly states.[8] The tract lacks Walwyn's customary perceptivity in that it fails to recognize that neither Parliament nor the army instigated or desired the 1648 war and is oblivious to the position of every revolutionary faction if the Royalists prevailed. These omissions suggest that the violence and slaughter of the renewed fighting so shocked Walwyn that, as his disillusionment with erstwhile allies was reinforced, his fundamental abhorrence of bloodshed was released.[9]

After eleven pages of negative criticism, *Bloody Project* reiterates the positive program of the Levellers as "the Causes to be insisted on."[10] The "Postscript" returns to the promise of the title page with expedients "for an happy Accommodation tending to the satisfaction of all Parties," and optimism and reasonableness emerge as the author adumbrates a solution which would come about in 1689: "If the Peace of the Nation cannot be secured without the Restauration of the King, let it be done speedily and honorably, and provide against his mis-government for the future; let his power be declared and limited by Law."[11] Parliament, too, as Walwyn states in *Helpe* and elsewhere, must have its privileges "be declared and power limitted, as to what they are empowred and what not."[12] The close is typical of Walwyn as it remains true to the concerns expressed in the body of the tract: "Let your Cause be declared, and just also, and let it be for the good of the whole Nation."[13]

The Bloody Project is reprinted as Walwyn's work in *Leveller Tracts*, ed. Haller and Davies, pp. 135–46, and in *Freedom in Arms*, ed. Morton, No. 8.

The Bloody Project, Or a discovery of the New *Designe*, in the present War.

BEING A perfect Narrative of the present proceedings of the severall Grandee Factions, for the prevention of a *just Peace*, and promoting of a *causelesse Warre*, to the destruction of THE KING, PARLIAMENT & PEOPLE.

Whereunto is annexed Several Expedients for an happy Accommodation tending to the satisfaction of all Parties, without the further effusion of blood.

By W. P. Gent.

Printed in this Yeare of dissembling, 1648.

The Bloody Project. OR New designe in the present War discovered.

In all undertakings, which may occasion war or bloodshed, men have great need to be sure that their cause be right, both in respect of themselves and others: for if they kill men themselves, or cause others to kill, without a just cause, and upon the extreamest necessity, they not only disturbe the peace of men, and familyes, and bring misery and poverty upon a Nation, but are indeed absolute murtherers.

Nor will it in any measure satisfy the Conscience, or Gods justice, to go on in uncertainties, for in doubtfull cases men ought to stand still, and consider, untill certainty do appear, especially when killing and sleying of men (the most horrid worke to Nature and Scripture) is in question.

Far be it from any man hastily to engage in any undertaking, which may occasion a War, before the cause he is to fight for, be rightly, and plainly stated, well considered, and throughly understood to be just, and of absolute necessity to be maintained; nothing being more abominable in the sight of God or good men, then such persons who runne but to shed blood for money, or to support this or the other Interest, but neither consider the cause for which they engage, nor ought else, but pay, interest, honour, &c. such are they who so eagerly endeavour to support the interest of a King, by the destruction of the Peoples Interest, the Interest of the Scots against the Interest of the English, the Interest of the Independents, by the ruine of the Presbyterians: and because it best consists with their present honour, profit or humours, make it their busines to pick quarrels, and encrease divisions, and jealousies, that so they may fish in the waters which they themselves have troubled.

But let such know, who ever they be, that though they may and do for a while brave it out, and flourish, yet a time is comming, and draw- [3] eth on apace, when for all the murthers they have caused, and mischiefs they have committed, they shall come to judgement, and then their Consciences will be as a thousand witnesses against them.

But especially let men pretending conscience take heed how they either engage themselves, or perswade others to engage to fight and kill men, for a cause not rightly stated, or not thoroughly understood to be just, and of necessity to be maintained; for it is one of the most unreasonable, unchristian, and unnaturall things that can enter into the mind of man, though it be to be feared that more than a few both in the Citie and Country, that have of late [been] and at present are active to engage in killing and sleying of men, cannot acquit themselves of this abomination.*

I beseech you, (you that are so forward and active to engage in the defence of the Kings, Presbyterian, or Independent interest, and yet know no just cause for either) consider, was it sufficient that the King

* The words in this sentence have been reordered to make sense. (Editors' note)

at first invited you in generall termes to joyn with him, for the defence of the true Protestant Religion, his own just Prerogatives, the Priviledges of Parliament, and the Liberty of the Subject; but never declared in particular what that Protestant Religion was he would have defended, or what Prerogative would please him, what priviledges he would allow the Parliament, or what Freedoms the People?

Or was it sufficient thinke you now, that the Parliament invited you at first upon generall termes, to fight for the maintenance of the true Protestant Religion, the Libertyes of the People, and Priviledges of Parliament; when neither themselves knew, for ought is yet seen, nor you, nor any body else, what they meant by the true Protestant Religion, or what the Liberties of the People were, or what those Priviledges of Parliament were, for which yet neverthelesse thousands of men have been slain, and thousands of Familyes destroyed?

It is very like that some of you that joyned with the King upon his invitation, thought, that though the King had formerly countenanced Popery, and Superstition, had stretcht his Prerogative to the oppression and destruction of his People, by Pattents, Projects, &c. yet for the future he would have been more zealous for the truth, and more tender of his People, and not have persisted (notwithstanding his new Protestations) to maintain his old Principles.

And so likewise many of you that joyned with the Parliament, who had formerly seen, felt, or considered the persecution of godly consci-
[4] entious people by the Bishops and their Cleargy, with the reproaches cast upon them, and their grievous and destructive imprisonment, did beleeve the Parliament under the notion of Religion, intended to free the Nation from all compulsion in matters of Religion, and from molestation, or persecution for opinions, or non-conformity; and that all Lawes or Statutes tending thereunto should have been repealed: But since you find (by killing and destroying their opposers) you have enabled them to performe all things that might concern your freedome, or be conducible to the peace of the Kingdome. But do you now find that they do mean that, or the contrary? And will your consciences give you leave any longer to fight or engage in the cause of Religion, when already you see what fruits you and your friends reap thereby.

And no doubt many of you understood by the Liberties of the People, that they intended to free the Commons in Parliament the peoples Representative, from a Negative voyce, in King, or Lords, and would have declared themselves the highest Authority, and so would have proceeded to have removed the grievances of the Common-wealth: And when you had seen Pattents, Projects, and Shipmoney taken away, the High Commission, and Starchamber abolished, did you ever imagine to have seen men and women examined upon Interrogatories, and questions against themselves, and imprisoned for refusing to answer? Or to have seen Commoners frequently sentenced and imprisoned by the Lords? Did you ever dream that the oppressions of Committees would have exceeded those of the Councel-table; or that in the place of Pattents and Projects, you should have seen an Excise established, ten fold surpassing all those, and Shipmoney together? You thought rather that Tythes would have been esteem'd an oppression, and that Trade would have been made perfectly free, and that Customs if continued, would have been abated, and not raysed, for the support of domineering factions, and enrichment of foure or five great men, as they have been of late times, to the sorrow and astonishment of all honest men, and the great prejudice of the Trade of the Nation.

Doubtlesse you hoped that both Lawes and Lawyers, and the proceeding in all Courts should have been abreviated, and corrected, and that you should never more have seen a Begger in England.

You have seen the Common-wealth enslaved for want of Parliaments, and also by their sudden dissolution, and you rejoyced that this Parliament was not to be dissolved by the King; but did you conceive it [5] would have sat seavn yeares to so little purpose, or that it should ever have come to passe, to be esteemed a crime to move for the ending thereof? Was the perpetuating of this Parliament, and the oppressions they have brought upon you and yours, a part of that Liberty of the People you fought for? Or was it for such a Priviledge of Parliament, that they only might have liberty to oppresse at their pleasure, without any hope of remedy? If all these put together make not up the cause for which you fought, what was the Cause? What have ye obtained to the People, but these Libertyes, for they must not be called oppressions? These are the fruits of all those vast disbursements, and those thousands of lives that have been spent and destroyed in the late War.

And though the Army seemed to be sensible of these grosse jugglings, and declared, and engaged against them, and professed that they tooke not paines as a mercenary Army, hired to fight for the Arbitrary ends of a State, but in judgement and conscience, for the preservation of their own, and the Peoples just Rights and Libertyes: Yet when they had prevailed against those their particular opposers, and accomplished the ends by them aymed at, all these things were forgotten, and those persons that appeared for the Peoples Freedoms, by them esteemed and proceeded against as Mutineers, or Incendiaries.

In like manner, the present Ruling Party of Presbyterians make a great shew of their apprehensions of the great slavery and servitude brought upon the People, by the exercise of an Arbitrary power in the Parliament, and by the jurisdiction of the Sword in the hands of the Army: They tell us that by this meanes the Trade of the Nation is destroyed, and that without the removall of these things, the peace of the Nation cannot be secured: And it is exceeding true: But I beseech you consider, whether they do not revive the same Play, and drive the same Designe, which was acted by the Parliament at first, and by the Army the last Summer.

First, they cry out against the exercise of an arbitrary power in the Parliament, and yet labour to invest it in the King, nay challenge the exercise of it by themselves: for what greater arbitrary power can there be in the world, then that a Priest or two, and a few Lay Elders, under the name of a Presbytery, should have power to bind or loose, bring in, or cast out, save or destroy at their pleasure, and enforce all persons within the limits of their jurisdiction, to beleeve as they beleeve, and submit to whatever they command, or else to be by them delivered over to Sathan. [6]

Nay if you looke into those of that party of the Magistracy of this City, that are the great promoters of the present worke: do there any men in the world exercise a more arbitrary power? Do not many of them act only by the Rule of will and pleasure, and have they not openly professed themselves to be obliged to observe no other Rule then Discretion.

And though they decry against the power of the Sword in the hands of the Independents, yet do they not with all their might, labour to get it into the hands of the Presbyterians? and being there, will they not do that themselves, which they complain of in others? will they not say that there are gain-sayers whose mouthes must be stopt, and with the Sword rather then faile, and though Royalists or Independents may not use the Sword to enforce their Principles, yet Presbyterians may, as if all knowledge of the truth were centred in a Presbytery, consisting of halfe Scotch, halfe English, part Puritan, part Cavalier, luke-warm christianity, neither hot nor cold, zealous for the truth which they know not, only by hearesay, and only because they love not Independency, that being to pure, nor Episcopacy, that being too prophane, they will be between both, (but not in a golden Meane, for that were well) but more zealous then either in outward performances, but for the power of godlines.— I cease to judge, but we say we may know the tree by the fruit, and certain I am that This-tles never bore Figgs.

But if you shall examine what grounds of freedome they propose in all their Papers; what equall Rules of justice they offer to be insisted on as a sure foundation for a lasting peace? Surely if you looke but seriously into the bottom of their design, you will find that the peace they aime at is only their own; not the Nations, and that their own ease, honour and dominion, is the only thing they pursue, and so they could enjoy ease and plenty, and stretch themselves upon Beds of Down, they would never care what the poor Country should suffer.

To be short, all the quarrell we have at this day in the Kingdome, is no other then a quarrel of Interests, and Partyes, a pulling down of one Tyrant, to set up another, and instead of Liberty, heaping upon our selves a greater slavery then that we fought against: certainly this is the Liberty that is so much strove for, and for which there are such fresh endeavours to engage men; but if you have not killed and de-stroyed men enough for this, go on and destroy, kill and sley, till your consciences are swoln so full with the blood of the People, that they [7] burst agen, and upon your death-beds may you see your selves the most horrid Murtherers that ever lived, since the time that Cain kild his brother without a just Cause; for where, or what is your cause? Beleeve it yee have a heavy reeckoning to make, and must undergo a sad repentance, or it will go ill with you at the great day, when all the sophistry of your great Reformers will serve you to little purpose, every man for himselfe being to give an account for the things which he hath done in the body, whether they be good or evill: Then it will serve you to little purpose to say, the King, Parliament, Army, Independents, Presbyterians, such an Officer, Magistrate, or Minister deluded me; no more then it did Adam, to say the woman whom thou gavest, &c. It being thus decreed in heaven, the soule which sinneth shall surely dye.

And though what is past cannot be recalled, yet it must be repented of, and speciall care taken for the future, that you sin no more in this kind, and either stand still or go right for the Future, to which end, let these following directions be your guide.

1. You are to know, that a People living under a Government, as

this Nation hath done, and doth, cannot lawfully put themselves into Arms, or engage in War, to kill and sley men, but upon a lawfull call and invitation from the Supream Authority, or Law-making power.

Now if the Supream Authority of this Nation were never yet so plainly declared, as that you understand certainly where it is, and who are invested therewith, you have then had no Warrant for what you have done, nor have any Plea in Law for your Indempnity, as some of all Parties have lately found to their costs.

And that this point of Supream Authority was ever certainly stated, is absolutely denyed; for according to the common supposition, it is 3. Estates, which till within these few yeares were ever taken to be 1. Lords Spirituall. 2. Lords Temporall. 3. The Commons in Parliament assembled.

Now if these three were essentiall and equall, as all former Times seem to allow; How could the Lords Temporall and the Commons, cast out the Lords Spirituall? For by the same rule, the Lords Spirituall, and Lords Temporall, might have cast out the Commons, but the casting out the Bishops hath both answered the question, and ended the controversie. [8]

Since when the supreme Authority is pretended to rest in the King, Lords and Commons; and if so, when did the King assent to your Proceedings in this War, which all the art in the world will not perswade him to be for him, but against him, and to ruine him and his? Or when did the Parliament assent to the proceedings of you that joyned with the King in the late war pretendedly raised for the defence of Religion, the priviledges of Parliament, and Liberty of the Subject; and if the supream power reside in all three, King, Lords and Commons, how can the King justly do any thing without the consent of the Lords and Commons, or the Lords and Commons without the King? May not the King and Lords as justly proceed to make Laws, War or Peace, without the Commons as they without the King? If they are not equal, which of them are supream, and declared and proved by convincing reason so to be? If any, that you are to observe? If none, what have you done? what can you lawfully do?

That there should be either three or two distinct Estates equally supream is an absurd nullity in government, for admit two of them agree, and not the third, then there can be no proceedings or determination, and if there be but two, as is now pretended, in Lords and Commons, whose Ordinances have served (how justly judge you) to make War and confiscate mens estates: admit they agree not, then also nothing can be done, which in Government is ridiculous to imagine, besides it is now a known case that their Ordinances are not pleadable against the Laws, and give no Indempnity, which were they the known supream Authority, could not but be effectual. That the King single and alone is the supream Authority himself never pretended to it, claiming only a negative voyce in the Law-making Power, by which rule nothing can be done without him, then which nothing is more un- [9] reasonable: The Lords also never pretended to more then an equal share with the Commons, which in effect is a negative voyce and as unreasonable as in the King: And when the Commons have been by Petitioners stiled the supream authority, they have punished the Petitioners, and disclaimed the supream Author- ity: and as two years since, so very lately they have voted that the Kingdom shall be governed by King, Lords and Commons; which is a riddle that no man understands; for who knoweth what appertains to the King, what to the Lords, or what to the House of Commons? It is all out as uncertain as at first; and if the trumpet give an uncertain sound, who shall prepare himself for the battel? If by all your endeav- ors you cannot prevail to have the supream Authority declared and proved, how can you lawfully fight, or upon what grounds with a good conscience can you engage your selves, or perswade others to engage in killing and slaying of men?

And if you should have the supream Authority rationally proved and declared to be in the Commons distinct from any other, as being the sole Representative of the people; you must note that you are a free people, and are not to be pressed or enforced to serve in Wars like horses and bruit beasts, but are to use the understanding God hath given you, in judging of the Cause, for defence whereof they desire you to fight, for it is not sufficient to fight by lawful authority, but you must be sure to fight for what is just: Lawful authority being some- times mistaken, and many times so perverted and corrupted, as to command the killing and imprisoning men for doing that which is just and commendable, and for opposing what is unjust and destruc- tive. Therefore as you are to forbear till you see the supream Author- ity distinctly and rationally stated; so also you are not to engage till the Cause be expresly declared, lest after your next engagement you [10] are as far to seek of a just cause as now you are; and after you have prevailed, in stead of finding your selves and your associates freemen, you find your selves more enslaved then you were formerly. For by experience you now find you may be made slaves as effectually by a Parliament, as by any other kind of Government; why then per- sist you to divide and fall into Factions? to kill and slay men for you know not what, to advance the honor and interest of you know not whom; the King, Parliament, great men in the City and Army can do nothing without you, to disturb the Peace of the Nation; upon you therefore both Soldiers and People, who fight, pay and disburse your estates, is to be charged all the evil that hath been done; if you on all hands had not been and were not so hasty to engage for the advancement of Interests to the prejudice of the Nation, it is very likely we had not only escaped those late bloody turmoils that have happened among us, but also might prevent greater threatned dangers, which like an inundation begin to break in upon us: And if you now stop not, your Consciences will be loaded with all that is to come, which threatneth far worse then what is past; Therefore, if ye are either men or Christians, hold your hands till you know what you fight for, and be sure that you have the truth of Freedom in it, or never medle, but desist, and let who will both fight and pay.

Certainly there is none so vile, considering what hath been said, that will again incur the guilt of murtherers, and fight before the Cause be plainly stated and published, and if that were done as it ought to be, possibly it may be attained without fighting, and might have been all this while, the difference not being so great as was imagined; Besides, where is the man that would fight against the supream Authority, and a just Cause? and certainly there is none of you (whether Royalists, Presbyterians or Independents) so wicked as to de- [11] sire to kill men without exceeding just grounds and upon the greatest necessity, it being the saddest work in the world.

For the preventing whereof, let us, I beseech you, examine what good things there are wanting, that are essential to the Peace, Freedom, and happiness of the Nation, that may not be obtained without fighting.

1. Is there wanting the certain knowledg where the supream Authority is, and of right ought to be; It is confest no one thing is more wanting, nor can the Nation ever be quiet, or happy without it.

But can it be any where justly and safely but in the House of Commons, who are chosen and trusted by the People? Certainly did men consider that in opposing thereof, they renounce and destroy their own freedoms, they would not do it for any thing in the world.

If the consideration of the manifold evils brought upon us by this House of Commons, deter them, the next thing that is wanting is, That a set time be appointed for the ending of this Parliament, and a certainty for future Parliaments, both for their due elections, meeting, and dissolving: And who will be so unreasonable as to oppose any of these? certainly the number cannot be considerable.

Is it also necessary That Parliaments be abridged the power of impressing men, to serve as bruit beasts in the Wars, who will be against their being bounded therein? a good Cause never wanted men, nor an authority that had money to pay them. [12]

Hath it proved destructive in Parliaments to meddle in Religion, and to compel and restrain in matters of Gods worship? Are they evidently such things as cannot be submitted to Judgment? Doth every man find it so that hath a living Conscience? Who then will be against their binding herein, though they be entrusted to establish an uncompulsive publike way of worship for the Nation?

Is it unreasonable that any person should be exempt from those proceedings of Law, unto which the generality of the People are to be subject? Who is there then that will not willingly have all from the highest to the lowest bound alike?

That Parliaments should have no power to punish any person for doing that which is not against a known declared Law, or to take away general property, or to force men to answer to questions against themselves, or to order tryals, or proceed by any other ways then by twelve sworn men, who would not rejoyce to have such boundaries?

Then, that the proceedings in Law might be rectified, and all Laws and the duty of Magistrates written and published in English: That the Excise might have a speedy end, and no Taxes but by way of subsidies: That Trade might be free, and a less burthensom way for the maintenance of Ministers be established, then that of Tythes; and that work and necessaries be provided for all kind of poor people. Certainly for the obtaining of these things a man may justly adventure his life; all these being for a common good, and tend not to the setting up of any one party or faction of men.

These then are the Causes to be insisted on, or nothing: And if the supream Authority adhere to this Cause, they need neither fear Scotch, French, nor English Enemies; but if they decline this Cause, they are to be declined; the just freedom and happiness of a Nation, being above all Constitutions, whether of Kings, Parliaments, or any other. [13]

For shame therefore (Royalists, Presbyterians, Independents,) before you murther another man hold forth your Cause plainly and expresly; and if any Adversaries appear either within or without the Land, reason it out with them if it be possible, deal as becometh Christians, argue, perswade, and use all possible means to prevent another War, and greater blood-shed; your great ones, whether the King, Lords, Parliament men, rich Citizens, &c. feel not the miserable effects thereof, and so cannot be sensible; but you and your poor friends that depend on Farmes, Trades, and small pay, have many an aking heart when these live in all pleasure and deliciousness: The accursed thing is accepted by them, wealth and honor, and both comes by the bleeding miserable distractions of the Common-wealth, and they fear an end of trouble would put an end to their glory and greatness.

Oh therefore all you Soldiers and People, that have your Consciences alive about you, put to your strength of Judgment, and all the might you have to prevent a further effusion of blood; let not the covetous, the proud, the blood-thirsty man bear sway amongst you; fear not their high looks, give no ear to their charms, their promises or tears; they have no strength without you, forsake them and ye will be strong for good, adhere to them, and they will be strong to evil; for which you must answer, and give an account at the last day.

The King, Parliament, great men in the City and Army, have made you but the stairs by which they have mounted to Honor, Wealth and Power. The only Quarrel that hath been, and at present is but this, namely, whose slaves the people shall be: All the power that any hath, was but a trust conveyed from you to them, to be employed by them for your good; they have mis-imployed their power, and instead of preserving you, have destroyed you: all Power and Authority is perverted from the King to the Constable, and it is no other but [14] the policy of Statesmen to keep you divided by creating jealousies and fears among you, to the end that their Tyranny and Injustice may pass undiscovered and unpunished; but the peoples safety is the supream Law; and if a people must not be left without a means to preserve it self against the King, by the same rule they may preserve themselves against the Parliament and Army too; if they pervert the end for which they received their power, to wit the Nations safety; therefore speedily unite your selves together, and as one man stand up for the defence of your Freedom, and for the establishment of such equal rules of Government for the future, as shall lay a firm foundation of peace and happiness to all the people without partiallity: Let Justice be your breastplate, and you shall need to fear no enemies, for you shall strike a terrour to your now insulting oppressors, and force all the Nations Peace to fly before you. Prosecute and prosper.

Vale. [15]

Postscript.

Can there be a more bloody Project then to engage men to kill one another, and yet no just cause declared? Therefore I advise all men that would be esteemed Religious or Rational, really to consider what may be done for the future that is conducible to the Peace of the Nation; If the Peace of the Nation cannot be secured without the Restauration of the King, let it be done speedily and honorably, and provide against his mis-government for the future; let his power be declared and limited by Law.

If the Peace of the Nation cannot be secured by the continuance of this Parliament, let a Period be set for the dissolution thereof, but first make certain provision for the successive calling, electing and sitting of Parliaments for the future; let their Priviledges be declared and power limitted, as to what they are empowred and what not; for doubtless in Parliaments rightly constituted consists the Freedom of a Nation: And in all things do as you would be done unto, seek peace with all men.

But above all things, abandon your former actings for a King against a Parliament, or an Army against both; for the Presbyterians against the Independents, &c. for in so doing you do but put a Sword into your enemies hands to destroy you, for hitherto, which of them soever were in power, they plaid the Tyrants and oppressed, and so it will ever be, when Parties are supported: Therefore if you engage at all, do it by Lawfull Authority, let your Cause be declared, and just also, and let it be for the good of the whole Nation, without which you will not only hazard being Slaves, but also contract upon your selves, and Posterities the guilt of Murtherers.
vale.

FINIS [16]

21

The Vanitie of the Present Churches, and Uncertainty of Their Preaching, Discovered

[12 March] 1648/9
Reprinted from a copy of the tract in the Thomason Collection in the British Library

The Vanitie of the Present Churches was published anonymously by J. Clows in 1649. The front cover (A1 recto) is blank. A short epistle "To the Reader" by the licenser, Theodore Jennings, is printed on A1 verso, opposite the title page, A2 recto. Jennings dates his epistle, and his imprimatur on the last page, "February 23. 1648–49." John Lilburne, in a tract published a few weeks later, observed that *Vanitie* had made some Independent preachers "very mad, . . . supposing it to be the Pen of some of our friends." Lilburne averred that he had first seen it a few hours before and considered it "one of the shrewdest bookes that ever I read."[1] Walwyn twice expressed his agreement with *Vanitie* without openly acknowledging it[2]—an understandable omission since he was in prison at the time. Haller concludes that Walwyn's allusions "point clearly to his authorship" of *Vanitie*, and Frank, Morton, and Murray Tolmie accept it as Walwyn's work without reservation or explanation.[3]

The attribution is supported by *Vanitie's* concurrence with Walwyn's attitude in 1648/9, by its extension of views expressed in his *Still and Soft Voice*, and by references characteristic of several of his known works. *Vanitie* is notable for its intensification of the disillusionment and bitterness that is discernible in *Still and Soft Voice*, written two years earlier, and accentuated in *Fountain of Slander* and *Just Defence*, which appeared some three months after *Vanitie*. Like *Still and Soft Voice*, *Vanitie* hints that its "tartnesse" is the result of harsh treatment by others,[4] and both tracts decry "wilde Notions and Opinions" that are not grounded in Scripture.[5] At the same time, *Vanitie* reiterates Walwyn's fundamental commitment to inclusive religious liberty, stressing the importance of concordance between conscience and religious practice,[6] and, echoing *Still and Soft Voice* precisely, *Vanitie* counts "all things as losse and dung" in comparison to the *unum necessarium* that Christ died for all men.[7] Other references that mark *Vanitie* as Walwyn's work are: the recollection of Demetrius and the Craftsmen;[8] the passage about the fallibility of human knowledge;[9] the emphasis on love.[10]

Unlike *Still and Soft Voice*, *Vanitie* is a polemic rather than an avowal of personal belief. Its criticism of the present state of religious diversity[11] is a departure from Walwyn's customary latitude, yet *Vanitie* concludes that men freed from "Church-bondage" will become true and loving Christians as they discover God within themselves through knowing and understanding the Scriptures.[12] It is a distinctive mark of Walwyn's indestructible optimism.

Vanitie is reprinted in *Leveller Tracts*, ed. Haller and Davies, pp. 252–75.

To the Reader

Although I dissent from some things in this Treatise, and other things seeme dark and doubtfull to me, yet there are many plain, clear, and evident Truths, of great use to all Christians. Therefore that the Truth may be manifest to all, And that all Believers and Churches of the Saints may be of one mind and may edifie the whole body in love. And in all their Doctrines, and Conversations, hold forth the truth as it is contained in the written word, the perfect rule of the spirit to guide us into al Truth, and to make us wise unto Salvation through that (one necessary thing) Faith, which is in Christ Jesus: which is by the Gospel, (the power of God to salvation) preached unto us. And that errour may be discovered, reproved, and corrected, and if possible, that the guilty may be convinced, and reformed.

Therefore I say to this Epistle, and the ensuing Treatise.

February 23. 1648–49.

Imprimatur
THEODORE JENNINGS.

To the Reader.

Although I differ: from some things in this Treatise, and other things I see me dark and doubtfull to me, yet there are many plain, clear, and evident Truths, of great use to all Christians. Therefore that the Truth may be manifest to all, And that all Believers, and Churches of the Saints may be of one mind, and may edifie the whole body in love. And in all their Doctrines, and Conversations, hold forth the truth as it is contained in the written word, the perfect rule of the spirit to guide us in all Truth, and to make us wise unto Salvation, through that (one necessary thing) Faith, which is in Christ Jesus: Which is by the Gospel, (the power of God to salvation) preached unto us. And that errors may be discovered, reproved, and corrected, and if possible, that the guilty may be convinced, and reformed.

Therefore I say to this Epistle, and the ensuing Treatise.

February 23.   Imprimatur
1648-49.   THEODORE JENNINGS.

THE
VANITIE
Of the present
CHURCHES,
AND
Vncertainty of their Preach-
ing, discovered.

WHEREIN

The pretended immediate teach-
ing of the Spirit, is denyed, and the all-
sufficiency of the Scriptures
teaching, is maintained

WITH,

A new and true Method of reading thereof,
for the peace of the mind, and rule of life.

Gal. 6.15.16 For in Christ Jesus neither Circumcision availeth any thing, nor uncircumcision,
but a new Creature. And as many as walk
according to this rule, peace be on them, &c.

London, Printed by J. Clows, and are to be sold
in Cornhill, and Poper-Head-Alley, 1649.

Title page of *The Vanitie of the Present Churches*, 1648/9.
(Folger Shakespeare Library)

THE VANITIE Of the present CHURCHES, and Uncertainty of their Preaching, discovered.

WHEREIN The pretended immediate teaching of the Spirit, is denyed, and the all-sufficiency of the Scriptures teaching, is maintained.

WITH, A new and true Method of reading thereof, for the peace of the mind, and rule of life.

Gal. 6. 15, 16. *For in Christ Jesus neither Circumcision availeth any thing, nor uncircumcision, but a new Creature. And as many as walk according to this rule, peace be on them, &c.*

London, *Printed* by *J. Clows,* and are to be sold in *Cornhill,* and *Popes-Head-Alley,* 1649.

The vanity of the present Churches, and uncertainty of their Preaching discovered, &c.

As there is nothing more commendable amongst men, then a true correspondency between the heart, the tongue, & the hand: so no thing is more lovely amongst Christians, then that the Conscience, the profession and the practice so universally agree; & though something be allowable unto frailty, yet when the defect or discord is continued, and that to the reproach of Christianity in generall, and to the prejudice of humane society; then certainly a reproofe is not only requisite, but the neglect thereof, a sinne of an high nature.

And so those, whom this discourse now deemeth worthy of reproofe did seeme to [1] judge, when they condemned the persecuting practices, of the new raysed Presbyters, whose positions and professions whilst they were persecuted by the Bishops, did clearly hold forth a full and compleat liberty of Conscience, in the exercise of Religion, and justly and truly did the Independents reprove them, as their many bookes, of that Subject, do sufficiently testifie: their reproofes were sharp, and their replyes driven home; whereby they put the question of the utmost liberty of Conscience, out of all question, accompting nothing more base, or mis-beseeming a Christian, then to question, or vex, or reproach any man for his judgment or practice, touching matters of Religion, and inciting all men to peace, unity, love, and true friendship, though of never so many severall opinions, or different wayes in Religion.

By which their ingenuity, they, (as the Puritan Presbyter had done before them) gained abundance of love and respect from all men: their Congregations multiplied, and in conclusion, obtained much countenance from authority: which they no sooner tasted but instantly, some of them began to pride themselves, and to dispise others; and to re- [2] proach and villifie all such, as upon tryall and examination of their Churches, their Pastors and Sermons, finding all to be but fained imitations, nothing reall or substantiall, forsooke their societies, and thereupon as the Presbyters had used them; so deale the Independant with these, and all that any wayes adhered unto these, raysing nick-names and bitter invective reproaches against them, sparing neither art nor paines, to make them odious to others, and their lives (if it were possible) a burthen to themselves; and though reasons have been offered, and conferences desired, that they might see their error, and forbeare to deale thus contrary to their positive, owned, and declared principles: yet have they persisted therein, and go on still without ceasing, manifesting a most destructive and persecuting disposition, not only towards these, but towards many others whom they now (as compleat Judges of other mens Consciences) judge to be erronious, or heriticall, and seeme to have placed their felicity in the ruine of those whom their own Consciences cannot deny to have been instrumentall in their preservations, and who have not thought their lives too precious, to purchase them that freedom which now they enjoy. [3]

And therefore it hath been conceived not only just, but of absolute necessity, to publish to the judgments of all impartial people, both of the Congregationall way and others: this their hard measure and unthankful usage of a harmlesse well-meaning people, and withall, to discover to all those who are conscientious, the error of their wayes, and emptinesse of the things wherein they glory, and to let all those who are wilfull or meere polititians amongst them, beare their shame openly, and since they are proofe against their Consciences, and can take up, and lay down principles, professions, and practices too, as stands most with their advantage, and like the Jewes in their worst estate, make no reckoning of oppressing all that are not of their tribes, it is but equall, that such should bear their mark in their forehead, that all men might be warned from conversing with such deceivers, and if any tartnesse appear herein, they are the occasion, it being no more then they deserve.

And not only so, but we have herein also indeavoured to support the weake, and by establishing them upon the sure foundation of the written word of God, (inclining them to give eare thereunto, as unto the only true infallible teacher of spirituall things in our [4] times) and by directing them in a brief and plain method, in the reading thereof, how to attain to that one necessary Doctrine and main design intended therein unto man, for his temporall and eternall comfort.

To which end, that we may neither seeme to wrong the one sort, nor to delude the other, and for full satisfaction of all that are, or shall be concerned herein: we affirm it to be most palpably evident, That ye of the Independant Congregationall, or of any Church-way whatsoever, have not that true essentiall mark of a true Church to be found amongst you, which only can distinguish the true from the false, and without which a true Church cannot be:— A true Church in the Scripture sence; being such only, as wherein the very word of God is purely and infallibly preached: that's the mark.

Now though it have been usuall among you in your prayers, to desire of God that your auditors may give eare to the word that you preach, not as unto the word of a mortall man, but as unto the word of the ever living God: and this too, with such solemn countenances, lifted up eyes and earnestnesse of expression, as if it were the sin of sinnes, for men to doubt it: Though this hath been [5] your course: do ye not tremble when you consider it, to think that you should so frequently practice so grosse an imposture, as openly to pray unto God, that your eronious, doubtfull uncertain conceptions, (for what other are your Sermons) shall be heard and received, as the word of the ever living God; what greater impiety, nay blasphemy, then to call mans word, Gods word, to counterfeit a Preacher an Evangelist, an Ambassadour of Christs, and to deliver a Word, a Message, a Gospel, mixt and made up of opinions and conjectures, as if it were the true reall word of the ever living God.

What is this but even to debase, belye, and offer despite to the spirit of God himself, for advancing your own false Honour and repute amongst men.

Consider this seriously, all ye that are captivated with the charmings of these Sophisters, that are intangled in their formes of godlinesse, that are drawn into their imaginary Churches, that are deluded into an opinion, that they are pastors, feeders, preachers of the word of God, and be so true to God, (whose honour lyes at stake) to your selves whose peace and comfort lyes at stake, and to your Neighbours, whose good name lye [6] at stake also: as to make a clear examination whether these pretended pastors, & Churches are taught immediately by the spirit of God, or not, as they pretend; try them by the word they preach.

And you shall find, however they have prepossest you to the contrary, that neither they, nor your selves, have any understanding at all of such divine or heavenly things, as bring peace of Conscience and joy in the Holy-ghost, by any other way or meanes, but only and solely by the Scriptures, and that neither they, nor your selves, are taught by the spirit, as they have long perswaded you, and whereby chiefly they delude you, into a belief that they are true pastors, and your Churches, true Churches of Christ. For Judge you, had they the spirit of God as you pretend? would they need, as they do; when they have resolved to speak to you from a Text of Scripture, to go sit in their Studies, three or four dayes together, turning over those authors, that have written thereupon; and beating their own braines, to find out the meaning and true intent thereof; no certainly, had they the spirit of God, it could in an instant, in the twinkling of an eye, inform them the meaning of his own writings; they [7] would not need to be studying, seven, ten, or twenty years, to understand the truth of the Gospel, and when they have done so too be as farre to seeke as they were at first for any expresse certainty therein; for do but observe, that when they have for some years preacht up a Doctrine, they are many times forst to preach it down again, as ye well know most of them have done, and that in very materiall points.

As for instance, are they not one while zealous for the baptizing of Infants, another while for the baptizing of Beleevers only, and then again for no Baptisme at all, for want of a true Ministry? do not the Pastors differ amongst themselves, and contentions arise not only between Church and Church, but in every Church within it self? are there not some that for many years have preacht up election and reprobation, and afterwards have as much preacht it down, and cryed up generall redemption, and, that man hath free will or a negative voice in his salvation, and this in a Church gathered and taught by the spirit, as they would make the world believe and those who by praying and preaching *ex tempore*, would be thought to have yet a more immediate teaching of the spirit; how [8] extreamly are they to seeke in the ready understanding of the Scriptures, what weake and indigested matter issueth from them, is too easily discerned, yea what contradictions, they huddle one in the neck of another, though through confidence in the speaker, and superstition in the hearer, all passeth for currant truth.

But consider, can it be of the true spirit to produce uncertain Doctrines; if the Trumpet give an uncertain sound, who can prepare himself to the battle; so if the preacher, preach uncertainly, how can he affirm his word to be the word of God; or how from such doubtfulnesse can true faith be begotten in the hearts of the hearers? is not a Church founded upon such uncertainty, founded upon the sand, and built up with hay & stubble, not able to stand the least blast of a reasonable opposition; and will ye that have Consciences towards God, any longer be instrumented in this mocking of him, and by your countenance thereof partake with them in this strong delusion?

What doth the Pope and his Clergy more then belye themselves, and blaspheam God, in saying, they have the true spirit of God, which leads them into all truth; whilst by [9] their lying miracles, by their art and sophistry, they lead the poor deluded people in the greatest errors, for maintenance of their own pride, covetousnesse, and luxury: The bishops they come, and by pretence of the true spirit, discover abundance of faults in the Pope and his Clergy, and make shew of great reformation; but advance only themselves and their uncertain Doctrines, for their own ambitious ends only, without any regard to the glory of God, or good of men: then comes the Presbyters, and they cry out against Common-Prayer (that was faulty enough) and studied Sermons, as stinters, and suppressors of the true Spirit of God in them; and they are no sooner in the Chaire, and their Prayers & preachings examined; but they also are found to differ one with another, to contradict themselves, & to mind only their own honour and profit; and to be possessed (as both the former) with a persecuting Spirit, which is abhorred of God, of Christ, and of all his true Ministers and Apostles.

Then comes the Independents and pretend to erect, a holy, pure and undefiled worship, according to the pattern, shewed unto them by the true Spirit indeed, pleading for generall liberty of conscience, void of all com- [10] pulsion or restriction, and professing the meeknes of the very Lambs of Christ, and humility towards all men; who now could have suspected what since hath been discovered? Namely, that they as the rest, belyed the Spirit of God, (pardon the harshnes of the expression, its for Gods cause and must be spoken) they being no more infallibly certain of the truth they raise from Scriptures then any of those whom they so much condemn; they as the rest, pray, preach, and do all for mony, and without it they do nothing, taking mony for that which is not bread, but flower, chaffe, and sand mixt together; that did not people swallow it whole, without chewing, or examination, it would be as gravell between their teeth, and they would spit it out of their mouths.

And since, they are increased in numbers, and have as it were, scumm'd the Parish Congregations of most of their wealthy and zealous members. Do they not fully discover a serpentine disposition hankering after persecution? Do they not dayly spet their venom privatly and publickly, against any that either seperate from them, or joyne not with them, and that in as foul aspertions, as ever the Pope uttered against Luther, the Bishops against the [11] Puritan, or the Presbyter against the Independents, are they not high and skillfull in rayling? making whom they please Atheists, Anti-scripturists, Antinomians, Anti-magistrats, Polligamists, Seekers, or what they will: and can these proceed from the true Spirit of God, or from the Spirit of Antichrist? Judge impartially Yee that are yet untainted in your consciences (going on in this Church-way as deceived, and not deceivers) whether yee can offer more dispite to the Spirit of Grace, then by your presence and society, to justifie this delusion; or to uphold this new idoll, this Apple of Sodome, seeming onely faire to the eye, but touch it, and it falls to powder, to the very earth, being nought but earth, like Dagon before the Arke, having neither hands nor feet, but to (discerning eyes) is a meere uselesse lump, an Idoll, which as the Apostle saith, is nothing in the world, and therefore let none, who minde the things that are of God, uphold it any longer.

It being hardly to be beleeved, the infinite evils which comes to the world by this false supposition and assumption of these Churches of having the Spirit of God, or being taught immediately thereby; for by occasion thereof, no sooner doth any one embrace any opinion [12] pretending to Religion, and beginnes to be fortified therein, and that after frequent hearing, prayer, fasting, or humiliation, he continues to be of the same minde, but presently he thinks himselfe bound to declare to all the world, what the Spirit of God (as he calles his owne imagination) hath made knowne unto him.

And hence it is, that at present, the World abounds with such variety of opinions, concerning life and salvation, that many a sincere heart, seeking for peace and rest therein, is kept in perpetuall suspence and doubtfullnesse, whereby their lives become a very burthen to them; and many sad, and wofull effects, follow thereupon.

Some by their confidence, and extreamity of zeale, and diligence, get their opinions (how contrary to Scripture soever they are) into halfe the people of a Towne, Village and Parish; and then there is nothing but wrangling, envy, malice, and back-biting one another, to the extreme prejudice and unquietnesse of the place.

Some of them crying up their owne experiences, and the teachings of God within them, affirming that they speak, not from Books, or Scriptures, written in Inke and Paper, and in [13] Letters and Sillables, but from the inward suggestion of the Spirit, induce multitudes to neglect the Scriptures, and to give credit onely to their wilde Notions and Opinions, and though they have no foundation in the plaine expression of the Scripture, or be contrary thereunto, yet are they satisfied, that they onely are in the truth, and all other Christians in errour, not examining their opinions by the Text, but urging that the Text is to be interpreted by their Opinions and experiences.

And hence it is, that in the esteeme of some, the Scriptures are of as small value as the Service Book: and to speak of a Christ crucified at Jerusalem, is carnall. Hence it is, that some, and those not a few, maintaine there is no sin, no evill, no difference of things, that all things are good, are one; and that all things are God, and that to see or judge any otherwise, is for want of the teaching of the Spirit; and this, though it quite contradict the whole tenour, and plaine open scope of the Scriptures, from the beginning of Genesis, to the end of the Revelation; yet passeth it for currant, and gets ground in all places.

Hence it is, that some men will neither stir, nor undertake any thing of any nature, Civill [14] or Naturall, but as they are prompted thereunto, (as they imagine) by the Spirit, or as some phrase it, by the drawings forth of the Father, taking all their inclinations, likings, or dislikings, to be immediatly from God, whereby grosse neglects and failings (to say no more) come to be excused; and not onely so, but expresly put upon Gods score.

Hence it is, that some after extreame fasting, and continuance in prayer, (beyond what their bodies could beare,) extent of minde, and intention of apprehension, have really beleeved, they have seen Christ standing by them, and heard him vocally speake unto them, that they have seene a light waving about their beds all the night long; at other times a black darkness intermixt: and in these extasies, as they call them, (but indeed fevourish distempers) they have been bid, as they thought, to doe such things as the holy Scriptures abhorre; and yet could never rest till they had done them.

And hence it is, that some presume to be so Goded with God, and Christed with Christ, as they affirme, they are in heaven, and upon the earth; that they are ever well, and that paine is not pain; that all things are nothing, and nothing all things, and glory that [15] they are contradictions; Prophesie of things to come, as the day of Judgement; name the time, the very day, see it false, and yet profess it true (in a sence,) and are beleeved; write bookes of the Germans madde mans Divinity,* of the occurrences and successe of the present distractions, in such unheard of expressions, concerning King, Parliament, and all Parties, that to a man that gives good heed to the Scriptures, nothing appeares more irreligious; yet through the generall supposition of the immediate teaching of the Spirit, the authors please not onely themselves, but others; and none speaks against it, or writes, or preaches against it to any purpose, least they should break the golden chaine of their own honour or profit; for whoever assumes, or maintaines himselfe to be taught by, or to have the Spirits mediate teaching, is lyable to hold any thing his Fancy presents to his Imagination, and dares not condemne the false assumption of Gods holy Spirit, in another, least he should thereby condemne himselfe; since they both have but their owne bare affirmations, for their foundation, neither being able to manifest, by any thing extraordinary, the reall possession thereof.

To this sad condition are men in these [16] times, brought by this fals presence of a Spirit, which once taken up, & insisted on, their credit becomes so ingag'd, and they are so exceedingly delighted, and lifted up, in being thought the darlings of God, that it is the hardest thing in the world, to make them see their mistake; offer but once to bring them into a doubt, or but desire them to examine how (amidst so many contradictory Opinionists, all affirming the Spirit of God for their leader in each) any one of them comes to know himselfe to be in the right, and they turne the head of one side, single [out] and condemn you as not enlightned, and pray not to trouble them; yet if you enquire, what at any time the Spirit immediatly hath made known unto them, they cannot tell one sillable, but recite some place of Scripture, which by serious intention hath imprinted it selfe in their minds.

If you demand a reall Demonstration of the Spirit, they can give you none, but (peradventure) will tell you, that you must awaite Gods time, and he will enlighten you. That their Spirit is as the White Stone in the Revelation, the name whereof no body knew, but he that received it; making use of false, darke, and misterious Scriptures (inten- [17] ded for another end) to prove that they are unable by any sound argument, or sensible demonstration to manifest: Whereas, were they really endowed therewith, they could not conceale it, nor we be unconvinced of its devine and supernaturall Power, but must needs bend our knees, and hearts in acknowledgement thereof.

* "The Germans madde man": may be Jakob Boehme. (*Tracts on Liberty*, ed. Haller, 1:45, n. 37).

If we urge the Scriptures against them, they tell us the Letter killeth, abusing, and that so grosly that place of Scripture, to the upholding their own vain imagination; nothing being more evident, then that by Letter, in that place of the Romanes, is to be understood the Law: and by Spirit: the Gospel.

And if men did not too much Idolize their owne fancies, it would soone appear, That now in our times we have no Preacher of the Gospel but the Scriptures; which being the infallible Word of God, *the Word of Truth,* Eph. 1. 13. *not the Word of man, but (as it is in truth) the Word of God.* 1 Thes. 2. ver. 13. *which was not yea, and nay, but yea,* 2 Cor. 1. ver. 18, 19, 20. *The Word of God that abideth for ever.* Is it not strange, that our pretended Preachers of all sorts, should so far prevaile upon the minds of men, as to draw them from giving eare, to what this Word of truth plainly [18] and evidently holdeth forth, for the peace of their minds, and direction of their lives; and take up their time and thoughts wholly, or principally, with their uncertain & fallible Sermons, making them in effect, forsake these living fountains, and digg to themselves broken Cisterns, that can hold no water.

Nay, a wonderfull thing it is, that it should be received for a currant truth, That this, the greatest blessing the World knows, this word of the ever living God, should now come to be esteemed, but as a dead Letter; this sword of the Spirit, that forceth it self into our dead naturall understandings, plants it self there, makes us one with it: and forms us new; this regenerating word, this immortall seed, should be so undervalued, as to passe but as a dead Letter.

Time was, that it was otherwise in England, when our fore-Fathers would have given any thing in the world; yea, many of them gave up their lives, rather then they would part with the smalest part of this precious Word, translated into English, by the first sincere professors of true Christian doctrins; but then Godlinesse was esteemed the greatest gain, and the iniquity of Learning, was not arived to so much impudence, as to make a gain [19] of Godlynesse, to make a trade of Religion, and to become rich by pretended preaching. Nor weaned they the people from the Scriptures, to give eare to their notions, and opinions; telling them they had the Spirit, and that the Scriptures were but a dead letter; but invited and perswaded all men, to a diligent consideration of the true scope and intent of them.

Neither did they preferr the understanding of men, with difficult points, or obscure doctrins; but (as Luther) insisted altogether upon the Doctrin of free Justification by Christ alone; and (in way of thankfulnes for so great a benefit) invited all men, to live righteously, Godly, and soberly in this present world; therein following the exam-

ple of the Apostles, and the very end, scope, and main design of the
Scriptures; which is that *unum necessarium*, and which, if people did
rightly and seriously mind, they would not so easily be drawn to follow such Teachers, or to give eare to such Sermons; whereby they are
alwaies learning, but never come to the knowledge of this one necessary truth.

For, how long work soever, Ministers and pretended Preachers,
make of it, to maintaine themselves, and families in wealth, plenty,
and [20] honour, necessary Doctrins are not at all hard to be understood, nor require long time to learne them; and if it did not concerne
their livelihood, and profession, to make men beleeve, they were
people who soone understand sufficiently for their establishment,
and comfort, and would fall to practice, that so they might become an
honour to their profession of Christianity; for the Scriptures, or word
of God, having once planted this truth in the understanding, viz.
That it is the bloud of Christ, which cleanseth us from all sinne; this
Evangelicall truth of its own nature, would instantly set man on work
to do the will of him, that hath so loved him, and constrain him to
walk in love as Christ hath loved: so that after this, all the care would
be, how to advance the Gospel, by making our light to shine forth
before men, that others seeing our good works, may glorifie our Father which is in Heaven.

But this is no profitable way, for any of our pretended Preachers,
this Doctrin is to soone learned; for if men once come to know that
this short lesson is sufficient; what will they regard? either printed
discourses, or Sermons, and if once they find them also full of uncer-
[21] tainty, contradiction, and unnecessary things, they'le not part
with their mony for such trash, when they may go to the two breasts
of Christ himself, freely at all times, to the Scriptures, and buy this
sweet milk and hony, without mony and without price; and if men
and women come once to understand this, they will not comber
themselves with many things but possessing this unvalluable truth,
will ever worship God in Spirit and in Truth; and declare unto others
this blessed one necessary comfortable way, and that not by preaching or long set speeches: which are apt to deceive; but by conferences,
and mutuall debates, one with another, (the best way for attaining a
right understanding) far excelling that which is called preaching. But
then, how shall Demetrius and the Craftsmen live? even by some
lawfull calling, this being the most palpably delusive [error] of any in
the world, and it is very strange, that all men do not discerne and
avoid it.

It is so, as cunningly as it is carryed, & as high in repute as it is, & hath long time been, having no foundation but in the weake credulity of men; for if men but once consider it, their Sermons will appear to be but as common discourses, full of mistakes, errors, and at the [22] least altogether uncertaine: and that all their preachings and prayings are only for mony, and that their greatest skill and labour, is to hold men ever in suspence; and upon pretence of truth, to give them a bastard Scholastick knowledge, which only serve to make men proud, wrangling Sophisters, and Disputers, vain boasters, talkers, busie-bodies, censurers, Pharisees, wise in their own eyes, and despising others, void of all true piety or reall Christian vertue: and no marvaile.

For such as the tree is, such ever will be the fruit; they boast to have the Spirit of God, & you see it is but boasting, or their own imagination only: and in the mean time, take the Scriptures for a dead Letter; and either reject them, or make them speak according to the spirit of their own Imaginations; and so instead of being reall, are at best but fantastick Christians, uncertain (if not false) Teachers: and such are their fruits. The greatest part of their time, wherein they should be imployed to feed the hungry, cloath the naked, or in visiting the fatherlesse & widdow, or in delivering the Captive, and setting the oppressed free, (all which are workes, so fully and plainly set forth in Scripture, as most pleasing to God) being spent in talking upon some hard texts [23] of Scripture, such are their Sermons, or in disputes & contests, upon some nice & difficult questions. And this exercising themselvs therein, week after week, and day after day, and in fastings and repetitions, and in writing of these doubtfull Sermons, is by them called a Religious exercise, and those who can but attain to so much boldnesse and utterance, as to speak and pray an howre, two or three, together, take upon them, and are reputed, guifted Christians, and principall religious persons, when as many of them get good estates by so doing, good benefices, and others who make not a trade of it, as many devout pastors do; yet gaine so much credit thereby, as doth much increase their Trades, and advance their Custom and dealing in the world, and now and then helps to a good round Office. And whilst any of this strain of Christians, may live in this kind of devotion twenty years, preach for twenty or forty shillings a year, and have the repute, of a most religious knowing Christian, from the testimony of the most grave, learned, and solemn pastors of all Congregations, if but a part of their religious disbursments be spent upon them, it is not to be wondered at, that so few are found to serve God sincerely in the way of pure and undefi- [24] led Religion, which would plume their Peacocks feathers, and cost them more in one year, then all their lip-service, and Church-devotion, doth many of them in their whole life-time.

Nay, so impudent are many of these proud boasting Churches, (who glory to follow precisely the pattern shewed in the mount) that contrary to all example of the Apostles and first Christians; they can content themselves to be known usurers, and those that are not such themselves, can allow it in their fellow Members, their Pastors, Elders, and Deacons can tolerate it, and why not, as well as for their pastors to take monies from such, as are of lesse abilitie then themselves; nay, do not many of them spend the greatest part of their time, either in making, buying, and selling of baubles and toyes, such as serve only to furnish out the pride, luxury, and fantasticallnesse of the world; yea, view them well in their apparell, from head to foote; consider them in their dyet and usuall feastings; in their furniture for their houses, even in these sad and miserable times; and then say, whether their silks, their fine and delicate linnen, their Laces, Beavers, Plushes; their Fancies, Plate, Rings, and Jewells; do not demonstrate [25] from what roote they are, that they are meere worldlings indeed, and Christians only in name and tongue, and not that neither, if they are well observed.

For there are many amongst them, for slandering and back-biting; for circumvention and an hipocriticall carriage, shall vie and compare with any sort of men in the world; they can play the part of Spies, Intelligencers, plot and betray, upon pretence of intimacy, of endeared friendship and familiarity, eat, drink, be merry with you, day after day, week after week, for months, year for many years and after al: professe boldly, openly, confidently, before their Church, to Neighbors, friends, or strangers, that all this intimacy, friendship, familiarity, was only and meerely to deceive, and to discover what might be, to mischief the parties with whom they held it: shall we aske which of the Apostles was a slanderer, a spy, an Intelligencer, a betrayer: certainly none but Judas, and the followers of Judas; let them henceforth professe themselves, at least, let all that know them, so account them, unles they manifest their speedy true repentance, for bringing such reproach to the profession of Christianity. [26]

But what will such men stick at, as have once dared to dissemble before God, to call themselves Preachers, and are not: to gather Churches, and to joyn and continue in the fellowship of meere mock-Churches, that dare attempt the Ordinances with prophane hands, without, and before Commission given from above, that dare pretend Commission, and yet can shew no seale, no letters of credit from Heaven, that dare affirm their own opinions and Sermons, to be the word of God: and all this after admonition, from such persons too, as out of Conscience have seperated from them, against whom also they persist to shoote their most sharp and poysoned Arrowes; even bitter words, false invectives, lyes, and slanders.

O therefore consider this! all ye whose Consciences are yet sound amongst them, or but a little taynted, and see into what a wretched condition ye may be led before ye are aware; there is no stop in wickednesse, but a progresse from one degree of evill to another, unlesse at first: therefore stop in time, and come out from amongst them, least ye soone partake with them in their sinnes; and neither approve, nor connive at what you see and know to be against the judgment of your [27] Consciences, least in time you become as the worst and vilest of them.

Study the Scriptures, that word of truth: blesse God for them, forsake them not for the vain traditions of men, for the uncertain notions, Doctrines, and comments of pretended Preachers; and be certain of this, that you may as soone as they themselves, come to a good and right understanding therein,——and that you may do so, Read them with these Considerations.

That although whatsoever is written, is written for our learning, and that we have great cause to be thankfull to God for vouchsaffing us the knowledge of the severall ways of his dispensations to man, according to the severall times, and ages, which were from Adam, (which was the first) unto the time of the descending of the holy spirit, (which was the last:) yet are we seriously to know, that this last dispensation of the holy spirit, is that which principally concerneth us rightly to understand, and to apply to our selves, both for our comfort and rule of life; for unto this time and dispensation doth our blessed Saviour himself referre us, saying, I will send you another Comforter, he shall lead you into all truth, he shall bring to remem- [28] brance the things that I have told you: and he performed his promise effectually to the Apostles, whose writings we have, containing what the same spirit taught unto them; the truth whereof, they were enabled, and did, confirm with miracles, so as it might be as truly said of them, as it was of Christ our Lord; that they taught as men having authority, and not as the Scribes, nor as the uncertain pharisaicall teachers of these times.

Unto which word of theirs, we are principally to give heed: but therein also, we are chiefly to discover and to mind, what that Doctrine was, which they by the spirit, were ordained to preach? because that being understood and believed, doth give the beleever thereof, the name and being of a Christian, how plain and brief soever it be; for we must note, that there are many things written by the Apostles upon occasions, that concerned only or chiefly, the times wherein they wrote, and the places and persons to whom they wrote, which is the true cause that many things are too hard for us to understand; but there was one universall Doctrine, which they were to preach to all Nations, [29] wherewith all their writings do abound, and which is very plain and easie to be understood.

And this is it, namely, that the same Jesus whom the Jewes crucified, was Lord and Christ: That he is the propitiation for our sins, and not only for ours, but for the sins of the whole world, That it is the bloud of Christ which cleanseth us from all sinne, That his love is so exceeding towards us, that even when we were enemies, Christ dyed for us: This was the Doctrine which begot people unto the faith, and made them Beleevers: and they used no other inducement, unto Beleevers, to walk as becometh this Gospel (or glad tydings of peace and reconciliation between God and us,) but this, ye are bought with a price, therefore honour God, both in your bodies, and in your spirits: their strongest Argument to perswade, being this and the like: That the love of God which bringeth salvation unto all men hath appeared, teaching us, to deny all ungodlinesse & unrighteousnes of men, and to live righteously, godly, and soberly in this present world: that we should love as Christ hath loved, who gave himself an Offering [30] and a Sacrifice for us: so that if we would try each others Faith, we are to consider each others love; so much faith, so much love; so much love, so much pure and undefiled Religion; extending it self to the fatherles and to the Widdow; to the hungry, the naked, sick, and imprisoned; it being evident, that he who hath this worlds goods, and suffereth his brother to lack, hath not the love of God in him, yea though he have never so great parts of knowledg, zeale, tongues, miracles, yet being void of love, he is nothing: plainly manifesting that all other Religions, are but as defiled and impure in comparison of this.

And these are the Doctrines, which make good the rejoyning of the Angels, bringing glory to God in the highest, in earth peace, good will towards men: These are sufficient, and in these do all sorts of Christians agree, and never had disagreed but for false Teachers, Wolves in sheepes Clothing; who crept in to devoure the flock: causing divers strifes and contentions, about genealogies, and about the Law, which made the Apostle abundance of trouble, crying out, *O foolish Galathians who hath be-* [31] *witched you;* telling them plainly, if righteousnesse came by the Law, then Christ dyed in vain; others, it should seem, fell to observe Dayes and Times, Sabaoths and Weeks, justifying themselves, and censuring others: provoking the Apostle to tell them, he was afraid of them, that he had bestowed labor in vain upon them, earnestly desiring them, to let no man deceive them, in respect of an holy day, or of the new Moon, or of the Sabaoth, &c.

The truth is, and upon experience it will be found a truth: that once exceed these plain indusputable Doctrines, and you will be ever to seeke; for though it be a kind of happinesse, to read in Genesis the proceedings of God towards our first Parents, to Abel, Cayne, Enoch, to Noah and the world that perished in the floud; to see his mighty power at the Confusion of Babell: his love to Abraham and Sarah, to Isaac, Jacob, and the twelve Patriarks, to see their way of worship, to observe his mighty wonders in Egypt, in the Wildernesse, and in the promised Land, under the Judges: Saul and David, Solomon, and the rest of the Kings of Judah and Israel: To know with what power he spake by his holy [32] Prophets in all times, even to John the Baptist.

Yet when we have done all, we must acknowledge, that very many things exceed our understandings, and that we draw no comfort like unto this, that unto Christ, do all these beare witnesse: and though we have great cause to blesse God, for those wonderfull things we read of the life of Christ, of his wisdom, goodnesse, and power; by which he beat down the wisdom, craft, and policy of the Scribes and Pharices, of the high Priest and great ones of the world: and whereby he made it manifest, that he was indeed the Christ, yet draw we no comfort like unto that, which the Apostles publish't by the power of the holy spirit, the comforter promised by Christ before his Assention: because by this dispensation of God, only, do we come to know the benefits of Christs death, and that he is the end of the Law for righteousnesse, and the propitiation for our sinnes; whereby we have peace of Conscience, and joy in the Holy-Ghost.

We Read, with thankfulnesse to God, the Acts of the Apostles, all the Epistles of Paul, of Peter, James, Jude, and the Epistles [33] of John, & the Revelat. to St. John: But we must still acknowledge, that there are very many things in them all, which wee apprehend not fully. We Read of Apostles, Evangelists, Prophets, Pastors, and Teachers, and of the ordering and regulating of Churches, and of gifts given to all these from on high; but not so plainly exprest, as to leave the Conscientious without dispute, and difference thereupon: nor so collected into any one Book, as to convince, that God now under the Gospel, so exactly enjoyned Church Government, as he did under the Law; where Moses was expressely commanded to write particularly all that was required, not leaving out so much as Candlesticks, Snuffers, or Besomes. And when we come to compare the Churches, or their Pastors, and their abilities of our times, with those we read of: or the infallible power by which they spake, with the uncertaine Doctrines of ours, alas we must lay our hands upon our mouths, and hide our faces, as children use to doe, when they are discovered by people of understanding, at their childish immitations, of Christnings and Feastings; where, in a low and miserable weake forme [34] they counterfeit things reall: so that if we shall deale plainely with our selves, we must confesse, wee are at a losse in these things, and that hence onely is our rejoycing. That wee undoubtedly know Jesus Christ and him Crucified, and knowing him, accompt all things as losse and dung in Comparison of him: and that we may be found in him, not having our owne righteousnesse which is of the Law, but the righteousnesse which is of God in him: so that the whole Scriptures to us, is as the Field mentioned in the Gospel, and this the Jewell, for which the wise Merchant, sould all that ever he had to purchase it.

And truely, if the Traders in Divine things, truely consider this, how learned soever they are in Arts and Sciences, in all kinds of Readings and Languages, and how mighty and skilfull soever they would be thought in the Exposition, opening, and interpretation of all places of Scripture, when they come to cast up their account, possibly; nay, certainly, (if they are serious therein) they will accompt all as nothing for this Pearle, which passeth value, they will sell All to purchase it; and rejoyce ex- [35] ceedingly in the exchange, as the most profitable that ever they made.

And this certainly would be done frequently by all who with honest and good hearts Read the Scriptures; were they not kept from it by false Teachers, who hold them in suspence for their own advantage, ever raising, and starting new Questions, and new Opinions, whereby men are ever learning, but never at rest in the knowledge of this one necessary truth: but are tost too and fro, with every winde of Doctrine: and all by giving eare to those that call themselves Preachers, but are not: that pretend to expound the Scriptures, when as they raise nothing but doubts, and darken them; that say they Interpret, when they are to seeke for the meaning; being altogether doubtfull and uncertaine in all they doe.

And therfore much more happy are they, who read with honest and good hearts, and only Read, and considerately lay to heart; giving no care to these charmers: these doubtfull Expositors, these mocke-Preachers, with their trumpery Sermons, stuft with naught but uncertainety and fantasticke doctrines, which in the day of the [36] necessity of mans Conscience, prove like a broken Reed, that instead of help, further wounds.

Nor let any man henceforth wonder, whence so many severall and strange opinions should arise, by which the world becomes even rent and torne in peeces? It is from this kind of Preaching, and false Exposition of the Holy Scriptures. It being so, in more ancient times, with the Law and the old Testament, as Petrus Cunaeus, (*de Republ.* Lib. 2. chap. 17.) brings to light: affirming, That howsoever the Law was Read amongst them in the former times, either in publicke or in private, yet the bare Text was onely Read, without glosse or descant, *Interpretatio Magistrorum nulla, commentatio nulla;* but in the second Temple, when there were no Prophets, then did the Scribes and Doctors (mock Prophets, as our mock Preachers) begin to Comment, and make their severall Expositions on the holy Text: *Ex quo natae disputationes & sententiae contrariae;* from whence (saith he) sprung up debates, and doubtfull disputations: and most probable it is (saith another upon him) that from this liberty of Interpretation sprung [37] up diversity of judgements, from whence arose the severall Sects of Pharisees, Essees and Saduces; who by their difference of Opinions, did distract the multitude, and condemne one another.

Even so in these times, when as there are no true Apostles, Evangelists, Prophets, Pastors, or Teachers, endowed with power from on high, as all true ones are; by which, they are enabled to divide the word of God aright, to stop the mouths of gainsayers, and to say, thus saith the Lord, thus speakes the Lord, and not I, And if an Angell from Heaven, preach any other doctrine, let him be accursed. In the absence of these, are crept in swarmes of Locusts, false Teachers, men of corrupt minds, making Marchandize of the blessed Word of Truth, and for that wicked end, dress it up in what shape their Art or Rhetorick can devise; and upon pretence of exposition, raise thousands of doubts and disputes, write millions of books, and preach innumerable Sermons; whereby the people are divided, and subdivided into Factions, Sects and parties; and whereby the end of the Gospel, which directs only to peace and love, is most un- [38] thankfully made use of, as a fire-brand of quarrells and dissentions.

In the mean time, the poor innocent Dove, that desirs to injoy the peace of his mind in this *Unum necessarium*, that little Doctrin of Christ crucified, and to walke in love, ever worshiping God in Sprit, and in Truth, dis-intangled from all formes, as things he finds uncertain, dis-ingaged from all false Churches (and cannot find a true one) that in all things gives thanks, and dares not pray, but for what he needs, nor joyn with any, where he is not before agreed what to aske; This innocent dove findes not a place to rest his foot in, but is become the game of these birds of prey, these Ravens, Vultures, and Harpies.

O that all ingenious men would lay these things to heart! that they would looke more exactly into these Churches, more boldly & firmly, trying, examining & weighing them in the ballance: that they would shake off that vaile of superstition, and reverend respect to mens persons; whereby they are over-awed into a high esteeme of meer vanities, empty shels without kernells, empty clouds that hold no water. That they would consider, how extreamly partial they are in judging of things; For, who is [39] he, that doth not exceedingly condemn the impudence of Simon Magus, in offering to buy the holy Spirit of God with mony, purposely to have made a gain thereof; and yet can daily see men counterfeit the having of the Spirit, and pretend to preach and to pray by it; when as it is evident, they have it not, and yet are no whit troubled at this, though they see it done also, even for filthy luchre, vain glory, or other vile respects, as he intended.

But all are not alike guilty, many through weaknesse, and a preposterous zeale, being carryed with the stream and current of the times; and many there are, who have run themselves quite out of breath, in searching after peace, and rest, in the various waies of these Churches, and from one Church way to another; but find none to comfort them, nothing to establish them; confessing, that instead of reall ordinances, they find only names; instead of power in them, they find only formes, fashions, likenesses and imitations, meere pictures, and Images without life, altogether dead and comfortlesse; and are held up meerely by the power of Art, craft, and pollicy of men, not without the counte- [40] nance of corrupt authorities, & oppressive States-men; who find it (as it hath ever proved) a notable means to devide the people, making use thereof, to their wicked and tyrannous ends; But God in these times hath had instruments, to lay all kinds of delusion open: so that henceforth, if men continue in these evill waies, they are altogether inexcusable.

Neither will men ever live in peace, and quietnes one with another, so long as this vaile of false counterfeit preaching, remaineth before their eyes, nor untill the mocke Churches are overturned and laid flat;

For so long as men flatter themselves in those vaine waies, and puffe themselves up with vaine thoughts, that they are in a way well pleasing to God, because they are in a Church way, as they call it, or because they are able to speak long together (which they call preaching) they are for the most part regardles of storing their minds with truths reall Christian virtue, little or nothing careing, either for publick Justice, Peace, or freedom amongst men; but spend their time in endlesse disputes, in condemning and censuring those that are contrary minded; whereby nothing but heats and dis- [41] contents are ingendred, backbiting and snarling at all that oppose them, will neither buy, nor sell with them, if they can chuse, nor give them so much as a good looke; but on all occasions are ready to Censure, one to be carnall, another erronious; one an Atheist, another an Heretick, a Sectary, Scismatick, a Blasphemer, a man not worthy to live, though they have nothing whereof to accuse him; which in the true Scripture sence, will beare the title of an offence, but are stirred in their spirits against him, because happily he speaketh against their Church-way, and frequently sheweth the vanity and emptinesse of those things wherein they glory, and by which they distinguish themselves from other men.

So that it were much better for the Common-wealth, that all mens mindes were set at Liberty, from these entanglements, that so there might be an end of wrangling about shaddows; for if men were once free from this Church-bondage, they would by reading the Scriptures with such like considerations, as are before expressed, soone come to be able to understand the intent, & substantiall scope there- [42] of; and become substantiall Christians; full fraught with true Christian virtue, and reall godlinesse, which would incline them to a tendernesse of spirit towards all those they saw in any errour; make them to compassionate mens failings, and infirmities; and be ready to help the distressed, and any waies afflicted: it would enlarge their hearts toward all men, making them like unto our heavenly Father, who causeth his Sun to shine on the just, and unjust: that giveth to all men liberally, and upbraideth no man.

Certainely, were we all busied onely in those short necessary truths, we should soon become practicall Christians; and take more pleasure in Feeding the hungry, Cloathing the naked, visiting and comforting of the sicke, releeving the aged, weake and impotent; in delivering of Prisoners, supporting of poore families, or in freeing a Common wealth from all Tyrants, oppressors, and deceivers, (the authors and promoters of all corruption and superstition) thereby manifesting our universal love to all mankind, without respect of persons, Opinions,

Societies, or Churches; doubtlesse there were no way like unto this, to adorne the Go- [43] spel of Christ; men and women so exercising themselves, and persevering therein, might possibly deserve the name of Saints; but for men to assume that title for being a Presbyter, an Independent, Brownist, Anabaptist, or for being of this or that opinion, or of this or that forme of Worship, or for being able to Pray, and Preach (as they call it) three or foure houres together, venting their own uncertain notions, and conjectures, or for looking more sadly, and solemnly then other people, or for dressing themselves after a peculiar manner: or for pretending to have the Spirit of God, though they are ever to seeke about the meaning of the Scriptures: or for sucking in, and sighing out reproaches, and slanders against their neighbours: proceeds from meer pride and vanity of mind; when as the best of these put altogether, amount not to so much, towards the making of a true Saint, as one mercifull tender hearted compassionate act, for Christs sake doth.

And therefore those who would truly honour God, let them not think, that he will be flattered with words, or be served with lip service, with that which costeth [44] little or nothing; but let them resolve that he expecteth to be served with no lesse then with all our heart, with all our might, and with all our strength, to be honoured both in our bodies, and in our spirits, for they are his.

It is most certain, that men are first to know and understand, before they can become practicall Christians, and though the Scriptures are very plain and full, as to necessary knowledge, yet the errors of weake and perverse teachers do so abound, that it is a difficult thing to escape them, and to fall into a profitable method of reading, and meditation of the word of God: wherein may the considerations aforementioned, prove as profitable, as they are conscionably intended; but doubtlesse the best way to perfect knowledge, is, and will be, by endeavouring after meetings of people to conferre and discourse together (in a discreet, quiet, and well ordered way) upon necessary points only: the way of preaching or long set speeches, being subject to abundance of error, and inconvenience: and therefore it would be happy, that all welmeaning people would seriously set themselves to procure frequent [45] and full meetings, for increase of knowledg in all sorts of people, and no longer to depend, either on the publique, or congregationall Sermons, for information of their understandings: it being evident, that they serve rather to dignifie the Speakers, and to sway the hearers into what they please, then to any just or necessary end.

And as every one increaseth in knowledge, let them know, that God

hath not vouchsafed his word unto us, to make us talkers, or discour-
sers only; as the manner of many knowing people is, who as soone as
they arive to a good measure of understanding, and are thereby freed
from the burthens and oppressions, which error and superstition had
brought into their Consciences, instead of being thankfull to God for
the same, by dilligence in the wayes of doing good; they become
carelesse, turning the goodnesse and truth of God manifested in his
word to Idlenesse, if not to wantonnesse, not caring what becommeth
of the miseries of the times, or other mens sufferings, but ever after,
live as in a pleasing dream; these who ever they are, are to be looked
upon as the most unworthy of men, because the most ungrate- [46]
full: the most opposite to the end of their being, the vilest of Creatures,
because sloathfull Christians: the best things, being the worst, if once
corrupted.

And therefore it will be very good, for every one to stir up the
knowledg of God that is in him, and to keep it alive by continuall
practice, upon all occasions: practice in good and just and charitable
things being that wherein the Conscience is most delighted; so that if
any propose to themselves any happines here in this life, it is to be
found only in doing of good: the more good, the better contented, and
the greater the happinesse, man being in nothing like unto God, but in
doing good, nothing is more acceptable to God, nothing is more pleasant to Conscience, his vicegerent in us; to do good therefore, and to
distribute, forget not, for with such sacrifices God is well pleased:
whilst we have time and oppertunity, let us do good unto all men.

Let us all strive to go on before another in love, and let there be no
other strife at all amongst us; we wish with all our soules that all
reproach, despites and envyings amongst men might for ever cease,
and that difference in judgment, may no longer [47] occasion difference
in affection; there being in our apprehension no cause at all; but that all
men going in their severall wayes of serving God, whether publique or
private, may neverthelesse be free to communicate in all civill Offices
of love and true friendship, and cordially joyne with any, for a publique good; but if notwithstanding all that hath been endeavoured, or
hath been said: this Generation of congregationall men shall continue
to puffe, and swell through pride of heart, & to lift themselves up into
the Chayre of the scornfull, and as the man in Peters Chayre assume a
power of life and death over all opinions and wayes not owned by
them: as if they were infallible judges of all controversies, making no
scruple of blasting mens good names and reputations, or of undoing of
whose Families thereby: they must then expect to be told their own,

and be made appear to the world—as they are,—not as they would be esteemed.

It being evident by what hath been said, that although they have boasted themselvs to be rich, and increased with goods, and to have need of nothing; yet, they are as the luke-warm Church of Laodicea, miserable, & [48] wretched, and poore, and blind, and naked—and for all their bigg and swelling conceipts of parts, of gifts, of Saint-ship, of the Spirit, & (in effect) pharisaically crying out, *Lord we thank thee, we are not as other men,* nor as those poore Publicans, that receive all their knowledge of Divine things from the Scriptures onely, and are taught onely thereby; Notwithstanding these bigg swelling words, their Peacocks feathers, being thus pluckt off, you see: and they, will they, nill they, must also see, that they must be content at last, to shake hands even with those poore Publicans; and acknowledge that they have no other infallible Teacher of Divine things, but the Scriptures; and that they partake no more of the Spirit, then what that blessed Word of the Spirit planteth in them.

And if their consciences are awakened, will be enforced to forsake their falling Churches: unlesse for politique ends, they shall stifle the power of these Truths within them; chusing rather to perish in the rubbish, then to seem to have bin so exceedingly mistaken; which will prove an unpardonable error; For, however the best of men may erre, yet they are the [49] worst of men, that persist in error, after the discovery.

And therefore, if there be any whose consciences shall be fully informed of the vanity of these Churches; and yet for any ends shall continue to support the reputation of them; let all such know, that those who dare be so impious, as to stop the continuall cry of their consciences, must necessarily desire in their hearts there were no God, whose Vicegerent Conscience is; which is the most sad and dangerous condition that man can fall into in this life.

And certainly they will find it far better to forsake their tottering immaginary structures: confess their emptines, & sinfull imitation, taking shame unto themselves and giving glory unto God, whose name and power they have much diminished, by affirming those to be Churches which are not, those Pastors and Preachers which are not, those Saints which are not: his blessed Word to be but a dead Letter: that to be his Word, which is but conjecturall Sermons; and in censuring those to be erronious and carnall Christians, who have more warrant for what they do then themselves; And then by a more considerate, [50] ingenious, and Christian-like carriage, to make amends for the future, which would very much rejoyce the hearts of all that love the Lord Jesus in sincerity, whose Truth and Glory will be advanced by the Scriptures; when all the roving, wild and wandring immaginations of mens spirits, shall vanish, and come to nought.

FINIS

Feb. 23. 1648–49,
Imprimatur
THEODORE JENNINGS. [51]

22

A Manifestation from Lieutenant Col. John Lilburn, Mr. William Walwyn, Mr. Thomas Prince, and Mr. Richard Overton

14 April 1649
Reprinted from a copy of the tract in the Thomason Collection in the British Library

A Manifestation was published over the names of Lilburne, Walwyn, Prince, and Overton and dated "From the Tower—April 14. 1649."[1] There is no imprint, but some copies include the imprimatur of Gilbert Mabbott.[2] Walwyn declared that "four heads, and hands were nigh equally employed,"[3] but neither at the time nor since has there been serious doubt that Walwyn was the draftsman.[4] At once conciliatory and firm, *A Manifestation's* phrasing and tone are as characteristic of Walwyn as they are unlike anything written by Lilburne or Overton.

"Intended for their full vindication from the many aspersions cast upon them," the prisoners' *Manifestation* vigorously denies that Levellers advocate anarchy or intend "an equalling of mens estates"—unless there be "universall assent thereunto from all and every one of the People"—and expresses sorrow that they have been disowned "by such as we took for Friends, our brethren of severall Churches."[5] The heart of the tract justifies Leveller principles and promises a final appeal to the nation in a revised Agreement of the People.[6] Calm and even-tempered throughout, *A Manifestation* may be Walwyn's most attractive and effective political treatise.

A Manifestation is reprinted as Walwyn's work in: *Leveller Manifestoes*, ed. Wolfe, No. 18; *Leveller Tracts*, ed. Haller and Davies, pp. 276–84; *Freedom in Arms*, ed. Morton, No. 12; *Levellers in the English Revolution*, ed. Aylmer, No. 13.

A Manifestation

FROM Lieutenant Col. *John Lilburn*, M^r. *William Walwyn*, M^r. *Thomas Prince*, and M^r. *Richard Overton*, (Now Prisoners in the Tower of *London) And others, commonly (though unjustly) Styled LEVELLERS.

Intended for their FULL VINDICATION FROM The many aspersions cast upon them, to render them odious to the World, and unserviceable to the *Common-wealth*.

And to satisfie and ascertain all Men whereunto all their Motions and Endeavours tend, and what is the ultimate Scope of their Engagement in the *PUBLICK AFFAIRES*.

They also that render evill for good, are Our adversaries: because We follow the thing that good is.

Printed in the year of our LORD, 1649.

A MANIFESTATION FROM Lieutenant Colonel *John Lilburn*, Master *William Walwyne*, Master *Thomas Prince*, and Master *Richard Overton* (now prisoners in the Tower of *London*) and others, commonly (though unjustly) stiled *Levellers*.

Since no man is born for himself only, but obliged by the Laws of Nature (which reaches all) of Christianity (which ingages us as Christians) and of Publick Societie and Government, to employ our endeavours for the advancement of a communitive Happinesse, of equall concernment to others as our selves: here have we (according to that measure of understanding God hath dispensed

unto us) laboured with much weaknesse indeed, but with integrity of
heart, to produce out of the Common Calamities, such a proportion
of Freedom and good to the Nation, as might somewhat compensate
its many grievances and lasting sufferings: And although in doing
thereof we have hitherto reaped only Reproach, and hatred for our
good Will, and been faine to wrestle with the violent passions of
Powers and Principalities; yet since it is nothing so much as our
Blessed Master and his Followers suffered before us, and but what at
first we reckoned upon, we cannot be thereby any whit dismayed in
the performance of our duties, supported inwardly by the Innocency
and evennesse of our Consciences.

'Tis a very great unhappinesse we well know, to be alwayes strug-
ling and striving in the world, and does wholly keep us from the
enjoyment of those contentments our severall Conditions reach unto:
So that if we should consult only with ourselves, and regard only our
own ease, Wee should never enterpose as we have done, in behalfe of
the Commonwealth: But when so much has been done for recovery of
our Liberties, and seeing God hath so blest that which has been done,
as thereby to cleer the way, and to afford an opportunity which these
600 years has been desired, but could never be attained, of making
this a truly happy and wholly Free Nation; We think our selves bound
by the greatest obligations that may be, to prevent the neglect of this
opportunity, and to hinder as much as lyes in us, that the bloud
which has been shed be not spilt like water upon the ground, nor that
after the abundant Calamities, which have overspread all quarters of
the Land, the change be onely Notionall, Nominall, Circumstantiall,
whilst the reall Burdens, Grievances, and Bondages, be continued,
even when the Monarchy is changed into a Republike.

We are no more concern'd indeed then other men, and could bear
the Yoke we believe as easily as others; but since a Common Duty lyes
upon every man to be cautious and circumspect in behalfe of his
Country, especially while the Government thereof is setling, other
mens neglect is so far we thinke from being a just motive to us of the
like sloath and [3] inanimadvertency, as that it rather requires of us an
increase of care and circumspection, which if it produces not so good
a settlement as ought to be, yet certainly it will prevent its being so
bad as otherwise it would be, if we should all only mind our particular callings and imployments.

So that although personally we may suffer, yet our solace is that the
Common-wealth is therby some gainer, and we doubt not but that
God in his due time wil so cleerly dispel the Clouds of Ignominy and

Obloquy which now surround us by keeping our hearts upright and our spirits sincerely publike, that every good man will give us the right hand of fellowship, and be even sorry that they have been estranged, and so hardly opinionated against us: We question not but that in time the reason of such misprisions will appeare to be in their eyes and not in our Actions, in the false Representation of things to them and improper glosses that are put upon every thing we do or say: In our own behalfs we have as yet said nothing, trusting that either shame and Christian duty would restraine men from making so bold with others good Name and Reputation, or that the sincerity of our actions would evince the falshood of these scandals, and prevent the Peoples Beliefe of them; But we have found that with too much greedinesse they suck in Reports that tend to the discredit of others, and that our silence gives encouragement to bad Rumors of us; so that in all places they are spread, and industriously propagated as well amongst them that know us, as them that know us not, the first being fed with Jealousies that there is more in our designs then appeares, that there is something of danger in the bottom of our hearts, not yet discovered: that we are driven on by others, that we are even discontented and irresolved, that no body yet knowes what we would have, or where our desires will end; whilst they that know us not are made believe any strange conceit of us, that we would Levell all mens estates, that we would have no distinction of Orders and Dignities amongst men, that we are indeed for no government, but a Popular confusion; and then againe that we have bin Agents for the King, and now for the Queen; That we are Atheists, Antiscripturists, Jesuites and indeed any thing, that is hatefull and of evill repute amongst men.

All which we could without observance pass over, remembring what is promised to be the Portion of good men, were the damage only personall, but since the ends of such Rumors are purposely to make us uselesse and unserviceable to the Common-wealth, we are necessitated to open our breasts and shew the world our insides, for removing of those scandalls that lye upon us, and likewise for manifesting plainly and particularly what our desires are, and in what we will center and acquiess: all which we shall present to publike view and consideration, not pertinatiously or Magisterially, as concluding other mens judgements, but manifesting our own, for our further vindication, and for the procuring of a Bond and lasting establishment for the Commonwealth.

First, Then it will be requisite that we express our selves concerning

Levelling, for which we suppose is commonly meant an equalling of mens estates, and taking away the proper right and Title that every man has to what is his own. This as we have formerly declared against, particularly in our petition of the 11 of Sept. so do we again professe that to attempt an inducing the same is most injurious, un-lesse there did precede an universall assent thereunto from all and every one of the People. Nor doe we, under favour, judge it within the Power of a Representative it selfe, because although their power is supreame, yet it is but deputative and of trust, and consequently must be restrained expresly or tacitely, to some particulars essential as well to the Peoples safety and freedom as to the present Government.

The Community amongst the primitive Christians, was Voluntary, not Coactive; they [4] brought their goods and laid them at the Apostles feet, they were not enjoyned to bring them, it was the effect of their Charity and heavenly mindednesse, which the blessed Apostles begot in them, and not the Injunction of any Constitution, which as it was but for a short time done, and in but two or three places, that the Scripture makes mention of, so does the very doing of it there and the Apostles answer to him that detained a part, imply that it was not esteemed a duty, but reckoned a voluntary act occasioned by the abundant measure of faith that was in those Christians and Apostles.

We profess therefore that we never had it in our thoughts to Level mens estates, it being the utmost of our aime that the Commonwealth be reduced to such a passe that every man may with as much security as may be enjoy his propriety.

We know very well that in all Ages those men that engage themselves against Tyranny, unjust and Arbitrary proceedings in Magistrats, have suffered under such appellations, the People being purposely frighted from that wich is good by insinuations of imaginary evill.

But be it so, we must notwithstanding discharge our Duties, which being performed, the successe is in Gods hand to whose good pleasure we must leave the cleering of mens spirits, our only certainty being Tranquillity of mind, and peace of Conscience.

For distinction of Orders and Dignities, We think them so far needfull, as they are animosities of vertue, or requisite for the maintenance of the Magistracy and Government, we thinke they were never intended for the nourishment of Ambition, or subjugation of the People but only to preserve the due respect and obedience in the People which is necessary for the better execution of the Laws.

That we are for Government and against Popular Confusion, we conceive all our actions declare, when rightly considered, our aim having bin all along to reduce it as near as might be to perfection, and certainly we know very well the pravity and corruption of mans heart is such that there could be no living without it; and that though Tyranny is so excessively bad, yet of the two extreames, Confusion is the worst: Tis somewhat a strange consequence to infer that because we have laboured so earnestly for a good Government, therefore we would have none at all, Because we would have the dead and exorbitant Branches pruned, and better sciens grafted, therefore we would pluck the Tree up by the roots.

Yet thus have we been misconceived, and misrepresented to the world, under which we must suffer, till God sees it fitting in his good time to cleer such harsh mistakes, by which many, even good men keep a distance from us.

For those weake suppositions of some of us being Agents for the King or Queen, we think it needful to say no more but this, That though we have not bin any way violent against the persons of them, or their Partie, as having aimed at the conversion of all, and the destruction of none, yet doe we verily beleeve that those Principles and Maxims of Government which are most fundamentally opposite to the Prerogative, and the Kings interest, take their first rise and originall from us, many whereof though at first startled at, and disown'd by those that professed the greatest opposition to him, have yet since been taken up by them and put in practise: and this we think is sufficient, though much more might be said to cleer us from any Agency for that Party.

It is likewise suggested that we are acted by others, who have other ends then appear to us; we answer, That that cannot be, since every thing has its rise amongst our selves, and since those things we bring to light cannot conduce to the ends of any but the publike weale of the Nation.

All our Desires, Petitions and Papers are directly opposite to all corrupt Interests; nor [5] have any credit with us but persons well known, and of certain aboads, and such as have given sound and undeniable testimonies of the truth of their affection to their Country: Besides, the things we promote, are not good onely in appearance, but sensibly so: not moulded nor contrived by the subtill or politick Principles of the World, but plainly produced and nakedly sent, without any insinuating arts, relying wholly upon the apparent and universall beleefe they carry in themselves; and that is it which convinces and engages us in the promotion thereof. So that that suggestion has not indeed any foundation in it self, but is purposely framed, as we conceive, to make us afraid one of another, and to disable us in the promotion of those good things that tend to the freedom and happinesse of the Common-wealth.

For our being Jesuits, either in Order or Principles, as 'tis severally reported of us; Though the easiest Negative is hardly proved; yet we can say, That those on whom the first is principally fix'd, are married, and were never over Sea: and we think Marriage is never dispenc'd withall in that Order, and that none can be admitted into the Order but such as are personally present. 'Tis hard that we are put to expresse thus much; and haply we might better passe such reports over in silence; but that we beleeve the very mentioning of them publickly, will be an answer to them, and make such as foment them asham'd of such generally condemned wayes of discrediting and blasting the Reputation of other men. For the principles of Jesuits, we professe we know not what they are; but they are generally said to be full of craft and worldly policy; and therefore exceedingly different from that plainnesse and simplicity that is apparantly visible in all our proceedings.

Whereas its said, we are Atheists and Antiscripturists, we professe that we beleeve there is one eternall and omnipotent God, the Author and Preserver of all things in the world. To whose will and directions, written first in our hearts, and afterwards in his blessed Word, we ought to square our actions and conversations. And though we are not so strict upon the formall and Ceremonial part of his Service, the method, manner, and personall injunction being not so clearly made out unto us, nor the necessary requisites which his Officers and Ministers ought to be furnished withall as yet appearing to us in any that pretend thereunto: yet for the manifestation of Gods love in Christ, it is cleerly assented unto by us; and the practicall and most reall part of Religion is as readily submitted unto by us, as being, in our apprehensions, the most eminent and the most excellent in the world, and as proceeding from no other but that God who is Goodnesse it self: and we humbly desire his Majesty daily more and more to conform our hearts to a willing and sincere obedience thereunto.

For our not being preferred to Offices and Places of profit and credit, which is urged to be the ground of our dissatisfaction, we say, That although we know no reason why we should not be equally capable of them with other men, nor why our publick Affection should be any barr or hinderance thereunto: Yet on the other side, we suppose we can truly say of our selves, that we have not been so earnest and solicitous after them as others: and that in the Catalogue of Sutors, very few that are reckoned of us, are to be found. We are very sorry that so general a change of Officers is proposed, which we judge of no small disparagement to our Cause; and do think it best, that in removals of that kinde, the ground should not be difference in opinion, either in Religious or Civil Matters, but corruption or breach of Trust; considering the misery which befalls whole Families upon such Changes; and that discontents are thereby increased: Whereas we hold it necessary that all wayes of composure and acquieting those storms which the preceeding differences and distractions have begotten, be with utmost care and prudence endeavoured. [6]

And whereas 'tis urged, That if we were in power, we would bear our selves as Tyrannically as others have done: We confess indeed, that the experimentall defections of so many men as have succeeded in Authority, and the exceeding difference we have hitherto found in the same men in a low, and in an exalted condition, makes us even mistrust our own hearts, and hardly beleeve our own Resolutions of the contrary. And therefore we have proposed such an Establishment, as supposing men to be too flexible and yeelding to worldly Temptations, they should not yet have a means or opportunity either to injure particulars, or prejudice the Publick, without extreme hazard, and apparent danger to themselves. Besides, to the objection we have further to say, That we aim not at power in our selves, our Principles and Desires being in no measure of self-concernment: nor do we relie for obtaining the same upon strength, or a forcible obstruction; but solely upon that inbred and perswasive power that is in all good and just things, to make their own way in the hearts of men, and so to procure their own Establishment.

And that makes us at this time naked and defencelesse as we are, and amidst so many discouragements on all hands to persevere in our motions and desires of good to the Nation; although disowned therein at such a time when the doing thereof can be interpreted no other but a politick delivering us up to slaughter, by such as we took for Friends, our brethren of severall Churches; and for whom with truth of affection we have even in the most difficult times done many Services: all which, and whatsoever else can be done against us, we shall reckon but as badges of our sincerity, and be no whit discouraged thereby from the discharge of our duties.

For the dis-satisfactions that be upon many good mens spirits, for that they are not ascertained whereunto all our motions tend, and in what they will center,

Though, we conceive, they may have received some general satisfaction from what we have formerly at severall times propounded; yet since they were not disposed into such a form and condition as to become practicable; we have, with the best care and abilities God hath afforded us, cast the same into a Modell and Platform, which we shall speedily present unto the view and consideration of all, as the Standard and ultimate scope of our Designes, that so (in case of approvall) it may be subscribed and returned as agreed upon by the People. And thus far, we conceive, we may without offence or prejudice to Authority, proceed; and which we the rather do, because we know no better, and indeed no other way or means (but by such an Agreement) to remove (as much as may be) all disgusts and heart-burnings, and to settle the Common-wealth upon the fairest probabilities of a lasting Peace, and contentfull Establishment.

The Agreement of the People which was presented by his Excellency and the Officers of the Army to the Right Honourable the Commons in Parliament, although in many things short (according to our apprehensions) of what is necessary for the good of the Commonwealth, and satisfaction of the People; particularly, in that it containeth no provision for the certain removall of notorious and generally complained of grievances: And although it hath some things of much hazard to the Publick, —yet, had it been put in execution, we should scarcely have interrupted the proceedings thereof, since therein is contained many things of great and important concernment to the Common-wealth. But seeing the time proposed therein for reducing the same into practice, is now past, and that likewise the generality of the people have not, or do not approve of the same, for the reasons (as we suppose) fore-mentioned: We have thought fit to revise it, making onely such alterations therein as we conceive really necessary for the welfare, security and safety of the People, together with additionall Provisions for the [7] taking away of those Burdens and Grievances which may without reall prejudice to the Management of publick Affairs be removed.

And because it is essentiall to the nature of such an Agreement to take its rise from the People, we have therefore purposely declined the presentment thereof to the Parliament: and conceive it may speedily proceed to Subscription, and so to further practice, without any interruption to this Representative, untill the season prefix'd in the Agreement, for the assembling another: By whose immediate succession, without any intervall, the Affairs of the Common-wealth may suffer no stop or intermission.

Lastly, We conceive we are much mistaken in being judged impatient, and over-violent in our motions for the publick Good. To which we answer, That could we have had any assurance that what is desired should have otherwise, or by any have been done; and had not had some taste of the relinquishment of many good things that were promised, we should not have been so earnest and urgent for the doing thereof.

Though we know likewise it hath been very customary in such heretofore as never intended any freedom to the Nation, to except only against the season, and to protract the time so long, till they became sufficiently impowred to justifie the totall denyall and refusall thereof. However, the main reason of our proceeding as we do, is, because we prefer the way of a settlement by an Agreement of the People before any other whatsoever.

And thus the world may clearly see what we are, and what we aym at: We are altogether ignorant, and do from our hearts abominate all designes and contrivances of dangerous consequence which we are said (but God knows, untruly) to be labouring withall. Peace and Freedom is our Designe; by War we were never gainers, nor ever wish to be; and under bondage we have been hitherto sufferers. We desire however, that what is past may be forgotten, provided the Common wealth may have amends made it for the time to come. And this from our soul we desire.

Having no mens persons in hatred, and judging it needfull that all other respects whatsoever are to give way to the good of the Common-wealth, and this is the very truth and inside of our hearts.

From the Tower,
April 14. 1649.

> *John Lilburne*
> *William Walwyn*
> *Thomas Prince*
> *Richard Overton* [8]

23

An Agreement of the Free People of England. Tendered as a Peace-Offering to This Distressed Nation. By Lieutenant Colonel John Lilburne, Master William Walwyn, Master Thomas Prince, and Master Richard Overton, Prisoners in the Tower of London

1 May 1649
Partially reprinted from a copy of the tract in the Thomason Collection in the British Library

An Agreement of the Free People was published without separate title page, signed by Lilburne, Walwyn, Prince and Overton, dated 1 May 1649 and printed for Giles Calvert.[1] There are two identical copies in the Thomason Collection with the imprimatur of Gilbert Mabbott, dated 30 April 1649.[2] Copies lacking Mabbott's imprimatur may have been printed after 7 May, when Mabbott was forced out for licensing "divers dangerous books."[3]

An Agreement, unlike *A Manifestation*, is largely the product of all four signatories. The thirty articles of the constitution include echoes and repetitions from the December Agreement published as *Foundations of*

Freedom by Lilburne.[4] The last *Agreement* is a synthesis of Leveller
ideals and concerns, although Walwyn must have had misgivings
about disabling Roman Catholics from public office.[5] The opening
"Preparative to all sorts of people," which is reprinted below, is almost
certainly Walwyn's work. It is marked throughout by the quiet appeal
and optimism that set Walwyn's writing apart from Overton's trucu-
lence and the clamorous style of Lilburne.

Publication of *An Agreement* accorded with *A Manifestation*'s promise of "a Modell and Platform" of government.[6] Extending the proposals presented in December, the May *Agreement* more than doubled
the explicit rights reserved to the people.[7] Less a constitution than a
manifesto impossible to effect, it was, as Walwyn's "Preparative"
promised, "the ultimate and full scope of all our desires and intentions."[8]

An Agreement is reprinted in full in: *Levellers in the English Revolution,*
ed. Aylmer, No. 14; *Leveller Tracts,* ed. Haller and Davies, pp. 318–28;
Freedom in Arms, ed. Morton, No. 13; *Leveller Manifestoes,* ed. Wolfe,
No. 19.

AN AGREEMENT of the Free People of England.

Tendered as a *Peace-Offering* to this distressed *Nation.*

by Lieutenant Colonel *John Lilburne,* Master *William Walwyn,*
Master *Thomas Prince,* and Master *Richard Overton,* Prisoners in
the Tower of *London,* May the 1. 1649.

Matth. 5. verse 9. *Blessed are the Peace-makers for they shall be
called the children of God.*

A Preparative to all sorts of people.

If afflictions make men wise, and wisdom direct to happinesse, then certainly this Nation is not far from such a degree therof, as may compare if not far exceed, any part of the world:
having for some yeares by-past, drunk deep of the Cup of misery and
sorrow. We blesse God our consciences are cleer from adding affliction to affliction, having ever laboured from the beginning, of our
publick distractions, to compose and reconcile them: & should esteem

it the Crown of all our temporal felicity that yet we might be instrumentall in procuring the peace and prosperity of this Commonwealth the land of our Nativity.

And therefore according to our promise in our late *Manifestation* of the 14 of Aprill 1649 (being perswaded of the necessitie and justnesse thereof) as a Peace-Offering to the Free people of this Nation, we tender this ensuing Agreement, not knowing any more effectuall means to put a finall period to all our feares and troubles. [1]

It is a way of settlement, though at first much startled at by some in high authority; yet according to the nature of truth, it hath made its own way into the understanding, and taken root in most mens hearts and affections, so that we have reall ground to hope (what ever shall become of us) that our earnest desires and indeavours for good to the people will not altogether be null and frustrate.

The life of all things is in the right use and application, which is not our worke only, but every mans conscience must look to it selfe, and not dreame out more seasons and opportunities. And this we trust will satisfie all ingenuous people that we are not such wilde, irrationall, dangerous Creatures as we have been aspersed to be; This agreement being the ultimate and full scope of all our desires and intentions concerning the Government of this Nation, and wherein we shall absolutely rest satisfied and acquiesce; nor did we ever give just cause for any to beleeve worse of us by any thing either said or done by us, and which would not in the least be doubted, but that men consider not the interest of those that have so unchristian-like made bold with our good names; but we must bear with men of such interests as are opposite to any part of this Agreement, when neither our Saviour nor his Apostles innocency could stop such mens mouthes whose interests their doctrines and practises did extirpate: And therefore if friends at least would but consider what interest men relate to, whilst they are telling or whispering their aspersions against us, they would find the reason and save us a great deale of labour in clearing our selves, it being a remarkable signe of an ill cause when aspersions supply the place of Arguments.

We blesse God that he hath given us time and hearts to bring it to this issue, what further he hath for us to do is yet only knowne to his wisedom, to whose will and pleasure we shall willingly submit; we have if we look with the eyes of frailty, enemies like the sons of Anak, but if with the eyes of faith and confidence in a righteous God and a just cause, we see more with us then against us.

From our causelesse captivity in the Tower of *London, May* 1. 1649.

John Lilburn.
William Walwyn.
Thomas Prince.
Richard Overton.

The Agreement it selfe thus followeth.

.   .   .   . [2]

24

The Fountain of
Slaunder Discovered

[30 May] 1649
Reprinted from a copy of the tract in the Huntington Library

The Fountain of Slaunder, "By William Walwyn, Merchant," was printed by H. Hills for William Larner, 1649. It was not licensed.

Fountain of Slaunder is primarily a defense of Walwyn's morality and conduct. Much of it had been written more than a year before his arrest; publication was deferred because Walwyn was denied a license and thought that his quiet life would vindicate him.[1] In prison, taking his distance from those associated with the petition that precipitated their arrests,[2] Walwyn did not join Lilburne, Prince, and Overton in their accounts of seizure and imprisonment in *The Picture of the Council of State,* which was secured by Thomason on 11 April. Instead, Walwyn completed the unpublished defense of his character, added a narrative of his arrest and cross-examination—and again deferred publication, hoping the jointly signed *Manifestation* and the May *Agreement* would make his case.[3] Publication and the title of *Fountain* were prompted by the appearance of *Walwins Wiles:* "the corrupt *Fountain of Slander,* such a foggy mist of lies, invectives and slanders, as would have choakt any but the spawn of envy and malice to have uttered them."[4]

Fountain is partially reprinted in *Leveller Tracts,* ed. Haller and Davies, pp. 246–51. It is reprinted in full for the first time in this volume.

THE FOUNTAIN OF SLAUNDER Discovered.

By *William Walwyn*, Merchant.

WITH Some passages concerning his present Imprisonment in the Tower of LONDON.

Published for satisfaction of Friends and Enemies.

LONDON, Printed by *H. Hils*, and are to be sold by *W. Larnar*, at the sign of the *Blackmore*, near *Bishops-gate*. M. DC. XLIX

The Fountain of Slander discovered, &c.*

From my serious and frequent consideration of the good-nesse of God towards man, the innumerable good things he created for his sustenance & comfort; that he hath made him of so large a capacity as to be Lord over other creatures; ever testifying his love, by giving rain and fruitfull seasons, feeding our hearts with food and gladnesse: That he hath made him, as his own Vicegerent, to see all things justly and equally done, and planted in him an ever living conscience to mind him continually of his duty; I could not but wonder that this should not be sufficient to keep mankind in order, and the world in quiet.

But when I considered the infinite obligations of love and thank-fulnesse, wherewith men, as Christians, are bound unto God, and yet how extremely averse all sorts of Christians were, to the essen-tiall and practicall part of Religion; so great ingratitude did quite astonish me.

And made me with much patience passe over the many injuries I have suffered for my own endeavours after common good; and to resolve within my self, that for any man to give good heed to the voyce of God in his own conscience, and vigorously to appear against the unrighteousnesse of men, is certainly the way to affliction and reproaches.

---

* The printer's corrections on p. 26 have been incorporated in this reprint-ing. (Editors' note)

And hereupon, when of late I have been hunted with open mouth, and could appear in no place, but I was pointed at, and frown'd upon almost by every man, I was but little moved; for why should I expect better measure than my Maker and Redeemer? And so with patience sate me down, and considered, whence so many undeserved aspersions should proceed against me at a time too, when I was most secure; all power being then in the hands of such, from whom I had merited nothing but love and friendship.

I was sure any man that had a mind to know what, or where I was, might easily trace me from my present habitation in Moor-Fields, to Newland in Worcestershire, where I was born of no unknown or beggarly parentage, as some have suggested to disparage me; but such as were both generous, as the world accounts; and ingenuous too, as wise men judge; and to whose exemplary virtue I owe more, then for my being.

I knew an exact accompt might be taken of me, in lesse then one daies time: and that this may gain belief, I shall refer the enquiry of my birth and [1] breeding to Mr Sallaway,* a Member of Parliament for the County of Worcester; and for my first eight years in London to Mr Crowder,** another Member of this present Parliament: The truth of whose relation, I suppose none will doubt, and I shall be obliged to them, to satisfie as many as desire it.

For 15 years together, after that, I dwelt in the Parish of Saint James, Garlick-hill, London: Where, for all that time, any that please, may be satisfied; since which time, I have lived in Moor-Fields, where now my Wife and Children are; and what my demeanour there hath been, my neighbours will soon resolve.

I have been married 21 years, and have had almost 20 Children; my profession hath been Merchandising, but never was beyond the Seas; but my Brother died in Flanders in my imployment, and cost me near 50 pounds, rather then he should want that buriall accustomed to Protestants; which one would think might suffice to prove me no Jesuite.

In all which time, I believe scarce any that ever knew me, will be so dis-ingenuous as to spot me with any vice; and as little of infirmity as of any other; having never heard ill of my self, untill my hopes of this

---

* Humphrey Salwey, M.P., Worcestershire, 1640-1652. (Editors' note)
** William Crowther, London merchant, elected M.P., Woebley, Herefordshire, 1646, did not sit after Pride's Purge. (D. Brunton and D. H. Pennington, *Members of the Long Parliament* [London, 1954], pp. 60, 211).

Parliament encouraged me to engage in publique affairs; being then 40 years of age, 20 of which I had been a serious and studious reader and observer of things necessary.

But then in short time, I heard such vile unworthy things as I abhorred, and made me blush to hear; and ever since, reproaches have pursued me, like rowling waves, one in the neck of another.

All which being groundlesse, as my conscience well knew, I soon concluded, they were devised purposely by some Politicians (whose corrupt interest I opposed) to render me odious to all societies of men, and so to make me uselesse to the Common-wealth, which my long experience and observation told me, was a common practice in all ages.

So as to me it is evident, that corrupt interests are the originall of Politicians; for a just course of life, or interest, needs no crafts or policies to support it: And it is as clear to me, that Politicians are the originall of reproaches, and the fountain of slander: for that it being impossible to defend an ill cause by reason; reproaches necessarily must be devised, and cast upon the opposers to discredit what they speak; or it were impossible for any corrupt interest to stand the least blast of a rationall opposition.

Most miserable unhappy therfore are those men, who are engaged and resolved to continue in any kind of corrupt interest, or way of living; since they are thereby all their life long necessitated to become meer Politicians, devisers of lies, slanders, falshoods, and many times to perpetrate the most dishonest actions that can be imagined, for supportation of their interest.

And upon this accompt I am certain, and upon no other, so much dirt hath been cast upon me; for when art and sophistry will not serve to vanquish truth and reason, aspersion generally wil do the deed.

Which hath made discreet and considerable men to make a contrary use of aspersions: For whereas the rash, and weak, when they hear either man or Cause asperst, they presently shun the men, and abhominate the cause upon little or no examination, as being affrighted therewith. Wise and discreet men, skilfull in the common rules and practises of the world, are so far from prejud- [2] ging either the man or cause of evil; that without prejudging, or partiality, they make an exact enquiry, how things are, and determine nothing but upon good and reall satisfaction.

And there is good cause for every man so to do; for if all stories be well searcht into, it will be found, That unjust, cruel, covetous, or ambitious men, such as were engaged in corrupt interests, or in some wicked designs, were ever the aspersers; and honest, just and publique spirited men the aspersed.

That this is a certain truth, examples need not be brought out of common histories, whilst the Scriptures abound therewith.

It was the portion both of the Prophets and Apostles, and of all the holy men of all times: yea, our blessed Saviour, who spent all his time on earth in doing good, was neverthelesse tearmed, a Wine-bibber, a Friend of Publicans and sinners, a Caster out of Devils by Beelzebub the Prince of Devils. And who were they that so asperst him, but the great and learned Politicians of the times, who with the Scribes and Pharisees, set themselves against him and his doctrines, because he gave knowledge to the poor and simple; by which, their delusion, pride, oppression and corrupt interests were plainly discovered.

So that let no man look to escape aspersions, that sets himself to promote any publique good, or to remove any old or new setled evil; but let him resolve, according to the good he endeavoureth, so shall his aspersion be: Nor let him thinke, when time and his constant actings have worn out, one, or two, or ten aspersions, that he is therfore free; but if he continue to mind more good, he shall be sure to find new aspersions, such as he never dream'd of, or could imagine.

Luther opposeth the delusions and oppressions of the Pope, and his Clergy, and the ruine of Emperours, Kings and great ones of the world, laies them all open and naked to the view of all men: and who was ever more asperst then he?

Cornelius Agrippa sets forth a Treatise, entituled, *The vanity of Arts and Sciences;* and is reputed a Conjurer for his labour.

How falsly and vilely were our Martyrs reproached and cruelly used in Queen Maries daies, for opposing the wickednesse of the great ones of that time? And how unjustly Mr Greenwood, Mr Penry, and Mr Barrow suffered in Queen Elizabeths daies for publishing unwelcome truths, is yet sadly remembred.

Yet how odious did the Bishops set forth those that pretended for the Discipline of Presbyterie? all along comparing them to the Anabaptists of Munster; affirming, that (whatever they pretended) they aimed to destroy all Magistracy and Government; to have plurality of wives, and all things common; saying any thing of them to render them odious to the people.

In like manner the Court reproached Parliaments upon their least shew of redresse of grievances, or abatement of Prerogative; calling them, a factious, seditious, viperous brood, that intended to bring all to Anarchy, parity and confusion.

And even so divers Presbyters of late have dealt with the Independents, Brownists, Anabaptists, Antinomians, and the like; stiling them Heretiques, Blasphemers, Sectaries; and comparing the Army and their Leaders to Jack Cade, Wat Tyler, and John of Leydon. [3]

And so about that time dealt the Parliament with many wellminded people, that petitioned them for removall of long setled, and new imposed grievances, tearming them factious, and seditious Sectaries; and burnt their just Petitions most reproachfully by the common hangman.

And just so now deal some most unworthy Independents with many the present Asserters of common freedom, stiling them Levellers, Anti-scripturists, Atheists; and devise such scandalous, false aspersions against them; and publish the same with so much bitternesse and vilenesse of expression, as if they resolved of all that went before them, from Rabshekah, to the unhappy daies of Mr Edwards, and his Contemporaries, none should come nigh them for invention, or calumniation; and that upon no cause, except for opposing the present corruption and corrupt interests of the times; wherein it should seem, many of them are now engaged, and taking pleasure therein, are as impatient as ever Demetrius and the Crafts-men were with Paul for preaching against the Goddesse Diana, by making of whose Shrines they lived, tis like, very plenteously.

And although nothing be more evident, then that Aspersers are ever deceivers, and asperse for no other end but for their own interest and advantage, yet are not men sufficiently cautious to avoid their wiles, but are ensnared perpetually; for let a man with never so much discretion and fidelity, make known a publique grievance, or an imminent danger, and propose never so effectuall means for redresse and prevention, yet if one of these subtil Politicians, or their Agents, can have opportunity to buz into the ears of those that are concerned, thou the proposer art an Heretique, a Blasphemer, an Atheist, a denier of God and Scriptures; or, which is worse to most rich men, that he is a Leveller, and would have all things common: then out upon him, away with such a fellow from off the earth; better perish then be preserved by so prophane a person: and in the mean time, who so seemingly pious, meek and religious as the asperser? Whose councel so readily harkned to as his? which yet leadeth to a certain bondage, or destruction, never feared till felt.

And truly but for these deceits in Politicians, and these weaknesses in the people, it had been impossible but these times must necessarily have produced much more good to the Common wealth: and it is wonderfull to consider, how powerfully this delusion proves in all times; no warning or experience being guard enough against it, though to a reasonable judgment, no deceit be more palpable.

For generally the asperser is really guilty of what he unjustly brands another withall: So, the false Prophets accuse the true of falsnesse: In like manner, the false Apostles accuse the true: The Scribes and Pharisees were, indeed, friends of Publicans and Sinners, reall friends of Beelzebub, as being the chief of Hypocrites: The Pope and his Clergie really guilty of all they fained against Luther: Emperours and Great ones of the world, cry out of perfidiousnesse, and breach of Oaths; who have broken so frequently as they? or make so little of it when 'tis done? Those who cry out against Community, Parity and Levelling, in the mean time enforce all to their own wils, both Persons, Estates and Consciences, and if resisted, fire and sword, halters, axes and prisons, must be their Executioners. [4]

The persecutor is for the most part the most desperate heretick, and those that cry out so much against blasphemy, neither regard man nor honour God, pretending Godlinesse onely for by, and base respects: Those who make so great a noise against Atheists, are they not such as say in their hearts, there is no God? denying him in their actions and conversations, back-biting, covetousnesse, pride, and usury being no sinnes amongst them, men that have a meer specious forme of Godlinesse, but no power at all: Those that raise fames of denying the Scriptures; you shall have them do it so as if they did it purposely to bring Scriptures in question, and write so in defence of them, as if they bent all their endeavours (though subtilly and obscurely) to weaken the credit and belief thereof; and have the impudence to call their uncertaine, doubtfull preaching and sermons the word of God, preach for filthy lucre, and take money for that which is not bread; so that if people had but any consideration in them, they would easily discover the fraud, policy and malice of aspersors, and be armed against their stratagems.

And although the people for some time may be deceived by their delusions, and do not perceive their devises: yet God in the end discovers them to their shame; setling their nakednesse and the shame of their nakednesse open in the sight of all men; and that garment of hypocriticall Godlinesse with which they stalked so securely, becomes a badge of their reproach.

The Scribes, and Pharisees, and Herod, and Pilat had their time; but are their names now any other but a by-word? and doth not the Doctrine of Luther, shine in despite of all his mighty opposers?

What gained the Bishops by bespeaking the Presbyter of so much errour and madnesse, but their own down-fall? what got the Courtiers by accusing Parliaments of intending Anarchy and Community but their own ruine? and have not these Presbyters brought themselves to shame by their bitter invective Sermons and writings against the Independent and Sectaries?

And are all these forementioned, acquitted of the aspersions cast upon them? and am I and my friends guilty? why must these scandalous defamations be truer of us then of them? in their severall times they were beleeved to be true of them, and its time onely and successe that hath cleared them, and should perswade men to forbear censuring us of evil unlesse the just things we have proposed, and Petitioned for be granted; and if we content not our selves within the bounds of just Government let us then be blamed, and not before: but what sayes the politician if somebody be not asperst, Mischief cannot prosper if these men be believed and credited, downe goes our profit. And truely, that enemies to the common freedome of this Nation, or enemies to a just Parliamentary Government, enemies to the Army, or men of persecuting principles and practices, should either divide or scatter these false aspersions against me, I did never wonder at: beleiving these to be but as clouds that would soon vanish upon the rising of the friends of the Common wealth, and prevailing of the Army; And so it came to passe, and for a season continued; but no sooner did I and my friends in behalf of the Common-wealth, manifest our expectation of that freedome so long desired, so seriously promised them in the power of friends to give and grow importunate in pursuit thereof, but out flies these hornets againe about our ears, as if kept tame of purpose to vex and [5] sting to death those that would not rest satisfied with lesse then a well grounded freedome: and since, we have been afresh more violently rayled at then ever, as if all the corrupt interests in England must downe, except we were reproacht to purpose.

And certainly there was never so fair an opportunity to free this Nation from all kinds of oppression and usurpation as now, if some had hearts to do their endeavour, that strongly pretended to do their utmost; and what hinders, is as yet, somewhat in a mistery; but time will reveal all, and then it will appear more particularly then will yet be permitted to be discovered, from what corrupt fountaine, (though sweetned with flowers of Religion) these undeserved clamours have issued against me and my friends.

But I shame to thinke how readily, the most irrationall sencelesse aspersions cast upon me, are credited by many, whom I esteemed sincere in their way of Religion, and that most uncharitably against the long experience they have had of me, and most unthankfully too, against the many services I have done them, in standing for their liberties (and animating others so to do) when they were most in danger and most exposed, never yet failing though in my own particular I were not then concerned) to manifest as great a tendernesse of their welfare as mine owne.

But in patience I possesse my self, such as the tree is such I perceive will be the fruit: and as I see a man is no farther a man then as he clearly understands; so also I perceive a Christian is no farther a Christian then as he stands clear from errour, and superstition, with both which were not most men extreamly tainted? such rash and harish censures could never have past upon me, such evil fruits springing not from true Religion; wherein, as full of zeal, as the times seeme to be; most men are far to seek: every man almost differs from his neighbour, yet every man is confident, who then is right in judgement? and if the judgement direct to practice (as no doubt it ought) no marvell we see so much weaknesse, so much emptinesse, vanity, and to speak softly, so much unchristianity, so many meer Nationall and verball, so few practicall and reall Christians, but busie-bodies, talebearers, serviceable, not to God, in the preservation of the life or good name of their neighbours, but unto polititians in blasting and defaming, and so in ruining of their brother.

If I now amidst so great variety of judgements and practises as there are, should go a particular way; Charity and Christianity would forbear to censure me of evill, and would give me leave to follow mine owne understanding of the Scriptures, even as I freely allow unto others.

Admit then my Conscience have been necessitated to break through all kinds of Superstition, as finding no peace, but distraction and instability therein, and have found out true uncorrupt Religion, and placed my joy and contentment therein; admit I find it so brief and plaine, as to be understood in a very short time, by the meanest capacity, so sweet and delectable as cannot but be embraced, so certain as cannot be doubted, so powerfull to dissolve man into love, and to set me on work to do the will of him that loved me, how exceedingly then are weak superstitious people mistaken in me?

That I beleive a God, and Scriptures, and understand my self concerning both, those small things I have occasionally written and published, are testimo [6] nies more then sufficient; as my *Whisper in the eare of Mr. Thomas Edwards;* My *Antidote against his poyson;* My *prediction of his conversion and recantation:* My *parable or consultation of Physitians upon him:* and My *still and soft voice* (expresly written though needlesse after the rest) for my vindication herein, all which I intreat may be read and considered: and surely if any that accuse and backbite me, had done but half so much, they would (and might justly) take it very ill not to be believed.

But when I consider the small thanks and ill rewards I had from some of Mr. Edward's his opposers, upon my publishing those Treatises, I have cause to beleive they are fraught with some such unusuall truths, that have spoiled the markets of some of the more refined Demetrius's and crafts-men; I must confesse I have been very apt, to blunt out such truths as I had well digested to be needfull amongst men: wherein my conscience is much delighted, not much regarding the displeasure of any, whilst I but performe my duty.

And in all that I have written my judgement concerning Civil Government is so evident, as (if men were men indeed, and were not altogether devoid of Conscience) might acquit me from such vanities as I am accused of; but for this, besides those I have named, I shall refer the Reader to my *Word in Season,* published in a time of no small need; and to that large Petition that was burnt by the hand of the common Hangman, wherein with thousands of wel-affected people I was engaged: and to which I stand, being no more for Anarchy and Levelling, then that Petition importeth; the burners thereof, and the then aspersers of me and my friends having been since taught a new lesson, and which might be a good warning to those that now a fresh take liberty to abuse us: but no heart swoln with pride as the politicians, but scornes advice, spurns and jeers, and laugh at all; yet for all their confidence, few of them escape the severe hand of Gods justice first and last, even in this world.

Indeed it hath been no difficult thing to know my judgement by the scope of that Petition, and truely were I as deadly an enemy unto Parliaments (as I have been and still am a most affectionate devotant to their just Authority) I could not wish them a greater mischief then to be drawne to use Petitioners unkindly, or to deny them things reasonable, upon suspition that they would be emboldened to ask things unreasonable, by which rule, no just things should ever be granted; wishing with all my heart that care may be speedily taken in this particular, the people already being too much enclined to be out of love with Parliaments, then which I know no greater evill can befall the Common-wealth.

Another new thing I am asperst withall, is, that I hold Polygamie, that is, that it is lawfull to have more wives then one; (I wonder what will be next, for these will wear out, or returne to the right owners) and this scandall would intimate that I am addicted loosely to women; but this is another envenomed arrow drawne from the same Pollitick quiver, and shot without any regard to my inclination; and shewes the authors to be empty of all goodnesse, and filled with a most wretchlesse malice; for this is such a slander as doggs me at the heels home to my house; seeking to torment me even with my wife and children and so to make my life a burthen unto me; but this also loseth its force, and availeth nothing, as the rest do also, where I am fully known; nay it pro- [7] duceth the contrary; even the increase of love and esteeme amongst them, as from those, whose goodnesse and certain knowledge can admit no such thoughts of vanity or vilenesse in me: one and twenty years experience with my wife, and fifteen or sixteen with my daughters, without the least staine of my person, putting the question of my conversation out of all question.

There are also that give out that I am of a bloudy disposition, its very strange it should be so and I not know it, sure I am, and I blesse God for it, that since I was a youth I never struck any one a blow through quarrell or passion; avoyding with greatest care all occasions and provocation; and although possibly nature would prevaile with me to kill rather then be killed; yet to my judgement and conscience, to kill a man is so horrid a thing, that upon deliberation I cannot resolve I should do it.

And though to free a Nation from bondage and tyranny it may be lawfull to kill and slay, yet I judge it should not be attempted but after all means used for prevention; (wherein I fear there hath been some defect) and upon extreme necessity, and then also with so dismall a sadnesse, exempt from that usuall vapouring and gallantry (accustomed in meer mercinary Souldiers) as should testifie to the world that their hearts took no pleasure therein; much lesse that they look'd for particular gaine and profit for their so doing: and I wish those who have defamed me in this, did not by their garnisht outside, demonstrate that they have found a more pleasing sweetnesse in bloud then ever I did.

Now some may wonder why those religious people that so readily serve the Polliticians, turnes in catching and carrying these aspersions from man to man, have not so much honesty or charity, as to be fully satisfied of the truth thereof, and then deale with me in a Christian way, before they blow abroad their defamations; or why the taking away of my good name, which may be the undoing of my wife and children should be thought no sin amongst them? but truely I doe not wonder at it, for where notionall or verball Religion, which at best is but superstition, is author of that little shadow of goodnesse which possesses men, its no marvell they have so little hold of themselves: for they want that innate inbred vertue which makes men good men, and that pure and undefiled Religion, which truly denominateth men good Christians; and which only giveth strength against temptations of this nature.

And as men are more or lesse superstitious, the effects will be found amongst them; nor is better to be expected from them untill they deeme themselves, no further Religious, then as they find brotherly love abound in their hearts towards all men: all the rest being but as sounding brasse and tinkling Simbals; nor will they ever be so happy as to know their friends from their foes, except they will now at length be warned against these cunning ways of Polliticians, by scandals and aspersions to divide them; and be so wise, as to resolve to beleeve nothing upon report, so as to report it againe, untill full knowledge of the truth thereof; and then also to deal as becommeth a discreet Christian, to whom anothers good name is as pretious as his own; being ever mindfull, that love covereth a multitude of sins.

But I have said enough as I judge for my owne vindication and discovery of the infernall tongues of Polliticians, that set on fire the whole course of nature, and am hopefull thereby to reclaime some weak wel-minded people from their [8] sodain beleeving or inconsiderate dispersing of reproaches; and so to frustrate the polliticians ends in this dangerous kind of delusion.

As for those who know me and yet asperce me, or suffer others unreproved, all such I should judge to be polliticians their hirelings, or favourers; and I might as well undertake to wash a Blackmore white, as to turne their course, or restore them to a sound and honest mind.

However I shall no whit dispaire of the prosperity of the just cause I have hitherto prosecuted, because (though at present I be kept under) yet I have this to comfort me, that understanding increaseth exceedingly, and men daily abandon superstition, and all unnecessary fantastick knowledge; and become men of piercing judgements, that know the arts and crafts of deceivers, and have abillity to discover them; so that besides the goodnesse of the cause which commands my duty, I may hope to see it prosper, and to produce a lasting happinesse to this long enthraled Nation.

A good name amongst good men I love and would cherish; but my contentment is placed only in the just peace and quietnesse of my own conscience, I may be a man of reproaches, and a man of crosses, but my integrity no man can take from me; I may by my friends and nearest alliances, be blamed as too forward in publique affaires, be argued of pride, as David was by his brother; yet I thinke the family whereof I am, is so ingenious as to acquit me, and to believe my conscience provokes me to do what I have done; but admit it should not be so, my answer might be the same as his, Is there not a cause? nay may I not rather wonder the harvest being so great, that the labourers be so few; if all men should be offended with me for endeavouring the good of all men, in all just wayes (for I professe I know no other cause against me) I should choose it rather then the displeasure of God or the distaste of my owne conscience, affliction being to me a better choice then sin.

And this my judgement (as necessary for that time) I put into writing about 16 monthes since or somewhat more, but deferred the publishing, because it was once denied the Licencing, (which by the way was hard measure, considering how freely aspersers have been Licenced or countenanced against me) but chiefly I omitted to Print it, because I thought my continuall acting towards the common peace, freedome, and safety of the Nation, would yet in time clear off all my reproaches, and for that I could not possibly vindicate my selfe, but that I must necessarily reflect upon some sorts of men, whom I did hope time and their grouth in knowledg would have certified in their judgements concerning me, and the things I ever promoted; But finding now at length, that notwithstanding all times since, I walked in an uprightnesse of heart towards their publique good; without any the least wandering and deviation, (as their Petitioners of the 11 of September will bear me witnesse) notwithstanding I can prove I have rendered very much good, to those that had done me very much evil, and from whom its known I have deserved better things; yet my aspersions after the last Summers troubles were over, flew abroad a fresh, (for in all that time I had very fair words) and no nay but Walwin was a Jesuite, and a Pentioner to the Pope, or some Forraigne State: but for proof not one sillable ever proved one while I was a Leveller, then on a sodaine I drove on the King's designe, and none so countenanced as those that were officious in tel- [9] ling strange stories and tales of me: Insomuch, as I found it had an effect of danger towards my life; divers of the Army giving out, that it would never be well till some dispatch were made of me; that I deserved to be stoned to death; All which, though I considered it to its full value, yet did it not deterre me from pursuing my just Cause, according to my just Judgement and Conscience; but this was my portion from too many, from whom I may truly say, I had deserved better: yet in all these things it was my happinesse to have good esteem from such as I account constant to the Cause, and uncorrupted men of Army and Parliament, to whose love in this kind, for many years, I have been exceedingly obliged, and who never shunned me in any company, nothwithstanding all reproaches, but ever vindicated me, as having undoubted assurance of my integrity; and believing confidently, that I was asperst for no other cause, but for my perpetuall solicitation for the Common-wealth.

But there is no stopping the mouth of corrupt interests, against which only I have ever steered, and not in the least against persons; being still of the same mind I was when I wrote my *Whisper in the ear of Mr. Edwards, Minister;* professing still, as there in pag:3. I did, in sincerity of heart; *That I am one that do truly and heartily love all mankind, it being my unfeined desire, that all men might be saved, and come to the knowledge of the truth: That it is my extreme grief, that any man is afflicted, molested or punished, and cannot but most earnestly wish them all occasion were taken away*————*That there is no man weak, but I would strengthen; nor ignorant, but I would reform; nor erroneous, but I would rectifie; nor vicious, but I would reclaim; nor cruel, but I would moderate and reduce to clemency*————*I am as much grieved that any man should be so unhappy as to be cruel or unjust, as that any man should suffer by cruelty or injustice; and if I could, I would preserve from both.*

And however I am mistaken, it is from this disposition in me, that I have engaged in any publique affairs, and from no other————*Which my manner of proceeding, in every particular businesse wherein I have in any measure appear'd, will sufficiently evince to all that have, without partiality, observed me.*

I never proposed any man for my enemy, but injustice, oppression, innovation, arbitrary power, and cruelty; where I found them, I ever opposed my self against them; but so, as to destroy the evil, but to preserve the person: And therfore all the war I have made, other then what my voluntary and necessary contributions hath maintained, which I have wisht ten thousand times more then my ability; so really am I affected with the Parliaments just cause for the common freedom of this Nation. I say, all the war I have made, hath been to get victory over the understandings of men, accounting it a more worthy and profitable labour to beget friends to the Cause I loved, rather then *to molest mens persons, or confiscate mens estates: and how many reall Converts have been made through my endeavours, reproaches might tempt me to boast, were I not better pleased with the conscience of so doing.**

Of this mind I was in the year, 1646. and long before; and of the same mind I am at this present; and, I trust, shall ever but be so.

And hence it is, that I have pursued the settlement of the Government of this Nation by an Agreement of the People; as firmly hoping thereby, to see the Common-wealth past all possibility of returning into a slavish condition; though in pursuite thereof, I have met with very hard and froward measure from [10] some that pretended to be really for it: So that do what I will for the good of my native Country, I receive still nothing but evil for my labour; all I speak, or purpose, is construed to the worst; and though never so good, fares the worse for my proposing; and all by reason of those many aspersions cast upon me.

If any thing be displeasing, or judged dangerous, or thought worthy of punishment, then Walwyn's the Author; and no matter, saies one, if Walwyn had been destroyed long ago: Saies another, Let's get a law to have power our selves to hang all such: and this openly, and yet un-reproved; affronted in open Court; asperst in every corner; threatned wherever I passe; and within this last month of March, was twice advertised by Letters, of secret contrivances and resolutions to imprison me.

And so accordingly (sutable to such prejudgings and threatnings) upon the 28th of March last, by Warrant of the Councel of State; I that might have been fetcht by the least intimation of their desire to speak with me, was sent for by Warrant under Sergeant Bradshaw's hand, backt with a strong party of horse and foot, commanded by Adjutant Generall Stubber (by deputation from Sir Hardresse Waller, and Colonel Whaley) who placing his souldiers in the allyes, houses, and gardens round about my house, knockt violently at my garden gate, between four and five in the morning; which being opened by my maid, the Adjutant Generall, with many souldiers, entred, and immediately disperst themselves about the garden, and in my house, to the great terror of my Family; my poor maid comming up to me, crying and shivering, with news that Souldiers were come for me, in such a sad distempered manner (for she could hardly speak) as was sufficient to have daunted one that had been used to such sudden surprisals;

---

* The italic passages reiterate the passages in *Whisper*, pp. 2–3. (Editors' note)

much more my Wife, who for two and twenty years we have lived together, never had known me under a minutes restraint by any Authority; she being also so weakly a woman, as in all that time, I cannot say she hath enjoyed a week together in good health; and certainly had been much more affrighted, but for her confidence of my innocence; which fright hath likewise made too deep an impression upon my eldest Daughter, who hath continued sick ever since, my Children and I having been very tender one of another: Nor were my neighbours lesse troubled for me, to whose love I am very much obliged.

The Adjutant Generall immediately followed my maid into my Chamber, as I was putting on my clothes; telling me, that he was sent by the Councel of State (an Authority which he did own) to bring me before them: I askt, for what cause? he answered me, he did not understand particularly, but in the notion of it, it was of a very high nature: I askt him, if he had any warrant? he answered, he had; and that being drest, I should see it.

The Souldiers I perceived very loud in the garden; and I not imagining then, there had been more disperst in my neighbours grounds and houses; and being willing to preserve my credit (a thing sooner bruised then made whole) desired him, to cause their silence, which he courteously did: Then I told him, if he had known me in any measure, he would have thought himself, without any souldiers, sufficient to bring me before them: That I could not but wonder (considering how well I was known) that I should be sent for by Souldiers, when there was not the meanest civil Officer but might command my appea- [11] rance: That I thought it was a thing not agreeable to that freedom and liberty which had been pretended.

That now he saw what I was, I should take it as a favour, that he would command his Souldiers off, which he did very friendly, reserving some two very civil Gentlemen with him; so being ready, he shewed me the Warrant: the substance whereof was, for suspicion of treason, in being suspected to be the Author of a Book, entituled, *The second part of Englands new Chains discovered:* I desired him to take a Copy of it, which was denied, though then and afterwards by my self, the Lieut. Col. John Lilburn (who was likewise in the same Warrant) importuned very much for.

Then I went out with him into Moor-Fields, and there I saw, to my great wonder, a great party of souldiers, which he commanded to march before, and went with me, (only with another Gentleman, at a great distance) to Pauls; yet such people was were up, took so much notice of it, as it flew quickly all about the Town; which I knew would redound much to my prejudice, in my credit; which was my only care, the times being not quallified for recovery of bruises in that kind.

In Pauls Church-yard was their rendezvous; where I was no sooner come, but I espied my Friends, Mr Lilburn and Mr Prince, both labouring to convince the souldiers of the injury done unto us, and to themselves, and to posterity, and the Nation in us: in that they, as souldiers, would obey and execute commands in seizing any Freeman of England, not Members of the Army, before they evidently saw the civil Magistrates and Officers in the Common-wealth, were resisted by force, and not able to bring men to legall trials, with very much to that purpose; and in my judgment, prevailed very much amongst them; many looking, as if they repented and grieved to see such dealings.

Then they removed to a house for refreshment, where, after a little discourse, we perswaded them to release two of Mr Davenish his sons, whom a Captain had taken into custody without Warrant: but that kind of errour being laid fully open, they were enlarged with much civility, which I was glad to see, as perceiving no inclination in the present Officers or Souldiers, to defend any exorbitant proceedings, when this understood them to be such.

So the Adjutant Generall sent off the whole party, and with some very few, took us, by water, to his Quarters at Whitehall (where after a while, came in Mr Overton) the Adjutant intending about nine of the clock, to go with us to Darby house.

But the Councel not sitting till five at night, we were kept in his Quarters all that time; where some, but not many of our friends that came to visit us, were permitted.

About five a clock, the Councel sate; so he took us thither, where we continued about two houres, before any of us were called in; and then Mr Lilburn was called, and was there about a quarter of an hour, and then came out to us, and his Friends, declaring at large all that had past between him and them.

Then after a little while, I was called in, and directed up to Sergeant Bradshaw the President; who told me, that the Parliament had taken notice of a very dangerous Book, full of sedition and treason; and that the Councel was informed, that I had a hand in the making or compiling thereof; that the Par- [12] liament had referred the enquiry and search after the Authors and Publishers, to that Councel; and that I should hear the Order of Parliament read, for my better satisfaction: so the Order was read, containing the substance of what the President had delivered; and then he said, by this you understand the cause wherfore you are brought hither; and then was silent, expecting, as I thought, what I would say.

But the matter which had been spoken, being only a relation, I kept silence, expecting what further was intended; which being perceived, the President said, You are free to speak, if you have any thing to say to it: to which I said only this, I do not know why I am suspected: Is that all, said he: To which I answered, Yes; and then he said, You may withdraw: So I went forth.

And then Mr Overton, and after him, Mr Prince, were called in; and after all four had been out a while, Mr Lilburn was called in again, and put forth another way; and then I was called in again:

And the President said to this effect, that the Parliament had reposed a great trust in them for finding out the Authors of that Book; and that the Councel were carefull to give a good accompt of their trust; in order whereunto, I had been called in, and what I had said, they had considered; but they had now ordered him to ask me a question, which was this: Whether or no I had any hand in making or compiling of this Book? holding the Book in his hand: To which, after a little while, I answered to this effect, That I could not but very much wonder to be asked such a question; howsoever, that it was very much against my judgment and conscience, to answer to questions of that nature which concern'd my self; that if I should answer to it, I should not only betray my own liberty, but the liberties of all Englishmen, which I could not do with a good conscience: And that I could not but exceedingly grieve at the dealing I had found that day; that being one who had been alwaies so faithfull to the Parliament, and so well known to most of the Gentlemen there present, that neverthelesse I should be sent for with a party of horse and foot, to the affrighting of my family, and ruine of my credit; and that I could not be satisfied, but that it was very hard measure to be used thus upon suspicion only; professing, that if they did hold me under restraint from following my businesse and occasions, it might be my undoing, which I intreated might be considered.

Then the President said, I was to answer the question; and that they did not ask it, as in way of triall, so as to proceed in judgment thereupon, but to report it to the House: To which I said, that I had answered it so as I could with a good conscience, and could make no other answer; so I was put forth a back way, as Mr Lilburn had been, and where he was.

After this, they cal'd in Mr Overton, and after him Mr Prince, using the very same expressions, and question to all alike; and so we were all four together; and after a long expectance, we found we were committed Prisoners to the Tower of London, for suspicion of high treason; where now we are, to the great rejoycing of all that hate us, whose longing desires are so far satisfied: And to make good that face of danger, which by sending so many horse and foot was put upon it, a strong Guard hath ever since been continued at Darby house, when the Councel sits.

And now again, fresh aspersions and reproaches are let loose against us, and [13] by all means I, that never was beyond the Seas, nor ever saw the Sea, must be a Jesuite, and am reported to be now discovered to be born in Spain: That because I am an enemy to superstition, therfore they give out, I intend to destroy all Religion; and (which I never heard till now) that I desire to have all the Bibles in England burnt; that I value Heathen Authors above the Scriptures: whereas all that know me, can testifie how, though I esteem many other good Books very well, yet, I ever prefer'd the Scriptures; and I have alwaies maintained, that Reason and Philosophy could never have discovered peace and reconciliation by Christ alone, nor do teach men to love their enemies; doctrines which I prize more then the whole world: It seems I am used so ill, that except by aspersions I be made the vilest man in the world, it will be thought, I cannot deserve it: And though I were, yet (living under a civil Government) as I hope, I ever shall do, and not under a Military, I cannot discern how such dealing could be justified: For, admit any one should have a mind to accuse me of treason, the party accusing ought to go to some Justice of the Peace, dwelling in the County or hundred, and to inform the fact; which if the Justice find to be against the expresse law, and a crime of treason; and that the accuser make oath of his knowledge of the fact; then the Justice may lawfully give out a Warrant, to be served by some Constable, or the like civil Officer, to bring the party accused before him, or some other Justice: wherein the party accused is at liberty to go to what Justice of Peace he pleaseth; and as the matter appeareth when the parties are face to face before a Justice, with a competent number of friends about him to speak in his behalf, as they see cause, his house being to be kept open for that time; then the Justice is to proceed as Laws directeth, as he will answer the contrary at his perill; being responsible to the party, and to the Law, in case of any extra-judiciall proceeding; and the Warrant of attachment and commitment ought to expresse the cause of commitment in legall and expresse tearms, as to the very fact and crime; and to refer to the next Gaol delivery, and not at pleasure.

Whereas I was fetcht out of my bed by souldiers, in an hostile manner, by a Warrant, expressing no fact that was a crime by any law made formerly, but by a Vote of the House, past the very day the Warrant was dated: Nor was I carried to a Justice of the Peace, much lesse to such a one as I would have made choyce of, where my Accuser (if any) was to appear openly face to face, to make oath of fact against me, if any were, but before a Councel of State, where I saw no Accuser face to face, nor oath taken, nor my friends allowed to be present, nor dores open; but upon a bare affirmation that the Councel was informed that I had a hand in compiling a Book, the title nor matter whereof was not mentioned in any law extant: whereas treason by any law, is neither in words nor intents, but in deeds and actions, expresly written, *totidem verbis*, in the law. And after, being required to answer to a question against my self, in a matter (avouched by Vote of Parliament to be no lesse then Treason) was committed Prisoner, not to a common County prison, (nor for the time) referred to the next Gaol delivery, by the ordinary Courts of Justice, my birthright, but to the Tower of London, during pleasure, preferred to be tryed by the upper Bench, whereas treason is triable only in the County where the fact is pretended to be committed. [14]

All which I have laboured with all the understanding I have, or can procure, to make appear to be just and reasonable, but cannot as yet find any satisfaction therin; being clear in my judgment, that a Parliament may not make the people lesse free then they found them, but ought at least to make good their liberties contained in Magna Charta, the Petition of Right, and other the good Laws of the Land, which are the best evidences of our Freedoms. Besides, I consider the consequence of our Sufferings; for in like manner, any man or woman in England is liable to be fetcht from the farthest parts of the Land, by parties of horse and foot, in an hostile manner, to the affrighting and ruining of their Families; and for a thing, or act, never known before by any Law to be a crime, but voted to be so, only the very day perhaps of signing the Warrent: And therfore that such power can be in this, or any other Parliament; or that such a kind of proceeding can be consistent with freedom, I wish any would give me a reason that I might understand it; for certainly the meer voting of it, will hardly give satisfaction: And now I well perceive, they had good ground for it, who asserted this belief into the first Agreement of the people; namely,

That as the laws ought to be equall, so they must be good, and not evidently destructive to our liberties; and I wish that might be well considered in making of any Law: And likewise, That no Law might be concluded, before it be published for a competent time; that those who are so minded, might offer their reasons either for or against the same, as they see cause: But I forget my self, not considering that my proposing of this, will be a means to beget a dislike thereof, and may possibly work me some new aspersions.

I am said likewise to have worse opinions then this; whereof one is, That I hope to see this Nation governed by reason, and not by the sword.

Nay worse yet; That notwithstanding all our present distractions, there is a possibility upon a clear and free debate of things, to discover so equall, just and rationall Propositions, as should produce so contentfull satisfaction, and absolute peace, prosperity and rest to this Nation; as that there should be no fear of man, nor need of an Army; or at worst, but a very small one.

But if I should declare my mind in this more fully, it would, as other good motions and propositions of mine have done, beget me the opinion of a very dangerous man, and some new aspersion; there being some, whose interest must not suffer it to be believed.

And yet it may be true enough; for I could instance a Country, not so surrounded with Seas as ours is, nor so defensible from Enemies, but that is surrounded with potent Princes and States, and was as much distracted with divisions as ours at present is, yet by wisdom so order themselves, as that they keep up no Army, nor dread no war, but have set the native Militia in such a posture, as that all the Countries round about them dare not affront them with the least injury; or if they do, satisfaction being not made, upon demand, in 48 hours, a wel disciplin'd Army appears in Field to do themselves justice; it being a maxim and principle among them, to do no injury, nor to suffer any the least from Forraigners; as also, not to let passe, without severe exemplar punishment, the least corruption in publique Officers and Magistrates; without a due regard unto both which, it is impossible for any people to be long in safety; and to hold authority, or command beyond the time limited by law, or Commission [15] amongst them, is a capitall offence, and never fails of punishment: So that this opinion of mine is not the lesse true because I hold it, but is of the number of those many usefull ones, that this present age is not so happy as to believe: Nor are we like to be happier, till we are wiser.

But as subject as some would make me to vain opinions, there is one that hath been creeping upon us about eight months, which yet gets no hold upon me; and that is, That the present power of the

Sword may reign; from this ground, that the power which is uppermost is the power of God; and the power of the Sword being now (as
some reason) above the civil Authority, it is therfore the power of
God: But the greatest wonder in this, is, that some Anabaptists who
are descended from a people so far from this opinion, that they abhorred the use of the sword, though in their own defence (to such extremities are people subject to, that think themselves to have all
knowledge and religion in them, when in truth it is but imagination
and Scripture). As for me, I am of neither of these opinions, but
should be glad once-again to see the sword in its right place, in all
senses; and the civil Authority to mind as well the essence as the
punctilio's and formalities, but neglecting neither; and that the People
would be so far carefull of their own good, as to observe with a watchfull eie, the right ordering and disposing both of the civill and military
power; we having no warrant to argue that to be of God, but what is
justly derived, attained and used to honest means; the ends, I mean,
of all Government, *viz.* the safety, peace, freedom and prosperity of
the people governed; whereas otherwise, Tyrants, Theeves, out-laws,
Pirats and Murtherers, by the same kind of arguing, may prove themselves to be of God; which in reall effect, perverts the whole supreme
intent of Government, being constituted every where for the punishment and suppression of all evil and irregular men.

But why spend I my time thus, in clearing mens understandings,
that so they might be able to preserve themselves from bondage and
misery, being so ill requited for my labour? Nay that might have
thanks, and other good things besides, if I would forbear? To which
truly I have nothing to say, but that my conscience provokes and invites me to do what I do, and have done in all my motions for the
Common-wealth; nor have I, I blesse God, any other reason; and
which to me is irresistible; unlesse I should stifle the power of my
conscience, which is the voyce of God in me, alwaies accusing or excusing me: So that whil'st I have opportunity, I shall endeavour to do
good unto all men.

But I have other businesse now upon me, then ever I had, being
now in prison, which (I praise God for it) I never was in my life before; where though I think I have as much comfort as another, yet it is
not a place I like, and therfore am carefull how to become free as
soon as I can, my restraint being very prejudiciall to me; especially
considering how the corruptions of some false hearted people doth
now break out against me, in renewed clamours and aspersions;
which whil'st I labour to acquit my self of it, it proves to me like the

laving of the ever-flowing *Fountain of Slander;* the invective brain of
some resolved Politicians; for I see I must be asperst, till honesty gets
the victory of policy, and true Religion over superstition; the one
being the Inventer, and the other the Disperser, as the fore-going discourse will, I judge, sufficiently demonstrate: And therfore henceforth let men say and report what evil they will of me, I shall [16] not
after this regard it, nor trouble my self any more in this way of vindication, hoping to find some other way.

Only one aspersion remains, which I thought good to quit here;
which is, that I am a Pentioner to some forraign State; which indeed is
most false, and is invented for the end, as all the rest are, to make me
odious: And truly if men were not grown past all shame, or care of
what they said or heard of me, it would be impossible to get belief, for
which way doth it appear? I think, nay am sure, that in my house no
man (bred in that plenty I was) ever contented himself with lesse,
which is easily known—and for the apparell of my self, my Wife and
Children, if it exceed in any thing, it is in the plainesse, wherewith we
are very well satisfied; and so in houshold stuff, and all other ex-
penses; and for my charge upon publique, voluntary occasions, I
rather merit a charitable construction from those I have accompanied
with, then any thanks or praise for any extraordinary disbursments:
and I am sure I go on foot many times from my house to Westminster,
when as I see many inferiour to me in birth and breeding, only the
favorites of the times, on their stately horses, and in their coaches;
and when I have been amongst my Friends in the Army, as many
times I have had occasion, I must ever acknowledge that I have received amongst them ten kindnesses for one; and yet (not to wrong my
self) I think, nay am sure, there is not a man in the world that is of a
more free or thankfull heart; and have nothing else to bear me up
against what good and worthy men (whom I have seen in great necessities) might conjecture of me, when as I have administred nothing to
relieve them—when was the time, and where the place, I gave din-
ners or suppers, or other gifts? For shame, thou black-mouth'd
slander, hide thy head, till the light of these knowing times be out; all
that thou canst do, is not sufficient to blast me amongst those with
whom I converse, or who have experience of my constancy in affection & endeavour to the generall good of all men, but to thy greater
torment & vexation, know this, they that entirely love me for the
same, are exceedingly increased, and many whom thou hadst deceived, return daily, manifesting their greater love to me and the pub-

lique, as willing to recompence the losse of that time thou deceivedst them.

And this imprisonment, which thou hast procured me, for my greater and irrecoverable reproach amongst good men; thy poyson'd heart would burst to see how it hath wrought the contrary, so far, as I never had so clear a manifestation of love and approbation in my life, from sincere single-hearted people, as now to my exceeding joy I find.

And possibly for time to come, these notorious falshoods with which the slanderous tongue hath pursued me, may have the same effect upon these weak people thou makest thy instruments, which they have had upon me; and that is, That I am the most backward to receive a report concerning any mans reputation, to his prejudice, of any man in the world, and account it a basenesse to pry into mens actions, or to listen to mens discourses, or to report what I judge they would not have known, as not beseeming a man of good and honest breeding, or that understands what belongs to civil society.

But leaving these things, which I wish I had had no occasion to insist upon, it will concern me to consider the condition I am in; for though I know nothing of crime or guilt in my self, worthy my care, yet considering how, and in [17] what an hostile manner I was sent for out of my bed and house, from my dear Wife and Children; the sense of that force and authors of my present imprisonment, shewing so little a sencibility or fellow-feeling of the evils that might follow upon me and them, by their so doing; it will not be a misse for me to view it in the worst cullers it can bear.

As for the booke called *The second part of Englands new chaines discovered:* for which Lieut. Col. John Lilburn, Mr Prince, Mr Overton and my self are all questioned: it concernes me nothing at all, farther then as the matter therein contained agreeth or disagreeth with my judgement; and my judgement will work on any thing I read in spight of my heart; I cannot judge what I please, but it will judge according to its owne perceverance.

And to speake my conscience, having read the same before the Declaration of Parliament was abroad; I must professe I did not discerne it to deserve a censure of those evils which that Declaration doth import, but rather conceived the maine scope and drift thereof tended to the avoiding of all those evils: and when I had seen and read the Declaration, I wished with all my heart, the Parliament had been pleased for satisfaction of all those their faithfull friends who

were concerned therein, and of the whole Nation in generall: To have
expresly applied each part of the book to each censure upon it, as to
have shewed in what part it was false, scandalous, and reproachfull;
in what seditious, and destructive to the present Government, especially since both Parliament and Army, and all wel affected people
have approved of the way of settlement of our Government, by an
Agreement of the People.

Also that they had pleased to have shewed what part, sentence or
matter therein, tended to division and mutiny in the Army, and the
raising of a new War in the Common-wealth: or wherein to hinder the
relief of Ireland, and continuing of Free-quarter; for certainly it would
conduce very much to a contentfull satisfaction, to deal gently with
such as have been friends in all extremities; and in such cases as these
to condescend to a fair correspondency, as being willing to give reasons in all things, to any part of the people; there being not the least
or most inconsiderable part of men that deserve so much respect, as
to have reason given them by those they trust, and not possitively to
conclude any upon meere votes and resolutions: and in my poor
opinion had this course been taken all along from the beginning of
the Parliament to this day, many of the greatest evils that have befalne, had been avoided; the Land ere this time had been in a happy
and prosperous condition.

There being nothing that maintaines love, unity and friendship
in families; Societies, Citties, Countries, Authorities Nations; so
much as a condescention to the giving, and hearing, and debating of
reason.

And without this, what advantage is it for the people to be, and to
be voted the Supreme power? it being impossible for all the people to
meet together, to speak with, or debate things with their Representative; and then if no part be considerable but only the whole, or if any
men shall be reckoned slightly of in respect of opinions, estates, poverty, cloathes; and then one sort shall either be heard before another:
or none shall have reasons given them except they present things
pleasing: the Supreme power, the People, is a pittifull mear helplesse
thing; as under School-masters being in danger to be [18] whipt and
beaten in case they meddle in things without leave and licence from
their Masters: and since our Government now inclines to a Common-
wealth, 'twere good all imperiousnesse were laid aside, and all
friendlinesse hereafter used towards the meanest of the people especially (if Government make any dissention at all.)

And truly I wish there had been no such imperious courses taken in apprehending of me, nor that I had been carried before the Councell of State; nor that the Declaration had been so suddenly and with such solemnity proclaimed upon our commitment, there being no harsh expression therein; but what through the accustomed transportation of mens spirits towards these that suffer, but is applied to us, so that we are lookt upon as guilty already of no lesse then Mutiny, Sedition, and Treason; of raising a new War, or hindering the relief of Ireland, and continuance of Free-quarter; insomuch as though now we shall be allowed a legall triall in the ordinary Courts of Justice: as certainly the times will afford us that, or farewell all our rights and liberty, so often protested and declared to be kept inviolable; and within these two years so largely promised to be restored and preserved: yet what Judge will not be terrified and preposest by such a charge laid upon us by so high an Authority, and attached by Soldiers, and sent Prisoners to the Tower: nay what Judge will not be prejudiced against us?

If they should be persons relating to the Army, we are represented as Mutineers: if to the present actings in Government, to such we are represented as seditious and destructive: if such as are sensible of the losse of Trade, who can be more distrustfull to them then those that are said to raise a new Warre: if any of them should be of those who are engaged in the affairs of Ireland, to these we are represented as hinderers of the relief of Ireland: and what punishment shall seeme too great for us, from such as have been tired and wasted with Free-quarter? who are pointed out to be the continuers thereof: if any Jurymen should be of that sort of men who stile themselves of the seaven Churches of God, what equity are we like to finde from them who have already engaged against us, by their Pharisaicall Petition, for though they name us not, yet all their discourses point us out as the princiapall persons therein complained of; an ill requitall for our faithfull adherence unto them in the worst of times, and by whose endeavours under God they attained to that freedome they now enjoy; and can Churches prove unthankfull? nay watch a time when men are in prison to be so unthankfull as to oppose their enlargement? what to wound a man halfe dead by wounds? a Priest or Levite would have been ashamed of such unworthinesse: what, Christians that should be full of love, even to their enemies, to forget all humanity, and to be so dispightfull to frinds? alas, alas, for Churches that have such Pastors for their leaders; nay for Churches of God to owne such kind of un-Christian dealing: Churches of God, so their Petition denominates them; if the tree should be judged by his fruit, I know what I could say, but I am very loath to grive the spirits of any welmeaning people: and know there are whole societies of those that call themselves Churches, that abhor to be thought guilty of such un-worthinesse; Mr Lamb a pastor at the Spittle, offering upon a free debate, to prove the presenters of the Petition guilty of injustice, ar-rogance, flattery, and cruelty: ye many members of these [19] seven Churches, that have protested against it; and many more that con-demn them for this their doing, to whom I wish so much happinesse as they will seriously consider how apt in things of this civil nature, these their Pastors have been to be mistaken, as they were when they misled them not very long since to Petition for a Personall Treaty, which I would never thus have mentioned but that they persist for by-ends, offices or the like (it may be) to obstruct all publick-good pro-ceedings, and to maligne those, who without respect of persons or opinions, endeavour a common good to all men. And truly to be thus fore-laied; and as it were prejudg'd by Votes, and Declarations, and Proclamations of Parliament, under such hideous notions of sedition and Treason; apprehended in so formidable a way, and imprisoned in an extraordinary place, no Bayle being to be allowed: and after all these to be renounced and disclaimed by the open mouthes of the Pastors, and some members of seven Churches assuming the title of the Churches of God; are actions that may in one respect or other, worke a prejudicate opinion of us, in any jury that at this day may or can be found.

So as I cannot but exceedingly prefer the ordinary way of proceed-ings (as of right is due to every English-man) in Criminall cases by Justices of the Peace, which brings a man to a Triall in an ordinary way, without those affrightments and prejudgings which serve only to distract the understanding, and bias Justice, and to the hazarding of mens lives in an unreasonable manner, which is a consideration not unworthy the laying to heart of every particular person in this Nation; for what is done to us now, may be done to every person at any time at pleasure.

Neverthelesse, neither I nor my partners in suffering are any whit doubtfull of a full and clear Vindication, upon a legall triall; for in my observation of trials I have generally found, Juries and Jury-men to be full of conscience, care, and circumspection, and tendernesse in cases of life and death; and I have read very remarkable passages in our Histories; amongst which the Case and Triall of Throckmorton, in Queen Maries time is most remarkeable: the consciences of the Jury being proof against the opinion of the Judges, the rhetorick of the Councell who were great and Learned, nay against the threats of the

Court, which then was absolute in power and tyranny, and quit the Gentleman, like true-hearted, wel-resolved English-men, that valued their consciences above their lives; and I cannot think but these times, will afford as much good conscience, as that time of grosse ignorance and superstition did: and the liberty of exception against so many persons returned for Jury-men, is so mighty a guard against partaking, that I cannot doubt the issue.

Besides since In Col. Martin's* Case, a worthy Member of Parliament, it is clear that Parliaments have been mistaken in such censures, as appears by his restauration, and razing all matters concerning his Sentence out of the House Book: And since the Parliament revoked their Declaration against the Souldiers Petitioning in the beginning of the year, 1647. as having been mistaken therein: since they have so often imprisoned Mr Lilburn my fellow Prisoner, and some others, and have after found themselves mistaken; yea since some of these Gentlemen who now approve of the way of an Agreement of the People, as the only way to give rest to the Nation; about a year since voted it [20] destructive to Parliaments, and to the very being of all Governments, imprisoning divers for appearing in behalf thereof.

I am somewhat hopefull, that a Jury will not much be swaied by such their sudden proceedings towards us; as not perfectly knowing, but that they may also have been mistaken concerning us now; for it was never yet known, that Mr Lilburn, or I, or any of us, ever yet had a hand in any base, unworthy, dangerous businesse: though sometimes upon hasty apprehensions and jealousies of weak people, we have been so rendred: But (be this businesse what it wil) I do not know why I should be suspected in the least, and can never sufficiently wonder at this their dealing towards me.

And as for any great hurt the Pastors of the seven Churches are like to do, by their petitioning against us, though their intentions were very bad and vile, yet considering how few of their honest members approve thereof, and that the high esteem of the Church-way is a most worn out, being not made (as the Churches we reade of in Scriptures) of everlasting, but fading matter; as the Book, entituled, *The vanity of the present Churches*, doth fully demonstrate: a little consideration of these things by any Jury, will easily prevent the worst they intended: Wherein also, possibly, they may deserve some excuse, as being (probably) mis-led thereto by the same politique councels, as drew them in, to petition for a Personall Treaty: Such as these being fit

* Henry Marten, M.P., Berkshire, 1640–1659/60. (Editors' note)

instruments for Politicians; as in the former part of this Discourse is evinced.

But, be it as it may, if I be still thought so unworthy as to deserve a prosecution, a fair legall triall by twelve sworn men of the neighbourhood, in the ordinary Courts of Justice, is all I desire (as being even more willing to put myself upon my Country, then on the Court, or any the like Prorogative way) and have exceeding cause to rejoyce in the sincere affection of a multitude of Friends, who out of an assured confidence of our integrity, and sensible of the hard measure we have found, and of the prejudice our present imprisonment might bring upon us, did immediately bestir themselves, and presented a Petition for our present enlargement with a speedy legall triall: whose care and tender respects towards us, we shall ever thankfully acknowledge: But the seven Churches were got before them, and had so much respect, that our Friends found none at all; but what remedy but patience? all things have their season, and what one day denies, another gives.

And so I could willingly conclude, but that I shall stay a little to take in some more aspersions, which are brought in apace still, and I would willingly dispatch them.

I and my fellow prisoners are now abused, and that upon the Exchange, by the mouths of very godly people; so it must run, That say, all our bustlings are, because we are not put into some Offices of profit and Authority, and if we were once in power, we would be very Tyrants: But pray, Sirs, you that are at this loosenesse of conscience, why produce you not the Petitions we presented to your Patrons? Why tell you not the time and place, where we solicited for any advantage to our selves? But allow we had done so, with what faces can you reprove us? For shame pluck out the beams out of your own eies, you that have turned all things upside down for no other end, and run continually to and fro to furnish your selves and Friends, thrusting whole families out to seek their bread, to make room for you. [21]

And how appears it, that if we were in any power and Authority we would be very Tyrants? We never sought for any, and that's some good sign; those who do, seldom using it to the good of the publique: And for ought is seen, we might have had a large share if we would have sought it; but account it a sure rule, that into Muse as they use: So generally true is it, that the Asperser is really guilty of what he forgeth against another: And that this may appear, let all impartiall people but look about them, and consider what and who they are, that seek most after offices and power, and how they use them when they have them; and then say, whether those that asperse us, or we who are aspersed, do most deserve this imputation.

Nay, we find by experience, that we are reproacht scarce by any, but such as are engaged in one kind of corrupt interest or other; either he hath two or three offices or trusts upon him, by which he is enriched and made powerfull; or he hath an office in the excise, or customs; or is of some monopolizing company; or interested in the corruption of the laws; or is an encloser of fens, or other commons; or hath charge of publique monies in his hands, for which he would not willingly be accomptable; or hath kept some trust, authority or command in hand longer then commission and time intended; or being in power, hath done something that cannot well be answered; or that hath money upon usury in the excise; or that makes title of tythes, and the like burthenous grievances; or else such as have changed their principles with their condition; and of pleaders for liberty of Conscience, whil'st they were under restraint, and now become persecuters, so soon as they are freed from disturbance; or some that have been projectors, still fearing an after-reckoning; or that have received gifts, or purchased the publique lands at undervalues.

And we heartily wish, that all ingenuous people would but enquire into the interest of every one they hear asperse us; the which if they clearly do, it's ten to one the greatest number of them by far, will prove to belong to some of those corrupt interests forenamed; and we desire all men to mark this in all places: And the reason is evident, namely, because they are jealous (our hands being known to be clear from all those things) that by our, and our Friends means, in behalf of the common good, first or last, they shall be accomptable; and if those who hear any of these exclaiming against us would but tread, their corrupt interests a little upon the toe where the shoe pinches, they might soon have reason of them, and they will be glad to be silent: and this is a medicine for a foul mouth, I have often used very profitably.

And now comes one that tels me, it's reported by a very godly man, that I am a man of a most dissolute life, it being common with me to play at Cards on the Lord's day; there is indeed no end of lying and backbiting; nor shame in impudence, or such palpable impostors could never be beleived; and I am perswaded the Inventers would give a good deal of money I were indeed addicted to spend my time in gaming, drinking or loosnesse; from which I praise God, he hath alwaies preserved me, and hath so inclined my mind and disposition, as that it takes pleasure in nothing but what is truly good and virtuous; the most of my recreation being a good Book, or an honest and discoursing Friend: Other sports and pastimes that are lawfull and moderate, though I allow them well to yet I have used them as seldom my self as any man, I think, hath done: But I [22] see, slander will have its course; and that a good conscience, and a corrupt interest can no more consist in one and the same person, then Christ and Belial.

And for a conclusion to all these scandals, it is imposed upon us, that we are an unquiet, unstaied people, that are not resolved what will satisfie us; that we know not where to end, or what to fix a bottom upon—and truly this hath been alwaies the very language of those, who would keep all power in their hands, and would never condescend to such an issue as could satisfie; such as would content themselves with the least measure of what might justly be called true freedom: But what sort of men ever offered at, or discovered so rationall a way for men to come to so sure a foundation for peace and freedom, as we have done and long insisted on, namely, by an Agreement of the People, and unto which we all stand: As for the way, and as to the matter, we have been long since satisfied in our selves, but our willingnesse to obtain the patronage of some thereto, instead of furtherance, procur'd its obstruction: Because we cannot submit to things unreasonable, and unsafe in an Agreement, shall any brand us, that we are restlesse, and have no bottom? Certainly it had been time enough for such an aspersion, if there had been a joynt and free consent to what was produc't and insisted on by others.

For till a bargain be made, both parties are free, and may raise the price, as occasion invites; so hath it been in our case: At first, the little short Agreement was by us thought sufficient; and had that been establisht, we had rested there: but that being baffled, as the burnt Petition had procured that Agreement, so the baffling of that usher'd in, and occasioned the fulnesse, the largenesse of that Agreement which Mr Lilburn publisht: and if that had been assented to, and established, we had rested then; and untill after contract, all complaints are unjust; and now if the baffling of this last, thorow further observation and teachings of necessity; the next in motion should exceed both the former in clearnesse of freedom, and removall of all grievances: would it not rather be a good improvement of this time of suspension, then deserve the aspersion of unsetlednesse: We wish those that upbraid us of unsetlednesse, would settle according to promise; and if after, we content not our selves, and stand to what is setled, then, and not before, let us be thus asperst: God knows, how exceedingly we long to see this Nation out of danger, misery, and poverty it is like to run into through losse of trade, and by reason of the enmity continued amongst us, for want of such a settlement as we desire; and which are defects, if by some mens policies it had not been prevented, had been long since setled, as we verily believe, to the contentfull satisfaction of all sorts of people, and to the restoring of that peace, amity, love and friendship, which hath been too long absent from us; and untill which be restored, this Nation will never flourish with that plenty of trade and commerce, which alone can produce the happinesse and prosperity of this impoverished and wasted Nation.

Lastly (yet I am out of hope it will be the last, for I see no end of this ever-flowing fountain) I am accused to have said, I never would petition the Parliament, if I thought they would grant what I petitioned for; which, I professe, is most false and absurd; for I never had any hand in any Petition, but I desired with all my heart it might be granted; and am perswaded, if those I and [23] my Friends have presented, had been granted, it had been much better with the Common-wealth then now it is; for we have been ever watchfull for the good of England, though now we are requited with a prison and aspersions for our labour: and if the present time should be so froward as to reject the light we bring, yet our comfort is, that our principles are of a growing nature, as having the power of truth in them: so that we cannot doubt, but England will be the better for our motions and endeavours to all generations.

I little thought when I began this work, that it would have drawn me out to such a length, much beyond my disposition; but if I can avoid it, I shall make amends, and never trouble the world any more in this kind: Nor had I done thus much, but that through my easily pierced sides, they wounded the cause, I shall promote whil'st I have breath; they wound the reputation of the Family whereof I am; and may too much wound with grief my dear and ancient Mother, whom I have the greatest cause to love; my Wife and Children also are deeply wounded in my reproaches, whom I value ten-fold above my life; and upon whom, whensoever I shall leave the world, I would leave no blemish: Nor should I, could my heart be truly understood; for how exceedingly short soever I may come of doing my duty in all cases, yet are my desires, inclinations, and intentions, as reall to the publique, as free from basenesse in my particular walkings and occasions; as the corrupt *Fountain of Slander* is full of malice, treachery and impudence.

Nor could I, as the case is now with me (this restraint being very much to my prejudice) bear up my spirit with that contentednesse, I bless God, I do; were it not for the integrity of my Conscience towards all men: And whereas long since I had concluded it for a most excellent truth, my experience now tels me, that affliction is ten thousand times better then sin; and that the innocent have more chearfulnesse in a Dungeon, then corrupt and wicked men have, though they are cloathed in Purple, and fare deliciously every day.

This Discourse being thus far furnished immediately after I came into prison, I did forbear to print it, because of its largenesse, far exceeding my inclination; and was much better satisfied to fall in with my partners in sufferings, in publishing our joynt manifestation of the 4th of April, 1649. wherein we conceived, we had given full satisfaction to all men, and stopt the mouth of slander it self; and after that, according to our promise therein, having upon the first of May, 1649. published an Agreement of the People, to take off that scandall then upon us, that we would rest or bottom no where: As my three partners did, so did I judge my writing work at end, as not knowing or conceiving that any thing remained in objection against me, that was not either expresly or impliedly cleared and resolved.

And thereupon began to take some more content, that I had not published this Discourse: When lo, on a sudden, just as I was to be made a close Prisoner, there belches out from the corrupt *Fountain of Slander*, such a foggy mist of lies, invectives and slanders, as would have choakt any but the spawn of envy and malice to have uttered them: But that venome which destroyes men, I see, is the life-bloud of such ingratefull serpents, as now for former kindnesses, watch this time of my affliction, to choak me with their pestilentiall breath.

But, I blesse God, I am proof against it, I have a certain antidote they are not [24] acquainted withall, that published *Walwyn's Wyles*; it's called, a good Conscience; which tels me, if that Book had been named by its true Father, and Father of lies, it would have been entituled (for he sometimes speaks truth) *Lies of Walwyn*: But it finds nothing in me, whereof to condemn my self; and why then I should take so much pains as to answer them, I cannot yet resolve: especially considering my causlesse close imprisonment, hath somewhat weakned me: and possibly, being so fully known as I am, and being now thus restrained, some may wish me so well, as to write in my vindication; if not, possibly I may do it my self.

In the mean time, the ingenuous Reader of this will be indifferently well prepared to a right understanding, whence all this filthy matter proceedeth; it being evident by what hath been written, that the Politicians of this world are Satan's chief Agents, by whom all discords and dissentions amongst men are begot and nourished: and that the Politicians chief Agent is his tongue, wherewith in an evil sense, and to an evil end, he speaks to every man in his own language, applies himself to every man's corrupt humour and interest, by it he becomes all things to all men, that by all means he might deceive some.

And whom by flattery and delusion he gains not, by slander he labours to destroy; his brain is the forge of mischief, the *Fountain of Slander,* and his tongue set on fire of hel (as Saint James speaks)

Yet his words are cool as the dew, smooth as oyl, and sweet as the purest honey, weeps and kils, smiles and stobs, praieth, fasteth, and sometimes preacheth to betray, shrouds himself under the finest cloak of Religion, takes on him the most zealous form of godlinesse, and in this shape securely casts his nets to catch plain-meaning people.

Such as himself are his associates; for without confederacy, much cannot be effected; and superstitious people, and their Idolaters, upon whose ignorant zeal they work, and by whom (as by men religious, not prophane) they disperse and send abroad their reproaches and slanders without suspicion.

Yet as godly as they appear, and as close as they keep, if you but once take the boldnesse to suspect them, they are discovered; for as their Father is said not to be able to hide his cloven foot, so neither can these hide their double dealing: do but never so little watch them, and you shall find they are made up of Contradictions:

Very Religious in shew, but very covetous in deed, given to usury and oppressive gain, can possesse the worlds goods in abundance, yet suffer their Brethren to lack necessaries, yea, to lie and starve in prisons through penury and hunger: they can be clothed, as in purple, and fare deliciously every day, but poor Joseph's and Lazarus's tears and cries are despised by them: Seemingly humble, but upon advantage, none more violent, imperious, inhumane or bloud-thirsty then they: obstructers of justice, and all good things, neither doing it themselves, nor permitting others.

In a word, observe them well, and you shall see Christ and Belial, God and Mammon in one and the same person; Christ in shew, the other in reality: —— Men they are, that have no ties or bonds upon them, letting themselves loose to lying, dissimulation, slandering, backbiting, and all kinds of circumvention; God, Conscience, Religion, Reason, Virtue, are but meer tearms and no- [25] tions in them, serving them to no other purpose, but to deceive the more effectually:

And to speak them all at once, they are the most ingratefull men in the world.

Their principall work is to make proselytes, to corrupt the best parted, and most able Wits to take part with them; shewing them all the glories of the world, if they will fall down and worship them; and if they can but get them to embrace any corrupt way of living, or but plant them in any corrupt interest, they are theirs for ever, and must not stop at any wickednesse, baits which have taken too many precious spirits in these warping times.

And if this Discourse of mine serve but somewhat to warn all well-meaning people, so as to beware of this kind of men, or rather Monsters; I shall have the utmost benefit I expect therein; praying God to blesse all my weak indeavours and sufferings to the information of men, and good of the Nation.

The Printer to the Reader

Mend the Printer's faults, as thou doest them espy,
For the Author lies in Gaol, but knows not why.

Pag. 1. lin. 1.r. *from.* l. 12. for *born* r.*bound.* p. 2. l. 38. for *honest civilities.* r. *dishonest actions.* l. 41. for *seein* r. *serve.* l. 47. for *and* r. *are.* p. 3. l. 38. for *mines* r. *wives.* l. 45. for *compared* r. *comparing.* p. 4. l. 7. for *poleth* r. *publish.* p.5. l.31. for *then were* r. *they were.* p.7.l.25. for *nor so* r. *but.* p.8. l.22. for *seem* r. *serve.* p.15.l.25. for *reward* r. *regard.* p.17.l.2. for *hope* r. *hoping.*

FINIS [26]

25

Walwyns Just Defence against the Aspertions Cast upon Him, in a Late Un-Christian Pamphlet Entituled, Walwyns Wiles

[June–July?] 1649
Reprinted from a copy of the tract in the Folger Shakespeare Library

Walwyns Just Defence, "By William Walwyn, Merchant," was printed by "H. Hils, for W. Larnar," 1649. Thomason did not secure a copy. The title, references in the tract, and Humphrey Brooke's opening paragraphs in *The Charity of Church-Men* indicate that it was drafted after the appearance of *Walwins Wiles*, which was acquired by Thomason on 10 May.[1] Lilburne mentions *Just Defence* in the second edition of *Legall Fundamentall Liberties*, which was published in late July or early August.[2]

Just Defence is Walwyn's direct response to the attacks on his character, conduct, and convictions in *Walwins Wiles*. John Price, principal draftsman of *Wiles*, regarded Walwyn, rather than Lilburne or Overton, as the essential leader of the Leveller movement.[3] Walwyn's reply is a roughly chronological narrative of his relations with the Independents conjoined with a defense of Walwyn's own attitudes and bitter condemnations of his opponents—particularly those in John Goodwin's congregation.[4] *Just Defence* includes a wealth of detail that is invaluable for information about Walwyn and the development of the Leveller party.[5] In 1649 the mass of minutiae can only have detracted from a pamphlet that is unleavened by the wit that marked Walwyn's refutations of Edwards in 1646.

WALWYNS
JVST DEFENCE

AGAINST THE

ASPERTIONS

CAST UPON HIM,

IN

A late un-chriſtian Pamphlet entituled,
WALWYNS WILES.

By *William Walwyn*, Merchant.

Proverbs 12. ver. 6.
The words of the wicked are to lie in waite for blood, but the
mouth of the upright ſhall deliver them.

LONDON,
Printed by *H. Hils*, for *W. Larnar*, and are to be ſold at the ſign
of the *Blackmore*, near *Biſhops-gate.*
M.DC.XLIX.

Title page of *Walwyns Just Defence*, 1649. (Folger Shakespeare Library)

Just Defence is reprinted in *Leveller Tracts*, ed. Haller and Davies, pp. 350–98.

WALWYNS JUST DEFENCE AGAINST THE ASPER-TIONS CAST UPON HIM, IN A late un-christian Pamphlet en-tituled, WALWYNS WILES.

By *William Walwyn*, Merchant.

Proverbs 12. ver. 6. *The words of the wicked are to lie in waite for blood, but the mouth of the upright shall deliver them.*

LONDON, Printed by *H. Hils*, for *W. Larnar*, and are to be sold at the sign of the *Blackmore*, near *Bishops-gate.* M.DC.XLIX.

Walwyns just defence against the Aspersions cast upon him, &c.

I should be glad for the good of humane society, that those seven men whose names are subscribed to the Epistle of that Book, would set down a certain rule, or declare what rule theirs is, wherby in civil Communication, a man may know, when those he keeps company withall are reall; and when deceivers, when they mean as they seem, and when they carry two faces under one hood, which amongst honest men is called double-dealing; and this not so much in respect of themselves, for I have not had much familiarity with any of these seven; but in respect of those from whom they seem to have had their false informations concerning me; there being not one of them that ever reproved me to my face for any thing that I ever said or did, or that ever applied themselves to me with Friends in a Christian way, to shew me wherein I walked erroniously or scandalously: but all they have done or spoken to my disparagement, hath been behind my back; whil'st, wheresoever they met me, they nevertheless saluted me as a Friend: How this kind of behaviour can be justified, I professe I understand not.

And upon what grounds these seven men subscribe this Epistle, I do not apprehend; for, as for Mr Kiffin, I never had an unfriendly word or countenance from him; nor from Mr Rosier, but kind respects wherever I met them: for Mr Foster, and Mr Burnet, I know them not by name, nor can't ghesse who they are: Mr Lordall, and Mr Price have been somewhat shy a good while, about our different judgment for seasons of petitioning; but especially, since at Kingston, before his Excellency,* I gave my reasons against the raising of a new Regiment for the Tower of London; proposing the place to be guarded with Citizens, as a means to preserve trade, and the affection of the City to the Army; which I still judge was honest and good councel: but their Friends pursued the contrary, and prevailed; and ever since, these have cast an ill eie upon me, and as I have heard, have reproacht me much behind my back.

And for Mr Arnald, just before the New Model, he groundlesly reported to the Lieutenant Generall Cromwel, that I held correspondence with Oxford, though at the same time I held daily meetings, and intimate Discourse with Mr John Goodwin, Mr Henry Burton, Mr Peters, Mr Hilsly, Mr Lilburn, and others, and continued so after with the best respect; but I could never get so much satisfaction among them for so grosse an injury, as to know his Author, I only was answered, that I saw none of them had an ill thought of me: but since he understood I knew of this his injury to me, [1] he hath ever hated me, and sought to do me mischief; giving out confidently, that I am a Jesuite; and he now fixes his name, I fear, malliciously, to things I am sure it is impossible for him to know or for any man in the world: for what is false hath no essence or reallity; but it is sutable to his practise towards me, and so I wonder not to finde his name there: though at others, I cannot sufficiently wonder:

In the yeer 1646, whilst the army was victorious abroad, through the union and concurrence of conscientious people, of all judgments, and opinions in religion; there brake forth here about London a spirit of persecution; whereby private meetings were molested, & divers pastors of congregations imprisoned, & all threatned; Mr. Edwards, and others, fell foule upon them, with his Gangreen after Gangreen, slander upon slander, to make them odious, and so to fit them for destruction, whether by pretence of law, or open violence he seemed not to regard; and amongst the rest, abused me, which drew from me *a whisper in his ear,* and some other discourses, tending to my own vindication, and the defence of all conscientious people: and for

* Sir Thomas Fairfax. (Editors' note)

which [I] had then much respect from these very men, that now asperse me themselves, with the very same, and some other like aspertions, as he then did.

Persecution increased in all quarters of the land, sad stories coming dayly from all parts, which at length were by divers of the Churches, my self, and other friends, drawn into a large petition; which I professe was so lamentable, considering the time, that I could hardly read it without tears: and though most of those that are called Anabaptists and Brownists congregations, were for the presenting of it; yet Master Goodwins people, and some other of the Independent Churches being against the season, it was never delivered.

But troubles still increasing, another petition, not so large, was prepared, and at length agreed to by all sorts of conscientious people, that were opposite to persecution: and all this while I was acceptable among them; only some grudgings I perceived in Master John Price, which I imputed to some weaknes, inclyning to emulation: and all the strife about this petition also, was the season: multitudes with me being for the presenting, and the Independents against it: in conclusion, a finall meeting there was, where before I came was disperst the most shamefull aspertion of me, that ever was uttered of man: and which did render me so obnoxious to that meeting, that all I spake was construed to the worst; and caused so great a clamour and discontent, that he who had the petition and hands in keeping, rent it in peeces; and so the meeting ended.

Towards the conclusion whereof, Major Robert Cobet pulls me by the arm to speak with me, so I took Master Davis, and Master Antrobus and others with me; and master Cobet told me before them, that one master Husbands a linnen draper in Corn-hill, being at Lieutenant Generalls house, there openly avouched that I was an Atheist and denier of Scriptures, a loose and vitious man, and that abusing my self with a lew'd woman, she puting me in mind of that place of Scripture, that whoremongers and adulterers God would judge, that I should make answer, what do ye tell me of that Idle book?

Telling me withall, that this report was gone all about the town, and was the cause I was so ill resented by the present meeting; I confess, I was amazed to hear this, but whilst he was telling me this foule story, he espies master Husbands, and calls him to us; telling him he was declaring to master Walwyn here, pointing to me, what he heard him declare at the Lieutenant Generalls, says master Husbands, I wish you had not spoken of it, for I find it is a mistake, the thing is not true

of master Walwyn, it is another; so he suffered himself to be thorowly
reproved by those pre- [2] sent, and he seemed then to be sorry for it;
but aspersions fly faster, then any man can fetch them back, and so
did this, to my extream desparagement: and it served their turn at
that meeting to blast all the reason I spake, and to destroy that petition:

And those who had made use of this reproach, and so made themselves guilty, as the manner of men is, resolved to disparage me to
purpose, and thereupon some leading people of master John Goodwins, set themselves down as a Committee, calling before them, all
they could finde had ever conversed with me, to inform whatsoever I
had said, that might tend to my disparagement: this is some three
yeers since: and so by way of articles, most of the aspersions now in
this book, were then collected, which I had continuall notice of as
they came in, and who did inform: and who would not, but declared
confidently they were perswaded from long and much familiarity,
that I was really honest and conscientious; amongst which Mr. Henry
Brandriff, Captain Chaplain, Mr. Weekes and others;

Neverthelesse the violent party, as Mr. John Price, and others,
would go on with their articles: me thoughts it was a strange work,
for a people who called themselves the people of God: but so they
did; and at length had possest divers, who formerly had well respected me, that I was a dangerous man and not fit for society;
whereupon it was desired by my friends, and agreed unto by theirs,
that a meeting should be on both parties; and their articles should be
heard, and I have freedom to make my defence, and the place appointed was the Dolphin in Corn-hill, where I and my friends kept
our time and continued there, but on their parts none came.

And Mr. Brandriff, my then intimate friend, perswaded me it was
not fit, things should come to such a height, that it would make but
rejoycing for our enemies; that he was confident, there was no real
enmity, but only causles doubts and jealousies, and that if I would but
vindicate my judgement concerning the Scriptures, and my owning
of them, I should find they had nothing to object against me, and that
they and I should be as good and as loving friends as ever.

Whereunto I was very inclinable, as having never born any man a
grudge for any injury ever done me, esteeming the doer by wounding
his own conscience; to be punished sufficiently; nor do I relate these
things in way of revenge, but only as to do my self right, and to free
my wife and children from the reproach of having so unworthy a
husband and Father, and the cause I honour, from having so vile a

servant as these would make me, I told him my whisper to Mr. Edwards and my other writings did sufficiently testifie I owned the Scriptures, and he confest it, but yet wisht me to do something particularly, to that end:

About this time upon occasion of Mr. Edwards, writings (I take it) came forth Mr. John Goodwins *Haggio-Mastix*, wherein to the apprehension of some eminent men: he in effect denied the scriptures to be the word of God, and much discourse, and great complaint there was about it, in so much as Collonel Leighs Committee had it brought before them, where it was my lot to be, when the passage concerning the Scriptures was read openly by one, that amongst others, informed against it: and where it was called a most impious, blasphemous Book, and ordered to be seized, all of them immediatly;

That Committee was of a most persecuting disposition, and dealt most frowardly with divers conscientious people; with whom, and in whose behalf, I continually appeared, as for Mr. Kiffin, Mr. Patience, and many others, I cannot now remember: and Henry, Mr. Overtons man the book-seller, that, as I am told, prints this unchristian book, called, *Walwyns Wiles*, might remember who it was that gave timely [3] notice of the order for seizing his Master's Books (for he printed *Hagio Mastix*) and in thankfulnesse for the courtesie done to his dead Master, might have forborn to have done me such a discourtesie: but it hath been my usuall payment for all my services to that sort of men.

Divers did observe a strange providence, that those who had so scandalized me for a denier of Scriptures, should from a pen, wherein they were all concerned, receive occasion of so great suspicion, and be put themselves upon a work of vindication on his behalf: And though they called it, *a Candle to light the Sun* (as esteeming it altogether superfluous) yet many still say, it needs to be more cleared.

And hence some of my Friends perswaded me I needed not to publish my Vindication concerning the Scriptures, for satisfaction of those, who had enough to do for their own Vindication: yet because I was willing to stand clear in the sight of all men, I published my *Still and soft voyce*, against which I never yet heard any objection: And one of Mr Goodwin's People, namely, Mr Davenish, meeting me a few daies after in the Court of Requests, saluted me kindly, and gave me thanks for publishing that Book; I told him, I was glad understanding men approved it, and did hope it would be profitable to the publique: he replyed, it would be so, and that he should make it his rule.

And so a good while after this, I had much respect from many of them, and not an ill look from any: but though Mr Leigh's Committee extremely perplexed honest people about their private meetings and doctrines, yet did this sort of men that traduce me appear very slenderly in comparison of others, that were thought to be lesse concerned.

In conclusion, that Committee and their Favourers in both Houses grew to so great a height, that the Generality of Congregations, and others, resolved to bear testimony openly against the same, as being contrary to the many Declarations of Parliament, and as doing the very same things they had condemned in the high Commission: and thereupon drew up a Petition, wherein they did parallel all the former practises complained of in the Star Chamber and high Commission, with the present proceedings; which Petition was drawn and debated by many persons chosen purposely thereunto, and indeed was the most serious of any that was presented (which the Author of this Pamphlet, I perceive, tearms sharpnesse and provoking) and imputes it unto me.

This Petition was taken before it was handed, and questioned as a scandalous and seditious paper, and committed to Mr Leigh's Committee to enquire after the Authors and Promoters; and Mr Lamb, at whose meeting place it was taken, ordered to appear there: this occasioned a very great appearance in the owning of it, by aboundance of consciencious honest people, and that occasioned some discontent in the Committee, which begot the commitment of Major Tulidah, and Mr Tue; and that occasioned another Petition to the House, and that another, untill the last and the first large one were ordered to be burnt by the common Hangman; in all which time of motion and trouble, most of the uppermost Independents stood aloof, and look'd on: whil'st Mr Stasmore, Mr Highland, Mr Davis, Mr Cooper, Mr Thomas Lamb of the Spittle, and very many more, for many weeks continually plied the House.

The Petition is yet to be seen, and is fraught with aboundance of good things, such as I really desired the House would have granted; and I think it had been happy for them that burnt it, rather to have granted it, and most happy for the Common- [4] wealth: So that it's an extreme mistake to imagine, that I, or any that I ever knew, petitioned for such things as we did hope the Parliament would not grant: Indeed, we had cause to doubt they would not, but we conceived they ought, the things being evidently just; and we conceived if they would not, 'twas more then we knew before we ask'd; and we knew it was our duty to ask, and that upon such evidence of reason and equity which that Petition holds forth, as should leave a testimony to

the world, that we understood our rights, and did in an humble petitioning way demand them.

But this bustling unkind dealing with Petitioners for many weeks
together, and the burning of a Petition so just and necessary, so
opened the eies of the people in all places, that it was both grieved
and wondred at; all men evidently seeing, that we were likely, though
the Common Enemy was vanquish'd, to be liable to the same, or
worse bondage, notwithstanding all the bloud and misery it had cost
to be delivered there from.

And when this was discerned, then some of my now Adversaries
began to approve of our motions, and they and I began to come a little
nearer together, and had joynt meetings and debates; and Mr John
Price may, and cannot but remember an evenings journey he and I
made into Drury-lane to the Lieutenant Generall, and what satisfaction we received; what aboundance of friendly discourse we had all
the way going and comming, and parted in a most kind and cordiall
manner; rejoycing on my part, as having no grain of rancour remaining in me, and thought it had been so on his; if it were not, God
forgive him.

But the effect was, we all, both his Friends and mine, joyned in a
Petition, the last and most sharp of any, as is yet to be seen; wherein
he knows was not only his and mine advice, but many others: so that
to say, I delight or design provocations to Authority, is a grosse abuse;
if there were any, it is, he knows, to be shared amongst he knows
whom, as well as us.

And, as unadvised, it is to lay to my charge the opposing of all
Authority that ever was: for let them tell me what Authority they
opposed not; the Kings and Bishops they cannot deny; and the Parliament and Presbyterian, I think, they will confesse; and truly I never
opposed since, except to insist for such just things as were promised,
when the Army first disputed, be called an opposition: and such as
are not only fix'd in my mind, but in the minds of thousands more
that then owned the proceedings of the Army, and ventered their
lives for them, when these that now revile me, stood aloof, seeing it
neither just nor seasonable.

And truly, that they have sate themselves down on this side Jordan,
the reason is somewhat too evident, for men that would not be
thought men of this world; it is but a promised land, a promised good
that I and my Friends seek, it is neither offices, honours nor preferments, it is only promised Freedom, and exemption from burdens for
the whole Nation, not only for our selves; we wish them peace, we

repine not at any mans honour, preferment or advantage; give us but Common Right, some foundations, some boundaries, some certainty of Law, and a good Government; that now, when there is so high discourse of Freedom, we may be delivered from will, power, and meer arbitrary discretion, and we shall be satisfied: if to insist for this, be to oppose Authority, what a case are we in? Certainly were these men in our case, or were they sensible of the price it hath cost this Nation to purchase Freedom, they would think it deserved more then the meer name thereof. [5]

And how I can be charged to make it my work to divide the Army, I cannot see; I only pursue the establishment of Freedom, and redresse of Grievances, I have ever pursued, and which are not yet obtained; so also have done many in the Army. It is in the Army, as it is between these mens Friends and mine; some content themselves with present enjoyments, others with the Commonwealth at more certainty in the foundations of Freedom; and for my part, I ever most earnestly desired their union, so it were in good, and for that Freedom and good to the Nation, for which, I believe, most of them have fought; and if they divide for want of it, they divide them that keep them from it, and not I, that wish with all my heart that cause of division were not.

The Lieutenant Generall well knows (for I visited him often in Drury-lane about that time that Mr Price was there with me) how much I desired the union of the Army; and though it then divided, it was not esteemed a fault in those that seperated themselves for good, but blameworthy in those that would not unite, except for evil: So that to unite, or divide, is not the thing; but whether in good, or evil, is the main of all; and by which, my Adversaries and I shall one day be judged, though now they have taken the Chair, and most uncharitably judge me of evil in every thing wherein I move, or but open my mouth.

And the Lieutenant Generall also knows, upon what grounds I then perswaded him to divide from that Body, to which he was united; that if he did not, it would be his ruine, and the ruine of the Generall, and of all those Worthyes that had preserved us; that if he did do it in time, he should not only preserve himself and them, and all consciencious people, but he should do it without spilling one drop of bloud; professing, that if it were not evident to me that it would be so, I would not perswade him; and that I would undertake to demonstrate to him that it would be so; and so, through God's goodnesse, and the zeal and affections of these mens now despised Friends, it came to passe: so far was I ever from advising unto bloud:

whereas these men would suppose me to be delighted with nothing more then slaughter and confusion.

Well, I had no shew of enmity from them all the time the Army disputed with the Parliament, but they would, divers of them, come home to my house day by day, and sit and discourse friendly, and chearfully, and seriously, of the present affairs, and refresh themselves in my Garden with that simple entertainment I use unto my Friends; and when they had done, I would bring them on their way, and they as kindly bring me back; and so joy'd was I really with this (as I thought) renewed affection, that I would often say within my self, and to some others, I now see, The falling out of Lovers is the renewing of Love.

Nay, so great a testimony I then had, from my continued Friend Mr Brandriffe, that greater could not be; for it was his lot to discourse with one Major West, a Gentleman, I take it, of Cambridge-shire, who was to have gone for Ireland: this Gentleman told him divers secret things, that rightly ordered, were very usefull at that time: Mr Brandriffe thinks me the fittest man to be acquainted therewith, tels me of it, and brings him to my house, to whom I was not altogether a Stranger, so he opens his breast to me in such things, that as the times were, if I had been base, or false-hearted, might have cost him his life; I say, as the times were: but I proved as Mr Brandriffe had reported me to him, and kept his councel.

Well, very good Friends we were all; and I was by very eminent persons of the Army, sent for to Reading, to be advised withall touching the good of the people, a study my Conscience had much addicted me to; and after this, no jarr appeared [6] amongst us till the Army had past through the City, nor untill the businesse of the Tower aforementioned befell: But then, instead of Arguments against mine, and my Friends Reason, aspersions were produced; and then afresh, we were Atheists, Non-Scripturists, Jesuites and any thing to render us odious. This, whil'st I remained there, begot a great falling out amongst our Friends and theirs in London; which upon my comming (looking upon it as a thing of very ill consequence) I prevailed for a reconcilement: so far have I ever been from dividing, that I believe all those with whom I have most convert, judge no man more deserves the name of a Reconciler.

But about this time I met with that Gentleman, Major West, in the street, and he looks upon me somewhat ghastly, saying, what are you here? yes, said I, why not? why, saies he, being at my Lord Mayors, you were there said to be the most dangerous, ill-conditioned man alive; that you seek to have the City destroyed; that you would have no Government, and all things common, and drive on dangerous designs: saies I, who is it that avouches this? why, saies he, Henry Brandriffe, who saies, he knows it to be true, and that he hath kept you company these seven years, of purpose to discover you: I professe, I was so astonisht to hear this from Mr Brandriffe, that I had no thought (nor did not then call to mind) how upon intimate intire friendship, he had brought this Mr West to unbosome himself unto me, in a matter of so great concernment; so I past it over, and parted with him.

But in a little ruminating of the strangenesse and horriblenesse of this dealing, the businesse of Major Wests comming to me with Mr Brandriffe, withall circumstances came fresh into my mind; and about a week after, I met with Major West in Bishops-gate-street, and after a salute, askt him, if he had seen Mr Brandriffe: he told me, he had, and that he was of the same mind, and would justifie it, for he had kept me company seven years to discover me: upon this I askt him, whether he did not remember, that Mr Brandriffe (upon pre-discourse) did bring him to my house to discover such and such things to me, as the fittest Friend he had? he answered me, yes: and were they not such things, said I, that if I had been base and deceitfull, might have been much to your prejudice, as the times then were? yes, saies he: said I, did he then know me to be base, and to carry on dangerous designs, and had kept me company seven years to discover me, and would he bring you to discover such things, and to unbosome your self to me? said I, whether was he most false to you, or to me? he makes a stand a little while; truly, saies he, he must be very false and unworthy to one of us: So I wisht him to consider, what strange kind of men these were, and how a man might come to know when they meant good faith in their discourse and society amongst men.

This Discourse I have set down thus punctually, because a person of so good credit as this Major West is, is ready, as he told me lately, to avouch this that Mr Brandriffe said of me; and because it is their usuall way to beget credit in the foulest aspersions they cast upon me, by saying, this is certain, I kept him company so long of purpose to discover him, and will rather injure their own conscience then want of belief; for I am confident Mr Brandriffe in all his society with me, had not an ill thought of me; if he did keep me company so long for ill and unworthy ends, to entrap and make the worst of every thing I said (which I cannot believe) he was the more unworthy; and cannot but lament his condition, or any mans else that useth it: I blesse God, I never was a minute in his company, but upon tearms of true hearty love and friendship; nor ever circumvented him, or any man else; nor have used to carry tales, or to make the worst of mens discourses, but have set my house [7] and heart open at all times to honest men, where they have had a most sincere and hearty welcome; and if any have turned my freedom and kindnesse to my prejudice, God forgive them.

Yea, so far hath it been from being my principle, or practice (as the uncharitable Subscribers of the Epistle Dedicatory to this vain Book, infer) to say or do any thing against him whom I thought engaged to destroy me; that both to those of the Kings Party, with whom I had some acquaintance, and those my old and many Friends of the Presbyterian judgment, in all times; I ever spake and advised them what I thought in my conscience was for their good; perswading with all men to place their happinesse so, as it might be consistent with the freedom, peace and prosperity of the Common-wealth; and, I believe, many will acknowledge they have found my councel good, and wish they had taken it; some having since confest, I have told them truth, when they did not believe it; nor can any of them justly say, and I believe will not say, that ever I abated one sillable of my principle of Common Freedom, nor ever discovered a thought to the prejudice of the Parliament or Commonwealth.

But would these men turn their sight inward, and look into their own hearts, there they would find such a latitude of dissimulation, as is hardly to be found in any sort of men pretending to Religion; as may not only appear by these mens fair carriages outwardly alwaies to me, and Mr Brandriffe's strange discovery of himself, but in others also of the same people, as Mr Richard Price the Scrivener, the Author of one of the most notorious false scandals contained in the Book.

My first acquaintance with this Mr Richard Price, was by occasion of our Parish businesse, in his trade, and that about our Ward; and after that, about a Remonstrance presented to the Common Councel, in all which I found him ingenuous, and so grew to intimacy with him: this was when Alderman Pennington was Lord Mayor, and before Mr John Goodwin had gathered his Church, or at least, before this Mr Price was a Member of it; and I took so much content in his company, that I brought such as I loved most entirely, acquainted with him.

I, through God's goodnesse, had long before been established in that part of doctrine (called then, Antinomian) of free justification by

Christ alone; and so my heart was at much more ease and freedom, then others, who were entangled with those yokes of bondage, unto which Sermons and Doctrines mixt of Law and Gospel, do subject distressed consciences: upon which point, I was frequent in discourse with him, and he would frequently come home to my house, and took much delight in that company he found there; insomuch, as we fell to practice arms in my Garden: and whither he brought his Friends; and Lords daies, and Fast daies he spent usually with us: As for Fasts then, some circumstances of the times and proceedings considered, neither he nor we were satisfied therein, nor hardly any of those that we called Sectaries (or Antinomians, which was then the beam in the eie) about the Town.

It fell out upon a Fast day in the morning, my Friend and I thought fit to give him a visit, to manifest our joy in his society: so comming to his house, he seemed to be exceeding glad, and hastned abroad with us, and we went at last to Basing-shaw Church, it being where my Lord Mayor was to be, as expecting to hear some excellent man there; being there some time, we found the matter so lamentable, as we were all three weary of it: For the truth is, whosoever is clearly possest with this one Doctrine of Free Justification, hath such a touch-stone as presently discovers the least contradiction either in Praiers, or Sermons, and what is gold, silver, drosse, [8] hay or stubble: so we all at once together went away, but so, as we could give no offence to the congregation, being not in the body of the Church; (so that the relaters, in saying we had been from Church to Church [are mistaken]) Mr. Cranfords being all we were at before, though he know it hath not been more usuall with any then with themselves, passing to and fro from place to place on the Lords, and Fasts dayes, 4 and 6 of a company spying, watching, and censuring of doctrines (as he* that wrote the Book called the *Pullpit incendiary*, me thinks should be asham'd to seeme ignorant of).

Being come out of the Church, we past the way home-wards; much lamenting the condition of a people under such teachers, being taught scarce any thing to make them either knowing Christians, or good and usefull men; imputing much of the misery of the times to the ignorance or preversnesse of preachers; the greatest part of their time being spent to uphold their interest against Antinomians, Anabaptists, and others, that fell off from their congregations, seldom upon any necessary or usefull doctrine, or if they did, before they had

---

* John Price. (Editors' note)

done with it, they contradicted themselves much or little, sufficient to spoil all they had done.

So in short time, we came to my house, where we went on discoursing, from one thing to another, and amongst other things, of the wisdom of the heathen, how wise and able they were in those things, unto which their knowledge did extend; and what pains they took to make men wise, vertuous, and good common-wealths men; how pertinent they were in the things they undertook, to the shame of such Christians, as took upon them to be teachers of others, when they were to seeke in the main principle of their science, with which kinde of discourse, he was very much affected, though it did not appear he had been accustomed to the reading of humane authors; which for twenty yeers before I had been, but I used them alwayes in their due place; being very studious all that time in the Scriptures, and other divine authors, as some of Mr. Perkins works, Mr. Downhams divinity, I had, as it were, without book, also Doctor Halls meditations, and vowes, and his heaven upon earth, and those peeces annexed to Mr. Hookers *Ecclesiastical pollicy;* hearing, and reading continually; using Seneca, Plutarchs *Lives,* and Charon *of humane wisdom,* as things of recreation, wherein I was both pleased, and profited; and truly, I do not see I have cause to repent me of taking liberty in this kinde, having never in my life, I blesse God; made an ill use thereof, amongst which Lucian for his good ends, in discovering the vanity of things in worldly esteem, I like very well, whereof I can read only such as are translated into English; such a wise Jesuite I am, that with all my skill, I cannot construe three lines of any Latin author, nor do understand any, except such common proverbs, as are more familiar in Latine then in English, which sometimes I use not to dignifie my selfe, but because of the pertinency of them in some occasions.

For as this author would infer of me, I do not think any man much the wiser for having many languages, or for having more then one, & though I wish I had the Latin, yet I think it not worth that paines, and time, as is commonly spent in learning; and do beleeve, I had been furnisht with it, (for my parents, I thank them, were not wanting) but for the tediousnesse, and impertinency of my teachers; which since I understand, I often blame in them, which is all I have to say against Latin, or any kind of learning; except that part of it, which puffeth up, and makes men scornfull pedants, despisers of unlearned and illitterate men, a humour, if I mistake not puffeth my present Antagonist:

I see wise, and inconsiderate men too, skillfull in languages, and in arts, and science; I have not much to do with them; my care is rightly to understand my self in my native language, being troubled with no other; and of all I chiefly thank these that [9] employ there charity in translation of well meaning authors, which I hope I may read without asking leave of these that through scrupulosity dare not.

Moses was skilfull in all the learning of the Egyptians, which the Scriptures testifie without reproof, and S. Paul certainly read the poets, and was not abasht to recite one of them; and I am certain most of the university men in England, and most of the liberaries are not without all Lucians works, some whereof, as I am informed, are much more offencive to Christianity then these in English.

And why then I might not without blemish read one of his dialogues to this, Mr. Richard Price, I cannot yet perceive? as I take it we read that which is called his tyrant; a discourse, though possibly not in all things justifiable, yet such as he might have made a better use of, being so pointed against ambition, pride and coveteousnesse as he might have been the better for it whilst he lived: as for me I count him a very weak man, that takes harm by reading it or any such like things.

The truth is, for many yeers my books, and teachers were masters in a great measure of me; I durst scarce undertake to judge of the things I either Read, or heard: but having digested that *unum necessarium*, that pearle in the field, free justification by Christ alone; I became master of what I heard, or read, in divinity: and this doctrine working by love; I became also, much more master of my affections, and of what ever I read in humane authors, which I speak not as Glorying in my self, but in the author of that blessed principle; which I did long before, and then (and do still) prize at so inestimable a value; that I was far from any such thought of impious blasphemy, as to say, here is more wit in this (meaning Lucian) then in all the bible: all our discourse was before my wife and children, and my friend,* and a maid servant that had dwelt with us then three years, and since hath made them up nine yeers; I dare appeale to them all if ever they heard me value any, or all the Books, or Sermons either, in the world Comparable to the Bible; so as, but that I have since had some experience of the easinesse of Mr. Price his conscience? I should even expire with wonder, at his impudence, and at his uncharitablenesse, that he and his friends, people of a Church, that call themselves Saints, and a

* Apparently Humphrey Brooke, who recounted the incident in *Charity of Church-men*, p. 4. (Editors' note)

people of God, should harbour this wretched slander six yeares amongst them, and be bringing it forth this time, and that time, but finde no time their season but when I was violently taken out of my bed, and house, and made a prisoner: if this be their way of visiting of prisoners, would not it make men think they had forgot the Scriptures; nay, might they not go to the heathens to learn some Charity.

Where is Charity? Where is love? that true Christian love, which covereth a multitude of sins; but that there should be malice, inventive, inveterate malice, in place thereof: certainly were your Church truly a Church of Christs making, it would deserve a heavy Censure.

Our Saviour sends the sluggard to the Ant: the over carefull and distrustfull to the lilies of the field, and may not I send these to heathens, to get some charity?

Mr. Price, I blush not to say, I have been long accustomed to read Montaigns *Essaies*, an author perhaps youle startle at; nor do I approve of him in all things, but ile read you a peece or two, that will be worth your study; though he be an author scarce so modest as our Lucian.

Speaking in his 12 chap. page. 244. Of Christian religion, he saith thus,

"If this ray of Divinity, did in any sort touch us, it would every where appear: not only our words, but our actions, would bear some shew, & lustre of it. Whatsoever should proceed from us, might be seen inlightned, with this noble and matchlesse brightnesse. We should blush for shame that in humane sects, there was never any [10] so factious, what difficulty or strangenesse soever his Doctrine maintained; but would in some sort conform his behaviour, and square his life unto it; whereas so divine and heavenly an institution, never marks Christians but by the tongue: And will you see whether it be so? Compare but our manners unto a Turk, or a Pagan, and we must needs yeild unto them: whereas in respect of our religious superiority, we ought by much, yea, by an incomparable distance outshine them in excellency, And well might a man say, Are they so just, so charitable, and so good, then must they be Christians. All other outward shows, and exteriour appearances, are common to all Religions, as hope, affiance, events, ceremonies, penitence, and Martyrdom; the peculiar badg of our truth should be virtue, as it is the heavenlyest, and most difficult mark, and worthyest production of verity it self: And in his twentieth Chapter, pag: 102. he saies, speaking of the Cannibals, the very words that import lying, falshood, treason, dissimulation, covetousnesse, envy, detraction, and pardon, were never heard of amongst them."

These, and the like flowers, I think it lawfull to gather out of his Wildernesse, and to give them room in my Garden; yet this worthy Montaign was but a Romish Catholique: yet to observe with what contentment and full swoln joy he recites these cogitations, is wonderfull to consideration: And what now shall I say? Go to this honest Papist, or to these innocent Cannibals, ye Independent Churches, to learn civility, humanity, simplicity of heart; yea, charity and Christianity.

This hath been an old long-rooted slander, and hath therefore cost me thus much labour to stock it up: As for my breach of the Fast, one would think Mr John Goodwin's playing at Bowls upon a Fast day in the afternoon, a while after this, and which he did not seem to judge a fault, but as it was an offence against the reputation of his faculty, might have stopt these mens mouths in that particular: Nor would I ever have revived the memory of it, but their triumphing thus in slanders against me, deserves their abasement and humiliation.

Of whom this Mr Richard Price receives instruction, I know not; but this is he that with knowledge, if not direction of their Church, undertook to betray the King into the hands of the Governour of Alisbury, under pretence of giving up Alisbury unto him, in lieu of Liberty of Conscience (that was the gold upon the bait) and did go, and spake with him; and how many untruths in such a case he was forc'd to utter with confidence, may easily be judg'd; and where he had a rule for this being a Christian, for my part I am to seek; the Apostle thought himself injured, that it was reported, he maintained that evil might be done, that good might come thereof.

And since treachery seems so slight a matter, with these Churchmen, I shall make bold to send them again to this Lord Montaign, in his third Book, and first Chapter, pag: 443. he saith thus;

"To whom should not treachery be detestable, when Tiberius refused it on such great interest? One sent him word out of Germany, that if he thought good, Arminius should be made away by poyson; he was the mightyest enemy the Romans had, who had so vilely used them under Varus, and who only impeached the increase of his Dominion in that Country; his answer was, That the People of Rome were accustomed to be revenged on their enemies by open courses, with weapons in hand, not by subtilties, nor in hugger-mugger: thus left he the profitable for the honest, in 447. As for my part (saith

Montaign) both my word and my faith are as the rest, pieces of this common body, their best effect is the publique service; that's ever pre-supposed with me: But as if one should com- [11] mand me to take charge of the Rols or Records of the Pallace, I would answer, I have no skill in them, or to be a Leader of Pioners; I would say, I am called to a worthier office: Even so, who would go about to employ me not to murther, or poyson? but to lye, betray, or forswear my self, I would tell him, if I have rob'd or stoln any thing from any man, send me rather to the Galleys; for a Gentleman may lawfully speak, as did the Lacedemonians, defeated by Antipater, upon the points of their Agreement: You may impose as heavy burthens, and harmfull taxes upon us, as you please; but you lose your time to command us any shamefull or dishonest thing. Every man should give himself the oath which the Egyptian Kings solemnly and usually presented to their Judges, Not to swerve from their Consciences, what command soever they should receive from themselves to the contrary. In 448. he saith thus, What is lesse possible for him to do, then what he cannot effect without charge unto his faith."

It will, I know, be wondred at, that I thus enlarge my self; but these things are so rich and excellent, that I cannot but insist upon them, and am in some hope to convert my Adversaries, which hath ever been my aim, equall to my own vindication; for I recite these pas-sages, because I am in love with them, wishing them also of the same mind, for I wish them no worse then I wish to my self: or if I fail of this, yet I am desirous and hopefull to better other men by the things I write.

These are the plainnesses wherein I have ever delighted; so far am I from that politique, crafty, subtil and hidden reservedness, which this Author would perswade the world I abound withall; exercising his wit so exquisitly in decyphering me out to be a man of so large capac-ity and ability, as for my part I do not believe there is any man in the world so; much lesse my self, who setting aside a little consideration and experience, united to an upright conscience, have nothing to please my self withall: Nor do I much desire those extraordinary parts, which are seldom employed to their right end, being com-monly tempted, to serve some Politicians ends; as may be seen rather in the abilities and application of them, in this Author; for he hath drawn such a picture of mans ability, as shews only his own parts in so doing; and applyes them to me, that have no part of them, of pur-pose to make me vile, lifts me up to the top of the pinacle, that he may cast me down to my greater ruine.

Truly, I never thought a good cause ever needed such workings as he exalts himself (not me) withall: and I dare appeal to those many my Friends, that I daily and hourly converst withall for some years now in publique businesses, whether ever they saw more plainnesse and open-heartednesse in man: Indeed, if I suspected any man inclinable to ensnare me, as these mens practises, made me of late somewhat wary; I had reason to be carefull. And whereas he taxes me of heightening mens discontents, I believe till now, they are pleased (not without particular morsels) none were more apt thereto then themselves: but the world is well amended with them, and every other mans mouth must be stopt on pain of Treason.

I am not more pleased with the former sayings of Montaign, then with what he saies in pag: 449.

"I have therfore placed Epaminondas in the first rank of virtuous men, and now recant it not: unto what a high pitch raised he the consideration of his particular duty? Who never slew man he had vanquished; Who for the invaluable good of restoring his Country her liberty, made it a matter of Conscience to take away any mans life, without a due and formall course of Law; and who judged him a bad man (how good a Citizen soever) that amongst his enemies, and in the fury of a [12] battail, spared not his friend, or his honor, lo here a mind of a rich composition."

And truly, I boast not, but these things have long since made so deep impression in me, that I have been extreamly mistaken by those, that gave out, there was a plot amongst us to murther the King, when he was at Hampton Court, and as much these that now start that other as base, of an intention to murther the Lieutenant Generall, they are wayes neither justifiable nor profitable; for where should such courses end, or what could more disparage that side that began it; I wish you would be but as carefull to preserve intirely, the due and formall course of Law to every man, without exception, friend, or foe, as we have been: and though at present you may please your selves with the sufferings of your adversaries (as you fancy them) yet you do therein but tread down your own hedges, and pluck up that Bank that lets in the sea of will, and power, overwhelming your own liberties.

But before I part with this Mr. Richard Price; I have another thing to lay to his charge, and that is; That he should say, I had a hand in that plot where Read, and Sir Basil brook were in question: in so much as my friends came running to me with tears in their eyes, and all from his unadvised speeches: was this like a friend, with whom you had eaten, and drunk, and discoursed familiarly, and from whom you had taken some small tokens of sincere affection; as the books entituled *Luthers Christian liberty, The benefits of Christs death, Freemans meditations,* and as I remember; *Christs Councell to Loadicea;* and since I was so far from retorting this injury upon you, as that after it, I chose rather to convince you by love, and as a testimony of my good respects to you, sent you the *Hystory of Thucidides,* wherewith I was much delighted, truly I wonder nothing could keep you from bearing me rancour thus long, and to watch this time of any, to slay me with your unjust report.

And truly, upon occasion lately, making my moan of this kinde of usage to one of their own people, that had received extream prejudice against me upon these, & the like false reports, which upon some discourse with a friend of mine first, and afterwards with my friend, and I together, he did professe much greef, for my hard usage; and told me that he did impute most of all this to pride, and emulation, from this Mr. Price, and in that my pen in Petitions (which otherwise was his work and trade) was many times accepted, if it be so it is a sad story indeed, his own conscience only knows whether it be so or not.

Yet I cannot but fear most of all the injuryes of this nature I have received, have proceeded from this ground, for otherwise I am certain, I have given no occasion to that Congregation, whereas most of my reproaches come from them. And since I am thus fallen upon Mr. Richard Price, there is yet another of that name of this congregation, and is this Mr. Richard Price his unckle, and Mr. Hilleslyes son in law: from this Mr. Price I heard the first aspersion, that ever I heard of my self, and it was thus,

Standing in Cornhill, at a Book-sellers shop, a man comes and looks me very earnestly in my face, I took little regard to it and went away, I was no sooner gone, but sayes he to the Book seller, You are acquainted with all the sparcks in the town; sparcks saies he, the man seemes to be a rational man: but, replied the party, I am told he is a notorious drunkard, and a whore master, and that he painted his face, but I see thats false: whereupon the Book-seller having some knowledge of me, became troubled on my behalf; and fell to be very serious with him, to know his author, and he honestly tells him, naming this Mr. Price a mercer; and the Book-seller soon after tells me the whole story, and the authors name, saying, he had been [13] abused himself with base reports; and a man might be undone by them, and never know it, till t'was too late, and therefore had resolved to hear no evil of any man, but if he could he would learn the author, and tell the party concernd of it: this Book seller is Mr. Peter Cole at the sign of the Printing presse, and I esteem my self obliedged to him, ever since for his plain dealing:

So away went I to this Mr. Price, for I was somewhat troubled having never heard, evil of my self till then: and I found him at Mr. Hilslies, and in a friendly manner made him acquainted, with my businesse; he did not deny but he had spoken as much; and that walking in Westminster hall, he was called from me, and bid beware of me for I was supposed to be a Papist, and a dangerous man: but he had not spoken any evil of me, as beleeving any of it to be true? so I told him he and I had come acquainted upon a very honest businesse, about the remonstrance presented to the Common-councel, and therefore why he should suffer such words to passe from him concerning me, I did wonder at it; I told him how with very little enquiry he might soon have been satisfied, that I was no such man; askt him if he knew any at Garlick-hill, where I had lived fifteen yeers together, in good and honest repute; and where he ought to have informed himself; and not so unadvisedly to disparage me: he seemed to be sorry for it: so I only desired him to let me know his author, he told me I must excuse him; he might not do it: nor could I ever get him to tell me: so being familiar with my then friend Mr. Brandiff, I askt, whether they had not some rule, or method in their Church, to give a man some satisfaction, that had received palpable injury by a member; come said he I know where abouts you mean; trouble not your self, nobody beleeves it: and this was all I could get in this case: wherein I yet stand injured, and since they are so desirous, more then truth should be beleeved of me: I think it fit this which is certainly true, should be known of their dealing with me.

Nor can any ingenious people now blame me, for being thus open, and particuler, since this sort of independents have made thus bold with my good name so long a time, and since it is evident [from] that manifestation dated the 14 of April 1649. Published by my self, and my other three fellow sufferers, that I was willing to have vindicated my self, from those common reproaches, they had asperst me withall without naming or reflecting upon any person, or any sort of men whatsoever, so carefull have I ever been, as much as in me is to have peace with all men; bearing, and forbearing to my own losse, rather then I would return evil for evil.

But their malice breaking thus fouly out upon me, in this vile book; I should be unjust to my self, if I should not do my best endeavour to manifest so detestable falsenesse, uttered to so bad an end, in so unseemly a time (the time of my affliction) which I shall do with as much truth, as I can remember, professing withall from my very heart, and conscience, that I take no more pleasure in doing of it, then I should do in gathering up, and throwing away Snakes, and Vermin scattered in my Garden; and do wish with all my soul they had not necessitated me, nor my other fellow-prisoners, to have exceeded our joynt *Manifestation*; but that we might all have been good friends thereupon.

In which *Manifestation*, is to be seen all our very hearts, and wherein all our four heads, and hands were nigh equally employed, though this capritious author (Mr. John Price, its said) be pleased to suppose me to be all in all therein; yet I must, and truly professe the contrary: and must be bold to tell them, where my friend Lieutenent Collonel John Lillburn, appeares otherwise in any of his wri- [14] tings; I do not impute it to passion, as his adversaries politiquely are accustomed; to take weak people off from the consideration of what he says: but unto his zeal against that injustice, cruelty, hypocrisie, arrogancy, and flattery, which he hath found amongst a sort of men, from whom of any men in the world, he expected the contrary virtues; being otherwise to my knowledge, and upon experience, a very lamb in conversation; and whom goodnesse, and love, and piety, justice, and compassion, shall as soon melt, and that into tears (I hope he will pardon my blabbing) as any man in the world: but he hates all kinde of basenesse, with a perfect hatred: especially that of ingratitude, which he hath found, I have heard him say, so exceeding all measure, in some of the subscribers of this pamphlet, that it loathes him to think of it.

And as for my friend, Mr. Prince, whom this self-conceited author, would make so weak in judgment, as to have no abillity towards such a work; it is his unhappinesse to be so exceedingly mistaken; yet I must tell him, he hath given him so true a character, for honesty, and sincerity of heart, towards the publick, which in my esteem, doth more commend him, then if he had attributed to him, all those parts & abilities, he falsly, and for an ill end, doth unto me: lifting me up to heaven, that he might cast me down to hell: making me an Angel, that he might make me a Devil: which parts are more abounding in himself, as is to be seen in this his unhappy Book, and for which he will one day sigh and groan, except he make a better use of them.

But Mr. John Price, Mr. Prince hath not a congregation to cry up his parts; amongst whom there is such a humor of flattery, as is not to be found the like again amongst any sort of men; Oh such a Sermon, such a discourse, such arguments, as never was heard of; when oftentimes 'tis meer lamp work, and ink horn termes; such as the three first yeers in the University; or the first yeer of a sound consideration, with a sincere conscience, would be ashamed of.

But were Mr. Prince of one of your congregation, & had but run with the stream, and turned with the times, as most of you have done; could he but have changed his principles with his condition; would he (as he was tempted by some of you) have belyed his friends, & betrayed his cause, Oh what a man of parts Mr. Prince had been; what could Mr. Prince have wanted, that those men had to give: but to their shame, let them know, Mr. Prince values the integrity of his conscience above his life, or any thing in this world; and for which he deserveth the love of all sound hearted men.

But Mr. John Price, you that make it so strange a thing for any man, to own in the substance, what another hath penn'd; there is a book with Mr. John Prices name at it, of no long date; and the subject of it is about the King-ship of the People: to me it seems not to be the stile of Mr. John Price: I am against examining you, upon questions against your self; but there are (Knaves and Fools in Folio, a book so called) that seems to claim kindred of Mr. John Price in that peice; and if you be but a God-father; (and it be now against your judgement to be such) yet since the childe beares your name, and tis a pretty handsome one, be not ashamed still to own it; but if you be, the childe shall not want, I'le undertake to finde the right Father: so much for Mr. Prince.

And for the complexion of my Friend Mr Overtons pen, truly it commonly carries so much truth and reason in it, though sometimes in a Comick, and otherwhiles in a Satyrick stile, that I do not wonder you shun its acquaintance; and you did wisely by this touch and glance, think to passe him by without provoking of him: [15] But look to your selves, and say, I gave you lawfull warning; for he, I assure ye, knows when, and when not, to answer such as you according to your folly: And truly, but that it is against the nature of impudence to blush, the complexion of the pen engaged in this your unseemly discourse, might well turn Cowler, in correction of his: but he is old enough, let him answer for himself.

But why come their lines from them, as through a Prison-gate, Mr Price? Are Prisons, in your Divinity, such ominous things? The Primitive Christians, and the Martyrs in Queen Maries daies, did not esteem them so. But it seems your Congregation is of a near relation to those that hold prosperity a mark of the true Church; and it will be good for those amongst you, that are yet sincere in their Consciences, in time to consider it, and to enquire amongst all those Churches the Apostles wrote to, where they find a Warrant for such slanderous and backbiting practises as you are accustomed unto, licking up the very foam and dregs of Mr Edwards his *Gangrena;* yea, your own vomit and poyson which then you cast out upon him.

But, I confesse, you have notable waies to escape imprisonments; you can be for a Kingly Government, and publish to all the world, that Kings are, as the Consecrated Corn, not to be reapt by any humane sickle; and when occasion serves, you can change your copy, and say, you are not bound to declare why your judgment altered: But pray, Mr Goodwin, are you not bound to undeceive those whom by your errour you deceived, as soon as you saw your errour? Sometime your strength is not in an arm of flesh, nor in the power of the Sword, but you no sooner get, as you think, the least hold of it, but the power of the Sword is then the power of God, and then the Saints (meaning no body but your selves) must judge and rule the earth. Indeed Friends, you manifest to all the world, that your waies are the waies rather to good Offices and Benefices too (for else, why are ye now so high for tyths, that some years since were so much against them?) and led to honours, and preferments, and greetings in the market places, rather then to prisons.

Yet are ye furnisht with waies enough to send other men thither; you have one way, is called, *Ah Lord! we thank thee we are not as other men:* A way to make them first odious, by vindicating your selves in those things whereof no man suspected you, that others might be thought guilty; as you endeavoured by your Declaration, wherein you vindicated your selves from being against Magistracy, or liberty of Conscience, nor for Poligamy, or Community; and this in a time when you had freshly & falsely asperst us, to be opposite to you in all these, purposely to get your Guard into the Tower: and for your abatement, it will not be amisse to let you know how a weak woman answered your strength spent in this elaborate Declaration, at first and in the reading of it; but it was my Wife, and she having been (as you will have it) a Jesuit's wife this two and twenty years, may have more wit then ordinary.

Saies she, *They against Magistracy? Who can suspect them, that hunt and seek for Offices as they do?* (now I am sure the City and Custome-house will cry, *probatum est*); and where you argued your selves to be for liberty of Conscience, saies she, *Who have more need? I am sure none use so great a liberty, to raise such vile and false reports as they do* (for she hears all you say of me, and about that time, that some of your tribe should report I used her very hardly, and used to beat her; whereas we both know and believe in our consciences, never two in the world lived more comfortably together then we have done, nor have more delighted in one another. And where you declared, you did not hold it lawfull to have more Wives then one, saies she, *They* [16] *that keep their Wives at such a rate as they do, had not need to have more then one apeice, they will find one enough:* And where you declared, that you were not for to have all things common, saies she, *No, I warrant you they know well enough how to hold their own: are not some of them Usurers?* And you know it to be true: but if you deny it, we will find you for this also a *probatum;* and thus was your mighty Sisera struck through the temples by the hand of a silly Woman: The truth is, ye overween your selves exceedingly, because ye are a little skilfull in talking and writing: But why went ye not on boasting? ye were no hypocrites, no slanderers, no backbiters, no envious, malicious persons, no spies or intelligencers, no covetous or ambitious persons, no hard-hearted or cruell persons: truly you took the better way to vindicate your selves of those things only, that no men accused you of.

Another way ye have to get men into prison, by suggesting fears and jealousies of them into the minds of such as are in power and authority; playing the pick-thanks by such unworthy and uncharitable courses; buzzing continually in their ears, that we drive on dangerous designs; that we are Atheists, Jesuits, and the like, which hath been your common practice: insomuch, as being with Collonel Martin, and another Gentleman, about a month before I was made Prisoner, at Lieutenant Generall Cromwels; and amongst other discourse, wondering why he should suffer me continually at his table to be reproacht, as if I were a Jesuit, and a man of dangerous principles; whereas none in the world could have more testimony of any man to the contrary, then he had of me; and why he did not vindicate me, when he heard me so abused: he told me, that he could not believe those scandals, that he had profest often and again he could not, but they were brought continually to them by Citizens, that were esteemed honest godly men: And truly I do believe in my Conscience, we never had been thus dealt withall as we are, but by your reports; and that we are prisoners more by your occasion then any other.

And what a way did Mr Kiffin, & his Associates, find out as soon as we were in, to rivet us in, with a Petition somewhat like your forementioned Declaration? the scope thereof being truly Pharisaicall: Another, *Lord, we thank thee, we are not as other men, &c. Nor as these Publicans. No Anabaptists of Munster* (defiling their own nest, as supposing that lying story of that injured people true) *and praying the Parliament to be carefull to suppresse all prophanenesse and licenciousnesse: as if we had been such a people:* But so justly did this mischief (intended on us) turn on their own heads, that most of their own people abhorred the practice, as Un-Christian; and Mr Thomas Lamb of the Spittle, offered to prove the promoters of it guilty of injustice, arrogance, flattery and cruelty, and to give them a meeting to that purpose; but sure they were asham'd, and durst not, for none of them would undertake him.

Besides these waies of holding Prisoners fast, my back-friend, Mr Arnald, hath a way of going from house to house, to discover matter (there being none at all in these very mens opinions of me) For they all conclude, *England's New Chains,* to be none of my indicting: I wonder why then they did not petition, or move for my enlargement. No, besides that I am not of their Church; 'twas good holding a man so hardly to be catcht, that needed horse and foot to catch and fetch him out of his bed: And therfore this Mr Arnald also sends Spies to ensnare and entrap us in our discourse: and for encouragement to those he sends, that they may not scruple, but think they do God good service therein; he professes continually, I am a Jesuit: And now, I believe, finding his errour (for it's very easily found) he dreads [17] my releasment, as believing I may have remedy at Law for so destructive a slander: and therfore hath thought even to overwhelm me with this floud of aspersions, that I should not possibly escape drowning. But the man's mistaken, and so are his Abettors and Associates; 'tis but a Vision, a false fantastick apparition; they are all Nothings, meer falsnesses, Serpents of Magicians making, the meer works of a malicious imagination, that by crosse working, forcing and wresting of words and sentences, and by fames and opinions, hath made a kind of crawling thing, that might possibly serve to fright Children, or to please a Church that would go a wool-gathering for a miracle, to confirm its reallity: But truth, which is Moses his Serpent, you shall see will eat them up, and devour them all: Many of them, if you well consider what you have here and elswhere read, being consumed already.

That which remains in generall, is, that I aim at the destroying of Religion, and at the subversion of all Government: But why should I do either? Where's the advantage? I have alwaies profess'd the contrary, and ever practised the contrary; as those that reade my *Whisper to Mr Edwards,* and my *still and soft voyce,* fore-mentioned, will easily believe. And I begge and intreat both young and old to reade them, before they give sentence in their own hearts of me, that I should be so irreligious, as to utter such profane language concerning the Book of Psalms, or Proverbs, or that horrid expression of the Book of Canticles, as that it was nothing else but one of Salomons *Epiphonemaes:* a word that I never spake, nor yet know well how to pronounce, nor ever did apply the meaning of it to so vile an end (speak the rest, whoso will for me) and if the Author had had any modesty or Religion in him, however it had come into his thought, he would have silenc'd it, rather then such blasphemy should be seen in print; I abhor the words should be in any of my papers; having never entred my thought, or past my lips.

As true, likewise, are all the other unworthy passages in the 9 and 10 pages of that shamelesse book; they have been all malicious snatchings and gatherings from some officious tongues, at third, fourth or tenth hand; there being nothing but mistakes and mis-applications in all of them, contrary to my judgment, or any thing ever intended by me, in my discourse of any of those subjects: And to shew some palpable token, that they are meer malicious smatterings, I appeal to all that know me, whether ever I were heard to commend Plutarch's *Morals* to any mans reading; it being a Book, that although I have had above these twenty years, yet I am certain, I never read forty hours therein; though I somewhat blame my self for my neglect, it being so generally commended by wise and judicious men: yet I could never perswade my self to take the pains in reading of it, it being somewhat too tedious for my expectation. And as for Cicero's *Orations,* I never had it, have only seen it; and (though very unadvisedly, as I was lately told by one whose judgment I love) am somewhat prejudic'd against his writings, as esteeming him a verball and vain-glorious Writer.

I have, indeed, bemoaned the breeding of the Youth of this Nation, as being bred so, as to be artificiall and crafty, rather then truly wise and honest, to be Sophisters, and Pedantick Disputers, and Wranglers about words, then of solid judgment: but as for feats of activity, it's a light expression, to be applyed rather to tumblers, and the like, then to be a part of Childrens breeding; and for Geometry, there may be much in it, and of use: but I have not so much skill in it, as that I could make it matter for my commendation. So that these Intelligencers being engaged in evil [18] designs, and knowing themselves guilty, are confused in their thoughts, their consciences ever flying in their faces; and so they hear otherwise then is uttered, and report different from what they hear, and so prove by a just providence destructive to those that employ them; and it were pity an ill end should be better served.

In the 11 page, because he would not want matter to disparage, he puls in I know not who, that, forsooth, must be of my acquaintance, and speaking absurd profane language, concerning things heavenly, and of God; that I professe I do not think any man in the world would utter, nor think them fit to be repeated, much lesse printed, to save a life: whereas this unhappy Author puts them in a particular character, lest they should passe un-observed; and that not to save, but to destroy me and mine: Who this should be, I cannot ghesse; but it seems, it is a man of parts, possibly, for to have made him an Intelligencer: if so you have given him your reward, slander him, and let him go; and 'tis well he scapes so, as the world goes.

For there are uses for Spies and Intelligencers, that few men dream of; and Mr John Price, and Mr Goodwin, and Mr Lavander, knows of the making of them, their instructions and oaths of employment and secrecy; an office and institution we never read of in all the New Testament: but what wonder if their practice be point-Blanck against the Scriptures, whose structure is not built upon (but borrowed, or rather forc'd upon) that golden foundation?

As for the next passage in the 11 page, that I should affirm the Scriptures to be, and not to be the Word of God; it is such a double way of expression, as I dislike in all men, and avoyd it in all my writings or discourse: but for this, or any thing relating to the Scriptures, I refer the honest-hearted Reader to my *still and soft voyce*.

And that I should perswade that Gentlewoman next mentioned, to ruine her self, is as false as ever was spoken, as her Husband, her Sisters, her Friend that was continually with her, her Servants and Children, I am confident are all ready to testifie, and some of them I am certain will witnesse, that I used my utmost skill to disswade her, and did manifest as much grief for her, as I never did more for any, except a Child I had, to whom she was Godmother, for she was my true Friend, and her Husband hath for these twelve years (as I have cause to believe) held me as dear to him as any Friend, and so hath continued to the time I came into prison; and her sister that hath been in the most extreme affliction for her, hath yet shewed so much respect to me (with the Gentlewoman that was alwaies with my distressed Friend) as to give me a visit in this my imprisonment, and so also hath two of her Sons: these are truths, and will be believed by all that truly knew both her and me; though Mr Goodwins whole

Church should swear the contrary; and from whom she deserved a better regard. I am sorry their hate to me should awake the remembrance of that sad disaster from sleep, where it ought to have rested; she being very religious after the way of Mr Simpson of Allhallowe's Thames-street, and no admirer of Mr John Goodwin: Insomuch as it was said to her, in her greatest extremity of pain in her head (the greatest, in my apprehension, and most continued, that ever was felt) you have a wise Religion, that cannot bear with a pain in your head: his profession that said it, required another remedy; but as he exceeded in his tongue, he was as short in his brain and hand: Not only she, but her Husband to this hour, being much distrest through such comforters: and it were well some skilfull man would administer [19] some matter to cure the man of his vain-glory, and flashing self conceitednesse, with which he abounds to the destruction of some native goodnesse, & acquired parts; which would otherwise commend him: I could not be more particular in this story, lest I should grieve my friends, who I know cannot but desire this were buried in oblivion.

As false also is that other passage, concerning King James, and King David: it having never been my manner, to use such opprobrious language towards any men; much lesse towards persons of such Eminency; but Generally reproove it.

I have from a serious consideration of Davids offences, and Gods passing them by, and not rejecting of him for them; observed a different way from God, in those of our times, that call themselves Saints, and would be esteemed his nearest servants; for if any man be overtaken in a fault; they are so far from restoring such a one by the spirit of meeknesse: or, reproving him privatly, or by love, as Gods way is; passing by multitudes of sins, and failings; that they make it their meat and drink, yea, they hunger, and thirst after evil reports; yea, send out into the high-wayes, and hedges, and as it were compell men to come in to witnesse, and article, against men too, that have hazarded their lives for their good: and with whom they have frequently, familiarly, and intimately conversed; never reproveing them in their lives to their faces: and keep things in boxes, three, four, six, yeers together, watching a season to divulge them to their ruin: as now in mine, & my friends cases.

They that are now advocates for David, if David lived in our dayes, and had not favoured Mr. Goodwins Church-way, and had been guilty of the matter with Bathsheba, and Uriah, where should David have found a place to have hid himself, who amongst them; (according to their present rule with us) would have pleaded for him? nay, had not Davids wiles (pardon the expression) been published in words at length, and not in figures: yet possibly (nay probably) Davids being King had altered the case with these men; especially, if he were supream in power: for they are ever carefull to row with, or not long against the tide: but what (think you) would they not give that they had such matter against me, that make so much to gather up false reports against me; what society should I keep; who would own me, no marvail? now I see, that David being put to his choice; chose rather to fall into the hands of God, then into the hands of men: for with him there is mercy, his mercies are over all his works; he delighteth in shewing mercy, he considers that we are but dust: and putteth away our sins out of his remembrance; as far as the East is from the West: whereas the mercies of men are cruelties: although I cannot so experimentally say it, of any other sort of men, as of these; for I have found the contrary from so many other sorts of people, upon divers of my particular occasions, that I have wondered to consider the difference.

For the next slander: that I should speak so slightly, of the sin against the holy Ghost; this I heard they have asperst me withall above these three yeers: and I have considered it seriously, and can professe, with a sincere conscience, that I do not know that I ever uttered a syllable towards it: sure I am it never entred into my heart: nor could I, till now I see it in their book, learn, to what woman they charged me to have spoken it: but yet, because I ghessed, they might mean the gentle-woman forementioned, she being well known to them: I have told her of the aspertion; and desired seriously if she could call to minde, whither ever any such unadvised speech had past from me to her; as I might meete her, and in a friendly manner chide her for not visiting my wife: and she hath very often solemnly protested, she [20] could not for her life remember, that I did ever speake any thing towards it. and truly, if I had known any such thing by my self, though it had been never so unserious, I should have taken the shame of it to my self; and have manifested my sorrow for it, as not in the least justifying a carelesnes in things of so high a nature: and do fear, they come neer to scoffing, that dare thus liberally publish in print, expressions so unsutable to so divine a subject, for they may remain upon a readers mind, to prejudice, longer then he would have them.

And concerning the next slander; I might blame her for her sadnesse, and fear, which sometimes she would expresse, as being con-

trary to the principle, of that love of God, she would constantly professe, to have assurance of: urging frequently that place, which saith,
we have not received the spirit of bondage to fear any more; but the
spirit of adoption whereby we cry, *Abba, Father*, and have boldnesse to
the throne of Grace, and the like; but that I ever discouraged her in
the hearing of Mr. Simpson; or in the wayes of religion, I utterly deny.

And being thus, as thus in truth it is, and no otherwise in all the
perticulars forementioned, let all impartiall, and judicious people
judge, whether it had not been more for the honour of God, the Scriptures and Religion; that this authour; his assotiats subscribers, his
abetters, and confederates; to have received in good part our clear
manifestation; wherein we justly vindicated our selves in generall,
from those aspersions that causlesly were cast upon us; without naming any person, or persons, as authors thereof; or reflecting, with the
least rancour upon any condition of men; as being willing, if possible,
to have buried for ever, all former unkindnesses, and evill offices
done to any of us in this kinde: and as far as in us was to have renewed our former friendship with those, in whom we had formerly
delighted, or at least to have expelled that enmity, which we knew
was exceedingly prejudiciall to the Common-wealth: I say, had it not
been much more Christian-like; then to have set their brains, and
credits thus upon the tenters (stretching them past the staple that
they will never in again) and to put upon record, so many unseemly
expressions, as if they gladly took occasion through my sides, &
friends, to give Religion, the scriptures, yea, God himself were it possible a deadly wound: for such I fear will be the effect; whither throw
their malice, or indiscretion, or both, I leave to judgment: and for
what cause, at best; but only to render me and my friends odious, to
discredit us in the things we undertook for the publick.

And then to cry out of violence in some mens writings, and yet to
abound, as here they do, with such new invented invectives, and
provoking language, as is hardly to be parallel'd: *Cheef secretaries of the
Prince of slander:* this *English man-hunter, this wretch:* this *wretched man
Walwyn:* this *wrothy Champion: the venison, which his soul doth so sorely
long for: as the serpent, that deceived our first Parents: this factor for the
Region of Darknesse, these Jesuiticall-whifflers: this artificiall impostor, in his
Satan-like work:* Good God, where is the cause, what hath moved them
to this high flown mallice, these bumbaste poetick raptures, fit rather
for stagers, then Preachers, for swaggerers, then Saints, (oh, but it
must not be so taken; it must be esteemed their zeal, their Jehu-like

affection to God, and his truth; yea, come see our zeal (say they in effect) which we have for God): why, be it so, ô Jehu, yet what's the cause?

The cause; why, heers *Walwyn* with his *Wiles* will overturn, destroy, and overthrow all Religion; and the Scriptures themselves? sure its not possible? no, have you ever heard such things uttered by man, as is recited in *Walwyns Wiles?* no, but he denies them to be true; gives reasons here; and refers to his *Whisper:* and [21] other writings: and particularly to his *still, and soft voice:* and those are extant, and to be seen; and surely if he intend to destroy Religion, to publish such things as these is not the way; besides, uttered by one, that you your selves say is wary, and sober, and discreet. But I pray, friends what a religion is yours, that fears the breath of one man should overthrow it? what? is it built upon the sand? if so, you may doubt indeed; but if upon a rock? let the winds blow, and the waves too beat; what need you fear? sure your faith is built but upon Reason; look to it; some say it is your tenent; if so, you had need indeed to bestir your selves, for you finde he is a rationall man, and thats a shew'd thing; against Diana of the Ephesians, though all Asia, & the world worship her: if your Churches have but an imaginary foundation then indeed you had need betake your selves to Demetrius his Arguments; and to tell all men these Walwynites every where, turn the world upside down; breathing strange, and unwelcome doctrines, such as your Churches and people cannot bear.

And so it seems, indeed they do, as these authors Complain in the latter part of their 13 pag. where they say, *I am ever harping upon the hard-heartednes and uncharitablenes of professors; and those that are religious men, how grinding they are in bargines: how pennurious: base, and backward in works of charity, and mercy, how undermining, and over-reaching they are in buying, in selling; how having and craving in the things of this life, how hardly any work of mercy, and charity comes from them; how they let their brethren starve, and dy, and perish, rather then help them; and how bountifull, free, and liberall the very heathens have been and how beneficiall even Papists, and many that do not so much as pretend to religion are to the poor; and herein (he confesseth) I speake too true:* yet immediately calls me devil for my labour (they pay their Pastors better, I beleeve, for worse doctrine).

But why devil? Why, say they, for speaking truth to wound, and destroy it; but say I, who art thou, ô man, that judgest another mans Conscience, forbear the chair a while, & it may be the chair of the scornful: for God and my own conscience knows, I never yet in my life spake, or uttered one of these truthes but to the end the Scriptures warrant.

But they go further, and say, by doing thus, I cunningly insinuate into the discreet, and beget a disparagement of *that that is called Religion amongst them.* page the 14.

This is very observable: for by this expression, all men shall easily understand the ground of their quarrell against me: if they can but finde out, *what it is that is called Religion amongst them:* do not these men call such a thing Religion; as the Pharises did; Ile deal so kindly with them, yet; as to leave the comparing the one with the other to themselves: only, *'twas much in words, and to be seen of men:* both which our Saviour reproves: and both by example, and precept invites to practice; possitively concluding, that not he that saith Lord, Lord, shall enter into the kingdom, but he that doth the will of my father which is in heaven: requireth, That our light so shine forth before men, that they, seeing our good works, may glorifie our heavenly father and at the last day, he will say unto those on his right hand, Come ye blessed of my Father, receive the kingdom prepared for you; for when I was an hungry, ye fed me, naked, ye clothed me; sick and in prison, and ye visited me; in as much as ye have done it unto these, ye had done it unto me: when to others, (that yet have to say, Lord we have prophesied, and done many great things in thy name) he will say; Away from me ye workers of iniquity, I know ye not, for when I was hungry, ye fed me not: naked, ye clothed me not; sick and in prison, and [22] ye visited me not; inasmuch as ye did it not unto these, ye did it not unto me.

And if now to invite to these, and to reprove the want thereof, be, to be a Devil, truly I'll bear it, and rejoyce that I am accounted worthy to suffer reproach for this cause of Christ: I am sure the Apostle Paul (that abounded with reall, not pretended gifts, or acquisitions rather) boasted not of them; but proclaims to all the world, that though he spake with the tongues of men and Angels, and have no Charity, that he was but as sounding brasse, or a tinkling Cymball; and Saint James, his pure and undefiled Religion, is, to visit the fatherlesse, and the widowes in their distresse, and to keep our selves unspotted of the world; and saith plainly, that he who hath this worlds goods, and seeth his brother lack, and shutteth up his bowels of compassion, how dwelleth the love of God in him? And truly, if I must be a Devil for insisting upon these most needfull doctrines, I had rather be these mens Devil then their Saint: And if the use and application of these, and the like, will overthrow that which they call Religion amongst them; certainly it is not pure and undefiled, and hardly of Gods making: I might enlarge my self upon this theme, but the little Book, called, *The vanity of the present Churches*, hath prevented me, unto which I refer the ingenious Reader, for satisfaction of what they call Religion among them.

And thus I think to all unbiassed men, I have acquitted my self from going about to destroy Religion; I mean, true, not false Religion, or superstition, too commonly dignified with the title of Religion.

And as for my designing, as the desire of my soul, the trouble, misery and ruine of this Commonwealth, it is so absurd a suggestion, that it seems not worth my answer; the utmost of my desire concerning this Commonwealth, being held forth and contained in the *Agreement of the People*, dated the first of May, 1649. And as a testimony of our acquiescence therein, is subscribed by Lieut: Col. John Lilburn, Mr Richard Overton, Mr Thomas Prince, and my self: so that all my designs are therein center'd; and if that imports the trouble, misery and ruine of this Commonwealth, I am extremely mistaken, and shall not refuse to acknowledge my errour when I see it: but till then, and whil'st I conceive it to tend to the good of all men, I cannot but wish it might be establish'd with contentment and security of all sorts of people: I know not the man in the world, whose finger I desire should ake longer then he pinches another; nor that any man should be reduced to any extremity, by any alteration it might bring with it: but that authority would provide rather a change of interests, and remove men from that which is not, to that which is consistent with the peace, freedom and prosperity of the Nation; it having been all along a sad thing to me, to see men of parts, and breeding, and eminency, upon reformation of interests, or their reducements, to be left to the wide world, without any care or regard of a livelyhood for themselves, their Wives and Children, in some measure answerable to their former condition: such extremities commonly begetting greater, and more mischievous to the Commonwealth; and it should, in my poor opinion, be the care of the supreme Authority; no desire being more forcible in man, then to live answerable to his breeding, or to what he hath been long accustomed; every one finding it an easie thing to learn how to abound, but to abate, most difficult: and, I fear, our late and present times suffer much under these two extremes. [23]

He upbraids me, that I find fault, that riches, and estates, and the things of this world, should prefer men to offices, and places of trust: but say that virtue, though in poor men, should be more regarded, as in Butchers, or Coblers: And truly I know some Butchers, though not many, as fit as some in your Congregations; and I think you do not exclude for that trade: And as for Coblers, there are trades more in credit, hardly so usefull, and Mr Price knows it well; and were he as busy in self examination, as he is in reproaching others, he would have little time to trouble himself about others motes: he who thought it no robbery to be equall with God, and yet despised not to be esteemed the Son of a Carpenter, and chose simple herdsmen for his Prophets, and poor fishermen for his Apostles, did certainly judge otherwise then these Churchmen judge. Besides, there was a time, when Samuel How, a Cobler by trade, and a contented man in that calling, was not ashamed to preach before your most learned Pastor, and printed his Sermon afterwards; and your Pastor hath chang'd his mind since, and is come somewhat nearer to his judgment; and had done then, as is said, and can be proved, could any have shewed him a livelyhood with credit, upon the exchange.

But by the way, I am not so strong as to talk usually after this rule, I know the generality of our times cannot bear it; I indulge exceedingly towards the weakness of men for peace sake: who ever heard me speak either in behalf of Butchers or Coblers, as to places of government? I professe, I know not where, nor when; though for their callings, I make no difference between them and my self; for the callings are honest, and mine can but be so.

And as for Riches, Saint James, whom I am exceeding in love with, had no great good opinion thereof: he demands positively, Do not rich men oppresse you, and leade you before the Magistrates? (the Magistrates, possibly, were no rich men) Nay, is there not such an expression again in Scripture, as, Go too, weep and howl, ye rich men, &c? But I shall be told anon, I have too much straw for this brick; truly, I wish I had none at all, and that you and your Associates had been more advised, then to have necessitated me thus to discover your weaknesse; but I comfort my self, that I shall turn it to your good. I hope you will say no more, that by these truths I shall destroy that which is called *Religion amongst you,* for this is a part of pure and undefiled Religion: And if you make one more change, and sell all that ever you have, all your uncertainties, vanities, and superfluities, for these reallities, it will prove the best bargain that ever you made; and, I believe, we should be Friends upon it; this difference being the only quarrell: And that Riches may no longer be a stumbling block in your way, reade, at your leisure, Montaign's 52 Chapter, of the Parcimony of our Fore-Fathers.

And where you charge me, that I find fault that some abound, whil'st others want bread; truly, I think it a sad thing, in so fruitfull a land, as, through Gods blessing, this is; and I do think it one main end of Government, to provide, that those who refuse not labour, should eat comfortably: and if you think otherwise, I think it your errour, and your unhappinesse: But for my turning the world upside down, I leave it to you, it's not a work I ever intended, as all my actions, and the Agreement of the People, do sufficiently evince, and doth indeed so fully answer all your remaining rambling scandals, that I shall pray the courteous Reader hereof to reade it, and apply it, and then shall not doubt my full and clear vindication: so far as that is, am I for plucking up of all the pales and hedges in the Nation; so far, for all things common. [24]

So far from wishing printing had never been known, that I have alwaies said, that printing (if any thing in this age) would preserve us from slavery; and you that know how much I have been against the stopping of the presse, methinks should blush to talk thus.

As for Mr Pym, and Mr Hampden, it's well known, I honoured them much, for what I saw was good in them, and never reproach'd them in my life; but was not satisfied, when they would make a war, that they would make it in the name of the King and Parliament; I could not understand it to be plain dealing, nor thousands more besides me.

As for any invectives against the Lieutenant Generall Cromwel, Commissary Generall Ireton, or Collonel Harrison, I shall refer this to be satisfied by one Mr David Brown, the Scotch Writing-Master, a man of integrity, and of a sincere Congregration, what I have done to the contrary: but I allow him not to be over-particular, in naming what particularly, that being inconvenient: And if Collonel Harrison would but remember my attendance on him at Collonel Fleetwoods, and but reflect upon a paper I then deliver'd him, methinks my integrity to my Country, and affection to all such as desire the liberty thereof, could not be question'd; and, I confesse, I have wondered, he of any man in power, hath not appeared more to my vindication: indeed, I have no fawning flattering waies to work upon men, nor have used any towards them, I have been reall and plain-hearted towards them; and though you may have courted them more plausibly into an opinion of your way in the affairs of the Commonwealth; yet is it conscience and time that proves all things, and I refer my self to both; and if you prove not to them (and the rest in power, that give ear to you) like Rhehoboam's young Counsellours, I shall be glad of it; I am sure you came in late to the work, and (to my apprehension) labour to build hay and stubble, if not worse, upon a golden foundation, laid by others for the Freedom of the Commonwealth.

But I must beware, for, as I hear, you much rejoyce in a new Act concerning Treason; so copious, that I may be in the verge of it, before I am aware; it makes me almost not sorry that I am kept close Prisoner, but that it's no good sign of Englands liberty which I have earnestly labour'd for: but truly I may rejoyce that I am kept from you, and you from me; for certainly, should we passe but one hours discourse together (in the mind you are in) and as the case and law now is, I should not escape an information.

And truly, that ye are so well pleas'd with this act proceeds, for that it serves your present turn, rather then any reason or consideration in you; for how soon the edge of it may be turned against your selves, you know not; and some who consider not how much ye have labour'd for it, wonder ye do not petition against it: for whil'st a Parliament sits, it is lawfull to petition against things, though establish'd by Law; and it's somewhat rare in the practice of Parliaments, for a law to take place, and be of force so soon as it is made, having commonly had a good distance of time, that men might digest, and consider and understand it, before the commencement or beginning of the power thereof; and that, at soonest, not before the end of the Parliament that made it: And there seems to be this reason for it, that the Parliament men that made it should be as soon, and as clearly subject thereunto, as any other persons whatsoever; otherwise they might make such, as might ensnare the people, and yet keep themselves out of danger. [25]

And certainly, if this caution be necessary in any case, it must be where mens lives are concerned, as in Treason and Felony; wherein our forefathers were ever very carefull; as Sir Edward Cooke doth sufficiently witnesse, some particulars whereof concerning Treason, are worth yours, and every mans knowledge.

"Briefly thus: he saies, The Parliament holden the 25th of Ed. 3. was called *benedictum Parliamentum*; because of its particular expressing what was Treason: and that except Magna Charta, no other Act of Parliament hath had more Honour given to it, as appeareth by the Statute of the 1 of Hen. 4. chap. 10 reciting, That whereas a Parliament, holden the 21 of Rich. 2. Divers paines of Treason were ordained by Statute, insomuch as there was no man did know how to behave himselfe; to do, speake, or say, for doubt of such paines: It is enacted, &c. That in no time to come, any Treason be judged otherwise, then it was ordained by the Statute of 25 Ed. 3. the like honour is given to it, by the Statute 1 Ed. 6. chap. 12. and by the Statute of the first of Mary, chap. 1. Sess. 1. —different times, but all agreeing in the magnifying, and extolling that blessed Act of 25 Ed. 3."

And speaking of the care of our Ancestors, in avoiding nice and extreame Laws concerning Treason: he saith, *And all this was done in severall Ages, that the faire Lillies and Roses of the Crowne (which now may be interpreted) the Government of England, might flourish, and not be stained with severe and sanguinary (bloudy) Statutes.*

He saith further, That the Statute for Treason, is to be taken strictly; and the *proofs to be direct and manifest; not upon conjecturall presumptions, or inferences, or straines of Wit: but upon good and sufficient proof, That none are to be proceeded against, but according to due course, and proceeding of Law, to be judged by men of our own condition; and not by absolute power, or other meanes, as in former times had been used; and affirmes it to be a received maxim, that bare words without an overt Act, could not make a Traytor.*

But if you can rejoyce that these strong holds, and safegards of our lives, shall now in the first year of Englands Liberty, with the Petition of Right, be accounted of no value; but that we must be so exposed to danger, that no man shall know how to behave himselfe, to doe, speake, or say, for fear of the paines of Treason: I believe your rejoycing is but matter of grief to us, and the rest of the plain-hearted people in England: it being not who doth it, but what is done, that most concernes all men: you use to talke of something still, in the bottome of what I, and my friends proposed; but when shall we see what lies at the bottome of your hearts, if such as those rejoycings are aflote already?

You think it strange, that we should object against Martiall Law, in times of Peace, for Souldiers or others; and yet if you read the Petition of Right, you cannot but confesse it to be expresly therein provided against; you deny us all Legall proceedings, and yet thinke the proceedings of the Swisse a horrible thing; a story kept in Lavander about seven years, and next to one that now is not, is due to him that kept it in sweetning so long, for so unsavoury a season, and whose profession is nearer cutting of throats, then mine is; and as I remember, was very merry at the thought of it.

I am of opinion, there is much, if not more need of another kind of Law; and I could wish some good people would consider of it, but I have no hope of your Congregation: It is a Law against Lying; you know what a sad condition the Scripture holds forth to him that lov-

eth, or maketh a lye: what thinke you of it? will our [26] trades bear it?
there needs no sanguinary punishment be annexed, but some easie
punishment: besides, if you hear one that is not of your own Congregation asperst, and runne presently and tell it to others, before
you are certaine of the truth your self, this need not passe for a lye, if
you can but remember your author; though he had it only from the
father of lies: being sure also, that you may confidently avouch, that
you had it from a very pretious Godly man; so are all your Church-
men: or if you do but thinke ye remember a thing right, and witnesse
it; this also had not need to be taken for a lie neither: and some such
other indulgences, as the time, and your occasions require; there are
some say, *pia mendacia*, those that are Learned amongst you, will expound the meaning; there may be a remission also for those, but certainly, yet a Law (though with allowance of a large latitude) were
absolutely necessary for these times, and it would honour you exceedingly to seeke for it; you may have also allowance, for all false
slanderous invectives, if once you have gotten them Licenc'd, and
Printed, such as are in *Walwyns Wiles;* all such shall not be doubted for
lies: but a Law would be wonderous necessary, though it were never
kept, you can bear with that, though we, as you say, cannot, but are
clamouring alwayes about the Selfe-denying Ordinance: well, pray
get a Law, and draw it up as large as will serve your seared Consciences, that durst subscribe such abominable ones, as that booke
containeth; it being a thousand pities, that you, who have ever been
so forward for the good of the Commonwealth, should stay till some
that are not of Churches, or some obscure inferiour Churches should
move for it, nay, and may occasion a greater strictnesse, then will
serve your turne.

Many considerations will be necessary in the making of it; for as
you know in wrastling, three foiles, are valued a fall: so it must be
exprest, how many mentall reservations shall make a lie; how many
feignings, how many times appearing as a spie; whether a spie under
an oath can lie, so long as he intends the service of his principals: how
many times a man may walke and discourse familiarly in dissimulation, before it amount to a lie; how many lies a years hypocrisie
amount to: that so, such as Mr Richard Price, Mr Brandriff and the
like, may be reckoned withall: and then to proportion punishments to
offences; you have time and leisure, and I perceive, meet together for
worse purposes, so I leave it to you.

Only thus much for encouragement; Almanzar the first (or third) of
the Sarazens Emperors, made use of such a Law, by which (above any

other meanes) a mighty people were kept in great quietnesse and prosperity, as you may read in a little Book, called the *Life of Mahomet;* and are we not in a low forme for Christians, when we are not so wise as such Schoole-masters? O miserable Reformation!

But I must take heed what I say, for it seemes the Petition of the 11 of September, is afresh come into their minds, and all the circumstances therein reckoned up, as matter of provocation to all interests, and of devision to the honest party; for of all Petitions, after that which was burnt, this conteined most particulars; and then, and long after, was that wherein the wel-affected from all parts, and Countries, did agree and center; so that it proved a Petition of the greatest power of uniting, as ever was: and was by the heads, and chosen men of these mens friends agreed unto, to be the substance of an *Agreement of the People;* as Lieut: Collonel John Lilburne, Mr Doctor Parker, and others can testifie: and yet now by this author, must be raised against me, as if but for me, that Petition, had never been seen; & as if his judgement were to be valued to the blasting of that [27] which received the approbation of many thousands of the most cordiall friends the Parliament, and Army had throughout England: I wonder of what honest party, this author reckons himself to be, if this Petition were so unworthy; an exasperating Petition, who did it exasperate? if this Petition did demonstrate my designe of mischief to the honest party, I say (as he saies) let any mans reason judge impartially and determine; certainly these people have resolved themselves to be, and have contracted some corrupt interest, that the matters of that Petition now so much troubles them: but why this must fall upon my accompt, more then upon any others, that I do not see; only he hath undertaken to try what work his wit can make of any thing; and out of the strength of his braine, presumes he can turne my promotion of the best things to my disadvantage, although (but that I will not favour his expectation with a blab) I could tell him how little I had to do in that Petition; but why should I take care to set that man right, that cares not which way he goes, to do mischiefe, and will not be disswaded? and whose ends are so unworthy, as to affright all men from Petitioning, without his, and his associates allowance?

I know not whether any body sets him to this unhappy work, or whether he officiously undertakes it of himselfe, but truely to me he seemes to be but an impertinent workman to his pretended ends; for as in the former part, no man (to my apprehension) ever more wounded Religion, and the honour of God and his Word, then he hath done, upon pretence of wounding me: so in this other part, which he pretends for the honour of the present Parliament; what man in the world would have made such a repetition of things? trumpeting out himselfe really such things, as I am confident, he never heard from me, nor any body else: it hath not been my use to stir much in what is past; but my way hath been to propose a passing by of what is gone, and laying a good foundation for the time to come; that there might be no need of such complaints, as he there more Rhetorically, then truly, reckons up as uttered against me.

"As how basely things go; what Oppressions, Taxations, and vexations, the poor people indure, how this poor betrayed Nation is bought and sold; how the cutting off some Tyrants, do alwaies make way for more, and worse to succeed them; how nothing is done for the Commonwealth; how basely the treasure of the Common-wealth is embezell'd; how Parliament-men Vote money out of the purses of the poor ridden people, into their owne; how they share the riches of the Nation among themselves; how to day, they Vote this Parliament-man into a great Office, and to morrow, another; and how they doe nothing for the Common-wealth, but Vote one another into places of power and profit; how that, though to abuse, and cast a mist before the eyes of the people, they made a Self-denying Ordinance, yet suffer no man to put it in execution; how they promote their Kindred and Allies, into great places every where; if any use be for men in the Custome house, in Excise office, or in any other places of profit, this, and that Parliament-man's friends, or brothers, or sons, or nephewes must be the men; nay, Parliament-men and their allyes, have place upon place, and office upon office; as if they had severall bodies, to be imployed at one and the same time: What's become of the infinite summes, the unconceiveable Treasure of the Nation; the late King's Customes, Ship-money, Coat and Conduct money, Monopolies, &c. were nothing to the Customes, Excise, Taxations, Free quarter, Sequestrations, Papists monies, Bishops Lands, Revenues of the Crowne; besides all the Plate and monies, lent freely by the [28] people, and yet nothing done: nay, how many for their zeal and good will to the State, have lent freely and bountifully, thereby beggering and undoing themselves, and now cannot receive one peny to buy them bread, but may lie begging, petitioning, and starving at their dores, and cannot be heard; nay, it may be, have nothing but course, hard and cruel language from them; how one Faction tears the Common-wealth, & share it among them one while, & another another while, neither of them regarding the ease or grievances of the poor people all this while: And what have they done since this purge, and that purge? they have voted the continuance of tythes, the laying of more taxes and rates, they imprison honest men, &c."

These he implyes, are my ordinary discourses, to the disparagement of the Parliament, and that too since the King's Death; for my part, I must deny it; and that if I should have in any place, or at any time, spoken, or directed others to speak all what he there recites, I had spoken what I do not know to be true; for I have never made it my work to take a Catalogue of the failings of Authority, but have frequently proposed a generall remission and security to all men, for what hath been past (as I said before) without which I never expected peace, or an end of wars and miseries: And this my back friend, Mr Arnald, may averr on my behalf; to whom I once gave a paper (upon his sight and desire) to that end: so far have I been from blowing such coles as these, that if any ever cast water or milk upon this wild-fire, I have done my endeavour therein.

But I must not be what indeed I am, but what this and these men are pleased to give me out; unto whose secret suggestions, and false aspersions continually whisper'd by them at Parliament, and Derby-house, I impute all the hard measure I have found (and which, I fear, will be the undoing of me, my Wife, and Children) there being none of the Gentlemen of either place, I am certain, have any thing against me, but what these men bring; and some of them, I am confident, have that experience of my integrity and ingenuity in all I have done in relation to the publique, that they would do as much for my deliverance out of this affliction, as for any mans in the world.

And truly, whether he wounds me or the Parliament more, in making such a Rhetoricall recitall of so many particulars, as, whether true or false, will be apt enough to be believed in these sad, complaining and distracted times; let any man that hath reason, judge.

So that if he meant not to wrong the Parliament, but me, he hath overdone his work, which generally befals such as take not their Consciences along with them in what they undertake; they over-do, do, and undo, ordinarily; as you may observe by his so many firsts, seconds, thirds, his doubling and trebling of them, and his running over one and the same thing again and again, as if he labour'd with the disease of multiplication.

But truly, when I consider with what a continued, but secret malice, they have pursued me, and that all their pretended reconcilements and friendships, have been but counterfeit, I can impute the same to nothing more then emulation: for before this Parliament, I was accustomed to discourse much with Mr Goodwins hearers, upon what

they and I had heard him preach; and my character of him usually was, that he spent much time (in my apprehension) to make plain things difficult to be understood, and then labour'd again to make them plain and easie to be understood; but he had so perplex'd them, as that he could not: this I know did sorely trouble them, though when they fell to congregate in a Church-way, they gave me good re-
[29] spect, as needing the help of every one, whose conscience (as mine did) led them out to stand and plead for liberty of Conscience.

I believe they were also not a little troubled, that I closed not with them, or some others, in their Church-way; for so I once perceived by one Mr Lamb, a Linnen Draper in Cornhill; to whom I having sold a good parcel of linnens, and taking it very kindly that he would deal with me, I would needs give him, and some Friends with him, a cup of beer and sugar one morning, and we were all free and chearfull: but Mr Lamb and I out-staid the rest, falling very largely into discourse, he putting all the questions and doubts he had concerning my opinions; which I answered one by one, upon condition that he would give himself and me time, then, and hear me out all I had to say, because (as I then told him) I never had received prejudice from any discourse that ever pass'd from me with ingenious men, but where they carried away things peece-meal, and by halfs: So in a most friendly manner he heard me, and, in conclusion, approved exceedingly of all I had said, even with abundance of content and rejoycing: but when we had done, he fetches a deep sigh, saying, O, Mr Walwyn, that you had a good opinion of Churches.

To which I answered, that I had no evil opinion of them; that rather I did rejoyce to see with what amity and friendship they enjoyed each others society in a comfortable way, assisting and supporting one another; that I was glad they so contentedly enjoyed the exercise of their consciences in a way that was agreeable to their judgments; that I had made it my work, as far as I was able, to preserve unto them, and all others, the enjoyment of that just liberty; it being a principle in me, that every man ought to be protected in the use of that wherein he doth not actually hurt another; and that were I satisfied in some particulars, I could not but joyn my self to some such society; that I thought, as I was, I wanted much of that intimacy with good people which they had, but yet must not purchase it upon a doubtfull conscience, or against my judgment; that I wish'd them all happinesse in their way, and was not willing to disturb any, and hop'd they would not disturb me; hoping, that they would have as good an opinion of me, as I had of them, though I did not joyn in a Church-way: and with this he then seemed to be very well satisfied.

And so we held very fair and serious respects a good while, I giving him some visits at his house, where he would reade to me with much admiration, some of Mr Goodwin's Books; the weaknesse whereof I made somewhat bold withall (as being never used to flattery, or to balk my judgment) which proved a *noli me tangere:* for Mr Goodwin is the apple of their eie, and in a short time, not only his familiarity ceased, but I was even slandered to death from this man's mouth; no place wherever he came, but his aspersions flew abroad; as if to blast my reputation, had been given him in commission from the whole Congregation: this was the fruit of my intimacy with him.

Nor can I imagine any other reason why Mr Brandriff should deal so unworthily with himself and me; for when we have been together, he hath discours'd to me much concerning his Wife, his Father, his Children, what he had done for his Kindred, how ingratefull they were, the manner of his trade; how, and by what means he got good store of monies, in the midst of the wars, by rising early in mornings, and searching in Inns, what goods were brought to Town (indeed, most commendably and industriously) how he many times ventered to buy goods he had little skill in, nor knew not when he had bought them, where he was like to vent them; yet how well he sped, with abundance of things, I will not repeat, these being sufficient [30] to shew the man, was not certainly feigned towards me so long a time as afterwards he pretended; only when we have been hearing Mr Goodwin together, and come from him discoursing, I have shewed suddenly some mistakes, and weaknesses, and drinesses in things which Mr Goodwin had much laboured to make good, but would not endure my touchstone; and Mr Brandriff hath been forc'd to confesse as much; sadly smiling and saying, well, what shall we say? where can we hear better? To which I would answer, that's not the thing, you see what this is.

Indeed, but for this, which can be nothing but emulation, I know not any cause I have given them thus to persecute me; they have thank'd me for Books I have written, as my *Whisper*, and others forenamed; and for a Book, entituled, *A help to the understanding of Mr Pryn*, which they would no nay, but it should be mine, though my name was not to it; so good an opinion they had of my integrity: Nay, their Church disbursed fifty shillings towards the printing of ten thousand of that little Book, called, *The word in season* (they then judg'd the dispersing of Books no sin) which Mr Batcheler can tell who was Author of, and they know well enough; so far were they from believing what now they subscribe to; that in all times I ever opposed the present Government; but it will be found only, that I

never flattered them by such undue expressions, as, by the womb
that bare you, and the paps that gave you suck, and the like, more
sutable to the liberty of Sycophants, then Christians: Nor did I ever
oppose any just authority otherwise then as I have opposed men: not
to destroy them, but their destructive errours and misapplications of
their power.

Well, ye are the most strange conditioned people that ever I met
withall, the most inconsistent; walking, not by any principles, but
meerly by occasion, and as the wind turns; and I am heartily glad I
have so nigh done with you, for I never shall be induced to bestow
the like pains about you again: only I have this farther to acquaint the
ingenious withall concerning you, *viz:* that you bear your selves very
high and confidently upon your ability of proving whatsoever you
alleadge by way of aspersion against any man: And indeed herein, I
can resemble you to none so properly, as to a people are called, Gyp-
syes (I must intreat pardon, if there seem any lightnesse or despising
in this simile) for if I could have found one more handsome so proper,
I would not have stained my paper with this: but just so have I found
them confederated together; if one but averr a thing, presently there
are a cloud of witnesses; and not in a slighting way, but such as will
take their oaths of it: Upon which accompt, upon the Exchange, all
their affirmatives concerning others, and there negatives concerning
themselves, are carried on; beating down, by this one trick, all their
opposers.

And so they dealt in a most filthy scandall concerning an honest
man I know abhorred such basenesse; and which was carried all over
the Town by this kind of Congregationall men: I reproving of it, and
saying, the party would not so put it up, but would seek for remedy
at Law; one of them rounds me in the ear, If you are his Friend, advise
him to be quiet; for I am told by as godly men as any in England, the
thing will be witnessed upon sufficient mens oaths: whereas, I professe, the thing was of so abominable a nature, as I do not believe
ever was, or ever could be proved by witnesses, all circumstances of
day, and light, and open-street considered: And truly they are as cunning at dispersing, as they are confident in avouching, that the resemblance may well hold; for generally all their aspersions, though
they are so vile, as, if believed, shall undo a man and his family, in
respect of the loathings they will beget in all that know him: yet you
shall ever have them such as [31] by law you shall hardly ever take
hold of them: so that they exceedingly presume, never giving over
railing and writing, that there is no possibility of silencing them:

shame they care not for, and no prejudice can come unto them; for touch one, and touch all; all have one purse for a common end, offensive and defensive; and if they should by these courses grow so odious, as that no body else would trust them; their Confederacy is so large, that by buying, and selling, and purchasing, and lending, they are able to enrich one another, so as they grow to a mighty interest, as distinct almost as the Jews in Amsterdam; and much to the same ends of gain, but have greater aims of power and dominion.

And I beseech God to deliver me out of their unmercifull hands, before they yet grow greater; for I look upon my self as their Prisoner, aspersed and imprisoned, and even ruin'd by their ingratefull, Un-Christian suggestions and machinations.

Mr Kiffin, I hear, since he hath subscribed *Walwyns Wyles*, desires I would give him a meeting, with others he will bring with him; and if proof be not then made of the truth of those things therein alleadged against me, effectually and sufficiently, he will then himself write against the Book: what an offer is here? he hath set his name already to the Book, as a witnesse, and published the Book (before ever he, or any man else ever spake to me of it) to my disparagement, and undoing (were men as ready in believing, as they are in scandalizing) and now he offers a meeting to have those falshoods proved.

Is this like the Pastor of a Congregation of Christians? Good God! what are befaln to Congregations, that they can bear with such Pastors! Truly, Mr Kiffin, although your people will not deal with you as you deserve, I shall be bold to perswade you to leave them; and take such with you as are of your own mind, and colour your faces of a tauny colour, and pursue the profession, you have begun the practice already; and cease to (can't, shall I say, I even tremble to think it is no better) to deceive, I will say, any longer, in the name of the Lord; for God is a jealous God, and will one day recompence it.

A man that looks upon these seeming Saints, no mervail if they take them for such indeed, they are so solemn in their countenances, so frequent and so formall in their devotions, so sad at others chearfulnesse, so watchfull over others tripping, so censorious over others failings, having a kind of disdainfulnesse at others, bespeaking them in effect to stand farther off, I am holyer then thou; it being a great scruple amongst many of them, the lawfulnesse of playing at Cards, or the like recreation, as being a vain expence of time.

Whereas all this is meer out-side, and but the washing of the out-side of the pot, a but appearing holy before men, to gain the repute of Godlinesse; shut but the dores, and let them but be sure of their company, and they are as other men for sports, and jigs, and jeers, and idle jests and tales, and laugh and love it, and even lie down again; for if they would do thus before me, and some other of my Friends, what will they do when they are alone one amongst another? Collonel Tichburn himself, at Mr Hunts house at Whitehall, telling so nasty a tale of a Scotchman that would teach a Lord to give himself a vomit, crooking his fingers, and thrusting them as into one place, and then into his mouth, and down again, and up again, acting of it with so much art, and delight, and laughter, as that other solemn man, Mr Daniel Taylor, and Mr Richard Price, were ready to burst themselves with laughter; Mr Taylor calling out for more jests and sports, being, as he said, extremely troubled with melancholly; I would he were troubled with no worse. [32]

For it was but a slippery trick of him, to allow of all I said against Excise, as an extreame burthen to Trades; and saying he felt it himselfe, and was at that time in question at the Office, and wishing it downe with all his heart, when at the very same time, or just upon it, he writes a Letter to the Commissioners of the Excise, advising them not to be so severe in dealing with him, for the times were like to be such, as they might need the least of their friends; whereas in an eminent place, he had appeared in no mean manner, in defence of the Excise, or to this effect; yet these, forsooth, must passe for the only holy, unspotted men of the times; so as a man that hath but a chearfull countenance is scarce fit for their company, and he that should be said in their company to carry two faces under one hood; O what a wretch were he! but these it seemes may do any thing; and as the proverb hath it, better steale a horse, then others looke over the hedge; but you must note, Captaine Lacy, and Mr Lamb, fellow members with Mr Taylor of Mr John Goodwins Congregation, have some hundreds of pounds in the Excise, which yeilds them good interest (what ere it doth the Common-wealth) and how many Congregationall mens cases it may be, they knew better then I, and so Mr Daniel Taylor, had more reason for what he did, then he would tell every body of: these relations are the tenter-hooks, upon which all oppressions hang, and cannot get off; if they but concerne one of a Congregationall way, you draw Dunne out of the mire, and none of that way will help, but hinder you.

And for Col. Tychburn's jest as they call'd it, and their other gibbish pratling, how long one had been from his Wife, and how long another; which was to me no better than catterwawling; I was wondred at I was no merrier, being somewhat dumpish by thinking, why those men seperated themselves from other men; and sadly considering, what a stroake this light easie people were like to have; through their seeming Godlinesse, in the greatest affaires of the Common-wealth, as soone after was, and hath been seen.

But its well knowne, I, and all that were with me, were so far from telling these things any where to their disparagement, or so much as speaking of it, that we agreed it should not be knowne, lest we should break those rules of society, which require honest men, not to talke to any mans discredit, whatever befell in company, where no evill to any man was intended; and truly, but that now these men seeme to stretch themselves and to walke on tiptoe, not only upon my ruines, but without all tendernesse of compassion, towards my dear Wife and Children; yea, and insult over our more dear Cause, and our Countries Liberties, bearing downe all upon an opinion of their godlinesse, and our licentiousnesse, which we more abhor then themselves; these stories had been buried in the grave of silence, but as they have borne themselves, not regarding our manifestation, but despising and jeering of it; and by their most uncharitable Book, raising up a whole legion of scandals and slanders against me; a necessity was upon me, to shew these men as they are, not as they labour by hypocrisie to appear unto the world.

I have onely one request to this sort of men, and I have done with them; and that is, That they would agree among themselves, to wear some very visible and remarkable thing, either upon their breasts, or in their hatts, in that company where they resolve to be sincere; and to make no perfidious use of that meeting, or conversation, whilst they weare it, and to keep it in their pockets, or concealed, when they intend to deceive; and it will be necessary in your next Book, to publish what this note shall be, that all men may expect it, and accordingly keep you company or not, and know how to behave themselves in their conversing with [33] you; in the observation whereof also, you must advise all those that have been used to deceive; especially those that have profest to have kept me company, purposly to turn all I did to my prejudice; that they be very exact and sincere in the observation thereof, for otherwise it will come to nothing; and no body will know where to have you, or how to confer with you.

It hath been others cases, who have used over-much dissimulation, as Lewis the 11th of France, who in his transactions with Charles Duke of Burgundy, concluding Peace, Truce, and Articles upon Oathes; and nothing proving of force to hold him; neither oathes, nor sacraments, nor execrations, nor covenants, nor any such bonds as should hold inviolable all contracts amongst men; in conclusion, he discovers the image of St. Claud, which he continually wore in his hatt; and after he had offered any other obligation, in a thing he was suspected not to intend, or keep; he urging him to swear by that St. Claud, he refused; as not daring to break faith upon that oath; this was something yet; and truly, when you shall consider to what a pass you have brought your selves, you cannot but conclude upon some such course.

And having thus turned your insides outwards, though with unpleasing paines to himself, and much trouble to the ingenious Reader (for I was hopefull I had done for ever with this kind of work, when our manifestation and Agreement of the People was once abroad) you may without spectacles, read in your own hearts, written in Capitall letters, what you through a great mistake intended to me, and my friends, in the first enterance of your Book: namely, "That the greatest hypocrisie, is often palliated with the most specious pretences of the plainest sincerity; and the chiefest use that some men make of Religion, and the language thereof, is (after the similitude of Satan with our first parents) to muffle the understandings of over credulous and flexible men, and then to cheat them, under a guilded bait of their seeming good, unto such actions, that are most conducible to their certaine misery": If this be not true of you, and due to you, it hath no true owners in the world.

And so I have done with you all, and all your Wiles; and henceforth, he that is filthy, let him be filthy still, and he that is ignorant, let him be ignorant still; he that is so fouly partiall in his Conscience, as after this my Just Defence, to believe your slanders of me, let him remaine so still; and he that through a perverse ignorance, shall henceforth doubt my integrity, let him remaine ignorant still: I would gladly be free from this Restraint, because I fear it will prove prejudiciall to many more besides my selfe, if not already, and I trust, God will open some just way; however, I have peace within, because in all that hath befallen me; my will is not to harme any man, nor to dishonour God; affliction being still to me, a better choice then sin.

William Walwyn

FINIS [34]

26

Juries Justified; or,
A Word of Correction to
Mr. Henry Robinson

[2 December] 1651
Reprinted from a copy of the tract in the Thomason Collection in the British Library

Juries Justified, "By William Walwin," was printed by Robert Wood, 1651. The title page states that it is "Published by Authority." It has no imprimatur and is not listed in the *Stationers' Register*.

Juries Justified was Walwyn's first tract since the publication of his *Just Defence* more than two years before. Walwyn broke his silence to refute Henry Robinson's proposal to replace juries "in the lesser divisions of a County" with judges appointed by Parliament.[1] Walwyn had advised Robinson of his opposition before *Certain Considerations* was published and expressed reluctance to oppose his friend publicly. However, "gratitude" (presumably for his own release after Lilburne's acquittal by a jury in 1649) and the conviction that trial by jury was England's "principal liberty" compelled him to publish a "gentle Correction."[2] In fact, the treatise is at once gently scornful and incisive. There are traces of Walwyn's earlier irony in denunciations of Robinson's proposal as "a humour for the most part got by travel" while denigration of the quality of jurors is indignantly rejected: "Consciences . . . have been as frequently found under Felt Hats and Worsted Stockings, as with people of a finer Stuff."[3] Walwyn concludes that his reply to Robinson is probably unnecessary, "for certainly Juries cannot in time of Parliament be in any danger."[4] It was a fair tribute to the republican government with which Walwyn had come to terms.

Juries Justified is reprinted for the first time in this volume.

JURIES juſtified:

OR,

A WORD

OF

CORRECTION

TO

M^r. HENRY ROBINSON;

FOR

His ſeven Objections againſt the Trial of Cauſes, by Juries of twelve men.

By WILLIAM WALWIN.

Job. 22. 28. *Remove not the ancient Land-mark which thy Fathers have ſet.*

Publiſhed by Authority.

London, Printed by *Robert Wood*; and are to be ſold at his houſe, near the *Flying-Horſe* in *Grubſtreet*. 1651.

Title page of *Juries Justified*, 1651. (Folger Shakespeare Library)

Juries justified: or,

A WORD of CORRECTION to Mr. Henry Robinson;

for His seven Objections against the Trial of Causes, by Juries of twelve men.

By William Walwin

Job. 22. 28. *Remove not the ancient Land-mark which thy Fathers have set.*

Published by Authority.

London, Printed by *Robert Wood;* and are to be sold at his house, near the *Flying-Horse* in *Grubstreet.* 1651.

Juries Justified: or, A Word of Correction, to Mr. *Henry Robinson.*

Though a silence had seiz'd me, equal to his that was born and continued dumb, till his father was in danger of being murthered; yet retaining still a sincere and vigorous affection to my Native Countrey, and seeing this mans Knife offering at the throat of our preservers (such I esteem our Juries) for Englands, and for this its fundamental essential liberty, I could not hold my peace; but must tell Mr. Robinson, he deals most injuriously with his Country, whereof he must either speedily repent, or be made ashamed: For how doth it appear, *That there is not a competent number of understanding and fit men to be had in the lesser divisions of a County, for trial of all causes upon all occasions?* which is his first frivolous objection. If by lesser Divisions, he means Hundreds, who doth not know it to be a most notorious slander? there being not the least in England, but affordeth a double competency of understanding and fit men; yea, should he mean Parishes, I verily beleeve, a [1] sufficiency might even there be found, for trial of all the causes of each Parish; but that needs not, the divisions of Hundreds being more commodious, and the Hundred Courts being of ancient continuance, might soon be reduced to the former use; in which Courts (before the Conquest) all causes or matters in question, upon especial penalty were finally to be decided, in every Month.

And though William the Conquerour was so unjust and unworthy
(indeed so perjured) as to alter this course so far, as to ordain that four
times in the year, for certain days, the same businesses should be
determined in such place as he would appoint, where he constituted
Judges to attend for that purpose, and others, from whom (as from his
own bosom) all litigators should have justice, from whom was no
appeal; and appointed others for the punishment of malefactors: yet he
never attempted to take away Juries, as finding by the resolute strug-
ling of the people against what he did, that they would never bear it. So
as this Mr. Robinson does what he can, to induce the present Parliament, to deal worse with us then the Conquerour did with our Prede-
cessors, not minding as it should seem, how heinous an offence it hath
been always judged, for any to endevour the subversion of the fundamental Laws of the Nation: nor regarding how frequently this Parliament have avowed to maintain inviolable, those fundamentals, in all
things touching life, liberty, and estate, with all things incident thereunto; so as he invites them to do that, then which nothing could be
more dishonourable. Insomuch, as it is a difficult thing to conceive,
whence it is that he should engage himself in such a subject, nor can I
imagin; except it be from his proneness to invention, a humour for the
most part got by travel, but proving very unhappy to this Nation; as
might be instanced, in our exchange of many of our substantial honest
plain customs, for Frenchified and Italianated inventions, which have
had no small share in our late distempers, new platforms of Government, sent from [2] English-fugitives abroad, to reduce us into the like
depth of bondage with our neighbours, having been received with too
great applause; but it is strange the ill success of the inventers & at-
tempters, few of which have escaped exemplar punishment, should
not as Land-marks warn travellers from such Shipwracks. And of all
our English travellers (I say) well fare Col. Henry Marten, who returned a true English-man, and continued so ever after; always manifesting a most zealous affection to his Countries liberties, and especially to this, of Trials by 12 men or Juries; as eminently appeared by
his demeanor upon the Bench at Redding, where it being his lot to give
the charge to the Grand-Jury, in the first place, he wisht them to be
rightly informed of their own places and authority, affirming it to be
judicial, when as their own (meaning the Justices) was but ministerial;
and therefore desired them not to stand bare any longer, but to put on
their hats, as became them, and not to under-value their Country,
which virtually they were; or words to this effect: which I the rather
mention, to set traveller against traveller; for had he been a meer

Country Justice, and not seen the world abroad, this our Anti-Juriman, possibly would have said it had been a vapour, sutable to one that had never been farther then the smoke of his own Chimney; for so our inventive innovating travellers, use to silence those that oppose their corrupt reasonings: And I have good hope our fear is our greatest harm, for certainly the Honourable Parliament would never have referred the care of the Regulating of Law and its proceedings, in so special a manner to Colonel Marten, but that they approve of his affection to Trials per Juries.

But it may be, he lays the most weight of his first Objection upon the word *Understanding;* that *there is not a competent number of Understanding and fit men:* Understanding indeed is very good, but as I take it, there is not so great a want thereof in England, as there is of Consci- [3] ence, a faculty that puts on to the doing of what is approved to be ones duty, and to the resistance of what is not: a little quantity whereof (in my opinion) were very wholesom for one that is troubled with the rising of such Objections. But as for understanding sufficient to judge between right & wrong, in any case, where proof is to be made by witnesses openly and freely to be examined, and where a man shall be sure to have the help of eleven more equally engaged under oath to be careful therein; truly I wonder, that (any man not suspicious of his own judgment, or not over-weening it) should so much as doubt, that a competency of such understanding fit men, are not in every lesser Division or Hundred to be found.

Indeed, understanding is in great reputation, and so is utterance too, but yet nothing is so precious as a true conscience; not such a one as is satisfied with, touch not, tast not, handle not; nor with saying Corbun: nor with observation of days and times, no nor with saying Lord, Lord; but with doing judgment and justice, in delivering the Captive, and setting the Oppressed free; in feeding the Hungry, clothing the Naked, visiting the Sick and the imprisoned; and in faithfully keeping all promises and compacts amongst men, without which civil societies cannot be maintained.

And certainly, any one that hath such a good Conscience, would make a Conscience of removing so ancient a Land-mark, which our fore-fathers have set, *Job.* 22.28. and more of such good Consciences I beleeve are to be found amongst our ancient English Gentry, and other our Free-holders, than among our sharp-sighted, smooth tongued Travellers; and such as (to the honour of our English nation) have in all times served their Country justly and faithfully, judging the causes both of rich and poor without fear or favour, as justly as can be expected amongst men, yea, without respect to persons or opinions, as truly honouring God in their hearts, and trembling at an Oath taken to deal justly; and who with [4] their lives and fortunes, in all times, have preserved this, the most essential Liberty of England.

For howsoever men in these days make bold to trample *Magna Charta* under their feet, making sport at the many absurd prerogative and superstitious things therein contained; it is to be noted, that these things are but as a French garb or cloathing, which the Conqueror and his successours, by main strength, forced our fore-fathers to put on: but yet, as an Englishman is to be known from a Frenchman amongst a thousand, though he labor to fashion himself as the most Frenchified Gallant; so are our true English Liberties, contained in Magna Charta, as easy to be differenced from amidst that superstitious and in some measure, tyrannical heap cast upon them, and which that worthy Parliament, in the third year of the late King, culled out to purpose, and reduced into that excellent Law (as this Parliament stiled it since his death) the *Petition of Right,* and wherein trials *per* Juries is the principal.

And therefore this is a strange kind of service or gratitude to the Parliament in Mr. Robinson, for so many profitable places and favours conferred upon him, to invite them to take away Juries, and to erect another way of trial of Causes, whereby he must necessarily render them more odious to the people, than the worst of those they have removed: for certainly, had either party when these publick differences began, proposed the taking away of Juries, they had never had a thousand men to have taken part with them; so as if his counsel should take place, I wonder where the Parliaments Cause would be, which they have ever, hitherto, held forth, for the concurrence of the People? is it not also as easie to judge for whom he labours to beget friends, as by his so doing, it being no new thing with him to play the Lapwing.

As ill also doth he repay the Army; for whereas they publish to all the world, That they esteemed all present enjoyments (whether of life or livelihood, or nearest re- [5] lations,) a price but sufficient to the purchase of so rich a blessing, *viz.* That they, and all the free-born people of England might sit down in quiet under their own vines, under the glorious Administration of Justice, and Righteousness, and in full possession of those Fundamental Rights and Liberties, without which, they could have little hopes to enjoy either any comforts of life, or so much as life itself, but at the pleasure of some men, ruling meerly according to Will and Power.

What more fundamental liberty than the trial of causes by Juries of twelve men? What more constant, more glorious administration of Justice and Righteousness? Yet this true or false lover of the Army, insinuates, nay, invites the taking of this away, as the end of their conquest, as if they had conquered, not for the establishment of our fundamental liberties, but for their extirpation: if these are his mites he so much boasts of, to cast into the work of Reformation, sure it is not for the English, but the Scotch Treasury; where if he should be as acceptable as (time was) one was at Oxford and Newcastle, the new Office of Addresse may serve turn for private parlies, with any body, and is a fit contrivance for him to be *hic & ubique* as formerly: What think yee of it? is it, or is it not? Is it not more likely, than that England should not be able to afford a sufficient number of judicious and conscionable men for Juries? for my part I professe I think it is.

And how I pray doth it appear, that *People are generally unwilling to be called upon for Jurie-men, whereby they neglect their own affairs?* Which is his second objection. What an unheard of grievance hath this tender hearted man found out! even the most insensible burthen of serving upon Juries; wherein his care appears above and beyond all that ever petitioned the Parliament: not one Petition of the well-affected, in all their large Petitions, so much as minding or desiring to have it removed; no, nor none of the ill-affected: manifestly shewing, that either he is [6] better then the best, or worse then the worst affected: say Scotch, or English, whether is it? (for he desires us to be tried by God and his Country) is it not right sterling. But certainly Mr. Robinson is troubled, the plain people should be put upon occasions to understand themselves in any measure, or be able to discern of one anothers causes, but would have them so wholly fixt upon their own particular affairs, that they might remain as ignorant of the laws of the land, as in time of Popery they were of the laws of God; then, knowing no more but what the priest pleased: and now he would have them put all their understandings (in the affairs of law) into the pockets of such Judges, as he in his own brain fancies, and would perswade them to it for their own good, then they might the better follow their more profitable callings; he finding, it seems that every man is born for himself, and not so much as a Jury-mans time to be spent for the publique: sure 'twill not be long but he will also find, Constables, Headboroughs, and all other Officers to their hands; but by the way, not without good pay, for so he carefully proposeth for his Judges, and so large as they may live upon it when they are out of their Offices: and thus he will devise waies to raise monies in such

sort I warrant ye, as shall be no waies burthensome to the people, no
so much as felt by them, if you will beleeve him, but so long till he
hath brought you into his fooles Paradice, when he hath you there,
beleeve or no, all is one, he will make you pay, and say too you feel it
not; to such an end drives his Mountebank promises, in all he hath
yet undertaken; for he hath made some believe, that he will shew
how all the vast charges of the Common-wealth should be constantly
defrayed without burthen to the people; but sure his meaning is, that
he would have them at such a passe, as they should not dare to say
the contrary, if he but say it is so; otherwise; where are the mountains
he hath so often promised, are they in his office of addresse, or are
they not? [7] 'tis like there's more, then such as truly love the Liberties
of their Country can imagin.

Well, all the Jurie-men in England shall be excused from any further
service, because they are generally unwilling: off with your hats,
Country-men, and thank him; he onely takes care of you and your
affairs: Not a Parliament man, God be praysed, hath had this wicked
care of you, as for a poor complement, a little drawing back from your
duty, to take you at your words, and smile you out of all your liberties
at once; for beleeve it, lose this and lose all: No more complements, I
beseech you; but upon the first call, pack up and be going, for if once
Mr. Robinson take you napping, he may chance to shew you a new
Florentine trick for it.

For he further objecteth, that *though they do come to avoid the penaltie,
they seldome take the course to be rightly qualified and fitted to judge of the
matter in controversie.* But doth it appear to be a truth, that they come
(only) to avoid the penalty? it may be some do so, & yet they may
bring their consciences with them; (which, some think, have been as
frequently found under Felt Hats and Worsted Stockings, as with people of a finer Stuff,) and then I hope, it is well they are there; but that
one Swallow should make a Summer, or one Woodcock a Winter, is
against our English proverb; and as ill reasoning it is, to imply (as he
doth) that none come, but to avoid the penalty, when as it is impossible for him to know it, or to think it, so as to beleeve it: but some say,
our decoy Ducks may twattle any thing, for what is this and all the
rest but twatling? They seldom take the course to be rightly qualified
and fitted to judge of the matter in controversie, What cours trow
hath he seen beyond the seas in his travels, that are wanting here? are
not our Juries and Jurie-men sufficiently known before hand, who
shall be upon this, and who upon that cause, that the parties concerned might apply themselves to them by great letters and gifts, to

make them sensible? What a horrible [8] defect is this, and it seems would be perfectly supplied by such Judges as he fancied; then indeed they might be rightly qualified to judg, as should be best for their own and their Patrons advantage: And truly, in this way sure he ayms to be a Judg himself, and no doubt would soon come to have a feeling of the Cause; but if he do, I hope his itch will not yet be cured, and that he shall scratch where it doth not itch, first, as he hath done formerly: though now provender prick him to spur-gal his Country, as now he doth.

For yet again he sticks them in the sides, with this; That, *Most commonly, one or two active and nimble-pated men over-sway all the rest of the Jury; and too often for the worst:* which is his 4th Objection. But truly, with us in England, our nimble-pated men are not in so great credit, as possibly they are in other parts, we are generally of somewhat a more dullish complexion, which renders most so considerate as to suspect those few nimble-pated men as are amongst us; and for the most part not without cause: so as the nimble-pated seldom carry anything, except they have reason and equity of their side, and then the more they sway therewith the better: And those dull men (as he accounts them now it servs his turn) were he to deal with them in buying, selling, letting or setting, I beleeve he would not think them so easily caught with Chaff or Nutshels: Nor is right and wrong so difficult to be discerned in Causes and Controversies, but that an ordinary capacity (careful to keep a good conscience, and that is tender of an oath) shall soon perceive the true state thereof; and be able to do right therein according to evidence: Nor will this nimble-pated Mr. Robinson with all his quickness of wit, be able to make this (the most desperat project he ever undertook, or was ever offered at in England) pass for currant Coyn with our dullest apprehensions; and in time may be made to know, that none are so apt to mistakes as the quick-sighted; nor any so sottish, as those that are conceiptedly wise.

[9] Another gird he gives Our good men and true, is; That, *Though never so many of them dissent in judgment from the rest, they must notwithstanding all concur in the Verdict, or be wearied into it;* which is his 5th Objection: And truly (how strong soever he beleeves it) nothing in my opinion is more commendable in the institution of Juries, than the provision that all must agree, and agree necessarily and finally in so short a time; for should it rest on a major part, there might be some won for partiality, and some won for complaint in the parties against whom the Verdict is given; and some cause of quarrel ever after amongst the Jury-men themselvs: but in that all 12 must be agreed, all

these michievous inconveniences are manifestly to be avoided; and in that it is provided that they must make an end before they shall either eat or drink, it supposeth (what is said before) that right and wrong are not hard to be discerned, and that those that are convinced of the truth and yet desire to carry it otherwise, wanting that strength of a good conscience, to bear them out in such a strait of time, will yeeld to the truth rather than die in it; which those that labour to keep a good conscience, even dare to die: besides, had they further time, what means would be un-assayed to corrupt their Verdict? So as all things justly considered, doubtless it is the best provision that ever was in the world.

But he hunts farther to finde matter against them, and hath found; *That if they give corrupt or erroneous Verdict, there cannot justly be any penalty inflicted on them, because they may pretend, they did at first declare themselves unfit for such employment; that they undertook it not willingly, but were compelled thereunto:* This is a long-winded Objection. But (if any part of it were true, as I do not see it is) may they not justly be unfit for a corrupt Verdict? what a vast difference is there in judgment between our fore-fathers and some of their white sons? They no doubt, in the time of the institution of Juries, fore-saw as such as this man objects, and yet provide the most heavie [10] and reproachful punishment for a false Verdict, found *per* Attaint, as ever the wit of man devised; As, that every one of their Houses should be razed to the ground, their Trees stockt up by the roots, and all their Ground turn'd up and made useless, &c.

And all this justly too, as being fully convinced, it could not be, except it were wilfully and wickedly done, and deserving to bee made exemplary; and is so good a provision against corruption, that very seldom hath such a case befaln: but either men have had consciences for right, or have been deterred from daring to be confederates in so high a wrong, as to give a false or corrupt Verdict; as knowing it in vain to say in excuse, as this man goes on: *That they undertook it un-willingly, and were compelled thereunto; and when they saw there was no avoiding it, they endeavoured to proceed therein according to the uprightness of their Consciences, if they be thought to have done amiss, it was but what they could not remedy, and are heartily sorry for it.* Such Childish toyes, as fitter for Children than men, were of no value with them; and therefore supposing every man, a Man, and bound to serve his Country in any place as he shall be lawfully called thereunto (willing or unwilling) and to discharge his trust judiciously and faithfully, or to suffer for it.

His last Objection is; That, *The keeping the Jury without Fire-light,
Bread, or Drink, as the Law requires may possibly make the major part of
them, if not all, agree upon a Verdict contrary to their Consciences, to be freed
from any of these exigencies; at least, some of them to strike up with the rest in
a joint-Verdict, since it is well near impossible for twelve men, all circumstances considered, much more in a doubtful case, to bee of one opinion; and
though the case were never so clear, yet one peremptory man of a strong
constitution, whether his judgment be right or wrong, may serve all the rest,
unless they will give Verdict as he will have them.* Certainly, he thinks
most men of such a [11] kinde of tenderness in conscience, as soon is
crackt a sunder; beleeve it Sir, a true English consicence is of more
solid stuff, and will endure every one of these, yea death it self, rather
then be so base and unworthy; and certainly, but from unworthiness
could not be supposed: For if a man were but resolved how base a
thing it were so to do, how could he once think of striking up with the
rest, in a joint false Verdict (conscience in this case being more powerful than the strongest constitutions?) And as for any absurdity in their
being kept without fire-light, &c. it supposes that they have had time
enough at the Trial (or might have had) to be fully satisfied from the
examination of the Witnesses, in the right state of the Cause; which
then they are to look to, and to clear all their scruples by what questions they please, and well to understand themselves and one another before they discharge the Witnesses or go together: And this
standing for good, what cause is there they should have any longer
time then is admitted them? Except to make them liable to corruption.

For my part, I have heard many discourses touching Juries, but
never any material exception against the way of Trials by them: Indeed I have heard divers complain and wonder, that the way of proceeding before Causes come to Juries, should be so tedious, so full of
charge, trouble, and perplexity; since in their accompt, there is very
little more requisite in any Cause, but a convenient time for preparation and appearance, as about a Month or two; and then one chief
Officer (a Judg or the like) Witnesses, and a Jury, and time for Trial,
and so an end: A dispatch as speedy, with less charge, and more
certainty, than any new thing proposed by this new Inventor; most of
the accustomed pleading, serving rather to perplex then clear the
Cause to the understanding of the Jury: Which ocasioned that at a
certain Trial (time was) after that the state of the Cause was set forth
in the Declaration (the Councel beginning to speak) the Foreman of
the Jury, cals to the Judg and tels him, he had an [12] humble suit to
his Lordship; well (says the Judg) what is it? My Lord (said he) it is,

that now the state of the Cause hath been set forth, that we may proceed immediately to the examination of Witnesses, and so to give our Verdict, whil'st we remember what is material, and that we may spare the labour of these Gentlemen the Councel on both sides, whom I see are prepared to speak largely thereunto; for truly (my Lord) if they shall fall to work as they use to do, our understandings will be so confounded by their long discourses, and many niceties, as we shall not be able so rightly to judge thereof as now we shall, this was his humble motion; but the Judg having formerly been a Pleader, laught at the honest man, and so did all the Court, except some plain people that had so little understanding as to think there was reason in it. But such was the sport of those times, and perhaps may make some merry now, but yet they may consider that mocking is catching, and that laughter oft ends in Lachrymae. 'Tis but a story, yet a true one, and may one day be acted to the life, and with a general applause, so it be well and throughly done: And do this man what he can, the many good mens lives and estates, that have been preserved by Juries, will never be forgotten whil'st England is England; and wherein I deem my self so much concerned, as in gratitude I justly owe my Country this service; but have done it gently, as judging gentle Correction to be the best; and the rather, because the Objector is of my acquaintance, which made me indeed unwilling to undertake him, lest it might be deemed disagreeable to friendship; but seeing no body else did, and since he knew my minde to be against his Propositions, and much more against his endeavour to deprive us of our Juries, and yet would publish them, to the prejudice of Common Right, (against which, in all his writings he hath uttered most irradicating expressions) I take it, this *Word of Correction* is properly bestowed on him; and I hope profitably for the Common-wealth, having indeed [13] been born withall too long: for whil'st the Husbandmen sleep, envious men will be sowing their Tares.

To Correct all the rest of the errours in his little Treatise, were an endless labour; nor will this my present labour (I hope) be absolutely needful, for certainly Juries cannot in time of Parliament be in any danger; and then, they standing, his project fals: Only I thought it necessary to appear a friend to this my Countries principal liberty, when any one should adventure to appear so palpable an enemy; wishing with all my heart, that hee may consider the nature of what he hath done, remembring that as there was a Law (amongst the Locrines I take it) that he that moved to have any new Law established, should appear as if he were going to Execution, and if that he moved were not approved, he was indeed to suffer: Even so among us, there is a Law called the *Excomengement,* wherein all are accursed, that shall move for any Law to be made, contrary to our ancient Rights; and to subvert the Fundamental Law, hath been always adjudged a capital offence; and though with help of a little Fasting-spittle, a man may play with Quicksilver, yet 'tis a fond thing to take fire into ones bosom, and venture upon a charm only to keep it from burning. It were much better to pray unto God to give no more wit, nor strength, nor power, than men have good consciences to make a right use of, to his glory, and their spiritual good: Which is and shall be ever, the hearty prayer of

William Walwin

FINIS [14]

27

W Walwins Conceptions;
For a Free Trade

Presented to the Committee of the Council of State for Trade and Foreign Affairs, May 1652
Printed from the manuscript in the Public Record Office, State Papers, Foreign, 105, vol. 144, fos. 68–74

Walwyn's "Conceptions" was presented on behalf of free traders in a dispute with the Levant Company.[1] Walwyn's paper begins with a characteristic definition of the "publique good" as synonymous with the "Common Right"—which has "ever proved to include what hath been most proper and commodious for the Common-wealth." From the "ancient and continuall Claime of Right unto a generall freedome of Trade," Walwyn proceeds to the practical economic benefits of competition: more goods; lower prices; better goods; more ships; more mariners becoming profitable citizens of the Commonwealth; smaller and less tempting convoys ensuing from increased numbers of ships; the diffusion of wealth among enterprising and creative men. The fairest course, concludes Walwyn, is the restoration of the people's Common Right to trade freely. Alternatively, Parliament could open trade for half the number of years the company has prevailed and the case for free trade will be evident. The paper is logically organized, clearly stated, and presented with Walwyn's customary tone of reasonable persuasion.

The company's presentation concludes with a reply to Walwyn's paper. The government stood by the company.[2]

Walwyn's statement is printed for the first time in this volume.

To the Honble Committe for Forraine Affaires Sitting at Whitehall

The humble conceptions of Wm Walwin referring to this Quere vizt whether the restriction and Government of Forraine Trade by Companyes: Or leaving the same equally free to all Englishmen would bee most profitable for the Comon wealth*

Humbly sheweth

That seing those who desire a continuance of forraine trade under Companies, and those that propose an absolute freedome therein, doe both hold forth the publike good, as **that which ought to be submitted unto: The first thing necessary towards a resolution, seemeth to be a discovery of the true way of discerning what is to be deemed a publique good in England: [68]

And that (if the voyce of experience have any Credit) is to find out what is Common Right in England; Those things which are of Common concernment alwaies adiuged and claimed as native right both before and after alterations (such are common Rights) having ever proved to include what hath been most proper and commodious for the Common-wealth and best for every particular person whose Interest hath not been opposite to that of the publique:

The which Rule of Discovery proving sound and good in this quere of Forraine Trade, the ancient and continuall Claime of Right unto a generall freedome of Trade by Parliaments and the most industrious people at all times, both before and since the alterations and obstructions made therein by prerogative, would necessarily conclude that for forraine Trade to be universally free to all English men alike, would be most advantagious to the Common wealth; Scarce any the most noted and knowne Right of the Nation (if Parliaments themselves) having been more constantly claimed as Right.

And though this way of discovery of what is to be deemed a publike good and best for the Commonwealth of England may at first appeare not so pertinent to the solution of the question before you; yet be pleased to favor it so farr, as to admitt a serious consideration whether in this and all other queries touching publique good, it be not the safest and speediest way affording and contenting it selfe with a moderate generall experienced good, such as at best men or Nations

* W. Walwins Conceptions; For a free Trade
** Comon Rights

are capable of, avoyding that uncertainty innovation and a possibility of ever changing for the worse, which either vaine hopes of perfection or pretences of greater good to the publique (the originall of most if not all Companyes) might strongly but pernitiously perswade unto.

For if it be thoroughly considered, it will (as is humbly conceived) apeare that the waveing of this Rule of Discovery of what is most good, by what is most antient certaine and continuall claimed Right, [69] (Except in cases of iminent & extreme danger) for any other way of Discovery, hath generally (if not ever) proved of sad consequence to the Comon wealth and hath been so apprehended in most of former ages; Motions or pleas against comon & knowne Right, though upon never so specious pretences, being hardly admitted, ever suspected, and sometimes deepely censured.

And seemeth to have been soe upon good and sollid grounds; for waive but this Rule, and admit but pleas and motions against knowne Right, upon pretences of better and more profittable things, and an entrance is thereby given and roome made for Art, Sophistry, and corrupt policy to practise upon and against any or all the ancient liberties of the Nation, to baffle Reason, hold Argument for ever, untill at length it hath prevailed (as in times foregoing this Parliam^t:) but never without glorious colour and glosses of publique good, to a Totall subvertion of Publique Right and an inundation of oppressions & grevances; amongst which the restriction of Forraine Trade by Companyes (in the beginning of this Parliament) was not esteemed the least.

So as the premises seriously considered, with what farther may arise in your grate wisdomes, possibly this breife way of discovering will conduce most to the good of the Common wealth in this case may appeare most proper and effectuall, and of it selfe so sufficient to prove this so antient a continuall claymed Right, as freedome to all English men in all Forraine Trade is knowne to be, as needs no other argument to prove it more profitable for the Commonwealth, then any way of a restriction on Companies whatsoever.

But least this way of proving should seeme too strictly & precisely fixt upon the poynt of Right (which yet is humbly conceived to be the best) to make it manifest that (as all other the knowne Rights of England) so this of freedome of Trade doth comprize that wealth & essentiall publique good which in reason can justly be expected, and far beyond what possibly can be attained by restriction or the Government of Companies:

It is farther humblie offered That if the good of the Commonwealth accruing by forraine Trade consisteth as surely it doth,

1. In the improvement of Land by the buying & transporting of Native Comodities

2. In occasioning profitable Labour for all industrious people, in buying and transporting all sort of Manufactures, and bringing of all sorts of unwrought samples & materialls of Gold & Silver: [70]

3. In keeping other Nations from making the like unto our home Manufacture

4. In the increase of Shipping:

5. In the increase of Marriners:

6. In being more secure from advantages of Forraine States:

7. In the increase of Wealth and plenty:

All these are (as is humbly conceived) manifestly to be proved be effected most certainly & substantially, by admitting an universall freedome in all forraine trades; and that by this undeniable produc-tion thereof, The increase of Merchants.

1. For as to Merchants increasing (as increase they must in few yeares) they will not continue plodding to one or two townes in a Nation or Province, Trading in a stately manner upon set Dayes, with Grossiers, in great quantityes, making up their gaines in the grosse; but will be dispersed in every Haven and Towne, furnishing (not Grossiers that gain great estates out of our Native Comodities, and soe render them deare to the last user) but the last sellers, and so will be able to give at home the better Rates, which in conclusion re-dounds to workemen of all sorts, to Farmers, Owners & Land.

2. The numerousness of Merchants will occasion a strife & emula-tion among them, who shall produce the best ordered goods; and so will be more exquisite in the workmanship of dyings and dressings & the like, and give greater prices for worke; whereas Merchants in Companyes have noe need of such diligence, none being at the places of their sale, but themselves, or very few others: what they have must be taken, there being no other to be sold and workmen must worke at what Rates they please, worke being generally scarce through the scarcity of Merchants: and by setting their owne time of shippings, they make their own Markets for any their Commodities which im-poverisheth the maker, worker, grower, growth & Land. The more buyers, the more is bought & sould, all corners of the world would be found out; noe good towne in any province, but where English Mer-chants would be resident; whence they would returne the Comodities

of their respective places from the first hand, and so upon cheaper Rates then to be brought from all parts to one or two Townes in a Nation through divers getting hands, and at great charges; and if any Money of Gold Silver or Bullion be in any place, it could not but find the way to England.

3. They being numerous, and so dispersed into every town & with their fresh goods upon a neat Charge, exempt from Companyes impositions, could be able to sell upon reasonable Termes, & to supply all occasions, as would necessarily beat downe the making of any goods like unto [71] Our Native Manufactures, and by their residence in all Creekes & haven Townes, their own Interest would bind them to watch against the bringing into any forraine parts either Wools or Fullers Earth, more carefully and certainely than any Officers can doe; the want whereof, and the Residence of Merchants in one or two set places, giving advantage & opportunity thereunto; they growing Rich notwithstanding; which hath been of infinite prejudice to this Nation.

4. The numerousness of Merchants would necessarily increase the number of Shipping; as may be seen amongst our diligent neighbours, and good & large & usefull Ships too; although hardly any Merchants ships are soe serviceable or to be trusted to, for Warr or for defence and protection, as those that are built purposely for these uses by the State.

5. Mariners would be exceedingly increased (a thing of very great moment) inriched and incouraged thereby; being free to make the best use of their longe, dangerous voyages to the East & West Indies, to Turky, Spaine, France, & all places; & to Trade and buy & sell with their small stocks, & to make their returne in jewells or any Commodities without that feare & danger incurred from Companyes: every ten shillings, as in some Countries, would be improveable; even servants would adventure their wages with them, and they would in shorter time become able & profitable members of the Commonwealth.

6. The numerousness of Merchants would occasion that as to long voyages and far distant places (as to East & West Indies & the like) many would joyne together for one place, & others for another, in waies forseen to be as secure as Companyes, whether to sea or Land dangers: but being in small inconsiderable bodies, States would have noe such temptations to worke upon them, they being of noe considerable capacity to afford them much at any time, unto which Companyes have been ever liable.

7. And although possibly for some few yeares this inlarging of Trade might not produce so many wealthy men, as have been in the same time by Companies, most of them being borne Rich & adding wealth to wealth by trading in a beaten Rode to wealth, wherein noe other had liberty to set his foote, yet it will produce Thousands more of able men to beare publique Charges or what other Publique occasions they may be called unto.

All which, & probably much more may (as is humbly conceived) be justly said in behalfe of an absolute & universall freedome in forraine Trade. [72] And where it is said on the other side, that Companyes merit much for finding out of Trades;* it is very doubtfull who were the first finders, commonly the first are after a time forgotten, and Companyes grow up after the Trade hath been Ripened and is worth the gathering; then upon Pretence of Reformation (the true ground being to hinder the increase of Traders that for their particular gaine might not be abated) they combine togeather into Companyes; this usually hath been their Originall; however the Law gives noe priviledge to inventions that are once discovered, and only fourteene yeares particular use for incouragement beyond discovery; soe as that in this Case is noe plea.

And for their being at great charges;** it being upon a Purchase from prerogative, and against common Right and Common good, the former rule being good is soe farr from deserving Encouragement, that it should not be so much as mentioned; & for having the benefit of mutuall Councells one with another, it is knowne that there is not that Union that is pretended, but that strife & contentions & circumventions doe abound amongst them, the greater lying more heavy upon the more moderate Traders, and the less heavyly complayning of their manifold burthens, by their many unreasonable Orders, Oathes, fines, Censures: soe that however through Custome & Tradition they are wedded ever superstitiously to continue in this way of a perplexed Society, pleasing themselves in spending very much of their time in Courts & meetings about others affaires, doubtless their Lives would be much more Comfortable, and their Trades as gainefull upon the score of Generall & equall freedome, had they hearts & Courages to prove it; Especially considering that their Consciences would not be burthened with taking away others Rights for their owne ad-

* Objections answd: Comp's discovery of Trade
** Their Charges therein

vantage, nor ly under so much hatred for the same as now for many yeares they have done; very many beleiving they have been much injured by them, and some undone.

But all being said that can be, there will not faile multiplicity of words to the contrary, and although the Right & the publique good both are conceived to be undeniably with generall Freedome of Trade; yet the Companyes have at present the advantage of possession, which (all things considered) is very hard on the other side; especially in that the one hath its foundation in Common Right, the other in prerogative, the Common Enemy; so as possibly it were but equall (prerogative being a kind of Forcecible entry) first to put the people into possession of this their Native Right; and then let Companyes or those who have a minde to be such, offer their merits & reasons for their Incorporations, as they shall see cause, if they can justly doe it. [73]

And truly it can hardly be discerned how this Controversy can ever come to a right & good end, so as the Parliam^t shall receive full satisfaction therein, except either they be pleased to proceed to judgm^t upon the ground of knowne Right, & thereupon resolve that Right shall take place as not counting but the yssue must be good: Or else that they will be pleased for Rights sake, to make an experiment of a free Trade for halfe the number of yeares that hath been made proofe of by Companyes; affording only attention thereunto, which is the only thing requisite from Authority. In which time, God preserving the Nation from the banefull interposition of prerogative & its money taking faculty, possibly so great an increase of wealth & strength & prosperity would be seen in short space of time, compared to the long continuance of the contrary Course, as would give a finall & happy solution to this Quere to the contentfull satisfaction even of those that have most contended for the continuance of Companies, & have most opposed Trades freedome; & to the universall good of all well minded people: which is the harty desire of the Author of these weake conceptions, & which with what also is in him, he humbly tenders to the service of your Honours, beseeching your favourable construction of all & every part

As (in duty bound) &c. [74]

Medical Writings, 1654–1696

28

Spirits Moderated

1654
Reprinted from a copy of the pamphlet in the Bodleian Library, Oxford

Spirits Moderated, "By W.W.," was published by J.C. for William Larner, 1654. Christopher Hill identified the pamphlet as Walwyn's in 1974.[1]

Spirits Moderated is almost certainly the first of Walwyn's medical writings. Opening with a statement of his long "Studie and Consideration" of health matters, Walwyn is more cautious than in his later treatises and advises those who fail to achieve desired results to consult physicians and surgeons.[2] At the same time, although he does not style himself "Physitian," Walwyn criticizes potions ordinarily prescribed. He notes the assistance he has had in his work from "a learned, able, and faithful friend" and describes the uses of nine "Vitae" and four aromatic spirits which may be purchased at the house of "Dr. Brooks" in Aldgate.[3] Clearly, the "friend" is Walwyn's son-in-law, Dr. Humphrey Brooke. It is also clear that the pamphlet is an advertisement for potions, some of which are described as useful for any conceivable ailment.[4] Walwyn's subsequent medical treatises further expound his concern for spirits attuned to "humane temperatures," elaborate his condemnations of current practices, and include wise advice about conduct in the presence of the sick. As there is little or no information about the contents of Walwyn's "moderate spirits" their curative powers are unknown, but it is probable that, unlike the drastic medicines dispensed by many seventeenth-century practitioners, Walwyn's potions did no positive harm. Neither a qualified physician nor a scientist, Walwyn conceived his "charitable intentions, sufficiently justified by the Text: The truly Christian Vertu of *Compassion*, being as essentially needful in a Physitian, as in the most tender hearted Samaritan."[5]

Spirits Moderated is reprinted for the first time in this volume.

Spirits Moderated,

And so qualified, as to maintain the true Natural Heat & Radical Moisture of the Body.

Varied and distributed to several Occasions and Necessities, under several Titles.

All pleasing to the Taste, and of great Efficacie in the preservation of Health, Strength, and Chearfulness; and in the Prevention of most, and Cure of many Distempers.

Being a middle, milde, and safe Course, between Diet and Medicine, yet in Aid of Both, by fortifying the Appetite and Digestion; and keeping off extremities, until the Physician can be had.

By *W.W.* a lover of all useful Studies:

And are to be had at Dr. *Brooks* his house in *Dukes Place* within Ald-gate, all the forenoons; and until two in the afternoons; and after sun-set, till bed-time.

Eccles. 3. *So I perceived that in these things there is nothing better for a man, then to be chearful, and to do good as long as he liveth.*

London, Printed by *J.C.* for *William Larnar,* at the Blackmoors head neer Fleet-bridge. 1654.

Being very intent and serious for many years in the Studie and Consideration of the things appertaining to the great Blessing of Health, infinite variety both of Simples and Compounds underwent the enquiry of my Understanding. In which Scrutiny, it hath been long time my constant use to compare their natures and efficacies unto the true Humane temperature, and to observe their agreement or disagreement thereunto, and so to make my Conclusions of the fitness or unfitness of any of them: And by many Experiments finding my Grounds of judging to be good, I have been the bolder therein.

What my Observations, according to this Rule, have been concerning Diet, I judge not much material to publish: for, besides that it would require a very large Discourse, it is more then probable, that it would work [1] but too much scrupulosity and doubtfulness in the Weak, mistrust things they either eat or drink: drawing on a distrust, where there is most need of confidence. For hardly would they turn any thing to true Nourishment, where their mindes misgive them. And when all were done, the custom of provision in most Families is so prevalent, that to endeavour to reduce that under Rules, or to hope for any material alteration therein, were no less a vanity, then to imagine the turning of the swiftest River. And therefore all I have to offer in case of Diet, is, To beware of much Variety at any one Meal; yet let every Meal vary somewhat from each other: To eat what the teeth easily grinde: To grinde slowe and small: and, To be sure not to exceed in quantity, either in Meats or Drinks: To beware of those things are most beloved, and that chiefly in times of mirth and delight: To rest, or be unserious, a small time immediately before and after Eating.

As little have I to say of what my Observations have been concerning Physick or Medicines, though therein also my thoughts have been much exercised: Onely thus much I think needful: That to my apprehension most Simples, as to their vertues and effects, are [2] very much over-boasted in Books, to the general prejudice and mis-guiding of inconsiderate people in times of their necessity. The like also may with too much truth be affirmed of most of the Compositions now extant in our casual Books: not one of a hundred of them answering what is with confidence avouched of them; and are in no measure to be trusted to. And as for those set forth and sent abroad in Books approved and regular, not many of them have due regard to mans proper Temperature: nor are they of so general and familiar use, as many do suppose them to be: Which puts the wary and judicious Physitian to continual additions and alterations of them, in all or most of his prescriptions; and without whose careful advice, they are but dangerously to be medled withal; as many sad Experiences have proved. Though in strong bodies, the inconveniencies and prejudices are sometimes overcome, or appear not but in after-times, and then haply are imputed to some other cause. And therefore when once the distemper goes not off with the help of moderate preventive applications that are certainly innocent and harmless, Tamper not, but in-

stantly to the conscionable and skilful Phy- [3] sitian or Chirurgion, as
the case requireth: It being not more true in any thing then this of
Sickness and Distemper, That without counsel, without sound and
good advice, the people perish. And, as you love your selves and
others, and hate Ingratitude, slight not, nor slightly reward, a Cure
speedily performed.

So, as for Diet, leaving every one to their own experience, with that
little I have advised: And for Physick, to the judicious and conscionable Physitian, in times of Sickness; my thoughts have been employed
chiefly about such things as are conversant upon the borders of both;
endeavouring to produce what might be of good avail to either, and in
the frequent use whereof, Health, Strength, Chearfulness, & Length
of days, might with God's blessing upon good grounds be hoped for.
And upon some consideration, I was not long in resolving, that the
way of Chymistry and Distillation was the most effectual of any, for
my purpose; because thereby I was certain it was possible so to unite
and incorporate things of several natures and temperatures, as to
raise their vertues to what height, and to adapt them to what end I
most desired. [4]

Nor did I set my self to this work out of Curiosity, but upon serious
consideration, That very much was wanting, which I conceived attainable, both for strenthening the Stomack, Heart, and the other Vitals, for clearing and chearing the various passages of the body, and
for preventing of Diseases, or rendering them less difficult to the
Physitian. It having fared in this Art of Chymistry, as in some others,
to have the Mean, the golden mean neglected; it hath scarce been
thought on; and hath been prosecuted without any regard to the true
humane temperature. Indeed, many high and Physical Rarities have
been produced; but they are so far from familiar use, that onely the
learned Physitians are safe disposers of them. And for those much-
famed Spirits and Cordial Waters, which were highest in esteem;
upon examination of their Ingredients, I found, that as in other Studies, so in this, Tradition and Received Opinions had swayed greatly
with their Authors; and that some Considerations and some Species
were wanting in them all; which I understood Sir Walter Rawleigh
valued as his *Magnalia* in all his productions, and through which (as I
have good cause to [5] believe) it was, that he wrought an effect upon
Prince Henry in his sickness, which none else did, or (as then appeared) could do: by which Star, my studies in this Mystery have
been much enlightened; and for want of which knowledg, and re-

spect thereunto, hardly shall the best productions in this kinde of Art (though they may work some present ease) go off without some prejudice to the body.

Those Strong-Waters which are ordinarily sold, I also examined, and to my grief found, that it hath befallen to them, as to most other things which come once to be publikely known, and to be made the common subject of Trade: That how noble and worthy soever they were in the first Inventers, yet Time had infinitely abated their worth; little regard having long time been had in their productions, but how to get Sale; and that not by making so good as they could, but so good onely as they could at the lowe prices they are generally sold for; and that truely is so lamentable, for the most part, as cannot but grieve those who are ingenious amongst the producers: it being impossible they can be ignorant of the uncertainty of the good it doth, and that much [6] better of every sort might be made, then is, if people respecting their own good would go to the price of it; and which doubtless they would do, if men did not strive, by that which is imperfect, to under-sell one another.

So that upon the whole, all things duely weighed, I had this encouragement to proceed towards my productions, That I aimed at a work not of Curiosity, or of Superfluity, but such as was really wanting, and necessary to the Health and Well-being of men, women, and children. With which encouragement, this Principle took impression in me: That to make good things grateful and acceptable, and to be desired, as well for their Pleasantness, as for their Use and Goodness, was in all to be specially aimed at; that as they were good, so people might take them with delight.

With my understanding thus furnished, and with a minde desirous of Divine improvement, I set my thoughts on work to the production of a Spirit of an universal vertue, and of familiar pleasant use. A task which proved of various and vast consideration, and fraught with nice difficulties, and wherein it was very long before I could give [7] my self satisfaction; though at length I did, in my *Radix vitae*.

But through all I aimed at, or have effected, it hath been my great happiness to have had the ready aid and judicious advice of a learned, able, and faithful friend, with whom I could communicate my thoughts upon all occasions: who, although at first he discouraged me from engaging in these Studies, as believing, the utmost had been attained long since by others; yet when I had given him my Objections and Reasons to the contrary, and the Grounds of my apprehensions, and how useful and beneficial my endeavours therein, once perfected, would be unto all sorts of people, he approved my Intentions, and strengthned me in all my Operations.

And that both he and I might rest confirmed, that we had not flattered our selves in ought, he put himself to no small charge, to purchase several sorts of Spirits, sold at very high rates; that by comparing mine therewith, the difference might clearly appear; and submitted the judgment to divers, who, as with one voice, gave sentence on my side. And since, some other Doctors in Physick, and Chirurgions, tasting of se- [8] veral sorts of mine, they have stood in admiration at the kindliness thereof; as if not the heat of the fire, but rather that of the sun had been the raiser and uniter of so clear and natural vertues. One (and he singularly vers'd in this Art) upon the taste of a Glass or two, (as is usual, in my entertainment of friends) professing, he did perceive it to be so qualified, as that he saw not but it might of it self cure a Fever. All which being real truths, I urge as arguments, that I have not run upon these things at adventure; and that what I have herein attained and effected, are not common, but of a peculiar nature, of singular use, and highly vertuous, as, through Gods blessing, I doubt not will be found by all such as shall have occasion to make trial of any sort I draw, Truth being still my refuge.

The several sorts of Spirits moderated which I have already produced, and intend to have always in readiness, are as followeth. [9]

1. Radix Vitae.

A milde, pleasant Spirit, universally useful, being fitly qualified for familiar entertainment, and may be taken to the third glass, two or three times a day: not a wine-glass, but such as I have caused to be made for the purpose.

If by the Healthful it be taken, it heightens appetite, strength, and chearfulness. If by the Weak, in faintings, or the like, it comforts and restores. In Colds, turning to Loosness or Vomiting, it is instantly to be taken, in large quantity, as six of those glasses in two hours time: for so it hath not onely abated, but discharged the Distemper. If heat and burning in stomack, heart, or liver, offend, two or three glasses cool and [10] quench thirst. A little taken as you enter into cold, raw, moist, offensive, or infectious Airs, prevents dangerous distempers and diseases usually following: and a little sipt as you pass out of such unwholsom airs, or out of sultry sweating places; or immediately after any violent stress of the body, infinitely refreshes, and prevents great inconveniences. If there be inclination to a Cough, taken freely, it generally fails not. If Tooth-ake be fear'd or felt, (before extremity, as is in all intended) hold a glass-full about the gums, and keep your breath the while, as long as you can: for so it hath often cured, or given ease. If the head be out of order, or be much opened by sneezing, hicket, or gaping, through winde and emptiness; a glass or two then taken, fills the open passages with a most acceptable flavor; [11] and so keeps Rheums from teeth and eyes. It is an excellent companion at beds head, being of a very digestive faculty, (yea, though of wine and fulness) and inclines to rest. Against Winde, and fits of the Mother, it is of special use, taken to three or four glasses in a short distance of time. Children, to half a glass at a time, take it with certain advantage, upon any distemper, or when Small-pox, Measles, Surfet, Fever, or other infections, are feared; and is also beneficial for clearing and healing those passages of the body usually troubled with gravel. Nor, indeed, can I think of any distemper, wherein, upon serious consideration of the properties of this Spirit, good may not be hoped for, so it be taken in time, and that reasonable distances of time are observed, and not left off too soon. For as where there [12] was cause, it hath stayed Vomiting; so, where cause hath been, it hath occasioned Vomiting: And it hath stayed Loosness, so it hath opened the body, where frequent obstructions have been burthensome. And both warms and cools as there is occasion, as with all sincerity I profess I have frequently and generally found. So that I conceive its Title to be as proper as can be given; being as true a friend to the Life of man, or to that which is the Life of life, his Health and Chearfulness, as the Root is to the Stock and Branches: in all cases, *Amicus certus*, doing all offices of love mildly, pleasantly, and without upbraiding; and in the most doubtful or dangerous, a good support, until the Physitian can be obtained. [13]

2. *Nutrix Vitae*.

Milde and pleasant, and referring principally to such as are troubled with, or fear Consumptions; to help decaying Nature, whether occasioned by age, or other infirmities; its influence chiefly regarding the brest, lungs, defluxions, and to strengthen the parts most liable to wastings. It may be taken in the same quantity, and as familiarly, night and day, by persons of any age, and of either sex, as the *Radix;*

and is a sure Cordial at all times, as carefully respecting true humane temperature, as the *Radix;* and as deservedly holds its Title of *Nutrix vitae,* the nurse or nourisher of Life. [14]

3. *Salus vitae.*

A milde, well-tasted Spirit, but, withal, a most high and effectual Antidote; and so more peculiarly then the *Radix,* attending cases threatning more danger: and therefore if a Surfet, Ague, Small-Pox, Measles, Yellow Jaundies, be suspected, a spoonful to a childe, and two to one of yeers, keeps off either the disease or the danger. But if Pleurisies, Fevers, Frenzies, Pestilence, be doubted; or that there be any wracking tormenting pains, by Gout or Collick, then double the quantity is requisite; and, if cause continue, may be repeated the third time, twelve hours time being allowed between every time of taking it: and in all such uses of it, the parties are to be in bed, and not [15] to drink for six hours after the taking; & when they do, it ought to [be] White-wine-Posset-drink, warm at first, but after as they like, and the more the better. It will procure a moderate Sweat, and dispose to Rest, and to Chearfulness, expelling those earthy damps which are apt to seize the heart at such times, and occasion Sighing. It obstructs not, as most, if not all powerful Cordials use, but leaves the body rather soluble. This was deemed necessary, because some persons may be far from Physitians, and for that I knew not any thing so effectual, so easie to be taken, even by children, and such as the least nauseousness distastes, and hinders from taking any Medicines, though there be never so great extremity. [16]

4. *Vis Vitae,*

Or, *The strength of Life,* being a great and peculiar Comforter of the Stomack, digesting crudities, and discharging all offensive vapors and windy humors; and so aiding the natural faculty, that the food is turned into sound and good nourishment, which is the original and continuation of health & strength. It hath also an appropriate vertue against the Dropsie, Scurvie, and Strangury; and may in quantity as the *Radix* be taken familiarly night and day; there being in this, as in any of the others, a most careful regard had to the true temperature of the body; and stands a real and good Cordial also. [17]

5. *Medulla Vitae,*

Or, *The Marrow of Life,* intended as a second to the *Nutrix Vitae;* purposely differed in taste, that where the one pleaseth not, or not always, the other may. Those who are much weakned by Consumptions, or otherwise, being for the most part nice of palate, and soon cloyed, and therefore are to be allowed some variety. It is a Cordial very precious and pleasant, and may be taken freely by all persons, at all times, being of a fix'd and clear nature, very much conducing to solid strength, and substantial firmness. [18]

6. *Delicia Vitae.*

Highly disposing to a lively Chearfulness, and an utter enemy to all sadness and melancholy; being of a quick and sprightly operation upon the Fancie, yet without any the least violence or disturbance to the Understanding. It also is both milde and graceful, and may be taken as plentifully as any other.

These of my own study, working, and composing, I judged absolutely necessary, for compleating my aims for Health; and in the advised use whereof, I am very confident very much and certain Good may be obtained.

And because divers may be addicted to, and finde comfort by such Spirits as are of ordinary denomination, whose uses are generally known; I have therefore thought good [19] to be furnished, after my own maner of qualification (ever respecting the right temperature) first, with a moderate Spirit of *Angelica,* so ordered, as to be free from its known quality of being somewhat offensive to the head. Secondly, with a moderate Spirit of *Cynamon,* freed also from an offensive dulness in the head and stomack, following the use of this Spice in all Compositions and preparations of it. Thirdly, Spirit of *Mint* moderated, and heightned to a most excellent vertue, being also corrected, as to its known quality of remaining with some harshness over-long upon the stomack. Fourthly, Spirit of *Rosemary,* so rectified, as to be a powerful opposer of all distempers of the head; singularly Preventive against Palsies, Apoplexies, Vertigo's, and the like: being also corrected, as to that long bitterness usually resting in the stomack upon its use almost in every thing. These are strong onely in their Ingredients, but very moderate in Spirit; and so may be taken in much larger quantity then such as are high and strong: the heat proceeding from them to stomack and vitals, being rather nourishing acceptable warmth, then heat; no ways oppressing, as all violent heats do, first or last; [20] but altogether cherishing and refreshing, and is better to be enlarged in quantity, when necessity requires (as in swoonings &c.) then to be higher or stronger in spirit: and it will be very happie for those that can to be satisfied with the use of the most moderate.

Yet because there may be some who through great infirmities and long Custom have been so inured to stronger Spirits, that they cannot without prejudice suddenly leave them, I shal therefore have also in readiness much stronger then my moderate, of every sort that so every one may be supplied as necessity shal require; the strong as well as moderate order'd with the same care of the true human temperature.

These, for the present, and always, are to be had. And if there be any other of the ordinary denominations, of which any person shall be desirous, upon reasonable time given, they may be furnished, with the like cautions and rectitude. So also, if any person be at any time troubled with any infirmity, and he necessitated to reside where he cannot have such accommodation of Physick or other help as is satisfactory; or for any other cause, would be furnished with a moderate, milde, or other safe Spirit, fitly qualified to his disease, they may be readily supplied, upon mature consideration, and skilful advice in any particular case: the accommodation by way of Spirits, being, both for their efficacious vertue, and duration, as commodious, if not more (especially to Travellers) then any other way whatsoever; and carries more life with it. [21]

The place where these are now to be had, is at Doctor Brooks his house, within Aldgate, in a Court over against the George-Tavern.

The time when, is, All the forenoons, and until two in the afternoons, and after sun-set till bed-time.

The Prices for which they are to be sold, are as followeth.

		£.s.d.
Delicia Vitae		01.00.00
Medulla Vitae		00.12.00
Nutrix Vitae		00.08.00
Salus Vitae	the Pinte	00.08.00
Radix Vitae		00.06.00
Vis Vitae		00.03.00

Spirit of Cynamon			00.04.00
Spirit of *Angelica*	the Pinte		00.03.00
Spirit of *Mint*			00.03.00
Spirit of *Rosemary*			00.03.00 [22]

Glasses also I have invented, and have in readiness, of the fashion of a round pillar with a globe neer the top, purposely strong. A servant may safely carry, with little care, two half Pintes, or two Pintes, if need be, and not be perceived to have any about him. One of four or six ounces is necessary for every one (mindful of health) to carry with them in any journey by Water or Land; especially women and children being in company.

Also, I have some small ones with scru'd tops; which one may drink out of in the streets as they go, or in any company, or throng of people, and not be noted, (if that were to be regarded.) And very compleat Drinking-glasses, that are very gracefully fill'd with little more then a spoonful: which are those I intend in my direction of the *Radix*, &c.

And whatever may be thought of these my Advices, by men of strong Constitutions, who are apt to despise all Counsel of this nature; yet since Experience proveth, that a small neglected occasion sends the strongest suddenly into dangerous Sick- [23] nesses, as a small spark neglected fires the strongest house. It may not be amiss, nor burthensome, even for the strongest, betimes, to bethink themselves, and to be provided against what daily befals. But certainly those of weak Constitutions shall be much indebted to themselves, if in some measure they provide not against undiscernable decays, and frequent inconveniences, ever attending frail Nature; wherein the charge is small, the benefit considered: for less then half a pinte of the *Radix Vitae*, served a Friend a journey of an hundred and fifty miles, and back again, refreshing him at all times; and saved him, as he professed, four times the value he should necessarily have spent otherwise, if he had not had it. Those who have much Writing, and are forced to sit long in colds or heats, dull'd and tyred with overmuch work, little imagine the benefit from a small quantity now and then taken, and how much it would enliven them in their business, and prevent Rheums and worse inconvinces: the like also for such as study much, or sit long in Council, tyring their hearts and brains, and subject to heats and colds; a small quantity of it at such times, takes away all tediousness and danger oft-times en- [24] suing. And so also, before, in, and after long speaking and straining of the voice, in places heated by the breath of people, and where one is much engaged and concerned, it hath been approved for chearing the vitals, quickning the Understanding and Memory, fortifying the Imagination and Resolution, without the least fuming trouble to the head, or burden to the stomack incident (at such times) to any other sustenance. Indeed, it may be truely affirmed of any of these Spirits, but especially of the *Radix*, that in watchings, or any stress of the body, or sadness of the heart, discreetly used, it comforts and restores, and resettles all the discomposed faculties both of body and minde; and gently prepareth and makes way for solid food and stronger nourishment. Nor is any danger to be doubted in the use of them; whenas, women with childe and in labour, young children, and people in the weakest condition, take of them, to their great advantage.

The truth is, I have seen, and known, and enjoyed so much good by them, in my family, and among my friends, that it is of great contentment to me, that ever I set my self to this study. Nor did I ever take so much sa- [25] tisfaction in minde, in any thing wherein I ever exercised my self, (next the things of everlasting concernment) as I have done in this employment: nothing of this world being more acceptable, then to be laborious in what is just, and may be profitable to present and future times: being very much blamed, that I had not made them and their uses publike before this time; which yet now, through vain modesty, I was hardly perswaded to.

Almighty God, who is the sole and gracious Author of every vertue in every creature; of the Understanding of man, of his ability with judgement and discretion to adde vertue to vertue, in incorporating, uniting, and qualifying them, so, as to make them profitable and beneficial to the health and comfort of the frail body: Bless these my faithful endeavours to the good of all such as shall make use thereof in his fear, and with submission to his holy will. To whom be glory, with thanksgiving, for ever.

FINIS [26]

Although the fore-mentioned Spirits are useful in most cases; yet, upon mature consideration, it was thought necessary to adde to the former, these peculiar Spirits following:

7. *Succus Vitae;*

Or, *The Juyce of Life:* Very milde, and of an acceptable taste; intended for strengthening the Nerves, and suppressing all stupifying Vapours; and is peculiar in cases of Cramps, Convulsions, Apoplexies, Catarrhs, Vertigo's, and Falling-Sickness. When any of these are onely feared, the small glass-full, (which holds a good spoonful) two hours afore dinner, and the like three hours after dinner, may suffice for Prevention; being so used for a season, as [27] there is cause: but if any of these Diseases appear, and are setled, two of those glasses in the morning, (fasting an hour after) and the same quantity three hours after dinner, and two glasses last at night, will be necessary; and to have a small hand-glass of it always about the Patient; that upon Neezing, or faint Yawnings, or any Vapours arising, any Shiverings or Qualms, a little of it may instantly be sip'd. For, besides the propriety of it to these Diseases, it is a very strengthening Restorative and Cordial also. The price of it is 5s. 4d. *per* Pinte.

8. *Lac Vitae,*

Prepared purposely against the Rickets and Worms in children; and is of special use against the Green-sickness, Stoppage of the Spleen, and diseases of the Mother; a fastener of all languishing parts, and purifier of Humours. To the youngest children, half a spoonful in the morning first, and last at night, may be very profitable; whether in cases of Rickets, or Worms, or both: To those of two or three yeers old, a good spoonful in like cases. Where the [28] Green-sickness is onely suspected, two spoonfuls in the morning, fasting two hours upon it; and the like last at night, will be very proper: But when the Disease appeareth, then not onely so, but two spoonfuls also three hours after dinner; and, if the diseased can be perswaded to have it always about them in a small Hand-glass, and when their appetite calls and importunes them to eat Coals, Clay, Chalk, and the like pernicious things, that feed and nourish the Disease, if then they would refuse those, and, to divert and satisfie their desires, sip a small quantity of the Spirit, it would be very profitable: and to continue this course for a good season; these and the like stoppages being not suddenly abated or removed. The like quantity and time is to be used and observed in the Diseases of the Mother, and to be continued; there being no danger

of any evil effects in the using of it; it being good for strengthning the
Stomack, and confirming the Vitals. The price is 5s.4d. [29]

9. *Sanguis Vitae:*

Provided for such as will not have of the higher rates: It is sound and
wholesome, though not quite so pleasant: an effectual Strengthener of
the Stomack, Heart, and Vitals; an expeller of Winde, clearer of the
Blood, a suppresser of all unnatural Vapours; and very Preservative, in
all Feverish and Pestilential cases. Half a spoonful to a young childe,
and a spoonful to one of three or four yeers, and two spoonfuls to one
of riper age, in cases ordinary; and double the quantity in cases dangerous, may be taken safely, and to great advantage; and so continued
(after two or three hours of distance) as cause shall require. The price is
2s. *per* Pinte. [30]

Note farther, that besides what is mentioned of the vertues and effects
of these Moderate Spirits; the *Vis Vitae* being well rubbed and chafed in
with the hand, in one night recovered a very grievous Sprain in the
small of the back: the party judging by the smell and taste, that it was
good upon such occasions.

Also, that one who received a bruise in his face by the fall of his
horse, that it bled very much, having a Glass of the *Radix* about him,
washing and bathing the sore places therewith, it kept them from
festering, & from turning either blue or yellow, as the manner is; and
without any other means, was perfectly cured.

Also, that a spoonful or two of the *Medulla Vitae*, taken in Red [31]
Cow's milk, or Goats or Asses milk, renders them far more nourishing
and pleasant, to those that usually take them.

And that the like quantity of *Vis Vitae* taken in Milk, makes it wholesome to such as are troubled with the Dropsie, Scurvie, or the like
brackish and waterish humors.

And, that the *Vis Vitae* alone, and the *Radix*, are very proper, taken in
good quantity, as two Ounces in twelve hours time, for such as are
burthened with fleshie or fat bodies, and reduce them to a mediocrity;
and for such as are troubled with shortness of breath.

But since the Ingenious, of themselves, are apt to make Experiments, and thereby further Discoveries of the uses of these milde and
safe Spirits, (in which respect they may safely do it) thus much shall
suffice at present. [32]

There is also newly studied and drawn, a lower sort of *Rosemary,* and Spirit of *Mint,* at 16 d. *per* Pinte; and of *Cinamon* and *Angelica,* at 2s. *per* pinte: which are very mild, sound, and wholesome. So as persons of all qualities may now be furnished, as they have occasion.

FINIS [33]

29

Healths New Store-House Opened

1661
Partially reprinted from a copy of the pamphlet in the British Library

Healths New Store-House Opened, "By Health's Student," was published by Jane Clowes in 1661. The prefatory "To the Reader" is signed by "The servant of your health, W.W." Jack R. McMichael identified the treatise as Walwyn's in 1965.[1]

Healths New Store-House is a twenty-six page pamphlet. The opening pages caution the young to secure health through moderation and wise diet and urge the use of humane physic to assist the infirm and "Elder sort." With some additions, the potions described in *Spirits Moderated* are listed for sale in Postern Street, joining little Moorfields.[2] Some ten pages of case histories with cures effected by Walwyn's medicines are followed by testimonials presented in verse.[3] The case histories suggest that Walwyn's medicines were harmless and he consequently achieved the customary success that results from inactive treatment. The first three case histories are reprinted here.

Healths New Store-House is partially reprinted for the first time in this volume.

HEALTHS NEW STORE-HOUSE OPENED,

Offering to Familiar Use Such Supplies as are Most wanting and Really needful to Humane Frailty.

By *HEALTH'S Student*

London, Printed by *Jane Clowes,* and are to be sold by *John Sweeting* at the *Angel* in *Popes-head-Alley* over against the *Royal Exchange* in *Corn-hill*, 1661.

To the Reader.

Is it uncivil to advise a Reader? possibly it is. And to little purpose to perswade an unbiass'd entertainment of these friendly Aydes: It being the unhappiness of most times, to put off the acceptance of new Discoveries, till 'tis too late, and to leave the benefit to be enjoyed by the next Generation: Jealousie, envy, fear of loss, being oft too strong for Truth: and, if these were not; or could be silent; yet Witt-it-Self is apt to droll away their use.

A Scoff is a leight thing, but often sadly paid for: the Mind highly disdayning to stoop to the embrace of what it hath once despised, though it would save its life: so close is every evil followed with its own punishment.

A merry heart, therefore, joyn'd with Prudence, considers seriously before it judges; thinks thrice before it speaks: and, though apt to jest, yet is most watchfull against injury to any thing, deeming due checks, no bondage.

Why should it be Imagin'd, amid'st so much weakness, that nothing's wanting: or, that things more pertinent cannot be supplyed? Or, why things proposed in nature of friendly and powerfull assistance should not be so indeed? These are tendered to familiar use, such as the weakest Women, and smallest Children, may safely take. In such a case as this then, what cause is there of suspicion, but to tast and try, and so put all, past all dispute? [A3]

Which may be done also without Charge: so confident is the present keeper of the Store-house, which now stands always open, for entertainment of the Ingenious; and to make good its Title: Read on therefore without scruple, and be satisfied with the reality of its provisions, and of the Integrity of

The Servant of your health,

W.W. [A3v]

HEALTHS NEW Store-House Opened.

Though the youngest and the strongest days of life, are the times to lay in for, and to secure, a long-lasting and healthfull Constitution; and the times of health, to provide against the frequent assaults of sickness and distemper, yet to most of either Sex, the voyce of Experience seldome seems better then a mockery. Tell them of their daily wast and expence of spirit, of their continual generating within them the seeds of sickness & diseases, they hear you not; they are for this Gamesom [1] sport, and t'other wild and violent Exercise, and if taken ill, do as others use to do, recover with difficulty, with losse of blood and Spirits, boast of danger escaped, little or nothing regarding how deeply their nature is thereby wounded, and so remain as unapt for counsel as before.

And yet, as it is the surest way to eternal bliss, to *remember thy Creator in the days of thy Youth:* so is it the most certain way, to the happiness of this Life, (which rests very much in mans health and chearfulness), to give diligent heed betimes, to those advices wch respect the well ordering of the Body, both as to Diet, Physick, and Refreshment; and to endeavour after so much skill, at least, as to be able to distinguish between pure and impure, proper and improper, unto man; who being of Creatures next unto the Angels, both in his intellects and constitution, ought to aim at so effectual and so refined a Diet, that the faculties of his Soul, may be accommodated with so exquisite a Spirit and so clear a Body, that there may be a perfect Harmony in the whole Man.

And as these Considerations are most needful in time of Youth, in which the most are apt to set light by all things which most concern them; so are they not to be neglected by those of riper years, who commonly are so much wedded to their customary wayes, that if they keep themselves but any thing hearty and free from pain, deem their Diet good, and themselves Well enough; though they are either sad and melancholy, fearful, superstitious, fretful, passionate, covetous, violent, and revengeful: All which may proceed (and doth commonly) from the impropriety of Spirits in what they feed on, or use for helps; and might be o- [2] therwise without difficulty, to the much more comfort of themselves and their relations.

Nor are the Elder sort unconcerned herein: it being too much from that scrupulosity which dwells in them, and their distrust of all new Discoveries; which makes the younger sort so unapt to give ear, or credit, to Counsels of this nature: What? (say they) have we lived to these years, and do we not know what's good for our selves? and this too, though they are full of infirmities, of which by new Aids they might be discharged; forgetting also that no mere man was ever yet too old to learn.

But hence it is, That although both Diet and Physick, in their best

and largest forces, do but weakly perform their offices; the first of
Sustentation, the other of Restoration; and, that mans health (which
is so great a part of his happiness) is so weakly defended that the
strongest are soon brought upon their knees, whil'st the weak and
sickly in their first illness (the time which makes or marrs the cure)
betaking themselves to dull putrid, and burning helpers (for want of
what's safe and kindly) instead of help betray themselves to further
mischief. Yet all Tenders of farther improvement either to Diet or
Physick, or other Ayde, though never so needful, pretious, and effectual, are hardly and sowerly entertained; and under such re-
gardlesnesse, as if there were nothing but delusion in men, or an
impossibility of adding any advancement to the imperfit Art of
Health.

Through which unpreparednesse, aversnesse, and indisposition to
receive with gladnesse and gratitude, the productions of the studious, it is, That although the defects in Physick, Diet, &c. are so
manifest, that the [3] most Skilful professe they believe, the far better
part lies undiscovered: yet to make any considerable supplies, it sufficeth not by Study, Labour and Industry, to produce things excellent
and necessary; except all possible means be likewise used, to make
their virtues and effects publickly and throughly understood, and
that in such sort, as to convince all scrupulous gainsayers.

These (and such like) are the causes of the present Opening of this
new Store-house of Health, the close keeping thereof being of little
more advantage then a Candle set under a Bushel.

The new Aids therein presented, are in an allowed and Physical
sense Spiritual, untainted, friendly and powerful, as being proposed
for an immediate assistance unto that natural spirit of man, by which
the Soul is united to the Body, and which maintained in its right estate and condition, sustaineth all its infirmities: so as this aid is proportioned for supply of those Forces and Powers, which both Diet
and Physick hath hitherto but faintly furnished; for though properly
they are neither Physick nor Diet, yet are they in aid of both, by
strengthening appetite and disgesture, by rectifying and quickening
all the natural faculties, by opening and clearing all the most secret
passages of the Body: and either speedily discharging the Distemper,
or laying a sure foundation for farther help: besides, by their benign
qualities, and true Humane Temperature, they are the most acceptable Food of the Spirit, the joy of the Heart, and delight of Life; and,
as the genuine heat of the Sun brought into the inward parts: such
and no other are their heat and comfort. [4]

And through whose variety and specifique vertues, hardly any distemper can befall, but there is amongst them for fit relief, even in all
distresses and occasions; and that with such safety and innocency,
that although they have been frequently used by the weakest, both of
men, women and Children, in their most weak and sickly estates; yet
never any thing but good was ever received from them: so as these
arrive happily to take place of all burning, drying, and impure helpers, so much complain'd of in former times, yea and warn'd against
(though little regarded): as in these and the like sensible expressions.
"I advise the healthy (much more the weak) to beware of those burning liquors, which beguile the unadvised World (chiefly in times of
mirth and refreshment): The Life of man (or his Spirit) is in the Blood,
which Blood is mild, and quickly dryed up with violent heat.

"Such as the Blood is, such are the Spirits (for they issue from the
Blood it self) and such as the Spirits are, such is the temper or distemper of the Brain and Heart; and such as the Brain is, well or ill
disposed, so also are the virtues of Imagination, Understanding, and
Memory."

Proper and true humanized helps to Diet and Physick (such as
these), are therefore of more moment then can suddenly and cur-
sorily be imagined: "For, as another learned one saith, The Meat and
Drink which we Diet on, or at least the better part, is terminated
into humours, and at last into Spirits, by whose efficacy, the Flesh,
Nerves, Bones, and all parts of the body are nourished, and augmented, and do, by the never-tyred work of supply, repair decaying
nature. Of so great use are Spirits to the body; and so [5] exceedingly beneficial are al kindly means, wch increase and improve
them: The truth is, in that warfare which is maintained all our life-
long, twixt health and sicknesse, the main Agents in our defence are
our natural Spirits; yea so material unto life, have the wisest ever
deemed them, that they have assigned them to be like little indiscernable Chains. To unite and fasten the Soul to the Body, and which
dissolving, the dissolution of the whole Fabrick soon followeth."

Which office and effect of Spirits, whoever duly weighs, will soon
perceive, that as nothing is or can be of greater importance to mans
health, than the plenteous contribution of Genuine and Benign Spirits; so also that the true Improving Virtue of all things taken into the
Body, dependeth upon their version to the true Humane Temperature. Which being the peculiar qualification and proper work of
those Moderate Spirits with which this little Store-house is furnished,
renders them most kindly and powerful assistants to Humane Frailty,

and an improvement of the Art of Health; of great importance, and not to be despised.

Having thus exprest sufficient to induce a belief, that they are such an assistance to man's Nature as is really wanting, needfull and effectual for supply of the daily wast and expence of Spirit, for heightning and rectifying of Diet, Medicine, and Refreshment; and for relief in all necessities and extremities: Take a view of them in their particular Titles, Vertues, and Uses, as followeth: And as [6]

They are alwayes to be had, at the Star in the Postern-Street, joining to little Moor-fields, *viz.*

	£.s.d.
1. *Amicus Vitae:* Good in all Surfets, Colds, Agues, &c. at the Pint.	00.01.00
2. *Sanguis Vitae:* In all Distempers of Stomach and Bowels, at	00.02.00
3. *Adjutrix Vitae:* To procure Appetite and Digesture: A pleasing Cordial.	00.02.00
4. *Vis Vitae:* For Dropsie, Scurvy, Spleen, Wind, Gravel.	00.03.00
5. *Succus Vitae:* For Convulsion, Palsie, Falling-sicknesse, &c.	00.05.04
6. *Lac Vitae:* For Rickets, Wormes, Green-sicknesse, Mother-Fits.	00.05.04
7. *Radix Vitae:* In Coughs, Shortness of Breath, Passions of the Heart, Vomitings, Looseness, Gripings, &c.	00.06.00
8. *Nutrix Vitae:* For Consumptions Defluxions; a great strengthner.	00.08.00
9. *Salus Vitae:* For all Cases, Infections, Pestilential, or Dangerous.	00.08.00
10. *Medulla Vitae:* For Wastings, and all Weaknesses.	00.12.00
11. *Deliciae Vitae:* Against Sadness, Melancholly; a great Reviver.	01.00.00
12. *Stella Vitae:* (Not so milde) in Swounings, and all Extremities.	00.12.00
13. *Ignis Vitae:* (Very high) in Lethargies, Dulnesse of sight, &c.	00.16.00 [7]

There are also divers others. As, Spirits of *Oranges, Lemons, Cinamon, Cloves, Rosemary, Angelica, Mint, Saffron, Bawn, Clary, Wormwood, Mace, Nutmegs,* &c. the vertues and uses whereof are so generally known, as needs no information.

All extracted with such special regard to the true humane Tem-

perature, as renders them of singular use in all conditions, especially
to such whose weaker Constitutions require Mild and Gentle Helpers; being called Spirits, not for their Heat, but from their sublime
Purity and Vivacity, which are more Spiritual Qualities, and through
which their Operations are not forcible and violent, but (like Benign
Influences) quiet, secret, sure, and most effectual.

So ye have here a large variety of powerful Assistances to humane
Frailty, with whose virtues, who ever throughly acquaint themselves;
may easily and pleasantly recruit their continual expence of Spirits,
and (in their familiar use) add strength and vigour to their usual diet;
solace and recreate themselves with real advantage to their healths,
and supply all sudden exigencies without fear of after-inconven-
iences.

Those now, who know not by sad experience, the difficulty of gaining credit to truths of this kind, might well suppose enough had already been expressed; to perswade at least a tast and tryal of these, if
not a fair and clear acceptation: But so great a prejudice against [8]
new Discoveries, remains upon the minds of the most by abuse of
Deceivers: That what hath been said in their behalf, will hardly prevail for such a reliance upon their use, as their virtues really deserve:
Therefore to silence all opposers, and to obtain their chearful em-
bracement; take here the sure testimony of some instances of their
happy victories and successes in divers remarkable cases and conflicts. Wherein though the Studier and Producer of them have much
to say for daily benefits to himself and relations (too numerous to
recount): yet knowing, whoever duly weighs the other instances, will
easily conclude, They must needs have been most serviceable, where
they have been most employed: he refers wholly to their other performances and cures else where.

The first of which shall be of a Child about four years old, that had
long time been extream ill through a Feverish Distemper: The Parents
using the advice of Physitians and all good means for recovery, yet
prevailed nothing; so that the Child was utterly wasted, and no hope
of Life remain'd; his Father hearing of these Spirits, desired he might
try some of them; so he took a Glass somewhat like a sucking-bottle,
holding about a quarter of a pint of the *Radix Vitae:* Which the Child
liking, kept it allwayes in his hand and fell to sucking of it a little and
a little continually, and grew somewhat lightsome upon it; the Father
seeing it, bestowed as much more upon him, which he took in like
manner; and after that as much again, with which, through Gods
blessing, he became perfectly well.

The second shall be of an Ancient weak Woman fal'n into a tedious fit of sicknesse, Feaverish, and so stuft in her breast, as she was even breathless. Much means [9] of physick by Counsel of physicians she had used, but left hopeless of all. She understanding of my spirits, sent for about a pint of the *Radix vitae:* and a while after that another; and soon after that another: by the use whereof continually a little and a little, she became hearty and well again. But near upon a twelvemonth after fell sick again, and then timely betaking her self to the same remedy, she with somewhat a less quantity recovered. And again about a year after that falling ill again, by the very same means again recovered and continued well for about twelve or fourteen moneths, as well as her years considered could be expected.

The third I shall instance, is a Young Gentleman a student belonging to Cambridge, in so deep a melancholly of minde, so disordered a body, and so dejected and perplexed a countenance, as can hardly be imagined: stomach, and head, and spleen, and liver, and bowels, and heart it self, all confounded: was quite wearied with physick and utterly hopeless of remedy; his understanding being exercised in nothing so much as in proving to himself an impossibility of recovery, and in thwarting all reasonings to the contrary. He was brought unto me by one who had a very good esteem of my spirits; he was very unapt to discourse with me, taking no pleasure to speak at all, so as I was fain to fall into a continued discourse for a good season, shewing some grounds of a hopeful progress towards such effects as in probability could not fail in some reasonable time, even insensibly and pleasantly to restore him to his native (or a better) temperature. It wrought quick and effectual with him, for he was of a sharp and suddain apprehension. We fell into [10] full discourses: and he became willing to tast my spirits which appearing above what he had conceived of them, he became suddainly full of hope, and so fell into the use, principally of the *vis vitae* and Rosemary which indeed were very proper for him: he used of them about three moneths time, yet in no great quantity; but such an alteration did it produce in him, so sprightly confident, discreet, and manly, strong, healthful, and chearful, that there could not be more difference between any two men, then was between what I saw him at first, and what he was at last, to the joy and comfort of himself and all his friends; for which the Author of all means of health be ever blessed and magnified. . . . [11]*

*Pages 11–26, here omitted, include: additional case histories, pp. 11–19; descriptions of conditions meriting prescribed potions, pp. 19–22; testimonial rhymes to "W. W." and his moderate spirits, pp. 22–26. (Editor's note)

30

A Touch-Stone for Physick

1667
Partially reprinted from a copy of the book in the National Library of Medicine in
Bethesda, Maryland

A Touch-Stone for Physick was printed by J.W. [J. Winter] for Benjamin Billingsley in 1667. The introductory "To the Ingenious Reader" is signed "W.W." The book is correctly attributed to Walwyn by S. Halkett and J. Laing.[1] Material in *Touch-Stone* is repeated in various editions of *Physick for Families,* and the opening pages of *Touch-Stone* are reproduced verbatim in the posthumous 1681 edition of *Physick,* which was published over Walwyn's name.[2]

Touch-Stone is a volume of 100 small pages. The title page asserts Walwyn's aversion to "Purgers, Vomiters, Bleedings," and other "disturbers of Nature," and the text describes the "Marks and Characters" that serve as a *"Touchstone* of Medicine" fit for consumption.[3] Unlike Walwyn's other medical texts, *Touch-Stone* does not list his medicines and prices but recounts many case histories which he concludes prove the value of his potions[4]—"even in the Pestilence," during which Walwyn finally retreated from London but received word of cures and prevention of the plague attributed to his medicines.[5]

Touch-Stone is partially reprinted for the first time in this volume.

A TOUCH-STONE FOR Physick,

Directing By evident Marks and Characters to such Medicines, AS Without Purgers, Vomiters, Bleedings, Issues, Minerals; or any other disturbers of Nature, may be securely trusted for Cure in all extreamities, AND Be easily distinguished from such as are hazardous or dangerous:

Exemplyfied By various Instances of Remarkable Cures performed solely by such Medicines.

LONDON, Printed by *J.W.* for *Benjamin Billingsley*, at *Gresham-
Colledge*-gate, near the Church in *Broad*-street 1667

To the Ingenious Reader.

Since the generous breeding of most Physitians, in reason
may be presumed to have freed them, more from envy and
partiallity, then less Phylosophical professions; though here and there
some few may appear perverse: yet now there seemeth no cause to
doubt their ready and cheerful entertainment, of whatsoever can be
proposed for support of humane frailty, or relief of distressed patients, and the rather because of their frequent, and free converse
with the most noble Virtuosi, those ample encouragers of all improving Studies. [A2]

The scruple being rather, how this Discourse will be digested by
those who are furnishers of all sorts of ingredients; and also by the
preparers of Medicines: for since self denial, may not like their *Semper
vivum* be alwaies green and florishing. If it cannot be proved, that
both shall be no losers; how can it be expected they should freely
yeild to such an alteration, as this Touchstone imports, though the
whole Society of practisers should deem it requisite.

For abatement therefore, of any proness to opposition, it may be
needful to give this assurance to all those, who furnish either forraign
or domestick materials, that in this [A2v] sublime and more refined
way of Medicine; not less but much larger quantities, are likely to be
used, in that where much can yeild but very little, much of necessity
must be employed.

Then for the preparers, and conveighers of Medicines, between
Physitians and Patients: were all expressly to be regulated, according
to the Marks and Characters herein specified, no loss at all appeareth;
for in this pure, liquid, powerful, pleasant and durable way; not one
spoonful would ever perish or decay upon their hands: neither Time,
nor Winters cold, nor Summers heat, in the least impairing their virtue or efficacy: a recom- [A3] pense far surmounting all objections, if
what they yearly lose by perishable ware, be but duely weighed.

Nor is this new way less vindicative of their reputation, not only
seldomer failing of their desired success in Cure, but not the least
quantity ever cast away by their Patients, being such as is serviceable

to them sundry waies, which how many hundreds if not thousands of pounds would be saved yearly in Patients purses, may be worth their consideration, nor is there many of their present preparations, but what by solicitous Study, and ingenious Art, may be converted into this clear stream of Physick. [A3v]

Besides, where one now in the present way of Medicine they are in, makes use either of the Physitians advice, or of any other preparations; and when they do, do it but meerly for necessity, as dreading the trouble, tediousness, and danger thereof, well nigh as much as sickness it: In this pure, pleasant, and safe effectuall way, twenty at the least would be frequent and familiar therewith, no time of the year being unseasonable, no scrupulosity in the dyet, no pains nor gripes in operation, nor tiresome confinement, to house or chamber, (unless when extreamity enforceth) nay when they are proper for all persons in all weaknesses, and distempers, from [A4] the Cradle to the oldest age: may be also taken in Dyet for improvement thereof, and in Recreation as the most pleasant and reviving refreshment, what infinite quantities must necessarily be employed.

So that they could not but be vast gainers every way, both in profit and credit, by so happy an alteration, bringing also to the Physitian, besides the respects and rewards usual, if not more and greater.

The inestimable contentment of a quiet mind, resting securely and calmly amidst all occasions and extreamities, with this sweet repository that he runs no hazard with his Patients, and yet supplies them with the utmost helps imaginable: so [A4v] that both the Physitian, the provider of Materials, and the preparer of Medicines, are all in an assured condition, unto whom I wish one more were added, so far am I from desiring the prejudice of any: And that is Studiers and Inventers of Medicine, known only by their faithfulness and the fruit of their productions: To be encouraged therein, and not to be diverted with any other part of Physick, or Practise; for if truly such, they will never be many, nor desire any other business, being not such by Education, but by Birth and Nature; for some Title whereunto I appeal, to the just restoration of the pallat, to its pristine jurisdiction, in discerning [A5] Virtues, and choise of Materials: And to the successeful conception and appropriation of the true humane temperature, that *Clavis Medicinae,* not consisting in the equality of the Elements or Humors (as most may imagine) but in the Proximity and Coherence of the spirit, and all parts of the Medicine, with the spirit of the true Humane constitution; without which, those who traffick for Medicine, may be as coasters; but no considerable new discoverers: This being to the Arts advancement, like Columbus his card to his discovery of the Indies, who though long seeming but as a vain boaster, yet those who first gave credit found it, far exceeding [A5v] his report; and so I doubt not it will prove here, the Medicines herein proposed for an example, never doing harm, but good where ever they were taken, many wishing they had known them sooner, never any repenting their use: And if the Body be more worth then Rayment, and Health to be preferred before Riches, it being not in Mountains of Gold, to give that exemption from the pains, fears and miseries of sickness, which resides in a benign powerful Medicine; your good acceptance of these overtures, will never blemish either that Virtue or that Prudence, for which you will be ever highly honored, By Your

Most humble Servant, W.W. [A6]

A TOUCH-STONE for PHYSICK, &c.

Though of all the Natural Sciences, that of Physick, and therein, the Medicinal part is of most Concernment to Humane Happiness: yet is there hardly any Art, Science or Mystery, whether for Delight, Conveni- [1] ence or Necessity, but what hath gotten the start thereof, by many degrees, of real Improvement; Whilst Physick, the chief of Arts, instituted for the preservation of Man's health, without which all his felicity in a moment is turned into gall and bitterness; hath so little to glory in, that notwithstanding infinite endeavours of the studious, with the utmost help of Chymistry; the most skilfull do ingenuously confess, They believe the far better part rests still undiscovered.

A Truth too evident, and the sad causes thereof too manifest to be doubted; yet so accompanied with unpleasing reflections, both upon the Speculative, Inventive and Practick part, that I willingly decline all repetition of whatsoever upon my enquiry fell into observation.

Onely as to the most Important, and which render'd the whole Fabrick craz'd and tottering: I must needs say, That [2] to my Apprehension, the aims of the Studious, Inquisitive after the Conservation or Restauration of Man, the sole Subject of Physick, had not been taken aright, nor in due measure proportioned to so peculiar and so refin'd a Being.

For, permitting my Understanding its free course throughout the

Wilderness of Physical Notions; at length my thoughts thus fixed: That the Original constitution of Humane Nature, being at first but One, however since deviated into various Temperatures and Complexions; and being far more sublimed, than any other Creature on Earth, to render his Body a fit Instrument for his Divine contemplative and discoursive Soul. The whole mass of assistants assigned by this Art, for his supportation or recovery, appeared either so weak and impotent; or else so course, casual, violent and dangerous; as seemed very unsuitable [to]* so sublime a Nature. [3]

Upon which, I conceived it undeniably requisite, that all provisions and preparations designed for help of Mankind, ought in special manner, both in purity, efficacie and pregnancy, to hold due and just proportion to the peculiarity of the true Humane Temperature or Constitution: and that all administrations of a gross, impure, or improper, unbenign nature, must needs produce cross and perverse effects; and could not but be the main occasion of the manifold failings and miscarriages so frequently and apparently discernable in Physick.

With which conclusion being very much satisfied; my hopes soon led me into persuasions of a possibility of raising new ayds both to Diet and Medicine, so refined, and so suited to the true Humane Constitution, and so appropriate to distinct Infirmities, Distempers, and Diseases; that, administer'd in any case, and to any complexion, though [4] never so far distant from the original: should really intend its reduction, and without any disturbance of Nature, by Loosners, Vomiters, Bleedings, Issues, Shaving the head, Clisters, Blisters; and without Minerals, or any hazardous or nauseous Ingredients; might rationally be relyed on in all extremities: And this solely from their powerful friendliness to Humane Nature, and efficacious virtue in extinguishing the venomous causes of Diseases.

In pursuance whereof, depending very much upon my palate, long exercised in determining of Virtues, (by which, Compounds, as well as Simples, became equally liable to my assistance;) and pressed thereunto by an express propensity in Nature: In process of time I proved so succesful in choice of materials, and in heightning and uniting of Excellencies; as by degrees to raise a large variety of so kindly and so powerfull Medicines, That not onely have ap- [5] proved themselves serviceable to the Healthful in Diet and Refreshment; and to

* In verbatim copy of the passage in *Physick*, 1681 edition, p. 3, "to" is inserted. (Editors' note)

the weakest women and children in manifold infirmities; but in greatest extremities, (all other means failing) have frequently been prevalent, beyond all hope or expectation; and this too (according to my ayms) without any outward Violence or inward Disturbance of the body, either by Vomiters, Loosners, Minerals, or any other Disturbers of Nature.

Insomuch that their various, weighty and remarkable performances have long time represented their peculiar qualifications, as so many evident marks and characters of Real Medicine, whereby to distinguish such as are (from such as are not) to be trusted in cure, or fit for Humane Constitutions.

And to my own particular; ever since I understood them, they have served me as a real Test or *Touchstone* of Medicine; using no other, for any that rely on me [6] in any occasion, but Medicines of their qualities; wherein having been succesful, to my own satisfaction, and others approbation, yea even to admiration: I have thence entertained some apprehensions, that it could not be taken amiss, but rather as a fair progress towards the Arts Improvement, to publish these Marks and Characters, as a competent *Touchstone* for probation of Medicine in general; especially of my own; and thereby possibly come to be somewhat better understood, as to my Physical Conceptions, than hitherto I have been; some having been over forward to imagine, all I aymed at, or had attained, amounted to no more, but onely some pleasant preparations and productions, serving merely for Refreshment and Recreation, without any material effect or prevalencie upon Distempers and Diseases. Whether it be so or not, and how far they are mistaken, who thus censure, the whole Discourse will [7] plainly evince: and haply may prove a safe and sure Guide to distressed Patients, what kinde of Medicines to avoid, and what to embrace, in any their necessities.

The Marks and Characters, with their Grounds or Reasons annexed, are as followeth.

As, First, I conceive, a benign kindly Medicine ought to be Liquid: and this, for avoyding that difficulty and disturbance incident in the disgesture of those of grosser substances; and likewise for the evil consequence of their remaining earthy parts in the coats, films and crevices both of the stomach and bowels, which generally so clog and tire the natural faculties to expell them; as instead of that quiet and ready help requisite in Sickness, makes Nature a new and tedious work in their avoidance; as whoever notes shall find in a [8] sad dejection of Spirit when they have done their best. Whereas things Liquid, if milde, disturbe no part, puts Nature to no stress in ordering them to its best advantage, nor leaves any remains for after Inconveniences: but through their gentle Vivacity, and insinuative Virtues, (like the Waters of Life) immediately prosecute the prime End for which they were taken.

II. I conceive they ought not onely to be Liquid, but transparently clear and pure, exempt from all grossness of residence or taint of rankness. It being possible to have liquid things as bright and clear as Chrystal, which yet in smell no carrion ever exceeded in noysomness; a tang whereof, any one that notes will find, in most of what is used for Refreshment or for Relief, in first Illness. Which should be heedfully avoided, because by things course, rank, or tainted, the whole sourse of Bloud and Spirits become insensibly to be corrupted; all [9] faculties debilitated; and the best and strongest constitutions, by degrees, betrayed into the worst distempers; therefore, like Virtues descending from above, they ought to be immaculately clear and pure.

III. Such Medicines as may be trusted in cure, I conceive, ought, as much as is possible, to be Pleasant, and to suffice in small quantity; that they may not in the least be burdensom, but at first touch appear like true and chearfull friends, that make the distressed heart leap for joy; no sooner tasted, but Nature bids them welcom, and easily disposes them to their proper service. *Bonum & jucundum,* as in Divine benedictions, being never to be separated in Physick.

IV. Such Medicines with the precedent qualities, ought especially to be highly virtuous and powerfull, and which at first tast, by their lively, sprightly, yet milde quickness, should [10] evidently appear such stout, long-breath'd valiant Champions, as are thoroughly qualified to tug, grapple with, and subdue the most violent, venemous, pestilential enemies of Mans Health and happiness: And yet withall so milde, gentle and manageable, (like our blessed Lamb and Lion couched together) as Children in greatest weakness may partake with safety; and for assurance that they are such, the prescribers, if desired, are to take the like quantity in sight of the Patient or Relations, for the more undoubted assurance of its innocence, and that it partakes not of any hazardous ingredient.

V. Such Medicines as may comfortably be relyed on in cure and in cases of extremity, ought to be so truly friendly to Humane Nature, that if taken by man, woman or childe, in health, shall no ways move their bodies, but shall nourish and strengthen them: and yet if by any in Sickness, the very same Medi- [11] cines, taken in the same quantity, shall in due time either open or binde, vomit or stop vomiting, sweat or restrain sweating, give sleep or abate excessive sleeping; as the instant necessity of the body most requireth, or most conduceth to recovery. And this, as the most distinguishing character, I conceive, is most to be noted by the Ingenious, and to be insisted on: For how can that possibly appear truly to deserve the Name of a Medicine, or real helper of the sick, or be rationally deem'd to work upon a distemper; which, if given to a well person, shall either binde or loosen him, vomit, or sweat, or lay him asleep, even as it doth those who are sick? and which if given to never so sound a person in larger quantity, shall purge him, or vomit him into his grave, sweat out his last breath, or sleep him past ever waking to this life; which are the known qualities of most things given in Sicknes: So as with much more likelihood they might [12] be stiled Disturbers of Nature, (for how else do they thus work upon the healthfull?) rather than Medicines and friendly Helpers, whose good qualities are with tenderness to cherish and retain all that's good in the body, and without the hazardous violences of Purgers, Vomiters, Bleedings, Issues, Shaving the head, Clisters, or Blisters; and without Minerals, or other nauseous or dangerous Ingredients, to exclude onely what is evil; and not, Bedlam-like, turn good to bad, and then madly throw out all together; which are the properties not of Heavenly and peaceable, but of Infernal wrathful Spirits.

VI. And lastly, Such Medicines as may be justly relyed on in cure, that they may be known to be compleat, ought not to be perishable Commodities, which argues such defects, as renders them unlikely to hold out upon a long march; being apt to tire, grow faint, sick, weak and heartless, before, or when [13] they come in sight of, or near the enemy, therefore they ought not to want this sure Mark, (Close stopt) to keep Good for Years (in all Climates) and in full strength and vigour without any the least diminution; much after the similitude of an endless life, which is no small assurance of their real virtue and efficacy. Then having all the other precedent qualities conjoyned in every medicine; and a large variety of them, (variety being singularly useful) you have medicines most Masculine and Heroick, such as may confidently be relied on for Cure, and be easily distinguished from those which are hazardous, or dangerous.

All which being neither difficult to remember; nor hard to be understood; and such as cannot be denyed to be both pertinent and suffi-

cient for proof and assurance of Medicine: Admit patients and all the
Ingenious every where should henceforth hold Practitioners [14]
strictly to these Characters; accepting or refusing; accordingly: what a
mighty Improvement would it soon occasion in Physick: By necessarily enforcing all Students and Practitioners, to set themselves to
that which the Noble Hippocrates made the chief Character of a Physician worthy Estimation *Viz. By Study and his own Industry, to bring to
light something that was not known before, and better known than unknown,
or at least to perfect something that was imperfect before.*

And then as Excellencies for real use in Physick could not but every
where abound; so would such a Test established, naturally tend to the
fixation of this too much uncertain Art; put a period to the many
Contrarieties and Contradictions of Practitioners, be an occasion of
less harm and danger, of more pertinency, certainty, and security in
Cure: and abundantly more enable them to perform with Comfort
[15] the infinite trust reposed in them, especially by their more Ingenious and Noble Patients in their extremities.

These are the Marks and Characters conceived requisite for the test
of Medicine; and the desirable Advantages which in good probability
would ensue upon such an establishment.

Nor let any suppose, as some may be apt to do, (who are loath any
thing should prove of weight, but what they themselves discover)
that these Characters or Marks of real Medicine are but meer imprac-
ticable notions, set forth to amuse the credulous with wonders that
never were nor never will be found in medicine: For silencing all such
slight suggestions, since such medicines are best known by their
Fruits: It will be best and most proper to let them speak for themselves in some of their manyfold instances of Cures performed by
them, in various [16] and dangerous cases: and are as followeth. . . .
[17]

. . . .
                                                                    *

These, though not neere the whole of what might have bin collected, of cures of this kind—much less of those who have cured
themselves by a draught or two in their first illness, and so escaped
fits of sickness, and courses of Physick; nor of such who have dayly
supplied their spirits, and fortified their natures, by their use in dyet
and refreshment, unto which they are essentially proper; yet I conceive are abundant proofe of their real virtue and effecacy: and that

* Pages 17–98, here deleted, are largely case histories of remarkable cures.
For examples, see *Healths New Store-House*, pp. 9–11. (Editors' note)

those marks and characters arising from them, are not irrationally proposed, as a test or Touchstone of real Medicine; and for distinction of such as may be thoroughly trusted in cure; from those which are not, and that with out, any outward violence, by Bleedings, Issues, Clisters, Blisters, &c. or any inward disturbance to the body, by Loosning, Vomiting, or other enforcements by Minerals, may suffice in all [99] cases and extreamities, to the comfort of all the ingeniuous, both persons and families, who taking this for their guide, need not hence forth be so much to seek for reliefe as formerly, in times of sickness and necessity. Every of those Medicines pointed at, being alwaies to be had,

At the Star in the Postern by little Moorefields, London, 1667.

FINIS [100]

31

Physick for Families

1669, 1674, 1681, 1696
Editions of 1669 and 1674 are partially reprinted from copies of the volumes in the National Library of Medicine (1669 edition) and the Folger Shakespeare Library (1674 edition). The 1681 and 1696 editions were consulted in the National Library of Medicine.

Physick for Families, 1669 edition, was published by J. Winter; the prefatory "To the Reader" was signed "W.W. Healths Student. At the Star in the Postern by little *Morefields, Lond.*"; the volume was licensed by Roger L'Estrange, 10 June 1669.[1] *Physick for Families*, 1674 edition, "By W.W. Healths Student," was published by J. R. The posthumous 1681 and 1696 editions, "By William Walwyn Physician," were also published by J.R.; the title pages are similar to that of the 1674 edition.

In 1944 Wilhelm Schenk, knowing only the 1681 edition of *Physick*, identified Walwyn the physician as Walwyn the Leveller.[2] Five years later F. N. L. Poynter described the two earlier editions of *Physick* and the 1696 edition.[3] The 1669 and 1674 editions have extensive overlaps with some emendations and include repetitions and extensions of parts of the earlier medical writings.

The 1681 and 1696 editions, after the preface to the reader and the index, open with fifteen pages taken from the beginning of *Touch-Stone* through the "Marks and Characters" requisite to good medicine.[4] The posthumous editions add nothing to the medical writings that Walwyn published in his lifetime, and the texts of the two editions are virtually identical. The 1696 edition adds running heads and there are three variations on the title page: the spelling of Physician as "Physitian" (1696); the misspelling of "Londn." (1696); the place where the volume is to be sold.[5] The 1696 edition eliminates the "Advertisement" on the last page, verso, of the 1681 unpaged index:

The Medicines are to be had at Mr. Richard Halfords being the Corner-house in Finsbury, at the Upper End of Little Moorefields, whose Assistance the Author of these Medicines, hath made use of for many years, in the preparation of them, and to whom being link'd by the tyes both of Nature and Friendship, he Communicated all his Secrets and Receipts.[6]

The extracts from the 1669 and 1674 editions are reprinted for the first time in this volume.

PHYSICK for FAMILIES,

DISCOVERING *A safe Way, and ready Means,* WHEREBY Every one at Sea or Land, may with Gods assistance be in a capacity of Curing themselves, or their Relations, in all Distempers or Extremities; WITHOUT Any the Hazards, Troubles, or Dangers, over usual, in all other wayes of Physick.

Prov. 9. 12. *If thou be wise, thou shalt be wise for thy self, but if thou scornest, thou alone shalt bear it.*

London, Printed by J. *Winter,* And are to be sold by *Robert Horn* in *Gresham Colledg* Court, 1669.

To the Reader:

Courteous Reader,

To love our Neighbour as our selves, though it be very good, yet since it signifies to make them as happy as our selves: Our judgments had need be right, both as to our own, and their good: Or we may soon render them very miserable, when we least intend it, by perswading them into the same path of ruine which (through mistake) our selves would have taken for our preservation.

And therefore, that every well-willer may be truly qualified to be a friend, nothing is more needful then to get Wisdom, and understanding in all the main occasions of this life, that so as our affections make us apt and ready to advise, our well digested Reason and Conscience may render our Coun- [A2] sel always good, and profitable to those we give it.

PHYSICK
FOR,
Families:

OR,

The new, Safe and powerfull way
of PHYSICK, upon conftant
proof Eftablifhed;

Enabling every one, at Sea or Land, By the
Medicines herein mentioned, to cure
themfelves, their Friends and Relations,
In all Diftempers and Difeafes.

Without any the trouble, hazzard, pain or danger,
Of Purgers, Vomitters, Bleedings, Iffues, Glifters,
Blifters, Opium, Antimony and Quickfilver, fo
full of perplexity in Sicknefs.

By *W. W.* Healths Student, At the *Star* in
the *Poftern* by little *Morefields*.

Prov. 9. 11. *For by me thy Dayes fhall be multiplyed, and the years of thy life fhall be in-
creafed.*

LONDON,

Printed, by *J.R.* and are to be Sold by *Robert
Horn,* at the South-entrance of the
Royal-Exchange, 1674.

Title page of *Physick for Families,* 1674.
(Folger Shakespeare Library)

And truly if in any thing these are useful Cogitations, they must needs be so in those of Physick; wherein as there are vast differences, and smallest Errours, often mortal, so unless those who in times of sickness are forward to perswade, are not also in good measure able to distinguish what's safe and powerful, from what's hazardous, painful, and dangerous both as to Methods, and Medicines, their friendship would much better be shewed in silence, than in speaking, or advising.

Which, yet, being but cold comfort; And that to get knowledge is every ones duty, that they may be helpful in time of need. None should either stand averse from endeavouring, or be discouraged in their hopes of obtaining so much skill at least: As in an instant, to make a safe and rational choice where the difference is so manifest; as in your serious reading of this Discourse will plainly appear, even in this (hitherto) much obscured Science of Physick.

The Scripture saith, a merry heart doth good like a Medicine: And if so, in true consequence, ought not the Operations and Effects of kindly and real Medicines, to resemble those of a merry heart? certainly it can be no absurdity to expect it.

Now, who knoweth not that a merry heart joyned with vertue and prudence (for such only the holy [A2v] Scriptures can intend) performeth all its good, by insensibly dispersing a most lively and benigne influence throughout the body, to the joy, contentment, and felicity of the whole man, without any the least disturbance, pain, or danger whatsoever?

And if Medicines are, or can be found, through whose friendly and powerful operations, all sadness, and sickness, may without pain or trouble be totally Expelled and Exstinguished, why should they not be known, sought after, and chearfully embraced?

But that there are such in being, having throwly perused this Discourse, you will be well assured; and that they are securely to be trusted to for cure in all cases. The manifold Instances of their real performances, will ascertain past all scruple. And which throughly read, & noted in all particulars, will soon enable you to cure your selvs, or friends, & to find what is most proper in those, or any other Distempers; and by their Marks you will really distinguish them from such as are improper, hazardous or dangerous.

Their particular Titles, Vertues, and Uses, where to have them, and how to order them, as necessity, or occasion requires, you will also clearly understand.

And though men for the most part seldom value any thing, though never so useful and precious, untill they immediately need them. Yet experience will tell you, it is neither safe nor prudent at such times to be to learn: But rather to be aforehand with all necessary knowledge; To give due and just regard to every thing according to its worth: And [A3] so to stand like wise and wary persons, always provided and prepared in every Exigence and Difficulty of Sickness or Distemper: To take the surest course, and to give the soundest and most assured advice to Neighbours, Friends, and Relations in all their extremities. It being in this as in all other parts of Wisdom, abundantly more happy, to be able to give, than to stand in need of Counsel.

And then, being rightly informed, if (as your judgments shall determine most proper) you shall furnish your selves for your Families, your Journeys, Voyages, or other occasions, with Gods blessing you may set your hearts at rest, as being better enabled to administer safe and effectual relief, to your selves, or Relations, then any other wayes you could either hope or imagine.

An accommodation and happiness of no mean degree, not known to Forreign Nations. And indeed, more worth than Jewels and richest Mines: for such in truth and reality is speedy Restoration from tedious sickness to inestimable health; without trouble, pain, or danger; the sole effect of these pure and powerful Medicines: And could not but be generally so esteemed, did not Collumbus still want a gown in England.

Despicit? Nescit.   W. W. Healths Student.

At the Star in the Postern by little *Morefields, Lond.* [A3v]

PHYSICK FOR Families, &c.

Though the Example of the good Samaritan, in pouring Wine and Oyl, into the Wounds of the half-dead Traveller, should not expresly warrant a sole reliance upon those Excellent Materials in all like cases, being not so determined by Divine Authority; yet being both of them blessings of high account, *Where their Wine and their Oyl encreaseth*, bringing gladness to mans Heart, and Chearfulness to his Countenance, of so safe, and so familiar a Nature, as to be both substantially nourishing, and most [1] delightful Diet. It cannot but imply and perswade, that whatsoever is administred in times of sickness, or extremity, should not only be highly vertuous, respecting the Distemper, but also of so benign, pure, and truly Humane Temperature, that they may be taken with as much security and delight, as the most wholesome and pleasant Diet: And which if admitted into Diet, may be as advantagious to the conservation of Health and life, as in the most venomous Distempers they are unto recovery: inducing also a belief, that until Medicine be so ordered, (let who will be the confident prescribers) Physick; the great sustainer of mankind, is not in its true exalted state, but in a sordid, low, and perplexed condition unfit for Humane Constitutions, and not to be trusted in times of sickness and extremity.

And from such Contemplations as these, it hath been that I have deemed nothing proper to be given in sickness to any person, old or young, but what may be safely, and profitably taken by those in health.

And if from hence, and out of my tender regard to the distressed and dismal times of sickness, I have indeavoured all I could, and bent all my Studies for the obtaining of such kindly, and Powerful Medicines, as thereby safely to avoid, and wholly to abandon all those troublesome, painful, hazardous, and dangerous ope- [2] rations, and Ingredients too to usual in practice; (It being too sad a time to add affliction to affliction) as I have much comfort therein; so I conceive my charitable intentions, sufficiently justified by the Text: The truly Christian Vertue of Compassion, being as essentially needful in a Physitian, as in the most tender hearted Samaritan: and without an eminent proportion whereof (what ever other parts or Arts abound) none ought, in justice, to be owned as a competent Helper, in times of such necessity.

Nor did I decline the common Road of Physick, for any other cause Imaginable, but for its manifest uncertainty in Principles, Roughness, Harshness, and Cruelty in Methods, Impropriety, Impotency, and danger in Medicines. Nor found out any way to relieve my understanding, when first at so great a loss, but by withdrawing my thoughts from out the wilderness of all the uncertain Notions and Guesses of Philosophy, and giving them free liberty in the walks of Scripture; Where the true Original of man, the sole subject of Physick (hid from Phylosophy) being apparent, and the sublimity of the true Humane Temperature thence deducible; I soon discerned that all miscarriages in Phisick, proceeded from the admission of gross, virulent, and dangerous materials into practice, together with other Rugged and

Boysterous handling; And for want of assimulating, all [3] Helps, and Helpers in times of sickness, more agreeable to the distinct purity of mans Nature.

Upon which, noting with great circumspection, every the least Glance, or Lustre, of this my surest Guider, the Scriptures, insinuating any spark of instruction towards the appropriation and power of Medicines. It was not long before I apprehended a possibility of obtaining all Effects attainable in Physick, solely by kindly and pleasant means, void of all noxious operations, or mischievous Materials.

In persuance whereof, I concieve it very conducible to my end, to confine every of my Medicines to such qualifications (of what specifick intention soever) as (being such) should necessarily answer all my aims and expectations; and which since, proving in their performance accordingly, I have deemed it a considerable advantage to the Science of Physick, to propose those their peculiar qualities, as sure Marks of Real Medicines, whereby to distinguish those which are fit and proper for Humane Constitutions, and Rational, to be relied on in all cases, from those which are not, as by the sequel of this Discourse will more fully appear.

An undertaking in the whole, of so strange a Difficulty, that I have many times since wondred I was not astonished, and utterly disheartned at the first conception.

Nevertheless, assisted as I have said, and (as I [4] verily believe) with very Effective Propensions in Nature, and with a Palate suitably exercised in the Discerning of the Spirits, and bent to the Discovery of the Vertues of materials, whereby all Compounds, as well as Simples, lay open to my assistance, with a mind thus furnished, and prepared, resolving neither to flatter, nor indulge my self in trifling insignificant Attainments, nor to be startled in so Worthy and Needfull an Attempt, by any Difficulties; with due Submissions, I proposed my End, made choice of Materials, wrought them into the consistence and Qualities of real Medicines, satisfied my Palate in their tast, proved them upon my self; and as cause required, either altered, or immediately fixt them for general Use and Practise.

In which way of proceeding, in process of time, I became so happy, as to satisfie my reason, in the Production of so large a variety of kindly and powerful Medicines, so Equally proportioned to mens Natures, and so peculiarly qualified for particular Distempers, as sufficed for all Occasions and Necessities: And which ever since they had a being, have with that constancy wrought so many remarkable Cures; that I now deem my self bound in duty to propose them as the

most proper *Physick for Families,* according to the Titles, judging I
should highly offend, if I should fail of my uttermost en- [5] deavour
to beget a right and thorow understanding of their performances.

And this, not only because of the manifest good they bring with
them, in their use (with safety) but also for that absolute exemption
from all those troublesome, painful, hazardous, and dangerous proceedings, with which the general course of practise is sadly and grievously encumbred.

A brief view of the particulars whereof, may here be needful, that
every one may see and lay to heart, how much more dreadful, painful, and Dangerous the afflicted times of sickness are thereby rendred, and what an unspeakable happiness it would be both to all
Conscionable, Compassionate Physitians, and all considerate Patients
to have such Medicines alwayes in readiness, by which all those Evils
and Inconveniences may Safely, and securely be avoided.

The first of which molesters of the sick, in the usual course of practice, are commonly Glisters; which how innocent and harmless
soever they are esteemed, are nevertheless attended with more Trouble and Danger then is considered: For besides their pressing over
hard upon the modesty of the more bashful natures, and so Disturbing their minds, by the odd position and Distastful handling of the
body; they also expose very much to the taking, or increasing of [6]
Colds, and exceedingly disorder, when Quietness and Sleep are most
desirable. But how they amaze with fears, when they one after another work not at all, as often befalls to extream prejudice, and how
dreadfully they affright when they work too much, as sometimes they
do, in my apprehentsion deserves very much consideration; Especially since in their mildest working, the state of the body and Distemper may be such, as they may prove no less then mortal, by divert-
ting and withdrawing the Spirits from their more needful combating
the venomous Cause of the Disease, to this needless operation, and
consequently leaving Nature destitute in her greatest extremity.

Nor is the very manual part, how slight so ever the most make of it,
altogether free from the most feared effect. It having been known
where a small errour in the Hand administring, hath occasioned an
incurable Ulcer; And therefore all circumstances duly weighed, it
must be deemed a very great advantage to understand the use of such
Medicines, as bring an absolute freedom from all those Troubles,
Hazards, and Mortal Inconveniences.

After Glisters, the next afflicter of the sick, is generally Bleeding, a
practice not so frequent in former, as in latter times, and both highly

commended, and every whit as much condemned by persons equally
Learned; So that in this, [7] their Trumpet gives an uncertain sound.
And some who are famous upon Record, Esteemed it the more
proper work of worthy Physitians to rectifie rather then draw and
wast it in times of sickness, when Nature most needeth its assistance,
of which cautious judgment also seem the Chineses and the Bannian
Physitians, but later times and Operators are at that pass, as if they
made little more of it then drawing of their breaths, and so they tearm
it but breathing of a Vein, though with their favour it be not so easily
recruited, and besides that many times the bleeders breath their last
by it, or by occasion thereof.

And truly, though those who usually order it, seldom make the
observation; yet for the most part, the persons concern'd, and their
Relations cast but Dismal looks upon it, and address themselves
thereunto, with much Dismay and Trembling (oftentimes swouning
away under the Bleeders hands,) as a thing of much uncertainty and
over much danger, the Event frequently so proving, not any one proceeding in Physick, being more complained of, nor any whereunto
the failing of patients is more imputed; and that with justice too, for
what worse can befall afflicted Patients, overborn, and oppressed
with the violent assaults of some Venomous Distempers; then to have
their main forces, their Spirits drawn off from making those [8] needful Defences whereunto by Nature they are assigned, and upon
which it most dependeth for her preservation?

And what wonder is it, if soon after a little flattery and shadows of
relief, suddain Dejections immediately follow thereupon, and sickness upon Nature thus betrayed, prevail beyond all possibility of recovery, as (were Records kept thereof) would be sadly seen in every
weeks experience.

And as it is but small relif to shew how many recover after bleeding; The Course in it self being so hazardous, and often Mortal: so as
little comfort it is to shew the ill, or rather odd Colours of the cooled
and congealed Blood, which is known to be but fallacious trifling, to
amuse bewailing and Disconsolate people, neither goodness, nor
badness being at all ascertained thereby.

And be it how it will, is generally the best friend the body hath, and
consequently never to be separated; nor indeed is ever needful where
such Medicines are in readiness, as are Effectually qualified for Extinguishing of the Venomous Causes of Diseases: And for Purifying
and Rectifying both of the Blood and Spirits, wherein chiefly consisteth the Worth or Ability of Physitians, and the Reality and Excellency of Medicines.

And without which, upon every Exigence [9] there is such Hurrying, Starting, and Puthering, one while with a Glister, then with Bleeding, sometimes the Arm, the Tongue, or other parts, and these suddenly again repeated, to the Extream affrightment of the afflicted Patient, and all his sad Relations; and all this upon meer Casual, uncertain Grounds, as to what the issue may be, or whether conducing to Life or Death: A hazard of a strange nature for Patients to adventure the parting with, and loss both of their Blood and Spirits, upon which Death so often follows, when the Physitian runs none at all, *Secundum Artem*, excusing even to the utmost scruple of Reputation, if not of Conscience, which possibly may yet often suggest that they ought to have been provided, and to have plyed those (who so highly trusted them) with such really powerful and benigne Medicines, as they cannot but have heard and been assured to have discharged the most, Violent, Venomous Distempers without this unmerciful Experiment of bleeding; which also in the very action, through a small miscarriage of the hand pricking a Nerve, hath lost the use of an Arm or Hand, and sometimes through an ensuing Gangrene proved utterly Destructive.

Why therefore, all these Particulars considered, this Bleeding, or bloody practice should longer continue in repute, especially since so pregnant Instances, are so generally discoursed, [10] *viz*. That after the many times bleeding of some persons, the last fits of their Distempers immediately before death, were (without any mitigation by all that wast of Blood) as vehement and Rigorous, as in any time of their sickness, which instances in reason ought to remind every conscionable Physitian, and every prudent Patient of this important Truth, that it is not this uncertain and uncomfortable course of bleeding; But the reality of kindly and powerful Medicines, that (under God) is most hopefully to be relied on for cure in all Extremities.

After bleeding, in the usual course soon followeth Purging, but very ill deserving, that plausible Title. Most of the mass of filthy matter, which it carrieth out of the body, being made by its own venomous qualities, and so in former times was deemed more an Enemy, then a Friend in all its loosening Operations, as working meerly by violence, and disturbance of Nature, and that also much alike upon the healthful, as upon the sick, and so could not be said to work upon the Disease directly, but at randome upon the body, and most often to its prejudice.

Advising accordingly, that for discharging of Crudities (the causers of many Diseases) recourse should be had to moderate Exercise and Recreation, rather then to Purgative Medicines. And that because not only of their pain- [11] fulness, their efficacy being contrary to Nature, and for the most part venomous, but also for that they are apt to root their poisonous qualities in the Body, and withall, divert and draw away from the Members those kindly Juices which the powers of nature require for their nourishment and subsistance; Yea and the vital spirits also which maintain and comfort life.

Thus hath this loosening way of Physick been frequently condemned; But if this be not thought sufficient to extinguish its unhappy use, let but every one concern'd refer to their own observation, and without partiality note, with what uncertainty these looseners perform their Office: As sometimes when but three or four stools are only expected, it gives eight, ten, nay twenty, and those frequently, with so much lothing to the tast, offensive nastiness to the Nostril, and to the Brain of patients and all about them, as also with such extremity of pains and gripings as are most intollerable, othertimes give never so many Potions, Pills, Powders, Electuaries of these loosening qualities, yet shall they not work at all to the terrour both of Physitian and Patient, yet otherwhiles run out into such loosnesses as are never stayed, but with the death of the taker.

And when working most kindly, and never so much ugly odd coloured stuff carried out, yet the Disease frequently not one jot abated, though the patient be thereby extreamly weaken- [12] ed, scarce able to stand: The body also drained, and robbed of almost all its Radical moisture, much more apt to obstinate obstructions, and so necessarily calls for more of such like miserable helpers, which by frequent use perverts the best constitutions, sow the seed of new Diseases, and confounds the whole course of nature.

And yet that this should be continued in perpetual practice, upon so very many and great disadvantages, perplexities and dangers meerly upon uncertainty, and be justified by the practisers, be the event never so sad and Dismal, this indeed is very mysterious, and too too like the mystery of*

For who now adays remains in so much ignorance as not to know that Disease is a more lively, active thing, then to reside amongst such muddy matter, as these Purgers can possibly reach, being indeed of a more sprightly and subtile Nature, then to be discovered by the Eye, Hand, or Knife of the most skilful Anatomists, and only liable to the disquisition of Reason, and an ingenious, intimate conception; And

---

*Word missing here. (Editors' note)

so, not to be attempted by such blusterers, but by Medicines issuing from the same Fountain, such as by their efficacious friendliness to Nature, with quietness and safety, Extinguish venoms, and enable her in all her faculties towards the clear discharge of all distempers; [13] And such being to be had, as in the sequel hereof will evidently appear, one would think there were no need to perswade either Physitians or patients to make an exchange where the differences of operation, and hopefulness of the Event, are so plainly manifest.

Now, if Purging (as they call it) be thus justly chargable with so many evils and mischiefs, what can be said in behalf of Vomiting the most Rugged, Churlish, and cruel of Physick, tearing and rending, and torturing, both Stomach, Bowels, Heart, Brain, Lungs, and Throat in so hidious a manner, as hardly any corporal punishment can be imagined to exceed it in pain and misery.

And yet though often reiterated, as it often befalls in many Distempers to intollerable torment, is never the less so uncertain in its Effects, as that no relief with any certainty can be promised thereby, but fills distressed patients one while with fears when it worketh not, and when it worketh, with greater fears of working too much: There being sad Examples of both, *viz.* where they have stayed in the body without any (expected) operation, and so destroyed the patient: And also where the working hath been so violent, and so continual, as hath never ceased, but with the Expiration of the sick.

And where these Extreams have not been, yet the failing of both men, women, and children is [14] so frequently ascribed to Vomits, that its wonderful they are not Excluded quite out of use.

Besides, where Minerals are the main Agents in this unhappy work, it is incredible how mischievous their present tortures, and after worse than mortal inconveniencies have proved, conveying and entailing most Horrid pains and distempers from Generation to Generation, to all Posterity without hope of remedy; which though in process of time are judged to proceed either from the Scurvy, or foul Disease, and to end in Consumptions, or Kings Evil, yet driving the inquiry back to its Root, generally it hath been found, that the Original Cause hath much more justly belonged to unwholsome Purgers or Vomiters taken in way of Physick.

And when with their violence they have thrown up never so great a quantity of ugly ropy or filthy stuff, which is often shewed to Patients, and friends, as if now the Disease must needs be wrought upon, and near its Extirpation, it truly proveth no more but the Venomous Nature of the Medicine; the Disease for the most part rather advancing than retreating, and receiving rather an addition of strength, then any mitigation from such mischievous helpers.

Seeing thus it generally is with Vomits; though sometimes they may perform what may be taken for a good Office, yet since they do it not through any benignity in them, but by di- [15] sturbance, and the consequence being certainly dangerous, why should so troublesome a mischief-working-operation be longer retained in practise, or be imposed as necessary upon distressed patients in time of sickness? and not rather gladly remitted for such truly vertuous Medicines, as through their powerful friendliness to Humane Nature, being taken into the body, perform with ease and safety, only, what the present necessity of the body requireth: so as if the Disease be such as requireth the emptying of the Stomach, throweth up, or carryeth downwards so much and no more but what is requisite for promoting the most speedy recovery, without any possibility of any after inconvenience, as hath been the constant prevalence of those real Medicines herein proposed; And in Reason may well deserve the serious thoughts of all ingenious persons, before they are further engaged in ways so uncertain and dangerous, though of never so long continuance.

The next prescription in Physick, is commonly Sweating, which is attempted, either with the vulgar Waters, Electuaries, or Powders, or else with Mineral Preparations, and had it not been for the known uncertainty and deficiency of the former, there had been no recourse to the latter, which instead of proving a sure Refuge in time of need, hath generally treated the distressed with like adulation, as hers who cut the [16] locks, or struck a nail into the Temple, frequently outsweating all the powers of Nature, or running madly out into salivation, or perpetual spetting, which are the ordinary Extravagant Effects of Quicksilver and Antimony, though under the most boasted Preparations, and whereof there are so many sad stories, as needs a Vail to cover their mischievous treacheries, and are more then enough, if but a little hearkened after, to induce all rational persons, for ever to renounce both the giving and taking of them into their bodies upon any occasion whatsoever.

Yet if there be any, who nevertheless will retain a confidence of the safety of their preparations, see them take them themselves before you take them, and then you have some assurance for your great adventure.

But for me who deem it irrational, that any thing should be given to the sick which is not safe, and good for the healthful, and who am undoubtedly assured; that there are Medicines as securely to be used in all Cases as Milk to Children, which yet in the most desperate Cases, are full as speedy and as certainly prevalent, as ever was pretended from those so extreamly hazardous and dangerous Minerals, and that too, with very little or no sweating at all, but ever without Exhausting the spirits, drying or binding of the body, or any other after inconveniencies, having always in readiness [17] plenty of such as these, and approved for such by continual performances, I hope I may pass without blame, though I retain my judgment, and press thus earnestly for an exchange, where the advantage to every one is so manifestly weighty and material.

The next sore troubler of the sick, are Vescicatories, or Raisers of small and great Blisters, by irksome fretting, if not venomous Plaisters, somtimes flaying off all the skin from the backs, otherwhiles the shoulders, leggs, or wrists, the neck, head, &c. to extream torments, especially when those raw places are rub'd and irritated, for diversion of venomous inflammations, hidious Curses and Excrations having been noted the impatient Effects of such cruelties; of which Nature also are the use of Cupping Glasses, drawing of Silk through the Neck-skin, Leeches; and Issues, all full of pain, hazard, and danger; And as the Event proveth them, frequently fruitless, as to the removal of any Distemper, so are they wholly needless, where real Medicines are in being, and must henceforth be accounted the more intollerable, since it is known so many notable Cures have been performed without any such tedious assistants, solely by such Medicines.

Then for cutting off the Hair, Capping and Plaistering the Head, they are all but troublesome Operations to the sick, very seldom pro- [18] ving successful, either in Consumptions, or for removal of invete- rate pains, for which ends they are most used, and with more advantage might be spared in liew of safe and powerful Medicines.

And so also were it happy if Patients in like manner were rid of *Opium*, let what will be said of its several Rectifications, for whether it be used in the *Ladanum*, or otherwise; the Event is oftentimes so suddenly, and so unexpectedly, and so unavoidably dangerous, that the knowledg of its aptness to miscarry, as it hath done with divers, is more then enough to make every Dispenser of it to tremble, during the whole time it is in the Patients body. And therefore in reason should gladly be left and abandoned for ever, having never since I have been furnished with the Medicines herein specified, though in the most violent distempers, seen any occasion for the use of so critical helpers, that instead of rest and sleep, like treacherous flatterers, stroak, and stab, and give Death it self in the same instant, to the horror and amazement both of Physitians and bewailing relations.

Which by truly good and real Medicines, might be safely avoided, such by their efficacious prevalence against the venom of the Distemper in short time, not failing to introduce an unenforced well proportioned sleep, not only void of all possibility of danger, but without [19] sickishness upon waking, after-dotages weakness of the Nerves, or any dispiriting of the Animal Faculties, Palsies, Vertigoes, Apoplexies, the frequent Issues of opumated Medicines.

And therefore though I am far from wishing so much evil to the Practisers with *Opium*, that every of them should be obliged to take the same quantity which at any time they prescribe: (which yet is one of the Rules I always bind my self to in whatsoever I advise) yet I do heartily wish, that the whole Old Method of Physick aforementioned in all the particulars of Glisters, Bleedings, Purgings, Vomitings, Sweatings, by Minerals, Issues, Cuppings, Blisterings, &c. were all so well and throughly opiated, stupified, and laid asleep for ever, that they might never more rise again in Reputation with Physicians, or ever more be readmitted by distressed Patients.

But that both out of a most powerful ingenuity which most good Consciences are full fraught withall; And out of a deep sense of the manifold mischiefs incident to that way, would freely and fully forsake them all; and exchange them for the use of such true, and real Helpers, as are known to perform the utmost in all Cases that can be expected from Medicine; and that with so much mildness and safety, as disturbs not, nor hazards the weakest in their Operations.

And which, both by Physitians and Pati- [20] ents: And all persons, and Families, may certainly be known to be such, and plainly to differ from all Medicines that are not such: By these Marks following.

1. A truly benign Medicine, fit for the Sublime Humane Nature ought to be liquid, transparently clear, pure and pleasant: (for reasons expressed in my touchstone of Physick) so powerful, as to subdue the most violent Distempers, and yet so mild, as the weakest women and children may partake thereof in any case without hazard: And for assurance, the Prescriber is to take the same quantity he gives upon any occasion.

2. All such kindly and real Medicines ought to be so qualified, that if taken by Men, Women, or Children, in Health, shall no ways move their bodies, but nourish and cherish them. But if by any in sickness, the same quantity from their effectual friendliness to humane Nature

in due time, shall either binde or loosen, vomit, or stay vomiting; sweat, or restrain excessive sweating, give rest in case of restlessness, or with-hold from immoderate sleep, as the instant necessity of the body needeth, or as conduceth most to Recovery.

3. And lastly, They ought to be no perishable Commodities, which prove but weak and defective helpers, but such as close stopt keep good for years in all Climates without any Diminution of their vertues, never failing or decay- [21] ing upon their hands, who furnisheth themselves therewith, either for Sea or Land, or that rely and depend upon them for relief in any their occasions or necessities.

These are the Marks which are sufficient for proof of the fitness or unfitness of all Medicines whatsoever; and for detection of all such as may, and no doubt will be counterfeiting of these, or at least some of them, as soon as they grow into any Estimation, and are called for by the sick; Then who that practises will be without some such spiritful preparation about them, that so it may be thought they are not wanting in any thing for their recovery; & well it were if it were so indeed: But being really such, they are then not to molest their Patients, either with Purgings, Vomitings, Bleedings, Issues, Glisters, Blisters, nor with any thing of Antimony, Quicksilver, or Opium, there being no need of such hazardous and dangerous operations or operators, but are all totally to be abandoned where there are Medicines of those absolute Marks and Qualifications; so as if in the least they tamper one while with a Glister, another-while with a Purge or a Vomit, &c. though now and then they should give a Dose, resembling such as these, it signifies just nothing, but that they would seem to have as much as any, when at the same time, it is manifest they themselves have no confidence therein, nor no dependence [22] thereupon, but according to their old Mode, are fain on all occasions to have recourse to their old perplexed medlyes; therefore its good to be wary, and to note all such Counterfeitters of Medicines, as but Counterfeit Practisers, more mindful of their own reputations, then of the recovery of their Patients: the Marks are few, easy to be minded, and to be applyed wheresoever, or by whomsoever any Medicines are presented and prescribed, and in reason should sway in every ones Election or rejection accordingly.

Or however for my self, I shall never be ashamed to acknowledge, that it is to these Marks solely that I have confined all my Medicines: And that for this way; This untrodden Path in Physick, so acquired as I have expressed, I have forsaken, and abandoned all the troublesome and dangerous courses, Materials, Operations and Practises foremen-

tioned; and still see good cause to bless God that ever I was Enabled
to make so happy an Exchange, for the benefit of mankind; at least to
so many as the difference of those two wayes, shall come to be inge-
niously and throughly considered. A difference so great, the one
bringing abundant troubles, pains, hazards and dangers, and attended with weepings, woes and lamentations: the other with quiet,
ease, safety, hopefulness and chearfulness: so that the profit of this
Exchange in it self rightly [23] understood, cannot but appear inestimable and unexpressible, yet so hardly (with many) are old ways
left though never so painful and perplexed; Or new ways embraced,
though never so safe, easeful and free from all disturbance (the avers-
ness being generally whetted by some sinister interest) that without
perpetual insisting in a full discovery of the Advantages and disadvantages, there would be no hope of Prevailing for such a condescension as in this weighty Cause is agreeable to Truth and Reason.

But all things have their season; Evangelical Doctrine bringing
nothing but peace, though long opposed by the Legal, which brought
nothing but terrour to the sin-sick Conscience, yet in time as truth
prevailed, became clearly victorious, both over the Law, and their Interest that would maintain it: And so in time I doubt not, but it may
also prove in this, as the difference once comes to be rightly understood; for however Custom and Interest may have so prevailed &
enchained mens minds, as almost in every sickness, to reckon no
other, but that there is a necessity of undergoing all those painful,
cruel, dangerous, and mischievous practises and proceedings afore
recited; yet certainly when they shall be serious in their thoughts, and
plainly see that there is another way in Physick Established upon
more sure Foundations and Principles, and another sort of Medicines
arising from these Prin- [24] ciples, which cure with much more certainty, and yet wholly exempt from all terrours, pains, and dangers,
and that may by every one be known to be such by Evident Marks
and Characters, and by abundant Instances of Cures performed solely
by such Medicines, as in the touchstone of Physick plentifully appeareth: There will then certainly be no place for opposition, nor need
of farther Arguments to perswade their chearful Entertainment, nor
to doubt a general adherence to their assistance, by all Persons and
Families.

For whose clear understanding, and more easy ordering of them to
their own, their Friends, and Relations, occasions in any Distempers
or necessities.

I shall here acquaint them with their particular Titles, Vertues, and Uses, with all requisite Circumstances as followeth. . . . [25]

. . . . *

These are the Medicines which upon all occasions I have found abundatly sufficient for all the Ends and Intentions of Physick, so that whosoever shall throughly acquaint themselves therewith, and furnish themselves with due quantities thereof, may not only easily and pleasantly add strength and vigour to their usual Diet, plenteously replenish their continual wast and Expence of Spirits, daily refresh themselves with real advantage to their health; Supply all suddain Illness or Exigencies, without all fear of after Inconveniencies; but are thereby firmly enabled, with Gods blessing, to grapple [33] with, and subdue the most violent and most inveterate diseases whatsoever, which make up the full scope of all Physical knowledge, and Medicinal performances.

And all these without any the hazards or dangers forementioned; Are alike useful at all times and seasons of the year, Winter, Sommer, Spring, or Autumn; safely and pleasantly to be taken by all persons in all states of health, or degrees of weakness from the very Cradle to Oldest Age, without any confinement to house, or Chamber (except in cases of Extremity,) without charge of visits, or tedious attendance, and with all possible quietness and hopefulness to the Patient.

All which are no feigned Delusions, but real Truths, as divers who have long time solely depended on their assistance, both for themselves and Families, with absolute good success can sufficiently testifie, reckoning withall, that all circumstances duly considered, they are not the dearest, but the cheapest of Physick.

Besides as never any harm could justly be imputed to any of them; so were they never known to fail of Cure, where time proportionable to the constitution of the body, and to the quality and degree of the Distemper, hath been allowed, and Directions followed accordingly.

But where Distemper hath taken fast hold [34] upon a body over worn with toyl, care, and business, aggravated by omission of timely medicines, and then tyred out, nay confounded with intricate and unwholesome Physick; and from one sort of Medicine to another, until the Medicines have proved more mischievous, and more inveterate then the first Disease; for Patients in such difficult Cases as these, to

* Pages 25–33, here deleted, list 32 medicines, 19 more than the list in *Healths New Store-House*, p. 7. (Editors' note)

think a moneths time (or so) sufficient for recovery, failing of their hopes, rather taxes their own reason, then the validity of the Medicines.

And yet even in such forlorn undertakings, I have in very few days seen so great and so good an alteration, that had it not been destroyed by too much presuming thereupon, and thereby taking cold anew, and so loosing all that was gained; There was sufficient to give assurance that time and perseverance in their plenteous use would have perfected their work; all after deviations from this course of Physick, and these Medicines never bringing the Patient to so good a condition; Nor did I ever know them laid aside for any others, but there was cause to wish they had not left them: But if ever it is in such cases as these, that this saying is verified, That there are some who will be sick too late, and well too soon: And makes me think of divers unhappy Patients, when I mind that saying, *He found no steadfastness, no not in his Angels.* Very few in inve [35] terate cases being apt upon utmost perswasive arguments to give a tenth part of time requisite; or having resolved to do it, that wil be constant for half the time; And this not always from an instability in the Patient, but most unhappily from the odd officious Medlings of Visitants and Relations, who though wholly void of true judgment in Physick, or in the differences between what is, and what is not to be trusted to, are ever censuring the present proceedings, and proposing one while this, another while that, boasting up this, and commending another, as having speedily cured divers in like cases with very small charge.

A sort of friendship might very well be spared, and should a little more then it doth touch the Consciences of all such well meaning disturbers, if not destroyers of these whom yet with all their hearts they earnestly desire should be preserved, affectionate and zealous: errors being always most mischievous.

For my part, I can clearly affirm, that I never gave the smallest quantity of those my Medicines to any person, in any case, but I heartily wisht it might prove a perfect Cure; And it is an absolute truth, that very many in a year have been cured of such Distempers, some for the value of 6 d. some 12 d. and sometimes a very little more, that probably in any other way, could not have escaped a tedious fit of sickness, or a chargable [36] course of Physick, and I am never more joyed then when it is so.

Yet this doth not argue that every one that falls ill should expect always the like success, there being so vast a difference in Constitutions, and in the nature of Diseases, in neglect of the instant use of means, and a while deferring as alters the Case beyond imagination, and which unavoidably enforces as great a difference in the difficulty and time of recovery.

But then, how Exceedingly much more doth the Case differ when the Disease hath been of many years continuance, and so many various Physicks used time after time, that it is very presumable some of it may have been venomous, and infinitely added to the malice of the Disease: Though in such Case I should not despair of prevailing, in this way of safe and powerful Medicines; yet I should blame my self excessively should I give any hope of success, but upon an absolute promise from such patients of perseverance for at least so many Moneths, if not twice the number, as they have been years afflicted, and admit the charge of such a condescension, should amount to 10, nay 20 Crowns a moneth, which I suppose would be the most, what a small thing were this to persons of means and quality, to adventure in a course so safe, and withal so hopeful, and after hundreds, if not thousands of pounds spent in vain, in ways [37] neither so safe nor rational, and in such hands as I am sure to gain the world, would not defer a Cure one moment; That Instance in the *Touch-stone of Physick,* Of the Gentlwoman that was left hopeless by all her Physitians, after a long time of using their utmost Endeavours, and she brought to nothing but skin and bones, and her Disease triumphing over her weakness, when her sad Husband came to me, desiring my assistance, had he scrupulously enquired whether I had ever cured any one in so hopeless a condition, or endeavoured to have confined me to time, or been solicitous in what time I thought some hopes might appear, or where about the charge of her Cure might be; It is very like I had never undertaken her, as abhorring nothing more then such huckstering in cases of sickness where there is ability: But he leaving all wholly to me, though by reason of some relapse, it was some moneths before she went abroad, yet both he and she were fully satisfied with all that was done, and God blest it to her wonderful recovery. All which I have thus Expressed, if possible to make all persons concern'd sensible how great a difference there may be in Distempers, seemingly alike, and how much more time may be requisite for recovery of one more then another; And to work them to a willing resignation to themselves, to whomsoever they shall think meet to trust, and with- [38] out scruple, or repining either at Time or Charge, stedfastly to persevere, especially being engaged in a way so safe, and with Medicines so kindly, and withal so powerful (as here are solely intended) and, which by the Marks foregoing may easily be tryed and proved, whether they are so or not; but being such, there is all Encouragement imaginable to persist with hope and chearfulness.

Withal, the Patient must be sure, both in his Diet, and shunning all hazards, to be helpful to his Physitian, and most careful to observe all Directions, Cautions and Circumstances advised, that being the only way to make the best of what is taken, and to keep and not loose the smallest degree of improvement obtained; for those who get and keep ground, though but by inches, are sure in the end of victory.

But without resolving to persist in their use, (whether they are governed by Patients themselves, or their relations on their behalf, or by Physitians) I would not encourage any to begin with any of these Medicines; It being my manner always to refuse the undertaking of any that I either doubt, or will not promise to persevere with them, and strictly to adhere to Directions; upon which being resolved, none need to fear success, Answerable either to the Instances mentioned in the *Touch-stone of Physick,* or to those Cures since performed by them. [39]

Some whereof to manifest that they are still the same both in Efficacy, and in Performance, I shall here recite as followeth. . . . [40]

. . . .   *

Many more instances of their performances I might here recite, were not these more then sufficient to satisfie the ingenious, that their virtues are still fresh, permanent, and prevalent; not of a dying or a declining nature, (as divers boasted Medicines have proved) but of so constant, lively, and efficacious performance, as gives just encouragement to believe they can never fail any rational expectation in any disease whatsoever.

And as it is from this undoubted assurance of their innocency and efficacy that I have thus frequently pressed their use, the very same reason still urgeth me thus far further to affirm, that in this important cause of health, or for the disconsolate times of sickness: It is not possible (in my appre- [100] hension) for any to do themselves or their Relations a greater good, Than to be constantly furnished with such of them, as in their rational observation of their vertues, They shall judg most requisite for their occasions: Yea even Practisers of Physick, how hardly soever they may bring their minds to it, ought in special

* Pages 40–100, here deleted, list 110 histories of cures, adding to the lists in *Healths New Store-House,* pp. 9–19, and *Touch-Stone,* pp. 17–98. (Editors' note)

manner throughly to consider their powerful benignity, and in tender respects to the weighty trust reposed in them, freely and fully to direct their use (thereby avoiding all the troubles and dangers of other Physick) untill from their own Studies they are provided of Medicines of like benignity: Which yet they are to know, will never be compass'd whil'st they give esteem to so many insignificant Notions, and Conceptions, referring to Principles, Methods and Medicines, set so high a value upon Antimony, Quicksilver, and Opium, are so little acquainted with the true humane temperature, and so regardless of the improvement of their pallats to the discerning the proprieties & Spirits of Materials, without serious regard, and conformation whereunto the Artist sails but by a bought or borrowed and imaginary wind without Needle or Compass, and never arive at any worthy production.

Besides, where Nature gives not promptitude, and as (one instances well) a Teeming Constitution though Art and Learning may abound, pertinent invention will be to seek, and new Discoveries fail, as the compleatest Laboratories do frequently manifest: The native genius, being the Artsmans Al- [101] kahest, and of more worth than that so much talk't of rarity was ever yet to any, for any commanding medicine as yet appeareth (except in boast) from its assistance. Or rather like unto the Archeus to one that had the Alchahest, in forming his pallat how to distinguish of every part lai'd open to view, and whereof rightly to choose, and regularly to dispose, for the advance of cure.

The want of which native Energie, hath in studens been the occasion that Chymistry hath lately abounded to its own disparagement, yielding nothing comparable to the noble countenance given unto it: For who now will not be a Chymist, whether Nature hath fitted him thereunto or not: So the famous Orator would needs make his son an Orator, but long labour in vain, Taught him his native temperature was not for it: And, if after his Father was gone, he should at any time need an Orator: He was to make use of anothers Fancy brain and Eloquence, and which he might do without disparagement, for no man makes himself. He that wants an Excellent Musitian seeks for one Naturally so adicted: And if the most Exquisite Mathematitian thinks no disparagement to make use of Instruments made by another hand, and invented by another head, why should a Physitian deem himself dishonour'd to make use of the long approved, safe Productions of another mans Invention, especially considering, that no Science (so material unto man) depends so wholly upon native promptitude as this of Medicine: There being no [102] Rule unto Conception, nor Instruction to direct the Pallats Election: Upon which the whole of all Improvements necessarily dependeth.

When all men are alike, every one will produce a like, but till then, one will still need anothers aid.

He that in this Warfare will use no weapons, but such as he knows how to make himself, would hardso venture upon a Combate were his own life concern'd: But I shall leave this to the sole perswasion of time, though I daily see manifest inconveniencies, for want of their general reception into practise. And so I return to my advice for Families.

Whom yet I would willingly, and fully possess of this important Truth, before I put a period to this Discourse: *viz.* That how ever it be taken (and justly) for a great happiness to be recovered immediately by safe means upon a suddain illness: And reckoned (upon good grounds) like life, from the death, to be raised to health and strength, from a tedious and dangerous fit of sickness, by safe and kindly Medicines, free from all hazards and disturbance (unto both which most remarkable ends in Physick, the Medicines afore proposed are effectually adapted) yet is there no benefit or advantage so desirable, or in it self so truly valuable, as where by a timely providence and foresight, you make use of them to keep you in constant health and chearfulness, whereunto I verily believe there is not any thing so proper, or so effectually prevalent, being used according as afore is specified: nor any thing that doth more [103] highly commend their qualifications, it being no common strain of Vertue, for the same particulars to be so powerful as to subdue the most violent Distempers, and yet so familiar as to be a most pleasant strengthner, and fortifier against all the ordinary assaults of time and accidents. And (which compleats the wonder of their vertue) as small quantity in sickness doth as effectually, and as speedily relieve one constantly using them in times of health, as it doth those who never before knew or took them: At so true an amity are they with humane nature, and so materially do they differ from all other Physical Preparations.

And as I have deemed these very worthy your serious notice, so also that you heedfully observe the vast difference between those who recover out of any considerable sickness, having run the usual Tract of Physick, and those who are raised from the beds of sickness by these kindly Medicines: How pale, weak, and crazy the one, long languish, liable to relapses upon every small occasion, if not to worse Distempers arising from the unhappy remains of unwholsome Physick: Whil'st the other are no sooner discharged from their main Distemper, but in a manner, immediately their Strength, Stomack, Courage, and countenance, return at once without fear of any after inconveniencies; And may well appear a circomstance of no mean consideration to manifest the difference of the means and Medicines.

And having thus far disburthened my reason of [104] so many important thoughts which I judged worthy the knowledge in this weighty cause of Physick, upon which mans happiness so much dependeth, wherein my principal aims have been, to make the differences of the usual Physick: And that which I here propose so apparent, that every capacity may be enabled to make their choice accordingly.

For perfecting this work, having been somewhat large in shewing the stilness, quietness, safeness and untroublesome way of cure by my really benigne Medicines, very much resembling the operations and effects, not of Terrestrial, but of Celestial Influences, for a more evident witness of their difference, and to put this main point past all dispute.

I shall here present the whole Entire Process (of no mean Physitian, but) of a most learnred Doctor Engaged in the undertaking of a Cure, and by himself published in Print, as what he deemed most laudable, though the success was doubtful.

And wherein is chiefly to be minded, what afore I have expressed. Touching the trouble, hazard, danger, and ill Events of Purging, Vomiting, Bleeding, Glisters, Blisters, &c. And the happiness of that way by which all those are safely and securely avoided. His own Relation verbatim, being as followeth. [105]

RIVERIU'S Observations, page 36, 37, &c. The Distempers Denominated; Tisick, Inflammation of the Lungs, and Palpitation of the Heart.

On the 8th of April 1632. The Widow of Monsi. Sejelory of Mon'Pelier, Starting out of her bed at midnight thinly clad to the window, was presently taken with great shortness of breath, like a Fit of the Tisick, with a Cough, spitting of blood, a Feaver, and readiness of Face; —I being sent for, caus'd a vein to be open'd in her right arm, and 8 ounces of blood being taken away, her shortness of breath presently ceased. Afterwards a Laxative Glister was injected, and a Julep given her of Red Poppy water, Sirrup of Violets, *Sal prunellae*, and *Confectio de Hyacintho*.

On the ninth day at ten in the forenoon, I visit her again, and find her in a Fever, troubled with a Cough, and spitting of bloody matter; also she felt a heavy weight in the middle of her breast with an inward burning, and pricking in many parts of her Chest. I cause her to be let blood in her left arm, and that the Glister, and Julep should be repeated, to anoint her breast with Oyl of Violets, and that she lick frequently some Sirrops of Violets; after the blood-letting she was presently eased & that sense of weight and burning in her Chest were abated. At five in the Evening the same day, conceiving that vapours arose from beneath, and humours into her Chest, which that shortness of breath did sufficiently declare; I cause her to be let [106] blood in the Saphena Vein, after which she was also better; The night following she took the foresaid Julep again, she slept but little.

On the tenth day in the morning she was better, her Fever and other Symptoms were very remiss. About the third hour of the Evening she had a coldness in her extream parts, with a light sweat in her Feet, and palms of her hands, after that an acute Fever, her pulse very much expressed, and the sense of heaviness in her chest very much augmented. Dr. Ranchinus the Chancellor was called to Consultation, who conceived, that it was a Pluerisie, arising from inflammation of the Mediastinum, and by common consent she was Let blood in her right Arm to seven ounces, after which also she was better. The other Medicines were continued, also Frictions, Ligatures, and Cupping-glasses were applyed to her lower parts.

On the eleventh day, which was the third of her sickness, moved with what I had observed in another Disease of the same patient, in which she was afflicted by turns, with a Flux of her Belly joyned with a Tenesmus, and a Catarrh falling upon her breast; So that as often as her loosness stopt, she was grievously afflicted with her Catarrh, and when her Flux recovered, her Catarrh presently ceased; The humour falling into her breast, being drawn downwards, I conceived that a Purge would do her most good, which I made after this manner.

Take leaves of Bugloss and Lettice of each one handful, Tamarinds half an ounce, Liquorice three drams, Violet flowers, one Pugil, boyl all to four ounces, in the strained Liquor dissolve one dram of Rubarb, infused in Bugloss water with yellow Sanders, Manna, and [107] sirrup of Roses of each one ounce, make all into a potion, which she took in the morning, and voided much Flegmatick, Wheyish, sharp, and stinking matter, nevertheless the Disease was more violent towards the Evening than formerly, yet her Pulse was not oppressed as before, and the weight in her breast was less; But she felt a pain about her right Chanel bone, which encreased by handling the same, she slept little that night, she took Emulsions frequently.

The fourth day of her Disease, and the twelfth of the moneth, when as in the morning her Fever and the pain in her Chanel bone continued. Dr. Ranchinus was again called to Consult, and besides the foresaid Symptoms, a great palpitation of the heart, which appeared also in her right Hypocondrium, also in her right side; but it lasted not long there. But about her heart it continued, and did beat like a Hammer violently, she was again Let blood in her right Arm. And an Oyntment was appointed for the part pained, and Remedies to revel the humours to the lower parts: About Evening the Disease was again exasperated, and the Palpitation continued, some hours after she did sweat a little all her body over, by which she was a little eased; But her Palpitation and Fever continued as before, when we began to suspect that Vapours did arise from her Womb, we prescribed her a Glister for the Mother, Frictions, Ligatures, and Cupping-glasses to be applyed to her lower parts, Emplastrum Hystericum was applyed to her Navel; and a Julep was given her, to assist her sweating, of Scabious and Carduus water with Bezoar stone, and half an ounce of Orange flower water in regard of her womb. In the night she had three [108] large stools of stinking corrupt matter: after midnight she slept quietly till morning.

On the fifth day of the Disease, I found her in the morning with a small Fever, without any oppression in her breast, or any pain, and with very little Palpitation of heart, about Evening she did sweat a little, and was better afterwards. After she had voided her Glister, her palpitation was augmented, her Fever became more intense, and she was pretty well in the Night.

On the sixth day, all things were as before, in the Evening Cupping-glasses were applyed with scarrification which did her good.

On the seventh day her Courses began to flow plentifully, by which means all Symptoms were very much abated.

On the eighth day she was better.

On the ninth day she had a light loosness joyned with a Tenesmus, by which she voided few Flegmatick excrements, and before that loosness, she vomited much bitter stuff, the Humours were prepared with temperate aperitives.

On the tenth day, which was the eighteenth day of the Moneth her loosness was less, at night it stopt quite, she had no Fever, and after that she plainly amended.

On the 29. of the said Moneth of April, when she felt [109] her self exceeding well, and was busy about her houshold occasions, as she was sitting in a Chair, she fell suddenly to the ground and died.

Her body being opened, her Mediastinum was found full of wheyish blood, which peradventure, the Membrane being broken towards the upper part of the Lungs, and pressing the same, and the Aspera Arteria, might suddenly choak her, moreover the whole substance of the Lungs was found full of purulent matter, exceeding heavy: Also her left Testicle was as big as a small Egg, of a blackish colour, and as it were Gangrenated, yea and as soon as it was open'd, there leapt out of the middle of her Testicle, a certain matter like a Nut-kernel, and very like a putrified clotter of blood; we conjectured that to have been the cause of her Mother-fits, to which she was very much subject, yea peradventure the Palpitation of her heart arose from thence, *viz*, From the filthy vapours ascending from that part.

Here you have a very smooth Story, yet of so unquiet, rugged, perplexed, and disconsolate a handling of a sick and Diseased body, that to one accustomed solely to mild and gentle ways in Physick, as nothing seems more cross to reason, so truly hardly any thing more grievous, or more justly to be lamented, for although the Relation of five times bleeding of one in her sad [110] Condition, and divers times Glisters, Ligatures, Cuppings, and Scarrifications, and purgings be here very plausibly delivered, as if the Fears, Troubles and Disturbances, these Attending were not at all felt, or thought on by the Patient, yet whoever sensibly considers the many tossings, and turmoilings this sick and tender person was exercised withal, during her ten Dayes sickness, can hardly avoid believing, but that it was even without any other Distemper, sufficient to have brought any weak person to their end, or far towards it, nor can I but firmly apprehend, That if any Patient taken as is here exprest, should for such a time be Discreetly plyed with *Refugium, Vindex, Salus, Vita naturae, Clavis* or *Radix,* being all strengthners of Nature, and of Power to subdue the venomous causes of Distempers, I say so plyed, I can hardly see it possible, but that recovery must necessarily follow.

And therefore, truly the course taken, was, and is still to be bewailed, and much the Rather because in this ye are to reckon, that (*ex ungue Leonem*) you have a full prospect of the generally approved Practice of Physick, The Essence, Quintessence, & master-piece, not of a learner, but of a Teacher, and most Reverent Author and Doctor in the Science, such as who ever [111] follows, may Authentically subscribe *Secundum Artem* to all their Prescriptions and Proceedings, for which they are both prais'd, and liberally pai'd too; And wherewithal their patients (speed how they will) must be contented.

And yet, who so blind, as with half an eye doth not see what extream uncertainty this Learned person was at, throughout his whole Engagement in this Distemper; how slenderly discerning of the Cause; how weakly judging of the alterations; how insensible of the Patients mollestations by Glisters, Blisters, &c. how regardless of her loss of blood and Spirit, which though very fruitless, yet often repeated, of how little use his Learning, and former reading seemed herein, how insignificant all his former opening and Anatomising of Bodies appeared here, where he was afresh fain to open his Patient to learn what her Disease was; And being open'd, how meanly he Guesses, taking notice meerly of apparent, defects of Parts, (which are but Effects) without any consideration of the cause thereof, which indeed is the Disease, and indiscernable, but by the Intellectual eye of the understanding: Also how poorly he was furnished with Medicines, of so mean, casual, and hazardous qualifications, as not in the least strengthened but [112] weakned nature, through which she fell. So that the whole considered, to any rational conscience I think there will appear a cause, for all I have said or done, In this weighty affair of Physick and Medicines; and cannot but judg that the World had been infinitely more happy, had it with the resignation of Judaism and Gentilism for Christianity, at the same time, both questioned, reformed, and exchanged, their groundless, hazardous, and rugged Physick, for what had been more pure, peaceable, and more suitable to that sublime and healing Doctrine.

But it doth not appear to have then been thought of, nor ever since to any considerable purpose, for though Chymistry hath struck in with large and full pretences, and fil'd our heads with new Bookish Tearms, and Notions, yet have they afforded us scarce any thing but vapouring Fancies, Mysteries, and Riddles, the proper issue of Vainglorious and Superstitious Reformers, who though very bad Leaders, themselves, being led by Quicksilver and Antimony, have had the fortune yet, to be both admired and followed by every Student in this useful Art; But with so little Fruit, not one Master Medicine yet appearing, that it would amaze ones Reason even to astonishment; But [113] that vain windy hopes, and ostentous shews or shadows, have ever been of more esteem then substances, and useful realities, but if hence forward it should be better, I to this place will deem my self a debtor.

And so in time I doubt not will others also acknowledge, for however some may still shamefully persist even against the testimony of so many instances, one while to fright people from their use upon pretense of their heat, and otherwhiles to accuse them of impotency by reason of their mildness, yet have I not found all Doctors so partially inclined. There being one, and he neither young nor mean, who having tasted all with very much attention and satisfaction openly affirmed, that in producing that Catalogue of Medicines, so qualified, as the particulars imported, and the instances manifested, I had done a more real service to Physick, then either Hippocrates Galen, Paracelsus, Vanhelmont, or any other he had ever Read or Heard of. And that could He Produce them in that perfection I did, he would not stay many dayes in England. I told him his meaning, and the place he aimed at, and he confessed I guessed right, but I thought the place that bred them best deservd them, though but for their sakes [114] who esteem them equal to this high Encomium, how Ironically soever given.

And to double this single Wonder, one also there is who for years hath laid the main weight of his Practise upon their Assistance, to his full satisfaction in all sorts of Distempers, and I believe would hardly be drawn to practice without them, yet never askt what one Particular was in any of them; his tast and assurance of me at first being his warrant, but now useth them with the same confidence and familiarity as I do; or as if they were his own preparations, suspitions, being poor and abject, in case of so great a trust.

Another Grave and Learned person of high Degree in Art, tasting and wondering at their so unexpected qualifications, to his extream contentment, did not, as others, vainly dignifie himself by spurting out Latine or Greek Sentences, Enquire whether I had travailed, or at what University I had studied. As if right Reason were not alike in every Language, and in every place on this side, or beyond the Seas, being indeed, more or less, as it is Diligently, Circumspectly, Pertinently, and Honestly exercised. But that grave Gentleman askt such a Question, not [115] of me neither, (so truly civil was he) but of a Bystander, which when I was told, pleas'd me abundantly, to find one prudent Question amongst so many others, frequently obtruded upon me, very much shewing the vast difference of the inward furniture of men, and ministring matter to me of very grateful contemplation.

Some other such like Congratulatory Testimonies I might further alledg, did I lay much weight upon them, but in this Case it being with Medicines as with men, if their performances commend them well and good, and for those the instances are throughly to be considered, if these speak in their commendations, all other praises, though thank-worthy, are but supernumerary.

However upon the whole, here is *Ars longa abbreviata,* a Physick tendered to general use, and fair Example that needs feel no Pulses, regards not Urines, Critical Dayes, Climacterical years, state of the Moon, or position of the Stars, sight of the Patient, visits, Diagnosticks, nor Prognosticks; That troubles not the head about Circulation, Chilification, or Sanguification, That values not Anatomy, as to the dis- [116] covery of Diseases, nor the four, nor the three, nor the five Principles, nor the Doctrine of Fermentation, nor the fine spun Thred of Atoms, as any whit advantagious to Cure. That is not beholden to any Book or Books of Philosophy, or Physick for its production, otherwise then to Discern the weaknesses of what had been so highly, but causelessly admired: That stands not obliged to any Chymical or Laboratory Instructers, nor esteems of their numerous tearms of Art, but as wit seldom fruitful in Excellencies, without which Chymistry like Honor without Vertue, is but a mere Name to bragge withal, as most make on't.

A Physick yet, which is the first hath dared to be brought within compass, and to be liable to be tryed whether true or false, fit, or unfit for the Sublime Nature of man, by certain and undeceivable marks, few & easie to be understood, Whose Principle is from above, in Qualification suited to the true humane Constitution, and powerfully Efficacious for Extirpation, and Extinguishing the venomous Causes of Diseases, that is not at any time either unsafe or unseasonable, and keeps good for years in all Climates.

And yet a Physick, as the Discourse plenti- [117] fully sheweth, that without any trouble or danger to the sick, may more rationally then any other, be confidently relied on for Cure, in all Cases and Extremities.

Why then, A Physick bringing so many large Exemptions to the Sick: And that acquits Physitians from so many encumbrances and perplexities, both in their studies and practise, should not with all chearfulness, and freeness be suitably entertained, Conscience in time will judg: with which being much satisfied, I shall here put a period to all farther Expostulation or Expectation: Referring the issue of all my Endeavours, To that Wisdom which governs the World; and which ought to bear Rule, above all partial interests, in all the Thoughts, Words, Actions, and Consciences of all Mankind, whether Rational, Learned, or Unlearned, Single, or in Societies: And whereunto most humbly, and most freely, I shall ever wholly submit.

W.W.

At the Star in the Porstern by little More-fields.

FINIS [118]

Licens'd June 10th 1669. Roger L'Strange. [flyleaf opposite p. 118]

PHYSICK FOR, FAMILIES: OR, The new, Safe and power-full way of PHYSICK, upon constant proof Established;

Enabling every one, at Sea or Land, By the Medicines herein mentioned, to cure themselves, their Friends and Relations, In all Distempers and Diseases.

Without any the trouble, hazzard, pain or danger, Of Purgers, Vomitters, Bleedings, Issues, Glisters, Blisters, Opium, Anti-mony and Quicksilver, so full of perplexity in Sickness.

By *W.W.* Healths Student, At the *Star* in the *Postern* by little *Morefields.*

Prov. 9. 11. *For by me thy Dayes shall be multiplyed, and the years of thy life shall be increased.*

LONDON, Printed, by *J.R.* and are to be Sold by *Robert Horn,* at the South-entrance of the *Royal-Exchange,* 1674.

Physick for Families.

Having now past through many years Practise in this my new way of Physick; And with Gods blessing, in, and upon my peculiar Method and Medicines, been most happily successfull, in abundance of very threatning, dangerous Distempers; And many of them after all the most hopeful means had failed; And some, so complicated, and confused, that ablest Consultations could give no name unto them: & hardly any such ever recovered by Physick. These Truths, being now generally known to the ingenuous in all quarters; I conceive I may reasonably expect, that whoever shall henceforth think it fit to advise with me touching any kind of Distemper, will neither doubt my [3] judgement, nor the efficacy of my Medicines: nor, after they have fully inform'd me all they know of the Disease, will trouble themselves with any other Question; But, whether I apprehend, That help and Recovery is to be hoped for, from my assistance.

There needing no more, It being a firm principle with me, never to engage with any, but where I have very good hopes of prevailing to their ample satisfaction.

Then for all those, who, through absence or distance from me, Are for their Directions in the use of these Medicines to depend solely upon what is herein expressed under every Title. I have for their sakes been as large, as the nature of the description of the vertues of such Medicines could possibly admit— The vertues of these kindly and powerfull Medicines, being indeed so largely comprehensive, and so diffusive towards real assistance, in so many, and so various cases: That [4] to be strictly conclusive, in confinement of their use, could not be done, but to the abridgment of their extensiveness in Cure.

So that, the Judicious have in these, a most spacious prospect for their contemplation, upon every occasion which calleth for the help or use off any of them.

And wherein, some living far of, and others neerer are grown so skilful, That what with the use of several sorts in a Cure: as also of divers mixtures of them upon occasion: and by knowing in the absence of want of the most appropriated medicine, which of those they have by them; is next best to be relyed on; by being studious, and ready in these and the like particulars, they have performed even to admiration.

The last of which distinguishing abillities (being of mighty use) I shall add a proof thereunto: sent me lately in a letter from the East-Indies: as followeth, [5]

January the 22 1672.

SIR, I have received yours of the 28 of November, 1671, and read the same, with much contentment; Heartily glad of your good health, which I pray God to grant unto you for many and happy years.

I thank God for good health at present: but had not the same so, at the arrival of our ships, that brought me your Cordial Medicines; very well conditioned, for which I return you my hearty thanks. Being visited by my former years Distemper, the Yellow Jaundies, But having received my

Cases after some dayes Arrival, and opened the same, I found none for
that distemper, as by your book I finde to be *Vita naturae:* yet not Discouraged, I took *Vis Vitae:* And continued until all the four bottles I had of it
were spent: which did my work, and restored me with Gods blessing to
my former health, I hope that with the next quantity, [6] you will send me
a proportion of *Vita naturae:* and also some *Ignis Vitae,* as I wrote in my last
years direction, &c.

Here you see, in the absence of *Vita naturae,* which my book expressly appropriated to the Jaundies: This Gentleman, with good judgement, and good success, relieth upon *Vis Vitae,* and very rationally,
for the yellow Jaundies, being a far degree of that Proteus, the inward
Scurvy, and arising from a peculiar venom, threatning the utter extinction of the chief Agents of life, The Spirits, *Vis Vitae,* being qualified for
the extinguishing of venoms, and appropriate to the Scurvy. It was
very presumable, the event could not but found a joyful probatum in
his happy recovery.

And may very well Instruct, and encourage the like free exercise of
Reason, where such a necessity calleth for it.

His two first, and his two last years [7] Cases contained each two
glasses of Vindex naturae, 3 of Salus vitae, 2 of Radix vitae, 3 of Sanguis
vitae, 3 of Adjutrix, 4 of Vis vitae, 2 of Flos vitae; all very mild of
temperature, 3 glasses of refugium, somewhat warmer, and 2 glasses
of Stella, hot in taste, but mild in operation.

Mildness: not flat and dull products of vulgar Art, but kindly im-
pregnated with benign power, and efficacy; perpetual mover in all my
Medicines, and unto which all their performances are real Debtors.

And from whence it is, That milde as they are, yet through that
secret lively power, plentiously dwelling in them; they as you see keep
good, and without any alteration, or diminution of their vertues; during so long a voyage, and in so hot a Clymate; where liquors far hotter
corrupt, perish, and become wholly useless: And is a secret belonging
to that benignity which gives them their efficacy against diseases, [8]
whether in the most inward or outward parts of the body whilst what
is of vulgar conception, flattens, and shrinks and sinks by the way; and
never reaches the distemper.

Nor need any to be startled from the free use of them by any supposed difficulty arising from the various differences of complexions,
and variety of Diseases.

For since Humane nature, rightly apprehended, is but one. And that
every of my Medicines are proportioned thereunto; well may my Medicines, reduce the excesses and defects of complections into better

temper (it being their proper office and nature so to doe) but are not liable to be frustrated in their vertues and operations, by any of the preternatural irregularities of constitutions.

And as to the variety of diseases, it being a known truth, that all disseases are comprised under certain tribes or heads, and those not many: [9] when any disease is proposed for cure though never so confused, or such as the most critical pretenders unto skill; can give no name to; (divers of which have happily past through my care:) in such cases it is but seriously noting unto which tribe the main disturber belongeth, and what touches of other tribes, the under-troublers have; and then it will be easie to discern with what medicines they are to be attempted.

And indeed as where the Iron is hard, the more strength is to be added, so where obstinacies and difficulties in cure doe appear, there is but one rule to be observed in answer to both objections, and that is to follow Patients with more frequent addresses, and larger Doses of appropriate Medicines, especially in the highest violence of fits; and then neither Physician nor Patient need to fear a comfortable issue; provided also, that a strict guard be kept upon many particulars which are apt [10] to destroy proceedings; chiefly against the admission of a sort of Artists, who finding this new way unshrines their Grecian Idol; will be visiting and censuring, and interposing such insinuations, as, if hearkned to, shall frustrate the most hopeful endeavors.

These carefully withheld, be sure to excuse the sick from over great and busie talkers, offerers of casual, trifling Medicines, sad, sighing, and dejected visitants; to withold all unkindness; gently perswading from all rash adventures upon wine; unusual doubtfull diet, hot waters, eagerness for drink, and too much thoughtfullness; but by friendliness, keep them in all quietness, and hopefullness, without any the least shew of fearing their dissolution; which with (what else prudence, upon the place may advise) heedfully observed. Hardly could any distemper resist this powerfull way of Physick: It being for want of wisdom, as much in sickness as [11] in health, that the dayes of man, are frequently shortned.

And which I thus particularly have urged, being earnestly desirous to infuse such thoughts into all those who either for themselves, or others, ingage in this way, as may preserve unto them the full and compleate benefit of my Medicines, without being deprived thereof by any error, weakness, subtilty, willfullness, or superstition of Visitants of attendants; through which the sick, frequently, and dangerously suffer.

Withall, I conceive it very requisite, that two at least of the nearest Relations to the sick: be fully satisfied of the safety and hopefullness of this way, before any the least proceeding be therein; without which there can never be any comfortable perseverance, nor good success to be expected.

And now that I have thus cautioned my observers; I conceive it requisite to represent unto them the mani- [12] fold troubles, hazzards and dangers, from which by this new discovery in times of sickness they are delivered; together with the important Reasons which induced me finally to reject all those disturbers mentioned in the Title; not without some hope, in time, of seeing them also excluded out of all practise, to the perpetual security, ease, and quiet of all Patients whatsoever. . . . [13]

. . . . *

Very many more instances, I could have added; and had done it; but that I conceive these well considered may suffice for instruction to any, in the use of my Medicines, both what, and what quantities, and at what times, to give or take any of them; and if any difficulty shall arise, I shall be always ready by word, or letter, to contribute my best councell and assistance.

And do presume, that by these it will manifestly appear (what was thought impossible) that where such benigne and powerfull Medicines as these, are in being and repute, there is no necessity nor need at all to trouble Patients with the long doted-on-help of purgers, vomiters, bleedings, issues, [105] glisters, blisters, Opium, Antimony, and Quicksilver, for though sometimes there may be a shaddow of good from some of them, yet are they generally attended with so many evil accidents, and pernicious consequences; and at best are so full of uncertainty and disturbance to the sick, that hardly any distemper can either be more tedious, or more threatning, scarce any one falling ill, though never so much pained grip'd and tormented with sickness, but presently the turmoile and hazzard of a glister must be undergone, then bleeding, and soon after that a purge, a vomit, a sweat, nauceous and loathsom, Decoctions, Apozems, fullsom Cordials, and insipid Juleps, and those over and over repeated, with sharp and painfull blisters, and where matters are difficult, both Opium, Antimony, and Quicksilvered preparations, are taken into service, and all these too often repeated: and though failing never so often, yet [106] other

* Pages 13–105, here deleted, include: pp. 13–67, similar to pp. 6–39 in 1669 edition; pp. 67–105, addition of "about half a hundred" cases to those described in previous works. (Editors' note)

course than this: hath not been provided for distressed Patients, till by the happy access of these Medicines, which in reason ought to be lookd upon, and thankfully entertained, as the greatest blessings of God, ever bestowed upon the sick, since the weakness and perversness of Physick hath been bewailed.

Which promps me to conclude with this farther advise.

That every one who approves of this way, will deem it of great convenience, to have some of these Medicines alwaies in readiness, what ever occasion may befall; nothing being of more hopefull importance towards a speedy and unchargeable recovery, than to give or take something of a benign and powerfull Nature, as soon as ever any illness appeareth.

And to be sure not to be over perswaded or deluded by what may hold some resemblance with these Medicines; partly in colour, and partly in [107] taste, which yet may as much differ in their effects, as thieves from true men, and as dangerous to take in times of sickness, as is the help of dissolute persons in times of trouble.

Therefore as it is requisite at all times to be seriously carefull what you admit into your bodies, so more especially in the first appearance of distemper: A good beginning being generally the happy preface to a good and comfortable conclusion.

And, as this counsel, well taken may be of continual advantage in all times, so more especially in times Contagious (which God avert) when Visits of Friends and Physicians are rendred dangerous; the Medicines here proposed being not only most proper and powerfull, but so easily managed either by the sick themselves, or any that attend them, that they may with comfort and much certainty partake the benefit thereof to their preservation and Recovery, without hazard [108] to any. And is a consideration of great importance to all, whose Offices, Employments, and Occasions deny their absence from Infectious places in those dismal times; many in the last great Mortality, under God, ascribing their freedom from Infection, and divers, their Recovery out of that threatning Distemper, to the prevalency of these benign and powerfull Medicines, observing the directions before expressed under the Titles of *Salus Vitae, Sanguis Vitae, Radix Vitae, Vita Naturae, Vindex Naturae, Athleta Naturae,* as most effectual Extinguishers of Pestilential venoms.

Think not then much of Counsel, nor be unmindfull of this Scripture, Prov. 9. 12. *If thou be wise, thou shalt be wise for thy self, but if thou scornest, thou alone shalt bear it.*

FINIS [109]

Appendixes

Appendix 1

William Walwyn's Canon

The thirty-one writings in this volume include fifteen that bear Walwyn's name or initials and are indubitably his work. Six of the signed pamphlets are largely statements of self-justification which would have been pointless if published anonymously: *A Whisper in the Eare of Mr. Thomas Edwards* (No. 9); *A Word More* (No. 10); *A Still and Soft Voice* (No. 18); *A Manifestation* (No. 22); *The Fountain of Slaunder Discovered* (No. 24); *Walwyn's Just Defence* (No. 25). Two others—*An Antidote against Master Edwards* (No. 12) and *A Prediction of Mr. Edwards* (No. 15)—convey their message with an inoffensive irony that not only permitted Walwyn to sign them without fear but secured the imprimatur of a licenser. Three signed works—*An Agreement of the Free People of England* (No. 23; cosigned with Lilburne, Prince, and Overton; the introductory "Preparative" is reprinted here as Walwyn's work); *Juries Justified* (No. 26); the hitherto unpublished "W. Walwins Conceptions" (No. 27)—are policy statements presented after the Commonwealth was established. Until the publication of the posthumous 1681 edition of *Physick for Families*, which bore his name, Walwyn's four medical works were published with his initials: *Spirits Moderated* (No. 28); *Healths New Store-House Opened* (No. 29); *A Touch-Stone for Physick* (No. 30); *Physick for Families*, 1669 and 1674 editions (No. 31).

Sixteen writings published anonymously are reprinted in this volume as Walwyn's work. Three were explicitly or implicitly acknowledged by Walwyn in 1649: *A Helpe to the Right Understanding* (No. 6); *A Word in Season* (No. 11); *A Parable, or Consultation of Physitians upon Master Edwards* (No. 17). Except for *A Parable*—the only one of five ripostes to Edwards that was not signed—the severity of Walwyn's criticisms of men in power in Parliament and the City readily explains his decision not to acknowledge his attacks at the time of publication.

Thirteen anonymous writings included in this collection have been identified as Walwyn's work by other scholars concerned with Leveller writings. Headnotes to these thirteen tracts cite the locations of the previous attributions and adjoin the present editors' reasons for concurrence.

The five tracts published between 1641 and August 1644 are primarily concerned with inclusive liberty of conscience and particularly urge toleration for the sectaries: *A New Petition of the Papists* (No. 1); *Some Considerations* (No. 2);

The Power of Love (No. 3); *The Compassionate Samaritane* (No. 4); *Good Counsell to All* (No. 5). All of them state or imply that the author is not a sectary and is a member of his parish church—a fact, as Humphrey Brooke noted, that describes Walwyn.[1] Walwyn's individualistic theology and unqualified tolerance were shared by few and disapproved by those in authority. A successful merchant and instinctively private man, Walwyn understandably published these five pieces anonymously.

Equally intelligible is the anonymous publication of the eight writings that were issued between October 1645 and March 1648/9: *Englands Lamentable Slaverie* (No. 7); *Tolleration Justified* (No. 8); *The Just Man in Bonds* (No. 13); *A Remonstrance of Many Thousand Citizens* (No. 14; two extracts are reprinted here as Walwyn's contribution); *A Demurre to the Bill for Preventing the Growth and Spreading of Heresie* (No. 16); *Gold Tried in the Fire* (No. 19); *The Bloody Project* (No. 20); *The Vanitie of the Present Churches* (No. 21). These works strongly oppose actions of men in positions of authority. Many of them propose radical alternatives.

Eleven anonymous tracts ascribed to Walwyn by modern scholars have been rejected. After 1645 ideas are a perilous guide. The presence of ideas and strategies alien to an author's known attitudes disqualify some writings from inclusion in his canon, but with few exceptions concepts that were novel in the first years of the decade were the common coin of countless radicals by the end of the first Civil War. Style, tone, and points of view provide more valid evidence of authorship, and distinctive references, phrases, and adjectives support attributions.[2] Walwyn's acknowledged works provide numerous keys to his distinctive approach and style, and while some of his later tracts are more passionate than his earlier pieces, none lacks echoes of his essential tolerance, optimism, and belief in reason.

Two attributions can be readily dismissed. C. H. Firth, in the entry for Walwyn in the *Dictionary of National Biography*, states that the contemporary suggestion that Walwyn "had a hand in" the first tract in favor of liberty of conscience refers "probably" to *Liberty of Conscience; or, The Sole Means to Obtaine Peace and Truth* ([24 March] 1643/4). However, in the entry for Henry Robinson, Firth includes *Liberty of Conscience* among Robinson's "certain" works, and Firth makes a definitive case for Robinson's authorship in an article published in 1894.[3] *Putney Projects; or, The Old Serpent in a New Forme*, "composed by . . . John Lawmind" ([30 December] 1647) is listed in Walwyn's canon by D. B. Robertson, who attributes the tract to John Wildman in the same bibliography.[4] The attribution to Walwyn may be a slip that Robertson failed to correct. "Lawmind" is a transparent anagram for "Wildman," whose attitude and tone are apparent throughout the tract.

The Afflicted Christian Justified. In a Letter to Mr. Thomas Hawes; . . . Now Prisoner for Supposed Blasphemy (18 May 1646) is an eighteen-page tract that includes a seven-page anonymous letter to Hawes. William Haller, noting that it was characteristic of Walwyn "to play the part of compassionate Samaritan," states that the letter "bears many signs of having come from Walwyn" and concludes that he was "probably the author."[5] Haller does not divulge the "signs" he detected, and while it was, indeed, like Walwyn to come to the aid of the beleaguered, in none of his known defenses does he present similarly narrow and legalistic arguments. The letter recounts the corrupt motives and false witness of Hawes's accuser, the malice and misconduct of the justices who tried the case, and contends that Hawes did not blaspheme because he acknowledged the Trinity. Concluding that "God hath still a quarrell with this Nation" because much injustice remains and "a subtill crafty, selfe-seeking" clergy "are most in favor and countenance," the last paragraph suggests that improvement may be possible as the present Parliament is bound "to heare our complaints." Finally, the letter urges Hawes to follow the example of imprisoned Marian martyrs and send letters abroad to advise good and godly people. The tone is largely accusatory with no trace of the charity, tolerance, and sweet reason that pervade *A Word in Season*, published by Walwyn the same week. No passages in the letter are distinctively Walwyn's, and the writer nowhere contends—as Walwyn surely would have done—that every man must be permitted to worship as he is persuaded in his own mind.

A Pearle in a Dounghill; or, Lieu. Col. John Lilburne in New-gate ([30 June] 1646) is attributed to Walwyn by Haller. Robertson, Joseph Frank, and A. L. Morton concur with the ascription.[6] Don M. Wolfe initially agreed, but subsequently concluded that "the fiery language and satirical sallies" in *Pearle* pointed to Richard Overton as the author.[7] The tract also has a coarseness that is unknown in works that are unquestionably Walwyn's, and some statements in *Pearle* do not accord with Walwyn's attitudes. He would not have attributed Lilburne's imprisonment to "a Popish and Episcopall party" and sarcastic comments about the Commons conflict with the respectful address in *A Word in Season*, which Walwyn published less than six weeks before *Pearle*, and in *Demurre*, which appeared in October.[8]

Vox Populi; or, The Peoples Cry against the Clergy ([25 August] 1646) is attributed to Walwyn by Haller. "Style, point of view and the imprint of Thomas Paine," wrote Haller in a footnote, "suggest that Walwyn came to the support of the citizens of Norwich in their resistance to persecution."[9] Paine's imprint is secondary evidence at best, and while Walwyn would have approved citizen opposition to a clerical Remonstrance pressing Parliament for a Presbyterian settlement, not only was he extremely busy in the summer of 1646 but he is unlikely to have known so many details about a city with which he had no connection. Moreover, although the tract has occasional references to "love, kindnesse and goodnesse" and a final plea to "all to follow the truth together in love,"[10] the style and specific attitudes are inconsistent with Walwyn's work. A meticulous account of the clergy's actions is accompanied by an aggressive attack. Ministers are rebuked for failing to move against "the knowne God provoking sins of the times, swearing, lying, defrauding, cozening and over-reaching." "Jesuiticall practises" are condemned in a manner certain to arouse anti-Catholicism and references to the *Solemn League and Covenant* do not replicate Walwyn's distinctive interpretation.[11] The evangelistic concern for the conversion of all non-Christians is at odds with Walwyn's gentle tolerance, while the absence of his fundamental precepts is notable. There is no word about inclusive liberty of conscience, the need for every man to be persuaded of faith in his own mind, or the sincerity of separatists and their steady loyalty to the parliamentary cause. Negative as well as positive evidence precludes the addition of *Vox Populi* to Walwyn's canon.

The *Poore Wise-mans Admonition unto All the Plaine People of London, and the Neighbour-Places* ([10 June] 1647) is attributed to Walwyn by A. L. Morton, who finds the tract notable for its "detailed class-analysis of the forces opposed" to the Leveller petitions of March–June 1647.[12] There is no doubt that Walwyn, who had guided the petitioning forces throughout the spring, was incensed by the Commons' burning of the petitions and accelerated his association with Cromwell and the army.[13] However, although it is possible to discover some references and attitudes in *Poore Wise-man* that are also present in Walwyn's known tracts—"yee shall judge the tree by the fruits"; "men by corruptions are growne rich"; a warning against "pretences of religion"; belief that the army's just cause triumphed "through Gods goodnesse"[14]—none of them is peculiar to Walwyn and the tract as a whole is unlike any writing known to be his. The "class-analysis" that attracts Morton describes opponents of the burnt petitions as corrupt war profiteers and secret Royalists in Parliament and the City, and the pamphlet urges "all the plaine People" to join the army in expelling "tyrannical and oppressive men" from the Commons and turning out London governors and a City militia that intend "the subjection of the plaine people."[15] Walwyn's ideal state included economic as well as political equality,[16] but neither by word or conduct did he seek to arouse one class against another. Nor does any of his acknowledged work include a threat of dire consequences—"the destruction of your selves, your wives and families"—if "plaine people" do not arise.[17] Four days after securing *Poore Wise-man*, George Thomason picked up *Gold Tried in the Fire*, a reprinting of the March–June petitions with a Preface that is all but certainly Walwyn's work. The tone is courteous, restrained, almost detached—from the opening to the concluding optimism that God will deliver the people, who should not sorrow.[18] It is all but impossible to believe that the same hand wrote *A Poore Wise-mans Admonition* within the same week.

Englands Weeping Spectacle; or, The Sad Condition of Lieutenant Colonell John Lilburne ([29 June] 1648) is attributed to Walwyn by M. A. Gibb for reasons that are nowhere stated.[19] Morton writes that Walwyn's authorship is "possible," although he dismisses the tract as "in any case unimportant." Frank, conceding that it is "possibly the work of Walwyn," points out that the "sentimentalism and stylistic exaggerations go beyond the manner of even his most religious writings."[20] If the deprecation of Walwyn's religious pamphlets is unjust, there is no question about the sentimentalism and stylistic extremism of *Englands Weeping Spectacle*. It is an emotional paean of praise for the imprisoned Lilburne, who, it is said, must be released and receive "full reparations for his foule injurious and unjust sufferings" before "any good is really intended to this Nation."[21] The plea for his release accords with Walwyn's view, as does the disillusionment with Parliament, which Walwyn had expressed in 1647. On the other hand, much of the content, like the style, is alien to Walwyn's known work. The tract lacks the calm expositions of justice that highlight Walwyn's earlier defenses of Lilburne,[22] while the harsh attacks on Cromwell and Henry Ireton and the sweeping condemnations of the Commons, lawyers, judges, clergymen, and apathetic people are contrary to Walwyn's innate civility. There is no appeal to charity and reason and no hint of the ultimate optimism that emerges in pieces as diverse as Walwyn's rebukes to individuals and institutions in 1646 and his denunciation of the second War in the summer of 1648. These inclusions and omissions, added to the absence of any mention of the goals of Lilburne and the Levellers, leave no reasonable doubt that someone other than Walwyn wrote *Englands Weeping Spectacle*.

The Humble Petition of 11 September 1648 is all but certainly among the petitions that Walwyn's adversaries had in mind when they described his masterly "craft and subtilty, viz. in the framing, ordering and managing of their Petitions."[23] Wolfe and Morton conclude that it is mainly Walwyn's work; Frank assigns it to Lilburne and Walwyn; G. E. Aylmer suggests Walwyn and Overton as the draftsmen. Haller and Davies state that the petition "was probably drafted by Lilburne in consultation with other leaders of the Leveller party."[24] The attributions to Walwyn in whole or in part are readily understood. The proposals for reform were common to all Leveller leaders; the conciliatory tone of the petition is very like that in petitions drafted by Walwyn in the spring of 1647.[25] However, Lilburne, recently released from the Tower, was in an unusually conciliatory mood toward Army grandees in the autumn of 1648 and subsequently wrote: "I was compelled in conscience to have a hand in that most excellent of Petitions of the 11 of Septemb. 1648. which (I am sure) was no small piece of service to Cromwel and his great Associates."[26] Walwyn, on the other hand, praised the content but stressed "how little I had to do in that Petition." Since Walwyn at the same time implied that he had drafted the Large Petition of March 1647,[27] there seems no reason to question his denial of significant participation in the later appeal. There can be little doubt that he was among Lilburne's close consultants, and he either contributed or later appropriated a phrase deploring beggary "in so fruitful a Nation as through Gods blessing this is." It is repeated without significant alteration in *Walwyns Just Defence*.[28]

No Papist nor Presbyterian ([21 December] 1648) is a plea for toleration for Roman Catholics. Frank states that "its views and its style" suggest that it "may well have been the work of Walwyn." Morton questions the attribution,

and Wolfe, who reprints the tract, doubts that the style is Walwyn's (or Overton's), noting that the stress on liberty for Papists is alien to the Levellers'
appeal for universal toleration.[29] The tract asks for additions to the second
Agreement of the People—which Walwyn helped draft—and is unlike Walwyn in its limitation of toleration to those "that profess Christ." Walwyn
made no exceptions, repeatedly writing that there should be liberty of conscience for "all professions whatsoever," including those who deny the existence of a Diety.[30] Walwyn opposed tithes absolutely, whereas the author of
No Papist proposed their elimination only for those who expressed scruples
against them.[31] Finally, although Walwyn occasionally mentioned successful
toleration in other lands, he never suggested, as No Papist does, that it was
practiced by "most Governments," and his primary appeal was always to
reason, Scripture, and the example of Jesus and the Apostles.[32] The presence
of viewpoints contrary to Walwyn's and the absence of his characteristic attitudes and language prohibit the inclusion of No Papist in Walwyn's canon.

The English Souldiers Standard to Repaire to ([5 April] 1649) is attributed to
Walwyn by H. N. Brailsford. Morton adds that Thomason's date of acquisition
one week after the imprisonment of the Leveller leaders—during which week
all but Walwyn worked on their defenses—increases the likelihood that the
pamphlet "was at least drafted by Walwyn."[33] There is no reason to doubt
Walwyn's concurrence with the tract's appeal to the individual consciences of
the soldiers, its stress on their need to gain civilian support, and its disapproval
of the Irish invasion. The caution to soldiers to "examine all things which shall
be proposed unto you to act upon" is also consonant with Walwyn's tone.[34] For
the most part, however, the tone, language, and underlying message are alien
to Walwyn. Contemptuous epithets—"uncircumcised Philistins" in Parliament; "Tyrant" officers; "ignorant" and "sottish" Papists[35]—are not only
unlike Walwyn but impossible to reconcile with his tacit acceptance of the
parliamentary republic before his arrest and the temperate argument in his
Manifestation, written during the first fortnight of his imprisonment. Attacks on
the general officers that pervade The English Souldiers Standard carry an incitement to mutiny that is at odds with Walwyn's aloofness from similar moves in
1647 and with his stated rejection of divisive tactics at any time.[36] There is no
evidence that The English Souldiers Standard was written after the four Levellers
were in custody, and it is probable that it is the work of someone who had been
participating in efforts to provoke an army mutiny during the weeks preceding
the 28 March arrest.

Tyranipocrit. Discovered with His Wiles, Wherewith He Vanquishes ([14 August]
1649) was published, according to the title page, in Rotterdam. In 1948 Harold
Laski declared that Tyranipocrit's "author was almost certainly William Walwyn."[37] Laski gives no evidence. H. N. Brailsford assumes that Walwyn is the
author and promises evidence in an Appendix that Christopher Hill, who
edited Brailsford's work after his death, did not find. Olivier Lutaud states
that Tyranipocrit is "probablement de Walwyn," but his extracts and analysis

draw no parallels with Walwyn's work.[38] Jack R. McMichael, considering the possibility of Walwyn's authorship, observed that the self-described author of *Tyranipocrit* reveals that he (like Walwyn) is a layman of some means, well versed in sacred and human writings, a believer in reason who hopes his readers will consider his ideas without prejudice and make their own judgments. McMichael also discerned ideas shared by Walwyn and the author of *Tyranipocrit* and detected a Walwyn-like irony in the style.[39]

Elements of Walwyn's style are consonant with aspects of *Tyranipocrit*, although it is more fervent than anything known to be Walwyn's and the marriage of "two Imps of hell"—the black devil, tyranny, and the white devil, hypocrisy—to create the monster, Tyranipocrit, is a great distance from the gentle symbolism employed by Walwyn in his controversy with Thomas Edwards.[40] *Tyranipocrit's* opening statement that God is speaking through the writer has a righteousness atypical of Walwyn, and the numerous Latin words and phrases interspersed throughout the pamphlet are at variance with Walwyn's practice and his contention that he knew no Latin but common proverbs that he occasionally used because they were pertinent. The emotional tone and relentless condemnation of those who practice tyranny and hypocrisy might be viewed as echoes of *The Bloody Project*, but while *Tyranipocrit's* author anticipates Utopia if men become equal, nowhere does he echo the pragmatic optimism that surfaces in the final paragraphs of Walwyn's denunciation of "causelesse War."[41]

McMichael identified a number of attitudes in *Tyranipocrit* that accord with Walwyn's convictions: condemnation of tyranny and hypocrisy; man's search for God within himself; the belief that God is love; the importance of loving one's neighbor and doing good works— although neither works nor faith can insure salvation for which the *"unum necessarium"* is the love of God in Christ.[42] Walwyn also concurred with the belief that the story of Adam is a revelation of repentance and forgiveness; with the detestation of war, concern for the poor, admiration for primitive cultures, and the communal society of early Christians; and with appeals for "the law of God, nature, and reason."[43] Walwyn rejected predestination for salvation through the gospel of love, but *Tyranipocrit's* all-out attack on the doctrine of predestination as "blasphemous" is unlike Walwyn's inclusive tolerance and none of his known writings fits "another worke" in which, concludes *Tyranipocrit's* author, "I have treated of this matter."[44]

The central proposal of the writer of *Tyranipocrit* is economic equality. God gave man "a sparke of his owne essence," which presumably will assist him to share his goods "consonant to the law of God and nature, and agreeable to the rule of Christ."[45] Thus far, there is no conflict with Walwyn's vision of sharing, equality, and brotherhood, motivated by love and impelled from within. However, *Tyranipocrit's* author, apparently distrustful of "the rich artificiall theeves [who] doe rob the poore, and . . . say and affirm, that Gods providence hath made them rich," asserts that "the Magistrates duty is, equally to divide and share . . . and yet that is not enough, but once in a yeere, or oftener, thou must examine every mans estate, to see if they have not made their goods uneven, and if they have, then thou must make it even againe."[46] The imposition of equality by fiat is a far cry from the egalitarian ideal envisioned by Walwyn. It is, rather, the style of "levelling" he expressly rejected in *A Manifestation*, *An Agreement of the Free People*, and *Walwyns Just Defence*, all of which were published within a few months of the appearance of *Tyranipocrit*.[47] Unless Walwyn dissembled in three publications that carried his name, he opposed the coerced equality advanced by the author of *Tyranipocrit*.

There are other difficulties with the attribution. In addition to the Epistle and the Preface, the pamphlet consists of four parts, and internal evidence indicates that the first and fourth parts were written at different times. The last section, "A Caveat for Princes," obviously was written after the execution of King Charles. The first and longest section—the "Tyranipocrit" division— apparently was drafted in the autumn of 1648: "Now at this present time," writes the author, "are assembled at Munster, the Agents of most of our su- preame christian Rulers."[48] Walwyn would have known this, as English newssheets of October and November carried accounts of the meetings and the peace treaty. However, it was an exceedingly busy time for Walwyn: he was a principal in the meetings of Levellers and other radicals that led to the Agreement of the People submitted to the Council of Officers in mid-De- cember.[49] If he were writing a long and complex treatise at the same time it is unlikely that he would have ignored the situation in England and concen- trated his fire on "Princes and Prelates" such as the Holy Roman Emperor, the Pope of Rome, "the Catholic, and the most Christian Kings," and "such false Christians as inhabit Europia."[50]

Throughout the pamphlet the writer reveals a preoccupation with Europe that is nowhere evident in works known to be Walwyn's. England's mistreat- ment of the Irish is condemned along with denunciations of cruelties by Hun- gary, France, Spain, and the Low Countries, and the target is always all "Christian Rulers."[51] The third and fourth sections—"An Intelligencer to the Reformers" and "A Caveat for Princes"—leave no doubt that the writer is an Englishman. "An Intelligencer" addresses the Lords and Commons, who are curiously termed "worthy Senators," condemning them for their failure to "maintain an equallity of goods and lands" or to set an example by parting with their own means in excess of £100 a year. In the same section the writer suggests his orientation by describing a year in accordance with the Gre- gorian Calendar used on the Continent: "from the first of January, to the last of December." "A Caveat for Princes" contends that the King's death is God's will and makes its broader point in warning that the entire Christian world "hath been pestered too long with ceremonial Kings and Priests, it is now time to casheere them."[52]

Tyranipocrit is a remarkable pamphlet which the text states is not the only work of the man who wrote it.[53] So far, however, there are convincing objections to every name that has been suggested as that of the author. Given the European emphasis of the tract and assuming that the Rotterdam imprint is authentic,[54] it is most probable that the writer was an Englishman residing in the Low Countries.

Publications of 1647–49 include a number that could have been written by Walwyn, but there is insufficient evidence that he did write them to include them in his canon. The Levellers' three Agreements of the People are works in which Walwyn was certainly involved. His collaboration in the Agreement of May 1649 was attested at the time and the opening "Preparative" is reprinted among his works in this volume (No. 23). He also participated in drawing up the articles of the constitution but neither the ideology nor the style is peculiarly his. The second Agreement, published in December 1648 as *Foundations of Freedom*, is another collaborative work and Walwyn was one of the four Levellers who dominated the committee that drafted it.[55] Again, while he could have written it, nothing distinguishes it as his work alone.

More tantalizing is Walwyn's part in the first *Agreement*, which was presented at Putney in 1647 as the proposal of "the Agents of the five Regiments of Horse."[56] Clearly, the ten agents who signed the *Agreement* did not draw it up by themselves, and it is variously attributed to one or more of the civilian Levellers—Lilburne, Overton, Walwyn, and Wildman—and possibly the soldier-agitator Edward Sexby.[57] There is a distinct echo of Walwyn's basic argument for religious liberty, and further reasons supporting Walwyn's involvement are set forth in the Introduction to this volume.[58] However, the proposals in the *Agreement* were widely held by the autumn of 1647, and while the style is very like Walwyn's known work there is no substantive reason to ascribe the *Agreement* to his pen alone.

Walwyn's adversaries observed that "one of the great Masterpeeces of his craft and subtilty" was the framing and managing of Leveller petitions.[59] Beyond the petitions he acknowledged and those that are attributed to him on the basis of internal and external evidence, it is probable that he was at least partly responsible for some others. Walwyn noted his part in petitions that were blocked by City Independents in the autumn of 1646,[60] and he may have influenced the petition urging the Commons to ratify the 1647 *Agreement of the People*. Presented to the House on 23 November 1647, the petition was published two days later with an aggressive appeal that is certainly not Walwyn's work.[61] The petition itself is quieter and more courteous, but there is no evidence that Walwyn participated in the drafting.

Walwyn may have written some of the leaders that appeared in *The Moderate*, a weekly news sheet published between July 1648 and September 1649. The paper soon became an unofficial advocate of Leveller proposals, publishing petitions, manifestoes, and sympathetic articles. A feature of most issues is the unsigned leader. Brailsford, suggesting that Overton was largely responsible for the better writing that enlivened the paper in the autumn, observes that "the well-to-do Walwyn might possibly have written an occasional contribution to help the party organ."[62] The content of the leaders is compatible with the views of all the Leveller writers at this time, and while Walwyn certainly could have written several of those appearing in October and November, there is nothing sufficiently distinctive about the language and style to support a conclusion that he did write any one of them.

The ascription of thirteen unacknowledged tracts to Walwyn, the rejection of eleven anonymous works previously attributed to him, and the classification of other writings as possible but uncertain have been determined after careful study of the known works of Walwyn and his contemporaries and respectful attention to the views of scholars who have considered anonymous writings of the Interregnum. No decision has been reached without acute awareness of the possibility of error. Writings that are now unknown may be identified as Walwyn's work and it is possible that information not yet discovered will compel reconsideration of some of the attributions included here. Evidence of the authorship of unacknowledged writings is usually imperfect. As Walwyn observed in 1642: "How ever each man concludes himselfe to be in the right . . . he may be mistaken, and upon better reasons which as yet he sees not may alter his judgement and be convinc't."[63]

BARBARA TAFT

William Walwyn's Last Will and Testament

Printed from the original proved in the Prerogative Court of Canterbury, 13 North.
The copy in the Public Record Office is Prob. 11/365.

William Walwyn's last will was probated in London on 14 January 1680/1, the same month in which the will was signed and witnessed.

Richard Halford, sole executor, is the son-in-law named in the posthumous 1681 edition of *Physick for Families* as the possessor of Walwyn's secret formulas and the man from whom the medicines can be procured.[1]

Thomas Exton, priest of St. Giles, Cripplegate, attested the probate of the will, and the St. Giles parish records include an entry for the burial of "William Walwin: Phisitan" on 16 January 1680/1. The cause of death is recorded as "Aged."[2]

Translation of the Latin probate:[3]

Proved in London before the venerable man Sir Richard Lloyd, knight, Doctor of Laws, surrogate etc. on the fourteenth day of the month of January A D 1680 [O.S.] by oath of Richard Halford Executor etc. to whom [administration was granted] he being sworn well [and truly to administer the same etc.].

14 January 1680 given to Richard Halford, Executor within-named, sworn before me.

Thomas Exton, Sacerdos [priest] St. Giles Cripplegate.

William Walwyn's Last Will and Testament

In the name of God Amen, I William Walwyn of Finsbury in the County of Middlesex physician; though weake in body yet God be praysed of sound and good memory, doe make this my last will and testament in maner and forme following that is to say first I give and bequeath my Soule unto God firmly believing that I have Redemption by Christ the foregiveness of my sins: Item I give my body to the Earth to be buryed according to the discretion of my Executor, herein hereafter mentioned provided that no mourning be worne for me: And for my worldly goods; in the first place I give and bequeath unto my sonn in law Mr. Francis Jenckes the two hundred pound he

hath in his hands, and should have beene returned back to me upon his
parting with my grandson William Halford: And I doe hereby make and con-
stitute my sonn in law Mr. Richard Halford my sole and absolute Executor of
this my last will and testament & with this desier That in the best maner he
can, and as soone as may be he will secure unto his three daughters Elizabeth
Anne and Sarah two hundred pounds a peece to be payd unto each of them
at the age of twenty yeeres or dayes of marryage: and if any dye before, the
survivor or survivors, to enjoy the portion of the deceased equally: And I
doe make my Loveing Friend Mr William Michell my overseer, In wittness
whereof I have hereunto set my hand and seale in the yeere of our Lord one
thousand six hundred and eighty:

                                                        William Walwyn

Signed sealed declared and published as my last will and testament (the word
the being only interlined) in the presence of J Best, Tho Hayward, Elizabeth
Pery, Elizabeth Michell. William Walwyn. January 1680. Roy E., Ech.

Probatum Londini coram venerabili viro Domino Richardo Lloyd milite
Legium Doctore Surrogato etc Decimo quarto die mensis Januarii Anno Do-
mini 1680 Juramento Richardis Halford Executoris etc Cui etc de bene etc
Juratum.

Dorse 14 Januarii 1680 juxta etc. Richardus Halford Executor intranominatus
juratus coram me.

                                                        Tho. Exton
                                                        Sacerdos
                                                        St. Giles Crippleg:

Notes

Introduction

Works by William Walwyn are cited by short title. The first citation to a title is followed by the number of the work in this volume.

1. Thomas Habington (1560–1647), *A Survey of Worcestershire*, ed. J. Amphlett, 2 vols. (Oxford, 1895–99), 2:179–80. The Parish Registers of Newland, Worcester Record Office, vol. 1, unpaginated, list William's baptism, 17 August 1600, and other Walwyn family records. For family arms, see *Victoria County History, Worcester*, 4 vols. (1901–24), 4:127. For William Walwyn, see: C. H. Firth, *Dictionary of National Biography* (hereafter *DNB*), s.v.; Joseph Frank, *The Levellers* (Cambridge, Mass., 1955), s.v.; *Tracts on Liberty in the Puritan Revolution, 1638–1647*, ed. William Haller, 3 vols. (New York, 1934), 1:33–45; A. L. Morton, *The World of the Ranters* (London, 1970), chap. 6; Lotte Mulligan, "The Religious Roots of William Walwyn's Radicalism," *Journal of Religious History* (Sydney, Australia) 12 (1982): 162–79; Wilhelm Schenk, *The Concern for Social Justice in the Puritan Revolution* (New York, 1948), chap. 3—which is essentially a reproduction of his article, "A Seventeenth-Century Radical," *Economic History Review* 14 (1944): 74–83.
2. Humphrey Brooke, *The Charity of Church-men* ([28 May] 1649), p. 10.
3. *Fountain* (No. 24), p. 1. *Alumni Oxonienses . . . 1500–1714*, ed. J. Foster, 4 vols. (Oxford, 1891–92), 4:1567 (s.v. "Harbart Walweyn"); the Parish Registers of Newland, vol. 1, record the 1598 baptism of Herbert Walwyn.
4. She signed her will with her "marke": Will of Elizabeth Dickins proved 9 September 1659, Public Record Office (hereafter PRO), Prob. 11/294 (Prerogative Court of Canterbury 418 Pell). The first bequest is "to my Sonne William Walweine tenne pounds in monie." The Parish Registers of Newland, vol. 1, penultimate page, record the 1616 marriage of Elizabeth Walwyn to John Dickins; cf. Habington, *Survey of Worcestershire*, 2:179.
5. *Just Defence* (No. 25), pp. 9, 18. See also Brooke, *Charity*, p. 5.
6. *Fountain*, pp. 1–2, 17, 24.
7. Brooke, *Charity*, p. 10.

8. St. James Garlickhythe Parish Register, MS 9139 (1622–66), Guildhall Library, London, 17 April 1627.

9. Walwyn entries run from 17 April 1627 to 1642. No sons, apparently, attained manhood; in 1649 Walwyn referred only to daughters (*Fountain*, p. 8).

10. Brooke, *Charity*, pp. 10–11.

11. *Fountain*, p. 2. St. James Garlickhythe Parish Register, MS 9139 (1622–66), 24 February 1629/30, 1633. *The Inhabitants of London in 1638*, ed. T. C. Dale (London, 1931), p. 74.

12. Vestry Minutes, St. James Garlickhythe, MS 4813, Guildhall Library, London, no. 1 (1615–93), fols. 54–55 (1639, 1640/1). Churchwardens Accounts, St. James Garlickhythe, MS 4810, Guildhall Library, London, no. 2 (1627–99), fol. 84; Walwyn's 1638 contribution to the poor is listed as £3.

13. *Whisper* (No. 9), p. 4. For church reformation, see Introduction, p. 9.

14. *Whisper*, pp. 5–6. For attacks on Walwyn's questioning ways, see: Thomas Edwards, *Gangraena*, pt. 1 ([26 Feb.] 1645/6), p. 96, pt. 2 ([28 May] 1646), pp. 25–30; John Vicars, *The Schismatick Sifted* ([22 June] 1646), pp. 23–24; William Kiffin et al., *Walwins Wiles* ([10 May] 1649), pp. 6–7.

15. *Fountain*, p. 22. Kiffin et al., *Walwins Wiles*, passim. Brooke, *Charity*, p. 11; cf. *Fountain*, pp. 11, 17, 24.

16. Will of William Walwyn, "physitian, Finsbury," Appendix 2.

17. *Fountain*, p. 14; Brooke, *Charity*, p. 10; *Just Defence*, pp. 6–7.

18. *Just Defence*, p. 9.

19. *Whisper*, p. 3.

20. *Power of Love* (No. 3), "To the Reader." *Helpe* (No. 6), p. 4.

21. *Just Defence*, p. 9. William Haller, *Liberty and Reformation in the Puritan Revolution* (New York, 1955), pp. 169–71, where Haller considers the probable effect on Walwyn of his reading.

22. *Petition of the Papists* (No. 1), pp. 6–7.

23. *Just Defence*, p. 13. [Benedetto da Mantova], *The Benefite of Christs Death; or, The Glorious Riches of Gods Free Grace*, trans. A.G., 3d ed. (London, 1633).

24. *Just Defence*, p. 13. *Vanitie* (No. 21), p. 20.

25. *Calendar of State Papers, Domestic* (hereafter *CSPD*), 1641–43, pp. 506–07. L.S., *The Fulnesse of God's Love Manifested* (1643). Samuel Eames, second bondsman for Sanders, was a founder of the Particular Baptists (Murray Tolmie, *The Triumph of the Saints* [Cambridge, 1977], p. 145).

26. *Just Defence*, p. 8.

27. Brooke, *Charity*, p. 5.

28. *Fountain*, p. 14.

29. Brooke, *Charity*, pp. 4–5. *Just Defence*, pp. 9–13.

30. *Just Defence*, p. 11. Michaell de Montaigne, *The Essayes*, trans. John Florio (London, 1603), bk. 1, chap. 30, "Of the Caniballes." See also Olivier Lutaud, "Montaigne chez les niveleurs anglais: Walwyn et les 'Essais,'" *Rivista di letterature moderne e comparate* 12 (1959): 53–58.

31. Pierre Charron, *Of Wisdome*, trans. Samson Lennard (London, pre–1612; facsimile reprint, Amsterdam, 1971), bk. 2, chap. 2, pp. 232, 239, 243–44. Cf. *Still and Soft Voice* (No. 18).

32. *Just Defence*, pp. 26–27. Sir Walter Raleigh, attrib. author, *The Life and Death of Mahomet* (London, 1637). Edward Coke, *Institutes of the Lawes of England*, 4 vols. (London, 1628–44).

33. *Whisper*, p. 3.

34. *Just Defence*, p. 10.

35. *Power of Love*, esp. "To the Reader" and p. 20.

36. *Still and Soft Voice*, esp. pp. 13, 16.

37. *Vanitie*, esp. pp. 12–18. *Just Defence*, p. 8.

38. *Vanitie*, esp. pp. 23–24, 29–35.

39. Ibid., pp. 30–31.

40. *Fountain*, p. 5. *Vanitie*, pp. 20–21. Martin Luther, *The Freedom of a Christian*, as in Luther, *Works*, 55 vols. (Philadelphia, 1955—), 31:358–77 esp. Walwyn apparently was unaware of Luther's harsh denunciations of Anabaptist sectaries.

41. *Whisper*, pp. 2–3; cf. *Fountain*, p. 10.

42. *Whisper*, p. 9.

43. *Prediction* (No. 15), p. 18.

44. *Parable* (No. 17), esp. p. 13.

45. *Power of Love*, pp. 1–2.

46. Ibid., esp. p. 3. See Introduction, p. 5.

47. *Power of Love*, pp. 7–8.

48. Nicholas Tyacke, "Puritanism, Arminianism and Counter-Revolution," in *The Origins of the English Civil War*, ed. Conrad Russell (London, 1973), pp. 119–43, esp. p. 128.

49. Anthony Fletcher, *The Outbreak of the English Civil War* (London, 1981), chap. 3, "Episcopacy and the Liturgy."

50. John Morrill, "The Church in England, 1642–9," *Reactions to the English Civil War, 1642–1649*, ed. John Morrill (London, 1982), No. 4, esp. pp. 89–95.

51. *Good Counsell* (No. 5), pp. 84–86. Cf.: *Power of Love*, "To every Reader"; *Helpe*, p. 4; *Tolleration Justified* (No. 8), p. 14; *Whisper*, pp. 5, 9.

52. *Demurre* (No. 16), pp. 4–6; cf. *Still and Soft Voice*, p. 16.

53. *Whisper*, p. 5; *Tolleration Justified*, p. 14. Walwyn repeated the golden rule many times; e.g.: *Compassionate Samaritane* (No. 4), title; *Helpe*, p. 4; *Prediction*, p. 16.

54. *Helpe*, pp. 3–4.

55. *Prediction*, pp. 15–16.

56. *Still and Soft Voice*, p. 3; cf. *Whisper*, p. 6.

57. *Compassionate Samaritane*, pp. 10–11.

58. *Prediction*, p. 4. *Parable*, p. 4. Cf.: *Compassionate Samaritane*, p. 53; *Helpe*, p. 4; *Whisper*, p. 14.

59. *Still and Soft Voice*, pp. 11–13. Cf.: *Prediction*, p. 3; *Demurre*, p. 3.

60. *Compassionate Samaritane*, pp. 6–7.

61. *Petition of the Papists*, p. 2; cf. *Demurre*, pp. 5–6.

62. *Parable*, p. 15; cf. *Still and Soft Voice*, p. 16.

63. *Prediction*, pp. 3–4. Cf.: *Helpe*, p. 4; *Whisper*, pp. 5, 9.

64. *Prediction*, pp. 13–14.

65. *Petition of the Papists*, pp. 3–4.

66. *Power of Love*, p. 43.

67. *Vanitie*, title page: Galatians 5:6 and 6:15, 16. In *Helpe*, p. 4, Walwyn cites Romans 14:3 on Paul's permissiveness.

68. *Petition of the Papists*, pp. 2–3. Cf.: *Compassionate Samaritane*, p. 46; *Tolleration Justified*, pp. 5–6.

69. *Some Considerations* (No. 2), esp. pp. 4–5, 8–9. Cf.: *Power of Love*, p. 43; *Compassionate Samaritane*, p. 79; *Helpe*, pp. 3, 7; *Antidote* (No. 12), pp. 9–11; *Demurre*, pp. 1–2; *Parable*, p. 15.

70. *Antidote*, pp. 15–16.

71. Ibid., pp. 11–14; *Demurre*, p. 7.

72. *Compassionate Samaritane*, pp. 42–43, see also pp. 53–54. Cf.: *Demurre*, p. 6; *Tolleration Justified*, p. 14.

73. *Word More* (No. 10), esp. pp. 3–6; cf.: *Tolleration Justified*, pp. 13–14. *A Solemn League and Covenant for Reformation and Defence of Religion*, taken by the Commons, 25 Sept. 1643, reprinted, *The Constitutional Documents of the Puritan Revolution, 1625–1660*, ed. S. R. Gardiner, 3d ed. (Oxford, 1906), No. 58.

74. *Whisper*, p. 6. Parliament had adopted, 8 November 1644, an ordinance "for the true Payment of Tithes, and such other Duties, according to the Laws and Customs of this Realm" (*Lords Journals*, 7:53–54).

75. *Gold Tried in the Fire* (No. 19), Petition of March 1646/7, Article 9.

76. *An Agreement of the Free People of England* (1 May 1649), Articles 23, 24, 26. Walwyn's agreement to the restriction on Papists is inexplicable.

77. *Demurre*, p. 3.

78. *Tolleration Justified*, p. 7.

79. Thomas Hobbes, *Behemoth; or, An Epitome of the Civil Wars of England, From 1640, to 1660* (London, 1679), pp. 20–21.

80. *Helpe*, p. 7.

81. *Whisper*, pp. 3–4.

82. *Petition of the Papists*, pp. 1–5. The pamphlet is probably the "book . . . upon that Subject" described by Humphrey Brooke, *Charity*, p. 11; Brooke noted that Walwyn was not personally concerned, as he was not a sectary but a member of his parish church (cf.: *Petition of the Papists*, pp. 3–5; *Some Considerations*, pp. 7–8; *Power of Love*, p. 22; *Compassionate Samaritane*, p. 4; *Good Counsell*, pp. 91–92; *Helpe*, pp. 3–4, 6; *Whisper*, p. 5).

83. Brooke, *Charity*, p. 11.

84. *A Petition . . . concerning the Draught of an Agreement of the People . . .*

Together with the Said Agreement ([22 Jan.] 1648/9), Article 9. Cf. *An Agreement of the Free People of England* (1649), Article 26.

85. *The Instrument of Government*, 16 December 1653, Article 37.

86. J[ohn] M[ilton], *Of True Religion, Haeresie, Schism, Toleration* (1673), passim.

87. John Locke, *A Letter concerning Toleration*, tr. William Popple (London, 1689), pp. 47–48.

88. *Tolleration Justified*, pp. 8–9; cf. *Demurre*, pp. 4–5; *Still and Soft Voice*, p. 16.

89. Thomas Goodwin et al., *An Apologeticall Narration* ([3 Jan.] 1643/4), esp. pp. 23–24. Tolmie, *Triumph of the Saints*, chap. 5.

90. *Certaine Considerations to Dis-swade* . . . ([28 Dec.] 1643), esp. pp. 3–4. Tolmie, *Triumph of the Saints*, p. 130.

91. For highlights of the controversy, see *Tracts on Liberty*, ed. Haller, 1:50–52, 59.

92. *Compassionate Samaritane*, pp. 1–4, 70. Thomas Bakewell, *A Confutation of the Anabaptists* ([21 June] 1644).

93. *Helpe*, esp. pp. 5–6, 8–9. William Prynne, *Independency Examined, Unmasked, Refuted* ([26 Sept.] 1644). William Prynne, *Truth Triumphing over Falshood* ([2 Jan.] 1644/5).

94. Richard Baxter, *Reliquiae Baxterianae*, ed. Matthew Sylvester (London, 1696), pt. 1, pp. 50–51.

95. Hugh Peter, *God's Doings, and Man's Duty*, ([2 April] 1646), esp. pp. 25–45.

96. For Parliament's attempts to achieve some religious indulgence for "tender Consciences," see *Commons Journals* (hereafter *CJ*), 4:428 (3 Feb.) and "A Declaration of the Commons . . . ," 17 April 1646, ibid., pp. 513–14. For the City, see Valerie Pearl, "London's Counter-Revolution," in *The Interregnum: The Quest for Settlement, 1646–1660*, ed. G. E. Aylmer (London, 1972), No. 1, esp. pp. 35–37.

97. Edwards, *Gangraena*, pt. 2, pp. 27–28.

98. *Just Defence*, p. 2.

99. Nos. 9, 10, 12, 15, 17. Introduction, p. 7.

100. *Tolleration Justified. A Letter of the Ministers of the City of London . . . against Toleration* (1 Jan. 1645/6). For a reply to *Tolleration Justified*, see *Anti-Toleration; or, A Modest Defence of the Letter of the London Ministers* ([16 April] 1646).

101. *Word in Season* (No. 11), Thomason's MS note on 26 May edition. *Word in Season*, Thomason's MS note on 18 May edition. *The Humble Remonstrance and Petition of the Lord Mayor, Aldermen and Commons of the City of London, in Common Councell Assembled* (26 May 1646). The *Remonstrance* had "circulated for at least a month before its presentation" (Pearl, "London's Counter-Revolution," p. 36).

102. *Demurre*, p. 3. For consideration of the ordinance in Grand Committee, see *CJ*, 4:659–74 (2–23 Sept.), passim; for passage, 2 May 1648, see Introduction, p. 33 and n. 163.

103. *Just Defence*, pp. 3–4. *Still and Soft Voice*, pp. 4–5, 7–9, 16.

104. Claire Cross, "The Church in England, 1646–1660," in *The Interregnum*, ed. Aylmer, No. 4, esp. p. 115. Morrill, "The Church in England, 1642–9," pp. 95–98. Tolmie, *Triumph of the Saints*, p. 4 and passim.

105. *Still and Soft Voice*, passim, esp. pp. 8–10, 14, 16.

106. *Whisper*, pp. 2–3; cf. *Power of Love*, pp. 39–41.

107. *Calendar of the Proceedings of the Committee for Advance of Money, 1642–1656*, pt. 1, pp. vi–vii, 1–2.

108. *Some Considerations*, pp. 4–5, 13–14. "Protestant," in this instance, refers to members of the established church.

109. *Slaverie* (No. 7), p. 5; cf. *A Manifestation* (No. 22), p. 3. J. C. Davis, "The Levellers and Christianity," in *Politics, Religion and the English Civil War*, ed. Brian Manning (London, 1973), No. 6, points out that "in most important respects, the Levellers never distinguished between natural and divine law" (see esp. p. 227).

110. *Whisper*, p. 4; *Just Defence*, pp. 8, 14. For the Remonstrance, see Valerie Pearl, *London and the Outbreak of the Puritan Revolution* (Oxford, 1961), pp. 260–61.

111. *Whisper*, pp. 4–6. For subcommittee at Salters' Hall, see Pearl, *London*, pp. 260, 267–73.

112. *Whisper*, p. 3; cf. *Fountain*, p. 10.

113. Pauline Gregg, *Free-born John; A Biography of John Lilburne* (London, 1961), esp. pp. 116–20.

114. *Slaverie*, pp. 1, 3–6.

115. Gregg, *Free-born John*, pp. 52–66.

116. John Bastwick, *A Just Defence . . . against the Calumnies of John Lilburne* ([30 August] 1645), pp. 16–17. Bastwick and Lilburne referred to Walwyn as "Worly" at this time (*Tracts on Liberty*, ed. Haller, 1:100, n. 109).

117. The name was used during the army debates at Putney, October 1647—John Lilburne, *The Legall Fundamentall Liberties of the People of England* ([18 June] 1649), p. 36; probably it had been current for some time. For an evaluation of studies of the Levellers, see J. S. Morrill, *Seventeenth-Century Britain, 1603–1714* (Hamden, Connecticut, 1980), pp. 41–42.

118. Kiffin et al., *Walwins Wiles*, esp. p. A3. For Overton, see: Marie Gimelfarb-Brack, *Liberté, egalité, fraternité, justice! La vie et l'oeuvre de Richard Overton, niveleur* (Berne, 1979); Frank, *Levellers*, s.v.; *Tracts on Liberty*, ed. Haller, s.v.

119. Lilburne was a member of Edmund Rosier's separatist church; Overton belonged to Thomas Lambe's General Baptist congregation (Tolmie, *Triumph of the Saints*, pp. 36, 151–54).

120. *Helpe*, p. 4; cf. p. 7.

121. *Slaverie*, p. 3.

122. *Word in Season*, esp. pp. 3–7. For the City *Remonstrance*, see Introduction, p. 18.

123. *Just Man* (No. 13).

124. Passages from *A Remonstrance* that are identifiable as Walwyn's are reprinted below (No. 14). The complete text is reproduced in facsimile in *Tracts on Liberty*, ed. Haller, 3:351–70; it is reprinted in *Leveller Manifestoes of the Puritan Revolution*, ed. Don M. Wolfe (New York, 1944, reprinted, 1967), No. 1.

125. [John Lilburne], *Englands Birth-right Justified* ([October] 1645), p. 45.

126. *Just Defence*, p. 31.

127. *CJ*, 4:561 (2 June 1646). Bulstrode Whitelocke, *Memorials of the English Affairs*, new ed. (London, 1732), p. 208. Edwards, *Gangraena*, pt. 3, p. 146.

128. *Just Defence*, pp. 2–3; Brooke, *Charity*, p. 10. For separatists, see Tolmie, *Triumph of the Saints*, pp. 147–48.

129. Kiffin et al., *Walwins Wiles*, passim.

130. Overton, imprisoned 11 August 1646, was released 16 Sept. 1647; Lilburne, imprisoned 16 June 1646, was given liberty on bail, 9 Nov. 1647 (*DNB*, s.v.).

131. *Just Defence*, p. 4; *Fountain*, p. 7.

132. Tolmie, *Triumph of the Saints*, pp. 150–53.

133. *Gold Tried in the Fire*, pp. 1–6.

134. *Just Defence*, pp. 4–5; *CJ*, 5:112, 119 (15, 20 March), 162 (4 May), 179–80 (20 May), 195 (2 June). For Independents and Baptists, see Tolmie, *Triumph of the Saints*, pp. 153–54.

135. *Gold Tried in the Fire*, preface, p. A2v. The March–June petitions are appended to the preface, pp. 1–12.

136. *Just Defence*, p. 5.

137. John Lilburne, *The Juglers Discovered* ([Oct.] 1647), esp. pp. 1–3, [12]. Cf.: *Two Letters Writ by Lieut. Col. John Lilburne . . . to Col. Henry Martin, a Member of the House of Commons, upon the 13 and 15 of September 1647* ([22 September] 1647), p. 4; John Lilburne, *The Just Mans Justification*, 2d ed. ([18 September] 1647), in which the appended address to "the Councell of Adjutators," pp. 24–28, is about nothing but his imprisonment.

138. Loder-Symonds MSS., *Historical Manuscripts Commission*, 13th Report, App., pt. 4, pp. 401–02.

139. *Gold Tried in the Fire*, p. 12.

140. *Just Defence*, p. 6.

141. *The Parliamentary or Constitutional History of England from the Earliest Times to the Restoration of Charles II*, 24 vols. (London, 1751–62), 15:342–44 (Army Appeal), 344–45 (Declaration).

142. Mark A. Kishlansky, *The Rise of the New Model Army* (Cambridge, 1979), chap. 7. Tolmie, *Triumph of the Saints*, pp. 155–61. Leveller proposals circulating in the regiments included: the Large Petition (*The Clarke Papers*, ed.

C. H. Firth, 4 vols. [London, 1891–1901], 1, 84–85—hereafter *CP*); "Heads of Demands to be made to the Parliament," c. 3 May 1647, Clarke MSS, Worcester College, Oxford, vol. 41, fol. 18.

143. Clarke MSS, vol. 41, fols. 105v–125, esp. fols. 109v (Cromwell's horse regiment), 116v (Fairfax's foot), 118v (H. Waller's foot), 120 (Hewson's foot), 124v (Lambert's foot).

144. *CP*, 1:111–12.

145. *A Solemne Engagement of the Army* (5 June 1647). *A Representation from . . . Fairfax, and the Army . . .* , St. Albans, 14 June 1647 (Cambridge: Printed by Roger Daniel, Printer to the Universitie); cf. *A Declaration, or, Representation from . . . Fairfax, And the Army . . .* , 14 June 1647 (London: Printed for George Whittington, 1647), which omits two paragraphs included in the Cambridge edition.

146. *Just Defence*, pp. 5–7.

147. Clarke MSS, vol. 41, fols. 164v–167v; the third paper is between appeals dated at Reading, 6 and 7 July 1647.

148. *CP*, 1:170–75 ("Representation"); 203–05 (Tulidah); 210 (Chillenden); 180–81, 189–94, 199–201 (Allen); 211–13 (Ireton); 213 (Allen). For religious affiliations of Allen and Chillenden, see Tolmie, *Triumph of the Saints*, esp. pp. 155–56.

149. *Just Defence*, pp. 1, 6–7. [John Lilburne et al.], *The Second Part of Englands New-Chaines Discovered* ([24 March] 1648/9), pp. 4–5. For the counter-revolution, see Pearl, "London's Counter-Revolution," esp. pp. 44–56. For Tower regiment, see Sir Charles Firth and Godfrey Davies, *The Regimental History of Cromwell's Army*, 2 vols. (Oxford, 1940), 2:571–72.

150. See, e.g.: *The Resolution of the Agitators*, with 41 subscribers (2 September 1647), esp. pp. 6–8. *CP*, 1: 229–32. [John Wildman], *A Cal to All the Souldiers of the Armie* ([29 October] 1647), esp. p. 7 (first part). Austin Woolrych, *Soldiers and Statesmen: The General Council of the Army and its Debates, 1647–48* (Oxford, 1987), p. 201, notes that from late September royalist newswriters frequently reported disagreement between the chief officers and agitators "described as wedded to Leveller notions of 'parity' and increasingly restless over the generals' persistence with the *Heads of the Proposals.*"

151. Lilburne, *Juglers Discovered*, p. 10; Sir Lewis Dyve's letter to the King, 29 September, "The Tower of London Letter-Book of Sir Lewis Dyve, 1646–47," ed. H. G. Tibbutt, *The Publications of the Bedfordshire Historical Record Society* 38 (Luton, Beds., 1958): 90–91.

152. [John Wildman], *The Case of the Armie* ([19 Oct.] 1647); for authorship, see *CP*, 1:356. *Papers from the Armie concerning . . . Their Dislike of the Papers from the new Agents of the Five Regaments of Horse* (23 October 1647), pp. 3–4; *Historical Collections*, ed. John Rushworth, 2d ed., 8 vols. (London, 1721–22), 7:849–50.

153. *Two Letters from the Agents of the five Regiments of Horse* ([28 October]

1647), p. 7; most of the last paragraph is reprinted in *Historical Collections*, ed. Rushworth, 7:857. *The Character of an Agitator* ([11 Nov.] 1647), p. 7, describes an agitator as a monster begotten of Lilburne and Overton and "counselled by Mr. Walwin."

154. *An Agreement of the People* ([3 November] 1647); presented at Putney 28 October (*CP*, 1:236).

155. *Slaverie*, p. 3; see also pp. 5–7 and *Helpe*, p. 4.

156. *Compassionate Samaritane*, p. 43. Cf., e.g.: *Petition of the Papists*, p. 2; *Helpe*, p. 4; *Whisper*, p. 5; *Antidote*, p. 3; *Parable*, p. 4; *Still and Soft Voice*, p. 16.

157. *CP*, 1:226–413, 440–42, esp. p. 240 (Wildman), 299–345 (franchise), 411–13 and 440–42 (3–8 Nov.); *A Letter Sent from several Agitators of the Army to Their Respective Regiments . . . with a True Account of the Proceedings of the General Councel*, signed by Edward Sexby and 14 others (11 Nov. 1647). Woolrych, *Soldiers and Statesmen*, pp. 214–63.

158. Woolrych, *Soldiers and Statesmen*, chap. 11.

159. Gregg, *Free-born John*, p. 223 and n. 42.

160. [Wildman], *A Cal to All the Souldiers*, esp. p. 7 (of second part).

161. Petition of 23 November 1647, printed with account of the Commons' action (25 Nov. 1647), reprinted, *Leveller Manifestoes*, ed. Wolfe, No. 7. *CJ*, 5:354, 367 (9, 23 Nov.).

162. Walter Frost, *A Declaration of some Proceedings of Lt. Col. John Lilburn* ([14 Feb.] 1647/8), reprinted with commentary, *The Leveller Tracts, 1647–1653*, ed. William Haller and Godfrey Davies (New York, 1944), esp. pp. 97–101. Norah Carlin, "Leveller Organization in London," *Historical Journal* 27 (1984): 955–60, and sources cited.

163. Petition of January 1647/8, reprinted, *Leveller Manifestoes*, ed. Wolfe, No. 9; *DNB*, s.v. Lilburne, Wildman. *Acts and Ordinances of the Interregnum, 1642–1660*, ed. C. H. Firth and R. S. Rait, 2 vols. (London, 1911), 1:1133–36.

164. *Bloody Project* (No. 20), title page, pp. 4–5, 14, 16 (Postscript).

165. Ian Gentles, "The Struggle for London in the Second Civil War," *Historical Journal* 26 (1983): 289–99 esp.

166. Petition of 11 September 1648, reprinted, *Leveller Manifestoes*, ed. Wolfe, No. 11. For Walwyn's comments, see *Just Defence*, pp. 27–28. For reprint of the Large Petition of March 1646/7, see copy in the British Library, E. 464 (19*), where Thomason's date is 19 Sept. 1648.

167. Barbara Taft, "The Council of Officers' *Agreement of the People*, 1648/9," *Historical Journal* 28 (1985): 170–71.

168. Lilburne, *Legall Fundamentall Liberties*, pp. 29–30.

169. Ibid., pp. 30–34.

170. Ibid., pp. 33–35. Henry Marten was the only Parliament man who attended regularly.

171. "An Agreement of the people of England & the places therewith Incorporated for a secure and present peace upon grounds of Comon right and

freedom," Clarke MSS, Worcester College, Oxford, vol. 16, fols. 31–35. For redistribution of seats, see *Foundations of Freedom; or, an Agreement of the People* ([15 Dec.] 1648).

172. *CP*, 2:78, 84, 98 (Lilburne); 91–92, 104 (Overton); 75–77, 112, 120–21, 131, 282 (Wildman); 282 (Walwyn). For an account of the debates, see Taft, "The Council of Officers' *Agreement of the People*, 1648/9," pp. 173–79.

173. *Foundations of Freedom. A Petition . . . concerning the Draught of an Agreement . . . together with the said Agreement* ([22 January] 1648/9).

174. [John Lilburne], *Englands New Chains Discovered* ([26 Feb.] 1648/9). Lilburne, *Legall Fundamentall Liberties*, esp. p. 35.

175. John Lilburne et al., *A Plea for Common-right and Freedom* ([29 Dec.] 1648). *The Humble Petition of . . . Presenters and Promoters of the late Large Petition of September 11, MDCXLVIII* ([19 Jan.] 1648/9).

176. Lilburne, *Legall Fundamentall Liberties*, pp. 43–44, 65–74.

177. [Lilburne et al.], *The Second Part of Englands New-Chaines Discovered*. John Lilburne, Richard Overton, and Thomas Prince, *The Picture of the Council of State* ([11 April] 1649), p. 2.

178. *A Manifestation*, p. 7.

179. *A Petition . . . concerning the Draught of an Agreement . . . together with the Said Agreement*, pp. 26–27 (corrected pagination).

180. *Vanitie*, esp. pp. 11–16, 23–27, 30–31, 41–46.

181. *Just Defence*, pp. 1, 17; cf. *Fountain*, p. 11.

182. *Fountain*, pp. 11–12.

183. Blair Worden, *The Rump Parliament, 1648–1653* (Cambridge, 1974), pp. 165–69. For officers' pressure, see, e.g., *CP*, 2:190–93.

184. *The English Souldiers Standard to Repaire to* ([5 April] 1649); See Appendix 1.

185. Lilburne et al., *Picture of the Councel of State*, pp. 20–23. Tolmie, *Triumph of the Saints*, pp. 169–72, notes that Baptists as well as Independents had been moving away from the Levellers since the autumn of 1647.

186. *The Humble Petition and Representation of Several Churches of God in London, Commonly (Though Falsly) Called Anabaptists* (2 April 1649); *CJ*, 6:177–78 (2 April 1649).

187. Lilburne et al., *Picture of the Councel of State*, pp. 24, 41–42.

188. *Just Defence*, p. 17; cf. *Fountain*, p. 21.

189. *A Manifestation*, pp. 4, 7–8; cf. *Fountain*, p. 19.

190. *An Agreement of the Free People of England* (1 May 1649). "A Preparative" is reprinted in this volume (No. 23); the complete text is reprinted in collections of Leveller tracts (Headnote to *An Agreement*).

191. *Fountain*, p. 21. For petitions, see *The Moderate*, Nos. 38 and 41 (27 March, 17 April 1649). See also *The Humble Petition of Divers Wel-affected Women-. . .* ([24 April] 1649).

192. Thomason's date is 10 May but the licenser's imprimatur is 23 April.

The absence of any comment about the 1 May *Agreement* suggests April publication.

193. Introduction, p. 25. For evidence that Price was the author, see *Leveller Tracts,* ed. Haller and Davies, p. 285.

194. Kiffin et al., *Walwins Wiles,* esp. pp. A3–A3v, 9, 11–13. For Ireland, cf. Edwards, *Gangraena,* pt. 2, p. 27.

195. Brooke, *Charity,* passim. See also Humphrey Brooke, *The Crafts-mens Craft* ([25 June] 1649).

196. *Fountain,* pp. 24–25.

197. *Just Defence,* passim, esp. pp. 12, 16. *A Declaration by Congregational Societies in, and about the City of London . . . in Way of Vindication of Themselves. Touching: 1. Liberty. 2. Magistracy. 3. Propriety. 4. Polygamie* ([22 Nov.] 1647).

198. *Just Defence,* pp. 23–24; cf. *Fountain,* p. 7. *An Agreement of the Free People,* Article 30.

199. *Power of Love,* p. A4v. Cf. Humphrey Brooke, *The Durable Legacy* (1681), p. 137.

200. *A Manifestation,* p. 4.

201. *Just Defence,* p. 24. Lilburne, *Legall Fundamentall Liberties,* p. 75; cf. *L. Colonel John Lilburne, His Apologetical Narration* (Amsterdam, April 1652), pp. 64, 68–70.

202. "W Walwins Conceptions; For a free Trade" (No. 27).

203. Richard Overton, *An Appeale from the Degenerate Representative Body the Commons of England . . . to the Body Represented, the Free People in General . . .* ([17 July] 1647), p. 38. *Compassionate Samaritane,* p. 37; [Lilburne], *Englands Birth-right Justified,* pp. 44–45; Lilburne, *Englands New Chains,* p. 15; *The Mournfull Cryes of Many Thousand Poor Tradesmen, Who Are Ready to Famish Through Decay of Trade* ([22 Jan.] 1647/8).

204. *CSPD,* 1649–50, p. 552 (8 Nov. 1649).

205. *Juries Justified* (No. 26), pp. 1, 6–8, 14, and passim. Henry Robinson, *Certain Considerations in Order to a More Speedy, Cheap, and Equall Distribution of Justice throughout the Nation* ([14 Nov.] 1651), esp. pp. 2–3. *An Agreement of the Free People,* Article 25; cf. *Bloody Project,* p. 13.

206. "W Walwins Conceptions; For a free Trade," esp. fol. 72. Reasons humbly offered by the Governor & Company of Merchants trading into the Levant Seas, PRO, State Papers, Foreign, 105, vol. 144, fols. 76–89. Walwyn's contribution is noted by Margaret James, *Social Problems and Policy during the Puritan Revolution, 1640–1660* (London, 1930), pp. 155–58; this section of James's study delineates the Rump's support of monopolies.

207. Gregg, *Free-born John,* chaps. 27, 28. John Lilburne, *The Banished Mans Suit for Protection* (14 June 1653).

208. *CSPD,* 1653–54, pp. 64–121 (August), esp. pp. 105, 107 (Lilburne), and 111 (Walwyn). See also *A Collection of State Papers of John Thurloe, Esq.,* ed. T. Birch, 7 vols. (London, 1742), 1:429, 441–42, 451.

209. Peter Cornelius, Van Zurich-Zee [i.e., Plockhoy], *The Way to the Peace and Settlement of These Nations*, 2d ed., with Richard Cromwell letter ([4 March] 1658/9). Peter Cornelius, Van Zurich-Zee, *A Way Propounded* ([28 May] 1659).

210. Schenk, *Social Justice*, pp. 144–46.

211. Leland Harder and Marvin Harder, *Plockhoy from Zurik-zee* (Kansas, 1952), pp. 40, 173.

212. *A Proposition in Order to the Proposing of a Commonwealth or Democracie* ([14 June] 1659); the broadsheet states that the proposal is presented "with Mr. Harrington's consent," but, as J. G. A. Pocock observes, the list of names is a hodgepodge that suggests that it is either an absurdity or "academically facetious" (*The Political Works of James Harrington*, ed. J. G. A. Pocock [Cambridge, 1977], pp. 110–11). For Nonsuch House see Maurice Ashley, *John Wildman* (London, 1947).

213. William Bray, *A Plea for the Peoples Fundamentall Liberties and Parliaments* ([Jan.?] 1659/60), esp. pp. 4, 9. *Biographical Dictionary of British Radicals in the Seventeenth Century*, ed. Richard L. Greaves and Robert Zaller, 3 vols. (Brighton, Sussex, 1981–84), s.v. Bray.

214. Statute 12 Car. II, c. 11. Lilburne had refused to serve as a High Court judge (Lilburne, *Legall Fundamentall Liberties*, p. 42).

215. *Spirits Moderated* (No. 28), p. 1.

216. In 1662 Walwyn and two others received Exchequer tallies for £159 in return for cash advanced to one John Beamont (*Calendar of Treasury Books, 1660–67*, p. 385).

217. *Spirits Moderated*, pp. 25–26.

218. Ibid., title page, pp. 2–4; cf. Humphrey Brooke, *A Conservatory of Health* ([13 June] 1650), esp. pp. 1–13.

219. *Spirits Moderated*, pp. 4, 10–33.

220. *Physick for Families* (No. 31), 1669 ed., pp. 1–3, 6–20, 113. *Physick*, 1674 ed., p. 11.

221. *Healths New Store-House Opened* (No. 29), p. 7.

222. *Touch-Stone for Physick* (No. 30), pp. 81, 100 (corrected pagination). Marriage license, 17 May 1666, of Francis Jenkes and Sarah Wallwin, consent of father William Wallwin, of Sutton, Surrey (*Allegations for Marriage Licenses Issued by the . . . Vicar-General of the Archbishop of Canterbury, 1660 to 1679*, extracted by Joseph Lemuel Chester and ed. Geo. J. Armitage [London, 1886], pp. 116–17).

223. *Physick*, 1681 ed., unpaged Index, last p., verso.

224. Appendix 2.

225. R.O. [Richard Overton], *Mans Mortalitie* ([19 January] 1643/4), title page and passim.

226. Kiffin et al., *Walwins Wiles*, p. 7.

227. Brooke, *Charity*, p. 4.

228. *Power of Love*, esp. pp. 20–28. *Vanitie*, esp. pp. 28–30.

229. *Power of Love*, pp. 15–25. *Vanitie*, passim.

230. *A Manifestation*, p. 4.

231. *Juries Justified*, pp. 2–5, passim.

232. For religious exiles, see: *Compassionate Samaritane*, p. 63; *Good Counsell*, pp. 83–84. For India and China, see *Physick*, 1669 ed., p. 8.

233. *Bloody Project*, passim; Headnote to *Bloody Project*.

234. *Vanitie*, passim; Introduction, pp. 16, 19.

235. *Fountain*, p. 18.

Headnote to *A New Petition of the Papists* (Number 1)

1. Theodore Calvin Pease, *The Leveller Movement* (Washington, 1916), pp. 256–57. Brooke, *Charity*, p. 11. C. H. Firth suggests that Walwyn "had a hand in" *Liberty of Conscience*, which appeared [24 March] 1642/3 (*DNB*, s.v. Walwyn), but Firth convincingly assigns this tract to Henry Robinson (C. H. Firth, "An Anonymous Tract on 'Liberty of Conscience,'" *English Historical Review* 9 [1894]: 715–17).

2. *Tracts on Liberty*, ed. Haller, 1:126. William Haller, *The Rise of Puritanism* (New York, 1938), pp. 266 and 396, n. 25.

3. S. R. Gardiner, *History of England . . . 1603–1642*, 10 vols. (London, 1900–04), 10:35, n. 2, dismisses *The Humble Petition of the Brownists*: "the largeness of its charity is rather suspicious, and it was most probably intended as a caricature."

4. Pease, *Leveller Movement*, p. 257. *Petition of the Papists*, pp. 3–5; *Prediction*, pp. 6–8.

5. *Petition of the Papists*, pp. 2, 5; *Helpe*, p. 4; *Whisper*, p. 5; *Prediction*, p. 6; *Parable*, p. 15; *Still and Soft Voice*, pp. 15–16.

6. *Petition of the Papists*, p. 2; *Word More*, pp. 5, 8; *Parable*, p. 16.

7. *Petition of the Papists*, p. 3; *Prediction*, pp. 13–14.

8. *Petition of the Papists*, p. 8; *Helpe*, p. 7; *Antidote*, pp. 15–16.

9. *Petition of the Papists*, p. 6; *Just Defence*, p. 9.

10. *Petition of the Papists*, pp. 3–5; *Helpe*, pp. 3–4, 6; *Whisper*, pp. 5–6.

11. Pease, *Leveller Movement*, p. 257.

Headnote to *Some Considerations* (Number 2)

1. *Tracts on Liberty*, ed. Haller, 1:122–23.

2. *Some Considerations*, pp. 7–8; Headnote to No. 1, n. 10.

3. *Some Considerations*, esp. pp. 2, 4–5, 8–9; *Helpe*, pp. 3–4, 7–8; *Antidote*, pp. 9–12; *Parable*, p. 15.

4. *Some Considerations*, esp. pp. 6–7; Headnote to No. 1, n. 5.

5. *Some Considerations*, esp. pp. 2, 8, 11–12, 16; *Helpe*, p. 5; *Word More*, p. 7;

Still and Soft Voice, passim; *Vanitie,* esp. pp. 21–22; *Fountain,* p. 5; *Just Defence,* p. 9.

6. *Some Considerations,* p. 12; *Helpe,* pp. 3, 5; *Whisper,* pp. 1–2; *Prediction,* p. 8; *Parable,* p. 15.

7. *Some Considerations,* p. 12.

8. Ibid., pp. 2, 6, 16; *Word in Season,* passim. See also: *Helpe,* p. 6; *Whisper,* p. 6. For Walwyn's own practice, see *Whisper,* pp. 4–6.

9. *Some Considerations,* p. 10; *Word in Season,* p. 7.

10. *Introduction,* p. 19.

11. *Some Considerations,* esp. pp. 6–7, 9–10, 13–14, 16; Headnote to No. 1, n. 8.

12. For Walwyn's pivotal stress on love, see *Whisper,* p. 2; *Antidote,* pp. 18–19; *Prediction,* pp. 4–6, 18–19; *Parable,* passim, esp. p. 13; *Vanitie,* pp. 30–31; *Fountain,* p. 14.

Headnote to *The Power of Love* (Number 3)

1. For the collapse of censorship, 1640–43, the ordinance of 14 June 1643, and subsequent censorship until the Restoration, see Fredrick Seaton Siebert, *Freedom of the Press in England, 1476–1776* (Urbana, Illinois, 1952), pt. 3.

2. *Tracts on Liberty,* ed. Haller, 1:123.

3. *Power of Love,* p. 43.

4. Ibid., p. A3; *Prediction,* p. 6; and see Headnote to No. 2, n. 12.

5. *Power of Love,* p. A5v, cf. p. 44; Headnote to No. 2, n. 6.

6. *Power of Love,* pp. A5v–A6, 48; Headnote to No. 2, n. 8.

7. *Power of Love,* p. A7; Headnote to No. 1, n. 5.

8. *Power of Love,* pp. A7v–A8, 10; *Prediction,* p. 3; *Still and Soft Voice,* pp. 11–13.

9. *Power of Love,* p. 2.

10. Ibid., pp. 2–3; *Just Defence,* p. 11; *Introduction,* p. 5.

11. *Power of Love,* p. 22; Headnote to No. 1, n. 10.

12. *Power of Love,* pp. 37–41; *Parable,* p. 14; *Still and Soft Voice,* pp. 9–10; *Vanitie,* pp. 30–31. For those who "walke not as becommeth the gospell of Christ," see *Power of Love,* p. 5.

13. *Power of Love,* p. 41; *Whisper,* p. 3; *Fountain,* p. 10 (which is taken from *Whisper*).

14. *Power of Love,* p. 43; *Helpe,* p. 4; *Whisper,* pp. 6, 14; *Word More,* p. 7; *Prediction,* pp. 3, 7, 15; *Parable,* pp. 4, 15.

15. *Power of Love,* pp. 48–49; *Whisper,* p. 1; *Just Defence,* p. 22; *Fountain,* pp. 4, 7; *Physick* (1674 edition), p. 11.

16. *Power of Love,* p. 50; *Word in Season,* pp. 1, 5.

Headnote to *The Compassionate Samaritane* (Number 4)

1. *Good Counsell to All* (No. 5).
2. *Tracts on Liberty,* ed. Haller, 1:123–25.
3. *Compassionate Samaritane,* pp. A3–A5v, 1–3. Introduction, pp. 15–16.
4. *Compassionate Samaritane,* pp. 4, 9, 10, 64–65; Headnote to No. 1, n. 10. For Walwyn's habits of inquiry, see *Whisper,* pp. 4–6.
5. *Compassionate Samaritane,* pp. A3–A3v, 3, 57, 65–66, 75–76; Headnote to No. 2, n. 3.
6. *Compassionate Samaritane,* pp. A4–A5, 39–40, 60–61, 78–79. *Just Defence,* p. 25. For the licensing ordinance, see Headnote to No. 3, n. 1.
7. *Compassionate Samaritane,* title page, p. 77; *Helpe,* p. 4; *Whisper,* p. 5; *Prediction,* p. 16; *Parable,* p. 15; *Still and Soft Voice,* p. 13.
8. *Compassionate Samaritane,* pp. 6–7; Headnote to No. 1, n. 5.
9. *Compassionate Samaritane,* pp. 10–11, 53; Headnote to No. 3, n. 14.
10. *Compassionate Samaritane,* pp. 20 ff. and passim; Headnote to No. 2, n. 5.
11. *Compassionate Samaritane,* pp. 32, 38; Headnote to No. 3, n. 15.
12. *Compassionate Samaritane,* pp. 43, 44; Headnote to No. 1, n. 5.
13. *Compassionate Samaritane,* p. 46; Headnote to No. 1, n. 8.
14. *Compassionate Samaritane,* pp. 54–55; Headnote to No. 1, n. 5.

Headnote to *Good Counsell to All* (Number 5)

1. *Tracts on Liberty,* ed. Haller, 1:123–25; Headnote to *The Compassionate Samaritane* (No. 4).
2. *Good Counsell,* pp. 79–80, 92; Headnote to No. 2, n. 3.
3. *Good Counsell,* pp. 80–83, 91–92; Headnote to No. 2, n. 6. Headnote to No. 1, n. 10.
4. *Good Counsell,* pp. 81–82; *Just Defence,* p. 8. For the cited text, Titus 2:11, 12, see also *Power of Love,* pp. 1, 14, 50. Cf. Headnote to No. 2, n. 12.
5. *Good Counsell,* pp. 84, 86, 87; Headnote to No. 1, n. 5.
6. *Good Counsell,* p. 85; *Helpe,* p. 4.
7. *Good Counsell,* p. 87; Headnote to No. 3, n. 14.

Headnote to *A Helpe to the Right Understanding* (Number 6)

1. *Just Defence,* p. 31.
2. *Helpe,* pp. 3–4.
3. E.g.: John Lilburne, *A Copie of a Letter, Written by John Lilburne . . . To Mr*

William Prinne, Esq. ([15 Jan.] 1644/5); John Goodwin, *Calumny Arraign'd and Cast* ([31 Jan.] 1644/5); [Richard Overton], *The Araignement of Mr. Persecution* ([8 April] 1645).

4. William Prynne, *Independency Examined* ([26 Sept.] 1644); Prynne, *Truth Triumphing over Falshood.*

Headnote to *Englands Lamentable Slaverie* (Number 7)

1. *Slaverie,* p. 8. H. R. Plomer, "Secret Printing during the Civil War," *The Library,* n.s., 5 (1904): 374–403, esp. 387–88, 399.

2. *Slaverie,* p. 1.

3. Pease, *Leveller Movement,* p. 116, n. 48.

4. *Tracts on Liberty,* ed. Haller, 1:125.

5. Introduction, p. 21.

6. *Slaverie,* esp. pp. 3, 5–6; *Helpe,* pp. 4, 6–7; *Word More,* p. 5; *Word in Season,* p. 3.

7. *Slaverie,* pp. 1–2; Headnote to No. 2, n. 3. Lilburne was a separatist and a Calvinist.

8. *Slaverie,* p. 2; *Fountain,* p. 2. Cf.: *Whisper,* p. 3; *Just Defence,* p. 9.

9. *Slaverie,* p. 4; Headnote to No. 3, n. 15.

10. *Slaverie,* p. 4; *Juries Justified,* p. 5.

11. *Slaverie,* p. 6; Headnote to No. 1, n. 6.

12. *Slaverie,* p. 7; *Helpe,* p. 2; for the text, Romans 3:13, see *Antidote,* title page. For Prynne and Lilburne, see Gregg, *Free-born John,* pp. 117–24, passim.

Headnote to *Tolleration Justified* (Number 8)

1. *Tracts on Liberty,* ed. Haller, 1:101.

2. *Tolleration Justified,* pp. 2, 7, 14; Headnote to No. 4, n. 7.

3. *Tolleration Justified,* e.g., pp. 5, 7, 9, 12, 14; Headnote to No. 2, n. 5.

4. *Tolleration Justified,* pp. 3, 5, 14; Headnote to No. 1, n. 5.

5. *Tolleration Justified,* pp. 3, 11, 12; *Word in Season,* p. 3; *Antidote,* p. 16; *Prediction,* pp. 7–8.

6. *Tolleration Justified,* p. 6; Headnote to No. 2, n. 12.

7. *Tolleration Justified,* pp. 3, 4–5, 6; *Still and Soft Voice,* pp. 4–5, 7–9; *Vanitie,* esp. pp. 23–26; *Just Defence,* pp. 3–4.

8. *Tolleration Justified,* esp. pp. 9–10; *Still and Soft Voice,* p. 11.

9. *Tolleration Justified,* esp. p. 8; Headnote to No. 2, n. 6.

10. *Tolleration Justified,* pp. 3, 13, 15; Headnote to No. 2, n. 8.

11. *Tolleration Justified,* pp. 8, 13; Headnote to No. 2, n. 3.

12. *Tolleration Justified,* pp. 14–15; Headnote to No. 3, n. 14.

13. *Tolleration Justified*, pp. 10, 11, 13; Headnote to No. 1, n. 8.

14. *Tolleration Justified*, pp. 8–9, 11; *Word More*, pp. 4–5, 8; *Still and Soft Voice*, p. 16.

15. *Tolleration Justified*, pp. 11–12, 15; Headnote to No. 7, n. 6.

16. *Tolleration Justified*, p. 15, cf. p. 13; Headnote to No. 1, n. 6.

17. *Tolleration Justified*, pp. 3, 6–7; Headnote to No. 2, n. 12.

18. *Tolleration Justified*, pp. 13–14; *Helpe*, pp. 7–8; *Word More*, throughout. Lilburne said he left the army because he could not take the Covenant (John Lilburne, *Innocency and Truth Justified*, [6 Jan.] 1646, p. 46).

Headnote to *A Whisper in the Eare* (Number 9)

1. For Paine, see *Tracts on Liberty*, ed. Haller, 1:122.

2. Edwards, *Gangraena*, pt. 1, title page and p. 96. For subsequent attacks on Walwyn, see Introduction, pp. 25, 40 and n. 14.

3. *Whisper*, p. 5. Cf. Headnotes to Nos. 1, 2, 4, 5, 6.

4. *Whisper*, esp. pp. 3–4.

Headnote to *A Word More* (Number 10)

1. Introduction, p. 13.

2. *A Briefe Discourse, Declaring the Impiety and Unlawfulnesse of the new Covenant with the Scots* ([26 Oct.] 1643), p. 11. Sir Henry Vane the Younger added two clauses to the Covenant at the meetings with the Scots: religion in England and Ireland would be reformed "according to the word of God, and the example of the best reformed churches." The Commons increased the flexibility of these clauses by refusing to describe the Church of Scotland as established "according to the word of God"—a clause omitted in Section 1 of the final version (Lawrence Kaplan, *Politics and Religion during the English Revolution; The Scots and the Long Parliament, 1643–1645* [New York, 1976], pp. xx–xxi).

Headnote to *A Word in Season* (Number 11)

1. *A Transcript of the Registers of the Worshipful Company of Stationers . . . 1640–1708*, 3 vols. (London, 1913–14), 1:230 (hereafter cited as *Stationers' Register*).

2. *Just Defence*, p. 31. *Fountain*, p. 7.

3. Another common bibliographical error is the attribution to Walwyn of an

earlier tract, *A Word in Season; or, Motives to Peace, Accommodation, and Unity, 'twixt Presbyterian and Independent Brethren* ([5 Jan.] 1645/6), which has the imprimatur of Joseph Caryl (ibid., p. 8). This tract does not include the commitment to Parliament that Walwyn states is evident in his *Word in Season* (*Just Defence*, p. 31) and does propose religious "accommodations" that are alien to Walwyn's fundamental beliefs.

4. Introduction, pp. 18, 23–24. Thomason's MS note on the 1st edition asks: "Was this booke Intended against the Remonstrance now in hand?" The City's *Remonstrance* had circulated for at least a month before its 26 May presentation (Introduction, n. 101).

5. *Just Defence*, p. 31. Thomason's MS note on the 2d edition. Introduction, p. 18.

Headnote to *An Antidote* (Number 12)

1. *Antidote*, p. 21. Stationers' Register, 1:233.

2. *Antidote*, pp. 1–16, esp. p. 10. Thomason's date for *Gangraena*, pt. 2, is 28 May—two days after the licenser passed *Antidote*—but it is probable that Thomason did not acquire *Gangraena*, pt. 2, until some days after its appearance: it was entered in the Stationers' Register under the Imprimatur of James Cranford on 4 April 1646 (*Stationers' Register*, 1:223).

3. Edwards, *Gangraena*, pt. 2, pp. 26–28.

4. *Antidote*, pp. 17–21.

Headnote to *The Just Man in Bonds* (Number 13)

1. *Tracts on Liberty*, ed. Haller, pp. 122, 126.

2. *Leveller Manifestoes*, ed. Wolfe, p. 9, n. 19; see also Don M. Wolfe, "Unsigned Pamphlets of Richard Overton: 1641–1649," *Huntington Library Quarterly* 21 (1958): 193–94.

3. Gregg, *Free-born John*, pp. 137–46. John Lilburne, *The Just Mans Justification* (6 June 1646), pp. 8–9.

4. *Just Man*, p. 1.

5. Ibid.

6. Ibid., pp. 1, 2, 4. For similar statements *re* Parliament's trust from and duty to the people, see Headnote to No. 7, n. 6.

7. *Just Man*, p. 3; *Whisper*, pp. 2–3; *Still and Soft Voice*, pp. 9–10.

8. *Just Man*, p. 2.

9. *A Remonstrance of Many Thousand Citizens*, [7 July], 1646; Headnote to No. 14.

Headnote to *A Remonstrance of Many Thousand Citizens* (Number 14)

1. Pease, *Leveller Movement*, p. 153, n. 39. *Tracts on Liberty*, ed. Haller, 1:111–12, 3:349. *Leveller Manifestoes*, ed. Wolfe, p. 111.
2. C. M. Williams, "The Political Career of Henry Marten" (Ph.D. dissertation, Oxford, 1954), pp. 226–27.
3. [Richard Overton], *A Pearle in a Dounghill; or, Lieu. Col. John Lilburne in New-gate* ([30 June] 1646). *Just Man* (No. 13).
4. The portrait is in the copy of *A Remonstrance* in the Thomason Collection. The copy of *A Remonstrance* in the McAlpin Collection at the Union Theological Seminary in New York City does not include the frontispiece.
5. *A Remonstrance*, pp. 7–8.
6. Introduction, p. 24.
7. *A Remonstrance*, p. 12; Headnote to No. 1, n. 5. Headnote to No. 7, n. 6.
8. *A Remonstrance*, p. 12; *Word More*, esp. pp. 3–6; Introduction, p. 13.
9. *A Remonstrance*, p. 12; *Helpe*, p. 4; see also Headnote to No. 7, n. 6.
10. *A Remonstrance*, pp. 12–13; Headnote to No. 4, n. 7.
11. *A Remonstrance*, p. 13; Headnote to No. 1, n. 8.
12. *A Remonstrance*, p. 13; Headnote to No. 2, n. 8.
13. *A Remonstrance*, p. 15; *Leveller Manifestoes*, ed. Wolfe, p. 111.

Headnote to *A Demurre to the Bill* (Number 16)

1. *Tracts on Liberty*, ed. Haller, 1:122, 126.
2. Introduction, p. 18.
3. *Demurre*, pp. 1–3, see also passim, esp. p. 7; Headnote to No. 2, n. 5.
4. *Demurre*, pp. 3–5; Headnote to No. 8, n. 8. Headnote to No. 5, n. 6.
5. *Demurre*, p. 3; *Prediction*, pp. 3–4; *Still and Soft Voice*, pp. 11–13.
6. *Demurre*, p. 7; Headnote to No. 2, n. 8.
7. *Demurre*, pp. 5–6; Headnote to No. 2, nn. 3 and 6.
8. *Demurre*, p. 6; Headnote to No. 1, n. 5.
9. *Demurre*, pp. 6–7; *Antidote*, pp. 11–14.
10. *Demurre*, pp. 7–8; Headnote to No. 1, n. 8.

Headnote to *A Parable* (Number 17)

1. *Fountain*, p. 7.
2. Introduction, p. 24; Headnote to No. 14.

Headnote to *A Still and Soft Voice* (Number 18)

1. *Just Defence*, p. 4.
2. Ibid., p. 3; for subsequent uncertainty about Brandriffe, see ibid., pp. 7, 27, 30–31. For hostility of Independents, see Introduction, p. 25.
3. *Just Defence*, p. 4.
4. *Still and Soft Voice*, esp. pp. 4–5, 7–10.
5. Ibid., esp. pp. 10–11.

Headnote to *Gold Tried in the Fire* (Number 19)

1. In the bound volume of the Thomason Tracts, E. 392, the petitions are separated from the Preface by tract E. 392 (20). Copies of *Gold* in the California State Library, Sutro Branch, and in Dr. Williams's Library, London, include Preface and petitions bound together.
2. *Tracts on Liberty*, ed. Haller, 1:116; *Fountain*, p. 7.
3. *Gold*, pp. A1–A2; *Just Defence*, pp. 4–5. The description of those who are presenting the Large Petition as men "earnestly desiring the glory of God, the freedom of the Common-wealth, & the peace of all Men" is a near verbatim repetition of the men described in *Good Counsell* three years before (*Gold*, p. 1; *Good Counsell*, p. 79).
4. *Just Defence*, p. 5.
5. Kiffin, et al., *Walwins Wiles*, p. 18.
6. *Gold*, pp. A2, 12; Introduction, p. 29.
7. *Gold*, p. A2v.

Headnote to *The Bloody Project* (Number 20)

1. *Tracts on Liberty*, ed. Haller, 1:126; Haller, *Liberty and Reformation*, p. 321.
2. *Leveller Tracts*, ed. Haller and Davies, pp. 15, 135. Frank, *The Levellers*, pp. 164–67. Morton, *World of the Ranters*, pp. 166–68; *Freedom in Arms*, ed. Morton, pp. 53–54.
3. *The Discoverer . . . The First Part* ([2 June] 1649), pp. 17–18; *Bloody Project*, p. 14. Lilburne, *Legall Fundamentall Liberties*, p. 66, states that the authors of *The Discoverer* were "commonly reported" to be "partly" Walter Frost, Secretary to the Council of State, and "principally" John Canne.
4. H.B. [Humphrey Brooke], *The Crafts-mens Craft; or, The Wiles of the Discoverers* ([25 June] 1649), p. 10. *The Discoverer . . . The Second Part* ([13 July] 1649), p. 54, again asserts Walwyn's authorship of *Bloody Project* in replying to *The Crafts-mens Craft*.
5. *Bloody Project*, esp. title page, pp. 3–7, 14–15.

6. *Some Considerations*, p. 13.

7. Introduction, pp. 27–31, passim.

8. *Bloody Project*, p. 6.

9. *Fountain*, p. 8; *Just Defence*, p. 6; *Just Man*, p. 2.

10. *Bloody Project*, pp. 12–13.

11. Ibid., title page, p. 16.

12. Ibid., p. 16; Headnote to No. 7, n. 6.

13. *Bloody Project*, p. 16.

Headnote to *The Vanitie of the Present Churches* (Number 21)

1. Lilburne, *Picture of the Council of State*, p. 24. *Church-Levellers; or, Vanity of Vanities and Certainty of Delusion* ([22 June] 1649), p. 4, implies that *Vanitie* is the work of John Wildman. Wildman's pen was flexible, but he moved away from the Levellers and toward the Commonwealthmen before the end of 1648 and religion was at no time his particular concern.

2. *Fountain*, p. 21. *Just Defence*, p. 23.

3. *Tracts on Liberty*, ed. Haller, 1:122; cf. *Leveller Tracts*, ed. Haller and Davies, pp. 25, 252. Frank, *Levellers*, p. 190. Morton, *World of the Ranters*, p. 172; *Freedom in Arms*, ed. Morton, p. 63. Tolmie, *Triumph of the Saints*, p. 185.

4. *Vanitie*, pp. 4, 26; *Still and Soft Voice*, p. 10. Cf.: *A Manifestation*, p. 7; *Fountain*, pp. 19–20.

5. *Vanitie*, pp. 12–15, 27; *Still and Soft Voice*, pp. 5, 7, and passim; Headnote to No. 8, n. 7.

6. *Vanitie*, pp. 1–2; Headnote to No. 1, n. 5.

7. "*Unum necessarium*" (*Vanitie*, pp. 20, 39) reappears in the same context in *Just Defence*, p. 10. The phrase from Philippians 3:8 (*Vanitie*, p. 35) is used in *Still and Soft Voice*, p. 16.

8. *Vanitie*, p. 22; Headnote to No. 3, n. 15.

9. *Vanitie*, p. 34; Headnote to No. 3, n. 14.

10. *Vanitie*, pp. 21, 30, 39, 47–48; Headnote to No. 2, n. 12.

11. *Vanitie*, esp. pp. 13, 37–38.

12. *Vanitie*, pp. 42–51; *Still and Soft Voice*, pp. 15–16.

Headnote to *A Manifestation* (Number 22)

1. *A Manifestation*, p. 8.

2. E.g., the copy in the Bodleian Library, Oxford, has the imprimatur. Copies in the McAlpin Collection and the Thomason Collection do not have the imprimatur. Thomason's date is 16 April.

3. *Just Defence*, p. 14.

4. Kiffin et al., *Walwins Wiles,* p. 2. Brooke, *Charity,* p. 12.

5. *A Manifestation,* title page, pp. 4–5, 7. For Baptists, see Introduction, p. 39.

6. *A Manifestation,* esp. pp. 4, 7–8.

Headnote to *An Agreement* (Number 23)

1. *An Agreement,* title page, pp. 2, 8.

2. *An Agreement,* p. 8. Thomason's copy E. 552 (23) has no MS date of acquisition. E. 571 (10), MS date 21 August, apparently is the reprint of the first run of *An Agreement* that was appended to *The Levellers (Falsly So Called) Vindicated*—E. 571 (11), MS date 21 August; in the bound volume of the Thomason Tracts the appended *Agreement* is separated and appears as a separate tract preceding *The Levellers . . . Vindicated.*

3. *CSPD,* 1649–50, p. 127; Siebert, *Freedom of the Press,* pp. 217–18. A copy of *An Agreement* that belonged to Godfrey Davies does not have Mabbott's imprimatur (*Leveller Tracts,* ed. Haller and Davies, p. 318).

4. For replication, see, e.g.: *An Agreement,* Articles 3, 10, 11, 12, 13, 20; *Foundations of Freedom,* Article 6 and Article 7, subheads 1, 2, 3, 5, 8. For publication of *Foundations of Freedom,* see Introduction, p. 36.

5. *An Agreement,* Article 26.

6. *A Manifestation,* p. 7.

7. *An Agreement,* Articles 10–30; cf. *Foundations of Freedom,* Article 7. Introduction, pp. 36, 39.

8. *An Agreement,* p. 2; cf. *A Manifestation,* p. 7.

Headnote to *The Fountain of Slaunder* (Number 24)

1. *Fountain,* p. 9. Cf. Brooke, *Charity of Church-men,* p. 1.

2. Introduction, p. 37.

3. *Fountain,* p. 24.

4. Ibid.

Headnote to *Just Defence* (Number 25)

1. *Just Defence,* pp. 3, 21, 27, 32. Brooke, *Charity of Church-men,* p. 1. See also, *Fountain,* p. 25.

2. Lilburne, *The Legal Fundamental Liberties,* 2d ed., p. [24]; the title page states that the 2d edition was "occasioned by the late coming out of Mr.

William Prynnes Book . . . , *A Legal Vindication,*" which Thomason acquired 16 July 1649.

3. Introduction, p. 40.

4. *Just Defence,* pp. 16, 19, 31–33.

5. Introduction, pp. 40–41.

Headnote to *Juries Justified* (Number 26)

1. *Juries Justified,* p. 1. Henry Robinson, *Certain Considerations in Order to a More Speedy, Cheap, and Equall Distribution of Justice* ([14 Nov.] 1651), esp. pp. 2–44. Introduction, p. 43.

2. *Juries Justified,* pp. 13–14. Cf. *Fountain,* p. 20.

3. *Juries Justified,* esp. pp. 2–5, 8.

4. Ibid., p. 14.

Headnote to "W Walwins Conceptions" (Number 27)

1. Introduction, p. 44.

2. Reasons humbly offered by the Governor & Company of Merchants trading into the Levant Seas, 21 May 1652, PRO, State Papers, Foreign, 105, vol. 144, pp. 76–89. Introduction, p. 44.

Headnote to *Spirits Moderated* (Number 28)

1. Christopher Hill, *Change and Continuity in Seventeenth-Century England* (London, 1974), p. 173.

2. *Spirits Moderated,* pp. 1, 3–5. Introduction, pp. 46–47.

3. *Spirits Moderated,* pp. 5–6, 8, 10–33, title page.

4. E.g., *Radix Vitae* (*Spirits Moderated,* pp. 7–8, 10–13).

5. *Physick,* 1669 ed., p. 3.

Headnote to *Healths New Store-House* (Number 29)

1. Jack R. McMichael, "The Life and Thought of William Walwyn: Seventeenth-century Englishman" (Ph.D. dissertation, Columbia University, 1965), pp. 352–53; cf. Hill, *Change and Continuity,* p. 173.

2. *Healths New Store-House,* pp. 7–8.

3. Ibid., pp. 9–26.

Headnote to *A Touch-Stone for Physick* (Number 30)

1. S. Halkett and J. Laing, *Dictionary of Anonymous and Pseudonymous Literature*, new. ed., 7 vols. (London, 1926–34), 6:65.
2. Headnote to *Physick for Families* (No. 31).
3. *Touch-Stone*, pp. 6–16.
4. Ibid., pp. 17–98.
5. Ibid., pp. 81–89. Introduction, pp. 47–48.

Headnote to *Physick for Families* (Number 31)

1. *Physick*, 1669 ed., p. A3v; cf. p. 118. For license, see flyleaf opposite p. 118.
2. Schenk, "A Seventeenth-Century Radical," p. 75 and n. 9; cf. Schenk, *Social Justice*, pp. 58–59 and n. 104.
3. F. N. L. Poynter, "William Walwyn, 'Health's Student,'" *British Medical Journal* (27 August 1949), pp. 482–83.
4. *Touch-Stone*, pp. 1–16. *Physick*, 1681 and 1696 eds. pp. 1–15.
5. The title page of the 1696 edition states that the volumes "are to be Sold by the Author," which may have caused some librarians to catalogue the medical works under "Walwyn, William, fl. 1667–1696" (e.g., the National Library of Medicine which possesses *Touch-Stone* [1667] and three editions of *Physick* [1669, 1681, 1696]). However, the 1696 edition reprints the anonymous "To the Reader" of the 1681 edition in which "this worthy Author" is praised in the past tense as if he were deceased (*Physick*, 1681, 1696 eds., p. A4v). Further, the will of "William Walwyn . . . physician" was proved 14 January 1680/1 and the records of St. Giles, Cripplegate, include an entry for the burial of William Walwyn, physician, 16 January 1680/1 (Appendix 2). Hesitant about his status in his first (1654) medical treatise, Walwyn evidently considered himself a physician by 1669 (*Spirits Moderated*, pp. 3–5, 8. *Physick*, 1669 ed., pp. 3, 64). The Walwyn family pedigree of 1682–83 erroneously describes William Walwyn as "M.D." (*The Visitation of the County of Worcester* [1682–83], ed. Walter C. Metcalfe [Exeter, 1883], p. 100).
6. Walwyn defended the right to keep medical formulas and arts secret (*Touch-Stone*, pp. 47–48), which was common practice at the time. Richard Halford was Walwyn's son-in-law (Introduction, p. 48).

Appendix 1. William Walwyn's Canon

1. Introduction, n. 82. Headnotes to Nos. 1, 2, 3, 4, 5.
2. Walwyn, for example, frequently: cited the golden rule (Headnote to

No. 4, n. 7); cited Romans 14 to support liberty of conscience (Headnote to No. 1, n. 5); referred to the story of Demetrius and Diana (Headnote to No. 3, n. 15); wrote of a "touch-stone," 1645/6 (*Whisper*, pp. 9, 10) through his medical writings (e.g., *Touch-Stone*, 1667; *Physick*, 1681 and 1696 editions, p. 6); used "ingenuous"/"ingenious" as a praise-word, 1644 (*Compassionate Samaritane*, p. 77) to 1674 (*Physick*, 1674 edition, passim).

3. *DNB*, s.v. Walwyn and Robinson. C. H. Firth, "An Anonymous Tract on 'Liberty of Conscience,'" pp. 715–17. For the "contemporary suggestion" about the first tract on liberty of conscience, see Introduction, n. 82.

4. D. B. Robertson, *The Religious Foundations of Leveller Democracy* (New York, 1951), pp. 160, 167.

5. *Tracts on Liberty*, ed. Haller, 1:92, n. 93 and pp. 125–26.

6. Ibid., pp. 107, 126; cf. Haller, *Liberty and Reformation*, pp. 284–85. Robertson, *Religious Foundations of Leveller Democracy*, p. 160. Frank, *Levellers*, pp. 79–80. Morton, *World of the Ranters*, p. 160.

7. Wolfe, *Milton in the Puritan Revolution*, p. 482. *Leveller Manifestoes*, ed. Wolfe, p. 9; cf. Wolfe, "Unsigned Pamphlets of Richard Overton: 1641–1649," pp. 193–94, and Gimelfarb-Brack, *Overton*, pp. 413–14.

8. [Overton], *Pearle*, pp. 1, 3. *Word in Season*, pp. 4, 7, 8–9; *Demurre*, passim.

9. *Tracts on Liberty*, ed. Haller, 1:92, n. 93; cf. ibid., p. 126.

10. *Vox Populi*, pp. C2, 19, 27.

11. Ibid., pp. 6, 7, 12–13, 25. Introduction, p. 13.

12. Morton, *World of the Ranters*, pp. 164–65, where three paragraphs are reprinted. The entire tract is reprinted as Walwyn's work in *Freedom in Arms*, ed. Morton, No. 5.

13. Introduction, pp. 25–26.

14. *Poore Wise-man*, pp. 2, 7, 9, 10; *Still and Soft Voice*, pp. 10, 16; *Fountain*, pp. 22; *Whisper*, p. 4; *Word in Season*, p. 8.

15. *Poore Wise-man*, esp. pp. 2–5, 9.

16. Introduction, pp. 41, 49.

17. *Poore Wise-man*, p. 4.

18. *Gold Tried in the Fire*.

19. M. A. Gibb, *John Lilburne the Leveller, a Christian Democrat* (London, 1947), p. 83, n. 2.

20. Morton, *World of the Ranters*, p. 165. Frank, *Levellers*, pp. 163, 314, n. 82. Gimelfarb-Brack, *Overton*, p. 365, argues that the tract is the work of Overton.

21. *Englands Weeping Spectacle*, p. 13.

22. *Slaverie; Just Man*.

23. Kiffin et al., *Walwins Wiles*, pp. 18–20.

24. *Leveller Manifestoes*, ed. Wolfe, pp. 281–82. Morton, *World of the Ranters*, p. 168; *Freedom in Arms*, ed. Morton, pp. 54, 181. Frank, *Levellers*, p. 167. *Levellers in the English Revolution*, ed. Aylmer, p. 131. *Leveller Tracts*, ed. Haller and Davies, p. 147.

25. Introduction, pp. 25–26. *Gold Tried in the Fire*.

26. Lilburne, *Legall Fundamentall Liberties*, p. 29.

27. *Just Defence*, pp. 4, 28; cf. *Fountain*, p. 7.

28. *Humble petition*, p. 5. *Just Defence*, p. 24.

29. Frank, *Levellers*, pp. 181, 317, n. 138. Morton, *World of the Ranters*, p. 196. *Leveller Manifestoes*, ed. Wolfe, p. 305.

30. *No Papist*, pp. 1–2. *Introduction*, p. 15.

31. *Introduction*, pp. 13–14. *No Papist*, p. 2.

32. *No Papist*, p. 4. *Introduction*, pp. 10, 13.

33. H. N. Brailsford, *The Levellers and the English Revolution*, ed. for publication by Christopher Hill (Stanford, California, 1961), pp. 498, 509, n. 3. *Freedom in Arms*, ed. Morton, p. 227. The other Leveller prisoners presumably were working on *The Picture of the Council of State*: statements were dated 3 and 4 April (Lilburne), 4 April (Overton), 1 April (Thomas Prince), and Thomason dated his copy 11 April 1649.

34. *English Souldiers Standard*, p. 10. *Introduction*, p. 38.

35. *English Souldiers Standard*, pp. 3, 7–8, 11.

36. Ibid., passim, esp. pp. 5–6. *Introduction*, p. 32; *Just Defence*, p. 6.

37. Harold J. Laski, *The New Statesman and Nation*, 25 Dec. 1948, p. 573; Laski was reviewing *British Pamphleteers*, vol. I, ed. George Orwell and Reginald Reynolds (London, 1948), which partially reprints *Tyranipocrit*. M. S. Knapton, a student of Laski's, has reported that Laski knew of a copy of *Tyranipocrit* owned by W. C. Abbott that had on a flyleaf a penned note in a contemporary hand: "This book was handed to me at Calvert's bookshop by William Walwyn who wrote it" (Knapton to Jack R. McMichael, 1959). Abbott's son, who inherited his father's Interregnum collections, found no copy of *Tyranipocrit* among them (Charles C. Abbott to Jack R. McMichael, 16 March, 1 April 1960).

38. Brailsford, *The Levellers*, p. 71, n. 1. Hill states that Laski apparently found Brailsford's arguments convincing (ibid., p. vi); Hill was not convinced (Christopher Hill, *The World Turned Upside Down* [London, 1972], passim), and Morton, *World of the Ranters*, p. 196, states that there is "insufficient reason" to attribute *Tyranipocrit* to Walwyn. Olivier Lutaud, *Les Niveleurs, Cromwell et la république* (Paris, 1967), pp. 81–90.

39. *Tyranipocrit*, pp. 6, 8, 18, 52. Notes in Jack R. McMichael's unpublished papers and his conversations with Barbara Taft.

40. *Tyranipocrit*, p. 31. *Antidote; Parable*.

41. *Tyranipocrit*, p. 3; *Just Defence*, p. 9. *Tyranipocrit*, p. 33; *Bloody Project*, p. 16.

42. *Tyranipocrit*, pp. 7, 20–21, 25–26, 35, 49.

43. Ibid., pp. 10, 16, 19, 24, 37, 50.

44. Ibid., p. 3, and the appended second section, "A Demonstration of Predestination," pp. 43–47.

45. Ibid., pp. 8, 19.

46. Ibid., pp. 16, 38; cf. 19, 35, 39, 41, 51–52.

47. *A Manifestation*, p. 4. *An Agreement of the Free People*, Article 30. *Just Defence*, p. 24. See also Introduction, pp. 49–50.

48. *Tyranipocrit*, p. 19.

49. *The Moderate Intelligencer*, 26 Oct.–16 Nov. 1648 (3 issues); *The Moderate*, 14–28 Nov. 1648 (2 issues). Introduction, pp. 35–36.

50. *Tyranipocrit*, pp. 22–23, 33.

51. Ibid., p. 35; cf. p. 13.

52. Ibid., pp. 47–48, 51, 54–55.

53. Ibid., p. 47.

54. A. E. C. Simoni of the British Library has stated that the word divisions at the ends of lines are not English style while the decorated initials are characteristic of seventeenth-century Dutch printing (Miss Simoni to Barbara Taft, 5 July 1985).

55. Introduction, pp. 35–36.

56. *An Agreement of the People for a Firme and Present Peace* ([3 Nov.] 1647), title page, pp. 10, 14. In *The Second Part of Englands New-Chaines*, p. 6, Lilburne reiterated the attribution to "the Agents."

57. Brailsford, *The Levellers*, pp. 260–61 (Walwyn probable). Frank, *Levellers*, p. 138 (Lilburne, Overton, Walwyn, Wildman). *Levellers in the English Revolution*, ed. Aylmer, p. 88 (Lilburne, Wildman, Sexby?). *Leveller Manifestoes*, ed. Wolfe, pp. 48–50 (noncommittal). Morton, *World of the Ranters*, p. 165 (Walwyn probably involved). Pease, *Leveller Movement*, p. 253 (Walwyn?). Tolmie, *Triumph of the Saints*, p. 166 (perhaps Walwyn).

58. Introduction, p. 31.

59. Kiffin et al., *Walwins Wiles*, p. 18.

60. Introduction, p. 25. See also *Just Defence*, p. 13.

61. *The Humble Petition* of 23 Nov. 1647, reprinted, *Leveller Manifestoes*, ed. Wolfe, No. 7. Introduction, pp. 32–33.

62. Brailsford, *The Levellers*, pp. 407–08, 416, n. 4. Gimelfarb-Brack, *Overton*, pp. 393–400, designates 19 leaders as Overton's work.

63. *Some Considerations*, pp. 9–10.

Appendix 2. William Walwyn's Last Will and Testament

1. Headnote to *Physick for Families* (No. 31).

2. St. Giles without Cripplegate, General Register, MS 6419/10 (1680–88), Guildhall Library, London, entry under January 1680/1.

3. Grateful thanks are due to Laetitia Yeandle of the Folger Shakespeare Library for her assistance with the translation.

Index